55524

2500

∞

MW00334239

KENTUCKY
Remembered

An Oral History Series

James C. Klotter
and
Terry L. Birdwhistell

General Editors

Conversations
with
Kentucky Writers

L. Elisabeth Beattie, Editor

Photographs by Susan Lippman

With a Foreword by Wade Hall

THE UNIVERSITY PRESS OF KENTUCKY

Copyright © 1996 by The University Press of Kentucky

Scholarly publisher for the Commonwealth,
serving Bellarmine University, Berea College, Centre
College of Kentucky, Eastern Kentucky University,
The Filson Historical Society, Georgetown College, Kentucky
Historical Society, Kentucky State University,
Morehead State University, Murray State University,
Northern Kentucky University, Transylvania University,
University of Kentucky, University of Louisville,
and Western Kentucky University.
All rights reserved.

Editorial and Sales Offices: The University Press of Kentucky
663 South Limestone Street, Lexington, Kentucky 40508-4008

03 04 05 06 07   5 4 3 2 1

Library of Congress Cataloging-in-Publication Data

Conversations with Kentucky writers / L. Elisabeth Beattie, editor ;
photographs by Susan Lippman ; with a foreword by Wade Hall.
    p.   cm.   — (Kentucky remembered)
Includes bibliographical references and index.
ISBN 0-8131-9017-7 (pbk. : alk. paper)
    1. American literature—Kentucky—History and criticism—Theory, etc.
2. American literature—20th century—History and criticism—Theory, etc.
3. Authors, American—20th century—Interviews. 4. Kentucky—Intellectual
life—20th century. 5. Authors, American—Kentucky—Interviews.
6. Kentucky—In literature. 7. Authorship.
I. Beattie, L. Elisabeth, 1953-   . II. Series.
PS266.K4C66   1996
810.9'9769—dc20   95-54206

This book is printed on acid-free recycled paper meeting
the requirements of the American National Standard
for Permanence of Paper for Printed Library Materials.

Manufactured in the United States of America

To the Memory of Leon Vinson Driskell
writer, teacher, mentor, friend
1932-1995
With love

Contents

General Editor's Preface

In the field of oral history, Kentucky is a national leader. Over the past several decades, thousands of its citizens have been interviewed. *Kentucky Remembered* brings into print the most important of those recollections, with each volume focusing on a particular subject.

Oral history is, of course, only one type of source material. Yet by the very personal nature of recollection, hidden aspects of history are often disclosed. Oral sources provide a vital thread in the rich fabric that is Kentucky history.

This volume is the third in the series and, unlike the first two works, focuses on several people rather than one individual. It is a much-needed book, for the Commonwealth's literary tradition is one of its strengths. For more than a century, from the time of James Lane Allen, Kentucky has produced and nurtured many major writers and poets. All too often their contributions have been overshadowed by colorful politics, feud violence, or other matters that have gained national attention. Yet writers have long been a vital part of the makeup of the Commonwealth, and the stories of their lives need to be told. *Conversations with Kentucky Writers* shows that, although variety may be a common feature among those interviewed, in the end they share a commitment to their profession and a talent for the written word.

These interviews tell of lives of hardship and success, of happiness and sorrow, of injustices and rewards. The accounts of these Kentucky writers, many of them national figures, help us to understand those who, through their exploration of the psyche of Kentucky, tell us also more about ourselves.

Foreword

Many years before I had the good sense to move here, I imagined Kentucky as a historical gallery containing the likes of Daniel Boone, Henry Clay, Floyd Collins, Alben Barkley, Abe Lincoln, and Jeff Davis. Furthermore, I knew that the state's wonderland of fiction included Mrs. Wiggs, Aunt Jane, Judge Priest, the Little Colonel, Private Tussie, and Mr. Belvedere. After I arrived and got to know Kentucky up close, I realized that my imagination was not nearly rich and broad enough for the wonders I found, in fact and in fiction.

What makes Kentucky so important historically and culturally? Perhaps it's the same limestone in the soil and water that produces superior Thoroughbreds. Perhaps it's the delightful climate, with four distinct seasons. Perhaps it's Kentucky's border-state location that has made it a crossroads of the nation—a place of division, decision, and sometimes violence. Perhaps Kentucky is a kind of no-man's-land where tension is the natural law that at once separates and unites, providing ultimately a glue that gives life and literature their texture and meaning. Whatever the reasons—and, of course, they are a combination of these and more—Kentucky has contributed a goodly portion to the nation's history and literature.

This gathering of conversations with Kentucky writers, expertly conducted and edited by L. Elisabeth Beattie, is good evidence that Kentucky's cultural resources are still abundant. Indeed, this sampling of Kentucky's many fine writers shows the continuing vitality of a literary renaissance that began in the 1930s and 1940s with such major figures as Robert Penn Warren, Allen Tate, Caroline Gordon, Elizabeth Madox Roberts, Janice Holt Giles, Harriette Arnow, Jesse Stuart, and James Still.

If there's anything writers like to do more than write, it's talk about themselves and their writing. In these conversations Beattie gives them that opportunity. All memory is selective and distorted, of course, and some people invent and reinvent themselves each time they tell their past. It's an invitation to become the hero of your own life. Whether writing novels or histories, writers are constantly dealing with the fine line between fiction and biography. When they become their own subjects, the blurring of fact and imagination can become more pronounced. As Chris Offutt warns us in his interview, "Once you remember one thing, then the next time you remember it, you don't remember the event, you remember the memory of the event. So if you remember something ten times, you know you're remembering a memory of a memory of a memory." The most recent memory becomes the truth.

Some people, of course, intend to reshape themselves into what they consider a more fitting image for public consumption. But the interview format, with follow-up questions and probes by a well-prepared interviewer, does not allow for elaborate charades. What you get in these conversations is essentially the truth, or as close to it as we are likely to get in autobiographical form. And the result is a colorful, living mosaic of human lives from people who are in the business of telling good stories.

Of the twenty authors in this collection, only two (James Still and Billy C. Clark) were born before 1930. Eight were born during the thirties, seven in the forties, and three in the fifties. Fourteen were born in Kentucky, three in Alabama, and one each in North Carolina, Georgia, and Maryland. Almost half were either reared on farms or had protracted rural exposure while growing up. At least thirteen are, or have been, teachers in some capacity, usually on college campuses. Almost all have college degrees, and most have degrees at the master's or doctoral level. Although few believe that it does much to help one become a writer, most have taken some formal instruction in creative writing.

All twenty writers have spent large chunks of lives in Kentucky—indeed, at least a fourth of them have lived almost their entire lives here—and they all agree that their books, obviously or indirectly, have been significantly influenced by their "Kentucky experience." Bobbie Ann Mason, James Still, Barbara Kingsolver, Sue Grafton, and Wendell Berry—to name a few—are read and respected wherever good writing is cherished. Betty Layman Receveur's recent historical novels about Kentucky have been translated into several foreign languages.

Most of the interviews are disarmingly honest and revealing. All of the writers say significant and fascinating things about their lives and their books. They talk about the family and community influences that molded them into the people and writers they were to become. We see writers in their youth and empathize as they suffer the traumas of dysfunctional families and environments that are insensitive to their needs. Some are almost confessional as they recall alcoholic, abusive parents, suicides, and broken relationships. For many of them, South Carolina writer Pat Conroy seems right on target when he says, "One of the greatest gifts you can get as a writer is to be born into an unhappy family."

These writers in their interviews cover the process of writing from the idea to the final draft to the frequent rejection slips, the occasional acceptances, and finally the reviews. They investigate the mystery of the imagination. They tell about the family members, places, books, and other writers who helped shape them into writers. They record the teachers and friends who led them to discover their talent, famous writers and teachers like May Sarton, Paul Engle, Walter Havighurst, and Donald Davidson, and Kentucky-based writers and teachers such as Robert Hazel, Hollis Summers, Guy Davenport, Jesse Stuart, Albert Stewart, and Leon Driskell.

Each interview is as unique as a fingerprint. Talking informally and off-guard, they reveal themselves honestly and vividly. Some are self-assured, almost cocky. Others are modest and self-effacing. Some you will admire as persons, some you will not. But no one will bore you. You will have your favorites. Perhaps it will be Billy C. Clark's moving tales of his impoverished boyhood in Catlettsburg, "the meanest river town along the Ohio," or Chris Offutt's quirky, comic adventures in publishing, or Marsha Norman's isolated, lonely childhood in Louisville, or Sue Grafton's gripping account of coping in an alcoholic family, or Fenton Johnson's brave, candid memories of growing up gay in New Haven, Kentucky, or Leon Driskell's off-beat vignettes of his life as a teacher and writer.

They also speculate on their reasons for writing. For most, writing is not a choice. George Ella Lyon admits that "If I don't write, I get mean." To natural-born storyteller

Clark, "Writing came like a hunger." For Offutt, "Writing is a form of rebellion." For Receveur, "Writing simply validates me in a way that nothing else in my life, perhaps, does." Most would probably agree with Mason that writing is "like a religious calling, a commitment that you devote your life to."

While each person is as different as the people you pass in the shopping center, there are traits that most of these writers share. All are from middle-class or working-class backgrounds. Although a few report happy, "normal" childhoods, most of them felt lonely and isolated and wanted desperately to flee a family or a community that was stifling and unsympathetic. Until that happy day when they would be free, most found solace and refuge in reading. Often their love of books was instilled in them by a relative, usually the mother, who read aloud to them before they could read on their own. In unliterate families, budding writers were frequently inspired and shaped by traditions of oral storytelling.

These interviews are filled with the sudden twists and surprises of conversation. In the middle of her interview, Mason launches into a delightful discussion of Western Kentucky dialects. Offutt tells of a hilarious incident involving his underwear during a visit to Simon and Schuster in New York. All in all, while recovering the experiences of their lives, they prove the truth of Henry James's advice to young writers: Be one on whom nothing is lost. Finally, the twenty voices heard in this volume are like a street choir directed by Walt Whitman, a gathering of voices blending in harmony to celebrate our diversity.

All twenty writers, whether native born or adopted, claim a special relationship to Kentucky. With some it is obvious. Alabama-born James Still celebrates the life and heritage of the Knott County mountains where he has lived since 1932. Wendell Berry honors the community life of the lower Kentucky River country. Billy Clark chronicles the hardscrabble life of the Kentucky-West Virginia borderland of Boyd County. Marsha Norman records the gritty urban life of Louisville. And Bobbie Ann Mason has made the world aware of the rural and small-town life of Western Kentucky.

At other times, the Kentucky connection is not so obvious. But even Sue Grafton, who has become one of the world's best known mystery writers with her "alphabet murders" set in California, began her career with fiction set in Kentucky. The books of Louisville native Michael Dorris have little to do with Kentucky, but he feels a close kinship with his hometown. "I always look at globes and maps to see if Louisville is on it," he says, "and if it's not, I don't buy it." After a nomadic life spent all over the country, Chris Offutt says, "Eastern Kentucky is the only place I ever felt truly comfortable, either at home in the hills or by myself."

All corners of the state are well-represented, and the writing genres are well-covered—from novels, short stories, and poems to plays, essays, and memoirs. This collection, although by no means exhaustive, is about as representative a selection as it is possible to put between the covers of one book. Indeed, there are many other excellent writers at work today in all parts of Kentucky composing the stories and poems and essays that will be published tomorrow.

Leon Driskell was supposed to write this foreword, but, sadly, he did not live to do so. All of us who knew him personally mourn his passing, and we miss his nurturing spirit and his unselfish love. We who know him as a writer, however, rejoice that he has left a legacy that will stand as a testimony to his vision and his talent. It is a fitting monument for a man who, in his words, was only "passing through"—as all of us are. Indeed, the works that we have written and talk about in these interviews are our efforts to leave behind the good parts of ourselves.

When Beattie asked James Still at the end of his interview if he had anything to add, he said, "No, I think I've said too much already. I believe I've told you more than anybody." It is to Beattie's credit that she got Still and the rest of us to reveal so much. But now let the writers speak for themselves. Prepare yourself for sudden epiphanies, charming surprises, shocking revelations, and great splotches of comedy.

Wade Hall

Preface

Some five years ago on the bitter winter morning that I agreed to direct the Kentucky Writers' Oral History Project, I failed to imagine that the commitment I made would soon assume a life of its own. It was then that I was invited by Terry Birdwhistell, the University of Kentucky's archivist and oral historian, to revive the University of Kentucky Oral History Program's interviews with authors initiated in the state's bicentennial year and abandoned soon thereafter. My primary goal was to capture on tape writers' speech patterns and reminiscences in order to add historical data to the archives of the University of Kentucky's Margaret I. King Library. Within a year, Terry requested me to edit a book of the interviews I conducted.

My own career as a writer, a reviewer, and an oral historian caused me to read and travel widely within the state, repeatedly encountering in print and in person Kentucky's diverse and significant authors. In 1990 I selected my first ten interviewees according to criteria emphasizing the writers' ages and geographical locations. My intent was to capture the memories of the state's senior authors from eastern Appalachia to the western Pennyrile. The more I learned about the Commonwealth's writers and their writing, the more I wanted and needed to know. Prior to each interview I read the available published and unpublished work of that author. As every writer I interviewed discussed his or her life, that individual also indicated to me affiliations with other Kentucky writers, with publications, and with geographical regions.

Thus, my project grew. I expanded my definition of "Kentucky writer" to include natives who've relocated outside the state and non-natives who've made Kentucky their home. From 1990 through 1993, I interviewed a total of fifty writers, realizing even as I completed my final taped conversation that many more writers are worthy of inclusion in such a project. Therefore, the twenty writers whose interviews appear in this volume are not definitive, but representative. It is useful to know who in Kentucky, and who from Kentucky, is publishing, and to note any parallels among people and their work that may indeed stem from common values, experiences, or perceptions.

Like letters or diary entries or even books themselves, oral history interviews capture particular moments—perspectives and lives—certain to alter in time. Indeed, most of the authors herein continue to write and publish. But also like letters and diaries and books, oral history interviews remain valuable for the very fact that they do catch people at a point in time, allowing scholars to study their subjects as those subjects once saw themselves and their worlds.

The Margaret I. King Library of the University of Kentucky houses the taped interviews and the transcripts from which this volume has been edited. The tape recorded interviews range from one to four-and-one-half hours; the average interview is three hours. The unedited transcripts average one-hundred-fifty pages. During the past year, I've edited the transcripts in the order I've received them from the Oral History Program of the University of Kentucky where the tapes have been transcribed. My editorial goal has been to preserve each interview's contextual integrity and tone. To focus on each interviewee, I've eliminated my questions where the interviewees' responses flow as narrative, but I've preserved every interview's sequence and precise wording, except in cases wherein the original phrasing might prove confusing. In those instances, I've added or substituted bracketed words or phrases.

As I conclude my work on this volume, it's another new year, and frost once again covers the creek near my house in sheets of ice that layer one another like the limestone at their base. This is a morning so similar to that of five years past that I can't help but regard my creek as a metaphor, the writers' interviews building on each other like rivulets of water, assuming a flow of their own.

Acknowledgments

A number of people's wisdom and work have helped me shape ten thousand pages of transcriptions into this volume of writers' interviews. I thank them all, but I'm especially grateful to the following individuals and institutions for their invaluable support.

Marion K. Stocking, my Beliot College mentor and beloved friend, is the individual who, in the mid-1970s, introduced me to oral history and who supervised my bachelor's degree in that field, the first to be awarded in the United States. To her I owe my impetus for even contemplating this project.

I appreciate the two interviewing and two transcribing grants I received from the Kentucky Oral History Commission, and I particularly thank Kim Lady Smith, executive director of that commission, for her support of my work.

Essential to this project and to its becoming a book is University of Kentucky Archivist and Oral History Program Director Terry Birdwhistell, who appointed me director of the Kentucky Writers' Oral History Project, who requested I edit transcripts from the interviews into a book, and who throughout the editorial process provided me cogent and always humorous counsel. Terry's assistant, Jeff Suchanek, supervised and aided the tedious transcribing task, and applauded the birth of this book.

State Historian James Klotter, coeditor with Terry Birdwhistell of the University Press of Kentucky's oral history book series, offered me encouragement. Art Jester, book editor of the *Lexington Herald-Leader;* Betty Arnett, formerly of the Friends of the Free Louisville Public Library; and Leon Driskell, a close friend and project interviewee, found me elusive authors' phone numbers and addresses.

Louisville author Wade Hall acted part cheerleader, part advisor, and part confessor to this interviewer-editor as *Conversations with Kentucky Writers* expanded, then eclipsed, repeatedly metamorphosing until reaching its ultimate form.

I thank my employer, Elizabethtown Community College—particularly its president, Dr. Charles E. Stebbins, and its dean of business affairs, Judy Wieman—for their vital support in the form of secretarial services. I also thank Gloria Garner Sneed Haynes, and especially Diane Marie Hess, for their dedication and for their quality work as typists. To my colleague Linda Mayhew, I extend my eternal gratitude for her indexing efforts.

For her devotion to this book, for her unstinting pursuit of images worthy of their subjects, and for her excellent work, I extend my gratitude to photographer Susan Lippman. I also thank the *Lexington Herald-Leader* for permission to reprint Marsha Norman's photo.

Of course essential to the interviewing and editing process has been the ongoing cooperation of each writer whose time, energy, and interest literally made the individual interviews, and finally this book itself, possible. Too, I am appreciative of each author's friendship, as discussing with them their lives and careers has, for the past four years, fueled my own literary interests.

Finally, my heartfelt thanks extend to friends who have leant their ears to my triumphs and travails, and to my family, especially to my parents, Elisabeth and Walter Beattie, whose crucial moral and financial support of this book have been surpassed only by my father's superb editorial suggestions.

Conversations
with
Kentucky Writers

Copyright © 1993 by Dan Carraco

WENDELL BERRY

BERRY: My name is Wendell Erdman Berry, and I was born August fifth, 1934. My mother's maiden name was Virginia Erdman Berry, and my father's name is John Marshall Berry. My father was a lawyer and also a farmer, and my mother is a housewife still. My father is dead.

BEATTIE: What was your childhood like?

BERRY: I had, I think, a wonderful childhood. I grew up in the little town of New Castle, Kentucky, where my parents moved in 1936. I went to school at New Castle School until 1948. But I also grew up on farms. My father continued to be a farmer, and both sets of grandparents were on the farm. I had what I think was a very free childhood, a lot of swimming and riding on horses and wandering about.

BEATTIE: Did you help your father much with the farm?

BERRY: Well, my father was often involved in things that he couldn't be helped with, but I helped other people on the farm. I helped my father sometimes. There would be days when he would take time off from his office, and we would work through a bunch of cattle or something like that. He was a good teacher. But my father was very busy in his law practice, and for fifty years he was involved with the Burley Tobacco Growers Cooperative Association as counsel, as vice-president, and then as president. So the opportunities for working with my father weren't all that available, but there were other people I worked for and with from the time I was very young.

BEATTIE: Did you think, when you were a child, that you might be a lawyer or a farmer?

BERRY: I thought off and on that I might be a lawyer. I always wanted to be a farmer from the time I was a little boy.

BEATTIE: What was your early schooling like?

BERRY: I had some good teachers. I wasn't a very tractable student, and after about the second grade, I began to cause a lot of trouble.

BEATTIE: In what way?

BERRY: Oh, being uproarious, doing the things kids do who are not very happy to be in school.

BEATTIE: Do you remember liking any subject better than any other?

BERRY: Not early. I liked to read from a very early age, but reading I did on my own. I had also found out very early what it was like to be at large in the countryside, and what it felt like to be at work in the countryside, and that made it difficult, I think, for me to be at home in school. I always thought that there would be a better place to be, and I'm not entirely convinced that I wasn't right. So I'm not sure that I had a favorite subject for a long time.

I loved to read from early in my life. I loved being read to, and my mother loved to read and loved to read to me. She really was the one who gave me a love of books, and who gave me books to read. It was a wonderful thing to be sick and home from school with her, because we would read. We read about King Arthur's knights and Robin Hood and other wonderful things.

BEATTIE: Do you remember other books that either she read to you or that you read yourself?

BERRY: *The Swiss Family Robinson* was a very big book with me. My mother read it to me, and then I read it over and over and over again for myself. And *The Yearling.* My mother gave that book to me, and it was another book that I virtually memorized. I didn't try to read a lot of books. If I found a book I liked, I just read it and read it and read it. A little later I read Mary O'Hara, *My Friend Flicka,* and *Thunderhead,* and later *Green Grass of Wyoming.* I nearly wore out *My Friend Flicka* and *Thunderhead.* I still know all about those books. So I took spells at reading, but I never much liked to read assignments.

BEATTIE: Because they were assignments or because they just weren't very interesting reading?

BERRY: Well, I don't very much like to read my own assignments. The sense of having to do it is damaging to reading, in a way. You ought to read freely, and I still do that some.

BEATTIE: That goes along with the psychology of reading with a flashlight under bed covers, doesn't it?

BERRY: I did a lot of that. The flashlight was a great boon to me. I read a lot of comic books that way, but also real books. My mother was convinced that we ruined ourselves with comic books, which, of course, made them irresistible.

BEATTIE: Did your sisters and brother read as much as you did?

BERRY: Not as much as I did. My mother read to us all, of course. I was the one who became a bookworm.

BEATTIE: What about athletics or other things? Did you do that sort of thing in school?

BERRY: There wasn't much in the way of organized sports for young kids at school. There was some organized play, and I did some of that, but mostly we played on our own. We played hours and hours of basketball in people's yards, throwing a basketball through old buckets and other makeshift hoops, but we played all the time. That was real play. I mean, it's real play when kids get together and play a game. It's not real play when they get together under supervision of adults and are made to do it the right way and all that.

BEATTIE: You just went through eighth grade in New Castle. Where did you go after that?

BERRY: I went to Millersburg Military Institute. It was very confining and military, of course. I never liked the military part of it. I did have some good teachers there, and I began there to read more seriously than I had before. In high school I began to have a favorite subject: literature.

BEATTIE: When did you start your own writing?

BERRY: I wrote a few poems and other things when I was in high school, but I didn't begin to write knowledgeably until I was well along in college. I had a very good teacher—who just died—at the University of Kentucky in my second semester, Thomas Stroup. He taught Milton and other seventeenth-century writers. But he also taught a course at that time called "Introduction to Literature." It involved reading and writing about poetry. He used that old textbook, *Understanding Poetry,* by Robert Penn Warren and Cleanth Brooks. It's still referred to, I think, as "Brooks and Warren." I would carry Stroup my awful poems, which he very patiently read and criticized and made fun of a little bit. But that was when I first began to write with the idea that there might be a way to do it that I needed to learn.

BEATTIE: Had you ever written poetry or done any kind of writing on your own in elementary school or high school?

BERRY: A poem or two, as I said, and articles for the school paper. I began to feel then that it would be a good thing to be a writer. I had been a bookish little boy. I would imagine how it would be to write about what I was doing. I would say it over to myself the way I thought a writer might write it. But there were times when I didn't read at all; my mind would be on farming or hunting. I wound up at military school because I was so much more interested in hunting and trapping and that sort of thing than I was in school. My parents thought something had to be done.

BEATTIE: Did you go directly from the military school to the University of Kentucky?

BERRY: Yes, the next fall.

BEATTIE: Why did you choose the University of Kentucky?

BERRY: I didn't give the subject very much thought; the University of Kentucky was just there, and I went to it. I had begun to think that I wanted to be a writer, and I had the rather naive assumption that the business of the University of Kentucky was to make me into a writer. Of course, that wasn't its business, but I found people there who helped me. Tom Stroup was the first, and then Hollis Summers, and after Hollis there was Robert Hazel—people who treated me very kindly and taught me a lot.

BEATTIE: Were you involved in any extracurricular pursuits there, such as the newspaper or literary magazines?

BERRY: I was involved with the literary magazines. They used to have a freshman magazine called the *Green Pen,* and I helped to edit that. Then I was involved in [the literary magazine] *Stylus,* as a contributor, and then as editor.

BEATTIE: Several other people I've interviewed for this project have talked long and fondly about their time with you at UK and at Stanford, Ed McClanahan and Gurney Norman and Jim Baker Hall.

BERRY: Jim Hall, oh yes.

BEATTIE: Even Bobbie Ann Mason.

BERRY: We were all together there. But Bobbie Ann Mason was Gurney's contemporary, and Gurney was just coming in as I was going out. I didn't meet Bobbie Ann until 1963 or '64, in New York. I stayed [at the University of Kentucky] five years and got an M.A. Jim Hall and I were friends from at least the time I was a sophomore. We got to know each other in one of Hollis Summers's creative writing classes, and we were very close friends. We were together all the time, talking about writing, poetry, T. S. Eliot, and Ezra Pound and the poets of that generation who were such monuments to kids in school at that time. Ed came as a graduate student in 1956, it must have been. He'd been to Stanford. Ed had been around quite a bit, much more than I had, heaven knows. We became friends at that time and stayed friends. I went, the next year after I was a graduate student, and taught at Georgetown [College]; and if I'm not mistaken, Ed was still working on his M.A.

BEATTIE: This is Georgetown, Kentucky?

BERRY: Yes. And Ed and Kitty, his first wife, were living out at Bryan Station Spring, in an old ice house. We visited a lot at that time. The next year Ed went to Corvallis [Oregon] to teach, and I went to Stanford as a Stegner Fellow.

BEATTIE: Your decision to go to Stanford, did it have anything to do with their having been at Stanford?

BERRY: Jim Hall went to Stanford as a graduate student the year that I taught at Georgetown, and he told me about those fellowships. Of course, I wanted to go where he was, and also my wife, Tanya, grew up in California. She loved it out there, and it was attractive to me to go out where she had been and was at home. It was a very fortunate thing, really, that I did get to know that part of the world that meant so much to her.

BEATTIE: When did you meet and marry your wife?

BERRY: I met Tanya at the University of Kentucky in the fall of 1955.

BEATTIE: What brought her from California to the University of Kentucky?

BERRY: Her father [Clifford Amyx] taught in the art department. Tanya and I got married on the twenty-ninth of May, 1957.

BEATTIE: What was your master's thesis on?

BERRY: I didn't do a thesis. That got me into trouble with some people, but Jim Hall and I had gone the year before, the summer of 1956, up to the School of Letters at Indiana University. We took a course in Joyce and Yeats from Richard Ellman, and a course in modern poetry from Karl Shapiro. I picked up six credit hours that way, you see. Then along in my year as a graduate student I found out that you could do six extra hours of credit in lieu of a thesis. I just took that option.

At Georgetown College, I taught three courses of freshman composition and a course of sophomore literature. I enjoyed the teaching a lot, but we were required to attend chapel and so on. I was the way a young man is supposed to be; I was rebellious, and didn't like to be required to do things.

BEATTIE: When you went to Stanford, I know you had Wallace Stegner as a major professor. You've written about what a wonderful teacher he is. Will you talk about your relationship with him? Also, you've described Stegner as a regional writer who has escaped the evils of regionalism. Will you describe those evils?

BERRY: Well, the evils of regionalism all have to do with thinking that special virtues come with your region, and that's something you have to get over. You're not going to be a better writer or a better person because you're a Kentuckian. The other evil is offering your region and people as curiosities. We've had a good bit of that in Kentucky, people offering Kentuckians as stereotypes, as what other people think they are, so that those other people can say, "Oh, look at the quaint, backward, ignorant Kentuckians."

BEATTIE: Would you say, too, that whatever a piece of writing is in terms of being regional, that it has to be universal to have any kind of real value?

BERRY: No, I don't agree with that entirely. It has value in itself. I mean, this is my assumption, that all creatures are uniquely valuable, individually. They don't get their value by virtue of belonging to a category. There has to be this appreciation, which is one of the most precious things in our tradition, this appreciation of the value that inheres in us by virtue of our being what we are individually.

BEATTIE: I agree with that. I just meant in order for other people to appreciate individuality, there has to be something . . .

BERRY: Oh yes, there must be recognition. If you're absolutely unique, you're absolutely lonely. So there is shared . . .

BEATTIE: Humanity?

BERRY: Yes.

BEATTIE: What about Wallace Stegner? What was he like in your relationship with him, the student-teacher relationship?

BERRY: Wallace Stegner was a man of great personal dignity and a lot of reserve. He wasn't the kind of professor who let you get to be his pal. You weren't going to drop in on him for an informal chat, or at least I wasn't. But implicit in that reserve was an expectation. I don't mean to say that he was not generous; he was absolutely generous, and he would help you no end. He's helped me, goodness knows, without reservation and without limit, so far as I know. Every time anything good has happened to me, he has turned out to be behind it somewhere, a letter of recommendation or something. But, he kept his distance. I always felt in his reserve an expectation that people ought to live up to what they'd been given, not just to a fellowship, but to the whole tradition of literature and culture in the West, in the world, even. He made me feel that there was no excuse for doing less than I could do, and no excuse not to give honor to the things that I'd been given.

BEATTIE: Do your classmates share your feelings about Stegner?

BERRY: I don't know. I never did ask them. We didn't gossip about him very much. If he had involved himself with us on a more familiar basis, we might have gossiped about him, but I don't remember very much gossip at all about Wallace Stegner, which is rather remarkable. I also had another wonderful teacher at Stanford, Richard Scowcroft. I have a large debt to him, also, and remain his friend.

BEATTIE: What sort of writing were you doing when you were in the workshop [at Stanford]?

BERRY: I was working on *Nathan Coulter,* my first novel. I had about half of it written when I went out there, and I just continued to work on it.

BEATTIE: I wondered when reading that novel if you, in your childhood, experienced the death of someone similar to the powerful scene in the book where the mother is in the parlor?

BERRY: No, I didn't experience anything like that. You mean the death of the mother.

BEATTIE: Yes.

BERRY: No. I experienced the deaths of loved ones early, but not of my mother. People immediately said that *Nathan Coulter* was an autobiographical novel, but it's not an autobiographical novel at all. Nathan, as I figured, was born in 1924. So his early experience was actually of a more unadulterated rural life than I ever knew.

BEATTIE: Ed McClanahan and Gurney Norman have talked about the good times they had living out in California. Were you ever part of that, with Ken Kesey and the psychedelic bus and all of that?

BERRY: Well, Ken Kesey was part of that seminar that I was in at Stanford, in that year of '58 and '59. Kesey was living on Perry Lane during those years. I lived in Mill Valley, though, and commuted, because Tanya's uncle and aunt had a little place there that they would rent to us. It was attractive to be there, so that's where we stayed. I guess it must have been '63 or '64 when Gurney or Ed made me aware of Kesey's exploits. But no, I missed that.

Gurney, Jim, and Ed came there as fellows after I left, so Kesey had flowered more fully during their time than he had during mine. I have always been friends with Ken, but I never was a prankster. Kesey and I are the only two people that Tanya and I knew in college who are still married to the same women. Very different styles of matrimony, I suppose, but it's a fact.

BEATTIE: What about your children? Were they born while you were in California?

BERRY: No. Mary, our oldest, was born in Lexington in May of 1958. She went to California with us as a little baby, in August of that year. Then Den was born, also in Lexington, in August of 1962.

BEATTIE: Where were you living?

BERRY: When Den was born, we weren't really living anywhere. We had come back from Europe. We were staying in a borrowed house that belonged to some friends of Tanya's parents.

BEATTIE: When you were in Europe, was that just vacation or were you studying there?

BERRY: I got a Guggenheim in 1961. We went to Europe that August and came back the next July.

BEATTIE: Where were you there?

BERRY: Mostly in Italy, in Florence, but we also spent two months in southern France and some time in Paris and London. I was writing a book, or so I thought, and I did work on it some, but not very effectively. I had begun *A Place on Earth* in California in January of 1960, and I carried it on in Europe as best I could. I wanted to write not so limited a book as *Nathan Coulter* had been, and I didn't know how to write a less limited book. There was a lot of awkwardness in the writing of *A Place on Earth*.

BEATTIE: But you were able to use parts of what you'd written?

BERRY: I believe I was. I don't think I wrote anything that was very good when I was in Europe, but I think I salvaged some of it.

BEATTIE: Then you went to New York to teach?

BERRY: Yes, at the University College, so called, of N.Y.U., which was up in the Bronx, in University Heights. I taught freshman English. I was the director of freshman English.

BEATTIE: How long were you there?

BERRY: Two years, until the spring of '64.

BEATTIE: What was the experience like?

BERRY: Well, I enjoyed all of it, pretty much, being up there. I learned a lot that has been indispensable to me.

BEATTIE: In terms of what sorts of things?

BERRY: Living in a great city and working in a great city and being used to being a part of a great city. Just knowing your way around and being equal to the things you had to put up with. We lived in an old loft on Greenwich Street, 277 Greenwich Street, down by City Hall and the Washington Market, an exciting part of town to live in. Then I got acquainted with museums and art galleries. The city offered a lot, and I took advantage of a good bit of it.

BEATTIE: But you decided you didn't want to stay?

BERRY: Yes, I got an offer to come back to teach at the University at Lexington—thanks, I later found out, to Wallace Stegner.

BEATTIE: Had you not gotten that offer, do you think you would have stayed in New York?

BERRY: I have no idea. I had assumed for a long time, because of the way I'd been taught by schools, that I would never amount to anything if I stayed at home. So when I got to New York I sort of assumed, well, this is what one does. Then when I got the offer to come back to Kentucky, we knew, first of all, that we wanted to come back. Also, it had become fairly plain to me that I was a Kentucky writer; I wasn't going to be a New York writer. I'd just lived in Kentucky too long. My mind and my life were formed here in Henry County, my allegiances were here. All my kinships were here, and several of my dearest friendships. So I wanted to come back, and teaching at the University of Kentucky would make it possible. So I did return to Kentucky. I certainly didn't feel that I wanted to spend a lot of my life living in New York. I liked it, it was exhilarating, it was wonderful, but I think a lot of my excitement depended on my understanding that I didn't have to stay, that I'd find some way to leave if I wanted to.

BEATTIE: You talk about realizing that you were a Kentucky writer and that you wouldn't be a New York writer. When you were in New York, did you write or attempt to write things that were centered in Kentucky?

BERRY: I worked on *A Place on Earth,* and, of course, always on poems. I've always written poems, off and on. They would come to me. But I was busy writing *A Place on Earth* all the time I was in New York. I finally sort of learned to write it when I was up there. I finally began to feel that I knew what I was doing. But, of course, *A Place on Earth* is about my part of Kentucky, and it was pretty plain by that time that what I really wanted to write about was this place here, these few square miles that I'd known all my life. What I loved most was this, and that was what I most wanted to serve. Of course, we had no idea what our life was going to turn out to be.

BEATTIE: Had you attempted to write stories or poems with other settings, such as New York?

BERRY: Oh, I wrote a few New York poems. I'd written a few West Coast poems, and I still occasionally write a poem about someplace else. But I don't have the permanence of commitment and interest elsewhere that I've always had here. My father had a commitment to this place and to small farmers, to the way of life that was practiced here, and I have followed him in that.

BEATTIE: Sounds like your father gave you the impetus to be what you are, and your mother showed you the way to be who you are.

BERRY: It would be hard to unravel my debts to them. My father, of course, thought that I was going to starve to death as a writer, and he didn't very much favor my choice. It was something that I now understand. If I had a child who came in and said he wanted to be a writer, I would be scared to death. It would not be something that I would want to encourage very much, because it's so chancy.

BEATTIE: Have either of your children wanted to write?

BERRY: No, my children are farmers. My daughter and son-in-law live at New Castle on a farm, and my son and his wife live near Lacie on a farm. Right here, ten miles away, and about four or five miles away.

BEATTIE: It's rare to be able to say that today.

BERRY: It is. It means we have our grandchildren.

BEATTIE: When you returned to the University of Kentucky, what were you teaching?

BERRY: I taught the writing courses, mainly.

BEATTIE: You have written about and talked about creative or imaginative writing being another form of good writing. How did you teach those classes, and don't you still teach at the University of Kentucky?

BERRY: I don't teach those classes any more, and I haven't since 1977. I quit in 1977, and stayed quit for ten years. When I went back, I started teaching other things. I don't like teaching so-called creative writing anymore.

I've been teaching, since the fall of '87, a course called Composition for Teachers, for people who are going to teach English in the public schools. Then I've taught, usually, a literature course of some kind. I taught a course called Readings in Agriculture, which is probably too complicated to explain this afternoon, and a course in pastoral literature.

BEATTIE: You didn't particularly enjoy teaching creative writing?

BERRY: I enjoyed it. I actually had a very good time doing it, but the course worried me all the time I was teaching it, because it was a little hard, given the assumptions that people came into the course with, to make them concentrate as much as they needed to on the technical issues of writing. I was always a little uneasy about the justification for such a course.

BEATTIE: Did you ever have any students that were very promising writers?

BERRY: I had some very good students. Lynn Hightower's the one I think of immediately, and I'm sort of out of touch with the people I taught all those years ago. It's been fifteen years now since I've taught one of those courses. I'm not sure what's happened to all of the students I had. Some of them were very good writers. But, you see, preparing people to be novelists and poets and that sort of thing, is hardly the same thing as preparing somebody to be a doctor or an engineer or a lawyer, or a teacher even, because there are just not any significant number of places that are dependably available. So really, in terms of the life of the student, you're working in the dark. You don't know what you're doing, and that's why I always insisted that I would rather make a good writer and a good reader than to make a published writer, because you'd be lucky, unless you were someplace like Stanford, to make very many of them.

BEATTIE: I'm always surprised at the number of would-be or creative writers who are not readers and who don't see why they need to be readers.

BERRY: Yes. Well, I can explain that, but I suppose there's not much use.

BEATTIE: I was wondering if you ran into that when you were teaching creative writing.

BERRY: I've run into people who were afraid that if they read any poetry, they would destroy their originality. You'd always find that such people were writing under the influence of cigarette commercials and that sort of thing. It's hard on people of romantic sensibility to face it, but the fact is that writing comes out of writing, just as talk comes out of talk. If you didn't hear other people talk, and study their ways of talking, you'd never get to be a good talker. The same goes for writing.

BEATTIE: In one of your essays you were quoting, I believe it was Adrienne Rich, talking about not needing to know Yeats's voice.

BERRY: Well, that wasn't an ignorant statement; it was a political statement, and I understand that. But there are people who think they don't need to read Yeats or Shakespeare or Milton. Some people who think those people don't need to be read are teaching literature in English departments.

BEATTIE: A lot of people think they shouldn't be read because they're "dead white men."

BERRY: They are dead white men.

BEATTIE: So that somehow negates them.

BERRY: Yes, and people who talk that way don't acknowledge their very considerable debts to dead white men who, after all, kept alive this idea of individual worth, and individual dignity, and individual freedom.

BEATTIE: It's replacing one prejudice for another.

BERRY: Yes, all that's very regrettable. The question of who is alive can't be settled by category. Some allegedly dead white men are more alive than some people who are allegedly living.

BEATTIE: When you were a student yourself, did you ever feel a need to choose a genre that you were going to write in?

BERRY: I sometimes wondered whether I would be a poet or a novelist. It didn't occur to me that I might be an essayist. But because you're in a school, you know, you're under the influence of specialization, and, without anybody ever telling you, you're made to feel, by the system itself, that someday you'll have to choose. I remember sitting around wondering, "Well now, what'll I choose?" But in practice the problem gets resolved fairly naturally. I've used the various genres that I've used simply because I've had a use for them. Occasionally, I'll get a review that makes me think, "Well, this person is really saying, 'What's this essayist doing writing a novel?' or 'What's this novelist doing writing a poem?' or, 'What's this poet doing writing about agriculture?'"

BEATTIE: I'm sure there are people who know you mostly by your writing and people who know you as a neighbor and farmer. Are your neighbors very familiar with your writing?

BERRY: I know that there are people in this community who read my books. But it's not a thing that I'd be very comfortable in trying to find out much about. You can't walk up to somebody and say, "Have you read my book?"

BEATTIE: They don't come up to you and talk about your writing?

BERRY: Occasionally they do, and occasionally I hear back things that people have said that they didn't say to me. But really, in a way, I don't want to be dealt with by my neighbors as somebody who publishes books. I don't want to be dealt with by my children as somebody who publishes books, or by my wife. And a fat chance there'd be of that. I want to be dealt with as a person who's living through the same life that these other people are living through, and dealing with the same difficulties and hardships and griefs and joys that they're dealing with. Being a writer has to be incidental to that.

I ought to say, though, that when I know that my neighbors read my books, or when they occasionally say they think I've done well, it's just an unspeakable pleasure to me.

BEATTIE: More than a *New York Times Book Review*?

BERRY: Yes, a lot more, because love is involved in it here. You see, it's a different emotion.

BEATTIE: All of your books—novels, essays, poetry—deal with your concern for community. Will you discuss that concern, and do you think it's probable or even possible that an increasingly urban and centralized and specialized society can return to or can achieve true community?

BERRY: Well, of course, willy-nilly, I've been part of a community. It hasn't been a thriving community since the end of World War II. Rural communities have been in rapid decline since about then.

BEATTIE: Port Royal [Berry's home]?

BERRY: Port Royal, New Castle, the little towns that I've known. The economic integrity of these communities has been destroyed. When I first knew them, you could hardly drive in these little towns on Saturday night. It would have been a problem to drive through Port Royal, as small as it was. The places were jammed with people who were talking together, visiting, doing their buying. You couldn't draw a line between the economic life of the community and its cultural life. It was all happening at the same time. Increasingly, that life has been destroyed. These little towns are dead as a wedge now on Saturday night.

I've been, in a way, a peculiar defender of community, because I'm pretty much a solitary person; I have never been a person who enjoyed institutional affairs or group activities much. But it affected me very much, especially after I came back here to live, to see what was happening to the communities.

Or, you can come to it in another way. You think, well, you would defend the small farm, the small family farm as a thing that's needful for various reasons. But then you finally see that the family is not an adequate vessel. Families deteriorate, or they perish altogether. So a larger container has to be proposed, and the only other one, of course, is the local community. The community survives the deaths of families, or it can.

So, in those various ways, I've slowly come to think of community. My novels and stories have all proposed a community that's more or less conscious of itself, its people conscientiously helping each other. I've learned a lot from the participation of my own family in community life. Tanya's involvement in the church up at Port Royal as member and musician matters to me and has taught me a lot.

I don't know, of course, what's going to happen, but it seems to me imaginable that a time could come when we will either have to achieve community or die, learn to love one another or die. We're rapidly coming to the time, I think, when the great centralized powers are not going to be able to do for us what we need to have done. Community will start again when people begin to do necessary things for each other.

BEATTIE: In your essay, 'Poetry and Place,' you argue that too often contemporary poetry lacks narrative, and instead focuses on autobiographical or psychological confessions, which you imply are self-indulgent and not universal. But I'm wondering if you think that sense of alienation—of geographical and spiritual hunger—expressed in so much contemporary poetry is universal? Is it a way of achieving an ironic sort of community between and among alienated poets and alienated audiences?

BERRY: There may be something to that. But the alienated are going to be a network at best. You can't start a community with that. Finally, it comes down to whether you want to be alienated or not, and whether you're willing to join yourself to the things that you have to join yourself to in order not to be alienated. This probably means that you're going to have to love people who don't have college degrees and who may appear to be not as smart as you, only to prove later, perhaps, that they are smarter than you, but in a different way. The community, you see, is a practical idea. The network is not necessarily practical at all. The community has to begin in practical matters. One of the things that a community has to do is make some kind of practical working peace with its place. If it's going to be a real community, a great diversity of people are going to have to know and cherish what they have in common, which of course would be their place, first of all.

This is what American multiculturalism is finally going to have to face. The question that is finally going to have to be asked and answered is not, what is your economic relationship to your place of origin, or what is your relationship to your ancestors, or what is your relationship to your old-world culture. The most important question, and ultimately the undodgeable question, is what is your economic relationship to this place where you are now? That would give us authentic cultural diversity, you see, because of the great diversity of places. Cultures and communities that were authentically adapted to their places would be authentically different.

BEATTIE: According to your definition of communities, a community has to be composed of different types of people, not, for instance, of people just in the same church congregation or people in the same school. It has to extend to include a variety of types of people and ways of life?

BERRY: Well, it would have to include a variety. Now, you have to go beyond that and say that it won't, maybe, work in the right way, or it may fail to work with absolute impartiality toward all its members. It may fail to love everybody that it includes. It may make it hard on some people and force them to leave. All kinds of bad possibilities inhere in the idea of community. But all kinds of bad possibilities inhere in human nature, and you have to do the best you can to correct them. My argument with these people who are by principle alienated from any kind of community life is that they're using inevitable human failings as a kind of escape. They're not facing up to these bad possibilities that inhere in human nature.

BEATTIE: In *What Are People For?* you write, "To be creative is only to have health," and in another place you say, "Order is the only possibility of rest." Both of those quotations interested me in conjunction with the question, "What is the nature of creativity?"

BERRY: I know less about creativity than I know about anything. It really is a mystery. I mean, where does it come from, how does it happen? I don't know. It's not rational, it's not subject to rational scrutiny. If you had only to think of what you wanted to think of, what you described to yourself ahead of time as a desirable thing to think of, there would be no such thing as so-called creativity. I wouldn't deny the involvement of my own history in what I have written, or my conscious reasons. Nor would I deny the absolute importance of workmanship, of technique, in the study of the art of writing. But I don't think that's all the story. It certainly isn't for me. Ruskin says that artists are moved by love for things that they want to preserve, or to preserve them at least in memory. That appeals to me. But I believe also in inspiration.

You have to have a routine. You've got to work. You've got to be able to work deliberately. If you write anything that's very long, you've got to work every day. But it depends, too, on serendipity, on felicity, on inspiration. When the poets invoke the Muse, or the Heavenly Muse, or the Holy Spirit, I take them very seriously, because I know that things come. Things come that you can't account for. When I write well, I'm writing, I think, far beyond anything you would expect from knowing me.

BEATTIE: Would you call it intense concentration when the writing just seems to come and you don't even know exactly what it's going to be until it's done?

BERRY: Occasionally the language itself will come. For me, it never comes in great quantities, but occasionally, something—a line or a sentence or even a passage—will come, and the sentences that come are the sentences that you really have to pay attention to.

BEATTIE: Do you find that sometimes you're in the middle of writing before you know what it is you're going to write?

BERRY: Not so much any more. Occasionally, I'll find that I've wasted a little work at the beginning. But I no longer try to write. I mean, I don't try to make myself think of something to write. If I don't already have something to say, I've got other things that I'd rather be doing. I don't ever ask myself, "Why don't you get an idea?" I just deal with what comes, and when it comes, then I try to do the best I can with it. But the essays I'm writing now are prepared for by years of other essays and thought and reading and worry, and the other things that go into essay writing. When I write stories, I'm apt now to be writing stories that I've had in mind for years, and wondered if I would ever be able to write. Sometimes the stories often come from thinking about real stories that I've known maybe for fifty years. In poems, I occasionally will wind up someplace that I didn't know I was going. You never have in your mind ahead of time, or in actual experience, a whole story. What has to come in order to make it a whole story is often a surprise. But I don't hanker enough to be a writer to write to see if I have something to write. I like the assurance of having a job of seeing the work pretty closely ahead of me.

BEATTIE: The meaning comes first and the form follows.

BERRY: For me it's words. I mean, the writing has to offer itself as something that can be said, that I'm now feeling close to having the power to say. As a young man, I had enough of the feeling that I had a wonderful thing to say and no ability whatsoever to say it. That's just a terrible fix to be in.

BEATTIE: *Fidelity*, the title of your most recent book of short stories, seems to me to describe an essential aspect of your character in relation to your community, your farm, your family, and your friends. Will you talk about what fidelity means to you?

BERRY: It just means making a commitment and hanging on, and never giving up. As long as you've got the life and willpower to continue, you continue. All that's based on a faith that my experience, to some extent, proves out—if you hang on, you'll see your way through whatever it is that's difficult—that there's going to be a reward. I believe that; it's my profoundest operating belief. Something will come. Out of the impasse, something will come that you'll be glad to know. I don't have enough faith in myself to believe the next choice I would make would be better than the ones I've already made.

BEATTIE: Or maybe you have more faith in other people?

BERRY: I have faith in God. I have no faith at all that I could find a better woman than Tanya, or a better place than this to live, or different work that I could do as well as the work I've already chosen. It just makes no sense to me to assume that I could. I'm not talking out of a life that I think is perfect, or that has been always easy and rewarding. I think that I've been blessed in all the choices I've made, but I don't think that I would have found out that I was blessed if I hadn't kept to those choices.

BEATTIE: It seems to me that so many people don't put time or energy into things that require work or effort.

BERRY: I would never, by the same token, have faith enough in myself to say to anybody that he or she absolutely ought to stick to any choice that he or she has made. Because you never know what the other person is suffering, and you understand that a fidelity that's imposed by somebody else's advice is not what fidelity is, anyway. It has to come from inside the person. So although you can lament the statistics of divorce and mobility and all the rest of it, you really can't say that in any particular instance people oughtn't to get a divorce or move to a new place. Or I can't. I know that things are happening to men and women, between men and women, now that are just awful, and the statistics are terrifying. The divorce statistics are terrifying. The impact on children is absolutely terrifying. Yet, you just can't go up to people and say, "What you're doing is, in your case, wrong."

BEATTIE: I think I've read recently that something like twelve percent of all families in this country are the traditional, two-parent households now, which *is* pretty scary.

BERRY: As a teacher, over and over again, I've seen young people who I thought must have needed their fathers at critical times in their lives when their fathers weren't there, and now I'm afraid we're going into a time when we'll see students who needed their mothers at such times. I don't think it's a great improvement for men to be working away from their families; having made that judgment, I can't say that I think it's a good idea for women to work away from theirs. It's just too clear that raising a child is not a job for one person. It isn't even a job for two people. It takes a lot of committed people. This is another argument for community. A well-raised child would be raised by the community, a community in which a lot of people feel privileged to correct that child. I think that was the great good fortune that I had in my growing up, that I had fathers and mothers wherever I looked. Some of them remained parents to me until they died. They would say, "Wendell, I think you're not right about that. I think you'd better think again about that."

BEATTIE: In your introduction to your 1975 book *Sayings and Doings,* you write, "Memorable speech is measured speech," and you indicate in several of your essays irritation with people who speak constantly. You also refer to a silent time returning home in a wagon with your granddaughter as a special time. Do you sometimes find more communion in silence than in speech?

BERRY: Oh, yes. And the inadequacy of language is the first thing a writer ought to know, or a speaker. The condition that language has to exist in and make the most of, be disciplined by, is it's own inadequacy. It just isn't adequate, and silence is the way we acknowledge that. Finally, you can't say all that needs to be said. To pretend to be able to say all that is necessary is what the modern reductiveness is all about. To think that when you name a person or a creature or a condition or a feeling, you have somehow done justice to it is foolhardy. I really resist and resent this claim that so many people make so readily now: "Oh, I understand." Mostly, we don't understand. We may know, but we don't understand, and can't prove that we do by talking.

BEATTIE: Maybe they really mean, consciously or subconsciously, "I want to understand it," or "I want to communicate . . ."

BERRY: Sure, or they mean, "I understand a little bit of it," or they mean, "I sympathize," or "I feel compassion," which is another matter altogether. That wonderful story "A River Runs Through It" is about that very thing, the necessity to love without understanding.

BEATTIE: Will you comment on your writing habits and on your views of the interconnectedness of all work?

BERRY: Well, if I *had* writing habits, it would be easier to comment on them. I have desires. The best way for me is to write half a day and work outdoors a half a day. But that's not always easy to do. Sometimes, other things have to be put first. But an ideal day for me in the winter would be to write through the mornings and get outdoors in the afternoon. In summer it would be good to do it the other way around, work outdoors in the morning and write in the afternoon. But, as I said, it's not always possible. I write with a pencil. I erase a lot and cross out a lot. Then, sooner or later, Tanya types a draft.

BEATTIE: You referred to Tanya as your best critic.

BERRY: She's my best critic, because she's my most faithful reader. I usually read my longhand drafts to her, and then she types them, so she knows what I've done. I don't agree with all her criticisms, but she's the first line of defense against my partialities and bad habits.

BEATTIE: Was she an English major as well at UK?

BERRY: Yes. She was also a music major for a while.

BEATTIE: Do you ever discuss what you write before you begin to write with her, or does she first see your work after you've completed it?

BERRY: Occasionally I have. We talked for instance, about that story, "Fidelity" before I wrote it. But I don't really like to talk about what I'm writing until I've finished my longhand draft. It's a bad thing to talk about what you're going to do.

BEATTIE: I've heard writers say that if they talk about writing beforehand that they can't write about it when they finally get down to doing it.

BERRY: I don't know whether that would be so with me or not, but I never have liked the idea of talking about what I'm going to do. The thing is to do it, and then talk if you want to. But if you do it, you don't need to talk. But I did talk about "Fidelity" a good bit with Tanya. Also, with my brother and sister-in-law, because it is a complicated plot and legal and medical issues were involved. My brother is a lawyer and my sister-in-law is a nurse, so I got some very necessary help.

BEATTIE: You have, in many places, written about the integrity of all types of work. Will you comment on that?

BERRY: If any kind of work is done well, it will have integrity. Work that's done poorly or done in fragments by various people who don't have responsibility for the result has no integrity.

BEATTIE: You've also talked about, or written about, craftsmanship having integrity if it's done for a useful purpose or if it's done for a purpose other than just for art's sake.

BERRY: Yes. I think that art comes about in answer to a need. At least, mine does. The community needs to talk about itself, needs to remember itself. It needs to recall the significant things that have happened, and to mull them over and figure out what the significance is. You see this working in the old ballads, in the Homeric epics, in the Greek tragedies. In my work, that need certainly figures. Not that the community has asked me to perform this function, but that I, as a member of the community, have these needs in mind. There's never a very direct correspondence, I think, between anything I've written and anything that really happened, or any actual place. But I write about an imagined community that's something like my actual community.

BEATTIE: What about the need for beauty itself, the human need for the aesthetic, even if it's not usable? I guess it's arguable whether a painting is *useful*.

BERRY: Well, you don't need to define use as utilitarian. All made things don't have to be commodities or tools. I mean a story, for instance, has no immediate utilitarian value, but it can inform the minds that use things. It's a part of the circumstance that finally determines how things will be used. A community is deeply dependent upon the stories available to it, and not just its own stories. The same thing would apply to painting, I would think, and painting had a carefully understood use for a long time. Paintings were a way to teach scripture. The churches of the Middle Ages were books in which the illiterate could read the stories of the Bible. Later, as in the Palazzo Veccio in Florence, the painters were painting their city's history to remind the people who held the public trust of the origins of that trust.

BEATTIE: Is there one piece of writing or one task that you would like to tackle more than any other?

BERRY: I have some projects lined up. I don't suppose it would be much fun talking about them. I'd like, before I die, to finish my series of Port Williams stories.

BEATTIE: Do you enjoy the type of writing, or the genre, in which you are engaged at the moment most, or do you have a preference?

BERRY: I never write without some pleasure. The pleasure of essay writing is diminished when you're trying to meet a deadline, or trying to fulfill an obligation that you're sorry you ever took on in the first place. But yes, I enjoy it. I like to meet the problems and work them out, and make the transitions, make the connections, figure out how I'm going to get two apparently disparate things into the same work.

BEATTIE: You've written repeatedly about your admiration for numerous writers from Homer, to Blake, to Yeats, to Gary Snyder. Are there Kentucky writers whom you particularly admire?

BERRY: My friends. I particularly admire my friends. I've learned a lot from them and things that they've done.

BEATTIE: Are you talking about Ed McClanahan and Gurney Norman and . . .

BERRY: And James Baker Hall. It would take a lot of talking even to acknowledge my debts to those three. James Still is a Kentucky writer whom I profoundly admire. I think he's one of the best short story writers that ever was. He's capable of such delicacy and at the same time such power, and he's a man who really has mastered the art, the craftsmanship. I admire Harriette Arnow, although not exactly for the same reason. I don't think she's as good a writer as James Still, but *The Dollmaker* is one of the great stories. It's one of the archetypal stories about our age, and one that everybody ought to know. Allen Tate is another Kentucky writer I admire, and one to whose work I often return.

BEATTIE: You refer to poetwatchers as the sort of people who hang onto poets' words as though poets are somehow more prophetic than other people.

BERRY: Did I say that?

BEATTIE: Well, something like that.

BERRY: People who see poets as privileged oddities.

BEATTIE: Even though poets may not be any more special or prophetic as human beings than are other people, don't you think that people are drawn to poets' particular articulations of the human condition, and often want to hear their own experiences voiced? And do you think that the act of publishing, of offering one's thoughts for public consumption, almost invites such recognition?

BERRY: Oh, it does. It invites it. The problem is that . . . Well, there are a number of problems. One is the problem of recognition that's not critical enough, that's too deferential. The other problem is that a poet is a maker of work, and the attention ought properly to be on the work. If more attention is paid to the person than to the work, then you've got an obvious absurdity. I think, myself, that writers are asked to talk too much. The thing that they are known for, if they're known, is writing. It seems curious to me that people who have already had something to say in writing should then be expected to talk, as if in talking they would make a contribution that they haven't already made.

BEATTIE: You've written strong essays on the lack of standards in education today and on the harm caused by teachers of literature attempting to remain objective. Do you see any hope that this will turn around in Kentucky or in the nation?

BERRY: Not very soon. The problem with the way literature is taught now is that people don't teach it as something that's of great importance. It's taught as a "subject" and as a specialty. I think a great change would come about if literature were taught by people who believed that it's of great importance to everybody, that it's necessary to everybody, that it says things that are indispensable to us.

BEATTIE: Morally as well as aesthetically?

BERRY: Yes. That it can be read for *both* instruction and delight. I've always read for instruction as well as for pleasure. It seems to me I've learned a lot from Shakespeare, Jane Austen, and other people, and not just about how to be a writer, but about how to be a person, how to conduct my life, how to be a husband and father and brother and son and friend and the other things that I've been.

The idea that education ought to be painless and fun all the time is something new. Nobody with sense and experience has ever believed that. Some things are hard to learn, and if they're going to be learned, the student has to submit to difficulty. And that, again, is an issue of faith. One teaches that way with the faith that a time will come when that student will be glad to have made the sacrifice. You can't learn a language easily. You can't learn to read Milton and Shakespeare and Chaucer easily. It takes some trouble, and there are rewards for that trouble. If there weren't, nobody would teach it. But you have to have authority as a teacher that does not come from an individual, but from a community that says, "These are beloved things, they must be passed on; these are the indispensably beloved, and everything will suffer if they are not learned."

I'm finding this dichotomy of objective and subjective less useful all the time. Literature does have a value that exceeds the value assigned to it by anybody out of whims or tastes. For want of a better standard, we have to use the standard of endurance. The so-called classics have meant a lot to a lot of people for a long time, and this is why we teach them. If they hadn't meant a lot to a lot of people for a long time, we wouldn't teach them, obviously.

My good teacher, Tom Stroup, told a class one time, "I love these things I'm teaching. If I didn't, why would I have devoted my life to them?" The justification of schools is the body of work that needs to be passed on to another generation. We claim now that we have schools in order to help all these people to have careers. But not much will get passed on in that way.

BEATTIE: In 1992 you received, from the University of Louisville, the Victory of Spirit Ethics Award. What did receiving that award and other such honors mean to you?

BERRY: Well, I'm grateful for honors. I don't know that they have much of an influence on me. I would have gone right ahead and done what I've done, whether I'd been honored or not, or so I hope. Honors warm your heart and make you grateful, and people are nice to you, and all that counts, but what interests you is not what you've already done. Or that's the way it is with me.

BEATTIE: Do you feel the same way about the process of writing a piece versus its publication? That it's much more exciting to write it than to see it completed?

BERRY: The excitement lasts a while. You have people you show your work to, and they're usually the people whose opinions matter the most to you. But by the time you've written a book and revised it and proofread the manuscript and gone over the copy-edited manuscript and read the galleys, you're pretty well worn out with it. You're very much ready to go on to something else. That is, if you're alive. I don't want to sound ungrateful for publication or honors, but if I'm ever going to amount to anything ever again, those things can't count very much. You don't say, "Oh, this confirms everything. Now I will live happily and then die happily." It doesn't work that way. If you're a living person, you're still underneath the same problems you were under when you started out, and you have the same obligation to work and get on.

January 3, 1993

BOOKS BY WENDELL BERRY

Nathan Coulter. Boston: Houghton Mifflin, 1960.

The Broken Ground. New York: Harcourt Brace, 1964.

A Place on Earth. New York: Harcourt Brace, 1967.

Openings. New York: Harcourt Brace, 1968.

Findings. Iowa City, Iowa: Prairie, 1969.

The Long-Legged House. New York: Harcourt Brace, 1969.

The Hidden Wound. Boston: Houghton Mifflin, 1970.

Farming: A Handbook. New York: Harcourt Brace Jovanovich, 1970.

The Unforeseen Wilderness. Lexington, Ky.: University Press of Kentucky, 1971.

A Continuous Harmony. New York: Harcourt Brace Jovanovich, 1972.

The Country of Marriage. New York: Harcourt Brace Jovanovich, 1973.

The Memory of Old Jack. New York: Harcourt Brace Jovanovich, 1974.

Sayings and Doings. Frankfort, Ky.: Gnomon, 1975.

The Unsettling of America. San Francisco: Sierra Club Books, 1977.

Clearing. New York: Harcourt Brace Jovanovich, 1977.

A Part. San Francisco: North Point, 1980.

Recollected Essays 1965-1980. San Francisco: North Point, 1981.

The Gift of Good Land. San Francisco: North Point, 1981.

The Wheel. San Francisco: North Point, 1982.

Standing By Words. San Francisco: North Point, 1983.

Collected Poems. San Francisco: North Point, 1985.

The Wild Birds. San Francisco: North Point, 1986.

Sabbaths. San Francisco: North Point, 1987.

Home Economics. San Francisco: North Point, 1987.

Remembering. San Francisco: North Point, 1988. 1990.

Sayings and Doings and An Eastward Look. Frankfort, Ky.: Gnomon, 1990.

What Are People For? San Francisco: North Point, 1990.

Harlan Hubbard: Life and Work. Lexington, Ky.: University Press of Kentucky, 1990.

The Discovery of Kentucky. Frankfort, Ky.: Gnomon, 1991.

Fidelity. New York: Pantheon, 1992.

A Consent. Monterey, Ky.: Larkspur, 1993.

Sex, Economy, Freedom, and Community. New York: Pantheon, 1993.

Entries. New York: Pantheon, 1994.

Watch With Me. New York: Pantheon, 1994.

Another Turn of the Crank. Washington, D.C.: Counterpoint, 1995.

The Farm. Monterey, Ky.: Larkspur, 1995.

BILLY C. CLARK

CLARK: I am Billy C. [Curtis] Clark, and I was born December the twenty-ninth, nineteen and twenty-eight, at Catlettsburg, Kentucky.

My mother's name was Bertha Gertrude Clark and my father was Mason Clark. Of course, my mother was a housewife, and my father was, among other things, a shoe cobbler in Catlettsburg.

BEATTIE: What do you remember about them growing up?

CLARK: Well, that's sort of a tough question. Of course, I left home when I was eleven years old to live alone in the City Building at Catlettsburg to put my way through the eighth grade and then through high school. If you ask what I remember, I think it was probably my dad's quietness and his tremendous talent that he had after only going to the first grade, and my mother for the tremendous heart that she had in wanting to do something for someone. The size of her heart, and Dad's talent with the fiddle and his quietness, are the two things I remember most about my parents.

BEATTIE: I remember a vignette in *A Long Row to Hoe* about your father making a shoe . . .

CLARK: For a clubfoot. When I grew up there, there were quite a number of club-footed people. I don't know why; I don't think that's still the case. But my dad was extremely gifted, not only in his mind, but with his hands, and he could make shoes. When people with club feet went to the store, they could only buy two pairs of shoes, because they couldn't wear one on their clubfeet. Dad, then, would make shoes out of leather, shoes that would fit their clubfeet. It didn't make a whole lot of difference to Dad; people could pay him in chickens or potatoes or whatever. Most people ended up wanting to pay, but they never had any money to pay.

BEATTIE: Was your mother that way as well?

CLARK: No, my mother was not. She was out of the Stuart clan, and is a great storyteller. She believed in spooks and omens, and in *A Long Row to Hoe*, if you read it, you know my mother was just the opposite of Dad as far as talking was concerned.

BEATTIE: You said she was from the Stuart clan. Any relation to any of the Kentucky writer Stuarts?

CLARK: Well, of course Jesse [Stuart] and I, we're blood kin. My great-grandmother was a Stuart, and my mother was the last of that Stuart clan to die. Uncle Mitch was Jesse's father.

BEATTIE: Did you know either set of grandparents?

CLARK: I only got to see one, my Grandma Clark. She was almost full-blooded

Shawnee Indian. I was young when she died. She died, the best I can remember, in either '41 or '42. We learned the thrill of the hills and the mountains from her. She knew all the herbs and all the cures. I have a very vivid memory of my Grandma Clark, but that's the only grandparent I got to see.

My mother had two sisters, and I got to know them. My father was one of seven children. He was the only boy, and I got to see all of his sisters but one. They're all non-living now.

There were four boys and four girls in my immediate family. I was the youngest boy, and now I have one brother living, and three sisters still alive. I have one sister still living in the Catlettsburg area.

BEATTIE: What was your childhood like? I know you talk about it in *A Long Row to Hoe*, but for anybody who hasn't read it, how would you characterize your childhood?

CLARK: Well, I've been told by so many people after reading my book and reading a lot of my other writings that I never had a childhood, but that's not really true at all. I had a very wonderful childhood, but I had a different childhood. It was a very difficult time. It was toward the end of the Depression, and there was little work for anyone, and I was the only one in my family to go to high school and finish and, as I say, I left home at the age of eleven and lived in the City Building. I spoke to a group of students in Catlettsburg yesterday, and told them that when I was there I walked a fourteen-mile trap line in the winter, seven miles up the creek and seven miles down, trying to stay in school. Then of the summers, of course, I ran trap lines in the Ohio and Big Sandy Rivers. Looking back, it was a hard, but an enjoyable, life. I have said, and I've been quoted many times—probably one of the great memories that I have—I really thought I'd rather starve to death before I grew up enough to earn my own keep. One thing I do remember about food, although I don't shop any today for food, my wife does that, was a loaf of bread cost seven cents and had twenty-one slices in it. If I could get one loaf of bread, I thought the world was all right. I could live. Today any weight that I gain it's because of bread. I love bread. I can live on a loaf of bread.

BEATTIE: What was your education like before you went to live on your own when you were eleven? What was it like going to school?

CLARK: Well, there were some enjoyable moments. It was hard in that I did not really have the clothing that most of the others had, and I was always ending up having lice. They were a great threat at that period of time, and it seems like I was always having to go to the principal's office, and he'd give me a little half of a gallon jug of coal oil. So, I always had the smell of coal oil on me, and those things were sort of embarrassing things that left marks on me. But I loved to learn, and I just had the great desire to remain in school. I was determined that I would go on. We were a terribly poor family, but we were a good, decent family. I saw so many like me that had dropped out, at even very early ages, and no one seemed to say anything. Just like they were not expected to get an education, and I was absolutely determined that I was going to go as far as I could.

BEATTIE: Where do you think that determination came from?

CLARK: I have absolutely no idea. I can only tell you that it was just as if I was born with that tremendous desire, not only to write, but to stay in school. I don't think I set out to prove anything, though I would be less than honest if I didn't tell you that while I was a Kentuckian through and through and wanted to go to the University of Kentucky and did, and graduated from the University of Kentucky, writing-wise, I don't think I learned a thing there, but I think the great thing was I was never expected to go, and I cannot separate even today whether I went for the great joy of actually learning, or whether it was just to show that I could go. I don't know how many people have gone through from Catlettsburg and up through the valley because they had read my autobiography, and they'd say, "Good golly, if Billy Clark can make it, I can make it, too." I think everyone is put on this earth to make a contribution to others, and maybe that's what it was all meant to be. I wish that I could know, or maybe I don't really want to know, but the desire was there as it was when they asked me how I came to write and I said, "You might as well ask me how I came to eat." That's the honest to God truth.

BEATTIE: Did either parent read to you as a child?

CLARK: My mother went to the second grade. My father went to the first grade. Their reading would have been tremendously limited. I never saw my father doing any more than sign his name. He may have been able to do more. I do know that they did not read any of my books, though they had all of my books.

I know that my mother could write some because when I was in Service and in the South Pacific, occasionally one of her letters would reach me; she got someone to address it. But I'm sure that anyone else, if they had gotten the letter, could not read it, because what Mom would do, Mom would write a sentence to say something as far along as she could go with the vocabulary she had. Now, if she got to the point where she didn't know how to finish it, she just quit, and she went on to something else. But knowing my mother, I could fill in the blanks, you know.

BEATTIE: When did you start reading on your own? Was that after you'd gone to school? Was that where you learned to read?

CLARK: Absolutely. There was no reading at home, or anything of that nature at all. As I say, I was the only one in my family to go to high school, so there was no great encouragement in academics.

BEATTIE: The elementary school that you attended, was this a one-room school?

CLARK: No. The school that I went to is Second Ward Grade School in Boyd County. It's one of the oldest still-standing schools in Kentucky. It still stands, but it's in terrible shape. It sits right up against the side of a hill there at Catlettsburg, and it's still standing because it's somewhere around two or three feet thick with bricks, and that's what makes it unique. It had eight rooms, one for each grade. They just had grade school from grades one to eight, and then high school from there on. Catlettsburg High School has been torn down, and it's all Boyd County High School now.

BEATTIE: When you left home to continue your education at age eleven, why age eleven? Was that a cut-off year from one grade to the next?

CLARK: Well, no. It really was not a cut-off at all. I don't know if you know Catlettsburg. It is historically probably the meanest river town along the Ohio. If you read some of the history of it, and of the Big Sandy Valley emptying Sandy [River] into the Ohio right there at Catlettsburg, that was flood country. You always had a flood every two years. There'd be a major flood. By major, I mean it would cover the town, and the people were always just so stubborn that they tried to ride the river out or they misjudged the rivers as long as they'd been with them, and think that this time it may not go that high. So the government would often send in skiffs or oaring boats to help move the people out of the water.

Well, I grew up on the river, and by the age of eleven I could handle what's known as a skiff. I hauled a joe boat [john boat] with the best of them, and everyone was needed, and so, I had a little job there with the city. They would let me use one of those boats at the age of eleven, and the only building in town tall enough that could not be totally covered with water was the City Building, and it was three stories high. They would let me stay on the third floor and I would tie the boat there outside the window on the third floor, and the water never got up into the third floor. So, it just occurred to me one time, and it happened to be at the age of eleven—it was very difficult for me to continue in school and to remain home where I was—I just thought, "I'm staying up here in this little concrete room and they may let me just stay here and do some work or something so I can go on and finish school." When I asked, they took it before the City Council, and agreed that they would let me live on the third floor. So, I stayed there and slept on a World War I army cot with one blanket. I stayed there . . . well, it's my home. It still stands—and when I go home, that's where I go. I go to the City Building, and the whole town recognizes that that's my home.

BEATTIE: Do you still have the same room there?

CLARK: Well, no, I don't stay up there in the room, but they have the little unique town clock, with four faces, and the place remains where I used to hang my muskrat hides. But when I look at it, it looks like it's home to me.

BEATTIE: It has to be highly unusual for an eleven-year-old to leave home. Were you self-sufficient, then, in terms of making your living?

CLARK: Well, sure. In the winter I trapped and got money from my hides. Also, it was a lively town. They had a men's jail in the first floor and a women's jail on the second floor, and I slept on the third floor. So, I had a little job of cleaning both jails, and they were always full with drunks. Then they had a volunteer fire department, and I made about a dollar-and-a-half a month by belonging to that, and then they had a town clock there that worked by weights. You cranked it up like a crank on a T-model Ford. You had to crank it till you cranked it up for almost three stories, and seven days, maybe, it would run. The clock had four faces, and every face had a different time, and when I hung my hides there, there were some times that they tied up the clocks so that they all stopped. Now, you know, it's a strange thing. It was quite all right that the clocks never had the correct time. That didn't bother many people. But if you let a clock stop, then there was trouble. The city paid three dollars for that job, but that job belonged to the fire chief. Now, he sublet it to me, and I did all the work and all the cranking, and he gave me a dollar-and-a-half a month, and he kept a dollar-and-a-half, so I got by all right.

They had one or two little restaurants in town, one in particular, where I would go over at night and mop the floors. Whatever they had leftover—sometimes from maybe a day, or maybe two or three days—whatever was leftover they left on a little table for me to eat. I'd take the beans that were sour or whatever it was, you know. If you're hungry, you take anything, and so I'd take whatever was left, and I'd take it up the third floor, and I sat up there and ate just as happy as I could be.

BEATTIE: Did you have friends or did you ever get to play when you were out on your own?

CLARK: I don't know what the connotation of play may be. From a very early age I was either on the rivers or I was in the hills, one or the other, either trapping or hunting. Then, of course, I was very active in school. I earned four letters at Catlettsburg High

School in basketball, baseball, and football, so I was very active in sports. But as far as just playing like I see children playing now, no, no, I had none of that.

BEATTIE: How often did you see your family during those years?

CLARK: Well, if my mother had had her way, none of us would have ever left home. It worried and grieved her, and if we would have all stayed there and died of old age, it would have pleased her. Looking back, she didn't stand in my way when I left home. Either she understood what I was trying to do, or maybe she'd been worn down with so many children in times so hard, and we were always all hungry, but for quite a period of time after I left she would come over in town in the evening and I would hear her. She would holler for me down on the sidewalk, and I would look out the window, and she would check on me, and sometimes I'd go down. What really worried Mom more than anything was that I might fall out of the third floor window. But I saw her all the time, every two or three days, or maybe once a week, and I always kept in touch. She always knew where I was.

BEATTIE: What happened after you graduated from high school?

CLARK: Well, I had, as I say, three brothers. Of course, the war [World War II] was over then—all my brothers had been in Service and been in the war—and I felt the obligation to at least go in Service. There was no draft then or anything, so I went in Service in the South Pacific, and then came back and went to the University of Kentucky.

BEATTIE: Gurney Norman, in his introduction to your book *Song of the River,* talks about your having written a book when you were fourteen.

CLARK: That's right.

BEATTIE: Did you write that when you were living by yourself?

CLARK: Yes. I wrote that really at the end of my freshman year in high school, almost at the end of my freshman year. Before I finished my sophomore year, I was through with the book. It really started as a short story, so, I'd written it even earlier than that. But, of course, I grew up on the river. I fished [in the area of] the catfish, the legendary catfish, Scrapiron. There were shanty boats all along the river then. I spent many, many a night on the shanty boats down there with the old people, and they're all gone, of course, now. But the story came to me, and I did write it at that early age. I've often said that it may be that of all the books and all of my writings, this may be the only book that I cannot rewrite. It's the simplicity of the book. It was written at a time when I was not conscious of writers or editors or the world outside of my own little world. The writing in that book expresses the total freedom of that. If the book has any strength, and so many say that it does have, it's within the simplicity of the language. I had written great numbers of short stories and poetry before I wrote *The Song of the River.*

BEATTIE: When did you start writing on your own?

CLARK: Oh, I've always been doing that. When I went to the University of Kentucky, I took I don't know how many manuscripts with me. This [*The Song of the River*] was one of them, and somehow a poem that I had written was published by the editor in the *Kentucky Kernel,* the newspaper [at the University of Kentucky] at that time. I was called in by Bill [William S.] Ward, and he said that he and others had seen that poem in there and wanted to know if I had any other manuscripts. I said, "Yes, I do have," and he said, "Well, would you have any objection to letting one of the professors here read them?" I said, "Well, no, I would not have," and then he mentioned the name of a beautiful human being, Hollis Summers. I met Hollis Summers then, and he wanted to know if he could take that manuscript, and I told him that that would be fine with me. He said, "How many have you got?" and I said, "How many do you want?" So I took him over batches of them, and he asked me if I had submitted them anywhere, and I told him no, that I had not. I had never submitted anything. He didn't tell me where to submit, but he told me that he thought that I should, and so I just thought, "Well, I'll do that." So, I just started looking in books and seeing the names of publishing companies. I sent the manuscripts out, and they just started being accepted, just like that.

BEATTIE: Where did you first send your manuscripts, do you remember?

CLARK: Mostly the first ones I submitted were short stories and poetry. A great number of poems appeared in the *New York Times,* and then the short stories seemed to be going about everywhere. Then I submitted *Song of the River* to one of the oldest literary publishing houses in the world, G. P. Putnam's, and they kept the book for so long that they finally wrote and told me that they regretted keeping it that long, but it was a terribly difficult decision, and they wanted to keep it a little longer. I was absolutely delighted. Well, they kept it maybe three or four more weeks, and then I got it back, and they said they were reluctantly returning it, and they wanted to know if I had any other book manuscript that I would care to show them. I told them I did have, and they said, "Well, we'd love to see it," and so, in three days and nights, I wrote the little book called *Trail of the Hunter's Horn.* I sent that and, of course, they got it, and they took it. In the meantime, I had sent this manuscript to another old, established publishing house, Thomas Y. Crowell. So, when Putnam's immediately accepted *Trail of the Hunter's Horn,* they said, "We would like for you to return *Song of the River.* We made a mistake. We'd like to have that book, too." Well, I never dreamed Crowell would take it, and I said, "Well, okay, I'll send it on along then." I waited around a couple of weeks, and I got a letter from Crowell saying they thought it was a classic, and that they wanted it, and so Putnam's felt very bad about that, and I did, too, and I told Putnam's that I had sent it to Crowell thinking it would be returned. They didn't return it, and Crowell had taken it, so, I felt rather badly. So, I sat down and wrote *Mooneyed Hound* and sent it to Putnam's, and they took it. I had three books coming out in that one year.

BEATTIE: How quickly was that third book written?

CLARK: Oh, that took me a little longer, about a week, and remember it was almost seven years before I wrote another. So, they all didn't come that easy, but at any rate, it created somewhat of a problem, a very happy problem. Crowell felt that they had the rights to my next book, and Putnam's felt they had the rights. The next book to come along, if memory serves me right, was the one that Walt Disney bought the film rights for, *Goodbye Kate.* In the meantime, I had worked on *A Long Row to Hoe,* and that was brought out by Crowell, and then *Kate* went to Putnam's.

BEATTIE: This was still when you were very young, wasn't it?

CLARK: I was still young. I wasn't twenty-seven, I don't think; I was just turning twenty-seven at that time. I had published a great number of short stories and poems before that period, but then I'd written *A Long Row to Hoe* for a tremendously long time, almost seven years. It was a tremendously large manuscript, a huge, huge manuscript. I sent it out, and I remember my editor, Bill Poole, told me how excited they were about the book. One of the editors of *Time Magazine* had read it, and wanted to review it before publication, and of course, they did, and they chose it as one of the best books of 1960. But Poole told me the book was so large. He said, "We'll be lucky to find someone that can carry it, let alone buy it. We're going to have to try to get it down to at least a hundred thousand words." Then came the great job of trying to cut and trying to cut and cut and cut, and I was worried that I might lose all the material I took out of there.

BEATTIE: You talked about having started writing when you were very young. Do you know what made you want to write?

CLARK: I did not have publication in mind when I first started, because I didn't have any conception of anything of that nature. I tread kind of light here, because I've heard so many people say, "Well, you know, I just write for myself." I think that's wonderful when they say that, but I've come to know that when you do say that, that's okay, but if you let someone else read it, then you're obligated to communicate, so I can tell you that first and foremost, I write for myself, as far as being pleased with what I do. Though I've never had any difficulty working with editors. I've never had a great deal of cutting on any of my works, but I knew nothing about publishing until I reached the University of Kentucky, quite frankly, and Hollis Summers was the one that encouraged me to submit material.

BEATTIE: Do you think reading when you were young helped give you a sense of the language?

CLARK: We had no library in Catlettsburg when I grew up. There was no library in the grade school. I did no reading whatsoever, other than just what we had in the little textbooks, and I cannot even remember what they were about. In high school, the library, as I remember it, was composed of just some books that maybe people in the town had given. So I really didn't do any reading that amounted to anything till I went to the University of Kentucky.

BEATTIE: And storytellers were important to you?

CLARK: Most of the stories I heard were ghost stories where the old people would gather at night, and we would sit around and listen to them. Of course, Kentucky is a land of storytellers. Anyone from Kentucky has heard stories and stories and stories growing up. Then we had no television and really, while there were a number of radios around, I can remember the first one we had featured earphones, and everyone was always fighting, trying to listen to something. Then we did have a radio without earphones, but I never listened to any, and so really, my great hunger for reading came at a later period. There was no influence anywhere from any writers, nor was there any teacher that said, "You ought to write," or anyone that said, "You know, you ought to write. You ought to do this or ought to do that." The only thing I can say to you is what I said earlier, that writing came like a hunger, like eating a meal, and that is the truth. When I saw something, I wanted to put it into words. I wanted to write about it and not just talk about it.

BEATTIE: Creativity, where do you think the instinct for it comes from?

CLARK: I remember Hollis Summers told me that I was the first and only natural-born writer that he had ever met. I'm saying that I do think good writers are born, just as Mozart composed a symphony at the age of four. Now, we both know that he didn't have time to get any schooling at the age of four to write that, and we both know people that cannot carry a tune in a bucket and others that can pick up any music or instrument you hand them and they can take to it, or they can do the same thing with an automobile. I think writing is the same way. I think that you can learn to write, but I think in storytelling and in writing, the great ones are born. You can learn techniques, but I think the gift is a given thing.

BEATTIE: You talked about going to the University of Kentucky. Did you major in English there?

CLARK: I majored in English only because they just pushed me into that. Several of my friends were over in engineering, and as rugged as I am, and with my rugged features, everyone thought I was in the College of Engineering. And when I'd say, "Well, I'm over in English," they'd say, "You've got to be kidding." It got to where it was kind of embarrassing for me. But my professors just all insisted—Hollis Summers and all the others—and, of course, I loved literature. So, I just stayed where I could read. That's where I ended up. I really didn't care what my major was.

BEATTIE: Did you have teachers that were particularly influential?

CLARK: No, not in writing. In fact, I remember a couple of professors there that told me that they should not even permit me to come into English composition class because there was no way in the world I'd ever be able to pass composition. On the other hand, I had one to tell me that I was the closest thing to Mark Twain that he had ever read, and finally a past president of the University said, "You're wasting his time by requiring 101 or 102. Exempt him from them."

BEATTIE: Why did those who thought you wouldn't do well in 101 say that?

CLARK: Well, I think their world consisted of semicolons and periods and commas, and things like that, the things that probably turned more writers away from writing by teaching them the fear of writing. I can't even remember if I went through composition there; I don't think I did. I never learned to diagram a sentence. I can't diagram a sentence today, and I must say, one should not learn to diagram a sentence. I'm not saying that no one should learn that, I'm just telling you how it is with me. The word comes first, and if I'm anything as a writer, I'm a storyteller, and you don't find a great number of storytellers. So much of the things that you see being written today have a hook, they have something to hang them on. Either at the end of a chapter they add their little bits of obscenity, or there's always some gimmick, there's always some hook. There are those out there writing, but it's difficult for them to get published. So, we've become a world of publishing commercial writers. That's what it amounts to, something that sure-fire sells for a short period of time, and then dies. The real tragedy is that there is no story, there is no heart, there is no spirit, there is none of that. Young people who watch television, I worry that they may never know what good stories are, and so, we may never get these young people or good stories back, because they don't read the classics. We don't require them to read the classics, and it worries me a great deal. Call this a plug or whatever you want to call it, but I say it because it's in my heart to say. The reason that I gave the Jesse Stuart Foundation permission to reprint and keep in print into perpetuity my works, is simply because by reprinting such work, the Foundation is bringing good literature, good stories, back.

People don't read much anymore. Look at the commercial magazines that are out there, and leaf through them and see how many of them take poetry now, or how many take short stories. The great tragedy in poetry in the educational systems is we're supposedly teaching poetry without teaching form. I don't care if a person wants to choose free verse, that's perfectly all right, but they ought to also know the form. They ought to know what a sonnet is composed of, what ballads are composed of, and what blank verse is. Today, teachers just tear into teaching poetry and turn students loose, and students think that the only thing that makes a poem is to separate sentences. I've been arguing forever that, at least in the high schools, we need to start teaching form. Teach and let students study Shakespeare and let them study Milton and let them study Keats and Shelley, and then along with that, teach students what the sonnets and what the variations of them are, and teach them about metric feet and all those other things. People ought to have the freedom to write any way they want to write, but at least they'll know what they're choosing and why they're choosing it.

If we could just say to young people, "Look, you're going to spend the first five years learning to do nothing but to study the forms of poetry before you're going to be permitted to put a line of poetry down," what a wonderful thing it would be. Trouble is, none of these young people seem to want to serve an apprenticeship. In education, we've lowered our standards to where it's frightening how little the standards are today. Students are not required to do a great deal, and I've been in education for many, many, many, many years, and we ought not to be lowering standards, we ought to be raising them up.

I used to, when I was teaching more than what I do now, like to walk into the classroom and say, "If your life depended on it, who in this classroom would be willing to know when and when not to use a comma? How many of you know that?" Not a hand would go up. I think this is one of the real tragedies in our teaching of English; we should never permit students to get through school without knowing how to use punctuation, because it's part of writing. The idea and the story is first, and then you need to know how to put it in some sort of order. Then I would tell students if you don't do something now, you're going to go all the way through life being whipped by a comma when you could take, say, a week, and say, "Okay, this week I'm going to learn how to use a comma." You should not permit students to get through school without knowing when and when not to use one, but I'm telling you, the standards are just not there. You don't teach content and punctuation separately; they're one and the same. They're all part of writing, the grammatical end, and the storytelling end.

I founded a publication for high school students for the Department of Education in Virginia, so I'm quite pleased with what the high school students are doing there. I'm getting some fine pieces of work.

BEATTIE: What is the program that you started?

CLARK: I founded *Virginia Writing Magazine,* and it's the number one educational publication in America today, and in Canada. It has won nine national awards. It is twenty-one years old. I publish prose and poetry and art work of high school students, and I use about five or ten percent of teachers' works in Virginia. I get hundreds and hundreds of manuscripts in a year, and some of these young people are really doing a wonderful job. I'm in touch with so many teachers. It's used as a supplementary text by almost two hundred high schools in Virginia.

BEATTIE: How do you think creative writing should be taught?

CLARK: If we're talking about writing stories and writing poetry, first of all, I think there has to be a desire with the student to do that. The best courses I've ever taught have been with graduate students, quite frankly, but when I think that I wrote this book at the age of fourteen, there's no reason why I should say, "Don't let anyone in a classroom that's younger than that." But first of all, I think there has to be a desire. I don't think everyone writes equally; maybe they might just not want to, that may be not their interest. So, I think if you have a creative writing class, you should have only students in there who want to be there. I think you need to turn them loose, and I think they need to know that all pieces of writing ought to be, to a great extent, autobiographical to be worth the paper they're on, and I think you need to let them know that most of the stories will end up being in their own backyard. When they learn that all the stories are basically about a handful of themes, when they learn that human beings do not cry in any given language, or are not hungry in any given way, that these things have a universality of theme, and when they learn that stories don't have to be written with the characters or a location in Boston or New York, then they may learn to write well. I can only share with students how it's been for me, and then I think if they're meant to write and want to write, they will go on and they'll write until hell freezes over; nothing is going to stop them. The rewriting, I think, will determine the writer in the end.

BEATTIE: Back to your experience at the University of Kentucky. What about reading? Did majoring in English open up worlds of literature for you?

CLARK: Oh, yes. I'd say probably the greatest thing I got out of college was reading, not so much what was assigned to me to read, but the availability of things to read. I could choose my own books. I had to read the ones they assigned, and I did do that, and learned from them, too. I tried to study why I didn't like a particular thing on my own. That's the great thing I got out of it.

BEATTIE: Do you remember books that you particularly liked, or authors?

CLARK: Oh well, of course, Melville and Twain and Kipling and Stevenson. I think Milton was my first choice, and, of course, a lot of Shakespeare and Keats. I think that still, today.

On the modern end, I read many of them, and my choice was Frost and then Albert Stewart, a great amount of Jesse Stuart. When he was at his best, he was as good as any of them.

BEATTIE: What about Jesse Stuart? Did you know him?

CLARK: Oh, yes, I knew Jesse. Jesse was the best man at my wedding, thirty-seven years ago. He never read a manuscript of mine. We were very, very close personal friends.

I got to know Jesse through his father, Uncle Mitch. Long before I even knew Jesse, Uncle Mitch made his pilgrimage at least once a year to see my mother, and I just knew that was Uncle Mitch coming out. When I was a young boy, Uncle Mitch took a shine to me, and always when he would leave, he'd say, "Now, Berthy, you let me take Billy home with me. I want Billy to come live with me." But, of course, Mom would have no part of that. I learned much, much later about Jesse, but I learned of Jesse through Uncle Mitch, and of course, even today, I favor their father, Uncle Mitch Stuart, more than Jesse or Jim or any of the Stuarts. My mother was the spitting image of all the Stuarts. Of course, her mother was a Stuart, and she just favored them all.

I guess it must have been when writing had become of great interest, maybe when I went to the University, when I first associated with Jesse, and when we became tremendously close and great friends. Uncle Mitch was still living then, and I would go visit Uncle Mitch in those years before he died, and Jesse and I would spend days talking. He was a tremendous man, a tremendous writer, and he produced a tremendous amount of work in all areas, and he had a heart as big as a mountain, and he went for many years without near the appreciation that he should have been getting.

BEATTIE: After you got out of college, what did you do?

CLARK: Well, when I got out of college, I returned home. I went to the university, and had to leave on two or three occasions, because I was trying to keep my mother and father at the time. They were both very old, and I was trying to earn a little money here and there to try to keep them. Sometimes it would get so tough that I would have to go home and work a little while and then come back, but after that, it settled down. I came home and I took a summer job with Ashland Oil Refining Company in their bottled gas department, and, of course, they knew of my writing, and they asked me to come into the publications department. So I did technical writing for almost seven years for Paul Blazer, who founded the company.

BEATTIE: How much had you published by then?

CLARK: Oh, four or five books, maybe, and I'd published poems and things quite frequently in the *New York Times* and some other newspapers and journals.

Boston University contacted me and was trying to get me to consider coming there to spend a little bit of time as one of the writers-in-residence on their campus. I can remember Dr. Howard Gotlieb there. We are very close friends now, of course. I chose Boston, as Boston University is the world's greatest repository for twentieth-century authors.

BEATTIE: Gotlieb called you one of the greatest southern writers.

CLARK: Well, what happened was, I'd asked Howard Gotlieb, "I cannot figure why in the world you people want me to come to Boston of all places." I said, "I'm so different from other authors you're interested in." He responded with one of the finest answers I've ever gotten in my life. He said, "Did it never occur to you that that may be just why we'd like to have you here?" They were always extremely high on my writings. I found out later that asking me to be a writer-in-residence might be one enticement to my making some sort of an agreement for my manuscripts, because they thought out of the twentieth century, that I would be one of those writers that would come out remembered.

At any rate, Paul Blazer knew about [Boston University's offer], and it worried him that I might leave Kentucky. A great friend of mine that's still living today, Dr. Frank Dickey, was president of the University of Kentucky, and so, Paul Blazer said, "Before you make any decision about leaving," he said, "I'd like to see you leave the company, because you're a writer, and here you have to give too much of your time. But before you leave Kentucky, would you talk to Frank Dickey?" I said, "Well, I'll be glad to do that, Mr. Blazer," because Mr. Blazer was the only genius I've ever had the privilege to meet. So, I did, and when I did, then of course, Frank Dickey said, "We don't want you to leave Kentucky. Come here as a writer-in-residence." And I did. I came there as the first paid writer-in-residence the university ever had.

BEATTIE: How old were you then?

CLARK: I was a young fellow. I may have been in my thirties. I was impressed with Dr. Dickey and his desire and the things that he said about me and my writing, so I told him that I would come. I was going to stay two years, and then I still thought I might sneak off to Boston. But two years after I came there Dr. Dickey took over the Southern Association of Colleges, and John Oswald came out of California to be the president, and the first week he was there he called me in and we became great friends. I was really impressed with him, and he asked me as a personal favor to remain there. So, I stayed there then, and so many things happened. John Oswald and Ellis Hartford were the fathers of the [Kentucky] Community College System, and Charlie Wethington, at that time, was a personal friend of mine, working on his doctorate, and I was doing some work for Ellis Hartford, and Dr. Hartford said, "Well, if you don't want to stay on the campus, what I'd like for you to do is to go from community college to community college building continuing education programs." He said, "Go wherever you want and do whatever you want to do," and so, I studied about it a long time, and I ended up as a full professor at UK, and I ended up spending eighteen years there, on and off campus, at Somerset Community College, and here and there for a while, wherever Ellis Hartford wanted me to go. So, I did a lot of PR.

BEATTIE: Did you get married during this period?

CLARK: I was married when I went back [to the University of Kentucky] as writer-in-residence. I married Ruth Bocook, who is from Catlettsburg, too, of course. I had already graduated from high school before she went; I was six years older than Ruth. She knew of me, but didn't know me at the time we met. I was working on *A Long Row to Hoe*. I'm not that good a typist—I still punch and peck—but I was looking for someone to do some typing for me. I was told that Ruth was a very fine typist, and she was a secretary at the Christian Church in Ashland. She often came in the evenings to this little restaurant in Catlettsburg, so I went in there one evening when she was there, and I was carrying the manuscript piles, huge things. I just thought, "Well, there will be no problem with those; she will be delighted to type." I had already published some books. So I asked her, and she turned me down flat. Out of disappointment I turned to go, and when I did, not on purpose, I dropped the manuscript, and the script went everywhere. She helped me pick it up, but she said she didn't think she'd be interested in typing for me. I managed to be there several evenings later, and she agreed to help me type it.

BEATTIE: What changed her mind?

CLARK: I don't know; maybe my being persistent. Then I asked her for a date, and, of course, she turned me down several times, and then finally agreed she would have a date with me. The first time I asked her to marry me I thought, "Well, there is no problem at all." I asked her, and she turned me down flat. I thought, "Gosh, there is no way," but she still dated me. I didn't ask her anymore for quite a while, and then finally when I asked her again, she told me that she would.

I was driving a little '47 Plymouth, and I had manuscripts everywhere. Where the sun had come through the window it had faded them; some of them had been there a long time. She kept fussing at me, and she'd say, "What are you going to do with them?" And I'd say, "Well, I don't know, I'll send them out one day." She said, "If I type them up, will you send them out?" I said, "If you type them up, you send them out, and if you have any luck with them, then you can keep the money." I don't know over what period of time, but she sold all twenty-one. All twenty-one of them were published, but I cannot remember who kept the money.

I've two children. I have a son and I have a daughter and I have three grandchildren.

BEATTIE: When were the children born and what are their names?

CLARK: Well, I have Billy Junior. Billy is thirty-four, and Melissa is twenty-five. Melissa has three children. I have two grandsons, one six, and one will be four in June. I'm grieving now that I've been away from them since last Tuesday. It just broke my heart.

BEATTIE: Do they live near you in Virginia?

CLARK: They're in Virginia. I'm like my mother; I want all my children around me. I eventually left the University of Kentucky because I had been contacted by the Virginia secretary of education. In Kentucky I had founded a little publication called *Kentucky Writing* that's still being published by Somerset Community College. I stayed long enough just to get it funded, not long enough to really bring it to where I wanted it. I was contacted by the secretary of education, Don Finley, in Virginia, in Richmond, because some people had seen or had heard of my philosophy. I had made a statement. It was carried by several national papers. An editor at the *Chicago Tribune* was talking to me one day, and I said that I was so grateful that I had just been given the gift to write and the great desire to write, and I had been so fortunate to publish so much. I said that I thought these things were all well and good for me, but if I really was that grateful, I ought to be in some way showing that appreciation by paying some of it back. So, I said, "You know, I'd like to try to devote more time to young people, to the ones that want to write so that they will not have to, as I did at their age when I sent my material out, compete against the finest writers in America, although they were much older than me." I competed against Hemingway, Steinbeck, Faulkner, and all of them, you know. So, I thought, why not come up with a literary publication then, for young people, that would give them an opportunity to publish? Don't expect finished work, but look at the ones that show promise, and have an outlet for them. My comment got around, and it got into Virginia. Then my first issue of *Kentucky Writing* came out, a nice issue, and I got a call from him wanting to know if I would come to Virginia to have a talk with him about something they had in mind there in education. I was really struggling for that first issue in Kentucky, I could not get the funding, and they told me that the funding was there in Virginia. I ended up going over there. I was told, "We'll fund you and we'll also create a position for you wherever you want to go." I chose Longwood [College] because of General Sam Wilson, the assistant secretary of defense under [George] Bush when Bush was head of the defense department before he became president. I knew General Sam, and General Sam came from Rice, Virginia, which is five miles from Longwood. I left UK in nineteen and eighty-five, and went into Virginia and founded *Virginia Writing,* and then I founded the *Virginia Writing* Creative Writing Workshop for high school students, which became the most prominent workshop in Virginia.

BEATTIE: How does that workshop work? Is it in several locations or one place?

CLARK: I'm headquartered at Longwood College. I'm also a writer-in-residence at Longwood College. The first couple of years or so I lectured all over Virginia. In Virginia I give an annual creative writing workshop one week for teachers and one week for high school students.

BEATTIE: What do you think has made *Virginia Writing* so successful? I mean, why is it successful where maybe similar publications in other states were not?

CLARK: For one thing, it is a top-quality publication. You can compare it with any magazine in America for the layout, for the paper, or for the printing. Nothing has been slighted. It's a beautiful publication. I have the funding to do that. I have the support of the school systems. So many of the teachers have their students working, they live and breathe with the hopes that they may one day make *Virginia Writing.* I will get five thousand manuscripts in two semesters. For one issue I may pick maybe sixty pieces, maybe four pieces of prose and the rest poetry. So, I'm taking the best of the best.

BEATTIE: Did you ever feel that you had to choose whether to call yourself a novelist or a short story writer?

CLARK: Sometimes you'll start on what you think is a short story and it ends up being a novel. Sometimes what you think may be longer may end up being shorter. I feel very comfortable with the short story, and I feel very comfortable with the novel. I feel very comfortable, quite frankly, with poetry. No, I have two new books coming out. They are *By Way of the Forked Stick,* and another one called *To Find the Bird Song.* I have almost finished another [book] that I just have a working title for. It's difficult to get a collection of short stories published on a national level with a major publishing company. Well, Putnam's only published three people in the short-story line: Pearl Buck and Nabokov and me were the only three that they ever published. I was in good company, and they brought out my *Sourwood Tales,* which was highly reviewed all over America.

BEATTIE: Because you had such good success just sending your manuscript off to publishers and then, I assume, got editors for those volumes, did you ever have to have an agent?

CLARK: No, I never did, because I had such close contact with editors. The real tragedy is that unless you have really proven yourself as a money-making or a publishable writer, you can't get to an agent. The top agents or the good agents that don't charge and have the contacts, they won't take on a new writer.

BEATTIE: What do you think distinguishes your writing, or what do you hope to achieve in your work?

CLARK: I don't know, except to say that I'm a storyteller, and I love to tell stories, so, I think all of my works do tell a story.

BEATTIE: What are your writing habits?

CLARK: I like to write poetry in longhand, but I type short stories and novels on a typewriter. Some days I can write and it's real legible, and I can read it easy, and then other times I cannot read a thing I've written, so on a typewriter I always can see what I write, and it's good and clear. I'm not a sleeper; three or four hours a night. I love to work early in the morning. Early in the morning you've got the entire world to yourself. I like to try to write two hours or better. If you want to write, you've got to write, and once I really get into a piece, sometimes I almost go around the clock. I'll go to my room, and it is not unusual for me not even to come out. Ruth will bring me sandwiches or tea or something, and I have at times even slept in my room, just working night and day. I just work feverishly that way, until I finish at least a first draft. I like to work on one thing at a time. I can totally lose myself in my work until nothing bothers me or interferes, noise or anything else. So, I'm very fortunate, and I appreciate that. I almost came into the world writing, and I certainly hope to go out of the world writing.

May 14, 1993

BOOKS BY BILLY C. CLARK

Song of the River. New York: Crowell, 1957.

Riverboy. New York: Putnams, 1958.

The Mooneyed Hound. New York: Putnams, 1958.

The Trail of the Hunter's Horn. New York: Putnams, 1958.

A Long Row to Hoe. New York: Crowell, 1960.

Useless Dog. New York: Putnams, 1961.

Goodbye Kate. New York: Putnams, 1964.

The Champion of Sourwood Mountain. New York: Putnams, 1966.

Sourwood Tales. New York: Putnams, 1968.

Tom Berthiaume / Parallel Productions

MICHAEL DORRIS

DORRIS: My name is Michael Anthony Dorris. I was born in Louisville, January thirtieth of 1945. My mother's name is Mary Bridget Burkhardt. She worked at Colgate Palmolive as a keypunch operator. My father's name was Jim Leonard Dorris, and he was in the army and was a first lieutenant at the time of his death, which was 1947, I believe. They met when he was stationed at Fort Knox, just after the outbreak of World War II. My mother's family is from Henderson, [Kentucky].

My grandfather [mother's father] was a carpenter, and he also worked for the Louisville and Nashville Railroad. They moved from Henderson up here [Louisville] when my mother was about five or six, and they lived in the West End. They were Irish and German and lived in the neighborhood where everybody else was Irish and German.

My father was born in the state of Washington. He was mostly a native American, a little bit French, a little bit English, but mostly Modoc and Coeur d'Alene tribes, and I think the first thing he did out of high school was enlist in the army. He was at Pearl Harbor when it was bombed, and then he was sent to Europe. On the way there he was at Fort Knox.

BEATTIE: What do you recall about your maternal grandparents?

DORRIS: Well, my grandmother, my mother's mother, whose name was Alice Burkhardt, originally Manion, I lived with throughout the time I lived in Louisville, and I recall her as being a very dominant person in the household. You always had to bring her something if you were a guest, or else she'd stay in her room. She was the loudest presence not in a room that you could ever imagine. I remember her being very affectionate as, you know, all the things you remember about a grandmother.

My father's mother is still alive, and still lives in the same house that she did all her life; she still lives alone. She is ninety-five, I think, and is also a very, very tough woman who has had a lot of hardship in her life. She has had three sons and two of them are deceased. But she was a nurse for most of her life and has a lot of friends, and dresses up in organdy formal gowns and marches around small, drafty VFWs.

BEATTIE: Your father died at a very young age. You were just two years old?

DORRIS: He died in an automobile accident in Europe. That was after the war was over. He had chosen to stay in Europe.

BEATTIE: What do you recall about aunts and uncles on either side of your family? I know you've written about your family's being very close, and of being raised by aunts in Louisville.

DORRIS: My mother's sister, Marion Burkhardt, still lives with my mother here in town, and she, for years, was the budget officer for the City of Louisville. She was a Democratic precinct captain, and was very involved in politics. She is a person that throughout my adolescence I fought with all the time, and we were equally matched, basically. My mother always tried to be a pacifist in the household, and my aunt was a very strong, opinionated thinker, as am I.

My mother is the youngest of four. The other aunt who lived in Louisville is deceased; her name was Katherine. My mother's oldest sister, Virginia Burkhardt, lives in New York, where she went at the age of forty, got a job selling tickets to *South Pacific,* and quit her job in an insurance company here [Louisville]. She made a whole career, and so for the next forty-five years she rose in the Schubert Organization and became the highest woman executive handling, oh, fifteen to twenty million dollars a year of business in sales, and she still lives in New York and I see her all the time. My mother and her sisters are all in their eighties now, and very healthy.

BEATTIE: I understand you attended St. Xavier High School here in Louisville, but where did you go to elementary school?

DORRIS: I went to a variety of places. I went to kindergarten at Holy Spirit Elementary School, and then I went one year, I think, to the Sacred Heart Model School. Then I went to Holy Spirit off and on for a couple of years, and when I say off and on, part of the time I went to the West End. I then went to a place that no longer exists; it's called Catholic Country Day which, I think, got absorbed into Louisville Country Day, and I went on a scholarship. I was there for three years, didn't like it at all, and then transferred to St. X, and ultimately graduated from there.

BEATTIE: What was your childhood like?

DORRIS: I was a very adult-oriented child, which is not something that makes you popular with other children. I didn't have many friends. My family always talked to me as an adult, and I did things with them, and we went to movies together and everything from a very early age, and I was a good boy. I was an adorable little boy. I think I felt a sense of responsibility for the hardships that my family had. We didn't have much money. My mother and I had a government pension from my father's death, and there was some insurance money that went towards buying our house.

My aunt worked for the city and then ultimately, after the Democrats lost, she worked as the executive secretary for Wilson Wyatt [former Louisville mayor and Kentucky lieutenant governor] until she and he both retired, well into their late seventies. So, you know, they struggled, and I was not oppressed by that, but very aware of our circumstances, and at the same time, I never felt deprived of anything. They always absolutely supported anything that I wanted to do, and thought that it was great, and they were encouraging, even if they didn't agree with it. So, in the respect of my family, I had a happy childhood.

In respect of social life, I wasn't very good at sports. I didn't have close friends. I spent a lot of time alone, read all the time, memorized poetry on my own. I used to write away for travel brochures all over the country. I also had seventy-five pen pals around the world. There was something called the International Friendship Week in Boston. For twenty-five cents you could get a pen pal anyplace, and I got very greedy and I had seventy-five, many of whom, again, I'm still in touch with. We're all middle-aged now.

BEATTIE: You were talking about reading books so much as a child: do you remember reading things that were your favorites? What sort of things did you like to read?

DORRIS: The first book I ever spent all night reading, and I was so pleased with myself for having done that, was *A Connecticut Yankee in King Arthur's Court.* I was pretty young; I would say I was maybe about nine or ten. But I remember stretching it out and taking my time, because I wanted to technically read all night, and it was part ego. I read everything. We lived, and my mother and aunt still do, within walking distance of the Crescent Hill Library, and I would go there certainly every day during the summer, and two or three times a week during the school year, using my aunt's library card so I could get adult books as well as children's books. I would say I made a fair dent in the collection that existed at that time.

BEATTIE: When you were a child did you like to or did you ever experiment with writing yourself?

DORRIS: Yes, I did all the time, and I have a lot of that stuff. It's kind of embarrassing to read now, because it certainly did not predict anything good. It was pretty pretentious stuff, but I always thought that I wanted to be a writer. That was my ambition.

BEATTIE: Before anthropology?

DORRIS: Oh, anthropology was a real afterthought. Anthropology came because I woke up one day, I think I was like a junior in high school, and I just woke up on a Saturday with the idea that I should improve my mind. So, I went to Taylor Drugstore in St. Matthews [Louisville suburb] and bought all of the paperback books that looked boring.

BEATTIE: Margaret Mead?

DORRIS: I did; it was Margaret Mead. It was *Growing Up in New Guinea,* and all the books I bought seemed to be anthropological. I just sat down to read them, and I did.

Then I went to college and majored in classics and English, with a minor in philosophy. I went to graduate school in history of the theater, and got a master's degree on the seventeenth century French public theater, and I just spent the summer on the reservation where my family and I looked in the Yale catalog. There was this course on contemporary North American Indian ethnography, and it never occurred to me that I could take a course on Indians before. I took the course, and the professor let me write my term paper on what I did last summer, which seemed to me the easiest thing in the world, so I immediately dropped out of history of the theater and entered anthropology.

That was a long, circuitous route, but I eventually met Margaret Mead and had dinner with her, and I thought, if I had only known back in those days in Taylor Drugstore, a twenty-five cent paperback . . .

BEATTIE: In reading your writing there's something that I see that I want to ask you about. Do you feel that writing, or English, or literature humanizes the study of the human character more than does the study of human groups?

DORRIS: Yes, absolutely. I mean, I think the way that human beings learn is by stories, and the best teachers are anecdotal teachers. I went through that system for years, and I wrote pieces that now I have to rewrite for this book of essays to make them readable, because I was writing for reference journals that demand such writing.

BEATTIE: Also, I think that was about the period in this century when social scientists, and I think they still do, feel that they had to compete with the hard sciences, and therefore be as objectively remote. It seems to me that what is essential to be human too often gets removed in order to study the human.

DORRIS: I agree. When I started writing the book *The Broken Cord,* it was initially going to be a scholarly article for a journal, and I started doing that, and I read all this stuff, and I was very insecure about my science. But then I started doing interviews, and there was just no way to encapsulate the reactions of the people I was talking to in some codified formula. At some point, I realized that it would also be dishonest to pretend that I didn't have a personal interest in this, and one step then was broken. A book came out that is very hard to classify. You go to some bookstores and it's in science, in some it's in psychology, in some it's in recovery, in some it is autobiography. In Doubleday, in New York, it was under music, because they were spelling *cord* wrong.

I've had various reactions from academics to that book. Some people are very patronizing and say, "Isn't that nice, it's readable," as if that's bad, and other people are pleased that a lot of these facts have been translated in a way that the people who have the greatest need to hear them are able to.

BEATTIE: That is, of course, true, but the step beyond that is you've almost turned a biography into literature. It has all of those elements in it, and I've read it a couple of times, and each time I'm moved again by it, not just because of the story, but because of the way the story is written.

DORRIS: Thank you very much. It was a very hard book to write. It was a strange writing time, because Louise [Erdrich] was pregnant, and we were having a lot of trouble with our older kids, all of them fetal-alcohol damaged. She would have insomnia and be up late writing poetry. She was working on *Baptism of Desire*. She would kind of stumble into bed at three o'clock or three-fifteen. I would get up and work on *The Broken Cord* until I got the kids up for school at seven o'clock.

So, it was a book written in the dark, and that, I think, was a very necessary time for it, because it was a place that was mixed with dreams, and where I could tap once again into the memories that were there. I don't think I could ever do it again. It's like a dream, to recall specifically what you had on, and what you were doing, twenty years ago. You can only remember it once.

BEATTIE: Your writing has the quality of prose poetry, and I think that's what makes it so literary. But *The Broken Cord* so easily could have been just an angry book, an "all this is what I've gone through" diatribe, or just sort of a warning treatise for other people.

DORRIS: Oh, it's such a hard thing to write autobiographically, because you're making your life a story, and you're doing the same thing that you're doing with any other story, fiction or nonfiction, and that is that you are selecting certain elements and trying to see a pattern in them that works out a certain way. The difference between doing it with fiction and nonfiction is, with nonfiction you know certain facts—how you got them to that place you don't know—and you follow this circuitous path of stimulus and response and consequence and motive and all this kind of thing. With fiction, you don't know what else ultimately is going to happen, and you just follow your character's experience line by line, and are surprised by what happens.

BEATTIE: Many writers I've interviewed say exactly that. They, too, are surprised by what will happen. Then there are those writers who have each of their works absolutely planned out from the beginning, and it seems to be sort of half-and-half, in terms of how people write. I think it's important for nonwriters to realize that writing is not a formula the way some people think it may be.

DORRIS: No, I think really when you're writing, you're telling yourself a story. If you know what's going to happen, it's not as interesting, and if it's not as interesting to you as a writer, it's not going to be as interesting to a reader. I couldn't ever do that.

BEATTIE: Do you think you're telling yourself the story for the purpose of understanding something yourself, something not only in your own life, but in human experience?

DORRIS: In human experience you get to a point, and we are at this point now in *The Bingo Palace,* in Louise's new book, where you know the characters so well and you've been through a lot with them, that even the slightest little nuance seems so significant, and you get worried about it.

Louise and I, we were taking a walk around the pond near where we were staying in New Hampshire, and there had been this nagging question for a long time about what happens to June's car that Lipsha is driving back at the end of *Love Medicine.* Is it going to be a high-speed chase, is it going to get this, is it going to get that? Finally, we solved this just by talking, maybe this, maybe that, maybe this, maybe that. We solved that, and I said to somebody later, that if anybody had seen the two distinguished Montgomery Fellows suddenly start jumping up and down and doing high-fives in the middle of a field, it wouldn't have looked like what you expect writers to do when the muse hits them over the head.

BEATTIE: Well, in twenty years, when a doctoral dissertation about that book . . .

DORRIS: It's very funny to read scholarship about one's own work, because a lot of times people find things that you think, "By golly, isn't that nice what I put in there, but I wish I had known that, and I'll certainly take credit for it, for what it's worth." In *Morning Girl,* one of the reviewers said that I had neatly paralleled the interaction in misunderstandings of siblings with the misunderstanding of two different cultures encountering each other. Did I?

BEATTIE: Yes.

DORRIS: That's something! Good for me!

BEATTIE: Going back for a minute to your life in Louisville through high school, did you think that you were going to be a writer then?

DORRIS: I didn't have any idea. Nobody in my family had gone to college, and most people in my family had not finished high school. So, there were no precedents. I had a couple of good teachers who were very encouraging to me, but then I was really not very good at science and math, and it was not at all clear whether I was going to go to college. I wrote away for a lot of catalogues because I liked to get mail. I was thinking of places like the College of Great Falls in Montana and, oh, New Mexico State, just different places. I sort of wanted to go to a place where I thought there would be other Indians. But then, lo and behold, I did very well on my SATs, and I'll never forget the day that the results came, and in those days there was no privacy. The teacher handed all the results out, and as he was handing them out, he would look at different people in the class and say, "Well, you did well," or "You didn't do so well," or something like that, and he got to me, and he looked at my scores, and said, "Oh, there is a mistake," and he didn't give it to me. He said, "Well, I have to call in, because it's a mistake."

I had to wait like two or three weeks, and then it turned out it wasn't a mistake. I had actually, by some miracle, done very well on the SATs, and that changed the complexion overnight about what my future was, because though my grades weren't all that wonderful, I did have good SATs, and on that basis, I got a scholarship to Georgetown University. Really, it was virtually the only place . . . I think I got admitted to Michigan State, because they somehow got wind of my SAT scores and wrote to people who had done well, but I had no idea about what to expect at college. I had no idea what to take except not math. That's the only priority that I had. I took Greek instead. You didn't have to take it if you took Greek. I had to struggle like anything with Greek, but because I went to a mission school also, on a reservation where I had a lot of Latin, I wound up having eight years of Latin and four years of Ancient Greek. So, I can do crossword puzzles like anything because I can make up the words.

BEATTIE: How did you like Georgetown?

DORRIS: I loved it. I was so happy. For the first time in my life I had friends who also liked the same things that I did, and we used to have political discussions and go to the movies, foreign movies, and talk about them. I was just absolutely wild about the experience of college, though I must say I came very close to not keeping my scholarship my first term. You had to get at least a C-plus average, and I made it by one one-hundredth of a point or something, because of Greek. Then I learned the technique of grades, and then I was fine from that point on.

BEATTIE: What about English classes there?

DORRIS: I had a wonderful, grumpy English teacher who had a reputation of being impossible to please, and my first paper I turned in, I was a freshman in English, we all had to write an essay on *Lord of the Flies,* a five-page essay. I wrote it, and I thought it was so profound, and I was used to getting good grades in English. So, I just whipped off this essay, and expected him to fall all over himself, and I got the thing back and it said, "E-minus. Please see me on question of plagiarism." I was just indignant to the point of madness. I went to his office and he came in and he said, "Well, I don't want to make an actual charge of plagiarism," he said, "but it just struck me odd that anybody who wrote as badly as you did could possibly have some good ideas, and there are some good ideas in this piece." To make a long story short, when I gave the two-hundredth commencement address at Georgetown three years ago, I talked mostly about him.

He is still there, still had on the same shirt, the same tie, still writing the same book on Trollope. He was like in freeze-dried form, but he really taught me how to write. He was the first person who taught me how to write. Louise [Erdrich] was the second. He taught me to be very self-critical, especially in criticism, to absolutely submit myself to the text.

BEATTIE: What is his name?

DORRIS: Roger Slakey, and I took courses from him the whole time I was at Georgetown. Every time he offered a course I would take it, because he was such a demanding person that making him pleased was a very strong motivator. He got me so excited about writing.

My freshman year, after that disaster story, I embarked on a project that I wound up doing for the whole year, and that was to read all of the plays and short stories and poetry of Tennessee Williams, and to plot out his characters' journeys on a chart, because there is a questing character in every one of Tennessee Williams's works. I plotted it out, and as a result of that plotting, I thought I had discovered that his most perfect and complete play was *Night of the Iguana,* because the character actually goes beyond the point where most of them die and survives, and I was so proud of that, I was proud of that paper, and I got it published. That was the first thing I had had published in a real place, and I sent it to Tennessee Williams, and he wrote back and agreed with it. It was just amazing. I suddenly had broken through into a different realm of possibility in which the writing could provoke a reaction.

But I got to the end of college, and again, because there were no precedents, I had no idea what I wanted to do with anything. So, I thought, "I will apply to a bunch of different graduate schools and a bunch of different fields, as well as law and journalism and business, and if I get into any of them that will be fate." I not only got into all of them, but I got a Woodrow Wilson Fellowship and a Danforth Fellowship that made it possible for me to go wherever I wanted. I turned everything down except history of the theater, because I didn't know what it was, and I had an insecurity about my education. I don't know why. I thought in history of the theater everybody would be starting from scratch, and it would be new. It was awful. There were only five people in the program, and the program's focus was two theaters in the seventeenth century in Paris that had burned down in the eighteenth century. I spent a year of my life on that, and the only real effect was that my French turned into Madame Racine's. I mean, I speak really old-fashioned French now. I have very flowery French.

I had interesting jobs all the time I was at Georgetown. I was on scholarship, as I said, and I worked at the medical records at the hospital every Friday and Saturday and Sunday night from midnight to eight. There are worse places, because a lot of famous people had been in Georgetown's medical records. They were just right there; you could just read them.

Then, in the summers, I worked back on the reservation. The first summer I worked for [Elsa Hoppenfeld's] Theater Party agency in New York. I worked in Paris the next year, and then I worked for the New York City Housing Authority after I graduated, and then got a job from that under the Lindsey Administration in the summers while I was in graduate school, running a bus program that took people in poverty neighborhoods to state parks for a day. I did that for three years, and the last year I did it I was twenty-three years old. I had seventeen people working for me, and we transported 535,000 people. Every day was just buses, buses, buses.

BEATTIE: What year was this?

DORRIS: This was 1969. I would go out to neighborhoods that were troubled, very troubled, and explain this program. I had a lot of tough, elderly women on my side, because one woman from Central Harlem had a grandson named Michael, and I somehow keyed into her consciousness. Ollie Wright was her name, and she was my champion, and basically, the idea was that if anybody picked on me, Ollie would beat them up. So, they didn't, and I had a real strange collection of young people working for me. I had a Comanche guy from Oklahoma, a Japanese-American from Idaho, a black woman from Mississippi (a student at Lincoln University), and we kept the city quiet. We would get a call from some higher up in the Lindsey Administration saying that there would be a riot at Coney Island, and we would send buses out there, pick these people up, and dump them on the beach.

BEATTIE: On the assumption that the water would cool them off?

DORRIS: It did. It really did. It was amazing.

BEATTIE: You've talked about going back to the reservation at times. Growing up, was your self-identity always that of a Native American?

DORRIS: Well, I think I was mixed-blood, which is a particular category of a person. It's somewhat schizophrenic, because you're never entirely sure what you are supposed to be at any given place, and there was a part of me that for years wished that I had a darker skin or straight black hair, as my first cousins do. Then, back here [Louisville], there was a part of me that wished that I didn't have that other complication of things that set me apart. Eventually, it either blows you away, that dichotomy, or else you learn its advantage. For me, it's been a real advantage.

My wife has the same background, almost identical, except that her mix is with Turtle Mountain Chippewa. So, I think one of the strengths we have in our friendship is that we understand this complicated mixture in which one day you are very, very happy to be walking down the street in the city and eating, you know, in a fancy restaurant, and the next day you're equally happy to be exchanging family stories or jokes and eating fry bread in somebody's house. It's a real advantage, it's a real plus, and I think, as a writer, it's a great plus, because you have to learn to observe society on its margins all the time. You learn how things work, because you're kind of imitating it to function with it. Vivian Twostar talks about this in *The Crown of Columbus,* about the advantages of originality, and I think it's true.

BEATTIE: Have you ever felt the need to choose an identity for yourself, or for the sake of other people?

DORRIS: Well, I think when you are growing up, sometimes, you do. I mean, you go through various points of rebellion toward one parent or the other, and there were times that I would very empathically introduce myself as an Indian and dare somebody to say, "But obviously, you're mixed." There were times there, especially after I had worked on a reservation for a long time and I would go back to Washington, I started glorifying in passing, in not having that complication.

BEATTIE: Talking about a writer needing to observe people constantly, don't you think that the more interests somebody has, the more adept they are at observing?

DORRIS: I think when people ask me what they should do to become a writer, I say: "Get a job. Don't be so self-conscious about being a writer, but accumulate a lot of experiences. The more diverse experiences you can have, the more diverse people with whom you can interact. That, eventually, is your treasure trove. That's what you draw from, not that you write about it, specifically. But it gives you a road to empathy with the character. And the road to empathy is what makes it a pleasure for you to get to know that character, and, I think, what makes the character real. So, keep a journal, that's number one. And write down all your first impressions when you're young."

BEATTIE: I tell my students to read anything, including the phone book.

DORRIS: Absolutely, cereal boxes, yes. We don't talk like we used to, either. I mean, it's all television talking to you or movies talking at you, and we are absorbing it without having to compete. In my family, everybody talks all the time, and you have to jump into any hole that you can find in the conversation and hold your own, basically.

My grandmother followed the Dorothy Parker maxim, and that is: any story worth telling is worth exaggerating. She never told the same story twice. I mean, we would hear her tell the same family story back-to-back to different visitors, and they would be different.

BEATTIE: What happened after graduate school? Your series of jobs?

DORRIS: Well, I went to Alaska to do field work among the Tanaina group of Athapaskan-speaking people. The tribe only had an oral language, nothing was written. I got a grant from the National Institute of Mental Health, and off I went. This is after working in New York very intensely with the buses and being very, very urban and fighting traffic every day.

Next thing I know I'm dropped on a beach by a sea-plane with my little bag of stuff.

A little boy comes and shows me where to go. Nobody would talk to me, and very few people spoke any English at all. It seemed at first that nobody spoke any.

I lost all of my grant money on the first night playing pinochle, and then the guy who had won it all from me saw me the next morning and gave it back and said, "When you get more competitive we'll play again."

I lived in a little cabin. I lived there for eighteen months, interspersed with which was my first teaching job at an experimental college in Southern California, called Johnston College, which was—remember this is 1970 in California—the faculty orientation was that we got to know each other through our feet. Everybody took their shoes off and shut their eyes and felt each other's feet to get to know each other. I left Johnston because they were going out to the Hopi reservation to help the Hopi harvest corn, and I said, "If you do that, I'm leaving, because the Hopi have been doing this for four thousand years, and they don't need a bunch of Beverly Hills High graduates who couldn't get into Stanford going there helping them," and they did, and I left. Then I went back to Alaska, and I was there for another nine months or so, and got a job. Over the radio telephone, which was the only communication, comes this voice from my past, Leon Botstein, who was a Danford fellow the same year I was, and who was the [nation's] youngest college president. He had just been appointed president of Franconia [College], and he remembered me in anthropology and he said, "How would you like to come and teach here? We'll fly you out for an interview."

I got a job there, and that was the weirdest college. You didn't have departments, you had divisions. You didn't major, you had contracts. One student was going to have a contract as to whether or not she wanted to major in fairytales and Spanish, so she could go on the good ship *Hope* to Brazil and tell fairytales and make the world a better place. I pointed out that they spoke Portuguese in Brazil, and that this might not work.

BEATTIE: Details . . .

DORRIS: It's weird how things worked out. We also had a community meeting that lasted until two o'clock in the morning to decide how we, as a community, felt about the fact that one of the students was running a prostitution ring for skiers. He was the son of a movie star, and nobody could decide how they felt about that.

BEATTIE: Enterprising.

DORRIS: It was. So, I stayed there one term or, no, one year, actually, and then I got a job offer from Dartmouth to come and found the Native American Studies Department, which sounded so normal after all this. So, I went down there, and it was funny because, well, I adopted my first child by that point. I started the process when I was in Alaska, and I adopted him from New Hampshire.

BEATTIE: Is this Adam?

DORRIS: Abel is his name, actually. I mean, he is called Adam in the book [*The Broken Cord*]. I went to Dartmouth with him; he was three-and-a-half, and I had a joint appointment. I was an instructor, I was only twenty-six, and I was instructor with half of my appointment in anthropology and half in Native American studies, of which I was also the chairman. I was the complete faculty, so I was chairman of half of myself. I would go to faculty meetings with, like, the chairman of the Economics Department who had, I think, twenty-seven faculty members, and then they would say, "Consult with your faculty and come back."

I was there, then, from—that was '72, and I was there until '88. I adopted Abel in

'71, and I adopted Sava in, I guess it was '73, and Madeline in '77, maybe '74 for him. Yes, '74, and she was '77.

BEATTIE: In addition to Abel, the child that you write about in *The Broken Cord,* you mention your other two adopted children also have Fetal Alcohol Syndrome.

DORRIS: Fetal Alcohol Effect. It was a less-obvious disability when they were smaller. I thought they were quite brilliant because, relative to Abel, they were quicker. But when they reached early adolescence, they sort of reached a plateau, and they have had pretty troubled lives ever since.

BEATTIE: Did they manifest some of the same symptoms as Abel?

DORRIS: Well, the symptoms of not understanding the relationship between an act and its consequences, and not learning from experience. I mean, they've both been in continual trouble with the law and with theft and drugs and alcohol and everything else, and they are both in their early twenties now.

BEATTIE: As when you adopted Abel, you didn't realize that they had Fetal Alcohol Effect until they were older?

DORRIS: No, not until they were older.

BEATTIE: You talked a little bit earlier about the process of writing that book. What did that do for you personally? Also, you've probably received lots of mail or information from people whom you've probably helped from writing the book, in terms of their identifying children or relatives with Fetal Alcohol Syndrome.

DORRIS: Yes, I wouldn't state it did anything for me. I wrote it because I thought that Abel—he was a very unusual person, very patient, very affectionate—and these were qualities that were not part of his disability. They were qualities that if he didn't have his disability would have made him remarkable. He had a charisma that everybody that knew him responded to in some way, ultimately with frustration, because they all thought they could make a difference. And when they didn't, they kind of dropped out of sight, almost always, except for Louise and our families. But all the care-givers just disappeared, eventually.

But you know, if his life was to have some meaning, it had to be through example, and I think the book was written partly out of the unfairness of it all, and partly to make a certain amount of sense out of things. But there really isn't any sense to it. It's unfair. It should not happen, it shouldn't have happened. So, writing *The Broken Cord* didn't act as a catharsis for me or anything. The book was finished and everything stayed the same way it was in our lives.

For a normal book, for *The Crown of Columbus,* which at last count had sold, in this country, six hundred thousand copies, I think, we've gotten about fifty letters, and that's what you normally get from a book. For *The Broken Cord* I've gotten five thousand letters from all over the world. It has been published in Korean and it's been published in Japanese and Russian and Dutch, Spanish, French. I think it had a part in making warnings on liquor bottles. I think it's had an impact on posting warning signs in bars. And I think for a lot of people when I come to a signing, just like around here the last few days, you know, I can recognize somebody in line who has this problem in their life, or this situation in their life.

BEATTIE: You mean with somebody else in their family?

DORRIS: Yes. I mean, I can just see it on their face as they're approaching in line, and sometimes they don't even have to say anything, and they come up and they just start crying, because they see their experience in the book, and the book does not offer a solution. You cannot create brain parts that never developed in utero, and, you know, we sort of look at each other as people who have this situation ahead of us for the rest of our lives about people whom we love. I think it helps people to know that they are not alone, and that it's a situation that no amount of extraordinary work on their part could have changed, because you always feel you should have done this, you should have done that, and then it would be perfect, and that's so whether the child is raised in an institution or by the richest, smartest family in the world. There is a kind of uniformity of deficit that happens when they reach puberty or earlier. Then that just transcends any environmental impact that you might have provided.

BEATTIE: Do you think you note any changes for the better in terms of anyone's halting the origin of the problem?

DORRIS: I think so. We decided to let *The Broken Cord* be made into a film for television, because it would reach the largest number of people who might not know about it. I worked very hard on the screenplay with the writer, Annie Becket, and very hard with Jimmy Smits, the star, and Ken Olin, the director, to make it a movie that we could be proud of, and not a disease-of-the-week kind of thing, and I think that succeeded. It was critically very well-received, and thirty million people watched it the first day. Well, thirty million people watched something because it's Jimmy Smits, and because it gets one little filter into the folklore of society that, like smoking, you're not supposed to drink when you are pregnant, and the difference is that there aren't textbooks out there that say, "It's a good thing to smoke during pregnancy," while there are textbooks still in circulation that say, "It's all right, even beneficial, to have a glass of wine every night." For some people that may not be damaging; for some people it definitely is. There was a real misinformation that had to be countered.

BEATTIE: Your son, Abel, died after the book.

DORRIS: He died about a year ago. He was coming home from his work as a dish-washer at a truck stop. He had had two brain surgeries the year before this happened to try and control his seizures, and they had been pretty successful. It was experimental surgery that separates the left and right hemispheres, so that when you have a seizure on one side, it doesn't go to the other side, and you don't pass out, because one hemisphere keeps you alert.

His life was about as good as it ever could have been. He had a good care-giver. He was living with a man who was in social services, and he [Abel] had a job that he had held for a year, and that he could walk to, and he was pretty happy. Somebody didn't look where he was going, and because he [Abel] was learning disabled, the police didn't charge the driver who said that Abel had run in front of the car, and I know Abel didn't run in front of the car. I mean, his greatest, perfected skill, along with tying his shoes, was crossing the street, because I had spent a year of my life training him with that. He was very vulnerable or potentially vulnerable, so he never crossed the street until the light turned red and then turned green again. He never regained consciousness, and I don't think suffered any pain. He probably had shock, initially, and it would have happened so quickly.

BEATTIE: Was that close to where you were living at the time?

DORRIS: We had just moved out to Montana, and he was going to come out and join us after a while, because it always took a lot of arranging to get him situated after checking with the local social service and everything, and he had this stable living situation, so it made perfect sense. I was actually in California with Jimmy Smits and Ken Olin talking about the making of the movie when the word came that he had this accident, and I had to wait with them for about six hours until I could get the plane back to New Hampshire. And out of that experience I think Jimmy and I have become pretty good friends. He did a beautiful job and he is a lovely man.

BEATTIE: When I heard that Abel had died, I thought, "Isn't it terrific that that piece that he wrote is included in *The Broken Cord,*" because that's absolutely wonderful, in its way, for what it is. It's incredibly expressive.

DORRIS: He was terribly exasperating, but there was something very special about him, which, unfortunately, is not true for everybody with that problem.

BEATTIE: Your children Sava and Madeline, are they living at home now, or are they in a group setting?

DORRIS: Well, no, they've been in and out of prison. She is in a locked facility now, and he is on the streets. We have three more children. Yes, three little girls, currently ages eight, seven, and three, and each very different than the other.

Persia is very emotional and dramatic and pathetic, and one day she came down to me and she asked if I had gone out in the evening and I said, "No, I could not find a baby-sitter." Her mother was gone, and I said, "I couldn't find a baby sitter." I had been going to go to the movies. So, I said, "I'll just stay home." She said, "Oh, I'm so sorry, so sorry. You should be able to go out and have fun." I said, "That's because I really like being a father; you don't have to be apologetic."

Pallas has been fascinated with bugs from the moment that she could identify them. She always has a spider on her hand or something. She loves bugs. I think she will be an entomologist, and she believes, or she used to believe, that she came from Venus and could speak Venutian.

Then Asa is Gertrude Stein reborn. She didn't sleep for the first two years of her life. She had a lot to say in no language, basically, and now that she's got language, she will not shut up.

To give you a picture of the three of them, I was out of town last week, and Louise said that Persia had said, "Oh, I miss Daddy," and Pallas had said, "I miss Daddy even more," and Asa said, "and Daddy misses me."

BEATTIE: You were talking about when you came to Dartmouth. That's also where you met your wife, Louise Erdrich. Would you talk about that?

DORRIS: Well, we both arrived on the same day. We were both in the Native American program. I was an instructor, and she was in the first group of women, and the first group of Native Americans, who had been actively recruited to attend Dartmouth. As a result of that, we were in the same orientation, met each other in '72, but, at that time, our eight-year age difference, especially when I was an instructor, and she was a student, seemed enormous. So we were friends in the same way that I was friends with a lot of students in that early group. I wasn't that much older than they and so forth, and then she graduated and we kept in touch, and she came back in 1979, after being away for three years. She had been a poet in the schools in North Dakota, and then she went to graduate school in creative writing at Johns Hopkins, and then she was the editor of the Boston Indian Council newspaper. She came up to Dartmouth to do a poetry reading, and I went to it, and I was just blown away, because it was so wonderful. We had a cup of coffee afterwards, and I had this strong impression about Louise, but it just so happened that the next week I was taking off for New Zealand with the three kids. I didn't know what she thought, but we said we would write, and we did, very oblique letters. Then by the time I got back nine months later, she had been offered a position as a writer-in-residence at Dartmouth for two terms, and so, once again, we arrived on the same day.

She was just beginning to write prose, and it was a huge, long manuscript that eventually got compressed into chapter two of *Tracks*. It was like a six-hundred-page manuscript that went into one chapter. We stayed up till three o'clock in the morning talking about this chapter, and then we talked about it some more the next night, and for the longest time everything was about the work, and then, I think finally, we looked up and saw each other and started going out, and we got married ten months later.

BEATTIE: This is a little bit of a backtrack, but especially in the seventies, it was unusual for single people to adopt, especially for males to adopt.

DORRIS: I was the first one.

BEATTIE: That was the first one in the country?

DORRIS: Right. To adopt a very young child.

BEATTIE: What made you want to do that?

DORRIS: I have no idea. I mean, I had always wanted to be a parent, and I finished my fieldwork in Alaska, and I thought, "Well, I've got a job. I've got an income making nine thousand dollars a year," and there was nobody on the horizon to marry, and why not? I got in touch with Catholic Social Services in Alaska, and they did home study and didn't know whether it would work out, but then ARENA, which was a national adoption agency, picked my file out and made the placement. To me, it wasn't so unusual, because my mother had been a single parent and her mother had been a single parent, and that was a context that was very familiar to me. Double parents is a much more complicated kind of thing, in that you have to share decision making.

BEATTIE: It sounds as though you found an extraordinary wife in a lot of ways in Louise Erdrich, because when she married you, you had three children.

DORRIS: I had been a single parent for ten years.

BEATTIE: And she has accepted everybody and everything?

DORRIS: Yes, she has been very strong, and it's not easy.

BEATTIE: What about your writing lives together? Much has been written about the fact that, even when you are not collaborating on a book, when you're writing your own books, that there is not only much collaboration, but critiquing, of each other's manuscripts.

DORRIS: Yes, there sure is. I mean, I think we know each other's work so well, I daresay we are each other's biggest fans. We believe in the work, and what each of us tries to do for the other is let the other realize what either she or I are trying to do in a particular piece, and sometimes that's a pretty brutal process, where you cut out everything but one sentence. Or when you ask, "Why don't you change this character in this direction? Or have this happen? Or don't have this happen? Or move this whole section to the beginning, and that to the end?" It's much more than an editor would ever do. Then, at the end, we read the manuscript aloud to each other, and basically concur on all the words, and that isn't an easy process. It takes a long time.

BEATTIE: You're both prolific.

DORRIS: It seems like that. On one hand, it seems to us like we never get enough done, because we are always squeezing in the kids' things and family things, and the responsibility of getting to a position of having an audience is that you have a forum, and that forum is there for issues of importance. And both Louise and I have been involved politically, so there is a lot of juggling, but you're right; when you look at the CVs, there is a rather consistent output in a wide variety of fields from children's literature to journalism to, in fact, I just had a play produced in L.A., the story "Groom Service" done for the homeless. It's a story about arranging a marriage in Athapaskan society, and it was done at the Met there in L.A.

BEATTIE: You talked about the fact that when you are writing something, you don't know what is going to happen to the characters until the end. So, how do you work with Louise in terms of discussing your books-in-progress, and hers with you?

DORRIS: We're doing well when one of us will go to the other and say, "You'll never believe what so and so just did," and one of us says, "Not possible." And if it really is impossible, then they won't do it. But if it's just on that possibility, they say, "Well, then this can happen, or that can happen," and, you know, you toss out a lot of different ideas, and it's like magic. The right one will appear. I don't know how you recognize it, or how it works, but it's there. Also, we're working in a lot of different fields simultaneously. Louise is doing a book of essays. I'm doing a book of essays. She writes a lot of poetry. I write a little bit of poetry. I've done a film treatment. We always have a lot of irons in the fire.

BEATTIE: And you are able to be emotionally and creatively involved with each other's work while working on your own?

DORRIS: Yes, it's a nice outlet. Right now we are in a real crunch, because I've got two deadlines January fifteenth, and she is at this point in the novel that really requires my close reading. So, basically, I made a decision that hers is the most important book right now, so I'm going to be late on my deadlines. I just put them aside. It may even push the essays back another season, but this is a real important book. What matters, ultimately, is the work, and not whose name is on it, and not who, at any one time, is getting more recognition than the other. It is really the work, because that's what's going to be there long after we're gone.

BEATTIE: That's true, but it's also an incredibly generous attitude. I know with all creative spouses it doesn't always work that way.

DORRIS: Oh, I think it would if the person that you're working with is your favorite writer, and, you know, you focus on the excitement of having another book of your favorite writer. I don't know, the privilege of contributing toward it is, it's not the same thing as writing it yourself, but it's right up there, in the good experience category.

I think we are fortunate because we've both been successful. Each of us have won what I consider to be the best writing prize, the National Book Critics Circle Award. That's the one given by people who read everything, the one that is not the province of a small group of committee members making a decision, like the Pulitzer or the National Book Award is. It's a real prize. I mean, it's a really meaningful prize, and I think the fact that we each won that early in our careers took all the pressure off, because whatever else happens, happens, and everything else is great.

This children's book [*Morning Girl*] has been such a surprise to me because not only is it the number one bestseller on the children's bestseller list right now for nonpicture books, but it got starred reviews on all five of the trade journals. That's the only book this year that got that. That even completely surprised the publisher, too. I mean, who knew that this was going to happen?

In 1988 I decided to take a leave of absence from Dartmouth and write full-time. We got the contract for *The Crown of Columbus,* which was a lot of money, and well, we had huge bills because Abel didn't have medical insurance, and he had two brain surgeries, which are not cheap, as you can imagine. But still, I couldn't do both. I couldn't keep getting up at four o'clock in the morning and going in to work and writing until my colleagues came in, and then teaching classes. So, I first took a leave to see how it felt and to see whether Louise and I could stand to be in the house together all day long every day, and then, to the utter incredulity, I think, of my colleagues, I gave up tenure. But the arrangement was amicable on all sides, and they replaced me with a man who is from the Soviet Union who is a specialist in Tlingit. It's funny to be replaced by a Russian in Native American Studies.

But nevertheless, I started writing full-time, and I never regretted it a minute. I had taught so much and so repetitively, because it was a small department, and I would teach the same courses year after year, with very little variation. I don't think I had anything left to teach. So, it's worked out well, and then Dartmouth invited us to come back as visiting fellows this fall, which really was remarkable, because I think I'm the first one who ever left who actually was invited to come back.

BEATTIE: How do you both write? Do you write every day or do you have separate writing places and times?

DORRIS: She really likes quiet, and I get up earlier. We have different writing times, styles, habits, everything like that. But when we get to a certain point in a book or a manuscript, then a kind of routine kicks in, in which we'll be reading it aloud or passing pages back and forth with great regularity.

BEATTIE: Had you ever considered moving back to Kentucky?

DORRIS: I thought about it. I think about it especially as this book gets closer, you know. I mean, I'll spend a lot of time down there. I spent about three weeks there year-before-last in Henderson, just nosing around in the archives and walking the streets, and getting a feel of the place, and that was very productive and very nice, and I'd like to do that some more. I don't know. I don't rule it out. I don't rule anything out. I have a lot of strong ties here, and I did a reading at Hawley-Cooke [Louisville bookstore] yesterday. All the parents of the people who were my friends showed up.

BEATTIE: I'm asking Kentucky writers about their sense of place in fiction, and although you write about distinct physical places with real presence, the sense of place that is essential to you is internal and collective more than physical, many times, and maybe spiritual or racial or truthful. Am I right, and has Kentucky, as a place, affected your writing in any conscious way?

DORRIS: It's a question I've thought of, because for Louise, it is so clearly the upper Midwest. She really needs to be there to write about it. I think you're right. I think it is internal for me. I have a very strong sense of attachment to Kentucky. It's going to sound strange, but it is always the first state I read in *USA Today*'s list of what's happening. I'm notorious for watching U of L basketball games. There is a sense of attachment that is very palpable when I'm here, walking about and knowing the story of each house and place. And though I don't write about it, my characters have that feeling, and it's a feeling that, I think, you can only have if you've experienced it. You can't write about it if you haven't experienced it.

I've had such a varied background, but it's hard to say that I'm exclusively Kentuckian. But I certainly am emphatically from Kentucky, and in Kentucky are places that I always identify with, in a way, because they always seem to be making crucial mistakes in terms of taking off. I mean, this Louisville should be a much bigger city than it is, if you look at the census. It let the National Basketball Association get away. It squabbled about the airport for years and years. It compared itself with the wrong places. It's this very plucky place that I always feel I have to defend in a strange way, but it makes it very vulnerable, too. I mean, from the first I can ever remember, I always look at globes and maps to see if Louisville is on it, and if it's not, I don't buy it. It's often there, sort of twirled around in a little curl.

The other thing is that the whole sense of identity of whether this is the South or the Midwest or the East or the West is something I could really identify with. I mean, when I was a kid, it was always very important that this was the South, this was the South, South, South, South, South, that's all it could be. And then when you look at the map and they have it classified with Indiana and Ohio or with West Virginia and Pennsylvania or something like that, there would be this sense of indignation, because it is a southern city, you know. My favorite sobriquet for Louisville was something called the Strategic City of the Seventies, in which there was—it was out on the telephone book cover, and there was going to be an international rocket or something that would connect Louisville to Helsinki.

BEATTIE: Instead they got UPS.

DORRIS: Yes, instead they got UPS. But still, still, you know, you see *Louisville Magazine* coming out with these little things, "We are the fourth busiest airport in the United States." Well, it all takes place between midnight and six in the morning, and there is nobody around. I don't know whether I'm making myself clear, but I could really identify as a marginal person, as a person moving back and forth trying to figure out an identity, that this was the perfect city for me to live in, because it was always trying to figure out its identity and it always shoots itself in the foot when it is doing that. It inspires a certain sense of competition. I mean, I've always kind of wanted to write and say, "Spend some money on this and not on this," but maybe Louisville is what it should be for its size and its everything else. It may have made all the right decisions; I don't know.

BEATTIE: What do you think the nature of creativity is? I could also rephrase that as, what gives you impetus to write?

DORRIS: It's not a question I've thought about. I guess I think if I think about it too much it might not work again. I think it is curiosity. It is an abstract kind of curiosity. It's like wanting to see what's behind you or on top of you and to expand your consciousness into the dark and turn on a light here and there. I don't know why we want to do that, why human beings want to do that, what it is that makes it so. It's sort of the mental equivalent of climbing a hill to see what's there, and then you want to climb it well, you want it to be neat and organized in some way. Whatever it is, it's a very basic human impulse that gets expressed in different people in different ways. But I think it's the same source.

BEATTIE: Do you feel that your writing is a drive or a compulsion? Do you feel it's something you have to do?

DORRIS: It's a pleasure. I mean, I don't think of it with me as therapy. When it's going well, it is like a cool breeze on a hot day. I mean it's this wonderful, satisfying sense, and I would say rather than creating things, it's sort of coloring things in. I have a very hard time talking about myself as an artist or anything like that. I don't know what it is. It's part technician. It is part daydreaming. It's amazing you get paid for it, but basically more than anything else, it's fun. I just feel fortunate to like what I'm doing; it's my job. I want to do it well. I go back and read things that I've written before, and I am sometimes pleasantly surprised to think where the writing comes from; that's pretty good. I mean, it is immortality. It's an urge to make something that will endure better than you do. And you know, the first time I had something that was in a library, I thought, "Oh, good; now I can die."

BEATTIE: Don't people often ask, "Isn't it nice to have this in the bookstore? Isn't it nice to have to do readings? Isn't it nice to have people wanting your autograph?"

DORRIS: Well, it is. That's really nice. Somebody said to me the other day, a student asked at some place where I was reading, "Would you write even if you didn't have an audience?" I said, "I did it for years."

BEATTIE: That's what I mean. You wrote when you didn't have an audience, so that there was something that . . .

DORRIS: But writing with an audience is a lot better, let me tell you. The case with Louise and me is that the key will be some little throw-away detail that's in a text. You go back and say, "Now why is that there, what does that mean?" And then you go from that to a deeper understanding, because the subconscious is somehow generating this very rich fabric that you have to pull the threads out of in order to see where they're fitting. That's a gift. I don't mean it's a gift in the sense that one is gifted; it's a gift that the human brain is able to do that.

I haven't been working on these short stories in a conscious way, but I know from past experience when I go back to them some part of my brain will have figured out some things, and it will be further along than it was when I stopped, even though I haven't been thinking about it.

BEATTIE: Your novel *A Yellow Raft in Blue Water* is written from three viewpoints of different women of three different generations. What made you choose to write from a woman's point of view?

DORRIS: Well, the answer to the first is the answer to the second. I started it out in a man's point of view, and it didn't work. If you want to see, there is a book called *The New Native American Novel in Progress* that the University of New Mexico Press put out, and I have a chapter in it when Rayona was Ray. It was going along and it just became this kind of boy's coming-of-age story and foreign; it was not what I wanted to write at all. So, I decided to switch genders and see if I didn't change any of the incidents after that point. And I switched genders, and doing so made that book come alive for me. At that point, I didn't know that there was a Christine or an Ida section or anything like that, and Rayona becoming a female suggested this whole sort of triumvirate of female characters, each pivoting around the age of fifteen.

As to why it works, if it does, it's, I think, because I was raised by strong women whose voices were the first ones I had to learn to listen to. But I think it's a false mystique about writing in another gender, because every character is imagined, and if you have interacted closely and observed closely another ethnic group or another gender or another age, I mean, you know, Morning Girl is twelve. I was never a twelve-year-old girl, I was never a

Taino, I was never an old lady like Ida. I was never Roger Williams, a Columbus scholar. I mean, I was not any of those people. But what you do, is try and find a key into a personality, and once you get that, everything sort of follows.

BEATTIE: I'm so glad Ray became Rayona, just because of the humor it adds to the novel. The little story about how she got her name, I think, is great. That is an extraordinarily accomplished first novel. What did writing that book do for you?

DORRIS: Well, to be melodramatic, it made me free. I had been so constricted in writing academic stuff, that actually writing without footnotes and so forth was almost illicitly pleasurable. I'm sure it was partly competition, you know. I mean Louise had written this wonderful book that I had been involved in, and she was finishing another one that I was closely involved in, and they were clearly her books. But I had been so daily interacting with the characters that it was frustrating not to be able to control them. I mean, not be able to really make them do what I wanted them to do and turn it around. The only way to do that would be to create my own characters and be in charge. It wasn't really until after *The Broken Cord* came out and was well-received that we were sort of on an equal footing. And oddly enough, I think we always are slightly off balance, because we each, maybe secretly, maybe not so secretly, want a little bit of what the other has. I mean, Louise has this unparalleled literary cachet, in Europe especially, and I am popular and journalistic. My writing is not literary, but there is just this edge of the different. When we do a signing together, there will come somebody who will be dressed in black and who has not washed her hair, and will say to Louise, "Your work is better than anybody's I've ever seen," and somebody will come up to me with a K-Mart bag and say, "I loved your novel," and I think we would each like to have the other happen every once in a while.

BEATTIE: I think it's human nature for people to love to categorize. People, if they cannot slot you as one particular thing, make your life extremely hard, no matter how much you can do.

DORRIS: Well, the only thing is, talking about slotting, is this business of an ethnic writer, a Native American writer, Louise being a woman writer. You know, we write American novels and so forth, and our characters sometimes happen to be Indians and sometimes not. But it's so condescending to put you into a slot.

BEATTIE: What do you think distinguishes your writing style?

DORRIS: Just what you just said. I don't mean to be a minimalist, because I'm not a minimalist by any stretch of the imagination. But I do not have extra words floating around. Every word should count for something.

BEATTIE: You count on nouns and verbs instead of adjectives and adverbs.

DORRIS: I almost never use adverbs. Adverbs are like parenthesis in my book, or exclamation points. If you cannot say it without an -ly or without a parenthesis or an exclamation point, there is something wrong with how you're writing. I find it very hard to read books written in dialect or to write characters speaking in dialect, because people don't think of themselves as speaking in dialect. They think of themselves as speaking very dramatically, and if you're in their voice, they're in charge. For instance, so many Native American books or books about Indian children seem as though they're bad translations of some foreign language, and if its their own language, they speak well, they speak dramatically. So, I'm looking for honesty. I'm looking for concision. I'm looking for surprise, not to be predictable from one sentence to the next, not to reconfirm truths, but to explore territory that maybe has been around a long time. But we just haven't looked at it closely enough. So, I say those are my goals, because those are my weaknesses.

BEATTIE: Identity is a strong theme in all of your books in one way or another, and usually in many ways. And going back to your own life in Kentucky, about identity, whether it's a cultural identity or your identity within the family, or writing from several people's points of views, you show that truth has more than one dimension.

DORRIS: It's a passing illusion, a temporary illusion, but when it happens, it just seems like gangbusters for five minutes and then life goes on. I mean, that's the terrible thing, it doesn't end at a certain point, which is why I did the *Yellow Raft* the way I did, because all endings are false endings, unless it's Armageddon. *The Crown of Columbus* ends with Roger having learned doubt. I mean, that's the beginning, and oddly enough, if I were analyzing what I just said, I would say that was a fairly typical Native American approach, not a linear thing, but a cyclical thing, where things are always beginning and ending at different points on the same circle. But I think that's the way things are.

November 23, 1992

BOOKS BY MICHAEL DORRIS

Native Americans: Five Hundred Years After. New York: Crowell, 1977.

A Guide to Research on North American Indians. With Arlene Hirshfelder and Mary Lou Byler. Chicago: American Library Association, 1983.

A Yellow Raft in Blue Water. New York: Holt, 1987.

The Broken Cord. New York: Harper & Row, 1989.

Route Two and Back. With Louise Erdrich. Northridge, Calif.: Lord John, 1991.

The Crown of Columbus. With Louise Erdrich. New York: HarperCollins, 1991.

Morning Girl. New York: Hyperion, 1992.

Rooms in the House of Stone. Minneapolis, Minn.: Milkweed, 1993.

Working Men. New York: Holt, 1993.

Paper Trails: Essays. New York: HarperCollins, 1994.

Guests. New York: Hyperion, 1994.

Amory Goes Wild. New York: Hyperion, 1996.

LEON DRISKELL

DRISKELL: My name is Leon Vinson Driskell, and I was born December sixth, 1932. My father's name was Dennis Halman Driskell, another family name. My mother's name is somewhat of a mystery. For years she claimed that her name was Mae Frances Driskell, but her brothers and sister teased her about that name, leading me to believe that she suppressed some other, awful name. My mother was reared in the hills of North Georgia. My grandfather owned a huge farm up near Clayton, Georgia.

My father was born in Forsyth County in Georgia, and went with his father and mother to Athens, the university town, when he was a quite small child. My grandfather on my father's side was a civil engineer and designed many of the roads in that area of the country.

The Depression was in full swing when I came along in 1932. I have the distinction of being one of the few people I know who, up to a very few years ago, could say, "There is the house, not hospital, in which I was born, and here is the room in which I was born, and here is the bed in which I was born."

My mother worked hard with every occupation my father entered. He was, fairly early on, involved in the experimental poultry department at the University of Georgia. He apparently had great skills and a great sensitivity for working with animals, knew a great deal about the breeding of fine chickens for various qualities.

I had the benefits, then, of living on a large farm outside Greenville, South Carolina. I recall, in particular, the van, the panel truck, that my father drove, and there were two others like it driven by other people, which advertised "Wilson's Red Farm—Eggs From Chickens Whose Feet Never Touch the Ground." Maybe that unnaturalness says something about the culture in which I had come of age.

BEATTIE: Can you tell what you remember about your grandparents or aunts and uncles, other relatives?

DRISKELL: Goodness. There are so many of them, and such fascinating ones. My grandfather Curtis, the farmer, was tall, with dark eyes, and was possibly a person of Indian extraction, though this I have never been able to document.

BEATTIE: American Indian?

DRISKELL: American Indian. My grandfather had gone off early in his life. His uncle, who reared him and cared for him throughout his life, was going to leave him his farms, but my grandfather took off going west when he was a young man, and ended up marrying a woman whom he met in Washington [state], and bringing her back to Georgia.

His pride, his humor, his patience with children, he combined hardness and softness, a heart that broke very, very, easily. Tears came easily to his eyes, and yet the strength with which he could chop wood, do all of the necessary things on a farm, that had to impress me.

My father was from a large family. He was one of six children, I believe. There was Uncle Julius, who amazed me early in life by going from a rather overinflated rhetoric, his preaching voice when he was running the small Baptist church in the area, to his other voice, which was the countryman farmer voice used talking to neighbors out in the front yard, and then to that other voice, which I had scarcely ever heard at that point in my life, the voice in which he read to me my first sounds of Greek and Latin in his cluttered study.

There was Aunt Carrie, the only sister in my grandfather's family, a woman very, very short with hair that I dare say, had I ever seen it down, would have actually dragged the ground, worn always in huge buns at the back of her head with, yes, knitting needles sticking out, which kept all that hair atop her head.

My grandmother—my paternal grandmother—was a tiny woman, not quite five feet tall, never I think weighed more than eighty-five, eighty-six pounds, but had a number of children. Five, I suppose, the number was. Her childlike qualities endeared her to me quite early.

BEATTIE: What about siblings?

DRISKELL: I have but one brother, an older brother, two years older than I. A person of great talents and abilities who, unfortunately, I think, failed to remain sufficiently in touch with those talents and abilities.

BEATTIE: What were they, the talents and abilities?

DRISKELL: He and I both began quite early in life as members of the staff of the daily newspaper in Athens, Georgia, where we spent the greater part of our childhoods and youth. He wrote for the newspaper from the time he was fifteen or sixteen years old. He was an awfully good, imaginative writer. He was writing short stories and even poems when he was in high school, which I thought were genuinely good. He introduced me to the writings of Joseph Conrad, telling me when I was possibly ten years old, "Here, Leon, read this story. It's so good it will make you smell your own armpits." A homely kind of metaphor, but I think a nice one. I read Conrad and marveled at what he had done. My brother had been the political editor, at one point, of the *Atlanta Constitution.* He was a Marine during the Korean conflict and possibly, during that conflict, lost some of the balance which made him such a good writer and such a good analyst of the social and cultural scene. His name is Curtis Halman, picking up, of course, my father's middle name.

BEATTIE: Talk a little bit about your childhood, what it was like, and where it was spent.

DRISKELL: My good fortune was nearly always to live with ready access to the country: fields, and streams, and animals. In South Carolina, where I went to second grade through sixth grade, I was living, of course, on a large farm, and attending a private school during the years that I was in Greenville. After I returned to Athens, when my father returned to employment at the University of Georgia, we lived initially in town for a very short period of time, and then we lived on the university farm, again a place where I had easy access to woods, and streams, and a great many animals. After my father left the University of Georgia and went into business for himself a few years later, I lived in a fairly far-out suburb, far enough from town that I still had the benefits of country.

BEATTIE: What do you remember about your early schooling?

DRISKELL: Goodness, the things that I recall from early schooling are fairly positive. My most important and formative year was eighth grade. That was the point at which I began the formal study of Latin. And the formal study of Latin told me things about English that I would have never known otherwise. The Latin has stuck with me over the years. I did three years of Latin in public high school in Athens, Georgia. I continued to be able to pick up a Latin text and make my way with it pretty effectively. After all these years I've never returned to the formal study of it. Getting Latin that year and going somehow toward that which would lead me into study of language and literature and culture, rather than more "practical" subjects, I think, was the most important event of my life up to that time.

BEATTIE: What about reading and writing, had those been favorite subjects prior to that?

DRISKELL: Reading and writing had been favorite subjects. I had been given a library card quite, quite early, and had been told, as had the staff at the public library, that I was not to be restricted to the children's section. I recall reading *Ivanhoe* by Sir Walter Scott at the point at which I had no notion, really, of what was at stake in that book. I asked my mother, on one occasion, what was meant by the statement that the Knight Templar seduced Rebecca, and she, caught off guard, said, "Well, he attacked her." You can see what kind of terrible notions I had about sex and sexual relations as a result of that.

BEATTIE: Were you read to much as a young child?

DRISKELL: I do not recall being read to a great deal except by two of my aunts. One woman whose name is Doyce, my father's sister, read to me regularly. She was lots of fun. I still recall silly jokes that she told me when I was five, six years old. But, alas, her idea of the appropriate material to read to a child, particularly I suppose before bedtime, was edifying Christian literature, which I did not think very highly of then or now.

BEATTIE: What about your education beyond eighth grade, and when did you start writing on your own?

DRISKELL: I had the, I think, good fortune of being on the cusp, as it were, in Georgia education. I was not required to go to twelve years of high school, and I completed high school in eleven years, and was, therefore, a freshman at the University of Georgia when I was fifteen, as was the woman I would later marry, Sue Driskell.

At the university I was a very young and precocious kid among the veterans who had come back in droves from the Second World War and were determined to get college degrees. I enjoyed my studies at the university. They were extremely eclectic. I worked at the *Athens Banner-Herald* throughout that period of time, and moved in a circle of people who were, I suppose, the demimonde of Georgia—people, sometimes, whose social backgrounds were, for then, scandalous. Much-divorced women, for instance. A couple, who were paving the way for later generations, living together for a longish period of time without benefit of clergy. A number of fascinating people, all of whom were either engaged in serious writing or were pursuing some other art and were using the newspaper as a convivial and genial way to support themselves while they did it.

My studies at the University of Georgia concentrated heavily on language and literature. I did what amounted to a major in French, as well as a major in English, and in the study of history, in which area also I could have taken a major had I chosen to do so. I stuck with the study of French and history, with my study of English, all the way through the Ph.D. degree, and feel that having some kind of historical frame, some kind of shape in which to place events, has helped me to know a little bit better who I am and what it is I'm trying to write about.

BEATTIE: You started working as a journalist while you were in college. Had you done any of that sort of thing before, or when had you really started writing on your own, other than just school assignments?

DRISKELL: I suppose I really began writing on my own during fifth or sixth grade. I was the class humorist, and I'm not sure what that means, in the private school from which I, quote, "was graduated from the sixth grade." I recall standing before an auditorium full of people, and delivering what I regarded then as a screamingly funny statement about my experiences in the school and all of my classmates that opened, I'm afraid, I must confess, "Ladies and jelly-spoons, I stand behind you to tell you of something I know nothing about." Well, those two lines give you a pretty fair sampling of where the piece went. I had been elected, at that point, to be class historian and also to make the class prophecies and to be funny at our commencement exercises.

I began working for the newspaper in Athens before I was fifteen. Actually, when I was about fourteen, I began proofreading at the newspaper, and frequently would simply be handed some notes and told to "write up this little story." I was also writing poems and short stories, neither of which I think I would allow into either genre now.

I was regularly in the *Thumbtack Tribune,* which was our high school newspaper. I was regularly represented with doleful and extremely socially conscious short stories and poems. That final aspect, I must say, I have not yet lost. My stories were, even then, nearly always about people who got the short end, about animals made foolishly to suffer. The social concern was extremely strong even then. The serious writing, I suppose, did not really begin to occur until I was out of high school and was reading slightly more sophisticated literature on my own, and talking to other people who were extremely knowledgeable about writing.

In my studies at the University of Georgia . . . it was a pretty big concession that I was allowed to take a couple of classes in American literature. It was assumed, in those days, that the British tradition was our tradition, and that was that, and that, of course, one kept up with American literature, but one did not make a serious study of it because, after all, it was so new, and we had no idea that any of it was any account, anyhow.

BEATTIE: You once told me about a woman in Georgia who was very influential in your literary development.

DRISKELL: One of the functions that I filled at the small, rather sleepy newspaper in Athens was to, quote, "cover the arts." Though I was writing political news as well, I was the one who went to the symphony when it came to town, if anybody went, and wrote something in the newspaper about it. I also wrote book reviews frequently and made a habit of interviewing people in the county who had published books or who had a relationship with the mysterious and magical world of publication.

One of my earliest interviews of a writer was, fortunately, with a woman named Aileen Parks. She was married to one of my professors at the University of Georgia. She was a very bright, highly educated woman who was a serious writer. She had devoted most of her time either to supporting her husband's career and scholarship and criticism, or to writing books that would sell and would sell fairly successfully. She had written just at the point at which a popular song made sure that the book would be a big popular success, a life of Davy Crockett, *Davy Crockett: Young Rifleman.* Her life of Davy Crockett I read, thinking, "Oh, well. After all, it's a children's book. There can't be much here."

When I went to interview Aileen and began talking to her about what she had done in that book, I began to learn all the kinds of things that no one had ever told me before, that one could control prose rhythm, that the rhythm of a passage had a great deal to do with the way in which the reader would receive the passage. She recommended books for me to read. I had never even heard, at that point, I suppose, of Gerard Manley Hopkins, but she told me about sprung rhythm and some of the things I might find if I read Gerard Manley Hopkins. She became a close, close friend, one of those supporting people in our life who would remain important until her death just a very few years ago. She continues to be important now. She not only believed in my gift, she thought I should do something with that gift. She would call me down when she caught me posing, and I had become a very adept poseur. After all, when you're a baby amongst war veterans, you have got to pretend that you're something other than a baby. Aileen and her husband, Edd Winfield Parks, remained important to me for, I suppose, all of my life.

William Davidson, the editor of the *Georgia Review* in those days, and one of my neighbors and professors, was equally important. And I got to know, through him, some of the greats of American literature, though I dare say none of them would have recalled that I was also present at some of those sessions.

Several of the greats came through Athens, and I was privileged to at least meet them and do some talking myself about reading and writing. Hugh Hodgson, who was then the head of the music department at the University of Georgia and later became dean of the fine arts school, brought every year to the university his old, old friend Carl Sandburg for a public reading. He also brought, every year, Robert Frost. So I was able to hear both of those men read from their work, at least attend parties with them, get to talk to them a little bit, and learn that poets are real people and that poets often are funny and could work and touch you in ways having little to do with the head, and having lots to do with the ear, and with your own capacity for imagination.

BEATTIE: Have you had people in your life who have been mentors to you in terms of writing? I ask that because you are such a mentor to, not only students at the University of Louisville, but to other writers in Louisville and beyond.

DRISKELL: That's really a wonderful question, and I'm afraid that I have to say I didn't really have one. I can't think of any person in my background to whom I have regularly shown manuscripts or confessed problems. I can say that I have trusted, for a long, long time, the good sense, the ear, the compassion, and the sense of humor of Sue Driskell. I would not want to send something out without her having read it. She's often able to tell me when a piece is a mistake from the start, and save me some time agonizing with it. She would never quite say, "Pitch that, it's not going to work," but I think that her manner of responding to a piece of writing would tell me that I ought to leave it alone, or go ahead and develop it.

BEATTIE: You mentioned that you met her in school in Georgia. Will you talk about that and about your marriage and family?

DRISKELL: Sue's family had come to Georgia from California, where her father had done his Ph.D. in German at Stanford University. We attended the same junior high school. In eighth grade we appeared in the same home room, the same Latin class, the same English class, and, of course, then were close friends throughout high school and into college.

Sue discovered that her interests really were in the sciences—geography and geology. She did a great deal of work in cartography, and then in making charts and designs for textbooks that the professors in those two departments were putting out.

After she left the University of Georgia with her baccalaureate degree in geography and geology, Sue went to work initially for the American Telephone and Telegraph Company, hoping that she would be actually in the field doing cartography and map making, charts, and all that kind of thing. But she discovered, alas, that women were kept in the home office, and they rendered the materials that the men did out in the field, and that was a no-win situation for her.

After we were married in 1955, she ended up pretty much taking a clerical job for the time that I was overseas in the later stage of the Korean conflict. After my return from the military, we went first to the University of Texas, where two of our children were born, and then to Birmingham Southern College in Alabama, where another child was born. At both schools she actively engaged in the visual arts program and also in the literary programs. She became a very proficient painter, and first began to show her painting professionally in, I suppose, 1960, while we were in Alabama. She was one of a very few painters who got into a juried show at the Birmingham Museum.

We had one additional child in Cincinnati, Laura. And then after moving to Louisville in 1964, we had our fifth child, Michael.

BEATTIE: Going back to your college years, after college, what happened? What did you do directly after graduation?

DRISKELL: I had continued throughout my years at the University of Georgia to work at the newspaper, and when time began to draw close and I felt that I had to go ahead and get my baccalaureate degree, I applied for various jobs in the state but was, by then, city editor of the Athens newspaper. I continued to hang on at the *Athens Banner-Herald,* taking additional classes at the university. And then I childishly got angry with a staff member of the *Athens Banner-Herald,* a woman who was sister-in-law to the publisher. Outraged that she had not taken my prerogatives quite as seriously as I did, I quit on the spot and was without work. I went to my chairman of the English department, and suggested that I apply for a teaching assistantship the following year. He dissuaded me from doing that, saying that I would go bonkers if I were to do nothing but teach freshman composition, that he would like for me simply to push ahead and complete my master's degree that very year, and accept an instructorship the following year.

I managed to take my final course for the baccalaureate degree simultaneously with taking two of my final classes for the M.A. degree, and I received both degrees simultaneously in a graduation exercise attended by thousands, in which scarcely anybody noticed that I was finally through.

I had, up to that time, done very little teaching, but I had been head tutor for the University of Georgia Athletic Association.

BEATTIE: Had you been an athlete yourself, ever?

DRISKELL: I had run cross-country track for a short period of time, and I enjoyed it a great deal and was really good. I was quite fast. This was in college. I probably would have made it as a cross-country runner and actually lettered, had it not been the case that coaches did not really tend to judge ability and performance quite so much as what they knew about the athlete. I continued smoking throughout this process and was finally told it was either cigarettes or track and I should choose, and I chose. I did not quit smoking in order to run track.

BEATTIE: How old were you when you received these degrees?

DRISKELL: Goodness. Oh, I was quite old enough to have done it, twenty-two. I had simply not been much interested in getting the degree, because I was convinced that I was either going to be a professional writer or I was going to pursue that first love of mine which was . . . it sounds pompous to use the term social justice. I was very much engaged in wanting the political, and social, and economic wrongs of our country to be addressed, and was actively engaged in politics at all levels, even when I was writing. The first election in which I was much involved was that election in which Henry Wallace, who had been FDR's vice-president, ran for the presidency on the Progressive Party ticket. Nearly everybody I knew and knew well was either continuing to support the Democratic Party, though they looked longingly toward the Progressive Party, or had actively joined into the Progressive Party activity.

BEATTIE: In talking about your strong interest in social justice, where do you, or how do you, think that interest developed? Was it an interest of your family or were you somewhat of a rebel in your family?

DRISKELL: It was certainly an interest in my family so far as racial relationships were concerned. My parents were quite intelligent enough to realize that the treatments of blacks in the Deep South and elsewhere was dead wrong. They did believe in the equality of the races; they did believe that one ought to be able to make one's way regardless of social background, parentage, lineage, all that.

BEATTIE: Did you find that your views were common where you were?

DRISKELL: No, my views were not common. I began debating civil rights, though we did not call them civil rights in those days, as early as the tenth or eleventh grade. We had education which was ostensibly separate but equal, one system for whites and one for blacks. I was cut off from knowing socially, or knowing personally, any black people in the community except through my family.

At the newspaper, of course, the editors of the papers were absolute segregationists. I got into slightly warm, if not hot, water once or twice when I insisted on writing an article about the birthday of Abraham Lincoln. He was one of those founding fathers, or important forebears, who was not much talked about in a community like Athens.

At the university I knew a number of people who agreed with my thinking and the thinking of other people with something like a social conscience, but even there, I discovered that the racial attitudes were so deeply buried that they had nothing to do with reason: they were simply knee-jerks.

I look back and recall the point at which one of the children with whom I had grown up and with whom I had always played stopped playing with me and began to call me, somewhat sullenly, "Mr. Leon." When I questioned my parents about it, they said that there was nothing I or they could do, that his mother had told him that it was time to stop winning when he wrestled with Mr. Leon. Consequently, he stopped wrestling with Mr. Leon, and began calling him Mr. Leon. We were maybe thirteen or fourteen. He was a very nice looking, obviously smart, muscular young black man with whom I could no longer be friends because our lives were totally separate.

BEATTIE: I assume that you came to the decision to pursue writing as opposed to any type of social service career because you could espouse your social justice views in writing and still be creative.

DRISKELL: I'd like to pretend that I made some kind of rational decision, but I don't think I ever made a rational decision about my career or my life. I think that my emotions led me in particular directions, and that's the way it was. Once I completed the B.A. and M.A. degrees at the University of Georgia, I felt that I did not want to return to newspaper work and that I probably was going to become an academic, so I applied for grants and fellowships and teaching assistantships for graduate studies. I got a number and then volunteered for the draft in order to get that over with before I began Ph.D. studies.

Then, of course, our next decision came when I returned home from Korea. Sue had received letters in my behalf from the schools to which I had applied for Ph.D. studies earlier. All of them were willing to give me the same grant that they had offered previously. I told Sue to make the decision of where she wanted to go based upon what we had talked about and my goals and aims. She accepted the one at Austin, Texas, and, literally, when I arrived home in April of 1958, I suppose it was, I said, "Where are we going?" And she told me Texas, which was my first choice.

BEATTIE: What was your time like in Austin?

DRISKELL: Delightful. It's the one city, I suppose, to which I would return, leaving Louisville behind. We were there at a particularly good time. The Cuban Revolution had just happened, and many Americans, I included, were extremely enthusiastic about what Fidel Castro might be able to do in that long-oppressed victim of imperialism. The Kingston Trio was out doing its thing. Protest had become endemic by that time.

BEATTIE: What about your academic work there at the university? What was it like? What was your concentration?

DRISKELL: I really enjoyed all the work I did at Texas. I cannot say that any of it was particularly rigorous or particularly inspiring. I did have the strong feeling that I was doing a job as thoroughly and well as I could, and being, alas, very competitive, I did well and, I think, prepared myself well, despite not having great, great intellectual experiences in the classroom.

I had decided years earlier to specialize in seventeenth- and eighteenth-century English literature, and I was allowed, at Texas, to present myself for examination in areas in which I felt competent, without doing course work. One simply tidied up all of the classes one had done, all the preparation one had done, and selected one's areas in which to be tested. If one wanted to take course work to satisfy certain areas of required courses, that was one thing. Consequently, I took the courses that were required of me by the university, and put myself up for examination in those other areas without benefit of course work. To the honor of the university, faculty did not ready my examinations with a snarl, thinking, "This wise-ass kid thinks he can get by without taking a course; we will show him." I really took good, hard tests and passed them, and was ready to pass them, and was not obliged to go back and do any further study.

I continued to write and did get some encouragement about my writing, but for the years in which I was at Texas, and later at Alabama, I had put imaginative writing pretty much on the back shelf, feeling that I had to earn my credentials, that I had to get enough scholarship and criticism behind me that I would be safe academically. At the University of Texas, I think that good graduate students taught one another, and we did it often without either the teacher or the learner knowing what was going on. We talked literature and social issues and ideas all the time.

I began getting my experience teaching at the sophomore and junior levels during that apprenticeship at the University of Texas. From the teaching I did there, I was literally set to go to Birmingham at the end of two years and teach survey literature courses and period and figure specialization courses without any difficulty. Like many an academic, however, I made the serious mistake of not completing my Ph.D. dissertation before accepting a full-time job as assistant professor of English. I had been offered, for my third year at Texas, a university fellowship, which would mean I had no teaching obligations, no obligations except to continue doing my research and my study. I decided that it was time for me to make more money, so I turned it down and went to Alabama instead. The next summer I returned to Texas with a grant from the University of Texas to complete my scholarship and research, but even then I did not buckle down and write the dissertation, because I was having too much fun teaching. I was having entirely too much fun being a young father and young husband, and also sticking my nose into politics any chance I got. I did not actually complete and defend the Ph.D. dissertation until 1964, the same year that I came to the University of Louisville.

I had received my degree just a few months before I began teaching here, in early September of 1964. My Ph.D. dissertation, at which I occasionally look, was much, much better than I thought it was at the time. It is a book that I would rather like some time or another to be able to prepare for book publication. It has to do with the shift in prose style in the seventeenth century. I argue, in that thesis, very hard against the school of critics who are convinced that the new science, the movement behind which, I suppose, most of English intellectuals were putting in their force. I argue with the Scientific Revolution, and ground the Revolution in two sources, one of which is pulpit oratory, and the other is the stage. And that argument, I think, is much better than the scientific explanation. I continue to be very much at one with the great neoclassical artist, the ancient-modern controversy, which would have it that somehow there was a golden age sometime or another intellectually and socially, but that we got off track, and we've been going downhill ever since. That is the ancient view. The modern view is that from the bestial we have risen and have risen, and that progress is real and change is nearly always progress, and we're going toward a real glory day in which we are, as Alfred Tennyson said, "little lower than the angels." I take my stand, I believe, as firmly with the ancients as I ever did. I think that the proliferation of print, the proliferation of entertainment, and the enshrinement of novelty and originality as being merits have, in fact, eviscerated the intellectual and spiritual life of the world, not just America. I regard myself, not in T. S. Eliot's terms, as a classicist in literature. I haven't the grounding to be his kind of classical, but I do think that I am classically oriented, and that my feelings are nearly always on the side of austerity.

From Austin we went to Alabama and I taught there for two years. We left Alabama deeply grieved at what we saw happening there. We had been convinced that it would be possible to return to the Deep South, and there would be quiet voices of moderation and reason. In the year 1960 the American civil rights movement was really getting started with a vengeance. We were, to some extent, persecuted in Alabama. We were supported by the college and by a wonderful circle of friends and artists and intellectuals, but I realized that I could not rear my children in Alabama, either expecting them to be physically safe, or expecting them to be untouched by what I witnessed around me. So, from there we went to Cincinnati, and there, too, I can tell you the racial climate was not much better than it had been in Alabama.

BEATTIE: And how many years were you in Cincinnati?

DRISKELL: Only two. I had the very good fortune of being officed for both of my years there with a man named Tom Ware, who was from Louisville and had studied with Harvey Curtis Webster, one of the greatest scholars who has ever been here; and with David Maurer, the sociolinguist; and also with Richard Kane. Tom and his wife, Judy, and Sue and I became close friends, and we had a wonderful circle of politically conscious and literarily attuned people in Cincinnati. Tom brought over, to the University of Cincinnati, his former mentor, Richard Kane, for a lecture, and went to all kinds of troubles to throw Dick Kane and me together. At a dinner party, for instance, he seated us next to each other. Though there were important scholars there, I was next to the guest of honor. We had a wonderful conversation. I had no idea what was going on until a few days later I received a telephone call from William Ekstrom, who was at that time chair or dean of the University of Louisville English department. He later became academic vice-president and acting president of the university. Dr. Ekstrom identified himself on the telephone and then said, "Well, I'm calling to find out why you haven't sent along your credentials." And I said, "I beg your pardon, if you want my credentials, ask for the bloody things. I didn't know you wanted them." "Well," he said, "we want you to come for an interview next Monday. Would that be possible?" I said, "Yes, but I don't know if I can get credentials to you that soon. I'll try."

It turned out that Dick Kane had recommended that I be appointed to take the place of an eighteenth-century scholar who was leaving Louisville. I arrived early in the morning on a Monday and, after our first round of interviews with various people on campus, we came by the English department and the secretary at that time—Sally Lowen, a woman we're still closely in touch with—held up two letters and said, "I got them, Dr. Ekstrom." And he said, "Oh, good. Those are your letters of recommendation." So, I came back, and he and Dr. Kane and a couple of other people were in there reading my letters. They then took me to lunch and gave me an opportunity to talk about my Ph.D. dissertation.

At the airport that afternoon, Dr. Ekstrom said what they were willing to offer and would I come? I said, "Give me a week," and went home knowing darn well that yes, we would go. That it was a job in which I would be with a distinguished faculty and would really be on that faculty someone whom they sought, someone they really saw as someone to help make the department what they wanted it to be. That was 1964, and here I am.

BEATTIE: Will you talk about your teaching experiences at U of L [University of Louisville], what you've taught, what you currently teach, and also about your founding of the magazine *Adena*?

DRISKELL: The teaching that I've done here has been almost universally exciting teaching. I was allowed, at Cincinnati, to design some courses which I wanted to see taught. I also discovered that that was a possibility at the University of Louisville, that one didn't simply live with the curriculum as it existed. One could stretch the curriculum a bit, one could use particular course numbers in order to try out subject matter and techniques that one had not previously tried out.

One of my greatest satisfactions came when John Dillon, a physicist, joined the University of Louisville as the dean of the graduate school. I called on Dr. Dillon with the suggestion that the University of Louisville mount a program for a summer institute for the humanities, which I had already designed and laid out. We asked for assistance in offering this institute from the newly founded National Endowment for the Humanities. We were the first institution nationally that had any such program funded. It was an enormous and good budget, allowing me and the other faculty involved to do things that we could never ordinarily have done. We could bring people in; we could take our participants elsewhere. We got our grant; we were operative.

Dr. Dillon insisted that he was going to be the chief executive officer for this institute and he was also going to teach in the institute. One of the really important things about working with John Dillon was that our participants, high school teachers and high school seniors, began to learn that, no, the arts and humanities and the sciences are not incompatible. Leon and John really admire and respect each other, and they can talk about all kinds of issues, agree and disagree, and still have respect for one another. That seemed to me an awfully, awfully good thing for them to learn. We had a wonderful time doing that for the institute, and I felt very privileged to have been able to set up a program of that sort.

I also began working very closely with Actors Theatre, almost from the time we arrived here, initially attending their performances in a loft downtown. Later, I was able to work up some nationally funded programs in which we were providing dramatic enrichment for students in all of the public, private, and parochial schools of Jefferson County and nearby counties, thus managing to subsidize the theater by tying it to the educational programs for students and for teachers. In the very recent past, Sandy Speer, who is the one remaining professional from the old days of Actors Theatre, said that had it not been for the dramatic enrichment program that Leon Driskell and Bob Neill put together, Actors Theatre probably would not have survived. It's a very rich feeling to think that one has had something to do with the maintenance, at least, of cultural activities of a good sort within one's community.

The regular teaching, I grieve the fact that full-time faculty no longer has its hands on composition in the way it used to have its hands on composition. We have so many students that most of the teaching of freshman composition is done by teaching assistants and is done by part-time faculty. Consequently, I think that there is a real chasm, a real division, between the real faculty and the part-time faculty. I should like to see us one faculty with one set of students, and I should like it to be the case that I could say I want nothing to teach but freshman composition from now until the time I retire, and continue to enjoy all of my benefits, my salary, and the respect of my colleagues. Unfortunately, I would be told that I was not carrying my proper weight in the department if I were to teach nothing but composition.

I discovered that my teaching in humanities gives me, in some ways, greater opportunities than my teaching in the English department does. I'm able to put together, under a topic like "The Modern Culture," readings that range from the hard sciences and social sciences to the occult, to the good, old-fashioned, well-made story, poem or play.

In the English department I have been in recent years teaching a good deal of American literature, though there was a time when the English department would not have admitted me to be qualified to teach American literature, since I took but one course in American literature throughout my experience as a student. Now, the 312 English, which is the second half of American literature, it's a course I enjoy a great deal. I have put together several fiction courses which reflect my interest in contemporary writing. One course I call the "Short Story as Lyric," and it enables me and a group of students to read all of the short fiction of Katherine Anne Porter and Eudora Welty, and then typically, at least one collection of short fiction by the late Flannery O'Connor, in order, partially, to use O'Connor as a foil to demonstrate some of the qualities that good fiction contains that Welty and Porter do not have.

I've also done one course the long title of which was, "Some Prose Fiction by Twentieth Century British Women I Like." That is the course in which we got to read some Stevie Smith and Muriel Spark and Iris Murdoch, Katherine Mansfield, Ivy Compton Burnett, a bunch of women who are no longer read, I think, with the attention that they ought to be given. I have very lately done a seminar, a 600-level class, in contemporary British fiction, in which I picked up a few more of the great British women writers who are at work right now. I also continue regularly to do a seminar in eighteenth-century fiction and also in eighteenth-century prose and poetry.

I'm certainly not tired of teaching. I would like it very, very much were it possible for academic departments to allow some of us to spend great portions of our time simply reading students' writing. I mean Ph.D. students, I mean M.A. students, I mean baccalaureate students in order to get them onto a right track to speak and to write a good, excitable prose, which is clearly about its subject instead of being about the methods of its discipline. The distinction I see as a very sharp and necessary one. Knowing the laboratory techniques is simply assumed in the sciences; in English one is likely to take courses three-quarters of which have to do with the theoretical frame which, if accepted, validates the rather stunted form of the essay. I'd like to be able to be a prose doctor and sit in my office and read papers on God knows what—whatever is brought into me—and do an evaluation of the manuscript in its substantive and formal, and in its mechanical, execution, and have the student be able to hear everything that I'm saying without fearing, "Oh, my, am I going to make a C in this course?" I suppose I could be totally happy simply as an editor, reading other people's manuscripts, being allowed to think about them, learning everything I need to learn in order to help that writer make the piece come off the page.

BEATTIE: I'm curious, in your teaching of creative writing, if you have found either the attitudes or the preparation of the students, especially undergraduate students, has changed very much in the last ten or twenty years?

DRISKELL: That's interesting, because I find myself really happy with the aptitude and the early productions of students in creative writing. I do not find myself so happy about their aptitude or their performance when they're writing analytical and discursive material. I think, in some ways, the culture has given some of these students real possession of their voices and their willingness to use language in a creative way. I do think that we have allowed skills in language arts to erode seriously in the past twenty, thirty years, but I find that the student in the creative writing workshop may come with a quirky and effectively thought-through poem, story, or dramatic monologue, and with a little help with conventions, they've got a strong, strong piece. That's encouraging. I'm not very patient with the teacher of creative writing who says, "We'll spend the first third of the term doing poems, the next third doing stories, and the next third doing plays." I'm receptive to anything you produce whenever you produce it, feeling that it all comes from the same place, and the quality of your dramatic monologue is going to affect your narrative voice in a short story. All of these things are feeding upon one another. I feel that it's artificial to say, "No, this is a course in poetry; you may not submit a story."

I mentioned a little while earlier my having been a poseur. I think nearly always that student who is insisting that his work stands all by itself and it doesn't need validation, I think that the poor soul is posing. I think that what they're really doing is calling out for some part of what they have done to have been affirmed, so that with some affirmation they can then maybe try to make it better. Proscriptions, prohibitions come very uneasily to my voice anyhow, but I would never dream of telling a group of students that they may not write the horror stuff, the fantasy stuff.

BEATTIE: Will you talk about your magazine, *Adena*?

DRISKELL: I owe a great deal to a former colleague at this university; his name was Bill Grant. He came here while Sue and the children and I were spending a year in Mexico, and he was appointed to the department as a kind of wonderful, fair-haired boy, a hard-working scholar, really out there doing great things. He wanted to start a magazine and I said, "Sure, let's start a magazine." So I helped. We decided that we would name it for some of the earliest inhabitants of the Ohio River Valley that we knew about, the Adena people, and that we would make it a journal of the history and culture of the Ohio Valley. This would allow us to use literary materials, visual materials, musical materials, folklore materials. It would also open us up to many of the social sciences, and to some of the findings of natural science. It would leave the door wide open for the regular inclusion of poetry, fiction, and drama.

We had a wonderful time editing the magazine. It was, I think, as important a voice in writing during those days as we had in the state. The arts council used to have an annual meeting at which the editors and staffs of the literary magazines came together and we were judged by outside experts. *Adena* was always judged either the best in the state or, on one occasion, it and the *Louisville Review* were judged the two best in the state.

That editing experience did a great deal for me. I was being supported in that work by the Kentuckiana Metroversity, the director of which at that time was John Ford, a philosopher. I did not want to have standard, printed rejection notices. I wanted every contributor to get a letter back, and I preferred that that letter be one I actually typewrote on letterhead stationery saying some of the things that I liked and some of the things I didn't like and why. I developed the habit of making a few pencil editing notes to contributors with each rejection. I discovered, alas, however, that this became an invitation to revise and resubmit, so I was often reading the same piece three or four times and still finding it not acceptable for the magazine. I did, however, develop genuine friendships and fairly deep relationships with several writers and artists as a result of working for *Adena*. It's something I value a great deal. When finally I allowed it to die, I did so with genuine grief.

BEATTIE: I also wanted to ask you about your Friday Group that's been going at the University of Louisville for twenty years.

DRISKELL: The Friday Group began, in part, simply as an expression of a need for more time to talk about writing than a fifty-minute class period would allow. So we were pretty heavily students and faculty at the beginning, and then, with older students who came back to the university and discovered that they enjoyed writing poems and stories, we began getting an increasing number of retired people and aging citizens.

Out of the Friday Group we quickly began to form some other groups. At one point, the Friday Group was no longer meeting on Friday, but still called the Friday Group it was meeting on Wednesday, and there was also a Tuesday Group comprised of the real hard-core Friday people. Each of the members of Tuesday Group would work over the manuscript given to them on one Tuesday, read all the accompanying materials, and then when gathered the following Tuesday, it would be open discussion without my reading my manuscript to the remainder of the group. Everybody would really have lots to say and lots to ask, helping me to understand where I was as a writer.

From the so-called Tuesday Group we then developed a performing group, and the performing group was called Minerva. We memorized our own work. We never sat down and planned a program; instead, we worked everything out improvisationally. We did sound circles, we did body movement. We did all kinds of concentration exercises and played inspirational games with one another. Then, once our energy was up at a high level, I might recite something I had just written, someone else might begin singing in the background as I recited, and then someone would say, "Well, that makes me think of something I haven't memorized. Let me get it. I'll read it." We would put together programs that we hoped were thematically and terminally integrated and coherent. One would not be able to say that fifty-minute program involved four characters with such-and-such a conflict, but that using, let's say, an African-American spiritual, "Nobody Knows the Troubles I've Seen," and using vocal imitations of emergency vehicles, we had put together a body of work which all went together and made connections that we were discovering even as we rehearsed.

BEATTIE: Your Minerva troupe performed all over Louisville.

DRISKELL: All over the state, really. It was a very exciting period of time. It was very heady stuff. We felt that a rehearsal session never began as work. It began sometimes with all of us feeling tired on this Saturday morning at nine o'clock, but once we began getting into vocal and body exercises, we would leave a rehearsal session at twelve-thirty literally high.

In terms of my writing, I've always been aware of an apparent dichotomy—I don't really think it is a dichotomy—my work which focuses upon people more or less like me, as you see me and experience me in my daily life. "A Gift of Time" is that kind of story. "The Note" is that kind of story. In some ways "Hester's Keep" is that kind of story. "The Other" is set in a socioeconomic and cultural group that is also part of me. I'm every bit as drawn to them as to these other, more nearly intellectual and educated, people. I was delighted when one critic compared me both to Eudora Welty and to Flannery O'Connor, and then said that she saw the affinity with Welty more deeply, because my affection for my people was obvious. Not always is O'Connor's affection for her people quite that obvious. She is looking with that unflinching ability of hers to see straight through the superficial to the essential, and would not regard the peculiarities and eccentricities of the character as being at all fundamental. They are simply trappings, and then one gets to the essential thing.

BEATTIE: If you're writing about emblems or you're writing about characters, those are two very different things.

DRISKELL: I don't think O'Connor's people really become emblems, but they are important to her for essential reasons, not those other reasons that I would accept and even love. I did, as you may know, a book with Joan Brittain about Flannery O'Connor, and it was a very important book to have done. I had met O'Connor on several occasions in Georgia. I had read her work and admired it a great deal. Joan Brittain is one of those wonderful, wonderful women I'm so glad I had an opportunity to work with. She was my student as an M.A. candidate at the university, I was encouraging her to publish critical articles and scholarly articles while she was still an M.A. candidate, and she succeeded wonderfully. She sold to several journals important pieces before she defended her thesis, which I directed, on O'Connor.

At the beginning of a Christmas holiday Joan showed up here [Driskell's home], and it was prearranged with Sue, though I did not know that Joan was coming. Joan said, "We're going to do a book." And I said, "The hell you say," and Sue said, "Yep, I think you're going to do a book." The two women had conspired, and we began writing.

We had been initially accepted for book publication at the University of Georgia Press, and we were asked to make changes in structure and format of the book, which would have rendered it little more than a Twayne series, useful but limited. I said there was no way that we were going to make any such changes, that the metaphor around which the book was based was simply of too much importance to me and to the subject matter for us to consider sacrificing it. We withdrew it from University of Georgia Press.

We submitted it without revision to the University Press of Kentucky, and it was accepted almost instantly. We did several additional articles. For the first time we collaborated on one article, which appeared in a magazine, and put the book out. The book is called *The Eternal Crossroads*. A couple of chapters in that book are as important, I think, as anything I've ever done or said as a critic. But meantime, Joan's wonderful overall grasp of the body of O'Connor's work was just invaluable. She was able to prevent my losing sight of one concern while pursuing another. It was the most joyous occasional collaboration I've ever had.

I have a little anthology with one of my first published stories in it. There was a magazine edited by a woman whose name is Ann Lewis, and it was called the *Atlanta Magazine,* and it was publishing work by the best Georgia writers around. At that time, I was not among the best Georgia writers around; I was a newspaper writer who also wanted to write fiction. I submitted to them and was accepted, and published several short stories with them back in, oh, 1950 to '53, I suppose. The one story has continued to remain in anthologies that the magazine put out at the end of twenty years. A twenty-year anthology of the best stories that appeared there, and then a twenty-five year anthology, and my little story called "Hoodwinked" made the cut for both of those and continues to be printed.

During my time in Texas, I continued doing some poetry and some fiction, but I was not submitting. I had one story accepted by Whit and Hallie Burnett. I judged a fiction contest with Whit and Hallie in Cincinnati, and it was wonderful. They had two motel rooms, so we sat in their motel rooms and read stories and talked about stories, and we finally picked our winners, and I learned a lot about fiction during that period. I submitted to them a story that I thought was the best I had done. They were both fond of me, and they both encouraged me to submit. They accepted the story for *Story Magazine,* and the *Magazine of Discovery,* saying "yes" to me. I thought maybe this was the beginning, maybe I was on my way. Then I received a letter from Whit that the magazine had gone under. I shipped the story off to another magazine, and I selected it for reasons that will be obvious when you hear the title. It was called *Phylon: A Magazine of Race and Culture.* I shipped the story off to them, and it appeared, and I was rather pleased and proud that I had got in. There was no reason that this magazine should accept me, except that the story was a really good one, I thought. Then blessed, blessed, wonderful Martha Foley, who was the editor of *The Best American Short Stories* for fifty years—Martha Foley picked the story up to list in her *One Hundred Distinguished Stories,* and to talk about in her introduction.

BEATTIE: This was the first story you had published?

DRISKELL: After the little *Atlanta Magazine* thing. I guess it was the second one I'd ever shipped off. I was thrilled with that inclusion and listing, and it's a story that I still believe in deeply, and would like to include in any collection that I ever do which in not thematically bound.

BEATTIE: What story is it?

DRISKELL: It's called "He Heard the Nickel Go Down," and it's patterned, in part, after Dante, and it is a story in which I went to some considerable effort to make my southern characters not quite distinguishable as either black or white. I wanted them to be people whose situation was a southern situation. The story was picked up by the Bobbs-Merrill people and that, of course, did not do me any harm. But then I was still very much involved in proving that I was an academic; therefore, I should get tenure and all that.

Things worked out very beautifully for me. I was accepted as a guest at Yaddo in 1970-71, the year in which I got academic tenure and was to be on a year's leave. So I went to Yaddo in July of 1970 and stayed until Halloween. Normally one stays for a week or two weeks, sometimes for even less time, but I was working productively, I was having a wonderful time.

BEATTIE: I remember your once telling me that you were called upon by other writers to critique their work while you were at Yaddo.

DRISKELL: Yes. And painters, too. I was writing a big article about a fairly unknown, at the time, abstract expressionist painter, and so that was part of what I was devoting time to while I was at Yaddo and I became, just by natural affinity, close to several of the painters and one sculptor—two sculptors, actually. I spent a good deal of time looking at, and talking about, painting as well as other work. That period of time that I spent at Yaddo gave me the thing I needed most. I didn't really need a place to be, and I didn't really need to have my meals served for me, though it was wonderful that they were, but I needed to have the sense that I wasn't just a school teacher who liked to write. I left there secure, in a way, professionally. I had achieved tenure, I had done my scholarly and critical publication so that the department would not have to be ashamed of me, and I was now going to attempt to write poems and stories. That was going to be what I did for a while.

BEATTIE: So, would you say your time at Yaddo, then, was pivotal in your own view of yourself as a fiction writer?

DRISKELL: Very much so. I began to think that it was not really self-indulgent to say, "I can't do that right now; I've got a story I have just got to stick to while it's coming." It was not quite a coming-of-age time, but it was very nearly coming of age. I was beginning to feel that I didn't have to explain myself, and I didn't have to have credentials.

BEATTIE: We may be getting out of chronological order here in terms of when you wrote various work, but your book *Passing Through,* that was published in the early eighties wasn't it? In reading that, there are two sentences or phrases that seemed to me pivotal for the book. One is, "There's no place to go but where you've already been." The other is, "What you do to balance your books is decide, once and for all, that the losses are really credits in disguise." Would you comment on your book and on those phrases?

DRISKELL: Oh, mercy, I'm just so pleased and so impressed. Of course, that's exactly what I'm up to and what this book is all about. The Buddhist term for what we do on the circle in the cycle of experience, from conception and birth through the joy, pain, sorrow, loss, and all the rest, to death and reincarnation, is translated frequently "passing through." It's what it's all about. And, of course, there is no place to be except where you've been before. I've done all this before, and am now getting a chance to do it a little bit better, a little bit more authentically. I am discovering myself in the process of becoming myself. Of course, that's precisely also what's behind the chapter called "A Fellow Making Himself Up." Rosco, in assigning himself his names and discovering his identity, there's a negation involved in that, in that story, as I think negations must always be involved in every story. He leaves the cafe and the woman who is his girlfriend in order to escape becoming the kind of joke that they are willing to make of him because of his origins, because of who and what he is. In negating and leaving behind, he begins a process of affirming. When he arrives in Kentucky and finds the love of a strong woman like Mama Pearl and a family that he may father and nurture, he recognizes that what one ought to do is to admit that one has been making oneself up all along, and cut some firewood so they can have hot biscuits for supper. That's what it's all about. That is a very, very important line for me.

Some people have felt that *Passing Through* turns after that opening story, "Dun-Roving," and the crazy kind of people that you see there with destructive impulses and all kinds of rather trivial qualities, that they suddenly become people instead of stereotypes or caricatures. It's not that I want to deny that they have stereotypical qualities in the opening story, but I think that those stereotypical qualities stick with them all the way through, that they are still struggling against all of the realities that formed them in the first place.

BEATTIE: I wanted to also talk to you about your story "The Blue You Thought in Kentucky," which features a character from *Passing Through*. When was that written, before or after the book?

DRISKELL: It has gone through, as nearly all of my stuff does, a number of metamorphoses. It existed at the time that I submitted to [Algonquin Books editor] Shannon Ravenel the manuscript for *Passing Through*. It got some serious and significant revisions thereafter. It is intended as possibly one of the stories in a sequel to *Passing Through*. I had saved several stories when I sent Shannon the manuscript, because I thought that the pieces I put together made sense. I would say that probably "The Blue You Thought in Kentucky" was initially conceived and written in '82 or '83, and that it took its final form in about 1986. And I have not changed it lately.

BEATTIE: In an introduction to a reading you did this past spring at Elizabethtown Community College, you quoted Katherine Anne Porter's introduction to *Flowering Judas*, "Art, like the human life of which it is the truest voice, thrives best by daylight in a green and growing world. For myself, and I was not alone, all the conscious and recollected years of my life have been lived to this day under the heavy threat of world catastrophe, and most of the energies of my mind and spirit have been spent in the effort of grasping the meaning of those threats, to trace them to their sources, and to understand the logic of this majestic and terrible failure of the life of man in the western world." You dedicated that reading to your wife, Sue, to Katherine Anne Porter, to Flannery O'Connor, to the poet May Sarton, and to your mother, Mae Curtis Driskell. I'd like to know if you believe your creativity or your creative vision derives in whole, or in part, from your effort to grasp the meaning of these threats, and I'd like also to know in what ways the women—and I think it's interesting that they are all women—to whom you dedicated your reading, share your quest or have somehow resolved or come to terms with it? Also, when Porter refers to the failure—"the terrible failure of the life of man in the western world"—do you believe she means man the gender or the species?

DRISKELL: That's really a great question. Let me go back to your preceding question just briefly. I responded to some of what you asked, but I didn't say what I should have said about Mama Pearl's saying late in *Passing Through*, "The losses are really credits in disguise." I think that I dedicate my work to those particular women and to women because I think women have the good sense to know that the losses are really gains in disguise, whereas the male generally is there, butting his head up against something he can't change, blaming himself for it and blaming everybody else around, and punishing people. Women, for the most part, say, "Well, that's one of the things we've got to bear. We take it from there and make the most of it," and generally, they make something pretty good of it.

Yes, I am very much aware that my world is Katherine Anne Porter's world. I think that we are seeing a terrible and cataclysmic failure of the Western, male-dominated civilization. I think that that failure has not everything to do with the gender "man." It may have a great deal to do with the general human qualities in the species. But, had there been a few more women in positions in which they could use that steady hand, that steady vision, and oblige us to stop and think and reassess before lashing out, we might not have lost quite so much as we have lost.

May Sarton, there's an enormous critical and creative capacity in that woman. The ability to make out of time spent alone, not time for brooding, for self-doubt, but time for building. Her capacity to make friends, to reach out to touch people all over the world, I admire and honor that very, very deeply.

Katherine Anne Porter, I suppose the consummate artist, always aware of the ways in which her own quest for human love was doomed to fail, partially because, as she said, she never fell a little bit in love, it was always the lightning stroke. And then she bumbled along. Yet the capacity of her vision in seeing in the Mexican Revolution the opportunities that were there and might have come to fruition had it not been for outside meddling. I think I've pretty well covered the several aspects of it.

BEATTIE: I've been asking writers what they think the nature of creativity itself is, and I'm wondering what you think it is.

DRISKELL: I've made, just lately, a few major discoveries about myself in that respect. I think that I am attempting to write and to do other things of a sort that we normally call creative, because of my need to fill an enormous gap, a void. I call it "The Hollow." I've written some surreal poems in which I tell all the things I've put into "The Hollow," and it's still not full. I imagine myself, on some occasions, as a kind of Henry Moore see-through sculpture with an enormous doughnut sitting there in the middle of my body, a transparency.

Sue did photographs the other night of me in front of her studio, Phoenix Hill Pottery, with shadows and shades, the picket fence, the foliage of Japanese maple, my long, skinny figure, and just miraculously, as the lights changed, there were large insets, cut-out areas in my body, in which one could see the foliage of the Japanese maple and part of the fence. And I thought, "What a wonderful metaphor for everything I am." I'm trying to earn something like humanity, and to fill those gaps, get rid of those animal instincts, temper and purify what I can, and get rid of the balance. I think that's the need to understand oneself through filling those gaps.

BEATTIE: Kentucky writer Jim Baker Hall talked about creativity being something that makes up for a loss in one's life, or a coming to an understanding. That instead of it being an added gift as some people regard it, it's something that makes up for a lack, that the creative person is actually lacking in something. Would you agree with that?

DRISKELL: Totally. I think that's what my hollow and my gap are all about, some kind of lack that I have at least recognized is there, and I have realized that the usual filler does not work in my case; the usual filler being lots of social activity, lots of busyness, alcohol, drugs. None of that will fill that gap. Now, this is not a constantly suffering, anguishing condition that one finds oneself in.

BEATTIE: So you don't believe the artist must necessarily suffer to produce.

DRISKELL: I think that all of us must necessarily suffer. I think it's what one makes of the suffering, or that one makes those losses into gains, or whether one just suffers and wallows in it, that makes the difference. I'm thinking of one of the gratuitous—I think that's the word I mean—achievements of that crazy book of freaks [one of Driskell's manuscripts] I've mentioned to you on occasion, the tattooed man and the male stripper and all that group of people. At the end of the book, the tattooed man still looking for his father, still trying to fill in some of his gaps, receives a very mean and spiteful letter from his daughter who is angry to discover that he's been publishing poems telling about all of the freakishness, perverseness, of the family. She tells him that she has changed her name, and that he will be glad to see that she has adopted the name of his old friend, "Though no matter how bad you say he is, I'd rather have his name than yours any day." And it's signed, "Sue Ann Blank," a negation, a nullity.

In the tattoo magazines which I have read occasionally, illustrated people, people who have been covered as my hero is with tattoo art, call other people "the blanks," people who have not been fulfilled, have not been decorated, have not achieved that kind of potentiality that I'm talking about. In some very significant ways then, I think that effort to cover oneself or to fill oneself in some way is what it's about. I did not know that Sue Ann Blank would mean someone not tattooed, someone incomplete, at the time I wrote it. I know now and feel that it's a perfect fulfillment of the kind of meaning that I'm after in that book.

BEATTIE: Your poem entitled "To Sue" is a real love poem in which you refer to her sustaining you in the season, "despite my sudden winter of thought." Would you discuss that winter of thought and how you have indeed transcended it with her help?

DRISKELL: I'm not positive that I have ever transcended it or ever can hope to transcend it, but I'll certainly tell you what I'm thinking about. That winter of thought is constant analytical process, the constant effort to understand everything and to push mystery aside, to penetrate the veil. It's what fouls us up nearly every time. That sudden winter of thought, if you recall William Blake, his character Urizen lived in the frozen North. That part of me which wants constantly to be busy, busy, busy figuring out, accounting for, understanding, that is the winter.

BEATTIE: But would you also say that's part of the creative drive, the need to understand?

DRISKELL: It is a part of the creative drive if one takes understanding to be something much more than cerebral or cognitive. I think that one really gets to the point at which one understands better with one's fingertips. If you recall, the poem's called "Signing Across the Dark," that notion that we're all really nothing more than fingers reaching out in the dark.

BEATTIE: Of course, sometimes understanding is also the same thing, as well as the opposite, of being understood. How much of the creative impulse do you think is to be understood by others as well as to understand yourself?

DRISKELL: How much of the creative impulse goes toward my wanting to be understood by other people? I think nine-tenths of it goes in that direction. If there is no communication at some level or another, it's a fatuous enterprise; one ought to hang it up right now. One doesn't necessarily hope that the person will be able to read a work and come up with a verbal assessment of what it is about and what it means, but if one has touched in some kind of secret way a secret part of the other, it's all been achieved. I was so very impressed a few minutes ago when you came up with those two sentences from *Passing Through* and said that you saw that so much of the book depends upon them. Those two statements and a few more—if you recall the little story called "Bright Star"—and one sees Mama Pearl looking out the window and it seems that Venus is penetrating her skull. I am seeing Mama Pearl as some kind of goddess, some kind of earth mother, if you will. It's that that Sue Driskell has in such enormous reserves, while I'm continually trying to earn a little bit of it. A student wrote a paper for me many, many years ago, the title was "No Matter How I Stand, My Head Keeps Getting in the Way." I don't want to go on record as an anti-intellectual or an opponent of cognitive things and learning, certainly not, but I would like to be able to get to the point at which my head and my heart are on talking terms, speaking.

BEATTIE: I'm interested in the notion of earning. You know you said that you're still trying to earn. Do you believe in the necessity of earning? Earning what? Earning your existence?

DRISKELL: I think that what one is able to earn is acceptance. I have been acculturated, I have been socialized, I have been taught to the point at which I question nearly everything, including myself, and to come to that really wonderful point at which I can accept, instead of trying constantly to change or to alter or to justify. I guess I do think that that has to be earned. I think it's easier for some people to earn than for others. I suppose that I would go along with the kinds of theologians who would argue that innocence not understood is scarcely innocence. And of course I'm back to William Blake.

BEATTIE: We've just talked about Flannery O'Connor. You conclude your poem entitled "To Flannery O'Connor, 1925-1964" with the line "Her darkness is the only light." Much of your work, particularly your story "Before Dinner," seems strongly influenced by O'Connor. Will you comment on how she has influenced your work and your philosophy?

DRISKELL: I think that she influenced my work most when she said unequivocally that the comic work is nearly always about matters of life and death. That gets rid of the kind of hierarchical structure that I had imposed upon me, in which I was led to believe that the epic which people no longer make, and the tragic which people no longer make, is somehow the superior, the better, the best. And that one moves down to such levels as comedy and satire—such modes as comedy and satire—and at that point, one is scarcely doing anything of any value at all.

No, I think O'Connor is important, and she does see that the comic spirit is, yes, a genial spirit, but it's also terribly, terribly important. I cannot imagine attempting to tell a story without seeing the potential for humor shot through all the fabric of the story. I don't always have a proper sense of limits and sense of restraint in my work, but I like very much for the story to be funny and to continue rattling along at a pretty good rate, continuing to be funny until the reader suddenly doesn't feel comfortable to laugh any longer. I think that at my best I achieve that.

July 27, 1992

Books by Leon Driskell

The Eternal Crossroads: The Art of Flannery O'Connor. With Joan Brittain. Lexington: University Press of Kentucky, 1972.

Passing Through. Chapel Hill, N.C.: Algonquin Books of Chapel Hill, 1983.

Turnabout. With Sue Driskell. Louisville: Beech Grove Press, 1995.

SUE GRAFTON

GRAFTON: My name is Sue Taylor Grafton. I was born in Louisville, Kentucky, on April twenty-fourth, 1940. My mother's name was Vivian Boisseau Harnsberger. She had a college education in chemistry, and I believe for awhile taught high school chemistry. My father's name was Cornelius Warren Grafton, and he was a municipal bond attorney in Louisville, Kentucky.

BEATTIE: Tell me about your grandparents on both sides of the family, what their names were and what you recall about them.

GRAFTON: I scarcely knew them. Both sets of grandparents were missionaries in China. My father was born in China and was educated there by his mother. My mother was born in Boston, West Virginia. We are not a close family, and while I was told many of these things often, I quickly deleted most of that from my memory.

I have a sister three years older than me whose name is Ann Warren Grafton. Her married name is Cox. She is the head of a branch library in Cincinnati, Ohio.

BEATTIE: What was your childhood in Louisville like?

GRAFTON: My parents were both alcoholics, so I was raised with what I'd consider benign neglect. My parents were educated and intelligent and caring and benign persons, but they had been raised in such a repressive environment, a church environment. When the two of them reached college age, my father discovered gin. In fact, it was his two older brothers who introduced him to gin, and I don't know that he ever recovered from that. My parents sort of acted out the textbook mythology of alcoholism, wherein my mother was the alcoholic and my father was the martyr. On my mother's death my father married a woman who then played the role of the martyr, and my father was the alcoholic, and thus everybody changed places.

I consider it the perfect childhood for a writer, because I learned early on to scan the environment. I always paid attention to what was going on emotionally. I learned to listen for the things that weren't said. Because I did not receive a lot of supervision, I used to wander Louisville from one end to the other. I would ride the buses from one end of the line to the other. I would wander in the park. I played with friends of mine in the neighborhood, and lived in my imagination for much of the time, so that I would consider that perfect training altogether.

BEATTIE: Were you aware at the time that your parents were alcoholics, or did you think that was normal parental behavior?

GRAFTON: I knew something was wrong with my mother and, obviously, I knew that she drank, but it's hard to put that in any kind of context when you're growing up. I remember being very unhappy, and in our family there were a lot of complex dynamics going on. I realize I'm very uncomfortable talking about this, not because I feel dishonest about it, but it seems too complex and complicated to explain for the purposes of an oral history. It's really very intricate psychological information, and while I've reached a point where I no longer feel protective of those two people, I despair at being able to describe it with any truthful content.

BEATTIE: I was just wondering if it was something that at the time made you feel somehow different.

GRAFTON: I felt probably somewhat isolated and somewhat estranged from other people, because I could tell, going into other households, that families did not live as mine did, and I found myself craving ordinary mortals. So I was in some ways very grateful to the parents of my childhood friends, because often they would sort of take me into the bosom of the family and they would invite me to stay for dinner, and I spent the night with friends a good deal of the time. My way of coping with the difficulties at home was to either imagine myself out of that or go somewhere else.

So I developed a lot of survival skills, and what I have found in later life is that those, then, became a prison of their own. A lot of the work I've done in terms of therapy and self-realization and reading and weeping and gnashing my teeth has been a process of coming to terms with all that and undoing some of the mechanisms I had to have about my person in order to survive my childhood.

BEATTIE: Did this make you closer to your sister? Was she going through similar things?

GRAFTON: She, in some ways, took the brunt of it, because she was older by three years, and what's curious is that I believe my parents loved each other very much, and they were very loyal to each other. In some ways, at the same time, they destroyed each other. So it was a curious relationship. I never doubted that they loved me, although my mother was difficult, and alcohol only exacerbated her problems. My sister, I have always felt, was more damaged by the situation than I, because she didn't seem to understand. She tended to take it head-on. She would head straight into the center of the storm, and I would just tap dance my way around the outside. I feel I had more inventive ways to escape. So in some ways, we were not closer because of it. In some ways, even now, it's as if in some respect my sister had a different set of parents, because she had a different set of coping skills.

The thing about alcohol is, the alcohol becomes the problem, and it, in fact, masks the real problems. So you never get around to solving the real problems, because you're so busy trying to cope with the side effects of alcoholism. So it's like you never get down to the real work, because you're always so busy coping with the devastation of people who are not sober.

BEATTIE: When did you start enjoying reading?

GRAFTON: My parents were very passionate about reading, and early on instilled in my sister and me a very deep and abiding love for books. One of the ways my family avoided dealing with its problems was by reading lots of books. So, for instance, my parents would sit in the living room, and my sister and I would sit in the living room, and we would all read. We did not speak to each other because we were so busy reading. In the evenings in the summertime we would often walk up to the Model Drug Store, which was at the corner of Eastern Parkway and Bardstown Road. In those days you could buy paperback novels for a quarter, and we would buy comic books and paperback books and bring them back to the house and read, which is really the way I was introduced, I believe, to the joy of books.

My sister . . . now, remember of course, since she was three years older than I, had always read more books, and I remember the frustration of never being able to catch up with her. She and my father would sit and discuss things that she'd been reading, and I can remember when I was still young enough to imagine that a book could not possibly be entertaining unless it had pictures, I would look at the book she was reading and think, "Ooh, this is so awful looking because there are no pictures." I can almost remember the day when it finally dawned on me that books were about stories, and that stories could be quite wonderful, whether there were pictures or not. That was a great leap forward for me.

BEATTIE: Were you read to before you went to school?

GRAFTON: Yes. I remember my mother teaching me the alphabet and how to write my name. Her alcoholism truly was exacerbated after the war. My father went off into the army, though he was actually beyond the age when he would have been required to do so, but since he had been raised in China, he had this fantasy that since he spoke Chinese, that they would send him back to China. In fact, this never happened. He ended up in India. He left when I was three and my sister was six, and my mother was responsible for the two of us and a big house on Everett Avenue, with rationing. I think it was very difficult for her. She also had some sort of thyroid condition and, in fact, went through menopause when she was thirty-three years old. There was a series of attempts to figure out what was really wrong with her. But much of the alcoholism was blamed on this mythical condition of hers. To this day, I don't know if there was some sort of chemical imbalance, or if that was just a euphemism for alcoholism.

But by the time my father got back from the war it was 1945, and there was a lot of drinking. I remember going to parties with my parents and people drank. That's what they did. They had highballs. There was an atmosphere of great celebration and great relief, because the war was over and people had survived. I was five or six at the time, but the adults drank. My mother began to show the effects of all this, and by the time I was five or six or seven, she was beginning a sort of downward spiral that nobody seemed able to save her from. In the family the mythology was, and my father perpetuated this, that he and Ann and I were the strong ones, and that it was our job to take care of her. So, in effect, my father infantilized my mother and made recovery impossible. Nowhere was there any mention of the fact that when she drank she was irrational and a tyrant, and that in fact my father had the luxury of going off to the office every day, leaving my sister and me in the care of this woman who was not always capable of raising young girls.

Usually there was somebody who would clean the house. My father had an ulcer operation in 1956. I was sixteen at the time, and the doctors refused to let him come home unless he had somebody cooking this special bland diet for him. So, at that point, my parents hired a woman named Carrie Glendenning who came into our household and cooked, and she became a sort of surrogate mother to me. But, in effect, it allowed my own mother to lie down and drink, because what little responsibility she had was no longer even hers to worry with. So, inadvertently, he made it possible for her to drink even more and do even less.

One of the things my father used to do was, when I was most miserable, he would sit down and explain to me that the doctors had told him that he had to choose between my mother or my sister and me. He would explain to us that, of course, he had chosen my mother, because he would tell me, Ann and I were strong and my mother was not, and therefore he had to choose to support her, because without him, she would die. So I would have to consent over and over again to my own abandonment.

I didn't understand how pernicious that was until I became a parent myself. Then I realized that the notion of sitting down with one of my children and explaining that a neglectful or abusive parent was being chosen over them, because they were strong and capable, and the abusing parent was not, just would be unthinkable. But what I think was true is that my father didn't know how to cope. He didn't know how to get help. He didn't know where to turn, and so he fumbled through on his own, and managed the whole thing very badly.

BEATTIE: It sounds as though you've done a great job of regaining self-esteem.

GRAFTON: In a curious way I did receive support in the world. Not always from my parents. I knew that my father loved me, and I knew that I was miserable, and I never in this world imagined to blame him. So a lot of the therapeutic work I've done has been in terms of recognizing the role he actually played in this whole drama, and recognizing the rage that I felt because of the position he put me in, and then getting to a point where I could forgive him for it. This takes thousands of dollars. I mean it is the most wonderful material for a writer, because my life has been spent understanding this—I was going to say, unusual growing up—but it's probably fairly common, if the truth be known. And that, in a way, has given me great power and great insight, and I would not change it for anything. You know, if I had to design a childhood for myself, it would look exactly the way it looked.

BEATTIE: What was your early education like, and where did you go to school?

GRAFTON: I went to Little I.N. Bloom, which sat at the corner of Cherokee Road and Bardstown Road, a little two-room school with a kindergarten and first grade. Then from Little I.N. Bloom, I went to Big I.N. Bloom.

I was always a sort of timid student and, for whatever reasons, I was always very worried about doing things correctly. I lived in mortal terror of getting bad grades or making mistakes or not getting it right. As a result of that, I did not really enjoy school. I did it well, and I was often a teacher's pet, because I was just such a worried little thing. I was just such a timid little creature. Kindergarten was the year of my first love affair. I fell in love with Nelson Helm, who sat next to me, and I'm sure we would tickle each other. When we had to have our little rest periods, you know, you lay your little head down on your arms, and we would conduct ourselves in a quite shabby fashion.

But I remember kindergarten very vividly. I remember so many things we did because it was like a fairy tale. It was like a great, frightening experience, and so it was planted indelibly in my imagination, and I probably still call on some of those feelings in order to write a scary scene in a book.

BEATTIE: What were the rest of elementary school and your junior high and high school years like?

GRAFTON: I remember grade school most vividly because of the melodrama, because it seemed so dangerous and so fraught with peril. For instance, if you were absent even one day, all the alliances would have changed in your absence, and you would come back to school and everybody's best friend would be somebody else, and you would be kind of shut out, and you'd be trying to figure out what had happened. I don't know what was going on, but I didn't feel I coped with that very well.

Junior high school I don't remember much of. I remember feeling very ugly. Well, actually, I felt pretty proud of myself. That same year I got braces and glasses and a bra. So I felt that was pretty wonderful stuff, because in those days, you had to wear a bra and a little slip. Girls had to wear a slip, and if you didn't have a bra, they would count the straps under your blouse and so everyone knew if you didn't have a bra on. So to get a bra was such a relief. Even if it was pitiful and small, at least now you were not one of the shunned. In many ways, I feel I was very imaginative and inventive, and yet I never felt I was part of the group that was popular and pretty and spiffy, you know, partly because at home, you see, this other melodrama was going down, so I never felt that comfortable bringing people to the house.

There was, by then, a very clear sense of the fact that my home life was not like other people's. The joy of going back to a high school reunion is that you realize everybody felt ugly and out of it, and then you begin to realize that that's what being fifteen is about. That helped me a lot when I began to understand that I wasn't really any different than anybody else. We were all ducklings instead of swans, and that's just the way life goes.

BEATTIE: You went to Atherton High School, right?

GRAFTON: That's right. And Highland Junior High.

BEATTIE: Were you writing at an early age?

GRAFTON: Yes, I was on the school paper in junior high school. I remember writing for the school paper when I was in I.N. Bloom School. Probably pitiful specimens of my work, but I did it.

BEATTIE: When did you start writing on your own, not school assignments, but things that you just wanted to write?

GRAFTON: I remember a poem I wrote when I was seven, and I'll recite it for you. The poem went as follows: "The new moon is on its way / the stars are shining bright and gay, / and if I close my sleepy eyes, / I can see my dreams come from the skies." That's sickening, but there you have it.

Another thing I did while in grade school was, for reasons that totally escape me, I used to memorize great long poems and go down to the principal's office and recite these, probably trying to ingratiate myself with her when she, in fact, scared the shit out of me. But my father in his upbringing in China was very much encouraged to commit things to memory, so it's possible that I was taking my cue from him.

But I remember I had begun to write probably in junior high school, and certainly by high school I was on the school paper there, too. On the school paper I worked . . . they had it divided into page one, page two, page three, and page one was sort of the news page, just as it would be in a regular paper. I think I worked on page two, which was features and that sort of thing. So I enjoyed journalism there, and was already doing some writing, with no particular aim toward a career as a writer.

BEATTIE: Do you remember when you first thought you wanted to be a writer?

GRAFTON: I remember early on, certainly by the time I was eighteen, I was obsessed with writing, but I did not imagine I would be a writer when I grew up, because that was not an option offered to girls in those days.

BEATTIE: Now, your father wrote books as well as being an attorney, correct?

GRAFTON: Yes, and I think that the reason I was attracted to writing was because he would talk to me about his writing process, and he was, of course, very encouraging of my writing. What he taught me was how to survive rejection as a writer. I remember he used to say that it was not my job to revise the English language, so he was very emphatic about the fact that I should spell correctly and punctuate correctly and not try to bend the English language into strange forms. He was very clear about how to cope with editorial comment and how to take editorial criticism, so that much of what he gave me was preparation for the life of a professional writer.

The problem was in those days many of the novels that were being published were of the Jack Kerouac sort, which is to say two men hitchhiking across America having adventures. Since I wasn't allowed to hitchhike, I knew that a life as a writer was totally impossible, so I imagined being a teacher, not a nurse, because I would faint at any approximation to a needle, and still I'm somewhat needle-phobic. So my choices seemed very limited, but I didn't resent that, because I didn't understand what the world had to offer other people, anyway. I just thought girls were nurses or teachers, and so I thought, "Well, I guess I'll be a secretary or something."

I went to U of L [University of Louisville] my freshman year, and then transferred to Western [Kentucky University], because I was dating a guy who had flunked out of the University of Louisville, and I just followed him down to Western. Then he and I broke up, and I ended up getting married my sophomore year at Western.

BEATTIE: So you married not the person you went to Western Kentucky University with, but someone else?

GRAFTON: Right. And I had a baby my junior year, and I divorced my husband my senior year. I found out I was pregnant at the same time and moved back in with my father.

My mother had since died. She died on my twentieth birthday, which, again, is perfect material for a writer. I was going, "My God, what does this mean?" I'm still not quite sure what the symbolism is, but she was diagnosed . . . she quit drinking in the summer of, it must have been 1959, and shortly thereafter began to complain of pain in the side of her head. Often with alcoholics, they are hypochondriacs also, and she had never paid any attention to nutrition. She smoked two or three packs of cigarettes a day for fifty years and she drank too much and she didn't eat well, so she was not a healthy person. When she began to complain of this pain, I remember we were all a little bit condescending. It was like, "Oh my God, what's this about?"

So she wanted to start going to doctors. She went to the family doctor and he couldn't find anything wrong, and she then went to an ear, nose, and throat specialist, and he couldn't find anything wrong. We were all sort of secretly rolling our eyes and being very obnoxious about it, because we just felt she was inventing. She finally went to the family dentist, and he discovered that she had cancer in the remnant of a tonsil. It was by then very far advanced, so they sent her up to New York to Memorial Hospital, and she had extensive surgery of the most horrendous sort. She had a hunk of jawbone removed, she had her tongue removed, she had her vocal cords removed. She was convinced that they had not gotten all the cancer, and I suspect she was correct. So she saved a hundred phenobarbitols and dissolved them. She had to be fed through her nose because she couldn't swallow anymore, so she took these hundred phenobarbitals and ran them through a tube in her nose and died, although it took her four days.

I was down at Western at the time, and I got word that she had fallen into a coma. Now, I didn't even know what that meant, really. But I drove up to Louisville. I knew she had the cancer, and I knew she had had this horrendous surgery. I also knew that she was not happy that she had survived that, but it took a little while for anybody to quite explain to me what had happened. They started pumping her full of medication, trying to counteract the phenobarbital, but there was no way to save her. She died on my twentieth birthday, as I said, and again, that is something that took me a long time to cope with, because I was not done with her. We had a very tormented relationship, and I had never processed it. It was very difficult for me to sort that out, because I realized, once she had died, that I had gotten married to get away from her. And she had died, and now the escape hatch I'd concocted for myself turned out to be a hideous trap. I had no business being married at the age of nineteen, so that began a sort of turbulence for some years, probably ten years, where I floundered around trying to get my balance and trying to cope with the legacy of the stress and confusion.

BEATTIE: Did you have two children from that first marriage?

GRAFTON: Yes.

BEATTIE: What are their names, and what was your husband's name?

GRAFTON: What was my husband's? I try not to mention these people by name. I was married to a man named James Leslie Flood. And my daughter's name was Leslie Kirsten Flood. She was born January fifth, 1960. She was about four months old when my mother died. Then my son, Jay Grafton, he was adopted by my second husband, so his name is now Schmidt. He was born April twenty-ninth, 1961.

BEATTIE: Did you get divorced in your senior year, and did you go back to U of L?

GRAFTON: Right. And my son was born in April of that year, and my graduation from U of L was delayed by, maybe, a quarter or a semester. I think we were on a semester system, because I had lost a little bit of time when Jay was born. So I think I graduated that summer instead of in June.

BEATTIE: And you had majored in English and minored in humanities?

GRAFTON: Yes, and a minor in fine arts.

BEATTIE: You said college was similar to high school in terms of your not liking it that much?

GRAFTON: Oh, I liked it pretty well, because I cut a lot of classes and played a lot of bridge, so I didn't find that nearly as stressful. I consider that I was brain dead till I was thirty-one years old, and then miraculously came to my senses, and sort of looked around and wondered how life had taken me to such a place. By then I was remarried, and by the time I was thirty-one, I had then had my youngest child. His name is Jamie Lee Schmidt, and it's very mysterious to me that I did not consider that I was an alert human being till very late in life.

BEATTIE: You've caught up fairly well.

GRAFTON: I think I was very pompous and impossible for someone who is not really conscious. I remember being very smug and judgmental for someone who had just screwed my life up desperately. Somehow I pulled out of it, and what was true was that the writing pulled me through. There was always the writing. No matter what was going on, writing was like a refuge to me, so I clung to it. I mean, writing is how I healed myself of my childhood.

BEATTIE: What did you do after college? Did you immediately start writing?

GRAFTON: Well, I decided to go to graduate school to get a little more bridge playing in, so I moved up to Cincinnati, and I was living with a friend of mine whose name is Pat Gray. Actually, we all called her "Torchy," and, in fact, *J is for Judgment* is dedicated to her. She and I were roommates in Cincinnati, and my son, Jay, was with me. My daughter, Leslie, I left with my ex-husband, James Flood, and he was raising her in Ashland, Kentucky. His parents helped raise her. So she and I were separated for many years, and we were reunited when she was about seventeen. I kept in touch with her, but I didn't feel capable of raising the two children, and he was very adamant that I could leave the marriage, but that she could not, so that was the agreement we reached.

So I got into graduate school, God knows how, because I don't think my grades were wonderful. But I hated graduate school. I couldn't bear it. I thought it was the most absurd thing, because there we were, dealing with English literature, which I dearly loved, but at the level of pompous analysis and absurd scrutiny. I remember being very offended that so much was projected onto a piece of prose, because I knew by then a little bit about what it felt like to be a writer, and I knew the difference between the choices a writer made and the interpretations that a reader inflicted, and I was just very offended. I think it was very clear to me at that point that my life was going to be about creating, and it was not going to be about analyzing other people's work. So I, for the first time in my life, became the bad girl of the department, and I refused to take my final exams, and so the university refused to pass me, and so I flunked. And oh, I remember feeling fairly delighted about that. It was the first time I had ever defied the system, really. Always before I had been the dutiful, timid, little creature, and I had just tried harder and harder, and I finally understood that it wasn't about that for me anymore, so it was a great and liberating juncture in my life. Actually, I think I flunked out fairly promptly. I did not waste time at this, and by then I had met and fallen in love with a fellow named Edward Allyn Schmidt.

BEATTIE: Was he in Cincinnati?

GRAFTON: Yes, when he was in Louisville he was introduced to me by a sorority sister. He was in the army at Fort Knox, and he was a somewhat eccentric fellow, and he didn't seem at all dismayed by me. I was, in fact, pregnant with my son Jay when I met him, and separated from James L. Flood. Phyllis Bader said to me, "Oh, I want to fix you up with this fellow." I said to her, "Dear, I am in just a world of hurt here. I'm pregnant and I'm separated from my husband. I don't think it's smart to date." She said to me, "Oh, he won't care. He'll think that's funny." I remember thinking to myself, "Al Schmidt is the ugliest name I ever heard, and why would you ever want to marry somebody with a name like that?" And sure enough, I ended up married to him, and truly he did not care that I was divorced and pregnant, and we dated the whole time I was pregnant with my son, Jay.

Al was in the army, as I mentioned, and word got back to his commanding officer that his girlfriend was pregnant, and so his commanding officer called him in to reprimand him, and Al said, "I didn't do it. It's not my kid, so I don't know why I should be blamed for it."

So, at any rate, it was a sort of a comical course of events. But in many ways, he was a very stabilizing factor in my life, because he apparently didn't realize how crazy I was. I was just looney-tunes by then, but he didn't get it, and so he kept treating me like a normal person. So because he treated me like a normal person, I did fine. He and I were married for nine-and-a-half years, and then we parted company.

After we married in the spring of 1962, we came out to California, to San Francisco, and I got a job with the Kern County Land Company as a file clerk. I worked there, and we left San Francisco fairly quickly, maybe four-to-six months later, because Al got a job with a company called Human Factors Research, which was based down in Santa Monica. So we moved down to the Los Angeles area, and I then got a job at St. Johns Hospital as an admissions clerk. I remember, at the time, Ben Casey was on television, and so was Dr. Kildare, and I decided I should enter the medical field right then in case a cute doctor was hanging around. So I pretended I knew medical terminology and got myself hired and quite enjoyed the work. I really liked hospital work, and I would do that again if I could. I would also be in the police department if I could, but I can't. Then, eventually, we moved to Santa Barbara, and I went to work for a general practitioner named Joe L. Atchison, and enjoyed that, too.

BEATTIE: All of these settings show up in your novels.

GRAFTON: Yes. In fact, I love medical stuff. What I love is the proximity to drama. With illness, as with homicide, you are looking at people who are under pressure and who are trying to cope with difficult situations, and I think that's where the truth about us comes to the fore. So I usually advise young writers, instead of becoming journalists, which I think is sort of redundant, I don't think you need to be a journalist and then go home and try to write a novel in your spare time. I think you're better off working in an occupation that gives you some insight into how the world works. Then your fiction is sort of a counterpoint to your ordinary life.

BEATTIE: I've heard that you've advised beginning writers to write mainstream fiction first and to then specialize.

GRAFTON: I believe that most writing is self-taught. We can have instruction and guidance and encouragement, but the job of writing is actually one that has to be generated from the inside out, and I think the best tool of instruction is the novel for anyone who intends to be a novelist, eventually. Many people start out as poets, and they're perfectly happy, and that's what they do. And many people write short stories, and that's where they intend to stay. But my progression, and what I have observed over the years, is that many writers begin with poetry and proceed to the short story, and from the short story then to the novel. But I was advised early on to get into the novel and I did that, and I feel it was very sound advice, so it's something I pass on to people.

BEATTIE: There seems to be a false premise that the quality of genres depends on their length, that there *is* a progression. You know, you're not a writer unless your work is *this* big.

GRAFTON: Really. Well, I think many people getting into this field have a natural concern with earning a living. If you love writing, your intention and your hope, always, is to reach a point where you can support yourself with the work. In my experience, the only way to do that is to move as quickly as possible to long form, which is nonfiction or the book-length novel.

I have seen people try to get into writing by way of the screenplay or the mystery novel, and I think it is a huge mistake, because those are really specialized forms. I think the first thing you need to do is learn how to tell a good story. You need to learn how to characterize and how to lay out suspense and how to pace yourself, all manner of things that are too much to cope with if you're adding the complication of suspense and being worried about planting and paying off clues and things of that sort.

BEATTIE: You wrote two novels, didn't you, before you began your alphabet mystery series?

GRAFTON: I did. The first novel I wrote while I was living in Los Angeles. I took a UCLA extension course from a man named Robert Kirsch, who was then the book editor at the *Los Angeles Times,* and he was the one who encouraged me to write my first novel, which was called "Miggie," which I don't even think I possess anymore. A quite miserable work. But I did prove that I could finish a book, and that's a huge victory. I was twenty-two years old at the time, and, of course, what I knew about the world was very limited, and it was not anything I could process at that point. So while I had the experience, I didn't have any wisdom whatsoever.

But I wrote a novel after that called "The Monkey Room," which was about a fellow who took care of the monkeys at Fort Knox, and I wrote a novel after that called "Sparrow's Field," about a man who ran a garbage dump somewhere in Kentucky. The fourth novel I wrote was called, in its original title, "The Seventh Day of Keziah Dane," which title became shortened to simply *Keziah Dane,* and that I entered in an Anglo-American Book Award contest, which I did not win, but I did receive a publishing offer for two-hundred-and-seventy-five pounds from a British publisher, and I used that publishing offer to get myself an American agent who got me an American publisher, and that publisher was MacMillan. So *Keziah Dane* was published in 1967 by MacMillan.

The book I wrote after that was called *The Lolly-Madonna War,* and the American publisher said it was too violent for American tastes, so it was only published in England. That book, the film rights were optioned by a British film producer who came to this country and asked me to help him with the screenplay because it was a novel about Appalachia, and because he was British he had no clear understanding of the mindset or even the use of language. So he taught me how to do screenplays for him. In about ten days we completed that screenplay, and then he took it to Hollywood. He was the producer on it, but it was actually filmed by MGM and it came out in 1973.

Meanwhile, I left Al Schmidt and moved in with this fellow, taking my two older children with me, and so he and I lived together for three years while the film was being made and while we were also trying to launch other works that we wrote together. But we never got anything else off the ground. And he was just such a wretched person, he was really a flim-flam man, and in the end that relationship broke up.

The film was wretched, but it did teach me the form. I have to credit the fact that it was a real break for me, because I got enough money to lose my husband, you see, and then I backed into the television business. Once the collaboration with this British film producer broke up, I was on my own, and I began to write movies for television.

I worked in Hollywood for probably ten or fifteen years altogether, but meanwhile, I wrote a novel called "The End of All Mourning," which was never published, and I wrote a book called "Diminished Capacity," which was never published. Then the eighth book I wrote was called *A Is For Alibi.* By then I was pulling out of Hollywood because I was totally miserable.

I was meant to be not a mainstream, but at least a solo writer, and I did not enjoy the process of working in Hollywood. For one thing, in Hollywood everybody is twenty-six years old, and they are put in positions of great power, and they will tell you how to do your business without any experience at writing whatsoever. And the older I got, the crankier I got, because I just couldn't bear being told how to do my business by these snot-nosed kids. So I found myself so angry so often I thought, "You know, if you don't like the game, don't take the money." I understood that if I was unhappy, it was my responsibility to get myself out of it.

I didn't feel it was healthy or fair to stay in a business for which I had no respect, working for people that I couldn't abide, and so I began to write *A Is For Alibi* as a sort of antidote to solve my distress and unhappiness at Hollywood. When I began my book, they told me that I would never make the kind of money from mysteries that I'd made in Hollywood, but I didn't care. I knew I needed to do it for my soul. I said at the time, "I'm not doing it for the money," but once I published several books I thought, "Well, now, let me prove my point. Now can I have the money?" So it's been very gratifying to watch that career come together.

BEATTIE: You were talking about a brief stint writing for television, about writing an episode of the *Rhoda* show.

GRAFTON: That was my first job in Hollywood. When the collaboration broke up, somebody said, "Well, you should write television." I said, "Well, how do you do that?" And they said, "Well, all you do is watch a show that you like." The only show I watched was *Rhoda,* so I watched an episode, and I figured out who the character was, and then wrote this episode for nothing and submitted it to the show, and again, they didn't buy it, but they called me in for a meeting and told me how to write for television, which I didn't really clearly understand. So I ended up writing a second show for nothing, and off that I got an assignment to do the episode of *Rhoda* that I eventually did. But I thought it was very hard work.

Comedy is very difficult. A thirty-minute script only allows you something like twenty-two or twenty-three pages of scripting, and they literally sit there counting the jokes. You were supposed to have like three pops [jokes] a page, and I really don't know how to be funny for money, so I was not happy doing that.

But in the meantime, an executive named Donald March of CBS remembered a script that this film producer and I had cowritten and, now, you understand that in Hollywood, nobody reads and nobody remembers anything. But this man read and remembered this joint venture of ours, and he asked me if I would be interested in writing a movie for television for him, which I did, and that was an adaptation of a book called *Walking Through the Fire,* by a woman named Laura Lee, who discovered that she had Hodgkin's Disease when she was six months pregnant with her third child. She was told that she would have to abort the baby and begin very vigorous chemotherapy, but she refused to do it, and so they did some radiation while she carried this baby to term. This book was the journal she kept throughout this life-threatening illness, and that's what I adapted for the movie for TV, and for that I won a Christopher Award.

Then I wrote, TV-wise, a teleplay called *Sex and the Single Parent* with Susan St. James and Mike Farrell. And I wrote one called *Mark, I Love You,* about a custody battle in Iowa, and I wrote a two-hour teleplay for *Nurse,* which became the series with Michael Lerned.

After that, Steve Humphrey, to whom I was by then married, had received his Ph.D. in the philosophy of physics at Ohio State, and I told him he was then perfectly equipped to write movies for television. What else is such an education going to equip you for? So he and I then wrote movies for television together, and among those were the two Agatha Christie adaptations we did, one of which was called *Caribbean Mystery* with Helen Hayes as Miss Marple, and *Sparkling Cyanide* with Deborah Raffin and Anthony Andrews. We also did a movie for TV called *Killer In the Family* with Robert Mitchum. We did one called *Love On the Run,* which was about a lady lawyer who busts a guy out of prison and runs away with him, and we coauthored one called *Tonight's the Night,* which is just a wretched exercise in popular culture that I prefer to forget.

BEATTIE: How did you meet your husband, Steve Humphrey?

GRAFTON: He and I were living in the same apartment building in west Los Angeles, and each of us had a little kitten, and we would let the kittens play together in the courtyard and make idle baby talk in their behalf, you know, and we ended up dating and we fell in love. He had been working as a waiter making, oh, minimum wage, probably three bucks an hour. This was before I really got launched writing movies for TV, and so I was working as a production secretary. In a pinch you can always fall back on those typing skills, by God.

I was working for Danny Thomas Productions. I worked on a pilot called *Fay* with Lee Grant, and then I worked on a movie for television called *Devil's Triangle* with Kim Novak and Doug McClure, and I was the one who put together the shooting schedule. I don't know what all I did, but it didn't seem difficult, and I made 175 bucks a week, which I thought was just a smashing amount of money. Meanwhile, Steve and I had started to date, and he had then been accepted for graduate school at Ohio State, so we were together for maybe seven or eight months, and then he had to go off to Columbus, Ohio, and I followed him a year later. I was there five years, he was there six, and we married in Columbus, Ohio, in 1978.

BEATTIE: Were you writing during that time when you were in Ohio?

GRAFTON: Yes, I was commuting to Hollywood writing movies for television, and by 1978 or '79 I had started just the early process of writing *A Is For Alibi.*

BEATTIE: What made you decide to write mysteries? Were they favorite things for you to read?

GRAFTON: Yes, my father had always loved mystery fiction and he, himself, had written and published three mysteries, so I remember it always seemed to me something I would do at some point in my life. And I thought, "Well, why not?"

BEATTIE: You've committed, I understand, to getting to the end of the alphabet, but you also said the writing is getting more difficult.

GRAFTON: Yes, partly because—and I suspect this is something many writers suffer from—when you're first beginning and you are nobody, there is something very liberating about that. I usually tell young writers that since they're unpublished, their reputations are intact. So I always caution them to be very careful about sending work out before it's finished, because when I started *A Is for Alibi,* how could I fail? I hadn't done anything, and I had no reputation, so I had nothing to protect, and the writing was a lark. I was doing that to amuse myself. I was sort of inventing the form as I went along. I was studying how-to books, and I was doing a lot of reading in terms of the technical end of it. But I had nothing at stake. I had no reputation. I was nobody, and that enabled me to work with great freedom. Where I am now, many people are looking over my shoulder, and often I feel they are waiting for me to fall flat on my face. It's like a little contest. There's nothing the critic enjoys so much as someone falling from grace.

BEATTIE: Not all critics.

GRAFTON: I know. They pretend to be so regretful that you screwed up, but the truth is, they adore it. So I know they are waiting for me to blow it, and I intend to outwit them. So that's part of the contest I'm involved in.

With writing in particular, when you begin, you have all your fresh material to deal with, and it's very easy when you first start out. But as you progress, when you've used up all those quick images, and you've used up all the ready insights, the only way to keep at it is to keep digging deeper and deeper into yourself, and that is not only painful, but it's very frightening, because I think we all worry that at heart we're shallow and trivial people. You think, "Well, we can all write one book," but it's book twelve and fifteen and book twenty-six that, in fact, are the test of your skills.

BEATTIE: Tell me about Kinsey Millhone. Is she your alter ego?

GRAFTON: She is an alter ego. She is also an extension of myself. She and I, as I describe it, we have different life lines, different biographies, but the same sensibilities. So I often say I think of us as one soul in two bodies, and she got the good one. She will never have to grow old and she will never have to be fat. She can eat junk food for the rest of her life and she'll always exercise. I have to suffer the indignity of failing senses and she does not, so she lives a much more adventurous life than I do, but mine is more glamorous. So there you have it.

BEATTIE: And you own more than one black dress.

GRAFTON: I personally do, and, in fact, it's funny, people are always surprised because I dress up. They expect to see me in blue jeans and a turtleneck, and I realize I really could tour in a pair of blue jeans. But I was raised, as I describe it, in the semi-South, and I was taught you dressed up in your Sunday best when you go out in public. So I would not wear those kind of clothes this woman [Kinsey Millhone] wears.

She really has informed my life. She has altered the course of my life. Because of her I had to learn how to shoot a handgun. I had to take a class in self-defense. I've taken a class in criminal law. I have gone into morgues, police stations, and I've done ride-alongs with a cop and God knows how many things I would never do as Sue Grafton.

BEATTIE: I think there's something about Kinsey Millhone with which most baby boomers can identify. We all identify with her diet of white wine and quarterpounders with cheese. Do you get letters from people referring to Kinsey Millhone as a real person?

GRAFTON: Oh, sure. Sometimes they actually write to her in care of me. I think they're sick. I get all manner of letters. I got a letter from a truck driver who had actually fallen in love with her listening to the audio tape, and so he wrote to her directly, and it was just very darling. I had to write back to tell him how big my husband was and I said, "He's in the other room, even as I speak, lifting weights." He wrote back, and he then assured me that his intentions were honorable, but it was amusing. So I generally try to write back to people.

BEATTIE: One thing I've noted in reading your books is that unlike the books by some male writers of mystery novels or detective fiction, you don't feel obligated to have your heroine engage in sexual liaisons in every book.

GRAFTON: No. What I have often thought is that the male private investigators, and the writer of the male private investigator, seem intent on persuading you that the hero is appealing to women, sexually accomplished. And the female private investigator and the writer of the female private investigator is intent on persuading you of her competence. So we are very careful, she and I, to make sure that you understand that she is a professional working woman and that she is not moving through the world on the basis of her back. I'm very particular about that, and it's one of the reasons I generally will tell you how much money she makes on a case, so that the reader understands she is a person who can pay her bills.

BEATTIE: I think that makes her someone with whom readers can identify more, too.

GRAFTON: Yes. Well, for one thing, we live in sexually dangerous times, and I feel she is too cautious a person, and rightly so, to be engaged in countless, frivolous sexual relationships or liaisons. Also I think, as most women will attest, there aren't that many good men in the world. So you come across one now and then, but my single women friends are always lamenting the fact that there are just not that many good men out there.

I feel I'm real clear with her, that she is very content to be by herself. She does not feel like half of something. She is not restlessly looking about for somebody to fill the gaps in her life. I think she enjoys her world and her life and her friends and her freedom and her independence, and I think it's really important for women to understand that there's nothing wrong with being by yourself. This is a treat. It is far superior to be by yourself than to be in a bad relationship. I do know women who are so determined to be connected to somebody that they end up in abusive situations, which I just think we need to look at from another lifestyle and another point of view, and certainly for me, Kinsey provides that.

BEATTIE: The whole way you've characterized Kinsey Millhone not only in terms of her not having excessive affairs, but in terms of her clothing, her lack of material things, etcetera, puts the emphasis of the drama on the action itself.

GRAFTON: She lives by outsmarting the bad guys, by figuring out the puzzle in life, which is truly just a metaphor for what all of us are doing. We're trying to figure out how to survive; we're trying to outrun the wolf.

March 28, 1993

Books by Sue Grafton

Keziah Dane. New York: MacMillan, 1967.

The Lolly-Madonna War. London: Owen, 1969.

"A" is for Alibi. New York: Holt, Rinehart & Winston, 1982.

"B" is for Burglar. New York: Holt, Rinehart & Winston, 1985.

"C" is for Corpse. New York: Holt, 1986.

"D" is for Deadbeat. New York: Holt, 1987.

"E" is for Evidence. New York: Holt, 1988.

"F" is for Fugitive. New York: Holt, 1989.

"G" is for Gumshoe. New York: Holt, 1990.

"H" is for Homicide. New York: Holt, 1991.

"I" is for Innocent. New York: Holt, 1992.

Kinsey and Me. Limited Edition. Hawthorne, Calif.: Bench Press, 1992.

"J" is for Judgment. New York: Holt, 1993.

"K" is for Killer. New York: Holt, 1994.

"L" is for Lawless. New York: Holt, 1995.

James Baker Hall

HALL: I am James Baker Hall, and I was born in Lexington, Kentucky, in 1935. My mother's name was Lurlene Bronaugh Hall, and she was a housewife and homemaker. My father's name was Walker Russell Hall, and he was a variety of things. Early on in his life he worked in his father's bank in Clay City, Kentucky, and was a wildcat driller in the Eastern Kentucky oil fields when they first began to open up. He was a military man in heart and in spirit. He was in the National Guard, and at the outset of World War II he went into the military and stayed until a couple of years after the war was over. He was in the army reserves until he retired.

I was born into the house of my paternal grandfather, whose name I bear, and of my grandmother, a big house on the Paris Pike outside Lexington, Kentucky, about a quarter of a mile down the road from the Lexington Country Club, where my mother and father moved in 1931, four years before I was born, with a one-and-a-half-year-old child, to live then for a number of years with his parents.

My mother died in 1943, and my grandfather died shortly after that, and then, in my grandmother's care, my sister and I moved into Lexington, where we lived with her for the rest of our dependency.

I never lived in a house with my mother and father as my parents; it was more nearly my grandparents functioning as my parents from the start. My grandfather was the manager of the Lexington Railway System—which was the precursor to what's now LexTran—during the period when it was transformed from the inner urban trolley to a bus company. My grandmother was a homemaker. They loomed very large in my childhood experience, much larger than my father.

I have one sister, who's five years older than I am. She is married with two grown children, and she is a long-time resident of Lexington. She has never lived elsewhere.

I went to a private school on Broadway—I don't remember the name of it—for the first two-and-a-half years, and entered public school at Bryan Station Elementary School for the first time in the third grade. As I recollect, I went to Bryan Station for one full academic year.

Then, with my grandmother, my sister and I moved into town. I went to public school first at Ashland Elementary School and then at Morton Junior High School, and then to Henry Clay High School, and then on to UK [University of Kentucky], and on to Stanford University after that.

I wasn't particularly interested in school, except as an occasion for sports, and as a way to organize my interest in sports. I did well enough in school, and it was never any particular concern to me. I did, in high school, have a liking for literature, at least for some things that we read in English class.

Edgar Allan Poe was my first great thrill with the written word. I know that I wrote a couple of imitation Poe poems when I was in high school, but that didn't represent anything that I would call an interest in writing. I don't think that really happened for several years.

What I was really interested in from the start was sports. Early on I played baseball and then, as soon as I could, basketball, and then when I got the chance, I was a member of the track team and the football team at Henry Clay. Until I got to the university and had a real experience of literature, my mind was taken over by sports, and by social activity, and by clothes, and by girls.

When I went to college there was nothing in my experience to suggest what I should become other than a businessman or lawyer or maybe a doctor if I wanted to. We were middle-class with very solid middle-class respectability, the values of respectability, and it was expected of me that I become a professional.

Well, I guess there was another real possibility. There certainly was the military. My father tried to get me an appointment to West Point and to Annapolis, and if I had gotten either of those, if he'd been able to get them, I certainly would have gone. I went into the university with these vague plans; I'd go into law school maybe, or whatever, and immediately on the experience of literature that I found in an introduction to literature class, I was taken over by the desire to write. A very specific experience turned me in that direction.

T. S. Eliot's poem, "The Love Song of J. Alfred Prufrock" sort of picked me up out of the nineteenth century and set me down in the twentieth century with a whole lot of experience that I'd never had before. A connection was made with parts of my mind and body that had been dormant and starved until that experience. It was riveting, it was mesmerizing, it was profound, and its impact on my life is beyond measure. I still am playing out the very life-enhancing consequences of that experience.

BEATTIE: Is it at all strange to you that you would have had such a profound experience without having some preparation for reading a poem like that, that such an experience might be difficult without that preparation?

HALL: Not really. I understand what you're asking, but that poem sounded to me, how to put this? I had never heard language before seeking the truth at whatever cost. I had never heard fearlessness before. I'd heard talk about such things, but I had never heard language spoken from the experience of fearlessness. And there was a very, very profound need in my life at that point for those very things, and for the possibility of honesty and directness to be among my chances in life. There was a great deal of trauma in my early childhood, and a family scandal that involved my mother's suicide. It went from a very ordinary scandal into a quite extraordinary tragedy right in front of me, and nobody in my family or elsewhere would talk to me about it. I had two or three years of my life blotted out by that trauma. I had a very great and profound need to hear someone's mind and language engage the possibility of facing whatever it is that life has brought him to. So, there was no need for an intellectual gloss on "The Love Song of J. Alfred Prufrock" in order to bring it home to me. It went right underneath my conscious mind into my soul, and what it was talking about I recognized immediately.

BEATTIE: That's what I was referring to. What had set you up to recognize it?

HALL: It was my life. My life had prepared me to need something that that poem had to offer as a matter of survival. Of well-being, certainly, and ultimately, survival. I was either going to find the truth of my life and of my sources, or I was going to live a lie. That poem presented me with the option. I didn't have the choice up until then. I didn't *know* there was any choice up until then. All I knew was that I was supposed to think about myself in a certain way, and I was supposed to act a certain way in order to protect the respectability of my name and my family. I didn't know that there was anything else possible.

BEATTIE: What was it that happened in your childhood that you found out about?

HALL: Well, it took me forty-eight years to find out the story that everyone else in my family and everyone else in our social circles knew. I was eight years old at the time of my mother's death, and the circumstances that surrounded her suicide were scandalous, and the scandal shut down everybody's willingness to discuss it with me. That was my life. I supposed for a long time, with my interest in fiction writing and with my imagination, I supposed and understood in a general way what had happened, but I wasn't able to have it confirmed until I was in my late forties, when I really was put on the spot where I had to find out about this and pin it down or never do it. And it involved some very, very serious confrontations with not only my family, but with myself and with the life I had made with myself up until that point. So, I had been on the track of finding out what my story was, and I had become a story writer, and I had written stories for thirty-five years before I actually was willing and able to track down the story of the scandal that proceeded my mother's suicide. But all that was implicit in the sound of "The Love Song of J. Alfred Prufrock."

BEATTIE: When you did track down the scandal, I know it was subjective for you, but were you able to look at the incident objectively enough to realize whether it was in fact as scandalous as it had seemed at the time?

HALL: Oh, it was every bit as scandalous as it was at the time, and the scandal continued quite consequentially in the silence that attended it. I mean, it was scandalous in every respect, and it involved me forgetting my mother and honoring my father, which was a terrible, terrible mistake, a spiritual mistake of enormous consequences. I forgot my mother, and didn't understand that she loved me, for most of my life. And I paid honor and respect to those who disconnected me from that experience. It was a terrible, terrible misunderstanding.

BEATTIE: So, this finding "The Love Song of J. Alfred Prufrock" was something that put you on the track to developing that understanding.

HALL: It created the possibility of wanting it. It created the possibility of honesty, of not living a lie, and my interest in literature was a bonfire from word go.

BEATTIE: Do you remember which year in college this was?

HALL: Yes, it was when I was a freshman, and I immediately started reading. I had never read until then. I had one period of reading when I was a kid, in junior high school. When I was in the eighth grade, I read a bunch of boys' adventure stories in a competition that a friend and I had constructed between ourselves, a competition of who could read the most books. We'd go to the library and get boys' adventure stories, and I did read during that period, but my reading then didn't have anything to do with the experience that I'm talking about that I had with literature. When I had the experience of "The Love Song of J. Alfred Prufrock," one of the first things I did was to find a record of Eliot reading Eliot in the Library of Congress. At that time there were no commercial records available. But I found out that there was this issue from the Library of Congress, and I got a copy of it, and

I didn't have any way to play it, but I had friends who had phonographs, and I would arrange for solitude in their houses, and I would go listen to T.S. Eliot read T.S. Eliot, and I had a protracted experience of the kind of concentration and the kind of trance that literature can get you in.

I began to read intensely and extensively in twentieth-century literature all of the things that Eliot led me to, and I began to pay real close attention to easel painting. I had been interested in practicing photography as a kid, all my life, and been very visually engaged from age twelve on. Easel painting spoke to me, and I understood it immediately, and I fired the interest generated by Eliot into a lot of reading and a lot of looking.

I became, as was the model of the day, a student of literature because of that, and I became what you call an English major, and then I went on to graduate school in English. But the fire in my belly had to do with writing, and with the experience of the few books that you find in your life that tell you how your life might deepen, and how your mind might become more clear. I wasn't really interested in becoming a student of literature. I went into the systematized study of literature on the energy of a love affair, and found an arranged marriage at the other end, by the time I got half-way through graduate school and got out.

The systematic study of literature, although I have pursued it all my life and am very interested in the literary history and the biography of the writers and read still with great interest and intensity in that area, is not the kind of energy that informs creative writing. It informs the writing of poetry and fiction. They're part of the same family tree, and they are often confused in their relationship. I mean, I have writing students who come to me who think that because they have studied literature they can back into the writing of a poem or a story. It's a terrible confusion.

BEATTIE: Appreciation and the ability to write are two different things.

HALL: They're coming from two different directions, and they cross at this one point.

BEATTIE: I understand that. What about graduate school? What sort of writing were you pursuing then?

HALL: Well, I didn't. I was in a Ph.D. program at Stanford in literature. I didn't have the time or the energy to do anything except what I was being asked to do as a graduate student in the Ph.D. program at Stanford. When I dropped out of the Ph.D. program, I did it in order to devote myself to my writing. I had, for five or six years, thought of myself as a writer, and I came to the point where I said, "Look, you've either got to put up or shut up. You've gotten all of the glamour and sucked all of the goody out of the idea that you're a writer or going to be a writer as you possibly can. You're a complete fraud now if you don't act like a writer." So I quit graduate school and I got a part-time job, and I was married by that time, and I had a professional wife who was able to help support us very significantly right from the start. I was able, then, to put writing first and to do it every day. After a year of full-time writing, I applied for a writing fellowship back at Stanford in their very prestigious writing program, and I got a fellowship in fiction. I then went back to Stanford in a whole other area of the English department, and I stayed as a fiction fellow at Stanford for one year, and then I stayed on and taught there for a while. Then my wife got a job in New England, and we moved to Massachusetts.

BEATTIE: When did you marry her, and what is her name?

HALL: Joan Joffe Hall. I married Joan in, I think, 1959. But I had been married briefly before that. I had a weekend marriage as an undergraduate that literally lasted about four months, and the divorce from that marriage was within a year.

BEATTIE: Was this to another undergraduate?

HALL: Yes. A friend, although an acquaintance more than a friend, from high school. A girl I had known. I'd never had much to do with her, but we ended up, to our mutual surprise and chagrin, getting married in the middle of our undergraduate days, and finding it very quickly unworkable. My marriage to Joan Joffe was my second marriage, and it lasted eighteen years.

BEATTIE: And this is while you were in graduate school. Was she another writer?

HALL: She finished her Ph.D. and has been a professional academic all of her life, and I was able to continue to be a full-time writer for years, because she was a professor at Wellesley College for a while, and then at the University of Connecticut, and she was making as much money as we needed to live on. So I wasn't under any economic necessity to work outside my study. I did, from time to time. I taught one place or another, part-time, during periods, but I was able and desirous of writing full-time, and that's what I did.

BEATTIE: At Stanford, did you end up with an M.A. degree?

HALL: I actually ended up with an M.A., but I wouldn't have, had I not gone back and done that last year in the creative writing program. They wanted a thesis from me to get an M.A. I was in the Ph.D. program. The M.A. was like a flunk-out degree, and in order to get it, I had to hand in a thesis, and I wasn't willing to do that. But then they accepted the first novel I wrote in lieu of a thesis, and gave me an M.A. But that was not something I pursued.

BEATTIE: Did you have any children from your first marriage?

HALL: Yes. I had one child from the first marriage, who was raised by my first wife's second husband, and I never saw the young man until recently. I mean, I saw him as a baby a couple of times, and then she went away and moved to Indiana and then to New York, and I saw him maybe once or twice while he was growing up.

BEATTIE: So, your divorce was soon after the baby was born?

HALL: Before the baby was born. Lois [Camack] was three or four months pregnant when we separated. So, I wasn't even invited to the hospital for the child's birth. I have had no connection with that son until, quite astonishingly, miraculously, very recently we've gotten together, finally. But I have two children from my second marriage, and I was the basic in-house parent for the first one for his first five years. Both of those children I brought up and am very close to.

BEATTIE: You're developing a relationship with the child from the first marriage?

HALL: I had two children, and I did have two children until recently. Well now, I've got a third, okay, who is like thirty-six years old. And my third child is indeed fully blown out of the drunken head of our experience.

BEATTIE: You were divorced from your second marriage in what year?

HALL: I was divorced in about 1978.

BEATTIE: Then what went on with your career and personal life? You said you were teaching part-time on the East Coast, is that right?

HALL: Yes. We went to Wellesley, Massachusetts, and were there for two years. I was living in a faculty apartment with my wife on the Wellesley College campus and writing full-time. When we moved to Storrs, Connecticut, she took up a job at the University of Connecticut. For about a period of eight years in there I taught part-time, sometimes at MIT [Massachusetts Institute of Technology] in Cambridge, sometimes in the English department teaching creative writing, sometimes in the photography department teaching photography. I taught, then, full-time in the art department at the University of Connecticut for two years teaching photography. I taught once at N.Y.U. [New York University], but those were on teaching stints laid in around a protracted ten-year period of fiction writing, and the story of my career during that period is as follows.

I published my first novel when I was twenty-six-years old. This was *Yates Paul: His Grand Flights, His Tootings.* It was the second novel that I had written. I wrote the first one, oh, basically when I was on the fellowship at Stanford. I started *Yates Paul* toward the end of that academic year, as a story, and its first form was a long short story, and then it went over into a novel. I didn't find this out until a few years ago, but the review copies of *Yates Paul* were not sent out. The guy in charge of that didn't do his job. The review copies stayed in the warehouse, so that I had a curious reception to the first novel. It got a few reviews in some very unlikely places, like the *New Yorker* reviewed it, but the *New York Times* didn't, and *Publisher's Weekly* did, and a couple of places that we wanted did, but then there was this silence, and I didn't understand it. The publisher obviously wasn't going to tell me what happened, and my good friend, the editor, wasn't going to mention it. It was a disaster for that to have happened to that book. But the one thing of consequence that did come with the publication of the first novel was that I got a really good agent. I got the hot-shot agent in New York at that time, Candida Donadio. It was a period in which there was a lot of ferment in the publishing world, and there were a half a dozen really hot-shot, so-called literary editors who were much in demand, and they were moving from house to house, and there were two or three agents, Candida being the foremost, who had a lot of power. She liked my first book, and she wanted me as her client, and I jumped gladly. She got me a really good two-book contract with one of these literary editors, who put off the signing of the contract for a year or a year-and-a-half, while he decided whether or not he was going to stay at the house that he was employed by at the time of the signing of the contract.

We signed the contract after much confusion and much waiting, and he immediately left the house where he signed the contract and went to another publishing house, left my contract in the hands of people who bought out this publishing house, who weren't literary people at all and wanted something to show for the advance that they had given.

When we'd signed the two-book contract I had what I thought was a nearly completed second novel, but I could never quite bring it off. I could never quite get it right. Well, when I found out what happened to this contract, I wanted out of it. So I gave that publishing house what is known in the trade as a contract breaker. I alternated the chapters of these two novels that I was writing, gave them an unreadable book, and it totally destroyed my career. I couldn't get my agent on the telephone for a long time after I did that. I ended up getting sued by my publisher, getting boycotted by my agent, and having what possibilities I had in a career as a novelist destroyed in that whole experience.

Well, I just went off into another option in my life at that point. I went into the photography world for about five years. I quit writing fiction for a while. Now, I was writing about photography and about photographers.

BEATTIE: Were these newspaper articles?

HALL: I was commissioned by *Esquire* to write a piece on Magnum Photos Incorporated, which I did. That was my only real, extended adventure in free-lance journalism. And I was a contributing editor for *Aperture, the* publisher, at the time, of photography books. I did two books for them, a Ralph Eugene Meatyard monograph, and then I wrote a biography of Minor White, who'd been a colleague of mine at MIT who was the publisher of *Aperture.* I wrote a biography of him. Then I wrote reviews, and I wrote profiles, and I wrote a bunch of different things. But I didn't really start writing again in the way that we're talking about now until . . . and this is another crazy story.

I was looking for a part-time job, and I went to the MIT English department and said, "Can you give me a course?" They said, "Well, yes." Denise Levertov was going to teach poetry writing the next year at MIT, and thousands of people had signed up for her course. Did I want to teach the overflow of Denise's poetry workshop? I said, "Why not?" I hadn't written a poem since I'd been an undergraduate. This was 1968, right? At Cambridge, Mass., MIT, you didn't profess anything. In order to teach MIT undergraduates poetry writing, I had to start writing poems, and that's how I got started writing poems. So, I got, in 1968, back into writing of the sort we're talking about now, but I didn't really devote myself to it again until I took the job that I'm in now at UK, in 1973. I got out of the photography world. I had been in it up to my eyeballs. I had owned a photography business in Hartford, Connecticut, and I had been teaching at MIT, and I had my own school. I had a photography venture in Hartford, Connecticut, that was a custom lab, a darkroom rental facility, a gallery, and a school.

BEATTIE: How long did you have that?

HALL: It lasted about two-and-a-half years. It was an absolutely brilliant idea, and it was an extraordinary place, but I'm a fool when it comes to business, and it was a few years ahead of its time.

BEATTIE: You talked about "The Love Song of J. Alfred Prufrock" being something that not only got you interested in writing, but in all the arts. Is that where you first developed an interest in photography, too?

HALL: No, when my grandmother and sister and I moved into town [Lexington, Kentucky], I went to work at age eleven and worked at two or three jobs right on through until I got out of college. One of those jobs was I apprenticed in the commercial business of my second-cousin who had the University of Kentucky athletic department account, and we made the first UK basketball films, the first UK football films, and it was quite an extraordinary job for a kid with my interests.

BEATTIE: So really, you were learning about photography from age eleven.

HALL: I learned about the technical end of photography from age eleven, and I was a functioning professional photographer when I was thirteen. I was sent out on jobs when I was thirteen, shooting weddings and dances and anything that came into the studio, at much too young an age, and I was on the sidelines and fifty-yard line of the UK athletic program in the era when Adolph Rupp was the basketball coach and Bear Bryant was the football coach. We'd have shooting sessions for UK all-Americans, and not all of them would show up. And I, as a young kid, had a press pass to the whole thing.

BEATTIE: When you were writing photography articles for various magazines, did this overlap your teaching poetry courses part-time?

HALL: It was all during the same seven-or-eight-year period. The connection that I had, the experience that I had as a kid in photography, was all in commercial photography, but in that studio I found some books that contained, I guess you'd call it art photography, and I got very attached to certain of those pictures. They gave me great solace.

BEATTIE: Do you remember whose photographs they were?

HALL: I fell in love with A. Aubrey Bodine, who was a pictorial photographer working for a newspaper in Baltimore, and who photographed a lot in the Chesapeake Bay and did seascapes like Poe's misty mid-regions in *Weir* in photography. Those pictures mesmerized me and spoke to those parts of my mind and heart that nobody else and no other thing was speaking to. They were like prayers for me. I stayed with them and meditated on them through hard times in my life. So, I had a very profound connection with visual images, even at the time that there was nobody to talk to or nobody to share any of those experiences with. So, when I got through the experience of "The Love Song of J. Alfred Prufrock," to some connection with other people interested in such things, I was led immediately into a lifelong connection with painting and into a lifelong love of certain painters, which has sustained me through hard times.

One of the first fearless things I ever did in my life was, between my sophomore and junior years of college, I packed up my bags, and took my savings from my paper route, and told Granny I was gone.

BEATTIE: How old were you?

HALL: I was twenty years old. It was the summer of '55.

BEATTIE: You were in college in Lexington at the time?

HALL: In college in Lexington. I had not a word of French, I didn't know anybody in Paris. I went to Hemingway's part of town, to Montparnasse, found me a little hotel off the boulevard, and holed up, and acted like a writer. But the first thing I did when I got to Paris was, I went to the cafes, and the second thing I did was, I went to the Louvre and I started going to the galleries and to all the museums in town.

BEATTIE: At that time, did you feel that the various media that you were interested in were feeding off one another in terms of your writing and your painting and your photography?

HALL: Oh, very much so. They were connected to the same part of my mind and soul. I understood, at the time, that the experience that I was having with literature and with painting was all of a piece, and that the connection I had with photography came in that context.

BEATTIE: Were you ever able to find a circle of friends or colleagues that shared your interests?

HALL: I have lifelong connections in the literary world with both poets and fiction writers. I have lifelong connections in the photography world, and I have connections with only a few painters. I mean, I've known a couple, and I've been in their studios, but I have never had the kind of work-a-day relationship with painters that I've had with poets.

I don't know about need, but I thrive on the connection that I have with my peers, with my writing colleagues, and with my photography colleagues. I would rather go into the studio of some of the people that I know and spend the day than just about anything. Extended conversations over a period of years and years with these people have been very fruitful to me. The writers that I'm close to now, our connection is basically that of friends.

We share a lot and talk about a lot of experiences we have as writers, but basically those friendships now are just friendships; they're not professional relationships.

BEATTIE: What caused you to move back to Lexington?

HALL: Well, my marriage was coming unhinged, and I was no longer comfortable with being supported by my wife. I wanted a full-time job, and the options that I had were to try to get one in Cambridge, or in New York, or in Lexington. The plan was, at that time, to try to save our marriage. I came to Lexington in order to live half the year around apart from the marriage that I'd had for thirteen years, and to see if it couldn't be worked out along those lines. But it turned out, history has shown me, that it was a much more complex move than that, and it was a precursor to a divorce, to the dissolution of that marriage, and that was the first step in coming back to face where I had come from and the trauma of my childhood.

I came to the University of Kentucky as a visiting writing teacher for a year, and the idea was that if I wanted to stay on and they wanted me to stay on, then it could turn into a full-time, or a continuing job, which it did. I wanted to stay, and they were agreeable, so I just hooked right in.

BEATTIE: What were you teaching?

HALL: Poetry writing and fiction writing. Sometimes I'm able to teach other things.

BEATTIE: Such as what?

HALL: Oh, I taught a graduate course in approaches to poetry a couple of years ago, and I'm going to teach a course, the first chance I get, in experimental film and poetry and dream. I've also become involved over the past eight years in filmmaking, and I have made some experimental films. I'm interested in things and have conjunctions in my experience that want me to make up courses that aren't there to be taught.

One of the reasons that I wanted to come back to UK was I know the kids here, I know where they came from. I know how their tongues have been tied, if they came from Eastern Kentucky or Western Kentucky. I know how to untie their tongues. And I know the feelings of provincialism that they're dealing with. I know not only the form of it, but the substance of it, the language of it. I know, in many cases, what they're scared of. I can lead them to their fears a lot quicker. Everybody knows what it means to have your tongue tied. Very few people want to face it very directly, and very few people want, when you get right down to it, to suffer the pain that's involved in untying your tongue. But everybody who's serious about the work knows exactly what you're talking about when you start talking that way, and they either take the challenge or they don't. And if the time's not right, they don't, and I don't push it. But if they do, then you've got the thread that you follow. If your tongue's tied here, where else is it tied? What else are you not supposed to say?

One of the ways that language acquires the intensity of literature is by passing over that threshold from what you can say into what you can't say. When language passes through that hoop, it acquires great intensity. It becomes necessary language, it becomes language that's charged with a job of work, the kind of work that literature does. It's only through the experience of those things as such that you can get the thread that you need. See, you find it very difficult to talk about the male authorities in your life. Okay, then let's follow it, let's follow it. And you get really close, then, to what they're afraid of. The minute you know what they're afraid of, you know, then you've got the basic *rite de passage*. That's what you've got to get through, that's what you've got to face.

My connection with my students, I think, is they have come with the ambition to write, and for me that's the desire, whether they understand it or not, to make a connection with parts of their minds that have been closed down all these years. That's my job, to make that connection for them. To help them make that connection, and to lead them into it. Some of my students have gone on to write and to publish and to prove themselves as writers, but that's not what our connection is about, and it's not the way I'm following them.

BEATTIE: Leon Driskell once said to me that he viewed his job as a creative writing teacher as freeing students to be themselves. That's pretty much what you're talking about, isn't it?

HALL: It certainly is, and it's based on the assumption that we're none of us very likely to know who we are. We're likely to know really well what other people want us to be, and to know everything that's expected of us. But usually people who want to write are responding to the fact that there's something down there that won't quite come out in conversation, that can't come out in conversation. The language of conversation won't deal with it; the language of an essay can't touch it or deal with it. There's something down in there that their communication in the rest of their lives has left alone, and they're suffering from it. They want some outlet, they want some expression. It's not like expressing their feelings. You can punch a punching bag and express your feelings, or you can go home and shout at the person you're irritated with. You're wanting to understand it, wanting to take that feeling to its source.

They've got something, but they don't know what it is. They've got something to say and they don't know what it is. So, writing is freeing them up to be themselves, but it's much more nearly freeing them up to discover themselves, to go where it takes to find out what that is that has no words, that has no voice. Writers are people who have experienced voicelessness, inarticulateness about things of critical importance. Having their tongues torn out and trying to get them back. That's a very private and it's a very delicate and it's a very explosive connection and endeavor.

BEATTIE: Would you agree that the truth is usually more complicated than a factual understanding of something, of an event or a situation?

HALL: Of course. A good deal more complex. The first thing I found out was that my experience was a good deal more complex than it seemed to be. It took about ten years to find that out, and then it took about twenty years to find out what that might mean, what the substance of that idea was. Then the next stage for me was to find out it's absolutely simple, that it's not complex. You find out there's an onion to peel and you peel it down, and you end up with something utterly simple, simpler than you ever thought it was to begin with, simpler than anybody ever told you it was.

BEATTIE: But there's a complexity to that simplicity, or else that would be all you had to say.

HALL: What the experience is is a deepening into your mind, and you find that there's a lot more going on the deeper you get. That's where the facts filter down into the feelings that generate them. That's all the parts of your body and soul at war with one another in a struggle. And as you deepen down into your mind and the connection with the felt experience, as distinguished from the facts of the matter, things get really wild and obscure and difficult, and very hard to face, very problematical. Like if you face this, you're liable to untie the neat little picture you've made of your entire life to that point, okay? I mean, I've got students all the time who can't write the poem or the story they're trying to write, because it would involve a divorce or a fight with their father or something they just simply don't want to go through. But what we're calling the complexity is, to me, a deepening into the feeling and into the censorship that has gone on.

BEATTIE: Back to your teaching at UK. You've known Wendell Berry for a long time. Was that from your undergraduate days?

HALL: We were undergraduates together, and had writing workshops together. Then we were together at Stanford. He went to Stanford as a fiction writing fellow three years before I did. We were together out there and had a very intense fifteen-year exchange of manuscripts, young writers trying to find out what they're doing. We worked very, very closely for years and years. And I knew Gurney Norman as an undergraduate at UK, and Ed McClanahan, and Bobbie Ann Mason. We were all at UK at the same time. Wendell was one year ahead of me, Gurney was a couple of years behind, Bobbie Ann was a year behind Gurney, and Ed came in as a graduate student, but we were all there at the same time. A good deal of the intensity that we were able to generate and sustain as young people with writerly ambitions had to do with the fact that there were several of us that had them.

BEATTIE: That's maybe what I was referring to earlier as a circle of friends.

HALL: I wasn't, at that time, thinking back that far, but indeed at the inception of my ambitions as a writer I had, in my immediate surroundings, several people, Wendell being the foremost, who were as interested as I was in engaging this possibility and carrying it through. In fact, when I got to Stanford, we had the most unlikely workshop that the Stanford writing program has probably ever had. We had Ken Kesey, who wrote *One Flew Over the Cuckoo's Nest,* and Larry McMurtry, who wrote *Leaving Cheyenne,* in the workshop in which I started *Yates Paul,* and in which Gurney started the stories in *Kinfolks.* Six other people in there were writing publishable work, and there was no competition in that group. We were all interested in one another's well-being, and we supported one another's careers. That's extraordinary.

BEATTIE: You have continued to mentor one another as you are now colleagues of one another.

HALL: We did that for years and years. There comes a point in mid-life as a writer where you don't need so much of that as you once did, and I have a mentor relationship with my wife, Mary Ann Taylor-Hall. We read one another's manuscripts, and she now provides the kind of help that I need, and there are a couple of other people as well. But during the period in which you really need a lot of it, I had a lot of it, and it was really good. Wendell is very good at that, and was exceptionally forthcoming at that time. Gurney's good at it.

BEATTIE: You've mentioned your current wife. When did you meet and marry her?

HALL: We met when I was a visiting writing teacher at UK in '68, I guess it was, '67-'68. She was teaching at UK at the time, and we met and had mutual friends and stayed in touch with one another over those years, but we didn't take up our friendship in this way until about 1979.

BEATTIE: What was she teaching at UK?

HALL: I think at the time she was a full-time freshman English teacher with a section of a survey course in British lit. She has taught creative writing on a part-time basis over the years since then. We took up in '79, and got married in '81, I think. So we've been together for about eleven years. She's a fiction writer and an extraordinarily good one, and a superb reader. I have in-house help with my work the likes of which you're not supposed to expect.

I have much more regular work habits than she does, and we have separate studies. In the new house that we're building we'll even separate them further. The study that we have now is two adjacent rooms down the hill from the house. She comes and goes as her psyche requires with her work. Mine requires that I keep a fairly regular schedule. I write, when I have my druthers and freedom in the matter, I get up very early, five or five-thirty, and go straight to my study with a cup of coffee. Depending on what I'm working on and what stage it's in, I can work for four or five or seven or eight hours, and do. I am completely happy doing that, either in the study or in the studio, depending on what I'm working on, or in the film room.

One of the things that I had to prove to myself when I left graduate school and decided that I was going to act like a writer, was that I had the discipline necessary to pursue such an ambition. And I didn't have it. My life was pretty chaotic, even as a graduate student. I did not have the discipline that a writer needs. I made an inviolable pact with myself that I would put in a certain number of hours every day, even if it meant just sitting there. It took about ten years of that before I was satisfied that I could get up and go if I wanted to. But I still am fairly formulaic about the discipline involved, and I like to sit there. My peace of mind hinges on sitting there, whether or not I'm able to do anything. So I work every day that I can for long hours, and she works almost every day, but not for such long hours.

BEATTIE: I wanted to ask you about your three books of poetry and two completed novels.

HALL: *Getting It On Up to the Brag* is a chapbook, I mean a short book, twenty pages or so, published by the Larkspur Press, which is in Monterey, Kentucky. Gray Zeitz is an absolutely brilliant printer and artist of very considerable achievement, and he has published a number of titles, mostly Kentucky authors, and in the mid-seventies, when Larkspur did that title, an apprentice, Vicky White, wanted to do a book of poems of mine, and we got together and did it. They printed it on a letterpress in the most exquisite and beautiful fashion. The next book, called *Her Name,* was published by a small press in Wisconsin called Pentagram, and Pentagram is a publisher. The difference is quite important. A printer is making a beautiful book, and what happens to it after he's printed it is of less concern than it would be to a publisher. *Getting It On Up to the Brag* was published, as I remember, in 1975, and *Her Name* in . . . God, I ought to be able to remember this, but like '78 or '9 [1981]. That was reviewed, but not widely. *Getting It On Up to the Brag* I think, had one review, and that was later on. It was an essay about me and my work that included *Getting It On Up to the Brag.* Then the third book was published by Wesleyan University Press, in Connecticut, in 1988? Is that right? *Stopping on the Edge to Wave.* That's the best of the three books by a long shot, and it includes most of my work in poetry that I think of as my mature work.

BEATTIE: What is it about that book that makes it the best, as far as you're concerned?

HALL: Well, I understood, in the poems in that book, much more clearly what I was writing about, and I was much more able to handle it. I had been writing poems for a number of years at that point, and I had written some poems that seemed to me re-readable. There're several poems in *Getting It On Up to the Brag* that I still read in public readings, and that I still read with respect and delight, and there are a couple in *Her Name*. But there are a number of poems in *Stopping on the Edge to Wave* that I always turn to when I read publicly, and that I go back to with some simple feeling and some abiding respect. The poems in that book are, in the main, free of what I call my private biography, or the life that began when I was born. They're free of that part of my life, and they hark back to the life that began a long time before I was born, my inheritances as a human being on the face of the earth.

I've had more success with my poetry in periodical publication than I have in book publication. I mean, *Stopping on the Edge to Wave*, for instance, has been out a couple of years now, and maybe I've seen a review or two. I'm not looking for them, but that book, although it was published by one of the best poetry publishers in the country and should, on the basis of the imprint and where the poems appeared in periodicals, have gotten reviewed in a number of places. I don't know whether it has or not. I doubt that it has. The periodical publication in poetry for me broke, and I started getting in all of the places that I wanted to get in, in the early eighties.

BEATTIE: And those periodicals are?

HALL: The *New Yorker, Poetry Magazine,* the *American Poetry Review, Kenyon Review, Hudson Review, Sewannee Review, Poetry Northwest*. I got in when I started writing poetry to one or two of those places and then, as the years went on, three or four, but I finally broke the *New Yorker*, which is the hardest of all of those places to get into, somewhere in the early eighties. That seemed to me to be a kind of fruition of the public part of my poetry writing.

BEATTIE: Many of your poems describe nature, or cultivate nature as metaphor. What is your view of the relationship between nature and human nature, and is nature, for you, an objective correlative, or something else?

HALL: I think the distinction between nature and human nature is a tricky, potentially disastrous, distinction. It seems to me that a good deal of the trouble that we're in in the world is a function of the fact that we think that human beings are outside or apart from nature. The natural world, which I'm living in the middle of all the time, is the life of all of the creatures on the face of the earth that aren't human whose well-being I feel deeply connected with, and the longer I spend out in the grass and among the creatures, the more deeply my connection and identification with them becomes. It is very much within its own terms, in that regard. It's not a metaphor for anything. I mean, it's this cat and that dog, and that cow, and that blade of grass. The experience of that cat, that dog, and that blade of grass, in my mind, is the experience of an ongoing transience that's very vivid and very inescapable. They live and die very quickly, you know. I mean, bugs come and go so rapidly and their tenure here is so thusly vivid, that the overriding experience of my own life is of transience, of being in an unstable state at all times. No moment is trapable; it's followed by the next moment, the next moment, the next moment. The essential experience is one of everything being taken away at the same time that it's given. The life of human beings and of rocks and of certain parts of nature is much more difficult to see dramatically played out than it is with the grass and with the bugs. It's another form of life that appeared and disappeared at the same moment in which its appearance and disappearance are breathtakingly simultaneous. In that regard, indeed, there's something more than each particular item. It's a mirror in which I'm seeing what I understand to be the essential nature of things, which is passing, death.

BEATTIE: In your poem "Tracings" you describe how photography captures the human spirit. What do you think are the similarities and differences between capturing that spirit in photography and in writing?

HALL: Photography has a very specific and curious and quite dramatic relationship with this whole subject of time and the passage of time. A still photograph is punching a hole in time. It is freezing a moment and taking one of these evanescent, transient experiences and making it stand still for a certain period of time. The spiritual drama of a still photograph for me is in the context of its extraordinary act in the flow of time. Fiction and photography are much more on a vertical axis for me. In lyric poetry and in photography, I can address myself more directly to the absolute than I can in fiction.

Fiction is a social activity. It's about characters in time and place, and the characters are the substance of a lot of the story and the situation. Their setting is right at the heart of the story, and those things are located in time. If a story involves a long period of time, then the passage of time is right at the heart of the story.

But the ability of the lyric poem and of the photograph to speak directly to what some people would call God or the Absolute, or to eternity, to timelessness, is much more direct. It's called upon, it's on that axis between the earth and the heavens. Fiction is on a horizontal axis, or wrapped around the earth.

My preoccupation, it seems, although I don't think in these terms or work in these terms, but the preoccupation of my vision seems to be with transience, with time. I mean, it's a time-preoccupied vision. The experience of arriving at the experience of timelessness, of the trance, of the meditative consciousness, is the experience that the nature poems are constantly trying to achieve. It's trying to achieve the meditative concentration on the subject that punches one through time into a kind of timelessness. And with photography, it's the same instinct. It's trying to find the image that will invite the connection between time and timelessness.

BEATTIE: Do you feel equally adept at all media, all genres, or is it simply a matter of whatever your vision is trying to relate, as you're talking about one being more suitable for a particular type of communication?

HALL: Well, that's a really good question, because my public career as an artist has been enormously complicated, and, some would say, destroyed, by my devotion to several different media, and you don't make film or photographs or poems or stories without a long apprenticeship. And it's unlikely that anybody's going to serve the necessary apprenticeship in more than one of those areas in order to achieve full potential. What I'm trying to do is to work in four different mediums. I feel, at this point, as though I have in the past several years arrived at my maturity as an artist, and I am able to do now the work I've been preparing myself to do. But I feel as though the apprenticeship that I have served in each of these areas has been responsible in its own terms, and that I understand what serious poets have gone through in the way of training, and what serious fiction writers have gone through in the way of training. The book that I'm writing now, *Saying Grace,* it's prose, but I could not have found the language for it had I not done the work I've done in lyric poetry.

BEATTIE: So you're really saying that work in the different media cross-pollinate one another.

HALL: Absolutely, and they've all been tracking the same subject. The writing of *Saying Grace,* this autobiographical meditation, has been accompanied by a parallel project in which I am rephotographing the Hall family albums. That has been another way in which I have gotten into the cave that was sealed off from me. I could not have verified my intuitions that language brought me to without the aid of those photographic images that came straight off the Hall family albums. It was not only a cross-pollination, but a whole process of mutual confirmation, that went on in those parallel projects. Now I am dealing with the lives of other people, not just myself, but my mother, and my father, and my grandparents, and so forth and so on. The things that I thought I had to say had to be verified somewhere in my experience. It took my work in photography, which was informed and brought to the place that it was by filmmaking, in order to verify the prose language that I came to, that I got to through the language of lyric poetry.

All of these things have been tools to track the same experience, to come into the presence of the images at the bottom of the cave of my mind. It's like back when my mother killed herself, the entrance to that cave was sealed off, and I had to find some way back in there. Then I had to be able to read the paintings that had been left on the wall. All of the training that I had looking at Gauguin and Van Gogh and Rothko and Matisse were part of the training of my eye that I was able to then elaborate on in my still photography, such that when I got into the cave and I had the light to shine on the wall, I knew how to get the image back outside.

But this has nothing to do with a career as an artist. As far as being on the public scene as an artist, what I have done through all of those endeavors is shoot myself in the foot, over and over and over again. I mean, here's Hall, who does he think he is? Is he a filmmaker, is he a photographer, is he a poet, or is he a fiction writer? That's an invitation to be treated like a dilettante in the professional world of art careers.

BEATTIE: Can you tell me a little bit more specifically about what happened to your mother?

HALL: Well, she was an extraordinarily beautiful woman from a lower middle-class background, who was pursued by a number of very eligible young men and chose to marry my father in part, I know, because it was a big step up on the social ladder. I mean, she went from where she was to money and to social prestige, and my grandfather was a big shot in the Lexington Republican Party, and he was a town father, and he was of a monied family. My mother married into fancy cars and clothes and trips abroad and all of that. She became imprisoned in that marriage, which ended them up in the house of my father's parents, and she became further imprisoned by those circumstances, until the only way she had out was to kill herself. She couldn't get herself and her children loose from that, and it brought her to her end. And it happened right in front of me. And it happened in my bed. And it was a brutal situation for everybody.

BEATTIE: Was it a shooting?

HALL: Yes. And I closed down, at that point; I forgot a whole lot. I forgot a whole lot of what had preceded that, and I forgot the several years surrounding that. It's been a lifelong charge as a spirit, as a soul loose in the world. That's the job of work the artist took up, was to see my soul through this life. It became the artist's job to cultivate and to deepen my soul, which involved going back to my childhood, and remembering what it was that had happened to me and to my family, and remembering where I came from, and remembering the circumstances of my origin.

That's the fearlessness that I heard in literature when I encountered "The Love Song of J. Alfred Prufrock," that has been the education that saw me through to that job. It provided me with the ambition, the possibility to imagine that kind of honesty and fearlessness, and the tools with which maybe to achieve it, if I was willing to learn how to use them. And that has been, I think, at the core of the experience that I've dealt with as an artist all these years. If you put it in its simplest possible terms, it's a very simple vision of the fact that your life comes from death, that that which gives you your life is death.

I was obliged to forget that there was any love involved in that. The mind that engaged that job of work found that a good deal of the world outside my own private little story is equally interesting and fascinating, and so I have gotten off from the core of that story, but even what I see on the ground glass of my cameras or in the language of a poem about nature is that very essential childhood experience of your life coming from death, and that she, the mother, and the mother earth, who gives you your life, takes it away. And that it all happens in your bed. And that it's your blood that you see.

What Eliot taught me was that I was a soul on a journey. I mean, that's one of the things you hear in "The Love Song of J. Alfred Prufrock." One of the things that I heard is that there is such a thing as a soul taking a journey through life. Well, once I understood that I was a soul taking a journey through life, my journey led me back to those childhood experiences, to the origin. And, were I not in the process of finishing this book in which I deal explicitly with all of these matters, I would wonder whether or not I had any business at all putting on the record any of these matters. But I'm putting them on the record, and this is a short and very oblique, very truncated description of the story that I'm trying to tell in *Saying Grace.*

BEATTIE: The book that you're working on, *Saying Grace,* is this the work that has freed you the most?

HALL: Yes. See, I did not understand that I was imprisoned until I got almost out. I mean, I don't think you can. I didn't understand that I had an inescapable lock on me and a preoccupation. I knew that this was a recurrent thought, my mother and my childhood, but I didn't understand what it was that I didn't understand until I understood it. I didn't know what it was that I didn't know until I knew it. And yes, in some respects, it was simply a matter of having it confirmed by other people that what I had always supposed to be the case was indeed true, which is that it was a scandal that preceded all of this.

But we're talking about the level at which you know things, and the responsibility with which you are able to engage what you know. I knew a lot of this all my life, but I wasn't able to be responsible to it. I did not have the ability to respond to it for years and years. I had to get a whole lot of the rest of my life straight. I had to get strong. I had to find some fundamental things in my life that were very elusive before I had the strength to respond to what I knew. Then it came back around at a different level in my understanding and it said, "If you're ready to understand these things, if you're ready to be responsible, then you have to respond."

BEATTIE: Would you say that creative people in any medium, in order to free themselves of any such experience, that their ultimate therapy is in something they create?

HALL: I should think so. What we're talking about is clarity of mind, and what a therapist can help you do is to clarify your thoughts. But a poem or a piece of fiction or a film leaves off thoughts. It delves much deeper into the experience, it deals in imagery, it deals in the embodied fact and the felt experience. And if you can shape the felt experience, if you take the image and shape it, if you can find the beauty in it, if you can create a beginning and a middle and an end that will release you from the experience, it seems to me that you're offered the chance there to deal with it at a much deeper level and be much clearer about it, much clearer.

I can think about these things and have thoughts that are nonetheless not as deep as the felt experience or the image. I think some people go through their lives without having the full range of their hearts, their souls, engaged. And I don't see anything wrong with that. People's lives work out differently. You have people all the time saying, "Is it really necessary to suffer to be an artist?" And, my God, I mean, if your head's clear and your heart's open, and you look around you, what do you see? It's suffering all over the place, right? Everybody is in anguish, everybody's dealing with a heartache.

People think that an open heart means joyousness or happiness, and that seems to me foolish. I mean, an open heart is a suffering soul. Joy and beauty and an embrace of life is the end of it if you keep it open, it seems to me. But right up and through that is a great anguish and pain.

July 11, 1991

BOOKS BY JAMES BAKER HALL

Yates Paul: His Grand Flight, His Tootings. New York: World, 1963.

Ralph Eugene Meatyard. Photography monograph, with text by Hall. Millerton, N.Y.: Aperture, 1973.

Getting It On Up to the Brag. Monterey, Ky.: Larkspur, 1975.

Minor White: Rites & Passages. Photography monograph, with text by Hall. Millerton, N.Y.: Aperture, 1978.

Her Name. Markesan, Wis.: Pentagram, 1982.

Music for Broken Piano. New York: Fiction Collective, 1982.

Stopping on the Edge to Wave. Middletown, Conn.: Wesleyan University Press, 1988.

Fast Signing Mute. Monterey, Ky.: Larkspur, 1993.

Orphan in the Attic. Lexington: University of Kentucky Art Museum, 1995.

WADE HALL

HALL: My full name is Wade Henry Hall, Jr. I was born February the second, Ground Hog's Day, 1934, in the same bed that my mother was born in some sixteen-and-a-half years before, in a farmhouse near Inverness, Alabama, which is near Union Springs, which is near Montgomery.

My mother was named Sarah Elizabeth Waters, and her mother was Tressie Grider, who married my mother's father, John Thomas Waters. They were all born in the community and were descended from families that had been there, I think, since that country was opened to white settlement in the 1830s and '40s.

My father was Wade Henry Hall, Sr. He was nicknamed "Jabo." My mother's nickname, and that was a name that I called her, too, was "Babe," only we pronounced it "Baibe." I called my grandmother "Momma," talk about confusion. My father was about four or five years older than my mother.

It's hard to imagine, if you knew my mother, but she married beneath her. She did not finish high school. She was the reader in the family. My father, to my knowledge, never read a book, never read a newspaper, never read anything. He could write his name, but it was a very crudely written name. He had six or eight brothers and sisters. My mother was an only child. Some of my father's brothers and sisters, who I think had gone to school, were functional illiterates. This was not a reading society, it was an oral society. We did not read, we talked. I had never had occasion to even think about it, until suddenly it hit me. I thought, "These people can't read and they're my kin, they're my aunts."

It was a farm family. My father kind of piddled around. He did lots of odds and ends and had a country store from time to time. He never did very much of anything. I don't know how in the world he supported five sons and a wife, but he did.

I have memories of my grandmother, my maternal grandmother, the one I called "Momma." In fact, I lived with her and she probably was the major influence on my life when I was very young. I lived with her until she married, just a year or so before she died. She married a man named Ellis, and moved away, and that was the most traumatic event of my childhood. I can remember it vividly, just as if it happened yesterday, when the car came to take her. It was like a hearse coming to take her away to her new home, which was about fifty miles south in a little place called Opp, Alabama, near the Florida line. Her death, her actual death, was not nearly as traumatic as that.

BEATTIE: You were how old when you started living with her?

HALL: I was an infant. I was born in my grandmother's house. That was her house where we were living. My father and mother, they never lived anywhere other than the county, but they kind of moved around, they were kind of county gypsies.

BEATTIE: How did it happen that you stayed with your grandmother?

HALL: Well, my mother was very young when I was born; I don't think she was quite seventeen. She was a child herself. My grandmother had just her, just one child, and I think my grandmother wanted to take care of me. A year and a half later I had a brother that was born, and his name is Jack.

I was the first child. Jack and I lived with my grandmother while my mother and father were out living in various temporary places around the county. Then when my grandmother married the second and last time, of course we had to live with my mother and father, which was a trauma, too, I'm telling you.

BEATTIE: Did you see much of her after she left?

HALL: We would go down occasionally and visit, but no, not very often. Once she had moved away it was death, worse than her actual death. I adjusted to living with my mother and father, which I never liked.

BEATTIE: What was living with your parents like?

HALL: My father drank, and for years I wouldn't have allowed a can of beer in my refrigerator, after I got grown. That was unpleasant, the fact that he drank. Sometimes, I think, he would abuse my mother. I realize now that probably it was her fault, too, when they had problems, when they had arguments and fusses. They never had really physical fights that I can remember, but it was just as bad. I would automatically take up for my mother, you see. I think sons do that, if they perceive their mothers are being threatened by their fathers. But I never had an Oedipus complex, I can assure you, because my mother and I didn't get along that well. But she and I got along very well after I moved away from home.

I left home at sixteen to go to college. That was a trauma, too, but I knew I had to do it, because I had to get away. I could not have lived at home. And that was good, because I was extremely shy. But it was a matter of options; either I stayed at home and had a nervous breakdown before I was seventeen, or went away to college, which was twenty-five miles away, and suffered for a while till I got used to it. I knew I had to do it, so I did it, and I've never been home again since then for more than two weeks at a time.

BEATTIE: Obviously you had an education through high school at home. How did it happen that you were interested in getting an education, when your family background had not had education in it?

HALL: Well, as I said, my mother was a reader. I can remember checking out books from the high school library to take home for her to read. Also, the only role models—we didn't know the word then—that I had were teachers. I mean, professional role models, because we did not know lawyers or doctors or dentists. We would occasionally use their services, but we didn't know them socially. There was no one in our community who was anything other than a farmer, or a moonshiner, or a bootlegger, and I didn't want to be a moonshiner or a bootlegger or a farmer or a preacher.

BEATTIE: But you did work on the farm as a child?

HALL: Oh, yes. My father usually had some little country store, and I would clerk in the store, too. My father couldn't sit still long enough to stay in a store, so my brother Jack and I would stay in the store while he was running around doing what he did, which was not much of anything. But he was not a role model for me, professionally, or any other way.

The only role models that I had were teachers. And I thought, "Well, teaching is something I can do and get away from home."

BEATTIE: What was your early education like?

HALL: It was very strict. I went to a public school, Inverness. This was the day of rigorous segregation, and the county that I grew up in was at least four-to-one black, and it still is. There were numerous little one- and two-room schoolhouses over the county that were black, but by the time I came along, most of the small white schools had been consolidated. So I went to a consolidated school. We may have had two hundred students from grades one through twelve in the whole school. We had two grades in each room, first and second, third and fourth, fifth and sixth. Even in my senior year in high school, we had the eleventh and twelfth grades in the same room. We had very small classes, but very good teachers, very strict. I literally went in one end of the school building, in the first grade, and came out the other end a high school graduate. But I skipped two grades in school, so that's why I was fifteen most of my senior year. I turned sixteen before the end of the year, in February. Most of my freshman year in college I was sixteen. I was always the youngest person in my class. I don't think I was that much smarter than everybody else. When I was getting ready to go to college at Troy State, which was a teacher's college then, they said, "Now, Wade Henry, you're pretty smart up here in Inverness, but when you get down to Troy, you're going to have competition." Didn't have any competition down there, either. Then when I went to University of Alabama for a master's they said, "Wait till you get up there to University of Alabama." No problem. Then I went to University of Illinois and they said, "Ah, you'll be in school with the Yankees then." Sometimes I'd hide my ignorance, you know. If I didn't know something, I knew enough not to open my mouth and show it.

BEATTIE: You say you went off to Troy to go to college. What was that like?

HALL: It was traumatic, too. You cannot believe how backward the community that I grew up in was. I mean, I knew that we didn't have a lot of things other people had, like telephones and electricity and so on—running water—but it was a shock when I got to Troy. It was about ten thousand people then, but to me it was a metropolis.

I had a great-aunt who lived in Troy, my grandmother's sister, my Aunt Emma O'Steen. Her husband had just died, and one time she was visiting us and I think she said, "Why don't you let Wade Henry come down and stay with me while he goes to school at Troy?" I thought that was a good idea because otherwise I couldn't have gone. It was very cheap to go to school at Troy in those days, but we just didn't have any money, and we didn't know how to apply for scholarships. There weren't many scholarships then, anyway. This is going to sound awfully sad and maudlin, but my great-aunt gave me a space about four-feet wide and about eight- or ten-feet long in her kitchen, where she put a little bed where I slept for three years. My aunt had a big boarding house and she turned it into apartments. So she was renting out everything else, all the other space. It was a big house. So she gave me a little space in her apartment. There was a little walkway right by my bed that went to her bathroom. So I had no privacy, none whatsoever. But when she offered the chance to live in that little space, I took it.

It was exciting because there was a picture show one block away. We always called the movie theater picture shows. When I was growing up we probably didn't go to the picture show more than once or twice a year, and we never checked to see what was playing because we knew we hadn't seen it. It didn't really matter, because anything on the screen was wonderful. But anyway, the Pike Theater was right down the street from my great-aunt's house, and I thought, "Gosh, this is like going to heaven to be able to go to the picture show when I want to."

I lived on about five dollars a week. But, you see, when you get what amounts to an allowance, which I'd never had before, then you can work within that. Working within an allowance of five dollars was better than working with nothing, which I had before, and it cost about a quarter, I think, to go to the picture show.

BEATTIE: Who gave you the allowance?

HALL: My father. But I worked around the house, I worked in the store. I'd come home on the weekends and work there, and I did things around the house and helped, so I kind of earned it, in a sense.

But of course, I had no car; I walked to school. And it was, I'm sure, at least two miles from where my aunt lived to the college campus. But I didn't mind that, it was kind of exciting living in town.

I remember that evening, the first night away from home. It was getting dark and I heard the phone ring inside, in the hall. It was a kind of a communal phone in the hall. I was sitting on the front porch watching people in the cars pass by and I thought, "Oh, Lord, they're going home and I want to be going home." And the phone rang and it kept ringing, and I thought, "Well, I wonder why somebody doesn't answer that telephone?" Then it dawned on me that nobody was there but me. So, I got up and I thought, "Lord, I've got to do it. I have got to answer that phone." I had never answered the phone in my life, never talked on a phone before. It was dark in the hall, and I saw the little table where the phone . . . it was one of those old-fashioned phones with the mouthpiece up on the pedestal, and an ear-piece. I went over, trembling. I picked up the earpiece, and I'd been to the picture show, so I knew that you were supposed to put a piece up here to your mouth, and I knew you were supposed to say, "Hello," a word that country people did not use. So I said, "Hello." And this voice, the first time I'd ever heard a voice on the telephone, this voice said, "Is this 4-6-2-J?" I panicked, because I didn't know my aunt's number, and I said, "I don't know." I guess she thought I was putting her on because she said something like, "Well, isn't it there on the telephone, what the number is?" I looked down and there it said, "4-6-2-J," and I thought, "Lord, she knows that I'm a hick."

That was my first experience. I was so homesick, so homesick. I adjusted, but I was so shy that I didn't have much to do with other students for the first year-and-a-half.

BEATTIE: What do you remember about your college classes, and did you major in English?

HALL: I started out majoring in math, because I was good in math in high school and I liked math. When I got to Troy, my best professors were in English, and they were colorful people, colorful characters. This was 1950 to '53. I went straight through; I went summers as well, so I finished college at age nineteen, and started teaching at nineteen. I went down to Opp. Now, I don't think there's any psychic connection between my selecting Opp as a place to teach, because that's where my grandmother had lived till she died in 1944. But I taught in the junior high school at Opp for one year.

BEATTIE: Had you written as a child at all?

HALL: I remember I had a pretty good English teacher in high school. Mrs. Lockwood, or as we said, Miz Lockwood, had us write themes. I remember one time I wrote a theme on a goat that we had. She read it to the class, which of course, thrilled me. This may have been in the eighth grade, or something like that, and she would read it to all of her classes. So that made me feel good. I thought, "Well, I can write." It was a little thing, but you know how little things, when you're that age, when you're thirteen or fourteen years old, are big things.

BEATTIE: Right after college you went to teach in this high school in Alabama. How long did you stay there, and how did you like teaching?

HALL: One year. I liked it very well. I was nineteen, and I was teaching seventh, eighth, and ninth graders. Not the best age to teach. The seventh graders, I rather liked. I had English and social studies and I don't remember what else. I had a seventh grade homeroom, too. I had the eighth-grade English class and a ninth-grade English class. After the first semester, I finally got one of the other teachers to take my eighth-grade section, because I said, "I just don't think I can survive." My classroom overlooked a cemetery and there were times when I envied those dead people out there.

I was drafted into the service and spent two years in the army, most of it in Germany, which was a good experience for me. I got to do some sightseeing.

BEATTIE: Was there anything that you were exposed to in Germany or Europe that influenced you to teach on the college level, do you think?

HALL: Yes. It was a gradual thing, but in my unit in Heidelberg I had friends who had master's degrees, and they were going to be college teachers, and I thought, "Well, shoot, I can do it, too, probably."

BEATTIE: What happened when you came back from Germany?

HALL: Well, by then I had decided that I wanted to go to graduate school, and I had the GI bill to help me. I applied at the University of Alabama for admission to the graduate program in English, and was accepted. I was discharged, like the fourth day of June, and three or four days later I enrolled at the University of Alabama.

I took Anglo-Saxon and Chaucer under the head of the department. His name was Brooks Forehand. I had never had a foreign language in school. I studied German and French in Heidelberg and learned enough to pass my graduate exams when I got to where I went after I finished at Alabama. I was at the University of Alabama for two summers and one whole academic year.

BEATTIE: And you received a master's.

HALL: A master's in English. By then I had decided I wanted to specialize more in American literature. But I didn't write a thesis. I took extra courses.

BEATTIE: What, especially, in American literature interested you?

HALL: The literature of the South. I had good history teachers at Troy, as well as good English teachers, and in fact, I took a double major in history and English. I took enough extra courses in history to have the equivalent of a major. I took Alabama history and southern history, and in those days, there were good teachers; there were gentlemen teachers and lady teachers. These were people who might not have written very much. Some of my teachers were writers, though not scholars. But they were excited about the history of literature. They had an enthusiasm which was very attractive to me.

BEATTIE: After you were graduated from the University of Alabama, what decided you on the University of Illinois as a place to get your doctorate?

HALL: Well, I had a friend who had been up there, and he said that he knew a lady that I would like to stay with, because he had lived with her when he was up there. He said he could get me a job teaching in the school of commerce; I could teach writing to business students, full-time. In fact, as it turned out, I made more as a graduate student at Illinois than I could have made teaching in the public schools of Alabama full-time. So I said, well, maybe I'll apply up there. So I applied at Illinois, and Vanderbilt, and Northwestern. I don't know why I applied at those three places. I was accepted at all three places, but Illinois came through with the best offer, a full-time instructorship, so I went there. And the lady that my friend had lived with—at 809 Illinois Street, right on the edge of the Illinois campus— accepted me sight unseen. It was in her own house, and she rented rooms, and she had one little apartment that she rented to one graduate student and I was the one, while I was up there. I later asked her why she would have rented to me sight unseen. She said, "You were from Alabama, weren't you?" I said, "Yes." She said, "Well, I like people from the Deep South." She'd had good experiences, she said, with graduate students from the South. Her name was Clarice Swinford, and she was a nice lady. A little brusque, but then that was Midwestern, you know.

I remember when I drove up to the University of Illinois. I had never really lived in the North. I mean, I had lived in Germany, when I was in the army, but I had never been in the North. I was driving through Kentucky, and it was getting late in the day, and I was by myself, and I thought, I don't know whether I want to drive into the North at night. I was on Highway 41, driving up through Western Kentucky, from Nashville, Tennessee. I got to Henderson, Kentucky, and you know, when you don't have a definite place to stop, you keep driving and driving, and you think, "Well, I've got to stop pretty soon or it'll be dark or I'll be exhausted." So finally I went through Henderson, and then I saw the Ohio River. I was in Indiana, and it scared me. I thought, "This is North. This is the North." So I turned my car around and went back south of the Ohio River into Henderson and spent the night in Henderson. I felt I was kind of at home, never dreaming that I'd be living in Kentucky most of my life, at that point.

The next morning I figured it was safe to go up North, in the daylight, so I went up to the University of Illinois. I loved the University of Illinois. It was a great university.

BEATTIE: How many years were you there?

HALL: I was there four. I was teaching full-time, you see.

BEATTIE: Did you have professors there that were influential?

HALL: I had some good professors. My advisor was John T. Flanagan, who was from Minnesota. He taught a seminar in Faulkner and Hemingway that I took. I decided that I wanted to do my dissertation under him, because I liked him. I said I would prefer to do it on some southern subject, and the University of Illinois had just acquired the Franklin J. Meine Collection of American Humor and Folklore at the time. Flanagan wanted me to devise a subject that I could research in that collection. He said, "It would be to your advantage, because all the material which you'll need will probably be here in this collection or in the library." Fortunately, he was on sabbatical, on a Fulbright, in Belgium and Germany, the year I wrote my dissertation, so he didn't bother me at all. I remember, the year that he was away and the end of the year when I was writing the dissertation, he wrote me that he was coming back to the States, gave me the date—we had corresponded while he was in Belgium—but he said, "I won't be coming to Urbana," he had a home in Urbana, "but," he said, "my wife and I will be going to my summer home in Chisago City, Minnesota," which is just north of St. Paul. His home was in St. Paul, Minnesota.

So he said, "Would you bring your dissertation up to Chisago City?" I took it up there, and we spent several days going over it, and that was it. He said, "I don't have any serious problems with it." It was on the humor of the South between the Civil War period and World War I. It was later published by the University of Florida Press as *The Smiling Phoenix,* the phoenix representing the South after the Civil War, rising from the ashes. I submitted the exact dissertation that I had turned in to Illinois. I hadn't thought about it being a publishable book when I was writing it, but when I defended the dissertation, one of my committee members said, "Wade, we think you've written a great book." I mean, not a great book, "a good book." He used the word book. And I thought, "Huh, maybe it is a book."

BEATTIE: It's lived on as a classic in its field, hasn't it?

HALL: It's kind of a standard book, yes.

BEATTIE: Could you comment a little bit about southern humor, from your dissertation, from the book?

HALL: I had taken courses in southern history, and I knew the period of the Civil War and the aftermath, Reconstruction. It was a period that hadn't been covered very much, literarily, because it was a dry period in southern writing. Southern literature hadn't had very much to begin with, before that. I decided to do a reflection of the South during that period through the humorous works, mainly through the literary humor, because, after all, I couldn't collect any folk humor. There was some indirect folk humor in the works of Joel Chandler Harris and the local-colorists. But for the most part, it was literary humor. It was humor that southern writers had gotten from the people that they knew, and the language, and so on. One of my conclusions was that humor had helped the South survive a very trying period of history, a period when the South was treated worse than any other conquered nation that this country has ever fought.

BEATTIE: What about the nature of the humor itself, southern versus northern, or any other regional humor?

HALL: Well, southern humor tends to be more kind of laid back and slow, as you might expect, not the wisecrack. To this day I don't like wisecrack humor, the Las Vegas stand-up kind of humor. The essence of southern humor is in the telling; it's the yarn, and that's why it's sometimes not easy to identify. I mean, you can identify a practical joke or a joke, but generally it's organic, it's in the story. It's in the short stories of John Fox, Jr., and James Lane Allen, Kentuckians. It's in Joel Chandler Harris' Uncle Remus stories. It's in Charles Egbert Craddock's [Mary Noailles Murfree] tales of the Eastern Tennessee mountaineers. It's not brusque; it's softer. It's not nearly as strident, I think, as Yankee humor. I think real organic humor is humor that arises from a situation. I think that's a mark of intelligence. I think you have to be intelligent to have a sense of humor.

Part of my dissertation was published originally as a monograph in the University of Florida Humanities Monograph Series. It was called *Reflections of the Civil War in Southern Humor.* We simply took out the Civil War material and published it separately. Then, when the book came out, we put it back in, so it was the total study. But, one of the points that I tried to make in that study was that during the Civil War, the southern soldier survived partly because he had a sense of humor.

In the meantime I had gone to Florida to teach, and I liked Florida very much.

BEATTIE: How many years were you there?

HALL: I was only there for a year-and-a-half, because a friend that I had known at the University of Illinois, who was from Kentucky, had given my name to the president of Kentucky Southern College, which was just about to open here in Louisville. The president of that school called me in the summer of '62. He said, "We want you to come up here and consider joining our new college." I said, "I don't want to come to Kentucky. I'm at the University of Florida. Everybody wants to go to Florida, you know."

He wouldn't take no for an answer. So, I flew up here. I have acrophobia, too. The second time I'd ever flown in my life. And I was so impressed with Louisville, I was so impressed. I had never been in a city this size before, to live.

My host was Dr. Rollin S. Burhans. He had been pastor of Crescent Hill Baptist Church. The Baptists of the state and the city had prevailed upon him to take over the presidency of this college that was aborning at that time, Kentucky Southern College, as it was going to be called. So, I was faced with a dilemma. Do I stay in Florida and be a little fish in a big pond, or do I come to Kentucky and be a big fish in maybe a cup of water?

BEATTIE: How long did it take you to make your decision?

HALL: Well, I didn't make a final decision until I got back to Florida, because I was already committed to going back to Gainesville for that fall. I called Dr. Morris. He was in charge of freshman composition down at Florida, was kind of my mentor, and I said, "Dr. Morris, what should I do?" He said, "Wade, you do what's best for you. We'd like for you to stay at Florida, but you do what you think you want to do." So, I talked with the people back up here, and they made me an offer that I couldn't refuse.

BEATTIE: The college was located where in Louisville?

HALL: It was located on Shelbyville Road. It's now the Shelby Campus of the University of Louisville. I was asked to be head of the English department. Here I was twenty-eight. I came here [Louisville] in December of '62 and joined Kentucky Southern the second semester that they were open. So, they were holding the slot open for me as chair of the department. We only had two other people in the department at the time. We got up to close to a thousand students before the college finally folded after seven years. It was a good experience. I enjoyed it very much.

In those days I was much closer to my students than I am now. I spent a lot of time with them, and I got the best students. The best students majored in English. One time we had about six hundred students in the whole student body, and almost a hundred were English majors. The school folded in '69.

BEATTIE: What year did you go to teach at Bellarmine College?

HALL: '69. They contacted me and asked me if I would like to join their faculty, and I did, because I liked Louisville. Louisville is a wonderful place to live, I think. It's big enough to have things that you want, and yet small enough to be accessible, to know people, to get around in. I have never regretted living in Louisville. I've never had a sabbatical, not one. So, there've been some negatives. But I've done pretty much what I wanted to do.

BEATTIE: How have you enjoyed teaching at Bellarmine?

HALL: Very much. I teach American literature, which is my field. I teach creative writing from time and time. I've always been interested in local history and local culture, and I think it's very important for people to know who they are. You find out who you are by finding out something about where you live and who came before you. That's why I was attracted to American literature to begin with, to southern literature, and more recently to

Kentucky literature and history. So I developed a course in Kentucky studies, and it's kind of an advanced undergraduate and graduate course that is a combination of history and literature and anything else we want to throw in.

BEATTIE: Does teaching energize you for writing, do you think, or does it have the opposite effect?

HALL: It used to. I do think that it's important for teachers to be professionally active, particularly in the academic areas, in English, and history, and theology, philosophy. You know, I think you need to write. You need to keep up with the literature, you need to go to professional meetings, and read papers, and write papers, and do books and things. It's hard for us when we don't have the funds for sabbaticals and grants to support your work, but it can be done. I've tried to do both, and I've enjoyed it.

BEATTIE: I know you publish the *Kentucky Poetry Review* [at Bellarmine]. Can you tell me how you came to edit that and how you've altered its direction since it was *Approaches* magazine?

HALL: Well, it was founded as *Approaches* by Joy Bale [Boone] in Elizabethtown, [Kentucky] back in '64, I guess. Joy founded it to nourish Kentucky poets, because Joy was a poet and she was interested primarily in poetry. I was asked to join the board of editors in the late sixties.

Joy's husband, Dr. Garnett Bale, died, and she didn't know what she was going to do, whether she was going to stay in Kentucky. So, she decided she was going to have to give up the poetry magazine. I offered to take it over and continue editing it. It didn't require a lot of work, and it was fairly inexpensive. It wasn't really paying for itself; we had to subsidize it with a little money from some patrons here and there. But we're talking about maybe a hundred dollars here and a hundred dollars there. It wasn't very much. It cost maybe three or four hundred dollars total for an issue in those days—printing, and postage, and everything.

I took over the magazine and changed the name from *Approaches* to *Kentucky Poetry Review*, which I thought would give it a sense of place, and then opened it up to non-Kentuckians, because I thought it had served its purpose in nourishing Kentucky poets. Joy approved of this. She said, "Go ahead and do what you think is best for it." She was four numbers a year, and I finally cut it back to two, but I increased the pages, so we're putting out more pages, but fewer issues a year. I hit upon the idea of doing special issues with a focus, dedicating each issue to a particular poet. The Jesse Stuart issue, the James Still issue, the May Sarton issue.

We've done issues dedicated to Reynolds Price, Wendell Berry, David Madden. We've published some of the best poets in the country. When I did the twentieth anniversary issue about six years ago, I just wrote out of the blue sky to some of the American poets that I admired. I would say more than three-fourths of them responded with poems. Everybody from W. D. Snodgrass to James Dickey, and William Stafford, people like that. So, it's been fun. It is really fun to edit a little magazine, and to have a personal relationship with these people. I like to discover young writers or new writers. I don't ask their ages. They may be eighteen or eighty; I don't care, if they're good. So, it is exciting to publish people I've never heard of. I think that's good, because I think beginning poets, or unknown poets, love to see their works in an issue with established poets. It gives them a certain credibility and prestige, and so I think it's a nice formula for doing a little magazine.

BEATTIE: As someone who is a writer and an editor and an interviewer and a professor, do you see any new directions for Kentucky writers or Kentucky writing?

HALL: I think it's an exciting time. I think Kentuckians have incredible materials to write about, and that's important. I think there's talent everywhere. And Kentucky, because of its unique history as a true border state, Kentucky's history as the first western state—the mother of the West—Kentucky's geographical location, its population mix, and the various sections within the state that are sometimes in conflict with each other, all of these things have made for a unique historical tradition and heritage in Kentucky. That's the stuff of good writing. And I think we're producing good writers. Bobbie Ann Mason is obvious, as one of them. Barbara Kingsolver is another. A lot of women are really coming to the front. I think they're doing a much better job, generally, than the men.

BEATTIE: You once mentioned meeting Eudora Welty last summer. What was that like?

HALL: Oh. It was a dream.

BEATTIE: How did it come about?

HALL: Well, I reviewed her masterpiece, *Losing Battles,* when it came out, for the *Courier-Journal.* That would have been about '72 or '3. Near the end of the following week I had a letter from her. It was a letter to my address at Bellarmine-Ursuline College, back when we were still hyphenated. She wrote, "Dear Mr. Hall,"—I almost have it memorized— "Mr. Jesse Stuart clipped your review of my new book and wrote across the top 'Excellent review,' and I just want you to know that I agree with him because I thought you got at, in your review, what I was trying to get at in my book." Well, of course, by that point I was on the floor, having convulsions of sheer ecstasy. So we started a correspondence. I tried for years to get her to come up and do a reading.

Last summer, the summer of '90, two friends were going to drive down to Alabama with me, to my home in Alabama, near Montgomery. One of the friends said, "Wade, could we drive back to Kentucky through the Mississippi delta?" I said, "Sure." I saw that we'd be going through Jackson, where Miss Welty lives. So, I thought, I'm going to write Miss Eudora and see if she will let us stop by for a brief visit. So, I wrote her and I said, "You know, I realize this is imposing on your time, but I would love to stop by just briefly to meet you, because I've admired you." I tried to sound sincere with my flattery. I gave her my Alabama address. Well, the day before we were to leave to come back to Louisville the mail rider said, "Wade, I've got a letter for you." And she said, "Dear Mr. Hall, if you will take me as you find me, I'd be glad for you to stop by."

We got to Jackson and I called her; it was easy to find her house. She was waiting for us. She opened the door, and we went in, and she said, "Mr. Hall, I must explain why I said what I did about taking me as you find me." She said, "I'm having trouble walking up and down these stairs and my doctor has said that I should move my bedroom and study down to the first floor, and things are in disarray."

They weren't. There were a few boxes scattered around the living room. We went into the living room, which looked like Miss Eudora Welty's living room, the way it's supposed to look, and we sat there. I'd planned to stay five or ten minutes. We sat there and talked and talked. She was so comfortable to talk to. We talked about the Public Broadcasting Service film that had been made based on "The Wide Net," her short story, which I loved.

Finally, an hour had passed and I said, "Miss Welty, we have got to go because I don't want to use up on any more of your time." But like most southern departures, you know, you don't leave immediately, you just plan to leave.

So, a half an hour later I said, "We've got to go. How would you like a jar of fig preserves?" She said, "Oh, I'd love a jar of fig preserves." I said, "Well, I have a jar in my car with your name on it." So, I explained to her that I had been at my mother's house and that I had gone out the day after I arrived and found the fig trees filled with figs that nobody had picked, and that I had made about six or eight quarts of fig preserves. So she said, "But can you spare a whole jar?" I said, "Miss Welty, I can spare a jar of fig preserves for you." So, I went out to the car, and got a jar of fig preserves, and brought them in, and presented them to Miss Welty. As we were walking on out, I said, "Miss Welty, may I take a picture of you with your fig preserves?" She said, "Well, of course." So I have these photographs of Miss Eudora Welty standing at the entrance to her house holding the fig preserves.

BEATTIE: You have met and known fairly well a lot of writers, haven't you?

HALL: Yes, mostly in Kentucky. I've fortunately been able to get to know most Kentucky writers since I've been living in Kentucky. I met Jesse Stuart when I was still teaching at the University of Florida, and we became friends, just within a few minutes. We got to know each other, and I visited him and Naomi Dean [Stuart's wife] many times at their home, W-Hollow. Of all the writers I have known up close, Jesse is my favorite. He was a wonderful person, a better person than he was a writer, which to me is a compliment, because a lot of writers are mean, low-down, ugly to people and to each other, to other writers. Jesse was not. Jesse was very affirmative of other writers. Jesse loved himself. He was very egotistical, but you know, you have to be sold on yourself or you're not going to be a good writer.

I loved Harriette Arnow, too. She was a delightful person. She was probably not five-feet tall, maybe four-feet something, just a little granny lady from the mountains. We had her on campus to do a reading, and she was quite good. She had a very low voice. I remember when I first met her I couldn't believe that that little lady had written that great book [*The Dollmaker*]. I mean, she created Gerty Nevilles, and she was so different from Gerty Nevilles. Gerty Nevilles was this big, raw-boned woman, and here was Harriette, a little, bitty, delicate woman.

BEATTIE: You've mentioned knowing James Still. What have your experiences been with him?

HALL: Well, Jim and I are both from Alabama, so we have a little common tie there. I like Jim very much. I think he's very intent on making himself into a legend before he dies, while he's still alive to enjoy it. I think he's always been a little bit odd and cantankerous, probably even when he was a young man. But living over in the Kentucky mountains, in a fair amount of isolation . . . I mean, he's known people and he's traveled a lot, so it hasn't been total isolation.

He visits me quite often here in Louisville, and I enjoy having him. He likes to come and stay here, and he's done readings at Bellarmine. He's enjoying his popularity now; he says he's the oldest living Kentucky writer, that's why everybody wants to have him. He's probably going to live to at least a hundred, because he seems to be in pretty good health. He's a very good writer, I think, a quality writer.

BEATTIE: I wanted to ask you about your book of poetry, *The High Limb*. I noticed in reading it that many of your poems in the volume concern your parents, your relationship to them.

HALL: Well, what's more intimate than your relationship with your parents? As I've indicated earlier, I had ambiguous relations with my parents. My father and I didn't get along very well, as you can probably guess. But it is ironic that the first poem I ever wrote, that I consider halfway decent, was a poem to my father, in which I kind of apologized to him for not being closer to him. "Ad Patrum," I think I called it.

I don't write a lot now, of poetry. I wish I had more time. For a long time I wasn't publishing any of my stuff in *Kentucky Poetry Review,* and I finally decided, "Shoot, I don't send poems out to anybody else; I think I want to stick one in here once in a while."

BEATTIE: Another of your poems in *The High Limb,* "The Terror of Loving," starts, "I will not love you again, any living thing that pulses toward death." What was the origin of that?

HALL: I don't remember. Well, you know, any time you love anything that's alive, you're going to be hurt. I think I was being a little bit sarcastic about the nature of love. I wasn't suggesting that we shouldn't have it, that we should do away with love and not love anybody, but I was referring to the dangers of loving. Because whether it's a dog or a human being, you're going to lose it sooner or later. It doesn't last; that's what I meant.

BEATTIE: Can you tell me about writing *The Rest of the Dream*? How did you first come to know Lyman Johnson, and what made you decide to conduct oral histories with him?

HALL: When I moved to Louisville, in the early sixties, Lyman was still very active, and you couldn't live in Louisville and be aware of anything and not know Lyman Johnson, because he was a black spokesman. The test case that opened the University of Kentucky to blacks had occurred in '49, and he had been the plaintiff in that suit that opened the University of Kentucky in 1949. But he was still very active in liberal causes. He and I had served on some boards together, and we got to know each other, and one day in the mid-seventies, the Friends of the Louisville Free Public Library had a meeting in the western branch, the traditionally black branch of the library, and Lyman was the speaker. While he was speaking, he was telling about his life, and he held up a document showing that his paternal grandfather had bought his wife from her owner. It was history right in front of me, and I thought, "My gosh, I can't believe it. Here's Lyman, his grandfather bought his grandmother. He owned her, and Lyman is still living. These are his grandparents he's talking about. This is American history." I realized that his life had spanned much of black American history, which is American history. I mean, blacks have had such an important influence in American history, particularly in the South, but nationally as well. And I knew he was a wonderful storyteller, which is important when you're doing an oral history.

So, I went to Lyman. I said, "Lyman, why don't you and I get together and discuss the possibility of doing an oral biography of you," I said, "with no obligation on either side? I may get into this and decide that you aren't worth it, and you may decide that you don't want to fool with me." So, he said, "Okay, that sounds good to me, Wade." So, we started meeting at his home on Mohammed Ali in the West End. Over a period of about six months I wound up with about fifty-five hours of taped conversations, and I realized that it was going to take a lot of time to get all those tapes transcribed and then make them into a book, because, you know, nobody talks a book. A book is a very conscious contrivance.

So finally, about eight or so years after I finished the tapes, I called Lyman up one day and I said, "Lyman, if I don't finish this book, one of us is not going to be around to enjoy it." So, I said, "It may not be you, it may be me. You'll be here, but I won't be here." So, I decided to focus on it and I finished it up.

I read the book to Lyman when I finished it. He had in the meantime moved to the Blanton House and he was almost blind. I wanted to make sure I got it essentially correct, in terms of facts. It took me a week to read the book to him, several hours a day. More than a week, I guess, it took. And Lyman was so moved by his own life. He was really moved by it, and he paid me the highest compliment. We've gotten some good reviews, but the best review was from him. He said, "Wade, nobody else could have done this book but you and me. You're a southern white man, I'm a southern black man. It took both of us to do this kind of book." In fact, when somebody asked me whose book it was, since it was a curious kind of book, you know, an oral biography, I said, "It's my book. It's Lyman's life, and for the most part his words, but it's my book. I did the book."

The book I'm working on now, my Alabama book, it's going to be an oral history of my home county in Alabama, and it's based on interviews that I've been conducting over the past seventeen years. Many of the people I've interviewed have died, and most of them are people that could not sit down and do a formal interview. So some of them, my own relatives, I had to kind of trick into doing interviews. I had to tape them surreptitiously, and I don't care. I mean, I think all's fair in love and getting this kind of thing down, so I have really taken liberties. See, I look upon oral history as a form of creative writing.

BEATTIE: How close are you to finishing your Alabama book?

HALL: I hope pretty close. I've done all the interviews I think I'm going to do. I have a friend who's working with me on it, a woman named Annie Mae Turner, who lives down there. She's done some of the interviews. I'm doing all the writing and putting it together as a book, but she did a few of the interviews. The Black Belt Press in Montgomery, Alabama, is planning to publish it.

I've also done a couple of scripts for one-person shows. I did a script for a one-woman show on Mary Anderson, the Louisville actress. Then I did a script for a one-man show on Abraham Lincoln. We've performed it around town, at the Arts Club and various places. But it hasn't been performed professionally. In fact, we did a performance of the Mary Anderson in the Mary Anderson Room at the Kentucky Center for the Arts a couple of years ago, as a benefit. I did that as a program for the English-Speaking Union. It hit me that Mary Anderson, who grew up in Louisville, and became the toast of the English-speaking stage and retired at age thirty, lived in England the rest of her life, but kept up a close contact with her Louisville family and friends—she would be an absolutely ideal subject for an ESU program. So I decided I'd write a script based on her career as an actress, mainly, and put together a script for a one-woman show, which I think is pretty good.

Most of the stuff that I have written has been published in one form or another, but those are two examples that have not been published.

BEATTIE: Are there other writing projects that you have in mind for the future?

HALL: When I finish this oral history of my home county I want to do fiction about the county. I want to take these people that I know really well and make them into fiction. I don't mean to suggest I'm going to try to do what Faulkner did, you know, but that ain't a bad idea. It seems to me that what you really know is what you learn before you left home. That's what you really know. Because when I tend to write creatively, whether it's a short story or a poem, most of the time I write about my first sixteen years. I've lived in Kentucky longer than I have lived anywhere else, but I tend not to write about Kentucky. If I ever become a creative writer of any significance, it will be as an Alabama writer. I mean, that will be the setting. Those are the people that I have to write about. What I'm trying to do is to write about them factually in the oral history of the county. Then, once I get that done, that'll be like laying the foundation for some fictional works. Almost all the poems in that little book of poetry are Alabama poems. Virtually all of them are. The ones that have a sense of place, the sense of place is almost always Alabama, not Kentucky.

BEATTIE: In talking about the things you feel most strongly about, how do you feel about creativity? What do you think the essence of creativity is, or where do you think it comes from?

HALL: I think that often there's something missing; there's a missing piece. I think a lot of creative people feel dislocated. They feel out of sync. You know, it's the old theme that Thomas Mann explores in so many of his stories, the supposedly happy, well-adjusted, kind of superficial, simple-minded people versus the tormented artist types. I think writers are looking for a place, and if it's not already there, they have to make it for themselves. I think most creative people are like that, so they have to play God, in a sense. They have to create something or some place where they can feel at home or feel satisfied.

BEATTIE: Do you think it's looking for a place or looking for an understanding?

HALL: Well, I was just using place to mean a place on earth, as Wendell Berry puts it in the title of his book, *A Place on Earth*, which can be a literal place, or maybe a more psychic place than anything else. A home, a feeling of belonging. We're all aliens in this world, anyway. If we weren't aliens we'd be here forever, so we're just passing through. I never liked the feeling of what we call in the army a casual or a transient. I always longed to be settled down. I think most people want that. Even the homeless want some place to settle. Or again, to use Wendell's title, a place on earth, a good place, a safe, comfortable place. And some people, it's easier for them to have it than others. I think for creative people, maybe there is something missing, for whatever reason, or at least they don't fit in. But some people, if Thomas Mann is right, are better adjusted to the world, and maybe if they're totally adjusted, they don't feel the need for anything else. You know, they don't feel a need to go out and create another place, to write plays, and write poems.

BEATTIE: I wanted to ask you about your television show, *Wade Hall's Louisville and Kentucky Desk*. How did you get started doing that?

HALL: I thought there should be some format in Louisville where you could talk to people in some depth, and there was none. They had a few little local programs then where you would give an author or an interesting person two or three minutes, or maybe five or six at the most, but nothing in depth. So, when John Robert Curtin came to be station manager at Channel 15, he and I were on the Community Arts Council together, and after his first meeting I said, "John Robert, there's something I've always wanted to do, and that is to have an interview series on Channel 15, which is the place where it ought to be." We chatted some more and he said, "Well, let's do it." I said, "That's what I like to hear," so we started it.

BEATTIE: What year was this?

HALL: I've been doing it for about eight years, I guess. I don't know how many we've done. I'd say between a-hundred-and-fifty to two hundred people, mostly people from this region. Occasionally I'll interview people who come through, but I much prefer to do interesting local people who are doing things that are worthwhile.

I would like to do a book, eventually, called *American Letters* and show American history in the letters, mainly of ordinary people. I have some letters of famous people, but I really think the best letters are the letters of ordinary people who never dreamed that I would be reading their mail a hundred years later. You can see, for one thing, the westward expansion of this country. I have letters written from a family starting out in New York State, and as the members of the family moved progressively westward, I have their letters. So, I have letters from New York, Ohio, Illinois, Missouri, Texas, Colorado, California, in the same family.

I have several thousand Civil War letters, too. Dealers save me things now and send them to me. I received five letters from a dealer in Ohio the other day, including one Confederate letter. He did not know it was a Confederate letter, so he priced it as a Union letter. See, Confederate letters are much scarcer than Union letters. This letter was written from Meridian, Mississippi, from a camp near Meridian to a lady in Demopolis, Alabama. He's thanking her for the socks that she gave him when he was in Demopolis, and he tells her that many of the men in his company don't have shoes. It's in November of '64, and they don't have shoes, and they can't work, they can't get out and do the work. He says, "Those of us that have shoes are having to do the work of those that don't have shoes." I mean, you know, that personalizes the war. It's the kind of thing that Ken Burns did so well with the Civil War [television] series. In fact, in one of my letters, a Union officer comments favorably on the black soldiers that he had come into contact with. That's unusual.

I just love to read, and I love diaries. I have diaries, too, a lot of them from Louisville. I did an article for the Sunday *Courier-Journal Magazine* some years ago based on a diary that was kept by a woman here in Louisville from about 1904 until she was an old woman. She wanted to be a writer and she never did. She had two plays published by Baker, but she never really became the writer that she thought she could have been and wanted to be, and she agonized over it in her diary. The irony is, in a Jamesian way, she was doing what she was lamenting that she was not doing, by writing about not doing it. So this kind of stuff will be, I hope, grist for writers' mills and historians' mills for a long time to come.

BEATTIE: In the setting we're in now, your house contains all of your antiques and your collection of African and American primitive art. When did you start collecting these items?

HALL: I think I got interested in primitive art because it's cheap and also it's honest. It's honest art. I think there is in every person some desire to create because, as you were saying earlier, no one is complete. Some people maybe feel more complete than others, or they don't sense the lack of completeness that other people do, so there's an instinct, I think, in all of us to create. I buy primitive art at flea markets, and I don't care if the pieces I buy are not signed, because they show this creative impulse.

I also collect quilts. I don't know how many I have now. I'd say between eighty and a hundred quilts. I like honesty in the arts, you know. Even if it's contrived honesty, I like it. I don't like anything fake, and quilts are honest works of art, I think.

BEATTIE: It seems to me all of the art in your home is so personalized it represents character, which is a real connection to your writing and to your interviewing, and probably even to your teaching.

HALL: I guess so. I hadn't thought about that, but it's probably true.

September 8, 1991

Books by Wade Hall

Reflections of the Civil War in Southern Humor. Gainesville: University of Florida Press, 1962.

The Smiling Phoenix: Southern Humor, 1865-1914. Gainesville: University of Florida Press, 1965.

The Truth Is Funny: A Study of Jesse Stuart's Humor. Terre Haute: Indiana Council of Teachers of English, 1970.

The High Limb: Poems by Wade Hall. Louisville: Kentucky Poetry, 1973.

This Place Kentucky. Louisville: Data Courier, 1975.

The Kentucky Book. Louisville: Courier-Journal Books, 1979.

The Rest of the Dream: The Black Odyssey of Lyman Johnson. Lexington: University Press of Kentucky, 1988.

Greetings from Kentucky: A Post Card Tour, 1900-1950. Lexington: University Press of Kentucky, 1994.

Sacred Violence: A Reader's Companion to Cormac McCarthy. By Hall and Rick Wallach. El Paso: Texas Western Press, 1995.

Conecuh People: Voices of Life from the Alabama Black Belt. Montgomery: Black Belt, 1996.

A Visit with Harlan Hubbard. Lexington: King Library, 1995.

Passing for Black: The Life and Careers of Mae Street Kidd. Lexington: University Press of Kentucky, 1996.

FENTON JOHNSON

JOHNSON: My full name is John Fenton Johnson, although you can drop the John. I don't use it much for any purposes except the Internal Revenue Service. I was actually born in Bardstown, Kentucky, although that was because my mother went to the hospital there. I grew up in New Haven [Kentucky], which is about fifteen miles to the south. I was born in 1953.

My father's name was Patrick Dean Johnson, Jr., generally called "P.D." He was a maintenance person at the Seagram's Distillery in Athertonville [Kentucky], which was an even smaller wide space in the road, about three miles south of New Haven. That's how he made his money. He was more a hunter, fisher, and storyteller, I think; those were his main occupations.

My mother's maiden name was Hubbard. Her name is Nan, Nancy Lee, and she was a homemaker who also started the library in New Haven, and who for probably twenty years worked part-time as the librarian for the branch library in New Haven. She also ultimately served on the State Library Commission for a few years. She's still alive. My father died in 1984.

My grandfather on my father's side died shortly before I was born. My grandmother lived to be just a few days shy of a hundred, and she died about five years or so ago.

On my mother's side, my grandmother died when my mother was eleven years old, I think. My grandfather remarried. I remember my step-grandmother. My grandfather on my mother's side died when I was in the seventh or eighth grade. In the generational chain of being, I am very close to the bottom of a very large generation of about thirty-five people, and of those thirty-five or so, I'm about the fourth from the bottom in terms of the people in that generation, age-wise.

BEATTIE: What was your childhood like?

JOHNSON: I'm the eighth of eight children. Actually, the ninth of nine children. My mother had a child that died quite young, before I was born. I don't think of myself as being unhappy as a child, although I was certainly very lonely, because of being gay, and because of figuring that out very early on. I didn't know what it meant or anything.

BEATTIE: How early?

JOHNSON: Oh, gee, as early as one has any kind of cognizance of sexuality, I knew that I was attracted to men. Probably by the time I was in the sixth or seventh grade I knew that that was forbidden and wrong, or thought of as forbidden and wrong, although I still hadn't attached a name to it.

I think most gay people share the experience that people who aren't gay wonder how you come by that knowledge when no one sits you down and says, "This is a terrible sin." The answer to that is expressed, at least obliquely, in *Scissors, Paper, Rock,* which is that children understand the holes in things, and when you look around and find that your place in the world is so appallingly bad that it has no correspondent, you know about even the worst things that can happen to people, like divorce and rape and murder. I had heard these atrocities discussed, albeit in hushed tones, by the time I was ten or twelve, but homosexuality wasn't even mentioned. Therefore, you figure out very early on that it must be a very terrible sin, indeed.

So there was that, but there was also, as Rose Ella says of the gay son in *Scissors, Paper, Rock,* "there was no place for this one around here." There was the problem of growing up in a very small town which had no library until my mother started a library. There were no books except the books that were in my house. My mother owned probably eighty percent of the books that existed in New Haven, which, of course, was a great blessing. But nonetheless, it was a very limited access to books, and I was just bored more than anything. As I look back at the main thing that characterized my growing up; it was just boredom. There wasn't enough to keep me occupied, and I wasn't particularly interested in hunting and fishing, which, if you were a male child growing up, was the main way you devoted your time.

My father was an expert hunter and he was a fisher. He was really an outdoorsman and very much gauged the masculinity and the success of his male children on their ability to do certain things, probably chief among which was hunting, and second among which was fishing. So it was a source of a lot of distancing, if not outright difficulty, between me and my father that I just wasn't interested in either hunting or fishing. I didn't have any particular moral qualms or objections to either. I didn't even mind cleaning fish or cleaning animals. I just wasn't particularly interested in it.

My next oldest brother is about as dramatically different a person from me as it's possible for two human beings who are genetically related to each other to be. He really does call forth fairytales of changelings and that sort of thing, because in every conceivable way from physical body type to emotional dent, my next older brother is my diametric opposite. My father very much enjoyed his company because he did, in fact, love hunting and fishing, and my father and he did that a lot. I was sort of given the option to tag along, and when I chose not to do it, I just sort of disappeared from the scene.

BEATTIE: You have four sisters and three brothers, is that right?

JOHNSON: I have four sisters and three brothers, yes. I always got along famously with my sisters in varying degrees. I think it certainly proved for me that I have a different relationship with each one of the siblings in my family. I've always been closer to my sisters, and I think part of the reason why I've been fascinated with writing from a woman's point of view, and whatever measure of success I can attribute to that comes, because I always felt very sympathetically close to my sisters.

One of my brothers I'm close to. My oldest brother was always bedeviled by a bone of solitude, actually. He was killed in an accident about six or eight months ago. Then there's my brother, Barth, who's the hunter and fisher, and we respect each other for what we've done, but he's very uncomfortable with the issue of sexuality. He knows that I'm gay, but we've never talked about it face to face.

At Christmas time several years back I was having a conversation, early in the morning, one of those white nights, with my nieces and nephews, in which I talked with them about issues of AIDS and HIV, and it became apparent in the course of that that no one had ever done that. No one had ever talked with them. They are the children of, in fact, my favorite brother, and I said to him later on that it was the mark of respect in which I held him that I was able and willing to talk to his children so openly, because I didn't think about this consciously, but I knew at some subliminal level that he would not be outraged and upset and, in fact, would welcome my talking to them.

BEATTIE: I was interested in reading in a recent interview with you that, as a child, you often sat in your house writing dialogue that other people were speaking around you.

JOHNSON: It's funny. My mother said in the *Lexington Herald* [*Lexington Herald-Leader*] interview that I was always scribbling away in a corner. And I thought, "Gee, what corner was that?" I don't remember that. The book, *Scissors, Paper, Rock,* of course, is partly about the ways in which we shape a life. We use memory to shape a life that we can have faith in. It would be a terrifying experience, surely, for all of us to have some sort of omnipresent television camera that would record everything that we did, and then hold that ten years later in our lives up to the mist that we have created for ourselves. We would have, actually, to see how we have constructed our lives. I don't believe in our lives. I don't believe necessarily that we whitewash our lives. Some people do, of course, but many people don't. But everybody engages in the process of molding memory to suit our own particular ends, whatever they might be.

As a child, I felt excluded both from the world of the men and the world of the women. Men, because I wasn't a hunter and a fisher. I mean, that was it at its most superficial level. But surely, at the more basic level, what was going on were some issues of sexual identity. I didn't belong to the world of the women because I was a man. I told someone once that the house that I grew up in had a kind of arrangement where the kitchen was one room. There was the living room, the room which is never lived in. The parlor, I suppose you would say, was next to that. Next to that was the family room or den, which was lived in quite a bit. The women always sat in the kitchen and talked, and the men always sat in the family room and talked, and I often sat in between the two alone, listening to the conversations in both directions, because I didn't really belong to either of those worlds and I just sort of observed them from afar. I'm sure that to the extent that I can create dialogue in stories, and certainly the roots of much of the dialogue in stories that I've heard, are in that listening process.

BEATTIE: You wrote an essay about feeling a bit alienated growing up Catholic surrounded by Protestants, and you write of your Protestant-born mother who converted to Catholicism. What was that like?

JOHNSON: I'm grateful to the Catholic church for that access to imagery and metaphor and mysticism. I respond to that at every level of my thinking and feeling process. I respond to it intuitively in a way that I don't find among most of, for example, my students in California. I can see the students that I teach grasping for, desperately wanting, some kind of structure, some sort of mythical structure in which to place the events of the world. We all understand, I think, deeply, that the universe is finally a mystery, and we need some acknowledgment, at least personal if not institutional, of that mystery. I see my students searching for that, grasping for that, and having no place to find it. And that, I think, is very sad. So I'm grateful to the church for having given me that.

Having said that about the church, it's an absolutely repressive and reactionary institution which is, in its insistence particularly on birth control policies, a leading factor, if not the leading factor, in the doom of the human race. I can't say that strongly enough. If we have people around two hundred years from now to catalog history, John Paul II will be seen as the villain of the twentieth century because of his insistence that we keep producing human beings on a planet in which there's simply no room for more human beings. And because of that, and because of any number of moral issues involved, I made a decision very early on, literally in the seventh grade, I made a decision to leave the Catholic church. I stopped going to confession in the seventh grade.

BEATTIE: Sounds as though you're self-awareness at all levels came very early, compared to most people's.

JOHNSON: It's pretty amazing. I realize that now when I talk to people. I talk to intelligent, thoughtful gay men, for example, who . . . it's more typical when you talk to women . . . lesbians who come to an understanding and acceptance or acknowledgment of their sexuality later in life. The pattern seems to be that women often come to it later in life, but they find it much easier to accept, and this is a generalization, but as a generalization I think it's true. Whereas men tend to come to it earlier, but have much more trouble accepting it for any number of reasons that have a lot to do, I think, with the place of men in this society, and how we deal with sexuality in this society, and so on and so forth.

But in talking both with men and women, I've come to understand that it's not unusual to find a gay man who was aware at some level or another of his sexuality by the time he was twelve or even, in my case, nine or ten or earlier. It is pretty unusual to find somebody who had pieced together the moral and social and whatever issues surrounding it as carefully as I had done by the time I was really quite young.

BEATTIE: So you stopped going to church in seventh grade?

JOHNSON: Well, I couldn't stop going to church, because that wasn't an option, especially in the Catholic church where, you know, you are required to go to church. It was a mortal sin in those days if you don't go to church. So I continued to go to church, but my mother, every month or two or three, she would say, "How long has it been since you've been to confession?" And I'd say, "Oh, a while." And she'd say, "Are you going to go sometime soon?" And I'd say, "Oh, sometime." And fortunately, because my mother was a Protestant and retains a very critical Protestant sensibility, she never pressed me on the subject very much. My mother retained the essence of Protestantism, which is that an individual may choose and shape his or her own religious tenets, as opposed to Catholicism, which posits that those tenets are largely directed from outside. Even though my mother is a devout Catholic and thinks of herself very much as a Catholic, nonetheless, whenever you get right down to discussing the issues, if there's anything in the Catholic church that the Catholic church is doing that she doesn't agree with, she just manages somehow to put it in a shoe box and stuff it in the back of the closet. It's a very endearing characteristic. It enabled me to escape the oppression of the Catholic church, which was very present in my town, because my town was one of these anomalies that you find in Kentucky, of rural towns that are solidly Catholic. In my town of roughly eight hundred or nine hundred people, there may have been ten or fifteen Protestants in town, if that.

BEATTIE: What was your early education like? Did you go to a Catholic school?

JOHNSON: I went to the Catholic parochial school through eighth grade, and then I went to a prep school in Bardstown for one year called St. Joe, and then that prep school closed, as many of the Catholic schools were doing in the late sixties. I went then to Larue County High School, the public school of the neighboring Protestant county, and I did that because my mother was from Larue County and had connections there. She had figured out what was obviously true at that point; I think it's much less true now, but at that point in the Catholic counties, the Catholics simply did not give any money to public educational systems because nobody sent their kids to the public education system. Everybody sent their kids to the Catholic schools. So if you were going to go to the public schools, it was much better to go to the public schools in the Protestant counties. They were much better schools.

Larue County did have a good system. While I was there, there were three or four teachers in subjects in which I was interested, who were really good teachers, and one or two who were really great teachers. It says something about the much-unsung, much-underrated profession of teaching that encountering one such person in the course of one's educational career is enough to transform one's life, and being fortunate enough in high school to encounter two or three of them makes one very lucky indeed. I was lucky in that sense.

BEATTIE: Who were these teachers, and what do you remember about them that was so good?

JOHNSON: Well, there was an extraordinary English teacher named Garland Blair, who is just about to retire now, and who was a complex and often difficult man, but a thoughtful and intelligent and perceptive man. He ran the debate program, and he had some sense of cosmopolitanism and the outside world about him. Not that he himself had seen that much of that world, but he had traveled a little bit, and he had a sense of humor. He was also Catholic, interestingly enough. Then there was a chemistry teacher named Roy Long, who was a great teacher. A geometry teacher named Phil Ackerson who was great. Those are the three people whom I remember. My aunt, Helen Hubbard, taught government, and she also was a quite good teacher.

Some of these people I'm talking about were good teachers, less in their command of their subject, although Garland Blair actually had a very wide range of command of his subject, than just in their sense that education was important, that learning was something to be praised and acknowledged and assisted whenever possible. The greatest gift that a parent or a teacher can give to a child is self-respect. Given that, a child can accomplish everything else. If a child wants learning, he or she can find his way to it. These were teachers who had an understanding of the basic dignity of human beings, and who conveyed that in every action in the classroom.

I think I survived and came to terms in a very comfortable way with my sexuality because I had been given enough self-respect at home that I was able to piece together the struggle and make it on my own, however difficult it might have been. I also had the combination of fortune, good sense, and encouragement from my family to go to California where, during those times, it was easier to achieve that there than in Kentucky. I will say that that's mostly from my mother. The subliminal issues of sexuality and personality conflict separated me from my father. There's no question about that. For better or worse or whatever, he did not make much effort to overcome that. But, again, that's why I'd love to get John Paul II and sit him down and lecture him, because when you have eight children, you just have too many damn chickens in the nest, and it is pretty easy to let the needs of one or the other chicks go by the wayside.

In *Scissors, Paper, Rock,* one of the sections that I liked the best is where the mother and the son are talking about if they could have helped each other when the son was growing up. What I like about that section is the way in which it underscores that, at the time that I was growing up, there was no language to talk about the fact that I was gay. I think my mother tells me that she sensed that very early on, and I'm sure she's right. But there simply weren't words. There were no words to use. "Gay" was still pejorative in those days. "Homosexual" was scientific and, in any case, not a word likely to be in currency in New Haven, Kentucky, in 1958 or '60 or '63. When words don't exist to talk about something, it's hardly surprising that it doesn't get talked about. So that was a barrier against which we were all laboring.

BEATTIE: Do you recall in school if you had a favorite subject early on?

JOHNSON: Well, I was always best in English. Geography was actually my favorite subject because I would spend days and days bored, looking at maps, plotting out where I was going to go once I got out of New Haven.

BEATTIE: Did you know how to read before you went to school?

JOHNSON: I'm sure I must have. There's no question that I did, again partly because I had older brothers and sisters who, as my mother readily admits, and which was not a bad thing at all, kind of saw me as a toy. I was a living doll, you know. I think all older brothers and sisters do that to younger kids when they come along, and so it was fun for them to sit down with me and, by way of playing with me, teach me to read.

BEATTIE: Do you remember when you started writing on your own?

JOHNSON: Well, there were various documents around the house of things that I was writing when I was in the fourth and fifth grades. I was scribbling away at something or another, and I was known even then as a sort of family bard or something. I would make up—what's the word I'm hunting for? Not jargon. Doggerel. I would make up doggerel for family occasions, birthdays or whatever. Little poems that would be read aloud and that sort of thing. I was doing that in high school. Garland Blair, one of the things that he did—that teacher to whom I was referring earlier—was, to require as part of his class that you undertake creative writing which, at the time, because I wanted to do it, made entirely good sense to me. But I look back now and realize that, in fact, that was a somewhat unusual thing to do for a junior English teacher in the mid- to late-1960s, at least in rural Kentucky. To not only encourage, but demand of his students, that they make up something in their own words, that they try to articulate their feelings and reactions about the world. I did that, of course, at much greater length and more diligently than anybody else in the classroom, because it was where my interest lay.

BEATTIE: You were on your high school debating team, is that right?

JOHNSON: Yes, I was significantly into debate, mainly because you got to go to other towns to go on debate tournaments. And for me, when I was fifteen years old, to go from New Haven to Madisonville, or from New Haven to Bowling Green, was quite an adventure.

BEATTIE: You won a scholarship, didn't you, from your father's company, Seagram's?

JOHNSON: Yes, Seagram's had a scholarship for a child, a son or a daughter of a Seagram's employee, that would pay anything anywhere you went to school. Until I got that scholarship, actually, I had been scheduled to go to Notre Dame because I needed financial aid. A lot of it. The school who gave me the best package was Notre Dame, and I was scheduled to go there. I had applied for a Seagram's scholarship, and I thought, on the off-chance that I'll get one, I want an ace in the hole. I figured if I get this I might as well A) go as far away as I can, and B) go to a place that is as expensive as I can possibly find, because if somebody's going to pay everything, I might as well get them to pay a lot as opposed to a little. In fact, I'd written to Stanford and told them that I wasn't going to come, and I was really dreading the prospect of reentering the Catholic educational system. Then the Seagram's scholarship, in a way that's sort of very Dickensesque, *Great Expectations,* this hand comes out of the sky and handed me a blank check and said, "Go away!" I called Stanford and said, "Can I change my mind?" They said, "Yes," and I changed my mind and went to California.

Coincidentally, that year the National Debate Tournament was at Stanford, and I was the boys' extemporaneous speaking champion for the state. I went to Stanford and saw it for the first time, and saw California for the first time, and it was a great experience.

BEATTIE: Were you the first child in your family to go to college?

JOHNSON: My parents both went to college briefly. Almost all of us have graduated from college. I am the only one who has any kind of advanced degree. I have a master's from Iowa.

BEATTIE: How did you find Stanford when you got there?

JOHNSON: It was a culture shock in ways that I'll only comprehend through all of my life. When you're seventeen years old, you tend to, whether you realize it or not, see all of the world in terms of your own experience, and it was a great source of shock and enlightenment, gradual enlightenment but immediate shock, to me to learn that the assumptions that I made about the world were almost, at least in urban California, uniquely mine. It was a very difficult process to go through in the time that I was there because, especially in my freshman year, people would make fun of my accent, and I had never thought of myself as having an accent.

I think the four years that I spent at Stanford were really a matter of learning how to live in an urban-suburban world, and that that was what the education was about as much as anything that I might learn out of books or in classes.

BEATTIE: Did you major in English?

JOHNSON: Yes, I majored in English.

Stanford generally does a pretty good job of taking care of people from foreign cultures, but I fell through the cracks on two counts. First of all, it didn't quite occur to them that someone from a small town in rural Kentucky would be from, essentially, a foreign culture. Now I think they realize that. Then, there was an accident that happened with the woman who was supposed to be my advisor. Essentially, she dropped out of school three weeks after she was assigned to me, and I knew so little about how college worked, I didn't know what an advisor was for. I didn't know that you were supposed to have one. I didn't know that there was actually someone to whom you might be able to turn to say, "What should I do about my college career?" So I just literally drifted through my college years very much catch-as-catch can. As it turns out, I don't suppose any great damage was done, because, as I say, I was really far more interested in learning about how big the world was and what constituted it than any particular thing I was learning in classes, and that was not necessarily bad.

BEATTIE: When did you start thinking of yourself as a writer?

JOHNSON: Well, I started taking creative writing classes when I was at Stanford. I worked as a press secretary for Ron Mazzoli, who was the congressional representative from Louisville in Washington. But the whole time that I was doing that, I was kind of within a goal of quitting and becoming a writer. It was right after college. It was the first job I had.

BEATTIE: How did you obtain that job?

JOHNSON: I wrote all of the Kentucky congressional delegation and said that I wanted to work for them for the summertime. Of all of the delegation, only, much to his credit, Ron Mazzoli responded. I interviewed with him just for a summertime internship. I had hair down to my shoulders and I went in and we talked for an hour about Flannery O'Connor and southern literature, and that was the interview. I just forgot about it until Mazzoli called me up one day and said, "Well, if you're still interested in this job, you can have it."

I don't know where the confusion happened. He thought he was offering me an internship. I thought he was offering me a full-time job. I did graduate in '75 a quarter early, and I moved to Washington with the assumption that I would have a job, and arrived to discover that I had an internship. But Mazzoli liked my work across the summer and hired me on full-time, and I stayed there for two years. It was a very good experience. I sometimes wonder, "What if I had done this instead of that?"

At the time the [*Louisville*] *Courier-Journal* had a pretty active Washington Bureau. The *Courier-Journal* was a more comprehensive and "better" newspaper in those days. The *Courier-Journal* reporter at the time in Washington asked me if I was interested in writing for the Washington Bureau, but I had this single-minded notion of going to California and being a writer and probably moving back to California. So I took the money I'd saved up and started writing full-time. It wasn't really, I think, until graduate school that I began seriously to think of myself as a writer. I think the main benefit that the program at Iowa gave to me was that it took me and everyone there seriously as writers.

BEATTIE: This is the Iowa Writers Workshop?

JOHNSON: Yes, the Iowa Writers Workshop. I could fault, in many ways, the way the program was structured at Iowa, but the one critical thing that it did and does very well is everyone who comes there is treated as a professional writer to the degree that they want to be treated that way. They take themselves seriously, the program and the town. Even outside the program treats you seriously as a writer, and that was a very good thing to happen because it began to make me believe that in fact I could become a writer.

BEATTIE: Did you go directly from Washington to the Iowa Writers Workshop?

JOHNSON: No, I went back to California and worked for a few years. I ran an independent film and video program, which, a number of years later, provided me a way to make a living during my first years after coming back from Iowa, because I edited a small journal for independent film- and videomakers in California and, ultimately, nationally. I became a consultant via that for various private foundations on spending money in the arts, specifically in independent film and video, which is something that I still do provisionally.

BEATTIE: Did you decide that the Iowa Writers Workshop was the only graduate program in writing you wanted to go to, or had you applied to several?

JOHNSON: No. One of the things that happened was that I was living in San Francisco, and I had been accepted both at the Stanford Program in Creative Writing, which is a very good program, and the Iowa Program, which is a very good program. And with their sort of narrow-minded superciliousness, people in San Francisco would say, "Iowa? How could you possibly go to Iowa?" But that wasn't enough. That didn't dissuade me. I was really trying to figure out which program was the better program. On the weekend on which I had to decide, my roommate invited a crazy man home with him who, to make a long story short, destroyed our apartment. Literally destroyed. Took a hammer and literally destroyed the apartment. When I woke up on Monday morning to that, the wreck of this dwelling, I thought, "Maybe it's time for me to get out of the city for a little while."

I decided to go to Iowa, and the reason why I think of that as significant is because had I stayed and had I gone to Stanford, I would have continued to live in San Francisco, and in the way of the chance and fate of things, it was the most sexually active period of my life, and it is difficult to imagine that I would be HIV-negative. When the consequences of your choices are so graphically portrayed to you, it's very difficult to ignore the element of chance and fate in the course of one's life.

BEATTIE: You said that there are some things about the Iowa Workshop that you didn't like. What were they?

JOHNSON: Well, the faculty, there's not much there, especially in the fiction program. Or at least while I was there, there was not much in the way of continuing faculty. People would come for one semester or at most a year. Those people were invited to teach, but there was very little else that was asked of them. At Iowa there tended to be a lot of people who were quite well-known, but whose teaching skills varied dramatically and often were not great.

But another problem that I had, again at Iowa, was that I didn't have a lot of money, and even though they were giving me financial aid, I had to work. I was a teaching assistant and I was also working as an editorial assistant at the University of Iowa Press, and occasionally doing other free-lance jobs on the side. I really had lots and lots of irons in the fire. I realized at the end of that summer that there were limits to how much one could work oneself, and that you had to respect those limits.

BEATTIE: What did you do upon graduation from Iowa?

JOHNSON: I got what they call a Michener Fellowship, which is endowed by [James] Michener to provide small grants to students graduating from Iowa completing first-time novels. I got that and I went back to San Francisco and attempted to live on that for a year, and I found that it just wasn't enough money to live on. But first of all, the Michener Fellowship reinforced the sense that I was a professional writer. Somebody was actually paying me to do this. It enabled me to write pretty much full-time for five or six months, and I began to understand what that process entailed. I began to learn about the real loneliness of writing at home alone all day long, and to figure out, that at least for someone like myself who is essentially gregarious, who enjoys social interaction, that I had to figure out ways to deal with that. I had to structure my life in a way that brought some kind of human contact into my life if I were to continue to write.

I know people laugh at me, but I have a very structured schedule where I typically get up at seven o'clock or so, and try to be at my desk by eight. I allow myself a cup of coffee at eight-thirty and a cup of coffee at nine-thirty. I look forward to those very much. Then, around ten-thirty, I start thinking about what I'm going to have for lunch. I can't imagine these people who don't eat lunch or who don't pay attention to what they have for lunch, because for me, it's such a ritual that I so look forward to, to break the day up. I usually reserve afternoons for correspondence or reading or something that is not as heavy-duty as the act of composition and editing. I'm not as disciplined as I would like to be, although I suppose almost every writer could say that.

Thinking of my novel *Scissors, Paper, Rock,* and the way in which I wrote it, the stories in the first half of the book are, I think, much more controlled and much more structured than are those in the second half of the book, when I get much more rambling, and that sort of longer novella that forms the heart of the book, and the stories that follow, those are much more impressionistic and less driven than the stories in the first half. It is a generalization to say this, but it is generally true that what happens between those two stories is that Larry [Johnson's lover] died. My brother died, and mostly as a result of that, and partly as a result of natural progression in my own work, I became somewhat more free-form, and I think that's been good.

I find sex difficult to write about, as I think most writers do. Anybody who is treating the subject seriously does. Also, there are issues very close to the heart that have a lot to do with the death of my friends and of my lover and of my father. I was worried that I was stepping over the line in those chapters towards sentimentality, which I think is one of my sort of sand traps as a writer. But in looking back at it now, I think that though they fail in some places, that on the whole, the success is worth the failures that happen, and that, in balance, they come out better. My hope, at least intention, is to continue more in that vein.

BEATTIE: It's difficult to be a humanist as a writer and not have sentiment. Not sentimentality, but sentiment.

JOHNSON: I explain to my students the distinction. I try to make the distinction between sentiment and sentimentality, that sentiment is noble and necessary, and sentimentality is gilding the lily, and I say that it's very difficult to know for oneself where one has crossed the line between those two. And, of course, the material that I'm working with is very loaded material.

BEATTIE: That's what I think distinguishes that book from being a book that could primarily be enjoyed by a gay audience, to a book that can be appreciated by a more universal audience, showing the likenesses of the human condition.

JOHNSON: When people ask me, as they have, why can you write from a woman's point of view, my response is that I think people are people before they're anything else, and that's not to minimize the differences in men's and women's responses, or for that matter, gay men and straight men's responses to various situations. But it is to say that the driving emotions of the human condition, which is to say fear and anger and grief and love, are emotions that we all share. My ambition had always been, from the beginning of this book, *Scissors, Paper, Rock,* to have a gay character as the principal character, but to present him integrated into the world, into the people among whom he travels in the world, among whom he lives.

BEATTIE: That's why I thought it was a much more human, caring, loving sort of book than so many that are angry.

JOHNSON: I think about that a lot, and I have to say, I understand exactly what it is you're saying. In defense of the people who have written the other kinds of books, two things separate my situation from theirs. The first that has to be pointed out, repeatedly, is just that I'm HIV-negative, and I always wonder where would I be if I were HIV-positive. What would my response be? And the anger that I have felt, it is certainly something that I think about. The measure of control that I am able to exercise comes in part from my nature, which is just that I am that kind of sort of mannered, controlled person. But also because of the fact that the issue, however much it has touched my life, is not as immediate for me as it is for someone who is literally facing the prospect of not just his death at a relatively young age, but a death that is likely to be an extremely painful and drawn out and difficult way to die.

The other issue at hand in my being able to write such a book is that I've taken more time. Paul Monette's books—and I know Paul and I admire his work—are necessary books. I don't think of Paul as a great prose stylist, but Paul hasn't the time to be a great prose stylist. Paul knew that he was dying and, in fact, as far as I know while he's alive—he is still alive— he's quite ill and probably not likely to finish another book. Paul is writing out of urgency of knowing that. I know that to a certain degree, but I would be fatuous if I were to claim that I could know, even as a writer or novelist, as intimately as someone who is HIV-positive, the condition of my own mortality.

Wendell Berry used a phrase in a letter to me that I have used again and again because I liked it so much. I think it was actually in a talk that I heard, and someone asked him if you live in the city and you don't have a yard and you live in an apartment and you commute to work and that sort of thing, how can you put into effect principles regarding the environment? Wendell said very wisely that one's responsibility is to act responsibly within the place where history has put you. And that phrase, "within the place where history has put you" is one that has a lot of resonance for me because it expresses the role of chance in determining our lives. It respects the role of history, of fate, in determining where we are, at the same time that it acknowledges our own responsibility to act within the bounds of what's possible for us within that place.

BEATTIE: I think the parallels you draw in *Scissors, Paper, Rock* between, say, the spinster schoolteacher and that kind of loneliness from lack of love, and the father who can't relate to his son, and the pain that causes on both sides, the mother who has a sort of ambivalence about love, and the brothers and sisters and everybody else in the community with their various lonelinesses, I think all of those examples bring the gay issue home to people in terms of universal loneliness.

JOHNSON: I think the lowest common denominator of the human condition is its loneliness. We are all finally alone in our journeys through history. The antidote to that, the lowest common denominator or antidote to that, is love. I do think that love comes in many ways, shapes, and forms. But the enlightened person respects love in all of its manifestations, no matter what way, shape, or form it comes in. It can come in some strange ways, shapes, and forms. Certainly what I have in my writing as its driving motivation, even when I'm not immediately conscious of that, is the duality of the essential loneliness of the human condition and the omnipresence of love, if we can but accept it in its various forms, which, incidentally, are not often forms in which we would choose to have it manifest itself in our lives. We have a vision that is too often molded by Madison Avenue and Hollywood as to ways in which love should enter our lives. It doesn't often enter our lives in that way at all.

BEATTIE: When you received the Michener Fellowship, was the book you were working on *Crossing the River*?

JOHNSON: Yes, and it shows the process of how long these things take, but I am getting a little faster. I got the Michener Fellowship in '82. I finished the first draft, and you couldn't even, in certain ways, say that I'd begun the book. I'd written a couple of preliminary chapters and that was it. So I really began the book in the fall of '82. I finished its first draft solidly by the summer of '83. I had a rough draft in place. But then I went to work full-time, and that slowed down the process enormously. I didn't finish the book until maybe fall of '85. Then it took a year and a half to sell, and sold, I think, probably in mid-1987. It wasn't published in hard cover until September of '89.

BEATTIE: When you sold *Crossing the River,* did you market it yourself or did you have an agent?

JOHNSON: I have an agent whose name is the wonderfully mellifluous name of Malaga Baldi. Her parents conceived her in Malaga, the city on the coast of Spain, and named her after that city. She's great.

BEATTIE: What are you attempting to do in your fiction, in general or specifically? Is there something overall that you are attempting to do other than tell a story? Something that's most important to you?

JOHNSON: Well, I think it's quintessentially important to entertain people. I do think that there is a direct line, a genealogical line, between what a fiction writer is doing today and the cavewomen and cavemen who told the stories around the fire ten thousand years ago. I feel very proud and lucky to be part of that. And, as any caveperson around the fire would say, your obligation is to entertain your audience. It is also to instruct your audience, and to the degree that someone who is thirty-nine years old is capable of instructing, to instruct the audience and to put forth a particular vision of truth in the world. I emphasize that it's a particular vision, and it grows out of where I am at a particular place in time. I probably won't feel the same way about certain subjects ten years from now as I feel about them now, but I aspire to a vision of truth.

Miss Camilla talks at great length in the final chapter of *Scissors, Paper, Rock* about the distinction between truth and fact, and she says that just facts are disputable at best, but it is possible to express truth. I always think of that as an interesting point of view because, of course, we are constantly told exactly the opposite, that it is possible to determine facts, but the truth is something that is shifting and ephemeral. I believe exactly the opposite.

I think that again, given the changing circumstances of times in one's life, at any particular time in one's life it is not only possible, but necessary, to have a moral code which can be expressed, which is the writer's responsibility and aspiration to express, and which aspires to express in the essential verities of her or his place in the world. That's what it's my ambition to do, and to express that in terms that are universal enough so that another person, whose experience of the world may be very different from mine, can nonetheless find resonance in my work. Someone who is from a small family with divorced parents, or who never knew his parents and is a straight man in central Missouri, I would like to think, if he is someone who is attuned to reading and enjoys reading, can enjoy this book about a large family with a gay son who dies of HIV.

BEATTIE: Your books are, would you say, largely autobiographical?

JOHNSON: Well, I think more so for *Crossing the River* than *Scissors, Paper, Rock.* I said to my sister once that I expected that for someone who was in my family, reading my books must be a little bit like walking into a fun house, mirrored with crazy mirrors where you would catch glimpses of details of the past, which you would recognize, or think that you recognize, but they would be distorted and changed so much, that you would catch a glimpse of it and you'd think, "Oh, yes, I know that," and then you'd realize that you didn't know it.

Joyce says that all fiction is autobiographical, and I agree with that absolutely. *Crossing the River* more so than *Scissors, Paper, Rock,* but both books have some detail which is drawn fairly directly from my life experience. At the same time that it interests me to observe that not only is my writing becoming less and less autobiographical, my characters who are the most successful, or the most successful parts of my characters, are often those that are least autobiographical.

BEATTIE: You referred earlier to your lover dying while you were writing *Scissors, Paper, Rock.* How has that experience affected your writing?

JOHNSON: Well, it transformed me as a human being which, of course, means that necessarily it must have transformed my writing. I think one thing I've already addressed is the way in which my writing is freer and less constrained now. I think probably because I have greater respect for mystery and the necessity of allowing the process to flow without trying to exert too heavy a controlling hand on it. I also don't think it's an exaggeration at all to say that Larry taught me how to love, and, in doing so, taught me a great deal about writing, even though we seldom spoke of it in those terms.

BEATTIE: One of your themes in *Scissors, Paper, Rock* is the importance of risk-taking to actually living, isn't it?

JOHNSON: Yes, and you know, while I was living with Larry, I lost a couple of very good friends because they said, "You're nuts. You're completely nuts." But at the point where it was clear that I couldn't persuade them of the rightness of what I was doing, I simply had to end the friendships, and I have great regret over that, at the same time that I have no regrets about my having undertaken the relationship with Larry. It was a risk, but it was a risk that was calculated, and I hate to put it in such crass terms, but it paid off.

All of us go through life calculating risks. It's just, I guess, that I'm willing to push the edges of the envelope a little bit more than most people. Also, there is a phenomenon which a few people have written about and which sounds absolutely nuts to people who aren't in the middle of it, but the fact is, and it has correspondence in history in other situations like the holocaust and the plague epidemics of the seventeenth century and sixteenth century, when you're in a situation where so many people that you know are sick and dying, you come to live much more immediately in the present than people who are not involved with that situation. Consequently, it is easier for you to make decisions that enrich the present, perhaps, at the expense of the future.

BEATTIE: What year was that, that he died?

JOHNSON: He died in 1990.

BEATTIE: How many years had you been together?

JOHNSON: Four years. I think of it as rather short in terms of, say, my parents' marriage of forty-five years. But what I came to understand across the course of that time was that the depth of a relationship does not necessarily depend on time. In fact, one thing I learned out of that, and that I began to talk about and will certainly write more about, is the elasticity of time. We tend to think in this society of time as moving in a linear fashion along a ruler where the three-hundred-and-sixty-five days of one year is exactly equivalent to three-hundred-and-sixty-five days of the following year. When in fact my feeling is that time is much more malleable than that, and there are periods in our lives where one aspect of our lives, say, in this case, emotion or the heart of intuition, we much more intensely experience that than at other points in our lives. I would be very comfortable with saying that in the four years of our relationship, Larry and I compressed sixty years of living together. It was that rich and that resonant for me.

BEATTIE: When did you start writing articles and columns for the *New York Times Sunday Magazine*?

JOHNSON: Well, because I was scribbling away in the corners, it's actually a good lesson for someone who wants to be a writer that what your task is finally is not to publish, but it's to write. I had gone home to spend the summer with my mother because my father had died and she was alone, and I thought it would be a good opportunity for us to get to know each other better, which it was. I planned to take the summer off, and I went and spent probably two months of it back in Kentucky with her. I wrote a three-thousand-word essay, which grew out of letters to friends, as many of my essays do, which talked about that experience, spending time with my mother. I had no idea what to do with it. It sat around on my desk for a year, and then my agent had lunch with an editor of the [*New York*] *Times* and she said, "I just had lunch with this editor who's taken over this column called 'About Men,' which is in the *Times,* the *Sunday Times Magazine,* and he's looking for material. Do you have anything?" I said, "Well, I wrote this piece about a year ago that doesn't really have anything particularly to do about men per se, but it's about a man, me, going home to spend summer with his mother." She said, "Well, send it to me and I'll give it to him."

He liked it, and then once they published that, an editor said, "Well, do you have any ideas for longer pieces?" I said, "Well, everybody that I grew up with in Kentucky who used to grow tobacco is now growing marijuana." He said, "Well, that sounds interesting. Why don't you go do a story on that?" One thing led to another. But it was all based on something that I had written not because I had any particular ambitions in publishing, or knowing where it was going to be published, but just out of the fact that I had the joy of writing it.

BEATTIE: I wanted to ask you about your teaching creative writing at San Francisco State [University]. How long have you done that?

JOHNSON: I taught there for two years before Larry died, and then I didn't teach for two years, and now I'm in the middle of my third year doing it. So I've done it four of the last six years, two semesters a year, and part-time each semester. Most semesters I've taught two classes.

BEATTIE: Graduate or undergraduate or both?

JOHNSON: A mix of both. Some undergraduate, some graduate. I love teaching. In fact, I wish I loved it a little less. I find it is gratifying, and it does satisfy that kind of gregarious aspect of my personality. If you teach well, it's very satisfying to one's ego in an immediate way, which writing almost very seldom is. Students really give me a lot of reinforcement for the work that I do with them.

BEATTIE: How do you think creative writing should be taught?

JOHNSON: I developed a very good motto, I think, which is the doctor's motto, which is "do no harm." I think that should be the creative writing teacher's first principle.

I had a teacher whose name I won't mention. He remains a good friend of mine and I respect him and admire him as a person. But in my first class at Iowa, I had a story that was written from two points of view. He was teaching the class and he started out the critique by saying, "Well, the first problem with this story is that it's written from two points of view.

No good stories are written from two points of view." I didn't know enough about literature to challenge him on that point, even though I thought that didn't make a lot of sense. Since then, I have read any number of really great stories that are written from more than one point of view.

"Well," he said, "in a novel, you can manage more than one point of view, but not in a story." As with many such pieces of wisdom, there's some truth in what he says. What he ought to have said was that the rule of conservation of energy applies, and when one has more than one point of view in a story, one is giving up something. You're giving up the power that you maintain by having the focus on a single character. What you have to decide as a writer is whether what you gain by giving up that power is worth what you lose. But it's not to say that a story can be written from only one point of view. It's to say that you are giving up certain power in having more than one point of view. Know that you're giving that up, and think about whether, in fact, you want to give that up in exchange for what you gain with the multiple point of view that you're presenting.

So my ambition, and I say this to my students right at the beginning of class, is to try to be as gentle as possible. I try to offer constructive criticism and I try to be firm when I think something is clearly wrongheaded. But at the same time I try never to make any kind of pronouncement that is absolute, because you simply can never know that this student is going to be somebody who is going to break the most basic of rules about dangling modifiers, for example, to some great effect. I think any teacher who doesn't respect that, particularly in this field, is treading on very thin ice.

BEATTIE: I'm wondering about what you think the nature of creativity itself is.

JOHNSON: Well, that's a big question. There is a purely selfish impulse to express oneself that bribes the writing process. There is no question about that. Maybe it's ingenuous of me, but I am always slightly mystified, and somewhat humbled, by the fact that anyone would go out and plunk down twenty dollars to buy two-hundred-and-fifty pages of my prose at the same time that I frequently plunk down twenty dollars to buy two-hundred-and-fifty pages of many other people's prose. So it isn't as if I don't understand what the process is about. At its most highfalutin' level, what I like to think of writing as being is the expression in words of the mystery of the universe. And put in those terms, what I have to say first of all is that given the fact that it's a mystery makes it a given that the end product is finally and necessarily inadequate to the cause. It is impossible to express the mystery of the universe in any human language. Chekhov ends a wonderful story called "Gusev" by describing a sunset in which the last words of the story are something to the effect that he describes the sunset as well as he can and then he says "and in colors and words, too, in colors too beautiful for the human tongue." He has the good sense to realize that he cannot express the beauty.

A cello that's being played next to another cello can set up a resonance in that cello that's not being played. I like to think that a writer can strike chords of response in a reader. The process is mysterious in and of itself, but in the very mystery of the process, the mystery of the universe is invoked. Through that the reader comes to experience some small part of the mystery of the universe, and in that sense, the mystery is, if not expressed, at least invoked.

BEATTIE: I know you've written a piece on sense of place in your writing, on how important that is. Kentucky and California—essentially what you are saying is that they are about equally important; you can't dismiss either one.

JOHNSON: It's true. I feel very lucky to have them both. I called them in that essay this small green apple and this large navel orange, and I thought that was a very apt comparison, because is it possible to say that apples or oranges are better, one than another? No. They're both wonderful in their very different ways, and that's how I think of Kentucky and California.

BEATTIE: Is there anything you can say about current or future work?

JOHNSON: The project that I'm working on is a book of essays about loss and love and grief. That, I see, as a way of expressing in nonfiction the richness of the experience of not just my years with Larry, although it will center around those, but of the whole time of the HIV epidemic. That's what I'm in the middle of, and I hope to finish it relatively soon. I haven't articulated this in any way beyond the description that I'm about to provide. I've not started on it at all. But what I would really like to write is a kind of García Márquez-type novel, set in the Southern Appalachians where there is sort of an application of a magical realism to the Appalachians that seem to me to cry for that kind of epic, and I like to think that my Catholic background would give me some access to that in a way that would be productive and rich.

BEATTIE: Since you are one of the few Kentucky writers and one of the few writers nationally who have the courage to call yourself a gay writer, is that how you would want yourself referred to, or do you prefer to simply be called a writer? Is the gay designation restricting or liberating?

JOHNSON: I don't think of it as restrictive. I think of it as descriptive. Toni Morrison is a black writer. I would never think of not describing her as a black writer, at the same time that I don't think of that description as limiting her in any way, shape, or form. If anything, it provides a touchstone from which then to open out one's comprehension of and understanding of her work. She is a humanist, above all and foremost. Above all and foremost she is a black writer, and any description of her that omitted that would be inadequate to the cause, and I would hope that they would say the same about my work. I don't object to being called a gay writer, and refer to myself as that, as long as that label isn't used to categorize and restrict, but rather is used, as I say, as a place from which to open out.

June 27, 1993

BOOKS BY FENTON JOHNSON

Crossing the River. New York: Birch Lane, 1989.

Scissors, Paper, Rock. New York: Pocket, 1993.

Geography of a Heart. New York: Scribner/Simon and Schuster, 1996.

BARBARA KINGSOLVER

KINGSOLVER: My name is Barbara Ellen Kingsolver, and I was born April eighth, 1955, in Annapolis, Maryland. My mother's name is Virginia Lee Henry Kingsolver. My father's name is Wendell Roy Kingsolver, and before he retired, he was a physician. He was in the navy when I was born, but most of my childhood we've lived here [Carlisle, Kentucky]. This is the house I grew up in. I have an older brother and a younger sister. My sister's name is Ann and my brother's name is Rob.

My father's mother lives two doors down—Mammaw. Her name is Louise Auxier Kingsolver. My father's father, Roy Kingsolver, died two years ago. My mother's parents, they were Henrys, and they died quite a long time ago—Arthur Raymond Henry and Nellie Henry. I was pretty young when she died.

BEATTIE: What do you remember about them?

KINGSOLVER: My mother's parents lived in Lexington in a place called Arcadia Park. It was sort of a very pretty urban neighborhood with big, old oak trees and lots of houses and streets. I loved going there. See, I grew up here, and now it might look like a neighborhood, but when we moved here, there were no other houses in sight. It was the middle of an enormous alfalfa field and, when you're a kid, you always want what you haven't got. I'm sure that all the kids on my grandmother's block would have died to live in the middle of an alfalfa field, because you could catch mice and insects, and pull their wings off and stuff. But I just thought the dream life would be to live in a neighborhood with sidewalks and to have roller skates, so it was really thrilling to visit Lexington.

I consider myself as having had a very rural childhood. The bookmobile was a big part of my life. My father's parents also lived in Lexington while I was growing up, and I really liked visiting them, too. There was a nice little house on the front of the lot, and all the back of it was a garden. It was just this wonderland of a vegetable garden that was my grandfather's and a flower garden that was my grandmother's. It was constantly a war, you know, through the bushes, kind of a Yugoslavia. I mean, they got along wonderfully, but the border between the flower garden and the vegetable garden was always being pushed one direction or the other. They had a whole farm packed into a half-acre lot. Here, we had gardens; that was no big deal. But there everything was jammed into this lot with all these fruit trees and flowering trees and chrysanthemums as high as my head, and it just seemed like a jungle. I live on the outskirts of Tucson now, but my back yard looks kind of like Mammaw and Pappaw's, except that I grow both vegetables and flowers, so I don't have to fight with anyone.

BEATTIE: Is your fascination with vegetables and flowers about the same as your character in *The Bean Trees* and in *Pigs in Heaven*, Turtle's?

KINGSOLVER: Absolutely. My favorite reading material is still the Burpee's Seed Catalog, I admit. I mean, Tolstoy and Dickens and Virginia Woolf are way up there, but Burpee's and Parks are on the top. I really credit my parents for raising me with an eye always to the natural world. I've always drawn a lot of comfort from growing a garden. It's the predictability of the natural that I find so comforting.

BEATTIE: So that's the metaphor for Turtle, who needed stability?

KINGSOLVER: Right. I was trying to think of an odd way for this child to be when she finally would begin to talk, because I knew that I wanted her to be lovable, but eccentric, and clearly marked by what had happened to her. I didn't have Camille [Kingsolver's daughter] when I invented Turtle. But I'd seen enough of kids and watched them carefully enough to know that they'll do things like that. It's not out of the realm of possibility for a child to start talking and say only, "vegetable." You know, only say the names of vegetables, especially if they're damaged in some way. You can kind of skew children into a direction where they seem to obsess. In an adult you would call it an obsession, but in a child it's more just finding . . .

BEATTIE: Focus?

KINGSOLVER: Something. Yes, focus, that's a really good word. Finding something that works for them and just doing it and doing it and doing it, because that's what gets them through. I like the idea of choosing as Turtle's focus garden vegetables, because for me it's the life force, kind of the living story and the predictability of what's going to happen there that I wanted to give Turtle, and also for that to reflect on who she would grow to be.

BEATTIE: What was your own childhood like?

KINGSOLVER: There are a thousand different truths when you talk about your childhood. But I guess the ones that come home to roost when I'm here [Carlisle] are both—I was very happy and very sad, both. I mean, I had a really enriched childhood. I had parents who gave me books and a love for books. TV was not a big part of this house.

BEATTIE: So your parents were both readers.

KINGSOLVER: Yes, and my father reveres books. There used to be a red leather chair there [pointing in living room], and I can remember sitting at his feet while he read Robert Burns to me and got tears in his eyes, which was not a common sight for Father, especially when he was reading poetry. I was seven, maybe, and my heart stood still, and I understood that words could have more power over people than any sort of physical object. So that, combined with kind of being a social misfit, I think, probably made me a writer.

BEATTIE: It's interesting that you remember the exact moment when words became important.

KINGSOLVER: A lot of my early memories are fixed with words. I can remember the first word I ever read. It was "orange." I was four or five, sort of on the borderline of being there, and I saw people reading, and I just kind of figured if I kept on staring at the words they would eventually . . . I had the idea. It was like Helen Keller; I understood. I'd had the breakthrough where I understood that these little things on the page were, in fact, words, and so I was staring hard at a full page of print, no pictures, just a full page of print in *Life* magazine, just staring at it waiting for the meaning to be revealed, and all of a sudden on the exact center of the page there was a word that started with "o," and I knew my letters, and I just said the letters, O-R-A-N-G-E. Then, boing!, "orange" came into my mind, and it was a breakthrough. That's when I got it, that actually every single one of these words would have a color inside it, or a meaning, or a sense. And, boy, it must have meant a lot to me, because I remember precisely how it felt for that to happen.

BEATTIE: Did you teach yourself how to read, then?

KINGSOLVER: I'm sure my mom taught me the alphabet. I knew how to read before I got to school, which was kind of a problem. I remember actually being punished for knowing how to read already.

Let me tell you about a memory. We had reading circles. There would be, maybe, eleven kids in little chairs sitting around in a circle, and we took turns reading this reader. It was Dick and Jane. "Dick sees the . . ." Then there's a little picture of a squirrel because, of course, we can't read the word "squirrel" yet. I mean, I was already reading, I don't know what. I was reading the "Raggedy Ann" books. I mean the original ones, not the picture books. I was reading chapter books, so I was supposed to be saying, "Dick sees the squirrel." Then there's a period of time and then, "Jane sees the dog." And I just said [says it fast], "Dick sees the squirrel. Jane . . ." you know, "Jane see the dog. Run after the squirrel, dog." I was reading in a regular intonation, and the teacher stopped me and told the other children, "Barbara doesn't understand that a period means to stop." I was reading too fast, in other words. So she said, "Whenever Barbara comes to a period, yell 'Stop!'" So I sat with ten children at the end of every sentence, of course, getting a big thrill out of screaming, "Stop!" at me, and I was mortified. So I learned to pretend that I was a slow reader. The things I brought to school were not nurtured there. I always felt like an outsider my whole life here, among my peers.

BEATTIE: Did any of your teachers appreciate your abilities?

KINGSOLVER: Some did. I had some glorious teachers. Ironically, some of the teachers that were generally considered less adept, or who were kind of considered to be the worst teachers, were the best in my book.

Our third grade teacher was notorious for just going off on these storytelling tangents and, you know, we kids knew it. We knew that after we came back from lunch, if we could get her started talking about something, she'd go till three-thirty, and we wouldn't have to have math. So we did, and she would just tell these wild tales that got wilder. My brother had this teacher two years ahead of me, and by comparing notes, we could tell that the stories had grown more expansive and colorful through the years.

BEATTIE: Were they supposed to be true stories?

KINGSOLVER: Oh, yes, they were supposed to be true, but they were just wild talk, and I loved it, and I loved the way she could keep us spellbound. I mean, even though we sort of thought we were taking advantage, she knew what she was doing. She was sort of exercising her right to enrapture an audience, and I really liked that. As a third grader, I knew these stories were not true, and I didn't care at all. I thought they were so much the better for being not true and, in fact, I have to admit that I was something of a liar in my childhood. I mean, my mom would tell you that I knew the difference between truth and fantasy, but partly because I never fit in, and my social life or lack of it was always painful for me all the way through, I never got invited to parties or had a sort of gang to run with. I used stories about myself to my advantage to . . . I don't think I was trying to fit in. If I had to be special anyway, I wanted to be special in a colorful way. You could call it a talent for sort of inventing a life of my own.

And the thing is, I did have a really colorful life, because we went to live in Africa. My dad worked as a physician in several places where people desperately needed medical care. That's a value of his that's really important to me that I know that I absorbed early on, that money is not the most important thing. The most important thing is what you can do for people that will make the world better in some way. So we lived for a time in central Africa; it was the Congo then, and then it was Zaire, and now, I guess, it's the Congo again.

BEATTIE: How old were you?

KINGSOLVER: I was seven. I turned eight there. It was, I think, less than a year. I missed part of the second grade. What a relief! Got back in time for third . . . We went quite a lot of places. I mean, odd places; this is not Club Med we're talking about. Just sort of outlandish, unusual places that were underdeveloped or whatever, we went to them.

We spent some time living in a convent in the island of St. Lucia in the Lesser Antilles. Nothing I write is autobiographical, but then again, all of it is. I mean it's not about my life, but it's from my life. Values, interests, settings, and occasionally incidents, all those things. So given that, and, of course, having been to these places and having lived in a place where lions might follow you home from getting the water, doesn't help you fit in, but it also kind of gives you license to see yourself as a little bit different.

I started keeping a journal when I was seven when we went to Africa. That's when I sort of officially began to write. I began keeping a journal with this conscious idea that I was going to write every day, and I began it on the plane going to Africa. My first sentence that I wrote, officially and self-consciously, was, "When I first saw Africa I thought it was a cloud," and it's kind of a nice sentence, you know. I've kept a journal ever since then pretty continuously. I won't say I've never skipped a day, but I have just a whole drawer-full of those little dumb diaries in my office in Tucson, and then I have a whole bookshelf of spiral-bound notebooks, which I started using after I got a little bit too sophisticated to use five-year diaries, three or four years ago.

BEATTIE: What started you, in second grade, with the idea of keeping a diary?

KINGSOLVER: When you ask something like what made me do it, I think it's pretty unusual for people to just, starting at seven, write and write and write every single day, even though what they're writing is real foolish and empty. But I know exactly what it is that makes me do it, and I've tried to articulate it, and it's not an easy thing to exactly pin down. What I feel is that writing is the thing that makes my experience real to me.

BEATTIE: I understand that perfectly.

KINGSOLVER: Yes, writers do, and it's always been that way. I've always had this sort of undercurrent of terror flowing through me when I think about time passing. When I look at a calendar I feel this profound urge not to stop time, but to stick pins in every inch of the way to make sure that it's attached to me, to make sure that I have passed through and will know that I've passed through that passage of time when it's over, and that it won't have just vanished. And writing is the way I do that, both journal keeping and other kinds of writing, and I've always felt that way. It just didn't cross my mind that I could be a writer. I didn't think these wonderful books I read were written by actual, mortal folk. I thought they were written by old dead guys from England, and I certainly wasn't growing up to be that. So it's that. It's that impulse, and I have always had a third-person voice in my head that comments on things. I just can hear words in my head, commenting like a sportscaster,

"Now she's fallen out of the swing. Oh, her knee is cut. Is anybody going to see? Oh, somebody sees. Someone's coming over." Just kind of a constant . . .

BEATTIE: Sort of a nonjudgmental voice?

KINGSOLVER: Exactly. I'm real aware of it, it's just perfectly neutral. It's just a commentator.

The interesting thing is, when I did begin to write seriously, I wrote almost exclusively in the first person, and it was kind of tricky. In fact, that's putting it mildly; the very, most difficult thing for me about writing this newest novel, *Pigs in Heaven,* was I was determined to get out of the first person and into the third. I tried to do it with *Animal Dreams.* I wrote an entire draft of that novel in the third person, but it just didn't work. First person comes really naturally to me, and maybe it's because, oddly enough, I mean, this kind of runs against what you would suppose intuitively, but for me, the third person is maybe closer to the bone. The first person is, for me, like a grand, magnificent lie, because I know it's not true when I'm writing. But I love to spin yarns, and say I did this and I did that, and so, for me, writing in the first person *is* once removed.

The other thing I do really like about the first person is that it's another thing about growing up here in Kentucky, which we all know is not the South, but if you leave, everybody else tells you that you're from the South, so I've just given up and say, "Okay. Okay, I'm from the South." It's what we have in common, I think, with the southerners, something about language. The way people say things can be just as important, or more important, than what they're saying.

BEATTIE: Is it Taylor who says that in *Pigs in Heaven?*

KINGSOLVER: Yes, she does. I think it's really true, and the things people choose to emphasize and the way they bring in extraneous information is so much a part of communication here, and I really like that. I especially love the way people will say a cliché, but get it a little bit wrong, like, "Don't go sticking your neck out on a limb." It's so revealing and so endearing, and it can create sort of an instant sympathy for a character who might otherwise not seem that interesting or appealing.

I think that has everything to do with growing up here where people from New York or outsiders might not see us as anything but ordinary. But we're all extraordinary. My third grade teacher who told the facts from the fabulous yarns when she was supposed to be teaching math was an extraordinary person, and so was the guy that pumped gas. All of us have lives that are worthy of literature, not just here in Nicholas County, but everywhere that the paint on the fences is peeling, and life keeps going behind them.

That's what I think took me a long time to realize, in terms of my own life history. I guess, growing up, I had spent so much time being sort of secretive and embarrassed about who I was because of not fitting in, and then when I went to college, well, I got a lot happier after I went to college because, lo and behold, I found other people who liked to read books. I found bonds of friendship that had to do with common interests and sort of the joy of shared intellectual discovery, and that was nice, because it was rugged going to high school in a place where the only things available for teenagers to do in the way of entertainment took place in the back seat of a car, or the front seat, if you were a boy and liked to drag race. That was it.

BEATTIE: Did you go to college directly after high school?

KINGSOLVER: Yes, I went to DePauw University in Indiana. It was a very happy experience. I didn't have to be embarrassed about having a life and a mind, and I could share friendships and an interest in books and ideas with other people, and that was really wonderful. But people made fun of my accent. It was a shock to me to go to Indiana—you know, that hotbed of intellectualism, Indiana—and be really killed for the way I talked. People I didn't know would stop me on the sidewalk of the campus and try to get me to say "hair" and "oil." It was kind of awful, and I never meant to change the way I spoke, but I just did, because of my lifelong habit of sort of being a chameleon, not morally, but socially—trying to blend into the wallpaper. I just changed. I dropped my accent. I never had bad grammar. For the most part, I just leveled out into speaking sort of a nonaccented English, in exactly the same way I sort of smoothly and gradually dropped my sense of having come from here.

I had written, by the way, in addition to keeping a diary, little stories and things all through high school, and I always outdid myself and, I always entered all these essay contests sponsored by the Fish and Game . . . "What Soil Conservation Means to Me," I would just become histrionic about soil conservation, go on for forty pages. I just really loved to write. So I had written fiction, if you could call it that. I wrote lots of stories about maimed little boys. They were protagonists. My protagonists were always boys, and they were blind or they had a club foot or something. I think that says something about my own self-esteem.

BEATTIE: Did you want to be a boy?

KINGSOLVER: Well, of course, I absolutely did, because boys clearly had a better shake. They got to do more stuff, and people listened to them a lot more. I very definitely did want to be a boy.

I was writing fiction in college, too. I wrote poetry and fiction. I didn't take a fiction class. Actually, I got to college on a music scholarship. I played piano and I had designs on being a classical pianist, and then about the middle of my second year in conservatory, which I liked pretty much, it dawned on me that there were about, maybe, eleven job openings a year in the United States of America for classical pianists, and all the others get to spend their lives playing "The Shadow of Your Smile" in a hotel lobby, and that wasn't for me. So I transferred out of the conservatory and majored in biology. I took some literature courses. I took one writing course. I took all kinds of courses. I was just a liberal arts kind of person. I just wanted to know everything. I'm still that way. I love to read the encyclopedia. So I took courses in East Asian history and anthropology and psychology and computer sciences and math and physics and chemistry and everything.

BEATTIE: Many times people who love literature and writing shy away from math and science.

KINGSOLVER: Which is a pity; I certainly couldn't do that. Having been raised to feel such a strong connection to the natural world, I think that biochemistry is absolutely as poetic as Shakespeare. You just have to know how to read it.

I didn't think I would ever be a writer, but I was still writing, because it was just I had to. I wrote lots of short stories and poems and things, and during that phase of my life my writing, which was still tripe, took on kind of this cosmopolitan sheen. And, at the same time I lost my accent, I lost my sort of thematic accent. I took Kentucky out of the girl, or tried to, and my writing became not only sentimental tripe, but deadly sentimental tripe, because it had no heart. It was heartless save for one story. I took one creative writing class in college, and I wrote this story that I don't know where it came from. Oh, yes, I do. It just poured straight out of my heart. It was like channeling, almost. I didn't try to impress anybody. I just poured the stuff straight out, and it was called "The Pilgrimage." I kept on revising that story for nineteen years, I think. How old would I have been? Nineteen when I wrote it, and about fifteen years later, it became the title story in this collection, *Homeland.* The title of it, ultimately, was "Homeland," and that is probably the most spiritually auto-biographical thing I've ever written.

But I think what that story's about is about this imperative that I feel to record, not just the past, but specifically, the voices of those who've had their voices taken away from them. The Cherokee grandmother in that story whose family made this pilgrimage back to her place of origin and found no trace at all. Found it so changed and so turned into a tourist trap that she sat in the truck and looked around and said, "I've never been here before." And the protagonist of that story, the first-person narrator, feels this burden as if she's carrying her grandmother on her back, but it's a burden of love. She feels like nobody else is going to remember, and she has to remember all those stories her grandmother told her. I don't know why, but that's how I feel, and that's why I dedicated *Animal Dreams* to Ben Linder, and that's why I write about Guatemalan refugees and Cherokee kids and single mothers living in seedy neighbors of Tucson, Arizona, and all of these people who have been left out of literature in the main, for hundreds of years.

My junior year of college I went to Greece, and then I went to France. I didn't want to come back. I liked it a lot. I was seeking my fortune. I was just living like a Bohemian, working on any job I could get to just pay the rent. I came back to finish up some things to get my degree, then I went back to Europe, and I was living in Paris. I liked it real well, but they kicked me out, unfortunately. It was just getting hard to keep my work visa, which is the French equivalent of a green card. So I had to come back, and I moved to Tucson for no good reason. I knew someone in Tucson, and I kind of had a theoretical interest in the Southwest. So it was a very interesting and sort of a high-profile period in my life, in terms of the experience gained in worldly wisdom.

BEATTIE: What year was that when you moved to Tucson?

KINGSOLVER: '77. I even wrote a novel there. Oh, boy, if I ever die, I hope some-one will burn that fast. I mean to say, if I die before I get myself to burn it. I was just writing very hideously uninteresting, happy stuff. But I think I was taking my writing more and more seriously and trying to reach some vein that I suppose I felt within me.

It must have been in 1981 I read *Shiloh and Other Stories,* Bobbie Ann Mason's first collection, and that was a life-changing moment for me, because I suddenly understood that what moved me about those stories was not so much the style or the execution: it was the respect that she has for her people—her characters who are her people—and the simple fact that she deemed them worthy of serious literature. My jaw sort of dropped open, and I just walked around for weeks thinking, "I almost threw that away." I have this wonderful thing, this place I come from, this life of mine, that I've been trying to ignore. Not just ignore, that I've been trying to pretend never existed.

I began writing stories about the people behind the picket fence with the paint peel-ing off it. The people who have lunch down at the Talk of the Town Restaurant [in Carlisle] you passed driving in. The people who drive too fast on Scrubgrass Road. The people who have never thought themselves worth very much, but whose lives are full of not just quiet desperation, but a lot of joyful moments. What moves me most about Bobbie Ann Mason's work is that when her characters speak, I hear them exactly. I'm hearing exact inflections, and it makes me homesick. I would say, for me, that's not what I'm trying to do as a writer. What I'm trying to do is the thing I said before about that burden of truth, of people who have had their voices stolen from them. The people I write about and the way they talk and the way they live and the way they think has to grow out of who I am. Otherwise, it's a hundred times more boring than real life.

BEATTIE: When did you start calling yourself a writer?

KINGSOLVER: In 1982, I believe, I wrote in my journal, just in the middle of a page with nothing else on it, "I am a writer." I didn't believe it, but it's the first effort I made to force myself to believe it. In the early eighties I began reading poetry aloud in public places. I mean, not at a street corner, but I was very cryptic about my writing. I was, to tell you the truth, embarrassed about it. All the things I wrote in college I never showed anyone, except for a few things to my closest friends, but I didn't think about going public. I was embarrassed.

The arts were never enormously valued in the social atmosphere that I grew up with. Being a poet would be sort of ridiculous. It's like saying you wanted to be Madonna when you grew up. So, I think it's a powerful ordering of things that was laid down in my brain stem that you can't change. I'm sure that's why I majored in biology, too. It seemed practical and sensible and reasonable, and I could support myself with that kind of knowledge.

BEATTIE: Intangibly, you know exactly what has been done and what there is to do.

KINGSOLVER: That's astute. It's a line between the tangible and the intangible, and the intangible stuff I'd always kept to myself. But I'd written just lots and lots of poetry, and I entered a poetry contest in, I think, 1981 and, to my absolute astonishment, won, and what that meant is that I had to come down to the university and read this poem and a few others.

That was the University of Arizona. I was not a student at that time, and the reading was held on the university campus. And, whew, boy, that was scary. Not the public speaking aspect of it, but just the public admission that I'd written these personal things and now was going to inflict them upon others. So I did that, and it sort of opened the flood gate. I was invited to other cities.

Tucson is kind of like a big, dry Soho. There are lots and lots and lots of artists there. There are a lot of established artists there, there are a lot of aspiring artists, and everything in between. So there are a lot of these regular reading series where people who aren't famous at all, but who are doing something decent, will be invited every month to read in this coffee house or that. I started giving readings, and I started sending things out to magazines, and to my surprise, they were accepted.

And I wrote a short story, "Where's Johnny?," in 1983, I think. That's the first fiction I ever wrote that was decent, and I sent that to someplace not too ostentatious, like the *Virginia Quarterly Review*, and they snapped it right up and sent me three hundred dollars.

I'm not cautious in any emotional sense. I'm a ridiculous risk taker emotionally; I'll give away everything I own and move to France because it's the right thing to do. But in the realm of writing, I'll wait until I'm pretty sure I'm on the right track.

So I don't want to say that the first poem I ever wrote I sent out, and it was accepted instantly. I wrote a lot of garbage, don't let's forget that. But by the early eighties I was starting to find that vein, pay attention to where I'd come from and listen to the voices that were really in my ear, and write things that had a little bit of emotional resonance, things I had to do to be a success publishing.

I went to graduate school in the early eighties; I got a master's in ecology and evolutionary biology.

BEATTIE: This was at the University of Arizona?

KINGSOLVER: Right. And that was in 1980 and '81, I think. I was in the Ph.D. program, but I just got disillusioned with all this effort I was devoting to a dissertation on the social life of termites. I didn't want that kind of ultracompetitive kind of very, very narrow focus, devoting myself to writing this dissertation that possibly eleven people in the universe are going to read. I didn't like doing something that was so hard, dedicating myself to something that it took about two hours to explain to your average, smart person on the street why anyone would consider this important. It shouldn't be that hard to justify yourself.

I do really believe in basic research, basic scientific research, and I think it should be supported, but it just wasn't for me. So I got my master's and I left the program, and I took this job as a scientific writer for the University of Arizona. That was great. That was just a real lucky thing that that job opened up and then I got it, because my problem all along is that I never quite understood how a person could make a living as a writer. There I was, sitting at a typewriter day after day after day, sometimes boring days, sometimes kind of fun days, but on Friday I got a check for it. Mostly what I did was, I took the research reports of scientists, and I translated them into English.

Then I began free-lancing, because I found that there is a wide-open market for people who have the background to understand scientific language, and who can translate it and who can speak English, too. As you said a little while ago, usually if people have a bent toward the humanities, they shun the sciences and vice versa. I happen to think that's a huge problem. I think that's really a big part of why we're in the mess we are in environmentally, because most people don't understand a thing about science, and they hated their high school chemistry course, and they've steered clear ever since and, therefore, they have this attitude that problems like that are not their problems. The scientists will fix it. "Oh, there's a hole in the ozone? Well, they'll think of something." The fact is, they *won't* think of something. I mean, not all problems are fixable with a technical fix. It takes a little bit of understanding of the sciences to understand which things are fixable through science and which are simply not. A lot of this stuff can only be fixed through massive individual action. You know, making changes in lifestyle, changing to a lower-consumption lifestyle, basically. It's something I care about, and I actually felt kind of a moral imperative to do this when I was doing it, and I felt pretty good. But the best thing is that I was writing every day, and I was getting paid for it, and I began taking on other kinds of writing assignments, too, and before I knew it, I had become a free-lance journalist mainly doing feature articles, interviews. I still did the scientific things. They always paid the best money.

In 1986, I became pregnant with Camille. She wasn't Camille at that time; she was just added weight. I developed severe insomnia right from the beginning. From the first week something chemical just went out of whack in my brain, and so I was up nights. I went to my doctor, because I was desperate after weeks of virtually no sleep. My doctor said, "Well, you shouldn't reward yourself for being up at night, so you should do something you hate. You should scrub the grout on your bathroom tile." And I said, "Heck, I'm up anyway, I think I'll write a novel." So I did. I wrote *The Bean Trees,* and it took nine months, fortunately.

BEATTIE: So that's how it was conceived!

KINGSOLVER: Yes, and interestingly, as I got farther and farther from my keyboard throughout this pregnancy, that part of *The Bean Trees* that's about the terror of becoming a parent, the emotional inadequacy that we feel facing the possibility of raising a child, all of those things became a bigger and bigger part of the book. I hadn't intended it to be that kind of book, but it was very much skewed by my pregnancy into a direction that I think made it more humane and probably more interesting to most people.

But it's also not accurate to say I wrote that book in nine months. After that was published, when people asked me how long it took me to write *The Bean Trees,* the most accurate answer I could say is nine months and thirty-two years, because that's a first novel. I think there's a charming thing that first novels almost always have in common. They're rarely some sort of elegant device. They're usually these sort of rambling, real-life, charmingly vocal sorts of collections, because they're a thing that somebody's been wanting to write all their lives. I think of it as your whole life long you've been carrying this big old purse, and every time you come upon something, a pretty rock or something, you put it in there. Then comes the day where it's too heavy, you can't carry it around anymore, and you sit down at a table and you just dump everything out. And kaboom!, there it all is, and that's your first novel. And obviously, you pick through, and the things that looked like pretty rocks at the time actually were pieces of plaster that fell out of the wall, so you throw those out. You pick and choose, you edit a little bit. Anyway, that was when I dumped out the big, old purse, in 1986.

BEATTIE: When had you gotten married?

KINGSOLVER: Technically, 1985, but Joe [Hoffmann] and I'd been together quite a few years before that.

So I just wrote that book because I wanted to, and to entertain myself, as long as I was going to be up all night. I had no ambitions for that novel. I didn't even call it a novel. Just as it was very hard for me to say, "I am a writer," it was very hard, even harder, for me to say, "I am writing a novel." I didn't tell anybody. I didn't show it to anybody. It just felt good. It was sort of like talking to myself on the phone.

BEATTIE: What about your husband or friends?

KINGSOLVER: Oh, Joe read it and a few close friends. Actually, the first chapter was meant as a short story, "The One To Get Away." A good friend of mine, Jan Bowers [Janice Emily Bowers], who's an author, read it and she loved it, but she said, "This is not a short story; it's the first chapter of a novel." I said, "No, go on." Then I looked at it and I thought, "Wow! If I could get that voice into this place in Tucson, then I could tell the story," because what had kept that novel inert for so long is I had all these characters, but I didn't have a point of view on them. What I needed was an outsider's take on this place that most people would consider a bad piece of real estate, but really it's this rich, lively, symbiotic, interconnected community of women. But only someone like me, who gets in the car in Kentucky and drives across the country and slams into it by accident, will really see, will recognize . . . I was really more of a nonfiction writer at that point. And I'd also begun what I thought might some day be a book that became *Holding the Line,* this nonfiction book about these women in this little mining town in Arizona, who took over their town during the mine strike in 1983.

BEATTIE: Did that book start as a magazine article?

KINGSOLVER: It did. Actually, I was covering the strike for a couple of different places, newspapers and magazines, so I was going down to these towns and just being a journalist, and what I began to see was quite amazing. It was just astonishing. The social order of these towns was completely turned upside down. These women who had never had a self-important bone in their bodies, they would introduce themselves to me as, "Hi, I'm Reggie. I'm a housewife." "No, I'm *just* a housewife," she would say. All of them mentioned, "Oh, I don't leave the house without my husband's permission." This is a Mexican-American Catholic little mining town. It's just the way it's always been. So these women just had no personal power whatsoever.

It was a very long strike. It went on for two years, and the first week of the strike their husbands were barred by an injunction from holding the picket line. In fact, a lot of them just had to leave town so they wouldn't get arrested, and also to look for other work, too, because there was no other work but the mine in a company town. So these women had the choice of seeing their communities disintegrate and losing the homes that had been their homes for generations. It was all they knew. It was their world. They could see that die, literally just vanish, or they could hold the line.

So they got up their nerve and they went up and stood on the picket line. Then they stood on the picket line some more. The governor sent in seven units of the National Guard and Huey helicopters. I mean, these are towns where there are four policemen and everyone calls them by name. People never locked their doors. So here comes the National Guard. Here come SWAT teams sitting on the hills following these women back and forth with their automatic rifles, and these women showed a degree of valor that I had not witnessed in my life. And I just kept going back and talking to these women to sort of chart the internal landscape. What in the world is going on in their hearts and minds as this is happening for two years? They changed so much and, believe me, by the end of that strike they were not asking their husbands' permission to leave the house. They were telling their husbands, "You may iron your own shirts, thank you very much. I have things to do." It was just a momentous thing, and I have hundreds of hours of tapes of interviews with these women, because I was so fascinated.

Someone who worked for a publishing house kind of queried me about writing a book out of that. I guess that person had seen some articles I had written or something. There was one article in the *Progressive,* that was the best one probably, and I thought, "Oh, yes. I should write a book." Actually I became known, mainly in the town of Clifton, that's where I went and spent the most time, whenever I'd drive into town, because, of course, everybody knows everybody. They'd all say, "Oh, it's that girl that's writing the book." So I had to at least pretend I was writing a book, and it occurred to me then that I would like to make a book out of that, but that I didn't know anything about book contracts or advances or anything at all. So I decided I needed to get an agent. I went to the library and I pulled down a big, fat book. It was *Literary Market Place,* I believe, that had a listing in the back of all the accredited literary agents there are, and I came to this listing, Frances Goldin. She was independent. What she said about herself was, "I do not represent any material that is sexist, racist, ageist, homophobic, or gratuitously violent. I realize this cuts me out of ninety percent of what's written, but at least I can be proud of all my authors." I said, "This woman is for me."

So I wrote to her and told her about this project that I was attempting to undertake, this was in about '84 or '85. It was years before I'd written *The Bean Trees*. I hadn't written much of anything but some short stories and articles. So I sent her this book proposal, and she wrote back and said, "This is just the kind of thing I love to represent. It'll probably never make a dime, but it sounds like a really worthy idea and I want to represent it."

So we had a brief correspondence, and I told her when I had the time to get more of it together, I would send her the manuscript. But I was really hustling. I was trying to make a living as a free-lancer, and I didn't really have blocks of free time to spend transcribing all these tapes and putting together a book, so it kind of went on hold. But three or four years later, after I'd written this novel in the night in my insomnia I got early in my pregnancy, I thought, "Well, what will I do with this?" So I wrote her and I said, "Well, I've written something. I am not sure what it is, but I think it's a novel. You might want to take a look at it. Let me know. Sorry for bothering you. Sincerely, Barbara." She wrote back and said, "Sure, send it." So I sent it, and she called me up at six o'clock, I think, the next morning after she'd gotten it, and said, "Yes, Barbara, it is a novel." "Oh," I said, "good." She said, "I'll get back to you. We're going to sell it."

She called me back a few days later to say Houghton Mifflin had made an offer, and I sort of fell out of my chair. The next thing she said was, "And we're going to turn it down." Then I stopped breathing. I said, "What? What do you mean, turn it down? I'll pay *them*!" She said, "No, it's not enough." It was not a huge amount of money, it's true, but it was certainly a much huger amount of money than I'd ever expected to make.

She gave me a little lecture, a very kind, succinct, intelligent lecture, on self-respect and the publishing world. She said, "If they pay you a moderately large advance, then they will put a moderately large amount of effort into promoting the book and insuring they get that advance back. You, the writer, are not the issue. The issue is their investment." "Oh, okay," I said, and she got exactly what she said she would for it, which was more than I'd ever made in a year. It was enough to live comfortably for a year, so I signed the contract with her, I think, twenty-four hours after I'd had Camille and brought her home from the hospital. So I became a mom and a novelist on the same day, and life has never been the same since then.

The really good thing about it is that I got this enormous external validation for writing fiction which, as you can probably guess, had been kind of a sticking point for me, to value myself as a fiction writer. Low self-esteem has a lot to do with it. Something fanciful is also difficult for me, though here I was sitting pretty with a publisher, Harper & Row, a big-time New York publisher saying, "Yes, you're a novelist. Here's the check to prove it." That's the only thing that allowed me to go on writing fiction and being a new mother. I think it's a problem for women anyway, for us to value the things we do, plus anything you do in your home is not valued as real work.

BEATTIE: Anything in the arts.

KINGSOLVER: Anything in the arts is not valued. Everybody thinks, to some extent, that they can do what you do. So at parties, people always, always, always say to me, "Oh, I always wanted to write a novel if I just had the time." I'm always terminally polite, but what I'm always profoundly inclined to say is, "You know, I've always wanted to do a little brain surgery if I just had the time."

Actually, Camille's father and I have always cooperated really well. He's a really good parent, and in the beginning, I would start at four or five in the morning and write until noon, and he would take care of Camille in the morning and then he'd go into work and work late. He'd work noon until nightfall or whatever, and we'd switch. Yes, we had the split shift. I nursed her until she was about six months, got teeth and a mind of her own, and then we brought someone in, this wonderful, wonderful, wonderful woman, a ninety-year-old woman named Ethel. I thought she was in her sixties until she started telling me stories about seeing the first car in Ohio, and then I started getting curious.

So, it's always worked out, but its working out has always been dependent, extremely dependent, on my willingness to value my time. So, anyway, that check from *The Bean Trees,* I bankrolled that, and I used the time to finish the copper-strike book, *Holding the Line.* So that was the second book I wrote. Then, since I was petrified of writing a second novel, because I just thought that everyone would say, "Well, her first showed promise, but now she has let us down," I wrote *Holding the Line.* Then I wrote a collection of short stories, *Homeland and Other Stories.* Then I thought, "Well, maybe by now they've forgotten that I wrote a novel, so maybe I can hazard another one." But it was pretty scary.

BEATTIE: Would you call yourself a humanist?

KINGSOLVER: Oh, sure. I would also call myself a social advocate, and an environmentalist, and a feminist, a lot of "ists." I'd be proud to claim them as titles. And I think that a great way to express a lot of those concerns or passions, and a great way to get information to people about these things, information about the environment, information about unfair labor conditions—whatever it is that I want to let people know so that they will think about it and maybe change their behavior somewhat, in accordance with making a better world—I think the best way to give that to people is fiction. Because in nonfiction, the fact that this book, *Holding the Line,* has been read by so few people compared to my other books, of which I was just told by my publisher there are a half a million in print, ninety percent of those are fiction.

The important part is, I like to make sure that all the information content of my novels is true. I really hate it when people just make up facts, either in life or in books. I would say that my motive is to change the world. I mean, let's face it, I would say that the meaning of life is contained in that old Girl Scout axiom of leaving the campsite better than you found it. That's what I aim to do, and writing is one of the ways I hope to do that. Raising my daughter in a humane and thoughtful way is another one of the ways I aim to do that, and there are other ways, too. So that's sort of the big picture.

But the smaller picture that takes place at my desk every day, what I pay attention to all the time, or what I try to pay attention to all the time, is the craft. That's what I'm thinking of. I don't write a story and think, "Oh, how can I inject some politics into that?" Life has some value and those decisions resonate somehow with my own life, and I hope will resonate with other people's lives. The reason that there are within these stories what could be defined as political issues, power struggles, struggles against discrimination, struggles against poverty and all kinds of inequities, the reason for that is simply that that's the world I live in. That's what I see. I don't know of a relationship that's positively equal, that doesn't contain within it some kind of a power imbalance. So how could I write about relationships and ignore those influences? It would be not only impossible, but glib.

BEATTIE: Was *Animal Dreams* then, your next published book after *Bean Trees,*

Holding The Line, and *Homeland*?

KINGSOLVER: *Animal Dreams* was the fourth.

BEATTIE: Will you talk about that book?

KINGSOLVER: I guess I was thinking about it for about a year while I was writing other things, and then it took about a year after I found the voice. I think I told you before that I tried really hard to write it in the third person, but couldn't. It's a triangle. It's a story of a father and two daughters, one of with whom I share a good deal of sympathy. Of all the characters I've written, I think she's the most like me. She's had a slightly different life, but only really because of accident. I could easily have been her. She went to Nicaragua.

Codi is the sister who stayed home, the sort of walking wounded who has never quite found the engagement with life that her sister has. Her sister accuses her of circling above the clouds waiting to land. And their father, when the book opens, is dying of Alzheimer's. I start every book, every novel, with a question that I can't answer. And my hope, and what keeps it interesting for me, is that I'll write my way to an answer. It has to be an important question. It can't be, "What did you have for breakfast?" It needs to be a question worthy of service of a year or two of my life.

The question that led me to write *Animal Dreams* was this, "Why is it that some people are activists who embrace the world and its problems and feel not only that they can, but that they must, do something about the world and its problems, while other people turn their back on that same world and pretend that it has no bearing on their lives? Why is it, moreover, that these two kinds of people can occur in the same family?" I have a friend, for example, who's an amazing peace activist, and her brother builds bombs at Los Alamos. It happens and it happens a lot.

So I invented a pair of sisters, Codi and Hallie, who personified these two different approaches to life, and I gave them a family history, I gave them a present, and then I worked back towards the past to find what it could be in their lives, in their shared family history, that could have sent one of them in one direction and one in the other. And, of course, I answered the question maybe not for perpetuity throughout the universe, or however that legal term goes, but I answered it specifically for this family, for these two sisters, why one went one way and one the other. I think that's the most we can hope for in fiction, a specific answer to a general question that will somehow shed light on specifics of every different reader's life. You can't answer questions in a general way, because if you do, what you've written is not fiction, it's a sermon, or it's something that falls flat. What we want is something personal and small enough to sort of fit inside a human right. So I had these very different sisters and their crazy father who was crazy before he had Alzheimer's.

BEATTIE: Unable to be too intimate.

KINGSOLVER: Right. Unable to show affection, to show the love that he actually did feel for his daughters. I think the way Codi put it in the novel, when he began getting sick, is that his mind had begun to roam in alarming new pastures, or something like that. So how to tell the story? I wondered. The natural thing for me to do would be to tell it in first person, from Hallie's point of view, because I identify with her so much. The easiest thing to know is that you can't do what's easy as a writer. Maybe in life. I used to have this poster that said, "Brooks become crooked when taking the course of least resistance." A good thing for a teenager to bear in mind, I thought. Not that I had any choice. There's another line, I was rereading *Animal Dreams,* I rarely read, even look in my books, once they're in print, because I just want to change everything and have a factory recall. But when I'm deciding what to read in a reading, I have to look through things. Codi is talking about her difficult adolescence and about her friend, Emelina, who was very popular in high school, and she says, "Virtue in a cheerleader is admirable, whereas in a wallflower it's gratuitous." And I thought, "Oh, yes. That's my line." I was a virtuous wallflower.

But anyway, when you're writing, you have to be the virtuous cheerleader. You have to choose the course of the most resistance. Do the difficult thing, otherwise it will all go to pot, and you won't have created anything very interesting.

I knew I couldn't tell the story from Hallie's point of view, so I had to tell it from the point of view of the other two characters, Doc Homer, the father, and Codi, and it was really tough for me to get into Codi's head, because she's cynical and I'm not. I'm one of the most ridiculously optimistic people on the face of the earth. The other one is my dad. I got it straight from him. I really avoid cynicism. I mean, you've got to be realistic and notice how bad things are, but cynicism, I think, is a matter of giving up and accepting what's on your plate and not hollering about it ever again. And that's so scary for me.

That's where Codi is when the book opens. I didn't like her much, and that was plainly evident in the first draft. It went through a lot of drafts, and I had to work pretty hard on making Codi a likeable, cynical walking-wounded type of person. And I always learn how to write by reading. I studied this in school. I think the best way to learn how to write good books is to read good books, so my teachers are always there on the shelf. When I get stuck, I pull down good books and I read them, and I'm always turning to great authors to figure out what to do next.

In the middle of writing *Animal Dreams* I read Margaret Atwood's novel *The Cat's Eye*. It's a fabulous novel, I think. An interesting idea phenomenally well-executed, and it's the story of a not very likeable, cynical, walking-wounded woman. So instantly I started dissecting it and trying to figure out how she made me care so much about that narrator. The trick is she very early on sent you back into this poor woman's adolescence, even her fifth-grade year where her little friends just persecuted her mercilessly, and she was subjected to the ordinary cruelty of children. That had never-ending consequences on her life, and I related to it deeply. I think that during my own childhood I thought everyone else is happy and I'm suffering. Now I know that almost everybody suffers at the hands of their peers in their childhood. Not all the time, but sometimes, and it's important, and it matters, and you remember.

So, I thought, if I can show you the particular ways that Codi suffered, and if I can get across to you that pain, you'll forgive her for whining a little bit now, or for being a little bit warped or being not quite together or being sad. You'll forgive her because you'll say, "Yes, I can feel that." That's what you have to do, I think, is find ways to make openings in your book that your readers . . . sort of slots that they can put their own hearts into.

BEATTIE: You've mentioned one creative writing course in college. Other than that, you had no formal writing instruction of any kind?

KINGSOLVER: No. I think there's a limit to how much you can learn about writing in a classroom. I think the main thing you have to do to become a writer is just write and write and write and write, and write a whole lot of junk. And learn that it's junk and be disheartened, but keep trying, and also read—I mean, read good stuff and write bad stuff until eventually what you're writing begins to approximate what you're reading, because in time it will, if you keep trying and if you can keep turned on and engaged. But I think there are, oh, seven or eight or twelve concrete things about writing that you can learn.

BEATTIE: What kinds of things do you think people can learn?

KINGSOLVER: I think it's an audacious thing to write a book. You're assuming that you have something to say that's so fascinating and important that somebody else is going to put their life on hold for you. Who am I to say that I can tell you something that you don't already know? It's very presumptuous. So you just better make sure that, number one, it's worth their time, and number two, that it's got enough in it on every single page to keep them turning the pages. How you do it is another story, but that you *must* do it is the main story.

And what else? Oh, this is one of the things Francine Prose told me that I really like a lot. The first sentence of a story or the first paragraph of a novel should make a promise that the rest of the book will keep. And it's really true if you think about your favorite books. Think of first lines like, "Call me Ishmael." That's a promise. It's a story of self-discovery and of what he should name himself, of who he is.

BEATTIE: Just more subtle than nonfiction. Your paper has to prove your thesis.

KINGSOLVER: Exactly, they're the same thing. And oh, the wonderful opening of *Anna Karenina,* which I always get a little bit wrong, must be because I'm from Carlisle, Kentucky. Oh, how does it go? "Every happy family is alike, every unhappy family is different it its own special way," or something like that. "It was the best of times, it was the worst of times." Or one of my favorites, this is the opening of *Household Saints* by Francine Prose. The first sentence is, "It happened by the grace of God that Joseph Santangelo won his wife in a card game." It's so promising. "It happened by the grace of God." I mean, you know already that it's going to be a legendary story.

BEATTIE: Have you taught creative writing?

KINGSOLVER: I do teach workshops two or three times a year in different parts of the country. I just teach week-long types of workshops. I like to keep teaching because it helps me to articulate my process to myself. When I have to teach it, it forces me to think it through and realize that there is a method. I do follow a series of steps. I do know what I'm doing. It's not just a magical mystery that falls onto my desk at the end of the day.

BEATTIE: How do you think it should be taught, creative writing?

KINGSOLVER: Oh, I don't know. Minimally, I think. I really believe the best criticism comes from nonwriters. It's helpful to have someone who can be sort of specific, who can say more than, "Well, gee, I didn't like it much." Every reader brings a different experience to the work, and takes away a different experience from the work, from having read the book, and that's fine. What I want is for the story to be good enough that you'll read it to the end.

Here's another piece of advice Francine Prose taught me. Keep a large trash can beside your desk. I count that among the best advice I've received. You've got to throw away a lot of stuff before you get to something good, and you're not going to get to the good stuff till you do throw away the bad stuff. So I don't know how creative writing should be taught, except maybe more kindly. I think the things that are helpful to writers are having access to good literature, and to a diversity of it. I think it's good that people are introduced to maybe Hispanic women writers like Anna Cisneros, or African-American writers, people that might be a little bit out of the mainstream. It's good that there are courses that introduce people to new sorts of writing and new sorts of experience. That's a good thing that happens in schools these days. I think the most important thing for a writer of fiction to have is a broad knowledge of other subjects besides writing, because all your characters—you're creating lots of people in your fiction—have to have jobs. They can't all be writers; how boring that would be! Nothing would ever happen. So they all have to have worlds of knowledge and you, the writer, you're God. You have to know everything they know and then some. You have to be the smartest person on your block. And the only way you're going to get all that—and we're not talking about horse sense here, we're talking about practical information like what does a truck driver do, what is involved in a job at a Toyota plant, what goes on in a bakery, what goes on in a tire shop.

BEATTIE: So your free-lance writing certainly would have helped in terms of giving you a variety of experiences?

KINGSOLVER: It did. I guess I've always been an information junky. In childhood I would just sit all day Saturday and read the encyclopedia. I would get from G to K maybe, on a good day, on a really rainy, long day. Even now, when I go to look up the Canary Islands, I keep going through *canary* the bird and then through *can* and all the way through . . . when I get to *dogfish,* I wake up and say, "Wow!"

BEATTIE: You're not going to ever run out of subject matter, I can tell.

KINGSOLVER: I don't know. I just really like knowing stuff, and I keep notebooks. I still keep journals. They're not so much about what happens to me, it's just they're repositories of fascinating things I come across every day.

BEATTIE: Do you ever feel compelled to categorize yourself, to choose a genre?

KINGSOLVER: I think, if I have to identify myself by genre, I would have to say I'm a storyteller. Everything I write is a story. My novels are long stories or bunches of stories all kind of bound together at the center with twine. My short stories are stories. My poems are little true stories, sort of emotionally intense stories. My nonfiction is always stories. Even when I do some travel writing for the *New York Times,* what I find is I can't write a regular, straight travel article: "Oh, there is this and there is that and this is beautiful and that is beautiful." I have to write a story. "When I first saw Africa I thought it was a cloud." Yes, I have this narrative drive I can't help. It's how I talk, too, as you might have noticed. That's how people around here talk. Everything's a big event. Nothing just happens. It has to have a beginning and an end and a moral and a theme.

BEATTIE: That's just what I was going to say about your fiction. I find that a distinguishing feature in your fiction is your ability to tell a contemporary, engaging story without sacrificing the rich complexity of the meaning, as so many slice-of-life fiction writers do.

KINGSOLVER: Well, thank you. I have to agree that there's been an abandonment of story. There's no judgment. There's an absence of judgment. It scares me. Sometimes I make these charts for a character, like what happened in her childhood, what sort of deficiency did that lead to, and what action has that led her to take in her adulthood. I do these sort of flow charts to try to make people consistent. It's scary to me to read fiction that is completely nonjudgmental. It's just this cold eye looking at everything as if all things are equal, and not passing any judgment on anything that happens.

BEATTIE: It seems, almost, that not passing judgment *is* a judgment. It's almost a sardonic, "Aren't we all amusing?"

KINGSOLVER: You're exactly right. There's this trend that's occurring in both literature and movies. I call it the "David Lynch Phenomenon," where it's the decline or the absence, really, of plot. It's just scene after scene after scene. A bunch of things happen and they aren't causally linked. Now, why do people watch this? Why do they like it? Why are they not disturbed by it? Why are they finding it satisfying? I think those are interesting questions to ask, because it's definitely a trend, and I've talked to filmmakers about it, and I've talked to writers about it, and it's happening in literature, too, a lot. I think the answer has something to do with an abdication of responsibility, of personal responsibility.

BEATTIE: I wanted to ask you what you think the nature of creativity may be?

KINGSOLVER: Oh, boy, that's good. Something about the right combination of construction and relaxation. Those aren't quite the right words, but two opposite things. What's the opposite of relaxation?

BEATTIE: Tension?

KINGSOLVER: Yes, I think that's it. I think that the secret or the gem of creativity lies in finding the right combination of tension and relaxation. You have to pull the line tight. You have to have something to hang it on. Then you have to be able to relax and let it happen. I think anybody could be creative, given lack of interference. I think that more than anything. I think people are born creative. All you have to do is look at a baby and then at a one-year old and a two-year old to see that. I think people become less creative as they go through school and age and learn to subject themselves and submit to judgment.

I think self-esteem has a lot to do with creativity, but not everything, because, as we've already established, most writers are riddled with self-doubt. So I don't think it's all of that, but I think at some level, giving yourself permission to connect . . . it has a lot to do with association. Allowing your mind to connect things that you've never seen connected in your life. You know, just allowing your mind to throw things together, and relaxing and living with the possibilities. But it can't be pure free association. There has to be the tension, there has to be the sort of taut line that makes things tow the line enough to be meaningful.

BEATTIE: Would you equate that with discipline?

KINGSOLVER: Yes, discipline and relaxation. Thank you. I think that's a better word than tension. Discipline and relaxation are the two things that have to be balanced, combined in the right measure, and at different times. The way I write a novel is, there's a back of the mind stage where things just simmer where I have an idea, and I just let it cook in it's own juices and don't try to force anything. Then, after a long time, maybe a year or two, it'll just slide to the front and it's ready to be manipulated and disciplined and rendered, the way metal is rendered into something useful.

BEATTIE: I think you used the word "drive" earlier. Do you feel that you have some kind of internal drive to write?

KINGSOLVER: Oh, absolutely.

BEATTIE: There are a lot of creative people who aren't driven to do any particular thing.

KINGSOLVER: Yes, and maybe that's where the sense of self-worth comes into it, too. I think you have to believe, at some level, that you have something that's worth saying or worth creating. I start to feel like I'm going to seed if I don't write. There are a lot of days when I don't write anything. I mean, there's this other part of my job as a writer that now— I never dreamed that this would become part of my job—but I have to spend a couple days a week just taking care of business. You know, sending faxes, reading faxes, talking to my

Hollywood agent, explaining why I don't want to do something or do want to do something and deciding whether I do. That's not even counting the days when I'm in Kentucky to give a reading or to teach a workshop, answer mail. I have an assistant to help me answer fan mail, but there's just this business end of writing that I never expected. And I still, to tell you the truth, resent it. It feels like an intrusion, because what I really want to do is write all the time. I organize my time. Right after I finish a novel, there will be a period of time given over to promotion, whether I like it or not. So I kind of just give in, and during that time I'll go and do things in a four-month period, anything that falls within that time that sounds interesting, I'll do, pretty much. After that, I'll set aside a long period where I'll say no to everything, no matter what.

BEATTIE: What about your writing habits?

KINGSOLVER: I use an old computer. I'm not on the cutting edge of computerdom, but certainly, I have a serviceable old IBM clone, which is grinding these days in an ominous way. I pretty much am a working stiff. I work from the time my daughter goes to school to the time that she comes home, eight to five. I don't write on the weekends or evenings, almost without exception.

BEATTIE: Do you give yourself a number of pages or words to write each day?

KINGSOLVER: Usually it's whatever happens each day. I try to push myself, but making myself have a page limit is not fair, because there are days when I can write ten worthless pages and days where I can write one good, great paragraph, and I would rather have the second kind of day than the first. I have, on occasion, come under deadline pressure. Writing the second half of *Pigs in Heaven* was like that. I sort of woke up with alarm at the end of last summer realizing that I had only about half of the first draft of this novel, which was due at the end of the year, so I mapped out all the rest of the novel scene by scene, and then forced myself to write five scenes a day. It was scary. I don't usually have to put myself to that kind of test, but I'm a hard worker.

BEATTIE: When you have completed a manuscript to your satisfaction, does anybody then read it before you send it off to your agent?

KINGSOLVER: I used to have quite a few people read things, but now I have a really close relationship with my editor at Harper, Janet Goldstein, who has been my editor for four books there now. All four of my books at Harper have been with the same editor, which is phenomenal in this day and time, and she's wonderful. I'm so lucky to have a wonderful agent and a wonderful editor. She's a very good critic. She's really good at identifying problems and letting me fix them. She doesn't tell me what to do about it; she just says what doesn't work. So what I turn in to Harper is usually very close to what's published.

I've never undergone any pressure from my publisher—from any of my publishers, actually. *The Bean Trees,* in fact, was submitted exactly as published. I think one sentence was changed from what I submitted over the transom. I know people say their publishers and their editors warp and truncate and deform their work, but I've been lucky. That's never happened to me.

BEATTIE: The book we haven't talked about is *Pigs in Heaven.* Would you talk a little bit about that book, and about how you see it in relation to *The Bean Trees?*

KINGSOLVER: After *The Bean Trees* had been published, quite a few people begged me for a sequel or they would write and say, "Oh, what happens next?" I had no intentions of ever writing a sequel to any book, including that one. A few years ago I was struck by this drama unfolding in South Tucson that replicated the drama I'd seen unfolding elsewhere, wherein a Native American child had been adopted informally by a white family, a white couple, and this adoption came to the attention of the tribe, and the tribe demanded the child back. It's sort of gripping; it's high drama. But what interested me about it was that in the newspaper or TV coverage of this event, you see these dramatic moments of the child being torn from the mother's arms, and everybody's saying, "Isn't that awful? Isn't that awful? How can that be in the best interest of the child?" And what the tribal officials who are the spokespeople for this endeavor keep saying over and over and over again to deaf ears is, "How can it be in the best interest of the tribe to lose its children?"

Well, who cares? Nobody cares. I mean, in the mainstream press and in the mainstream Anglo-Saxon society, nobody hears that, because our fundamental unit of good is the individual, is what is best for the individual. Well, in the tribe, the fundamental unit of good is what's good for the community. So it occurred to me that this is a dialogue where there's no point of intersection, because people's most basic assumptions are different. That interested me a lot, and I thought, "That would be an interesting thing to write about." And as I told you earlier, all of my novels begin with a question. So the question I was asking myself is, "In this dialogue, is there any point of intersection?" because that seems important to me. It also goes back to the thing I always write about, which is individualism versus community. How to balance community and autonomy. So I had to write a novel about this.

I started thinking about inventing, sort of dreaming up the situation in which we had a Native American child informally adopted by a white mother, and then I said to myself, "Oh, I did this." I set it up precisely in *The Bean Trees,* but I swear to you this is the truth, I had completely formed my idea and my goals for this novel before I realized that I'd already set up the situation perfectly with *The Bean Trees.* So then it seemed to me two things were true. One is I could make a lot of people happy by writing a sequel to *The Bean Trees,* because there's this whole moral dilemma that I set up without paying any attention, or without answering to it at all. It seemed irresponsible to me. I mean, I felt like I had kind of a responsibility to bring that up and settle it, so I did in *Pigs In Heaven.*

So that's how that happened, and I had some difficulties getting it into the third person, but I had to do that, because I really wanted to give absolutely equal weight and moral authority to both Taylor's point of view and the tribe's. That was the most difficult thing about writing the book.

The other thing is, I'm a person who avoids conflict at any cost. You know, raise your voice and I'll be under the desk in an instant. So it occurred to me—actually, it was pointed out to me—that in all my books so far up to *Pigs in Heaven,* the villain was always off-stage and usually institutional, like the Stitch 'n Bitch Club versus the Mine Company, or Taylor or a mother versus poverty. It was very hard for me to write about direct conflict between characters. I don't mean that they have to have a shootout at the OK Corral, but it seemed to me that I might mature as a writer if I forced myself to write about two people who have a conflict of interest who have to work it out within the page. On the page, not off.

Another thing my editor pointed out to me before I wrote *Pigs in Heaven,* she said, "You never write bad guys." And that's true, too. My characters, none of them is just really rotten-to-the-core bad. I determined that in this book I was going to have conflict between people. I was going to have a bad character, I mean someone who was really bad. And I did.

I'm pretty sure you know who I mean: Barbie. I found, actually, once I got into it, it was really kind of fun. So I think maybe my next novel will have lots of bad people in it. I do consider myself optimistic, and I think my characters tend to be, too. But I think, for my characters, it's because they have no choice.

BEATTIE: What projects are you currently working on or what writing do you have planned?

KINGSOLVER: The mother of all book tours, I'll tell you that. I'm doing a pretty thorough promotional tour when this book [*Pigs in Heaven*] is released, and I'm trying to keep a good attitude about it. I'm really lucky that Harper promotes my books to the extent they do, and nowadays, unfortunately, the author has to be a performer. If you want your books to be widely read, you have to go and do the sound bites and readings and signings, and I think I'm gong to twenty-five cities in twenty-five days, essentially. Right now I'm in the promotional phase. When I finish a novel, I always go into a little bit of psychic collapse, and it's actually a difficult time for me. I have something that feels exactly like postpartum depression after I finish a novel. So I knew that would happen, and I planned a lot of activities to keep myself occupied.

BEATTIE: Do you work on one project at a time, one book?

KINGSOLVER: I'm pretty monogamous as that goes. I like to be. When I really start to get cooking on a novel, I turn down everything else. But what I say is, "Call me in January. This novel's due in December, so call me in January."

I'm doing a bunch of book reviews and travel articles. Oh, I went to Africa in February. The next book . . . I suppose saying it on tape might hold me to it. For about half my life I have wanted to write a novel about and set in Africa, owing to the piece of my childhood that I spent there. And I have written something that feels like the first chapter of that novel, so I've been saying to my publisher and other people in the privacy of my own home that my next book will be the Africa book, that I'm finally ready to do that. It feels like it's going to be real different from anything else I've done.

April 17, 1993

BOOKS BY BARBARA KINGSOLVER

The Bean Trees. New York: HarperCollins, 1988.

Holding the Line: Women in the Great Arizona Mine Strike of 1983. New York: ILR, 1989.

Homeland and Other Stories. New York: HarperCollins, 1989.

Animal Dreams. New York: HarperCollins, 1990.

Another America. New York: Seal, 1991.

Pigs in Heaven. New York: HarperCollins, 1993.

High Tide in Tucson: Essays from Now or Never. New York: HarperCollins, 1995.

GEORGE ELLA LYON

LYON: George Ella Lyon is my name. I was named for my mother's brother and sister. I was born in Harlan, Kentucky, in 1949. My mother is Gladys Fowler Hoskins, and my father was Robert Hoskins, Jr. My father, when I was growing up, was a dry cleaner, and eventually became a vice-president of the savings and loan.

My mother was very active in community affairs when I was small, all kinds of civic efforts, and then she became secretary for the Chamber of Commerce when I was starting high school. She still has that job. She's involved in both local and regional and statewide civic concerns. She was on the Human Rights Commission in Kentucky for quite a while, and she's influential in getting money for flood control in Eastern Kentucky and for low-income housing.

I have one brother, Robert, who is seven years older than I am. He's an English professor at James Madison University in Virginia. We come from a family of storytellers and readers, and I think that that influenced us a lot toward being so amenable to literature. My direction was writing, although I did go to graduate school in English, so I was interested in studying it, as well.

I grew up in the same town with both sets of grandparents. They were precious to me, although I didn't see that so much at the time. But also, they were really instructive to me in lots of ways. They gave me wonderful stories, and they helped me see my parents as somebody's children.

My mother's father was a lumberman, like the daddy in *Borrowed Children*. They had a big family, seven children, six surviving children. My father's father was a house builder and was building the coal camp at Lynch when my father was born. He built the house I grew up in. He built many of the houses around us, and he built the Methodist church.

I grew up spending a lot of time at both sets of grandparents' houses. My father was an only child, so I didn't have aunts and uncles and cousins on that side, but on my mother's side, there were lots, and that provided an important sense of family.

BEATTIE: What were your grandparents' names?

LYON: J.D. Fowler and Ruby Lane Fowler, my mother's parents, and Robert Hoskins and Josephine Wilder Hoskins, my daddy's parents.

BEATTIE: What was your childhood like? What kinds of things do you remember?

LYON: I remember being a listener to the talk, to the stories. I was a real outdoors kid, and at that time and in that place, we had a lot of freedom. You had the run of the neighborhood, you knew everybody, backyards just sort of flowed together, and houses, too. Not at all the way it is now. Likewise, it seems to me that because of the neighbor-hoods, the way they were, your stories were more woven together. So when I was small, I had a real sense of freedom that I wish I could give my children, but I don't think I can, not a physical freedom in that same way. It's just not the same world.

BEATTIE: What was your early education like, and what was your school, itself, like?

LYON: I went to kindergarten in Harlan, in the basement of the hotel, which I thought was wonderful, and I went to Loyall Elementary School, a small school.

BEATTIE: What made the kindergarten so wonderful?

LYON: I don't know. I just liked school. It was fun; there were other kids. I was the youngest. There weren't any other children at home, so I really liked that, I liked being with other kids. I liked getting to do things. I liked tasks.

BEATTIE: Could you read before you went to school?

LYON: I couldn't read, and one of my big disappointments was that I didn't learn to read the first day at first grade. People kept saying to me, "Go to school; you'll learn to read." So I thought, with my great capacity for patience, that I would get it the first day, you know. I was sorry to find out it didn't work that way. But reading was a big thing in my house, and I was read to a lot. I can see now that I have had children of my own, and also now that I've worked with adults learning to read, how much I was learning to read long before I could sound out the alphabet. I knew the music of the sentence read aloud.

BEATTIE: Who read to you as a child?

LYON: My mother and my father. They often read poetry, sometimes after dinner, just sitting around the table, which sounds very quaint, but it didn't seem a bit odd at the time. I just thought it was wonderful. I often didn't understand it, but I loved the sound of it, and I could feel the emotions conveyed in the rhythm and sound of the language, even if I didn't understand the content. And I memorized a lot of songs, and my daddy sang to me, too.

BEATTIE: You said there were a lot of storytellers in your family. Who were they?

LYON: I can't think of who they *weren't*. I can't think of anybody who didn't. Most often they're things that really happened, which, over time, may have been improved upon. In fact, quite a few of the incidents in *Borrowed Children* come out of some of those stories that I heard as a child. They may not have happened in that way or to those people, but for instance, the boys charging their lunch at the hotel, my uncles did that. I'm always grateful for that habit of seeing your life in stories. I think that's mountain and rural, small town, also southern. There's the southern love of good talk, and then there's the mountain sort of storytelling, and they come together. I thought growing up that everybody did that, but I found out it's not true. You know, when Suzuki developed his theory about teaching music, and of course he wasn't talking just about music, but he used that as the example, he theorized that children learn first by ear. They learn to play without reading at all. I think you learn storytelling by ear, you hear it, and you learn about the possibilities of the language, and it's years and years before you could write down a sentence like that, but you have the resonance for it.

BEATTIE: Did you have favorite subjects in school, and were reading and writing among them?

LYON: Reading was always my favorite. I don't remember writing for class until probably seventh grade, but I started writing poems early on, in second or third grade. It seems like as soon as I could write, I started trying to make poems. But nobody ever asked us to do that for school. Reading was something that, if you finished all your work, you could go do in the back of the room. There was not an elementary school library, but there were books available. So, I was always rushing through everything to get back to the books.

BEATTIE: And this is something you enjoyed doing at home on your own as well?

LYON: We didn't have very many children's books. I think, generally, people didn't in the fifties. I had a fairytale book and some Golden Books that you'd get at the supermarket. But that was another thing that made school especially attractive, that they did have them. They might just have been discarded readers, but I thought they were wonderful.

BEATTIE: Do you remember teachers who particularly influenced you?

LYON: I had a wonderful first grade teacher. I think the biggest thing she did was make me welcome, make me feel at home in school. I always felt secure in her presence. She was happy to be there, and I was happy. And I had a really good fourth grade teacher, and a wonderful seventh grade teacher, the first male teacher I had. He was really very good.

BEATTIE: What were your junior high and high school years like, and were you writing then?

LYON: I was. I remember in seventh grade trying to write a novel in code, in numbers, so that no one would be able to read it. It's pretty funny, since now I just hope someone would want to read it. But the funny thing was, I lost the code and then I couldn't read it myself. I don't know how much of it I actually got done.

I think seventh and eighth grade were pretty hard. We didn't have a separate junior high, but those years were harder for me than high school, I think. All of a sudden, as a girl, I had kind of a gender crisis. I was not supposed to be interested in anything except boys, and I thought they were really stupid. But my interest in school and in learning things all of a sudden was a real negative, as far as school itself was concerned. I felt really on the outside, which is not unusual for that age, and I worked in a religious crisis. I just questioned everything.

BEATTIE: How had you been raised, religiously?

LYON: I grew up in the Disciples of Christ church. But as I began to learn about other religions, then I wanted to know how this all fit together, and also, like lots of kids, I think I was a real idealist, and when I began to see that people were human, people in my church, for instance, I realized that everybody was not out there living the Gospel like I thought I ought to be. That was a struggle.

BEATTIE: Did you rebel by not going to church?

LYON: No. I just anguished about it. I don't think that not going to church occurred to me as an option. I left that when I went to college. I didn't go at all for a while. Then, when I was in graduate school, I converted to Catholicism. I really responded to the liturgy and to having more of a sense of church history. Then, I couldn't stick with that, because I was conflicted about a lot of the big issues: birth control, abortion, ordination of women, for starters. So, there was a long stretch in there again where I didn't go to church. But I longed for that kind of community, and for some kind of ritual. Now I'm in an Episcopal church here [Lexington].

BEATTIE: What was the rest of your high school like?

LYON: Well, when I look back on it, I can see that I was kind of bored, although at the time I was so busy I didn't realize it, because I was active in a lot of clubs and so forth, and edited the newspaper for a while, the classroom newspaper. But I was not very often challenged as a student. I didn't think I wanted to go to college. I thought it would be just like high school, only worse, more of the same. I wanted to go to New York and be a folk singer, to Greenwich Village and sing at the Purple Onion. There's my guitar right over there, I still have it. I was writing songs and singing around and about, but I realized that I couldn't just go do that. I thought of the kinds of jobs I could get, and I knew they were not what I wanted. So I thought I'd better go to college and figure something out. I wanted to go to Columbia University then, so I'd be near the Purple Onion. I also had this fantasy of being a simultaneous translator at the United Nations while singing at the Purple Onion. I'd be near both my jobs. But my parents didn't want me to do that right out of Harlan. They suggested that I go to a Kentucky school for a year, a small school. It didn't have to be Kentucky, but a small school for a year, and then if I still wanted to do that, okay. So I went to Centre College, liked it so much, and found good friends, so going to New York was no longer what I wanted to do.

But also, in high school, I was in the creative writing class, and that's where I really started to identify myself as someone who wrote. I wouldn't have said I was a writer, but someone who wrote. And the teacher was herself a poet, and offered to look at my work after the class was over, so I could bring her things.

BEATTIE: Who was this?

LYON: Kathleen Hill. Her name is Kathleen Sterling, now. We're still friends after all these years. She was a tremendous support and influence and gave me a sense that somebody else cared about it, how you arranged forty-three words on a page. Also, I didn't think of this at the time, but she was married and had a family and had a job and, she was a sort of a model, too, of a woman who was doing this. I'd go over to her house sometimes on a Sunday afternoon. So, she was very generous.

Also, I read about poets. I was especially interested in Dylan Thomas, and Edna St. Vincent Millay, and Carl Sandburg. That was sort of my poet stew when I was in high school. I read about their work, and I knew that you worked, and worked, and worked, and worked on it.

BEATTIE: What else did you do in college? Did you do extracurricular activities, such as the newspaper or literary magazine?

LYON: I was a coeditor of the literary magazine one or two years, and I had worked on it before that. And I did some writing for the *Cento* [college newspaper], and I wrote some music for one of the drama productions.

I forget what it was called now, but we had a big sister-big brother program out in the community, so we didn't have classes on Wednesdays, and I had a little sister who then spent Wednesday mornings with me. Sometimes the whole group did things together and sometimes it was just you and your child that did things together.

BEATTIE: What did you do with her?

LYON: She was five. Or five and six, it was two years. She was a wonderful child. She taught me all kinds of things. I'd never had a little sister or little brother. I hadn't had that experience. We'd go for walks. We'd color, we'd do bubbles, we'd go to the public library, we would go get ice cream, we'd go jump in puddles, climb trees, whatever. So I was involved in that. I was in college from '67 to '71, and I was involved in the peace movement, and there wasn't a lot of civil rights movement in Danville, but what there was, I was involved in.

BEATTIE: Did you get any opportunity to play your guitar and sing folk songs?

LYON: I did some of that, too. In the one play I was a musician for, I played guitar and sang. But that was a time when almost everybody had a guitar.

BEATTIE: What did you do right after college, and did you major in English?

LYON: I majored in English, and I almost had a minor in music. I took a lot of music courses, which is how I met my husband, who's a musician.

BEATTIE: Did you marry in college?

LYON: No, I went to graduate school for a year before we married. He was a year behind me in school. He's two years younger, but he skipped a grade.

BEATTIE: And your husband's name is?

LYON: Steve Lyon. He's a keyboard player and composer. He plays on weekends here at the Marriot, and then he has a radio jingle business. He writes and produces ads for radio and some for TV. We're both free-lance people.

But at the end of college I knew that I wanted to go into writing; I wanted a writing program. So I applied all over, everywhere they had an M.F.A. [Master of Fine Arts] in creative writing. There weren't nearly as many such programs then as there are now. I did not get accepted anywhere except I.U. [Indiana University], but I needed to be able to pay my way. I.U., at that time, didn't offer teaching fellowships unless you already had an M.A. [Master of Arts]. So, I went to the University of Arkansas in a fellowship program, and I taught for a year and got an M.A. and then went to Indiana. I got married during that time, too. But, when I got to Indiana, it turned out they wouldn't let me get another M.A., because I already had one, and they didn't have an M.F.A. They just had an M.A. with a concentration in writing. But they said, "Well, you go into your Ph.D. program and take the writing courses; you just can't do a thesis, you'll have to do a dissertation." So, that's what I did. I wrote my dissertation on Virginia Woolf. But I really did not set out to get a Ph.D. This is kind of comical, since lots of people set out to get it and don't.

BEATTIE: How did you like that program?

LYON: I liked it. I don't think I would have been happy had I just been in the academic program. The thing I loved about my time at I.U. was the community of writers I found in the writing program. Many of my writer friends were musicians, too, so it was great for me and Steve, because he wound up having a band with one of the poets, and it all fit together. But I found some of the academic approach to writing and teaching very confusing. And the politics, I knew I didn't like that.

I envisioned myself as getting a full-time teaching job in writing. That's what I thought I would do. We were in Bloomington for three-and-a-half years. I finished my course work and took the exams, then Steve got a job writing country music in Nashville. So, we moved to Nashville and he was writing country music and I was writing my dissertation. Then we decided to have a baby, and the day that I discovered that I was pregnant, he found out that he wasn't going to be paid anymore. He was perfectly welcome to stay and write songs, but they reorganized and decided they couldn't employ somebody just to write songs. So, that's when we moved to Lexington.

BEATTIE: What year was that?

LYON: '76.

BEATTIE: And you had the baby in Lexington?

LYON: Yes. His name is Ben. He's now playing the electric guitar across the hall.

BEATTIE: So he, too, is a musician?

LYON: Yes, and he's very much interested in music and drama.

BEATTIE: Tell me about your dissertation.

LYON: I proposed to write a creative dissertation. I wanted to write a book of stories and poems set in the mountains. Creative dissertations had been done a couple of places, not at I.U., but they turned that down. So finally I asked myself, "Well, what am I really enjoying reading right now?" The answer was Virginia Woolf and E.M. Forster, so, I cooked up this project, and that's what I did.

BEATTIE: Has that ever been published?

LYON: Not that, but I've gone on to publish things about Woolf, which grew out of that. I have an essay in a collection of centennial essays about Woolf. I also have a sequence of poems about Woolf that was published.

BEATTIE: When you moved to Lexington, what was your husband doing? And after the baby, what were you doing?

LYON: When Ben was born, my husband was working at the Ramada Inn. I had to call him at the Ramada. He had to come to the hospital in his tuxedo, in this dark red brocade jacket and this ruffled shirt. I remember the obstetrician saying, "You certainly dressed for the occasion." And I was trying to finish my dissertation. I don't know that I ever would have finished it if I hadn't gotten pregnant. I don't recommend that as the best strategy, but for me, all of a sudden, I realized, "I have to quit reading and start writing. Never mind if I don't know that I know enough to do this." Plus, I knew I was going to have to go to work. So, I finished all but the last chapter of my dissertation before Ben was born.

BEATTIE: After your dissertation was completed, what did you do?

LYON: I started teaching at UK in '77, part-time, and this was really where I began to think about teaching full-time. I didn't want to put Ben in daycare, so I thought, "Well, I'll just start out part-time." Then I didn't see how I was going to have a full-time job and raise a child and write. I just didn't see how to do it. So, I tried to juggle different kinds of part-time work, and for a while I went on the job market for a full-time job, but I didn't get one.

BEATTIE: Did you like your first teaching job, the part-time teaching?

LYON: In some ways I really enjoyed doing it, and in other ways I didn't feel I was very good at it. I always found it hard to understand that people didn't have much interest in writing or much feeling for it. Also, when you're only teaching freshman comp., which is what I did for years and years, all you're finding out, at least all I found out, was all the things that didn't work. But I had gotten to teach one creative writing class at I.U., and I knew that I enjoyed that. So I was hoping that eventually I would get to teach creative writing, which eventually I did. But it took years.

While teaching creative writing I found something which I hadn't encountered before, on anything like this scale, and that is that there were a number of students in the fiction classes who wrote really violent, sensationalist things that were very disturbing, and that I know were gleaned in part from film and television and what's popular. I found that they took no responsibility for the impact of these images, that they were just something to manipulate and they thought "Hey, people will buy this stuff," or this was their idea of what happens. When something happens, it has to happen in a huge, catastrophic and disgusting external and x-rated way, and this was really hard to deal with. When I tried to talk about the writer's responsibility, not to censor what's in the story, but to deal with the moral implications of what's in the story, one student said, "Oh, you're talking about that moral fiction shit," like that was a little compartment off somewhere. You can write horror fiction, you can write moral fiction shit. So this was very distressing, and there was an extreme amount of violence against women in these stories, too.

BEATTIE: Mostly by male writers or by both male and female writers?

LYON: All by male. All by young men. Not all of them college age, some were returning students. But murder, mutilation, rape. Even stories supposed to be funny—the guys at the truck stop kill and eat the waitress, you know. So this got to be a drag, as they say. No, this was really a disturbing course of events, or events of course, I guess you'd say.

In one of Flannery O'Connor's essays, she responds to the question of whether students should set the curricula, and whether as a teacher you should appeal to their tastes, and she says the students' tastes should not be consulted, their tastes are being formed. I think my strongest convictions in teaching are that you take each student where he or she is and try to work from there, without ever singling out two or three students in the class who are the stars of the class, because I don't think that's productive for anybody, not for the stars and not for the rest of the students. I think you work at having a community and play down the competitive model in education, which I don't think works well. I don't think it nourishes the spirit. I don't think it makes good citizens. That's my biggest concern. It's very hard to do by the time people are in college, because they're so set. By the same token, I don't judge competitions of school-aged children. I'm often asked to do that, to be a judge. A contest produces a winner or maybe three winners, but mostly what it produces is losers, who then think the writing wasn't worth anything.

BEATTIE: The people who hold contests, I guess their argument would be, isn't that what publication, or life itself, is like?

LYON: I know. In fact, someone just said that to me the other day, when I turned down a request. She said, "But, honey," or "dear" or something, "isn't that what life is like?" I don't think that's what we want to nurture. I'm not saying you don't run into it. I'm not saying that there is not a competitive mode operating in the writing world, or the poetry world, that it's not political. But that's not what I think matters, and that's not what I'm interested in, and that's not how I'm going to set up my classroom.

BEATTIE: Or even so, you'll get more people to continue to pursue writing at an early age. At least if they're cut off eventually by an editor or a publisher, they will have had that much more time to grow in their writing and their work.

LYON: To grow and enjoy it. And the thing is, I think writing, the greatest value of it, is how it enriches your life. Of course you want to try to publish, and it's wonderful if you can and can share it in that way, but there are other ways to share it in reading to people and giving people copies. And you don't get validation for your writing from out there somewhere that certifies you as a writer. And people want that. Our whole model of success is fame and money. Not many people get either, or a lot of either, so I think we miss the richness of our lives by waiting for something to happen or by thinking, "Well, it won't happen, so I'm not even going to try."

BEATTIE: What about your career history? You started off, you said, teaching part-time, and then you were looking for full-time jobs that didn't come to pass. So then what did you do?

LYON: I've done a little bit of everything in the verbal mode. I did editing, free-lance editing for the U.K. Med. Center. And I worked for something called Rational Behavior Therapy. I edited their newsletter over at the Med. Center. I worked for the Kentucky Arts Council, I coordinated the visits from writers to colleges and universities. For two years I did that and helped with one of the Kentucky writing conferences. All of this was part-time. I worked for Appalshop in Whitesburg [Kentucky] writing a script for their history series. I was executive secretary of the Appalachian Poetry Project, which came through a grant at UK, and we coordinated workshops in five states in the mountains. That was what put me in touch with other Appalachian writers, and I received that position through Gurney Norman.

After that, I got a grant from the Kentucky Humanities Council to work in Eastern Kentucky in five counties, encouraging and teaching teachers to use writing from the region, poetry from the region, to teach writing. I did workshops with teachers, and then I did workshops with students, and then I brought writers in to read to the kids, so that was a year-long project I worked on. And I taught through community education at Transy [Transylvania University]. I taught at Transy and Centre. I used to have classes around my dining room table. I would just call people up and say, "You want to take a class in revision?" Then students from one class would call up other people. I didn't keep a list of all those classes, but I must have done four or five.

Then gradually, as I started publishing books for children, it became possible for me to get jobs going into the schools and working with kids, and gradually I've done more and more of that.

BEATTIE: Have you, yourself, done that through the Kentucky Arts Council?

LYON: I started out doing some through the Arts Council, but now I do it just myself or through my publisher.

BEATTIE: Speaking of publishing, what about your writing during all this time, your own writing? What were you writing and publishing?

LYON: Until 1984, I wrote and published mostly poetry and some essays and reviews. But, every once in a while I would come down with a short story, sort of like a virus, and I would write a story, but I never knew what to do with it. I never could get past the initial impulse, somehow. I didn't know how to work on it.

But in the summer of 1984, I decided that I would not take any jobs, which I had never done. I would write whenever I could; that's what I would do. I would give myself that permission, because it finally occurred to me that nobody was going to give me that permission. I turned thirty-five that spring, and I just said to myself, "The phone is ringing; either you're going to answer it and write, or you're not going to answer it. And if I'm not going to answer it, then I ought to do something that will make my life more coherent, get some kind of job that will make my life more coherent. And if I am going to do it, then I'd better do it so that it can start to amount to something." Well, that was April, and in May I got a letter from Richard Jackson, who is my editor, because I had some poems in an anthology that he published. The editor of the anthology had written, wanting to know where I got such a strange name. I wrote him back and told him. He liked my letter and he sent it to

Dick, and Dick wrote to me and said, "I wonder if you write for children, and if not, would you?" "If you have something, would you send it in? If not, would you think about it?"

So, I started working that summer on picture books, and I started writing *Borrowed Children,* and I wrote a play. So, once I committed myself in that way, it made a big difference. Also, once I started writing prose, the wonderful thing about prose, about fiction, for me anyway, is that once I have something going, I can come back to it whenever I can. It's not like poetry, where you're always starting over. There's some continuity, and I like that a lot.

BEATTIE: Since you're thought of primarily as a children's book writer, but you've written in so many genres, do you see yourself as primarily any one type of author?

LYON: I guess I think of myself first of all as a poet, because that's my starting place, and also I think that's really my sensibility, metaphorical, with my writing having a lot to do with the music of language. But, I think it's regrettable that we categorize writers so tightly. I'm always finding that Eudora Welty wrote a picture book or somebody else wrote a play, but we never hear that they wrote a play. We only hear that they're this kind of writer, or that kind of writer. I don't see why we need to be so restrictive. I have a novel for adults that's out at publishers now, and if that gets accepted, that would make a difference. I've had two plays that have been produced. The trouble with plays though, is that unless they're in print, or unless they really are picked up, which probably won't happen unless they're in print, then they sort of don't exist.

BEATTIE: But that summer, when you first started writing full-time, is that the first time you considered yourself a full-fledged writer?

LYON: I thought of myself, for myself, as a writer. I should say, though, that in '83 I won a contest, a chapbook contest, so I had a book of poems called *Mountain* come out in '83, and that was a real affirmation for me. I think that went into my being able to say to myself, "Okay, go on and take the plunge."

BEATTIE: After that chapbook, and after you started writing that summer, how did the publications come?

LYON: Well, the first picture book that I wrote was accepted, which gave me a very false idea of how it was going to be, because then I wrote, oh, ten or so picture books that were rejected before the second one was accepted. But I started working on *Borrowed Children,* and I was working on *Braids,* the first play I did. A friend of mine, Ann Kilkelly, decided it was a play. I didn't even realize it was a play to begin with, and she wanted to get a grant to produce it. She got the grant before I even finished the first draft, which was a little startling. The grant was from the Kentucky Arts Council. We performed the play at the Kentucky Women Writers' Conference in 1985. I started it in July of '84, and it was produced the first time in April of '85.

I was involved in working on the Kentucky Women Writers' Conference from its first year, when I was teaching part-time at UK, and that's been a really nurturing thing for women in this area, in this region, because it draws on quite a large area for attendance.

BEATTIE: That brings up a question. In terms of categorizing writers, as you were just talking about categorizing them as fiction writers, or poets, or novelists, do you believe in categorizing writers as women writers, as African American writers, as Jewish writers, as whatever? I mean, do you think that that provides them with something that they need to grow, or do you think such labels can also be diminishing?

LYON: I think it depends on who's using the term. Because for some people, a woman writer is a pejorative, regional means minor, Appalachian means hillbilly or a stereotype. Black means a certain kind of writing, or it means, "I don't want to read that," you know. "If this is an Appalachian writer, or something by a woman, I don't want to read that." So, language, labels, a label can be a weapon. So it depends. I think there's value in looking at Appalachian literature together. It's certainly important for me to know other writers from the region, and to read their work and be involved in writing that comes out of the region. I feel very identified with the region, but I don't feel limited by that. It doesn't mean that everything I write is based there, or even that that's the border of my interests or imagination. I think we can lose sight of what we all have in common; I think it's important to think about what it means to be from a region. It's also important to think what it means to be a North American writer, your relationship to your material, your relationship to your history, your relationship to your upbringing, which includes all those facets of your identity, your gender, the place you come from, your relationship in your own family and community, but also your relationship with the country and with the world.

BEATTIE: Since you published your first children's picture book, you have published how many?

LYON: The one that comes out this spring will make ten picture books, and then I have two novels for young readers, and I have a book of stories for adults learning to read. And I have the chapbook of poems, which is out of print now, and the plays.

BEATTIE: How were your plays received when they were produced?

LYON: *Braids* got a real good reception here, and then we produced it also at Appalshop. We've done readings of it other places, staged readings. So, it was well-received. We did it as a radio play, too, through WEKU [public radio station]. The second one, *Looking Back for Word,* is still getting produced. We're doing that ourselves, Steve and I and another friend. Steve, my husband, wrote the music, and another friend and I are in it, so it's sort of a cottage industry. We've done it, oh, fifteen different places, probably.

BEATTIE: Was that your first collaboration with your husband?

LYON: We've made up songs together, but it's the first thing we've done that we made public in some way.

BEATTIE: Are you planning to do other things together now?

LYON: We'd like to. We're doing a reading and music together at the Literacy Center next month.

BEATTIE: Is he a critic of your work before you send it to editors?

LYON: Oh, yes. He reads for me and he tries things out on me, too, things he's working on. So, we're important critics for each other.

BEATTIE: I'm wondering what you think distinguishes your work, or what you would like to have distinguish it. What are you most interested in in your writing?

LYON: I think that I'm very concerned with voice, whether it's first person or third person, or second person, for that matter. But I'm concerned with what makes a voice distinctive, a voice of a character or of a piece, with what that says about the relationship to the material and how, as a reader, where that places you in relationship to the speaker or to the material. The novel that I'm working on now, I just mailed it off yesterday, it's called *Here and Then*. I'm not at all finished with it. This is the first time the editor will have seen it, but it's alternating chapters taking place in 1991 and 1861. Two girls, the same age, in the same place, they don't meet, but they converge. They don't trade places or anything. But Abby, who's in the present, is in third person, and Bernetta, who's in the past, is in first person. So, that has been real instructive to me, to see what happens. I don't know if it works, but that's what I've tried to do. I don't know if that's going to be a problem for a younger reader, making the switch, but once you see what's going on, I don't think it will be.

BEATTIE: I know you've been very involved with literacy in Kentucky. Will you talk about that and about the adult literacy book you wrote?

LYON: I worked on something called the New Books for New Readers project through the Kentucky Humanities Council. Five writers each met with a literacy group and worked on a book. I worked with a group in Harlan County, which is my home county, to write a book that they would want to read. Mine is the only book of fiction.

I've spent this morning with students and tutors at the Literacy Center here who have read the book and who had questions, and who wanted to hear about writing it. Then I made suggestions for things that they might write, and I'm going to meet with them again next week and see how that goes.

BEATTIE: Has your book *Choices* been very successful?

LYON: It has, in the literacy program in Kentucky. They've had to reprint it, and also some other states have used it. Some high schools, I think, are using it now, in Kentucky. UK Press has published the series. The whole series has been well received, and there are now additional books, after the first five. It's a sort of pilot project, really.

BEATTIE: And in the midst of your career, you did have another son.

LYON: Right. I have a six-year- and a sixteen-year-old.

BEATTIE: And his name is?

LYON: We call him Joey. His name is Joseph.

BEATTIE: You did a wonderful job at the Elizabethtown Community College writers' workshop last year. I know you do other writers' conferences and workshops. Do you enjoy doing those, and do you think those are worthwhile for writers?

LYON: Oh, I do. For me, the biggest thing, both as a participant in workshops and as a teacher in workshops, is the community of writers, is finding other people who care about the same thing, being able to share your work, developing friendships that last beyond the week that get you through the unelevated times. And learning from one another. I don't see us as competing with one another, but as sort of laboring in the vineyard out there together. That's what's valuable to me. I also do conferences with teachers and librarians, talking about children's books, talking about teaching writing.

BEATTIE: That brings me to the question about what you think the nature of creativity is.

LYON: In my experience, what it involves for writing is being able to let go of the surface of my life, which to some extent includes the surface of the personal, and go inside to a deeper level where I feel connected, not separated from other people, but connected in a way that allows me to draw on voices and images and experiences that are not mine, but that are mine, too. I think that for me, I had to write through a lot of really personal material before that was possible. I think it is sort of the same kind of thing, that you need to go through all that and sort of tell your own story or stories. But then, for me, part of what is so rewarding about writing is that dissolving of borders between the personal self and the larger self. I don't know if that's collective unconscious or what it is, a more spiritual or psychic world, but for me that's really freeing and exciting and generative.

BEATTIE: Several people I've talked to have talked about feeling driven to write, or use the term obsessive-compulsive in terms of not thinking that being a writer was a choice with them—not having to do with the quality of the work, but just with the act of writing itself—that they felt driven. Several writers have also referred to it as a physical need as well as an emotional or an intellectual need, or a fulfillment of that need. Do you feel those things?

LYON: If I don't write, I get mean. I'm miserable if I don't write. I don't know what's happened. I don't understand things if I don't write. I don't mean that I'm necessarily writing about what's going on, but that writing brings things together for me, and it also forces me, if it's going well, into some kind of authentic relationship with things. I can't pretend, I can't posture, I can't be up on stilts or wherever. So it's centering in that way to write, whether it's journal writing or working on a piece. And I love to draw the words. That's very healing for me. I'm not a typist. Some people do that, but all I need is a pen and a piece of paper. And I don't have to be here. I can write anywhere. I just can't write and drive; that's my limit.

I think the need to make something out of experience is very strong, whether you do it in a story, or whether you do it in music, or whether you do it in painting, or whether you work with numbers and try to make it come out right, whether you build something with your hands and make it fit together. When I'm here [home], I write every morning as soon as I get the kids off to school. I work until noon, and then I may continue working on the writing in the afternoon, or there may be business things connected with writing that I have to do in the afternoon. Right now, I earn about half of my living from the books themselves and half from being a writer in the schools or at conferences, so my writing gets broken up by having to go off and teach or read.

BEATTIE: You have quite a circle of Kentucky writer friends, I know, Gurney Norman being one of them. How did you get to know most of them?

LYON: Well, a lot of that was through Gurney, because when we worked on the Appalachian Poetry Project in 1980, he took me down to Hindman to the writers' conference, the Appalachian Writers workshop. He said, "You've got to come down and meet people," and Gurney creates communities. So, I've gone ever since, except for one pregnant summer. That has brought me in contact with lots of writers in the state who either teach there or who come there. Then, when I worked coordinating the writers' residencies, I met people, and at the Women Writers' Conference I've met people.

One of the talks I've given this year is called "Voice Place," and it's about the relationship of place to story and speaking point.

BEATTIE: It seems to me you have a real sense of truth or veracity in your work related to sense of place. That is, it's almost a spiritual thing with you. Many writers, their sense of place is absolute and physical. Many are exclusively internal, no matter where their stories are set, it doesn't matter; that's just a backdrop for what is going on psychologically. You seem to me to combine the two; they're very interwoven.

What about writers who have influenced you?

LYON: Virginia Woolf has influenced me, especially as a model of a woman who wrote and who wrote all different kinds of things, and who wrote in some real difficult circumstances. I've just been nurtured by her work, her diaries and letters as well as by her fiction and essays and so forth.

In Kentucky writing, Gurney has been very influential, his writing as well as his generosity and guidance. James Still's work, Harriette Arnow's, Bobbie Ann Mason's. I admire Barbara Kingsolver immensely. Jim Wayne [Miller]'s work is important to me, and I've learned from him as a teacher as well.

BEATTIE: Is there one particular project that, more than any other, you would like to do in the future?

LYON: I guess, for a sense of closure, I would really like to have "Little Splinter Creek" [published in 1996 as *With a Hammer for My Heart*], the adult novel, accepted with a good editor so that I could fulfill the possibilities in that book and let it go. It's been a four-and-a-half year labor, and I'd like to see it born.

BEATTIE: Do you work on several projects simultaneously?

LYON: Usually I do. In the time I wrote "Little Splinter Creek" I wrote *Looking Back for Words,* the play, and I wrote *Red Rover, Red Rover,* another young adult novel, and picture books.

BEATTIE: Does that method of working break your concentration?

LYON: It does, and that may be one reason that "Little Splinter Creek" has that image of splintering in it. It's got ten different narrators in it. But because that's the nature of that book, I could let it be. I could let it be written that way, too. The advantage, too, of working on several things at once is that when one thing isn't going, I can turn to something else. Also, I never know when working on one thing is going to lead to something else. Gurney once said that his motto is "One thing leads to another," and I always count on that. Recently, I've been working on a scripting of videotape for the Markey Cancer Center, so that's a whole different kind of work I've been involved in, but as a part of that process I've been learning some about video. I don't know that I'll do more in that direction, but it's very interesting.

BEATTIE: Do you have advice for beginning or would-be writers?

LYON: I think to quote Rilke in his "Letter to a Young Poet," I would say don't look to other people to answer the question of whether or not you should be a writer. Rilke says look in your heart, and if that's what you need to do, then do it, and arrange your life accordingly. Don't expect it to be easy, and accept it as it's own reward, because that may be it.

January 23, 1993

BOOKS BY GEORGE ELLA LYON

Mountain. Hartford, Conn.: Andrew Mountain, 1983.

A Regular Rolling Noah. New York: Bradbury, 1986.

Father Time and the Day Boxes. New York: Bradbury, 1985.

Borrowed Children. New York: Orchard Books, 1988.

A B Cedar: An Alphabet of Trees. New York: Orchard Books, 1989.

Choices: Stories for Adult New Readers. Lexington: University Press of Kentucky, 1989.

Red Rover, Red Rover. New York: Orchard Books, 1989.

Together. New York: Orchard Books, 1989.

Basket. New York: Orchard Books, 1990.

Come A Tide. New York: Orchard Books, 1990.

Cecil's Story. New York: Orchard Books, 1991.

The Outside Inn. New York: Orchard Books, 1991.

Who Came Down That Road? New York: Orchard Books, 1992.

Catalpa. Lexington, Ky.: Wind, 1993.

Dreamplace. New York: Orchard Books, 1993.

A Gathering at the Forks: Fifteen Years of the Hindman Settlement School Appalachian Writers Workshop. Edited by Lyon, Jim Wayne Miller, and Gurney Norman. Wise, Va.: Vision, 1993.

Five Live Bongos. New York: Scholastic, 1994.

Here and Then. New York: Orchard Books, 1994.

Mama Is A Miner. New York: Orchard Books, 1994.

Old Wounds, New Words: Poems from the Appalachian Poetry Project. Edited by Lyon, Bob Henry Baber, and Gurney Norman. Ashland, Ky.: Jesse Stuart Foundation, 1994.

A Day at Camp. New York: Orchard Books, 1996.

A Wordful Child. Katonah, N.Y.: Richard Owen Publishers (Meet the Authors Series), 1996.

Ada's Pal. New York: Orchard Books, 1996.

With a Hammer for My Heart. New York: Orchard, 1996.

BOBBIE ANN MASON

MASON: I am Bobbie Ann Mason, and I was born in Mayfield, Kentucky, May first, 1940. My father was named Wilburn Arnett Mason. Arnett was his mother's last name. My mother was named Bernice Christiana Lee, and she's known as Christy.

BEATTIE: What did your father do?

MASON: He was a dairy farmer. My mother worked on the farm. She worked off and on a few years at a clothing factory in Mayfield. I'm the oldest. My sister Janice is four years younger. My sister LaNelle is twelve years younger, and my brother, Don, is seventeen years younger. So there were two sets of children.

I grew up with my grandparents. We lived with them, first in their house, and then in the house we built right next door on the farm.

BEATTIE: Was that your father's parents?

MASON: My father's parents. So I was with my grandparents until I left for college, and my mother remains on the same place.

BEATTIE: What was your childhood like?

MASON: Well, we were on a farm. It was quite close to town, but it was a small dairy farm, fields and corn and blackberries and gardens, so I spent a lot of time rounding up cows and doing my farm chores, and, in the summer, picking blackberries. I remember it as a happy and very free time, except that I was always frustrated because I felt very isolated and I wanted to go places and see the world and do something important and go to town at least.

I went to the school out in the county and rode the school bus until I was in high school, and then I transferred to the school in town. Mayfield itself is very isolated from the rest of the world. The nearest big city is a-hundred-and-fifty miles, I guess.

BEATTIE: That's which city?

MASON: Probably Memphis or Nashville, I'm not sure. They're about a-hundred-and-fifty miles. St. Louis is two hundred miles, Louisville's two hundred miles, so that little area of land down in Western Kentucky has been off on its own, it seems like, for a long time.

BEATTIE: What did you do in your childhood to compensate for the isolation?

MASON: Read books. I read the Bobbsie Twins, Honeybunch, Nancy Drew, the Dana Girls, Trixie Belden, Judy Bolton, Cherry Ames, and Vickie Barr. Those are all series books, and I didn't have anyone to guide me into reading anything a little more substantive. In fact, when I got to high school and we started reading literature, I didn't relate to it very well and didn't like it.

BEATTIE: Were you read to much as a child?

MASON: I don't think so.

BEATTIE: Your love of books developed, do you think, in school?

MASON: I'm not sure. I think my parents encouraged me, and they saw that I had that kind of inclination to be quiet and off in a corner. I must have just taken to books right away, so they encouraged that.

BEATTIE: What was your early schooling like?

MASON: Well, I went to a county school. Cuba School was the name of it. I went there in grade school and junior high, and there were between thirty and forty children in my grade. It was the kind of school where the teachers didn't have college degrees. They were working toward them. The library in high school and junior high consisted of a few shelves of books. The students were all from the country and a lot of them were poor, and the education, I remember, was nothing but getting your lessons out of the workbook and reading little books and memorizing things. And we had art. Art consisted of the teacher making a simple drawing on the occasion of a holiday. She would draw a pumpkin for Thanksgiving and run it off on the ditto machine. Then we would all have a pumpkin to color.

BEATTIE: Did you have to stay within the lines?

MASON: Oh, yes! There was no question about that. But when I was in first grade I had this marvelous teacher who was very creative, and I just have dim memories of this, but she would take colored chalks, and on the blackboard on those holidays she would draw a beautiful picture. Maybe I got my love of books from her, I don't know. Then my sixth grade teacher was very good and very devoted to the children, and she knew I liked to read. Those are my dominant memories, and other than that, it was a kind of exotic experience to go to school. Before first grade I had no playmates whatsoever. It's a wonder I could have functioned.

BEATTIE: What did you do by yourself most of the time before you could read?

MASON: I did jigsaw puzzles. I was always busy with something, and in those days they didn't teach you to read till you were in school. But I think my mother says I learned my ABC's before I went to school. I tried kindergarten the year before that, and it was too traumatic, and I came home. I suffered a great deal from shyness and still do, but at least it's not such a trauma as it used to be.

BEATTIE: Did you have, then, after you were in school, playmates you would see after school?

MASON: Well, because I rode the bus to school, I didn't really have anybody to play with after school, and it was a rare occasion when I would go home with some other play-mate and spend the night.

BEATTIE: What about junior high, as it was called then, and high school?

MASON: Seventh and eighth grade. Well, that was basically like grade school, and then I switched to high school where I was just a mile away from school, and I was taken in the car. People who went to Mayfield High School declared that it was a great education, and I still rebel against it because there was nothing creative or encouraging about it, it was all so institutional and regimented. And if you did try something creative, it wasn't re-warded. I don't remember trying anything particular, but . . . well, there was the time I wrote the essay and got accused of plagiarism. Well, the story is this. The senior English teacher, Miss [Florence] Wyman, was famous in Mayfield because she'd taught everybody in town for several decades, and some people remember her with fanatic devotion, because they loved her so much, and other people had a hard time with her. She was very strict in her standards, and she didn't treat me very well. I wanted to go to college and wanted to apply to several schools and wanted to apply to Duke University and the University of Houston and a couple of other places, and she wouldn't write me the recommendations. She was the person in charge of getting us all off to college, I guess. She told me that the schools that interested me were too far away, and I should go to the University of Kentucky. Then I wrote an essay, toward the end of the year, on agnosticism, and she called me to her office and accused me of plagiarism because she couldn't believe that I could have written this or could have known anything about agnosticism, and she wanted to know what philosophers I read. I think I said, "Well, I've read John Locke," which was probably not true. That may have been when she decided that I had to go to the University of Kentucky and I couldn't go to Duke University and study parapsychology with Dr. J. B. Rhine. He was doing those famous experiments then, and I was really intrigued by that. So it may be when I wrote that paper that she decided I needed to be reined in, and she told me that I had to forget all this stuff about philosophy and writing, that I ought to stick with math and science. So I did.

I started out majoring in math my first year, and I switched to journalism and then to English as I got further away from her. It was only a few years ago that I discovered something that links back to that episode. I found out that she had contributed one of my earlier essays, an essay on national security during the Eisenhower administration, an essay that she gave me an A-plus on, she had contributed that to the *Bulletin* for English teachers as a student essay, and it had gotten published, and I never knew this. She never told me. I only found out because a few years ago somebody informed me that the NCTE [National Council of Teachers of English] was publishing a special anniversary issue and was going back through and collecting some of the best student essays that had been contributed over the years, and they wanted to put my essay in it.

BEATTIE: So it was years before you knew?

MASON: She never told me. I guess she thought it might encourage me to go into writing. She's long dead now, and it's too bad, but I think I showed her, didn't I?

It probably wasn't my first publication, because I had been very busy for several years publishing the *National Hilltoppers Topics*. I was the national president of the Hilltoppers Fan Club, a fan club for the singing group called the Hilltoppers, who came out of Western Kentucky University, and were named after the sports teams there. They were a singing quartet in the fifties, and their first record was released in 1952. They started to fade when rock and roll took over. But I was devoted to them when I was in junior high, and then I formed this fan club, and then I got appointed national president because I was the most active of all their presidents. I was just really fiercely loyal and very busy with all my presidential duties. It was all by correspondence. I wouldn't have dared to even speak to anybody in my class about this, but it was my way of getting out of Mayfield.

BEATTIE: But nobody around you knew what you were doing?

MASON: No. Oh, well, sometimes they did, or I would be on the radio. I would go on the disc jockeys' shows and talk about the Hilltoppers, and my mother would take me to their concerts whenever they came nearby, like in Dexter, Missouri, or Blytheville, Arkansas. We traveled quite a bit, and I went to Detroit and Cincinnati.

BEATTIE: So you met them?

MASON: Yes, many times, and got to be friends with them. I mean, this is a groupie's dream, except it was all extremely innocent at the time. I loved them so much, and so I published the fan club news and a little journal, which was like a little magazine that I put together one time. I continued this when I was a freshman at UK [University of Kentucky], but they disbanded soon after that. They came to the UK homecoming my first year there.

BEATTIE: When did you first write?

MASON: I started writing when I was about eleven or twelve, and I started writing imitation Nancy Drew books. I wrote several chapters of a couple of them.

BEATTIE: When you were at UK, what kind of experiences did you have there?

MASON: Well, one of my problems is that I didn't go to an advisor, and I just kind of made my own way through the maze of the catalog, and I graduated with more credits than I needed. My freshman English teacher was the greatest influence I had there. That was Sheldon Grebstein, and he later helped me get into graduate school—kind of guided me into graduate school to study English. I had, my freshman year there, two courses from him, and he turned me onto books, to reading literature. I hadn't really been exposed to it before, and hadn't read anything except some popular novels. So then I read Hemingway, and Thomas Wolfe was my freshman-year devotion. I took a literature course from him later, so I really got turned on to J. D. Salinger and Scott Fitzgerald, especially.

But also, I was very interested in journalism and worked for the University of Kentucky *Kernel*. I did a lot of writing for the *Kernel*. I started on the *Kernel* when I was a sophomore. Mainly I wrote a column on the op-ed page. I was influenced to do that by a columnist they had during my freshman year named Hap Cawood from Harlan, Kentucky. He's now editorial page editor of the *Dayton Daily News* in Ohio. He wrote satirical columns in the *Kernel*, and he was very talented—such a good writer—and he influenced me quite a lot. Also, he was a boyfriend at the time.

I should backtrack and tell you that I did have two creative writing courses from Robert Hazel, who also taught Wendell Berry and Ed McClanahan and Gurney Norman and James Baker Hall.

BEATTIE: When you took the creative writing courses, did you begin to think that fiction writing is what you would be doing?

MASON: Yes, I wanted to do that more than anything. Robert Hazel's influence was that he was very glamorous and he made writing seem very glamorous. He also confirmed, somehow, in his attitude toward it, that writing was a calling. I think for a lot of writers in the South it was like a religious calling, a commitment that you devote your life to. I think he was impressive because he would talk about writers, he would talk about Bill Styron and Phil Roth and acquaintances of his. So that was very impressive. And he had published novels and poems, and that was impressive.

BEATTIE: What did you do right after college?

MASON: I went straight to New York by myself and lived in a hotel and got a job working for a movie magazine. I wrote those stories about movie stars and TV stars that are so tantalizing and amount to nothing.

BEATTIE: Which magazines?

MASON: *Movie Stars* and *TV Star Parade* and *Movie Life*. I didn't know I could get a job in journalism. I thought that since I didn't major in it I'd better not apply at the *New*

York Times. I had written a column, a little promotional column for *Life* magazine, which was an interesting thing to do. I had written it for the UK *Kernel* as a promotion for *Life* magazine, and *Life* magazine would send me its issue about two days early and I would read it and review it for the *Kernel,* and the column had my picture reading *Life* magazine. So I collected all my columns and marched into the Time-Life Building in New York at the age of twenty-two and said, "Here I am! What have you got?" They didn't have anything for me. I worked for those magazines for a little over a year.

BEATTIE: What made you stop writing for the magazines, and what did you do after that?

MASON: I thought, "Am I going to do this the rest of my life? I want to read books." I just by chance got into graduate school, so I could read. I had applied to creative writing programs, but there were only about three in the country at the time, and I didn't get into any of them.

I went to a place called Harper College in Binghamton, New York. It became SUNY [State University of New York]-Binghamton. It was a small, isolated place with a small graduate department. Very high-powered. I was terrified. I experienced quite a bit of culture shock going to the North. I switched to the University of Connecticut in midstream.

BEATTIE: Was that because you weren't finding what you wanted at Harper College?

MASON: Well, it was very rigorous academically, but socially it was very isolated, and I didn't know what was going to become of me.

BEATTIE: What was the University of Connecticut like?

MASON: Well, that was a lot looser, and I just had to pick up a few credits and then work on my dissertation, so I actually took courses for only about a year. Having no play-mates until first grade was traumatic; trying to teach a group of freshmen was even more traumatic. It was the worst experience of my life.

BEATTIE: And that was at both institutions?

MASON: At both. I don't know why I thought I could continue this.

BEATTIE: How many courses were you teaching while you were taking classes?

MASON: Two.

BEATTIE: And this was basic freshman English?

MASON: No, it wasn't. At Harper College it was Western Civilization. It was called freshman comp, but the reading was literature of Western Civilization. The reading started with Homer, it stopped before Chaucer, and it picked up with Chaucer again in the second part. But I never taught the second part, I only taught the first part. It was very hard and I had no background in it. I had no background, no guidance, no insight, no historical perspective. I had no idea what I was doing. Then, at the University of Connecticut, I taught the freshman comp course, but there it was looser, and I got to choose my own texts, and I did more contemporary things.

BEATTIE: Did you ever teach creative writing?

MASON: No.

BEATTIE: Do you think you would have liked that any better, or was it just the teaching experience itself you didn't care for?

MASON: It was the teaching. Well, it was the situation. As I said, I suffered from culture shock, and I think I had a very poor educational background, and I wasn't prepared to do what I did. I was so terrified that I think my terror set up a mental block that was so big that I couldn't fight through it. It took me a long time to learn how to speak in semicoherent sentences in front of the students, so I did nothing creative in those years.

BEATTIE: You were not writing on your own at this time?

MASON: No. For the master's I just wrote three term papers, and that counted as the master's thesis, but my dissertation at the University of Connecticut was about Vladimir Nabokov, whose work I got interested in when I was at Binghamton.

BEATTIE: And your dissertation became a book.

MASON: Published by Ardis of Ann Arbor in 1975, *Nabokov's Garden.*

BEATTIE: That was your first book publication.

MASON: Yes.

BEATTIE: What did you do after graduate school in Connecticut?

MASON: I moved to Pennsylvania where my husband had a job teaching. I finished up my dissertation and simultaneously started rereading my childhood reading. It was a kind of, I don't know how to describe it. I just felt such relief that I was through all the schooling, and I was starting at that time to examine my childhood and my past and to learn about myself and to know that I didn't want to live in the city and I wanted to live on a farm. So I just started back at the beginning reviewing my life and rereading my childhood books. And out of that came a little book I wrote called *The Girl Sleuth,* which was about girls' detective fiction.

BEATTIE: You were referring to your husband. When did you meet and marry him?

MASON: We met at the University of Connecticut in probably 1968, and we were married in 1969.

BEATTIE: And his name is?

MASON: Roger Rawlings.

BEATTIE: You went to Pennsylvania because he had a teaching job there? Was he also an English major?

MASON: He had a master's degree. I had a Ph.D., but at that time a Ph.D. could not get a job.

BEATTIE: What kind of teaching job did he have in Pennsylvania?

MASON: Freshman English at Mansfield State College. It's now a university.

BEATTIE: How long were you there?

MASON: About nine years. Some of the time he was the college's public relations director, and I taught part-time journalism there. I liked journalism, and I learned a lot more confidence and ability to get up and deal with students, but I don't think it was what I had in mind to do with my life.

BEATTIE: When did you start writing your novels and short stories? While you were living in Pennsylvania?

MASON: Yes, basically. When I was at Binghamton I did do an independent study for credit by writing some stories once, and when I was at the University of Connecticut I spent one summer writing a novel, and then I abandoned that. Then, after I finished all the schooling and got more situated and knew where I was and knew more about myself, I gradually got focused on fiction writing, and it was in Pennsylvania. I started writing a second novel, and then I revised that first one, and then I wrote some stories.

BEATTIE: How did you start getting published in the *Atlantic* and the *New Yorker*?

MASON: In 1978 I started sending stories to the *New Yorker* and immediately getting encouraging responses from Roger Angell, senior fiction editor there, and that was enough encouragement to get me really excited and get me to working very hard. For about a year and half I just wrote one story after another, and just sent them in as fast as I could. As soon as they'd send one back I'd have another one to send. They could hardly keep up with me, but it would take about two or three weeks to send one and get it back and then I'd send another one.

BEATTIE: How many do you think you sent them before they took one?

MASON: Oh, well, they took the twentieth one.

BEATTIE: You know exactly which one?

MASON: Oh, yes, and it was odd, because Ann Beattie had had the same experience.

BEATTIE: With exactly twenty?

MASON: With exactly twenty. Then I ran across the fact that James Thurber had had the same experience. This is all a coincidence. That period was probably the most exciting period of work I had ever done on anything, because I was getting encouragement from the top literary magazine in the country, and from a very kind and helpful editor who saw something in my work that excited him. I wasn't sure what it was, but I just kept going.

BEATTIE: Did he write you analytical letters saying what it was he liked?

MASON: They weren't very long letters. They were very kind letters, usually, giving some subjective reason why they weren't able to take that story, and then giving me a lot of praise about it and encouraging me toward the next one. So there wasn't any specific, detailed direction. It was all up to me, but he had a way of saying it so I'd have something to think about, and then it would be up to me. So it was just the best kind of advice.

BEATTIE: The first story they took was which one?

MASON: "Offerings." I just had a very exciting period there where I felt like at last somebody was encouraging me and giving me some hope, and it happened to come from the very top.

BEATTIE: Then you became a nationally and internationally known name from those stories in the *New Yorker.*

MASON: Well, I guess so, and the association with the *New Yorker* has been very solid and good. That's all I can say about it.

BEATTIE: Did you start publishing in the *Atlantic* simultaneously?

MASON: Soon thereafter. So by the time an agent called me, I had published a few stories. Her name is Amanda Urban, and she was a relatively new agent. She'd been working a year or so, and since then she's become virtually the top literary agent in New York, and she's very talented.

BEATTIE: As soon as your first collection of fiction, *Shiloh and Other Stories,* was published, what kind of reaction were you getting?

MASON: I think it went kind of slowly, because Harper didn't promote it especially, it being just a first book of short stories. So the notice for it grew gradually. First of all, it got very good reviews, and it was reviewed by Ann Tyler in the *New Republic.* So it just kind of grew by word of mouth that way, and then it got nominated for, I think, three or four prizes, and it won one prize, the PEN-Hemingway Award for First Fiction of 1982.

BEATTIE: In many of your stories it seems that you're showing readers what is extraordinary or important in the ordinary.

MASON: Right. I imagine my characters don't always see that unless they've been through something, because they're restless. The old ways and the past, to link up with vanished history, that's very important to me. It's partly looking for stories. It's like you can never be really literally accurate in history, so what you find is stuff that excites your imagination. The thing that interests me most about genealogy, which I've become interested in, is that I think a lot of people want to trace their ancestry so that they can prove that, yes, by God, they *are* related to George Washington, or their ancestor was in the Civil War, and they want to feel important somehow. I was always more interested in the prisoners and the criminals in the background. To me, it's not so I'll feel important, it's so I can exercise my imagination and share in all these incredible threads that led to my existence.

BEATTIE: I would see it as a similar instinct to the writing instinct, the need to understand where people and behaviors come from, what things are about.

MASON: Well, I started doing genealogy the same way I didn't follow the advisor at UK, just on my own, traipsing through the library. I'd get bogged down in whole histories of whole communities for days at a time, and I'd be tracing all these people who were, if they were ever related to me, so remotely related that they didn't count. This library genealogist gave me a little lecture and said, "You're not doing genealogy! You're doing history!" And I was saying, "Well, it's very interesting!"

BEATTIE: Are you still doing genealogy?

MASON: Not so much at the moment, because I'm writing a novel, but I'd like to get back to it, and I think the most productive way of doing genealogy that way is really to learn the history of a region and a time, and this is what I'm getting out of Harriet Arnow's books, *Seed Time On The Cumberland* and *Flowering of the Cumberland,* because she's writing about the very pioneer ancestors that my people come from. She did this enormous amount of research and painted a picture of those pioneers and the lives they lived. I can read her books and say, "Yes, that was my great-great-great grandfather Mason. Yes, he went through this."

BEATTIE: Your current novel you once told me you're working on that's set at the turn of the century, does that include any of the information you've gathered?

MASON: Not exactly. It's helped inspire it, but I think to write about the turn of the century in a farm family in Western Kentucky, I only have to remember my grandparents and my own life in the forties, because not a huge amount had changed. I'm especially interested in the language, and probably that's what inspired me to write about the turn of the century in the first place. Also, my love of the language and the way people talk and the way they sound is really the impetus for the stories, too, in other novels.

BEATTIE: Talk about your other novels or your books after *Shiloh and Other Stories.*

MASON: After writing *In Country,* I felt an enormous satisfaction at having written it, and I was very proud of it, and I felt like I had created some characters that really could stand on their own. I was very proud of them and I loved them. Sam and her Uncle Emmett and their situation was just very meaningful to me, and it was a book that was hard to grope toward in the writing of it. But when I finished it, I felt it had been such a challenge, and I felt like I was very proud that I had actually written a novel.

BEATTIE: That's one book that several years after having read it, one can still remember specific scenes, which is unusual to do for a reader of many, many novels. And especially, of course, the scene at the wall, the Vietnam Memorial . . .

MASON: Yes, there's a whole lot of emotion triggered by that situation. I guess I did feel like I had done something.

BEATTIE: Did things change for you in terms of more people coming to you, being interested in your work, or your being contacted then?

MASON: I did a lot of readings, and I went to a lot of universities.

BEATTIE: Do you like to do readings?

MASON: I do like to do readings. It might come as a surprise, after what I've told about my childhood and my shyness and my inability to stand in front of a group of freshmen and feel their hostility, but I enjoy the readings because it's always to an audience that wants to be there. The faces beaming up is like approval and applause right there, so it makes me feel very free to read the voices that I hear when I'm writing, and so I become a kind of actress or a medium for them, and as I said, the language and the sound of the language is as important to me as anything in what I write.

BEATTIE: That leads me to a question about your work habits. When you write, and you say the sound of the language is important to you, do you revise as you write?

MASON: No, I just write as fast as I can, and as recklessly as I can, and then I revise. I revise a lot. Till it sounds right. I just try to find the muse, try to activate it, try to take advantage of it, try to get it out as quickly and as painlessly and as intensely as I can, and then I've got something to work with. Then I will laboriously work on it again and again and again, over and over and over for years, if necessary.

BEATTIE: Do you have a specific time that you write, or do you try to write every day?

MASON: Well, in writing you're not always writing. I just described two different phases of the process. One is writing, which is the creative phase where you're just letting your mind go free and getting things out, and the other is a kind of editorial phase where you're reading your work critically, and then you send it back in to the creative phase to see what will happen, and then you go read it again and try to revise it some, and then it needs the imagination, so you close your eyes and try to relive it. I mean, there's just a whole lot of stages there, so it's not like you're always creating or always writing. Sometimes you're just editing or rereading. My best work time is late in the afternoon and early evening.

BEATTIE: A movie was made of the novel *In Country*, and that was well-received, too.

MASON: It was critically well-received, but it didn't get the box office it might have. I think they made a lot of marketing misdirections or something.

BEATTIE: You weren't all that involved with the making of the movie itself? Were you on location watching it?

MASON: No, the movie makers wouldn't let me anywhere near my hometown. I helped out in the early phases of developing the script. I gave my responses and also answered some questions and wrote up some notes for production details. I was kept informed of every stage of what they were doing, but once the director got started, I wasn't permitted to look over his shoulder. That's understandable. But toward the end of it, they let me come and watch some scenes being filmed. I was very pleased with what they did. The whole crew from the producers, the directors, the actors on down to . . . I even heard the caterers were so happy to be working on a serious movie that they could believe in, that they were very dedicated to it and very proud of it, and they took it so seriously. They really were respectful, and they tried to make it as close to the book as they could. They were trying to make it accurate. I certainly think they were more attentive to that than most movie productions would be. I was very well-treated in that regard, and I couldn't complain. I just wanted to be in it myself. I wanted to be in the background in the drugstore scene. Ann Beattie was in her movie. She got to be a waitress in *Chilly Scenes of Winter.*

BEATTIE: After *In Country,* then you published . . .

MASON: *Spence + Lila.*

BEATTIE: And you're working now on a book that you say should be done about the first of the year, 1993? Does it have a working title?

MASON: *Feather Crowns,* and it's supposed to come out in the fall of '93. It's a long novel. It's a narrative straight through about a family, and a great deal of my impetus for it comes from my memories of my grandparents and my knowledge of their language and my parents' language. It seems to me that the way farm people talk in Kentucky sounds exotic to outsiders, but this language is still there. And my grandparents, the way they talked, is the way they talked in 1900, so I can write about 1900 by just creating my grandparents' language, and my parents' language is much the same. I hate for this language to be lost. I'm interested in the way my grandparents' language came from the Carolinas and Virginia and through Tennessee. Most of the people who settled in west Kentucky took that route. They either came from Virginia or from North Carolina, and they may have settled in Tennessee for some time before going on up the Cumberland River and the Tennessee River to west Kentucky. I'm finding a lot of connections between the way they talked and the way people in Eastern Kentucky talk and the way they talked in the Carolinas. Like my grandparents would use the word "ye" instead of "you," and my parents did, too. "Did ye get yer crop out?" "Have ye had any rain?" "Thank ye, kindly." My grandmother would say "now and directly." "When are you gonna do that?" And she would say, "Now and directly," meaning soon. It's the sound of it, but it's also the expressions. You ask them how they're doing, and they would either say they were "poorly" or they were "tolerable-well." And they'd say "oughter." I ought to, "oughter," and "soughter" instead of "sort of," and "taters" and "maters" and "a right smart while," and the way they pronounce the piece of furniture you sit in is a "cher." When they say, "I ain't got 'ner one" or "n'ary a one," I never knew where that came from. I mean, I never knew what they were trying to say, and I think I finally figured out—this is in Elizabeth Madox Roberts' book, *The Time of Man*—I think when they say, "I ain't got 'ner one," they're saying "never a one." And when they say, "That 'ere" . . . "bring me that 'ere cher over there," they mean "that there." They use prepositions abundantly.

BEATTIE: At the end phrases and sentences.

MASON: Yes, and they use several in a row. "Get down off of that 'ere cher." But this one seems reasonable, "Reach me that book down from up off of that chelf over yonder." I love that stuff, and in my novel I use quaint words like "boresome." You ever hear "boresome"?

BEATTIE: Is that "boring"?

MASON: "Boring." And I ran across one the other day, "gigglesome." "The children were so gigglesome," which I think is just wonderful. Also, tobacco is such "toilsome" work. These are just wonderful words. It seems to me turn-of-the-century characters wouldn't say "I think"; they would say "I believe," "I reckon," "I expect," or "I'd allow" or "I imagine" or "Do you figure?" but they wouldn't say "I think." They use language in a not-very-economical way. It's a kind of rigged-up affair. They don't have the names for things, so they'll use a complicated long phrase as a substitute. My mother doesn't say "forsythia bushes," she says, "those yellow bushes out yonder." Then there are expressions like "mad as an old wet hen" or "my feet hurt, it's trying to weather and can't." My grandfather always said, "by jubbers!"

BEATTIE: What's a jubber?

MASON: I think that must come from Jupiter, and it's an oath, "By Jupiter!" Well, anyway, there're just lots of things like that in the way they talk and the sound of it that I wanted to explore and to study the history of, and which enter into my book. And also just plain Anglo-Saxon informal words that I find so much more interesting in all my fiction than Latinate formal words, like "stuck a stob in his shin."

BEATTIE: Which means?

MASON: A stob is a small piece of wood, or where a weed has broken off and dried and made something, so that if you fall on it, it would hurt you.

I was going to tell you, also, that the first word I said when I was little, my first word was "soocow," which is the way you call the cows. "Soocow!" It comes from Scottish or Gaelic Scots, Lowland Scots, I believe. And "soo" comes from "suc and suck cow." Scottish farmers called the cows that way, and so did the people in Western Kentucky, I guess. One of my favorite words is "barbware." My husband has now mastered that.

You know, it's not the accent that you can translate into fiction or on the page into words, it's the rhythm and the cadence, the sound of it. And it's not the quaintness of it or the meaning so much as just the poetry of it, the sound of it.

BEATTIE: Which makes me wonder if you've ever written poetry?

MASON: No, never. I don't actually read much poetry, although I think I go about writing in the same way. My problem with poetry is that it's not in complete sentences, and it seems to dwell on very heavy thought. I'm not that serious.

BEATTIE: You moved back to Kentucky in 19-what?

MASON: '90.

BEATTIE: What brought you back to the state? You had been away for how many years? Since college?

MASON: Yes, since college, whenever that was, '62. I came back to be nearer my parents.

BEATTIE: And you plan to stay in the state for a while?

MASON: I think so.

BEATTIE: I wanted to ask you what you think the nature of creativity might be?

MASON: I think it's a mixture of temperament and circumstance. I'd ask the question a different way in a way that links back to something we were talking about before. If I had lived in 1900 and I was myself, who would I be? If I had the same mind but in different circumstances, much more limited circumstances, circumstances that required me to live according to different conventions where I had to be in a large family and do all the "women's" work and work very hard on the farm. Given my desire to bust loose and see the world that I feel now, what would I have felt then? What would I have known? Was it the radio that I listened to so much when I was growing up? Is that what made me want to make my music? I think about that a lot. I think you can't answer the question, and maybe I wouldn't have been me. Maybe I would have been shaped so differently that I could have adjusted to those circumstances, or if I was frustrated by those circumstances, I would have had a different way of expressing it or reacting to it than I have now. Maybe I'm luckier now. Maybe then

I would have gone crazy. I think that writing very often is selfish and self-centered, and what you're doing is that you're playing with your toys by yourself and not sharing until you get finished and then you give them away.

BEATTIE: But it becomes a public gift after that.

MASON: Yes, you can do it then, but the act of doing it and what you want to do with your life is really a retreat from other kinds of living. To me, it's having your own life on your own terms and doing what you want to do, and it's a measure of independence, and, also, it's just a failure to interact with society and live the way normal people live. A normal person grows up and leaves his childhood behind and goes into the new adult role and matures and then grows old. A writer is always looking back and trying to understand what went on to make him this way, and then I find that once you have written about it, then that becomes your occupation, so then you become even more obsessed with it because that's what you do.

BEATTIE: Other than the novel that you're currently completing, do you have plans for future work?

MASON: I'm eager to get back to short stories.

BEATTIE: Do you prefer writing short stories to novels?

MASON: At the time I do. It's a lot more efficient and less time-consuming and less risky, but it's not as satisfying in the long run as having written a novel.

BEATTIE: What haven't we discussed that you think might be important for people to know about you?

MASON: I'm not very sophisticated or I don't live in a very literary world, and I don't talk literature and I don't talk on a university level with adults. My main interests are animals and plants, and I'm alone much of the time, and I read as much nonfiction as I do fiction.

BEATTIE: What kinds of nonfiction do you like to read?

MASON: Oh, magazine pieces and books about science and the world, nature.

BEATTIE: You obviously love cats. You have how many now?

MASON: I have four cats, and I have had many more. And I have three dogs.

BEATTIE: You say you love plants. Do you raise particular kinds of plants?

MASON: Not at the moment. I usually have a garden, but I haven't been able to get one since I've moved to Kentucky. I will, eventually. I like to know about plants. I like to know the names of things. I went to California and couldn't find a single person who could identify a single plant, tree, or flower. I think they know lemon trees.

BEATTIE: So this is something that is not only true in your writing but throughout your life, naming things?

MASON: Writers have to know the names of things. They have to have words. It really puzzles me that words are so important and the sound of words. It must be something from the womb or music or something. You go to an English class and the teachers and the students are always talking about what something means. Or you read a piece of literary criticism and they're talking about what the story means, and the writer is thinking, "Well, is the character's name Nicholas or Michael?" "Which sounds better?" And they're always dealing with all these piddly little details. Writers always put the names of trees in their stories if there're any trees in the landscape. It's only later that the meaning will emerge, and the meaning won't be worth anything unless all those words are right. It's mysterious to me that words are so important, and they are important to all people, not just writers. And wordplay is so much the source of our humor and advertisements and child's play.

BEATTIE: Is there work that you would like to experiment with beyond novels or short stories, whether it's screenplays, plays, or writing of any other genre?

MASON: No, the only other kind of thing I like to write is journalism. Not essays and not long nonfiction things, but I've written a number of things for "The Talk of the Town" in the *New Yorker*.

We humans love words, and they're just arbitrary. It's odd. It's something in our brains. I haven't studied linguistics, so it's all quite murky to me. That's the kind of writing I really enjoy, and my columns for the UK *Kernel* were of that order long, long ago.

August 15, 1992

BOOKS BY BOBBIE ANN MASON

Nabokov's Garden. Ann Arbor, Mich.: Ardis, 1974.

The Girl Sleuth. Old Westbury, N.Y.: Feminist Press, 1975.

Shiloh and Other Stories. New York: Harper & Row, 1982.

In Country. New York: Harper & Row, 1985.

Spence + Lila. New York: Harper & Row, 1988.

Love Life. New York: Harper & Row, 1989.

Feather Crowns. New York: HarperCollins, 1993.

With Jazz. Monterey, Ky.: Larkspur, 1995.

TAYLOR MCCAFFERTY

McCAFFERTY: My name is Barbara Taylor Taylor McCafferty. I was born in Louisville, Kentucky. My first husband's name was Taylor, and my maiden name is Taylor, so for a while there my name was Barbara Taylor Taylor. It sounded like I had a stutter.

I was born in 1946, October 15th. My mother is a homemaker, and her name is Marjorie Ozie Meador Taylor. My father's name is Charles Allen Taylor, and he is today a retired foundry foreman for the International Harvester Company, which is no longer in Louisville.

BEATTIE: Did you grow up in Louisville?

McCAFFERTY: I did, in various parts. Valley Station is the area that I remember the best. I graduated from Valley High School, and then I took the bus from Valley Station to the University of Louisville. The only time I have not lived in Kentucky was for a year when I lived in Georgetown, Indiana, on an eighteen-acre farm.

BEATTIE: What was your childhood like?

McCAFFERTY: It was actually very wonderful. I have an identical twin sister, so it was like being born with your best friend. I always had somebody to play with. Only my sister and I, when we were growing up, we'd constantly complain that we were not triplets, because we wanted somebody to turn rope. We had to tie it to a tree. I have a brother who is three years older than me; his name is Charles Eugene Taylor.

BEATTIE: And your twin sister's name is?

McCAFFERTY: Beverly June Taylor Herald, and my name is Barbara Jo. So it was like, "Beverly June and Barbara Jo!"

BEATTIE: Did you play the usual identical twin tricks as children?

McCAFFERTY: We didn't do that so much. I've seen pictures of us. We looked unbelievably alike when we were growing up. We went to our twenty-fifth reunion, and people were still calling us "the Taylor twins," which we thought was such a hoot, because we haven't heard anybody call us "the Taylor twins" in years.

BEATTIE: You were always referred to as a plural, right?

McCAFFERTY: Yes, we were, and when we were growing up we had—this is pathetic—we had these diaries. Actually, every page says, "Dear Dairy," because I couldn't spell. "Dear Dairy, We got off school. We went to . . ." and "Our favorite television program is . . ." I mean it's all plural. It's awful.

BEATTIE: You had those identical attitudes about everything?

McCAFFERTY: Very much. I mean, even now, because I guess genetics does play an unbelievable part in your life. It's great, though, because it's like you've got somebody out there being a first reader or a first looker at television and movies, so if Beverly calls up and tells me that there's a great movie on, I know I'll think it's a great movie. And if she says, "I've read this book and I love it," then I'll know I'll read and I'll love it, because we have very, very, close to the same tastes.

BEATTIE: Were you ever involved in the University of Louisville twin studies?

McCAFFERTY: We were. We were there and we loved it, because it got us out of class. They gave us I.Q. tests, and those things were fun to take.

BEATTIE: Did the test results end up fairly close together?

McCAFFERTY: Oh, yes. Our I.Q. is the same. It was two points different, and the difference for an individual is six, so it's the same. Everything we were or did was very much alike, very close. We were only in the studies for maybe a year or so, and my mother decided they were treating us like guinea pigs or freaks or something, and it bothered her. We could care less, but it bothered her, so she took us out of them. We were very disappointed.

BEATTIE: Of course, what they say about twins is, you have the same predispositions, the same likes, dislikes, talents, etcetera, so I was wondering if your sister has any proclivity for writing?

McCAFFERTY: I have always wanted to write since I was about in the third grade. I mean, I won a creative writing contest in the third grade and the prize was a twig.

BEATTIE: A twig?

McCAFFERTY: It was a twig. They said it was a crabapple tree, but it was a twig. They cannot fool me. I know what a twig looks like. Awfullest twig, didn't particularly grow once you set it in the ground. But it was for Arbor Day. Remember Arbor Day when they used to give you trees? Everybody got a tree. Well, our school had budget cutbacks, so they gave only one twig to each grade, and you had to win it by writing a short story, and I won it for the third grade. I remember standing up there. I stood up there with a twig and I thought, "I want to be a writer. This is something I want to do."

Bev does not remember wanting to be a writer that long back, but for English—remember, when they had television English and they would read your papers over the air? Beverly got her stories read, six of them in one year or something, and I got, maybe, four. But it's great having a twin, because Bev was always making a little bit better grades than me. So that kept me focused; otherwise, I probably would have had a much better time.

BEATTIE: Was there, then, a healthy competition between you?

McCAFFERTY: Actually, I don't think Bev and I feel at all competitive now. As we've grown older, we find it odd that people say things that lead us to believe that they expect us to feel very competitive with each other, and I think a lot of twins must. But we don't at all.

BEATTIE: Is she making her first stab at writing?

MCCAFFERTY: She has written what she wrote in school and all that, and she majored in communication, but she's written more sporadically than I have. I just decided to write when I was forty, the year I turned forty, and I took a course from Kentucky writer Betty Layman Receveur. It was one of those weekend things, a hookup with Sidney Sheldon. He was supposed to be able to answer questions at the University of Louisville, and I was around forty then, and Betty Receveur stood up there and said, "If your book is accepted today, it will be two years before you can go into a book store and see it on a shelf." And I thought, "Oh my God, I'm going to be forty-two!" I was thinking, "I'm going to be forty-two," and I was. I was forty-two the day I walked into a book store and saw *Pet Peeves* on the shelf. But it turned out I wrote the book faster and got it published faster than in two years. It got published in a matter of months.

BEATTIE: You said third grade was when you won the writing contest. Is that when you started writing on your own? I mean, other than class assignments?

McCAFFERTY: I have always written on my own, and you know something? I've almost never met a writer that writes just for himself. I wrote things like those diaries, "To Dairy." "Dear Dairy" we kept, and we started keeping, when I was six, so that would have been before the third grade. Then I remember, in summer I would have this sheaf of paper, of poems. I thought, "Oh, a typewriter is so wonderful because you get to see the print on the page," and all that was so great, and I was really surprised. I always wrote. I think it was a way of organizing my thoughts.

BEATTIE: What kind of things did you do as a child?

McCAFFERTY: I wore my brother's clothes. He had great outfits. He had a cowboy outfit, and back then we didn't have boots. I really wanted cowboy boots real bad, and I wanted one of those fringe outfits with Annie Oakley's picture on it. He had a great gun that would shoot, and Bev and I mainly played with Gene's toys. Oh, we climbed trees, and now when I look back, I realize we really took some chances. Near where we lived there was this ravine, and we would swing out on these old, dead roots hanging off trees. It was great fun, but we could have died.

BEATTIE: Did you read much as a child, or were you read to as a child?

McCAFFERTY: Well, believe it or not, when I was little we didn't have books. Mom and Daddy didn't have any books except religious books. They had the eternal struggle between Daddy, who was a Baptist, and Momma, who was the Methodist. Someday I'm going to write this story, because they'd have these huge arguments about which church was the best.

BEATTIE: Which were you raised in?

McCAFFERTY: Methodist. It was Momma's, and Momma was not going to raise her kids Baptist. Yet I think Momma was raised in a Baptist church. Anyway, we were raised Methodists. It was the best, for some reason. So we had *The Book of Life.* The only good book in *The Book of Life* was the pictures of the paintings, which was the Madonna and things like that. Then my parents had a children's book that was *The Children's Stories in the Bible,* and that had pretty pictures, too. It was that and the Bible: the Bible was a little heavy reading for a third grader.

Bev and I remember the day we found out about libraries. We didn't realize there were such places. We didn't go to kindergarten. We just started in first grade and our teacher, Mrs. Gray, walked us down to the library.

BEATTIE: It was a community library?

McCAFFERTY: Uh-huh. You kind of walked like ducks, the big duck and then the little ducks. And we went in, and the lady was telling us about the library. Bev and I are standing right next to each other—we must have been a pathetic sight—and she's telling us everybody's going to have this card and stuff like that, and Bev and I look at each other after she's finished her little speech and go, "Did she say we get to take them home?" Then we could go back . . . and we got three . . . you got to choose three, and you got any of them. You could take any of the books home. We got six. It was just unbelievable. I have always been a reader. I think my kids have always been readers, too. The best stories are in books.

BEATTIE: But you don't know who fostered that love of reading in you, or if anybody did, or if you just sort of had it in you anyway?

McCAFFERTY: My mother didn't read until lately. My father doesn't read much now. My mother now reads just greedily. Her bedroom is lined with bookcases, and she reads everything. I mean everything, from *Anna Karenina* to whatever drips blood all over the page, the latest *True Crime* or whatever. She just reads and reads and reads and reads. But when I was growing up, I don't recall her reading. I read fairly fast, and I picked it up quickly in first grade. But it wasn't like I was reading when I was three or anything.

BEATTIE: Do you remember favorite subjects from elementary school?

McCAFFERTY: In elementary school even I read Agatha Christie. I read all the Agatha Christie's in my high school. When I was little, I read my brother's books. Some of the guys' books back then were a lot more exciting. Gene had one called *Champs on Ice*. It was great! I didn't even know how to play hockey. I'd never seen anybody play hockey, and it was about ice hockey. It was the best book, and I'd love to find that book now.

And I read stuff about magic. I loved magic. Maybe that's why I like mysteries now, because of the illusion. In school I experienced what is kind of like that Advanced Program, but it was a class that you took called Exploratory. You got selected to go to this in probably about the seventh grade. In Exploratory you got to do whatever you wanted to do, which was, for me, write. And I did magic. I did this huge notebook on Houdini and I included all these little tricks on how to do it and all that. I just thought that was fascinating.

BEATTIE: What about junior high and high school? What do you remember about those years?

McCAFFERTY: I was a geek.

BEATTIE: I assume your sister was, too.

McCAFFERTY: Yes, we were twin geeks. We'd be Geek One, Geek Two. The Geek set. Perhaps I'm still a geek; I don't recall being popular at all. They made fun of us for everything. Bev ruined the curve. Well, we both ruined the curve. Everybody was making fifty percent on a test, and Bev would make 103 percent, because she'd make the extra credits, so you had to hate her. And if it wasn't for Beverly, they would have hated me, because she only made three points ahead of me. I wouldn't get the extra credit. I would just get the hundred, so if it wasn't for her, I would have really ruined the curve. But our classmates were mad, because since the top score was 103, then they got minus three. And they made fun of us, because we had glasses. They went around calling us four-eyes. Anyway, they went around, just teasing us, and we were real skinny and all that. One of our major torturers was this girl who had freckles, so Beverly called her Spatter Face. So people started calling this classmate "Spatter Face."

BEATTIE: Don't you have your character Haskell Blevins being called that by somebody?

McCAFFERTY: That's right. That's from high school.

BEATTIE: True life pays off.

McCAFFERTY: Oh, yes. You know, almost every little detail in your life eventually shows up in your books, I think. It's a well that you kind of dip down into or something. And I identify somewhat with Haskell, because he is judged a great deal on his looks; in high school you are judged on your looks. Particularly in high school. I think a lot in our society you're judged on your looks.

BEATTIE: I think all through life. I think adolescents just don't know how to contain their judgments in high school. Getting back to talking about your high school years, was English your favorite subject?

McCAFFERTY: No. Now, isn't that odd? I had an English teacher by the name of Mrs. Warren who read to us some, and I hate being read to. She read Shakespeare, and at the time I wasn't into Shakespeare. I learned to like Shakespeare once I got into U. of L., but in high school I didn't like it.

I really didn't start liking English until I went to the University of Louisville, and then I found all the courses that I took as electives were English. They just got to be more and more English. I really loved it. I remember telling the Shakespeare instructor that Shakespeare, to me, was like reading a mystery story, because you went through and picked up clues as to what Shakespeare was really saying and what he was trying to get across, and I decided that some of the plots were inverses of each other, like *Romeo and Juliet* is really the inverse of *Hamlet,* because *Hamlet* is the revenge story with the love story in the background, and *Romeo and Juliet* with the love story in the front has the revenge theme in the background. It was like the twist. So I did a whole paper on that. He loved it. He gave me an A+, and I'd never thought about Shakespeare's works being mysteries, but it helped me. You know, you went through and could pull out all the things that would substantiate your arguments for one thing or another.

BEATTIE: So literary analysis was something you really enjoyed.

McCAFFERTY: I loved it.

BEATTIE: You went straight from high school to U. of L., is that right?

MCCAFFERTY: Yes, I did, only I only went there for two years at first. I got a President's Scholarship. You had to take a test, the entrance exam. They gave it to a bunch of people that qualified at every school in Kentucky, and the top twelve got a scholarship for that year. Bev and I were among the top twelve, so we both went. When she got the letter and opened it first, I thought, "I'm going to have to absolutely scream!" And I did. We had to talk our parents into letting us go to college, because my mother went to school through the seventh grade, and my father went through the ninth grade.

They're wonderful country people, you know. They're terrific, but they did not see at that time that an education was something that a woman needed. As a matter of fact, my father told me—he has since recanted all of this—that a woman didn't need a college education. She barely needed a high school education, didn't need a college education because her husband was going to support her. Women, he believed, also didn't need a driver's license. I didn't get my driver's license until I was twenty-three. I was already married. My husband taught me to drive. It's probably how come the marriage didn't last.

Anyway, I went to the University of Louisville for two years on scholarship. We couldn't qualify for finances, because by that time my father was doing very well as a foreman, so we could only qualify as academics. You had to be in the top four to get your scholarship renewed . . . to get a Trustee's Scholarship, and Bev and I were third and fourth. So we got that renewed for the next year, and then the next year Beverly did not. She was fifth or something, and I did receive the scholarship. They gave me the scholarship, and I turned it down to get married to a man that I was to divorce twelve years later. How dumb can a smart girl be?

BEATTIE: Do you remember professors who most influenced you in college?

McCAFFERTY: I started taking English when I went back. When I got my divorce in 1980, I had one more year to get my degree, because I had taken courses off and on to complete my third year. When I got my divorce, I realized that I had three children to support at that time, ages eleven, nine and two, and I thought, "If I don't finish this degree, I will be working for the rest of my life, and will never, ever finish it." I got a grant for a Displaced Homemaker, because I'd been at home for so long. The grant title sounded like somebody had shouldered their way ahead of you in line, you know, like, "Get out of my way! This is my spot!" Anyway, but I got a grant and went back to school, and when I went back to school that second time, I was older, and I had changed my major from elementary education.

By that time, it was like, "What can I get a degree in fast, because I have these kids, and I can only . . ." I had enough maintenance [alimony] . . . I love the term *maintenance*, too. It sounded like you were on life support, with a tube or something. So, the quickest thing for me to get a degree in was art, by that time, because I had finished up most of the requirements, but all the electives that I took were in English, every one of them. And there was an English teacher, my Shakespeare teacher, that I really, really liked, because about a month into the class he asked everybody to raise their hands as to who was having difficulty reading these plays. I did not know what the plays were saying, and I raised my hand. I mean, it was like I was reading a foreign language. And my professor said, "Keep on reading," and he was right, because in a matter of weeks, all of a sudden Shakespeare's writing was beautiful and interesting, and complex, and you started noticing all the humor. Everything that was in Shakespeare, I really enjoyed. I wish I had been able to hang around longer. I thought about going back and getting a master's degree just so I could play with Shakespeare some more. I was twenty when I got married.

BEATTIE: What was your husband's name?

McCAFFERTY: Richard Clark Taylor. He was from Schenectady, New York. He was twenty-two.

BEATTIE: Did you meet him at the University?

McCAFFERTY: At the University of Louisville. He was very tall, had red hair; he looks just exactly like my son. He's about 6'5." Actually, to show you how incompatible we were, if that's a word, he had no sense of humor at all. Almost none. He had an inability to laugh at himself or others. Particularly at himself, though. He was brilliant. He taught himself computer programming and was a programmer at General Electric, and then he became the vice president for Marshall Fields in Chicago doing their computer things. And his sons, our sons, one looks just like him. They're both 6'6," and both of them are fascinated by computers. Both of them are studying programming now, and if they're at all intelligent, it's because of him.

BEATTIE: When you divorced, all the children remained with you?

McCAFFERTY: Yes. And they expected meals, a roof over their heads, the whole thing. They're so picky . . .

BEATTIE: What happened when you left U. of L. the first time?

McCAFFERTY: I went to get married. I figure that I have led every role for women in this society. I have been single, and then I have been young married with no kids, what is it, double-income-no-kids? DINKS. I was a DINK very briefly, and then I was a working mom, after Geoff was born, and I did that for about three years. I was a secretary and editorial assistant at General Electric. Then I went home and had two more children, so then I was a homemaker and mom.

BEATTIE: You didn't work during that time?

McCAFFERTY: Not at all. So that's how I got misplaced. The children grew up, and then when they were about . . . well, they weren't really very old—eleven and nine—Rachael was just, she was probably still toddling around in diapers when I got the divorce. We were living in Indiana then, and I moved back into Louisville and went back to school. It took me a year. I had an art degree with an English minor, and I started working as a copywriter for an ad agency, Schneider, Demuth Advertising, in downtown Louisville. I worked there until one day they came in to me and said, "You're the only person in this office who has an art degree, so why don't we make you art director?" I worked as an art director-copywriter for, all told, eight years there, and then I had been telling myself that writing all those words in ads was the same as being a writer, and eventually, I realized I was lying.

BEATTIE: Is that work you enjoyed?

McCAFFERTY: Very much. I still keep up with it, because now I enter contests. I enter a lot of writing contests, like twenty-five words or less, and I have won a lot of them. I win them frequently. I've won one with *Woman's Day,* I've won one with Amore Cat Food. I won second prize, which was a mere thousand dollars, for writing why I can't eat just one Lay's potato chip. But I think it helps to win these things to have been a copywriter. That part of the job I enjoyed very, very much.

BEATTIE: When did you start writing short stories on your own?

McCAFFERTY: I published my first short story in *Alfred Hitchcock* magazine in '86. I had sent in about four or five stories to them before they accepted one. When Christopher was a baby when I was home the first time, it was just before my divorce, and I started sending things in. I was typing them—it wasn't even on a word processor, it was a typewriter. I got a letter from the editors at *Redbook* that was encouraging, and all of a sudden everything went up in the air, because I got a divorce, and I had to actually go out and make money. Oh, that nasty stuff. So I just put everything on hold, and then when I started working and everything sort of settled back down, instead of going to the Galleria at lunch time and spending my money, I decided to stay in and start writing, and I almost had a heart attack when *Alfred Hitchcock* finally accepted one of my stories. Then they started accepting them more and more, so by the time that I got one story in *Redbook,* I had about five in *Hitchcock.* And I hadn't written that many, because I didn't have a whole lot of time.

Anyway, so I went home and I wrote this manuscript, and then I saw this ad for a private eye novel, and I had had a story rejected from *Hitchcock* that was the plot for *Pet Peeves.* It was written from the viewpoint of the murderer, and I got a letter from the editor that said she liked a whole lot of the colloquialisms, but she didn't buy it. She didn't believe it. I thought the reason why she didn't believe it was because it was only fifteen pages, and if I had two hundred pages, I bet I could sell her. So that's what I did. Then I saw this private eye, I thought, "Well, it would be better if that story was told from the private eye's viewpoint, rather than from the viewpoint of the murderer, because then you're not put in the position of trying to be sympathetic with somebody who has killed somebody." Then I added all of the humor and made up Haskell Blevins and sent him in to the Private Eye contest, and got him back without even so much as a rejection slip or anything, after months. By this time—this is a long story—the short story had come out in *Redbook* and, unbelievably, a literary agent wrote me through *Redbook* and asked if I had a novel, and said he was impressed with the short story that had been in *Redbook*. I sent him *Pet Peeves,* and he sold it for me. The only trouble is, by that time, I was looking for a job.

BEATTIE: What was your *Redbook* story?

McCAFFERTY: It was called "Momma Was Right," but that was not my title. It appeared first in *Hitchcock.* It was picked up as a reprint. Mine was called "Motion Sickness," and it was about a woman who was like Yuri Geller. She could move things with her mind, and it became an illness for her. It ended unhappily. I mean, anybody that's ever read it, they would repeat the last two words in the thing, or the last sentence, which was, "And I bent them." They would go, "I read your story, and 'I bent them.'" And I thought, "Ooh, that did have an impact."

BEATTIE: Is it a mystery?

McCAFFERTY: Yes, and it was in the October issue, I think it was their Halloween issue, because it wasn't a solving-type logic mystery; it is just a sequence of events.

BEATTIE: The agent that picked you up, is that the agent you have since been with?

McCAFFERTY: Uh-huh. He's a good guy. His name is Richard Parks. He used to be with Curtis-Brown [publisher], and he went out on his own, so he was looking for new, beginning writers, and he got me an option on *Pet Peeves* with John Ritter's production company, and for a while there they were going to make it into a television series. Now I think that project's dead, because John Ritter's doing another television series. And Richard Parks has just been very energetic, and from what I hear from other people, very attentive, as far as an agent is concerned.

BEATTIE: Did your getting an advance for *Pet Peeves* alleviate the necessity of having a full-time job?

McCAFFERTY: Well, what was nice about it was that I got enough from *Pet Peeves* as an advance, and then they gave me a contract for the next book all at once. So I knew that each step of the way I'd be getting a little bit more, because they divide it up. It's sort of like carrots they hold out for you. So far, it's just like there's always been another book to do, there's always been another advance. Now I've decided that I wanted to write as a woman, and I want to have more income, so I've started this new series. Pocket Books is no longer doing any more series. Jane Chelius is my editor. She's a wonderful editor. I found out that she's terrific from dealing with other editors. But she told me that they're not doing any more series. That she kind of hated, but she knew it was going to sell, because I met her at a mystery convention, and she asked, "Who did you sell that book to?" It sold to Dutton the first time out, right away.

BEATTIE: In the meantime you had remarried.

McCAFFERTY: Right. I got married in '82 to John Alexander McCafferty. He's got a graphic design business now. When we met he was a freelance graphic design artist, and he now has John McCafferty Advertising and Graphic Design. It's in Louisville. He has two buildings, side by side. One sort of an apartment building that has some offices in it, and then one is a complete office business that's on Floyd Street.

He came in the agency I worked for when I was art director, and as art director a lot of times you freelance, and I met him through that. In fact, I met him almost the first day I started working in 1980.

BEATTIE: I assume the book contracts and the fact that you were remarried helped you think that you could write on your own full-time.

McCAFFERTY: Right. And now what I'm making is just about the same as I was making at the ad agency, which is unbelievable. If I ever thought that I could have done this at home and been home with the kids, I would have tried it a lot earlier. Of course, then, at one time there weren't word processors like there are now, and now I've got a laser printer that kicks it out pretty fast and all that, so it's like all this technology you get to take home with you.

BEATTIE: Do you find that you miss just seeing other people in an office environment?

McCAFFERTY: I think occasionally I do feel bad, I feel somewhat isolated, but not lately, because my publisher has been sending me to these conventions, and there are book fairs and things like that, that they send you to. Then you get inundated with people. I'm very comfortable being by myself. I've been a part of a group my whole life. I've always had somebody there, so I think maybe my other need to have somebody has been very well satisfied. Also, my sister and I are very close, and I think that being a twin spoils you a lot, because you meet somebody when you open your eyes that understands perfectly how you're feeling, because that also happens to be the way she feels. Whatever you say to her she understands. I think I could tell Bev, as a mystery writer, "I shot somebody," and she'd say, "I understand." As a matter of fact, there really isn't enough time to get all my work done. Time goes by extremely fast when I'm writing. It just sails by. I've often said that writing is a lot like dreaming, only your eyes are open. It's like all of a sudden you wake up and it's four to five to six to eight hours later, and it just went by very, very quickly.

BEATTIE: What are your writing habits?

McCAFFERTY: I generally get up and start writing, sometimes still in my robe. It is not a pretty sight. Right now I'm on a deadline, because I have a book that's due June 15th, so I am writing from about, oh, 7:30 in the morning to nine, ten at night, but that generally isn't the way it goes. I have the book completely in my mind.

BEATTIE: Plotted but not written?

McCAFFERTY: Yes. I read that Agatha Christie said, she was with a friend, and she turned to her and she goes, "I just finished the book I'm working on." And her friend goes, "Oh, then you've sent it to the publisher?" And she goes, "Oh, no; I haven't written it yet." That's me. I finished this book, but I haven't written it yet. I write while Rachael's [McCafferty's daughter] in school, generally, and sometimes I sleep late. Usually you can tell from looking at me. I work 9:00 to 3:30, something like that. That's ideal. I don't give myself hours to write, so much as I give myself words to produce. About two thousand a day.

BEATTIE: What is the process of your revision? Do you do that as you write or after the fact or both?

McCAFFERTY: I write, and then I go back over it and, I've told my sister, it's like dough. It's like bread dough. You push it out and then you go back and you push it out and you get it stretched out. With mine I write, and then I go back a little bit and write forward, and everything that I don't feel comfortable about I go back and rewrite. Right now I've got the first part of the book that's fine that I will not read again until it's over, but about one chapter back of where I'm at right now, I will read again today. Then halfway through the book sometimes I want to change something, and I want to fore- shadow something or add something, so then I'll go all the way back and put it in.

BEATTIE: Is Pigeon Fork a thinly veiled Lebanon Junction, Kentucky?

McCAFFERTY: Well, not really. I live between two small towns. I live off the road between Lebanon Junction, but I moved some of the buildings in Shepherdsville. The Main Street of Shepherdsville . . .

BEATTIE: It's a combination of the two towns, then.

McCAFFERTY: Uh-huh. And yet, some of the stores have closed since I wrote about them. They're still open in Pigeon Fork, but they're gone in Shepherdsville. Like there was a "Somebody's New and Hardly Used Furniture" that was there in Shepherdsville, and it's gone. They used to bring all the furniture out on good days so that you had to stumble around them on the sidewalk.

BEATTIE: Are beehive hairdos still rampant in both places?

McCAFFERTY: Well, they're not really, although I have said that you see clothes there that you haven't seen since the '50s.

BEATTIE: Because they *are* '50s clothes.

MCCAFFERTY: Yes. I love Pigeon, I love Shepherdsville, because, you know, you can look really terrible and there'll be somebody that looks worse! I love that place! I'm just crazy about it!

BEATTIE: Would you tell me about how you came to create your protagonist, Haskell Blevins, and why you chose to write from a male point of view?

McCAFFERTY: I was trying to come up with somebody original, and I wanted somebody that was unlike any of the detectives that I had ever read about before, so that was Haskell, somebody that looked like Howdy-Doody and that was not drop-dead handsome and did not know how to behave with women, because the detectives on television always knew what to say, and I got so sick of that. So that was one reason.

Also, I wanted somebody that you could more identify with than all these people that are perfect, and then I thought that it would be interesting to have him be divorced. I also wanted to say something about judging people solely by appearances, because if you looked at Haskell you would think that he was a country bumpkin, but he is not. He is a very intelligent man behind Howdy-Doody's face, and really kind of a sweet and caring man.

The reason why I gave him the dog, Rip, is because I realized after I'd started writing that Haskell was going to do pages and pages and pages of complaining. I thought he might sound like he is whining all the time about what happened during the divorce: nobody likes him, he can't get any work, and he lives over his brother's . . . and he's having to mope. I just thought he would get to be such a whiner that I wanted to show a part of him in which he was being really a caring human being. I thought I could do that with the dog. Here is a dog that is a waste of breath, but Haskell obviously loves him, loves him enough to run home, and to carry him in and out of the house. I hoped that you would see Haskell as being really pretty much unselfish.

BEATTIE: It gives him another outlet to whine about the dog, too.

McCAFFERTY: Well, it does. He does whine about the dog, but you can kind of tell that he loves this dog. Also, I loved Rip, and I wanted to make Rip a personality, too. He has the same neurosis as my dog, Hector.

BEATTIE: Is your house similarly situated to Haskell's?

McCAFFERTY: It is. I live in Haskell's house. Well, I was writing this real fast. I wrote *Pet Peeves* in eight weeks for this contest, so I had no time to do any research or anything, so I used everything that was around me. My whole thing was trying to come up with originality, and so I looked in my living room and I had a dog that was afraid to go up and down stairs. He's afraid of linoleum, he's afraid of kitchen cabinets, he was born in this house.

BEATTIE: Fear of linoleum?

McCAFFERTY: Yes, I don't know what his problem is. He got over the going up and down stairs after about a year, but about the time that he learned his name, I think it's because his brain is so small, once he found out what his name was, it shoved out his being afraid to go up and down steps. It's sort of like a little cup that sloshed over the side. So about the time he finally figured out that his name was Hector, then he stopped being afraid to go up and down steps. So I had him, and then I live in an A-frame with a deck around it, and I live up a real steep hill that everybody complains about, and although my house is bigger, because I live with more people than Haskell, it's much the same, and I hadn't read of any detectives who lived in an A-frame up a hill.

BEATTIE: Do you, as does Haskell, refer to your house as the Bermuda Rectangle?

McCAFFERTY: No. I used to call my husband's office that because it is the worst. John put it on his bulletin board that, "This is the Bermuda Rectangle. Enter at your peril," so I just put that in my book. It was like everything that I thought of that was funny, I put in *Pet Peeves*. Then when my publisher wanted a new book, I thought, "Oh, my God!"

BEATTIE: You were talking about writing *Pet Peeves* for a contest. What contest was it?

McCAFFERTY: It was the Private Eye Association of America. It has a contest every year, and it's for a new private eye novel. I don't know if they still do it, but it was with St. Martin's Press, I believe. I'd heard it was so difficult to get your novel read that, I thought, "Well, entering a contest would make it definite that you'd get your manuscript read. But they were looking for a hard-boiled novel, and Haskell's not hard-boiled. In fact, he's not even soft-boiled. In fact, I've told people . . .

BEATTIE: Scrambled maybe.

McCAFFERTY: No, he's poached. He's a poached detective.

BEATTIE: We've discussed the fact that Haskell Blevins notices everything about everybody, what they're wearing, what they look like, how they speak, etcetera, and of course his character comments with a constant, sardonic sense of humor. I'm wondering if you regard people the same way, or do you see that as a stereotypically feminine trait?

McCAFFERTY: Well, I think that the nice thing about writing is that you can put in words what you've always thought, but what you would never say.

BEATTIE: And ascribe those words to somebody else.

McCAFFERTY: Yes. It's kind of like an outlet, because you know how when you're in a conversation, and you're thinking something that you don't want to tell, sometimes it's complimentary, but sometimes it isn't. It gives me an outlet for my nasty side or something. I have never really thought about whether women are more observant than men until you mentioned it, but I think you're probably right, that women notice more.

BEATTIE: More personal things, perhaps.

McCAFFERTY: I notice more details when I'm looking for details, because details define character a lot. My editor told me that I am very good at characterization, and I think it's because I notice things about people that are unique to that person, and that's what I try to find out. When I'm trying to come up with a new character, what I do is I walk around, or sometimes I sit around in a mall, and I watch people go by. I mean, it's easy to find somebody that's different, and yet who sort of represents a stereotype at the same time. Haskell probably is more observant than I am when I'm not writing.

BEATTIE: In what ways are you like Haskell, or do you identify with him?

McCAFFERTY: He and I have the exact same sense of humor. The exact same. The things that he thinks are funny, I think are funny. I do have a sense of humor, and my family has a sense of humor. I think what I got from my parents is that my mother and father are funny people, and they are funny all the time. My sons now have girlfriends, and they go visit their houses, and they say, "You know, other people's houses are not full of laughter like our house is." Or Bev's kids have gone and visited her in-laws, and they then come and visit my parents, and they go, "Your mom and daddy are always joking and laughing." I think that my parents have given me a view of the world that sees things humorously, even really sad things.

BEATTIE: Your writing style is the swift, clipped, declarative sentence style of the mystery writer or, as you say, of poached instead of hard-boiled detective fiction. Is that a style that comes naturally to you, or is it a style you developed in order to write in that genre?

McCAFFERTY: I think it comes naturally to me, because I know that the difference between the character that I'm writing now and Haskell is that this woman, she doesn't have as many colloquialisms in her vocabulary, but she has the same sense of humor, and she writes. I would say my books are humorous mysteries, because Haskell is so unlike a detective, a private eye. He's almost like an ordinary citizen doing investigations rather than a private eye. He does have a little bit more technical background that would help him, but it doesn't help him, really. I've tried to come up with cases that are, to start out with, bizarre. Like break-ins that don't have anything taken, or a kidnapping victim and she's still there, or the triple homicide in which two of the victims are pets, and the fourth one is a taxidermist that comes running in to Haskell Blevins and says, "The animals in the woods are trying to kill me because they're mad at what I've done to their relatives!" So Haskell thinks he's crazy and doesn't want to take the case, because he thinks the taxidermist could use his money better to get psychiatric help. It's always something like that, and the violence is off-screen for the most part. I'm very close to what they call a malice-domestic writer, rather than a writer of private eye novels. Haskell Blevins doesn't quite fit in, and the people that really like him are generally people that read Joan Hess and Charlotte MacLeod, writers I've been compared to. They're kind of folksy; the private eye is almost a misnomer.

BEATTIE: The fact that you didn't write your first novel until you were forty is certainly a good role model for women and writers who feel as though if they haven't tried something by the time they're forty, they might as well not do it.

McCAFFERTY: I know, that's so absurd. That is just so absurd. People come up to me, and most of the people that are writers or would-be writers want me to tell them there's an easy answer. I wish I could say at forty I just decided to sit down and write a book. But for me to do that at forty, I had to do a lot of studying and reading and finding out how to write up until I got to be forty.

BEATTIE: Who or what was your best educator for writing?

McCAFFERTY: Reading other people's things, the English courses that I took. There are so many unbelievable writers out there that are great, you know. Sylvia Plath for one, she was funny. I mean, for a woman who committed suicide, *The Bell Jar* is a funny book. It is hilarious. In fact, that's what really breaks your heart, is that that woman with that kind of sense of humor would have killed herself.

Anyway, people never want to hear this, but I read every single writing book in the library. I read every one of them.

BEATTIE: Is that how-to types of writing books?

McCAFFERTY: Uh-huh. 801.2 is where it is in the library. I read everything on how to write, and then once you've read all that, such books start repeating themselves, so then you start reading other people's novels and seeing how they use the information in those how-to books. How all the little rules, how they broke them or how they didn't break them, how they work. One of the best books is *Techniques of Fiction,* which my dog tore up in my backyard. I got to keep it, because I had to buy it from the library. But it was great, because it would say different ways of doing things. Then it would have authors you could read, like Faulkner.

I liked *The Great Gatsby.* I went on a Fitzgerald kick for a while there, massively. I read everything that he wrote, and then I started reading Zelda Fitzgerald. I started reading everything that she wrote. I did a kick with Sylvia Plath, too. I went back to the libraries and went to when she was first writing for *Mademoiselle,* and I read the first short story she got published. I read all of the things she wrote when she was looking like a hopeful, young person. Her life was so fascinating. It really was. I have a feeling that living it was nowhere near as fascinating as reading about it. I read everything that I could.

BEATTIE: This was all in your thirties or twenties?

McCAFFERTY: It was in my thirties. I read a lot of nonfiction, too, and I read strange books like *Life After Life,* you know, Raymond Moody, and the Kubler-Ross book, *On Death and Dying.* All of that stuff is fascinating.

I like to read the bizarre, and then I like to read what they call "classics." I always wonder about classics, because what we consider classics today may not be classics tomorrow, because what they considered classics yesterday, quite a few of them are no longer classics today. So mainly, it's, "Read this book." Some of the books that are classics I have really incredibly enjoyed, and some of them, like *Moby Dick,* I did not. Well, I read all of *Moby Dick,* and I was beginning to cheer for the fish.

BEATTIE: How do you come up with your plots, and how much of your plots are planned?

McCAFFERTY: Oh, I have an outline.

BEATTIE: You do outline everything before you write?

McCAFFERTY: *Pet Peeves* was a short story, so I knew exactly what that was. Then I had to come up with an outline for the second book, and you send it in and they approve it. Once I'd done *Pet Peeves,* I just sent in outlines. I could not believe it. It was such a scam. My outlines are very detailed, or else I'd probably panic. But I have about a thirty-page outline that's everything that happens, almost, and some description of the characters and everything, and even a little conversation is in these chapters. It reads almost like a short story, only it's all in present tense.

BEATTIE: And if you didn't need that outline to sell the book?

McCAFFERTY: I'd probably still do it. I'd probably do it writing mysteries, because the fun for me is not . . . a lot of people say they don't like doing an outline because it spoils the book, but for me, it's a map; it's not the journey. It tells me where I'm going, but it doesn't tell me how to get there.

BEATTIE: Mysteries are so plot-oriented, it would be hard to let the plot evolve if you didn't know it from the beginning.

McCAFFERTY: I've only written one short story that I didn't know how it was going to end. I had an ending, but as I was writing it, another ending occurred to me almost at the end, and I changed the whole thing and had to go back to the beginning and change it a little to accommodate that ending.

BEATTIE: You talked about your new book series.

McCAFFERTY: It's going to be written under a pseudonym, because Pocket Books had a kind of window in which they own the name Taylor McCafferty three months before and three months after each published book, and it's too much to schedule another book around that window. So, they're going to publish two of this new series, and the new name's going to be Tierney McClellan.

BEATTIE: Did your publisher come up with that name, or did you?

McCAFFERTY: My agent did. Actually, I came up with "T" names and "McC" names, and he put the two together for me. The reason why I use Taylor McCafferty is because Barbara Taylor Bradford was already Barbara Taylor, so I dropped Barbara Taylor. I dropped Barbara and just used Taylor. Besides, I thought it would be like Taylor Caldwell.

BEATTIE: Do you ever go by Taylor, other than professionally?

McCAFFERTY: No, never have.

BEATTIE: But friends and family call you . . .

McCAFFERTY: Barbara.

BEATTIE: Are you having to switch between writing projects for your different book series, or do you finish one and then start another?

McCAFFERTY: I find it a lot easier to try to get one done. Also, the Schuyler books are not quite as funny, or are not meant to be quite as funny, as the Haskells. I started out writing Haskell as entertainment, and meant him to be entertaining. The Schuylers are . . . she's a little bit more crabby. She's sort of like . . . you know how Sue Grafton's books are not funny, but they have funny moments?

BEATTIE: Are there other types of books you would like to write, or do you have any desire to write in other genres?

McCAFFERTY: Well, I have thought about writing just a mainstream novel. I still will write short stories. I probably will get back to that. In fact, I'd like to write a few, maybe. The bad thing about a short story is you get to where you really like a character, like I like this character that owns the store, and she's gone in fifteen pages. Whereas, if you write a book about her, she's around for two hundred and fifty pages.

BEATTIE: What about sense of place in your writing? Of course, you set your books in Kentucky, and a lot of the colloquialisms and that sort of thing depend on your settings. How important do you think sense of place is in your writing?

McCAFFERTY: Oh, I think it's very, very important, particularly now, since they're publishing regional mysteries. I think one of the reasons why *Pet Peeves* was picked up to be published in the first place is because it was not set in California or New York or, now, Chicago, that already have a lot of mysteries set in those areas. When they put out a map for Sisters in Crime, an organization I'm a member of, an organization of women mystery writers, they put out this big map, and everybody that has a series was dotted on it, and I was the only dot in Kentucky. I think that's great. I mean, to be able to write about this area is terrific, and I think Kentucky is charming. I think it's a beautiful state. I'm proud to be from here.

I'm not sure whether I'm doing this, but I want, in my writing, to dispel the notion that Kentuckians walk around without shoes, and that we're all illiterate. Haskell may be a country person, but he is an intelligent country person. And Schuyler, she lives in Louisville and she's from Kentucky, but she is a fairly aware woman with very definite opinions. She does not have to be dragged kicking and screaming into the twentieth century. She lives here. It's just so irritating to have . . . it's a kind of a prejudice. It's another way of separating people. So much of how we define people is we define our differences rather than come up with our samenesses. I don't understand that.

I do have people call me because I'm in a small town. I'm the only McCafferty there. They can look me up. So they call me and they say a few words, or it's somebody who wants to write, and my heart goes out to anybody who wants to write. I know how difficult it is to break into this field. I know what the odds are, I also know how much effort you have to put in. I can talk to somebody for five minutes and tell you whether they'll be able to write or not. It's how much they want to do it. You can see it in their eyes.

BEATTIE: A lot of people want to have written, but they do not want to go through the work of writing.

McCAFFERTY: People don't even want to have written. They want to be a writer. They want to have that persona. They don't want to do any of that other stuff, and some of them, you think they want to do something that they perceive makes you a great deal of money, and sometimes it doesn't, or they want to do something they perceive makes you famous and gets you a lot of attention. But as far as being alone with only yourself and a piece of paper, there are a lot of people who don't want to have to go through that part at all.

BEATTIE: I wanted to ask you what you think the nature of creativity itself might be.

McCAFFERTY: You know what I think it is? I kind of rail against the word "creativity," because it sounds like you can do something God-like and make something from nothing, and I'm not sure that anybody can do that. But I think for me, what I write is being able to make connections; one thing reminds me of another. So the humor that I bring out, I hope, if it's funny, is to make a connection between one thing and another, like so-and-so looked like somebody. All that meaningless trivia that I never thought I would use I can now use in my books.

I think everybody makes connections, and everybody tells stories. Conversation is stories. Some people sit down and put it on paper and organize it a little better and read about how to do it, and they eventually start making money from it. But if you run into anybody, they will tell you a story. They'll tell you a story on an airplane and they'll tell you a story at parties, and they'll tell you a story if you run into them anywhere. They'll tell you what they did, and sometimes their stories are boring. Sometimes their stories are fascinating, and everybody gathers around, and sometimes their stories are funny.

Our television is nothing but stories. Our movies are stories. Everything that we do, the way we communicate with each other, the thing that sets us apart from the rest of the animal kingdom is sitting around telling each other stories. It's the way we relate to each other.

The whole thing is tales. It's tales and tales and tales until we die. Even at our funerals, they will tell a story. They will get up and tell a story of our life, and it will probably be terribly boring.

BEATTIE: Do you think that is to give order and meaning to life?

McCAFFERTY: Uh-huh, and I think it's because we are all isolated. It's a way to make a connection with each other. My books are about the connections that I make when describing somebody like somebody else, and I want to bring out humor in connections. I think that's what fiction and all of it is about, to try to connect with each other, and ultimately, hopefully, one day we'll try to understand and not be so intolerant, and maybe not emphasize our differences like we do now.

May 21, 1993

Books by Taylor McCafferty

Pet Peeves. New York: Pocket Books, 1990.

Ruffled Feathers. New York: Pocket Books, 1992.

Bed Bugs. New York: Pocket Books, 1993.

Thin Skins. New York: Pocket Books, 1994.

Hanky Panky. New York: Pocket Books, 1995.

[McClellan, Tierney.] *Heir Condition*. New York: NAL/Dutton, 1995.

[McClellan, Tierney.] *Closing Statement*. New York: NAL/Dutton, 1995.

[McClellan, Tierney.] *A Killing in Real Estate*. New York: NAL/Dutton, 1995.

Herald, Beverly Taylor, and Taylor McCafferty. *Double Murder*. New York: Pocket Books, 1996.

ED MCCLANAHAN

McCLANAHAN: Edward Poage McClanahan is my name, and I was born in Brooksville, Kentucky in 1932.

My father's name was Edward L. McClanahan. He was a Standard Oil distributor most of the rest of his life. In the late 1940s he got into the river towing business, and he owned portions of tow boats, barges, and so forth. My mother is Jessie Poage McClanahan. She lives right now in Campbellsburg, Kentucky. Both my parents were from Bracken County.

My grandfather, Jesse Poage, was a kind of closet writer. He only had about an eighth grade education, but he had read for the law. He was a Shakespeare fan, and he read Shakespeare a lot. He attempted to write epic poems. I still have a few little fragments of them. He once undertook, for a while, to write a history of Bracken County, and I still have some bits and pieces of that. And, although he died when I was four, he has always been a kind of shining example to me. He raised eight children on a salary that never rose above eight hundred dollars a year, and all eight of his children got a year in college. He said that was the best he could do, and then they were on their own after that. He was a grand man, I think.

I never really knew too much about my father's father. He was a farmer. My father's people were farmers, basically. My paternal grandfather died, as did my other grandfather, when I was very young. Both my grandmothers lived to a great age. Both of them were ninety-two when they died, so I knew them both very, very well. They were wonderful old ladies; they were just great. But my aunts, especially my aunts on my mother's side, were a really major influence on me, because of the six girls in that family, five were school teachers. I was an only child, and oddly enough, although my grandmother had eight children, she only had two grandchildren, me and my cousin, who was born when her mother was well into her forties. So for many years, for all my formative years, I was the only nephew or niece, and consequently, I got a lot of attention, and from a bunch of school teachers, too.

I had one aunt, who just died a year ago—my aunt Leila—who was something of an intellectual, and a literary intellectual at that. She had a master's degree in English education, from UK [University of Kentucky], and she also had a law degree from UK. She never practiced law and never took the bar. She was a high school English teacher, but also, for several years, a college English teacher. When I was a very small child, she used to read to me a lot. She read Shelley and Keats even, I think, before I could read myself. She used to read me to sleep at nap time. I can remember even now.

BEATTIE: Did your mother read to you as well?

McCLANAHAN: My mother did read to me, but it's my aunt's reading to me that I specifically remember. You would never think so to look at me now, but I was puny when I was little, and consequently, I didn't start first grade until I was almost seven. The year before that I had my tonsils taken out, and then I became anything but puny. But, by the time I started school, thanks to all these aunts and to a mother who was also an elementary school teacher, I basically could read before I ever started school, which was very unusual in a rural, small-town school like Brooksville. Being an only child, I guess reading was my entertainment.

Most of my early childhood was spent in Brooksville, although we did live for a few years in Augusta, Kentucky. I do a little writer's conference up in Augusta every October. But anyway, I grew up in Brooksville, and there has been a time in my life when I thought about that as a terrible burden. In fact, the town shaped me in ways that were hugely important to me. In retrospect, I loved my childhood. It wasn't necessarily all that delightful at the time, but if you're bookish in a community like that, you get heat.

By the time I was in the eighth or ninth grade, I was really coming out a lot. I got a lot taller and I made the basketball team, and things were really looking up. Then, just at the beginning of my sophomore year in high school, we moved to Maysville. And, I mean, it was like moving to Paris, France, from my point of view. I thought Maysville, which of course was only twenty miles away from Brooksville, was just a metropolitan paradise. I found a whole new identity in Maysville. Oh, you know how it is when you're a new kid who comes into school, and you're suddenly more popular than you ever dreamed you'd be. I had a great time in Maysville. High school was a wonderful time for me. For two of the three years that I was in high school in Maysville, we lived right downtown, less than a block from the high school, less than a block from this wonderful movie theater there, straight across the street from the drugstore where everybody hung out, and where I worked as a soda jerk for a couple of years.

I had a car, and that enhanced my popularity. I played basketball when I was a sophomore. I wasn't really any good, and Maysville was good. They had an absolutely red-hot basketball team then. I made the team my sophomore year, and then I got cut in the first week of practice in my junior year, and I was secretly relieved. I never was really an athlete at all. But I had a good time in high school. It was wonderful.

BEATTIE: From elementary school through high school, do you remember favorite teachers, or did writing emerge as a favorite subject early on?

McCLANAHAN: I literally have wanted to write all of my conscious life. I mean, I've toyed with other ideas. I used to like to draw, and I thought maybe I'd want to try to be an artist or a cartoonist or something like that. But I started off wanting to write. I tried to write a novel about a caveboy, when I was in the third grade. I undertook to write a book. I've always been a kind of word freak. I like language; it excites me. So it's always been a kind of pursuit of mine.

BEATTIE: Do you remember teachers from elementary school?

McCLANAHAN: I had good teachers and I do remember them, but I was so different from most of the other kids in that particular respect. I mean, I was crazy about books and words, and this sounds incredibly arrogant, but I think, in a way, I was a little much for them, in that sense. So, for the most part, they just sort of let me go. I never got anything but A's in English, and I was really just encouraged to follow my own leanings.

In high school, I had two really good English teachers at Maysville. A woman named Frances Bogie and another lady whose last name was Wallingford; I can't remember her first name. They were both good teachers, and they did care about literature. I went through a period, along about then, of wanting to go into journalism. In fact, I went to college thinking that I was going to major in journalism. I had a job in high school, for a while, as the sports reporter for the Maysville newspaper.

BEATTIE: How did you get that job while you were still in high school?

McCLANAHAN: I had a predecessor in the job, a friend of mine who was a year ahead of me in high school, a very bright fellow named Bill Perrine. The paper sort of tried this idea of having a kind of internship. Billy had a really successful career at it, but I bombed out completely. The atmosphere of that newspaper office—it was a small-town daily—was just so frantic and hectic, and the idea of trying to write anything in that kind of circumstance just overwhelmed me. I just simply couldn't do it. I was never cut out to be that kind of journalist.

BEATTIE: Did you feel as though you learned any discipline from writing journalism?

McCLANAHAN: I think any writing that you do is valuable. I took a journalism class in high school, and that was kind of fun, because there weren't deadline pressures and so forth, so I could do well in that. But through all of high school, and certainly through college, really right straight through my master's degree, I was a "bull-meister." On exams and things like that, I could write well enough that I was often able to successfully disguise the fact that I didn't know anything. I had good teachers, certainly in graduate school at UK I had great teachers, but I did not get a good education. It wasn't their fault; it was my own doing. I just weaseled my way through.

BEATTIE: Did you go directly from high school to college?

McCLANAHAN: I graduated from Maysville in 1951, Maysville High, and went, as a freshman, to Washington and Lee University in Virginia, which I did not enjoy. It was an all-male school at the time, and besides that, it was a very conservative school then. I had a couple of absolutely marvelous teachers there, teachers whom I still remember with great affection. But I didn't like the school, and it was very much a fraternity school. I was in a fraternity, and I didn't find myself enjoying that very much. In a casual, nonvirulent way, it was a very racist school. In the fraternity you had to take a pledge never to let any person of black or Hebrew descent darken the door of the fraternity. I found myself in stout resistance to that and became a kind of rebel against it. You had to wear a coat and tie every day, and I did, but you should have seen my coat and tie. My own fraternity brothers told me that I was a disgrace to the house, which gave me great pleasure.

BEATTIE: Did it raise your consciousness of racism, that experience?

McCLANAHAN: It did.

BEATTIE: Had you always felt that way?

McCLANAHAN: Well, I had always been a kind of skeptic. I was the only atheist in Maysville High School, I'm sure of that. At least, the only declared one. I was searching for ways to distinguish myself from everybody else.

BEATTIE: Do you think it was more the adolescent need for that distinction, or were you really trying to find your own values at that time?

McCLANAHAN: Oh, I think, to some extent, it was both things. I mean, at that stage in life I was quite capable of being a flaming Commie one day and a Nazi the next, just looking, to some extent, for ways to shock my contemporaries.

BEATTIE: How had you been brought up in your family, in terms of religion?

McCLANAHAN: We were regular churchgoers, especially in Brooksville. But my father was a poker player, and he liked to drink more often than now and then. We lived on Church Street, and next door to our house was the Methodist parsonage, and next door to the parsonage was the Methodist Church. Next door to the Methodist Church was the Catholic rectory where the priest lived. Although we were staunch Methodists, my father was a very good friend of the Catholic priest there, who used to come to the poker games. He was a wonderful man, Father Linehauser. My buddies and I used to go and snoop into his trash can and find beer cans. So we were a church family, and I went to church and Sunday school every week, and in fact, for a long time I had to go to church on Sunday evening, too. I can remember making mad dashes from the church to the movie theater to see the Sunday evening movie after the Sunday service. The movie started at eight and church started at seven. If I got real lucky, the preacher would cut it off just a minute or two early, and I could get there.

BEATTIE: You said you went to college your first year at Washington and Lee. Where did you go after that?

McCLANAHAN: I transferred to Miami University of Ohio, where I had a really close friend. He had gone to Miami of Ohio ahead of me, and there were several things that I liked about Miami. The first thing was that he told me, to my utter amazement, that you could actually take a course in creative writing at Miami. I hadn't known there was any such animal.

Miami was a Yankee school, and it had a lot of black students, and they had a very progressive sociology department, which I ended up majoring in, largely for the iconoclastic value of it. The man who taught the creative writing course there became a wonderful friend to me, and I did get in that class just as quickly as I could. I took it for the first time the second semester of my sophomore year.

The professor's name was Walter Havighurst, and he was a beautiful man for a creative writing teacher. He was very tweedy, and had a salt-and-pepper mustache, and was really a gentleman of the old school. He wrote several novels, and I never read very much of Mr. Havighurst's work; it was more his personal style. So I took his creative writing class, and on the first story I wrote for him, I got a C-minus. I still have it.

BEATTIE: In retrospect, would you have given it a C-minus?

McCLANAHAN: I think a C-minus was about right. But I keep that story, and sometimes when I teach, I read it to classes without telling them who wrote it. When I have a new class of students, beginners, I read them this and I say, "Here's a story by someone who wrote this story at approximately your stage of development, but who is not here today, so you can criticize this as heavily as you want to and be free about it." I let them just jump all over it. Then, I tell them that I wrote it. It's a pretty good strategy, somehow.

Anyway, I stayed with it in Mr. Havighurst's class, and the first story that he gave me a B on, I sent to the *Atlantic Monthly* right away. But before I sent it to the *Atlantic Monthly*, I got a subscription to the *Atlantic Monthly*, because I thought, well, obviously they wouldn't publish a story by somebody who didn't even subscribe to their magazine. But actually, it was kind of amazing. I got a written response from the *Atlantic Monthly,* a personal response. They, of course, turned the story down, but a nice note came with it.

BEATTIE. Were you encouraged or discouraged by that?

McCLANAHAN: I think at the time I was probably discouraged, but pretty soon I began to realize that this was a pretty nice thing. Anyway, although I continued to major in sociology, I also continued to write all the time I was there, and to think of myself as a writer. I was majoring in sociology on the supposition that, well, I didn't want to be bothered reading all those old dead white guys, as they say nowadays. I took a minimum of English literature courses. But my notion was that I would major in sociology because I was going to be a writer, and sociology was all about people, and I would learn about people. Of course, you know, there's probably no worse place in the world to go to learn about people than a sociology class.

But I continued to take Dr. Havighurst's courses all the time that I was there. He arranged things so that I could stay in the class, even though I was repeating it, basically. They had an annual writing contest, a short story contest, and in my junior year I won it. Then again in my senior year I won the contest.

At the end of my college career, Dr. Havighurst got me a fellowship, or a scholarship—I can't remember which they called it—to a writer's conference at Boulder, Colorado, in the summer of 1955. That was when I was just fresh out of college. I had decided to go to graduate school in English, because I had done so well on these writing courses and had won these contests. I always wanted to pursue the writing in some fashion or other. I didn't know quite what else to do. Certainly nobody was going to hire me as a writer. I had a friend who was going to go to law school in New York, and we decided that we would live together in Greenwich Village, and he would go to law school and I would go to graduate school. Then I applied for, and was admitted to, Columbia, to the graduate program.

When I was in Colorado, my roommate at this conference, Vic Lovell, who was a sophomore at Stanford University at the time asked, "What are you going to do in the fall?" And I said, "Well, I'm going to Columbia to go to graduate school." And he said, "Well, you know you ought to think about coming to Stanford, because, you can get a master's in creative writing at Stanford." I said, "The hell you can." So I called Stanford from Boulder and got them to send me an application to graduate school. This was in July, I guess. I filled out the application and sent it in from Boulder, and went back to Kentucky after the writer's conference was over. By the way, my teacher at the writer's conference was May Sarton, and she was very encouraging. She made me feel real good about the possibility that I could do something with writing.

I got back to Kentucky and started assembling myself for going somewhere in the fall. The summer wore on and I hadn't heard from Stanford, and I had literally begun packing my car to drive to New York, to Columbia. I called the graduate office at Stanford and said, "I need to know whether I'm going to get in or not," and they said, "Well, as a matter of fact, you've just been admitted."

The next day I got in the car and headed west instead of north. When I got there I roomed with Vic; we lived in a big old house with ten or twelve other guys. I signed up for a lot of graduate literature courses and the graduate seminar in creative writing. We met once a week, three hours in an afternoon, in a place called the Jones Room up on top of the old library, a wonderful room, which was reserved strictly for creative writing courses. They had a big hi-fi in there with a lot of spoken-word albums. You could go in there and listen to, oh, Robert Frost read poems on those old albums. A lot of books were there that you couldn't find any place else in the university, in the libraries, and in that room was this wonderful big seminar table. The first day in the class, the first reader was Tillie Olsen reading "Hey Sailor, What Ship?" Of course, that's an absolute knock-out of a story, and I thought, "Oh, my God, I'm miles over my head here," and indeed, it turned out that I was.

I was over my head in the literature classes as well, because, suddenly I was in with these graduate students, and I had no background in English literature at all. I didn't know anything, and all these people really understood the history of English lit. I mean, all these graduate students were bright to start with, of course, being Stanford students, and my writing skills no longer stood me in nearly as good stead as they had before, because I was revealed as a fool too often. So I did not do well as a graduate student. I got a letter from the head of the department at the winter break saying, if I would like to come in and talk to him about my deficiencies as a graduate student, he'd be glad to see me. I didn't go.

But I did go back for the second quarter; they were on the quarter system there. The second quarter, Malcolm Cowley ran the writing seminar. I never did have Wallace Stegner, the head of the program, during that first period that I was at Stanford. But Mr. Cowley let me into the creative writing seminar. It was an incredible act of generosity on his part to let me into either of these courses, because I really wasn't good enough to be there. But he also let me into his graduate course. It was called a course in criticism, but what we did was read Proust and Henry James and Faulkner. But see, Mr. Cowley's book, *The Viking Portable Faulkner,* which was credited with restoring Faulkner to literary credibility, that book had just come out, so he was full of these wonderful anecdotes about his association with Faulkner. I just loved Mr. Cowley. He was wonderful. I also took a third course in modern American fiction from another teacher there, which I knew I could do okay in, because I didn't need background for it. I managed to get myself, that term, three B's, and I quit.

What happened was, I came back to Kentucky that spring from Stanford, thinking that I was going to get drafted at any minute. I had already taken the physical, and Korea had cooled off by then, but they were still drafting. So, in the spring of '56, I came back to Maysville where my folks still lived, and spent the rest of the spring and early summer working on a construction job. When it came time to go to summer school, I kept thinking I was going to be drafted at any minute, and I hadn't been, and it came time for UK summer session to begin, and I thought, "Well, why not?" So I came up here [University of Kentucky] and signed up for two graduate courses that summer. And damned if I didn't get A's in both of them. I took a Shakespeare course from a wonderful UK teacher named Ben Black, and a course in eighteenth-century literature from Dr. [Arthur] Cooke.

After summer school, I thought, "Well, I'll get drafted before school starts in the fall," and I didn't. So I came back in the fall and signed up for some more graduate courses and did well again. I continued to do well, and then in the spring of that year I still hadn't gotten drafted. I got married. I met a woman from Lexington who was an undergraduate in the English department. Her name is Kitty [Katherine] Andrews, Kit Andrews. She lives three blocks away from here right now, and we're great friends. We got married in the spring of '57.

I took the master's oral that spring and flunked it cold as a wedge, because, again, my checkered past caught up with me. I had done well in all these individual courses, but I had no sense of the history of English literature at all. I never had put all this stuff together. I never had taken the sophomore surveys like everybody else. Then I got into the master's oral and all three of the people on the committee were great friends of mine. They were wonderful faculty people and all of them had given me A's and had been my friends and defenders and supporters right through, but I just couldn't handle it. Then they started trying to ask me easy questions to kind of carry me. And the easier the questions got, the more befuddled I got. I just blew it sky high.

So, Kit and I stayed here, and I still hadn't gotten drafted. This was getting on into late '57. What I was doing during that subsequent year was what I should have done years ago, which was I hung around the university and sat in on a bunch of sophomore survey courses, and memorized the rhyme scheme of the sonnet, and so forth. So, in the spring of '58, I finally did get drafted, and I discovered that I had these blessed allergies that kept me out of the draft. I got drafted and was 4-F, which was wonderful, because at the time, Korea was basically over with, and it would have meant just two years of marking time.

Anyway, I took the master's oral again in the spring of '58, and did fine on it. Somehow, I heard about a teaching job—an instructorship in freshman English at Oregon State College—it was then in Corvallis, Oregon. I'd been dreaming about going west again ever since my stay at Stanford. So, in the fall of '58, Kit and I drove out to Corvallis, Oregon, in my brand new MGA, the first one that was ever sold in Lexington, my graduation present.

I taught four years at Oregon State, where my most noted colleague was Bernard Malamud. It was basically a vo-tech school. When I was teaching there, they offered no degree in humanities at all. If you evinced an unhealthy, unwholesome, insalubrious interest in the humanities, you were advised to go elsewhere after your sophomore year. But despite that, Bern Malamud, who had already won a National Book Award, they didn't understand what they had there. I mean, there were certain people who did, but the administration didn't realize that he was the powerful figure that he was.

At the end of my second year, I had begun trying to write again. I had pretty much quit writing. I did take writing courses at UK, by the way. I should have mentioned that, because I had two marvelous teachers there, too, Robert Hazel and Hollis Summers. They were both good friends of mine. In fact, just a couple of weeks ago, Bob sent me a new book of poems. He's still writing. He lives in Florida now. Of course, he retired long ago.

BEATTIE: Weren't some of your classmates Kentucky writers, too?

McCLANAHAN: Well, I never did know Bobbie [Bobbie Ann Mason] at that time. I certainly know her now. We've become friends. But she was younger and, of course, I was a graduate student. But I did get to know Gurney [Norman]. Gurney and I were in a couple of Bob Hazel's classes together. Wendell Berry and I became friends. We weren't in creative writing classes, but we were in a couple of lit. classes together. I don't know that Jim [James Baker Hall] and I ever were in the same class, but we became friends, because he was Wendell's good friend, and I got to know him through Wendell. All four of us, at one time or another, were editors of the literary magazine during those years, a literary magazine called *Stylus*. I still have my copies of it.

BEATTIE: Were you all represented in the magazine?

McCLANAHAN: I think all four of us are in there two or three times.

BEATTIE: Did the style you were writing in then, or that everybody was writing in, stay? Can you tell now whose writing you're reading?

McCLANAHAN: You can. You can certainly tell that we are who we are from what we did then. Wendell more so than anybody, because Wendell was already developing his themes. But, anyway, eventually, all four of us landed at Stanford again. We reconnected there, and then we all landed back here again.

BEATTIE: Did you go back to Stanford after Oregon?

McCLANAHAN: Well, about the end of my second year of teaching at Oregon State, I was teaching freshman comp., huge quantities of freshman comp. I decided that I just had to find some way out of that situation, because the school was just such a dead end. It just looked like the world would end in freshman composition. It was not a pleasant situation. So, I started writing again, and I wrote a story called "The Little-Known Bird of the Inner-Eye" that I sent to *Contact* magazine, which was a San Francisco literary quarterly that was basically run in competition with the early *Evergreen Review.* To my utter astonishment, they took it. It was the first publication that I had that really counted. I'd had stuff in literary magazines, college literary magazines, but this was a nationally distributed literary journal.

And as luck would have it, at the same time that that happened, Bernard Malamud wrote an absolutely scathing novel about Oregon State and quit. And I had just published this story, and I had let it be known that I was interested in being a writer. The day Bernard Malamud quit—he had this big-time job at Bennington—the head of the English department stuck his head out in the hall and said, "Anybody want to teach creative writing?" I said, "Yes, Herb, I do." So I got to be Bernard Malamud's successor, and I got the one creative writing class that they had at Oregon State. I taught that class for the next two years and continued to write.

In 1962 I got a Stegner Fellowship to go back to Stanford. At that time, Jim [James Baker Hall] had finished his term at Stanford and had gone to Connecticut, and Wendell had left Stanford and gotten a Guggenheim. He went abroad for a year and then came back and taught at NYU [New York University]. Gurney [Gurney Norman] had finished his time at Stanford, and then he had an ROTC [Reserve Officer Training Corps] obligation, so he finished his time at Stanford and went into the army and they sent him to Fort Ord, California, which was about fifty miles south of where I was. Palo Alto's just right down the road from Monterey, so Gurney was in Palo Alto every weekend. When Kit and I and our new baby moved back to Palo Alto for my year on the Stegner Fellowship, the first thing I did was go look up my old friend Vic Lovell, who had become a member of this community called Perry Lane, which was where Ken Kesey was. I had, in fact, met Kesey in Oregon once. I went over and sought him out one afternoon and spent some time with him, because at that time I thought I was going to get a Stegner Fellowship. I wanted to meet him because I'd heard that he knew some old friends of mine down there. So Gurney was up every weekend, and Kit and I rented a house that wasn't exactly on Perry Lane, but was right up the street from it, within easy walking distance, and we became immediate members of this bohemian community which got freakier and freakier. Then I started in the fellowship classes at Stanford, and the first friend I made in those classes was Bob Stone, Robert Stone, who is still my dear friend. Then I introduced Bob to the Perry Lane bunch, and we all become running mates, and life picked up quite rapidly at that point.

I had a great year at Stanford that year, and at the end of the year, Mr. Stegner asked me if I wanted to stay. They had a teaching position called the Jones Lecturer in Creative

Writing. It was a job with no tenure prospects attached to it; it was part-time. You needed some outside income, really, to live on it. But I had some by then. My father had died and left me a barge, as a matter of fact.

BEATTIE: A real barge?

McCLANAHAN: A genuine barge, which gave me some income every month, and allowed us to stay on. At the end of that year, Mr. Stegner took me to see the chairman of the department, to meet him, and he was the same man, Dr. [Virgil] Whittaker, who had written me a note asking if I'd like to come and talk to him about my deficiencies as a graduate student seven years before that.

BEATTIE: Did he remember that?

McCLANAHAN: Yes. Mr. Stegner took me in to see him and introduced me to him as "the young man that's going to be on our staff here." I was secretly patting myself on the back at a furious rate.

I ended up staying on another nine years, connected in one way or another with the writing program at Stanford. Of course, those were great years to be at Stanford, and I got completely involved in the free university movement and in the antiwar movement and the civil rights movement and the free ed movement. We lived a good deal of that time in a big, old house in downtown Palo Alto that was like living in Penn Station. It was a constant parade of freaks, and we had a great time.

BEATTIE: Some of the people from your book *Famous People I Have Known*?

McCLANAHAN: Yes. All of that happened then.

BEATTIE: Was this before Gurney Norman started writing for the *Whole Earth Catalog*?

McCLANAHAN: During that time. He and I were soul mates and brothers, really, during all that time. Meanwhile, Jim [James Baker Hall] was in and out of there. I think he came back once to teach for a little while, and then he made trips out there and, of course, we would all make trips back here, too, and he would land here in Lexington when we did and so forth. So we were all still in touch.

Meanwhile, Wendell [Berry] came out in the late sixties and spent two quarters in Palo Alto teaching in the Stegner program. So although we were never all together at the same moment, we continued to be friends. Then, in '71, Wendell took a year off, and I came back to Lexington and taught for him. My marriage was coming apart at that point, and by the end of that year it did come apart.

At the end of that year I went back to California just for the summer, and then went to Montana, where I was involved in a new relationship, and I taught at the University of Montana for the next two years, '73 to '75.

BEATTIE: Were you at the University of Montana before or after Sena Naslund was there?

McCLANAHAN: I came just after she left. She was Sena Callaghan at the time that she was there. In a way, I suppose, I probably replaced her. In the spring of '76, my teaching there was over, and by that time my wife and I embarked on our honky-tonk adventure [a cross-country journey to write about "honky-tonk" bars in the U.S.].

BEATTIE: What is her name?

McCLANAHAN: Cia White. She's a school teacher in Louisville now, and we're not on good terms.

BEATTIE: Well, back to your first marriage. You had children?

McCLANAHAN: I had three children by that marriage and two by the second marriage.

But, anyway, at the end of mine and Cia's honky-tonk adventure, we landed back in Port Royal, and lived there for the next fourteen years. When we first went back there, I was dead broke and out of work. The first four years that we were in Port Royal, I did eventually get some teaching at UK, but I spent a lot of time working as a farmhand, working in tobacco. I raised calves during that time, for beef, and we gardened a lot. That lasted until 1990. In the course of that time, I published *The Natural Man* and *Famous People I Have Known*. Then, that marriage crashed and burned. We separated in 1990.

A year ago, in the bitter throes of that divorce, I went to a Derby party in 1991, up by Versailles [Kentucky]. It was a party I didn't even intend to go to. I was going to go to a different one, but that party didn't transpire for some reason, and so a friend said, "We're going to a party; why don't you go with us?" I didn't even know the woman who was having the party. I went to this party and met this absolutely wonderful woman, met her on the front porch at this house, and three months later we got married on the same front porch. I met her on May second and we got married on July thirty-first.

Her name is Hilda. She's Belgian, and she is a graduate student [at UK] in English. She's a classical pianist. Her [full] name is Hilda Van Eggermont. She started as a freshman at the age of thirty-nine, and she graduated in four years with honors. So she really did very well. Then she went into the graduate program, and she is still working on a master's in music, and she teaches piano, too.

BEATTIE: Going back to your publishing career, could you talk about the history of that?

McCLANAHAN: Well, I got the Stegner Fellowship in the spring of '62, but the submission had to be made in the fall of '61. What I submitted to them was a ninety-eight-page novella which was, for all practical purposes, *The Natural Man*. It was the exact same story, same characters. The story line is really, essentially, identical.

In the summer of '61, with the first twenty pages of that novella, I went to an incredible writers' conference at a place called Wagner College on Staten Island. It was an amazing event. They had three workshops: poetry, fiction, and drama. The poetry workshop was run by Robert Lowell, the drama workshop by Edward Albee, and the fiction workshop by Saul Bellow. That ain't bad. The director of the conference was Rust Hills, who was, and still is, the fiction editor of *Esquire*. It was absolutely incredible, and while I was there, I met an agent in New York who had happened to see my story in *Contact*. This is a woman named Elizabeth McKee, who is an old-time New York agent. She's been my agent ever since, thirty-two years now. She was Flannery O'Connor's agent and William Styron's agent, and Erskine Caldwell's agent, and, you know, she's just been there and back. She took my finished novella, which I'd finished in time to apply for the Stegner Fellowship, she took that and sent it to the Dial Press, and they gave me a contract for a book. It was going to be a novella and five stories to go with it. That was what I had projected.

When I went to Stanford, I spent that whole year working on what I thought was going to be the first of these stories. It was going to be short stories. In the course of that year, it turned into a longer novella than the first one, and it wasn't any good. It had its moments, but it was a novella about a school bus wreck; it was based on an event that happened in

Kentucky in the fifties, down at Prestonsburg. A man had a heart attack and drove a bus full of kids into the Big Sandy River.

By that time, I had begun to harbor a lot of doubts about my other novella. I spent the next three or four years at Stanford trying to doctor these two things and trying to write a third novella that would go with them and make a book. The longer it took, the more apparent it became to me that there was something wrong with this stuff, that the point of view was skewed in such way that it just didn't feel right.

In the meantime, I got involved with the Free University of Palo Alto, which was publishing, in the beginning, just a newsletter. There was a marvelously talented fellow named Fred Nelson who was the editor of it. He was multitalented; he could write and he could also draw, and he had a sense for design and layout and so forth, and he began turning this little thing into a genuine magazine called the *Free You*. Fred asked me to become an editor of it. Well, what it meant to me, at least, and we quickly defined this as our editorial policy, was that we never turned down anything. Everybody who was editing it tried to write for it. We tried to guarantee that there would be something readable in each issue that way, and then we also took it as our task to go out and hustle our writer friends into contributing good work. It was a tight community of people. We were all antiwar, we were all hippies, we all shared a great many enthusiasms. So you really felt like you were writing for a known audience. Besides that, it was liberating, because it was not only a known audience, but they knew you well enough that you didn't have to feel any constraint about what you said.

So, I began writing for the *Free You* and began finding a new voice for myself, a much freer, looser, less-constrained voice. The first piece that I wrote for them that really worked was a piece that was called "Highway Fifty-two Revisited." That piece turns up in *Famous People I Have Known* as a trip back to Kentucky that I made, when I went into a tavern over in southern Ohio, and nearly got taken apart by a bunch of young toughs who thought I was a hippie, and they were, of course, correct. Then I wrote a follow-up piece to that about an episode that happened in Palo Alto when three hippies stole my typewriter, and that also turns up in *Famous People*. Those two pieces kind of gave me a whole other handle on a way to write, and on a way to write what passed for journalism.

Then I wrote some book reviews for *Rolling Stone,* in its early years. *Esquire,* in the meantime, had published a short story in 1970. I kept going back to this old material, the fiction, and especially to the story that eventually became *The Natural Man.* Rust Hills, had asked for, and I had sent him, a chapter of one of my many endeavors to rewrite that story. He published it as a short story in *Esquire,* and that was a sort of breakthrough for me.

Then I wrote a piece about my college years encounter with Jimmy Sacca and the Hilltoppers down in Bowling Green, when I got drunk and passed out in their car, and I wrote this piece for *Esquire* called "Famous People I Have Known," which was the germ of the idea for this other book. Meanwhile, my life was undergoing all these alterations.

Then in '72 my old friend on the *Free You* staff, Fred Nelson, and I put together this anthology from the old *Free You* which, in the meantime, had itself crashed and burned. We put together this anthology, which we titled *One Lord, One Faith, One Cornbread,* after a line that we'd stolen from Wendell. Doubleday Anchor published that in the early seventies in an Anchor paperback, and sold about three hundred copies. It's now worth about eighty-five dollars a copy. Both of my two pieces that I mentioned, the typewriter piece and the tavern piece, they're both in there. There were some pieces by my old friend, Vic Lovell. There were pieces by Kesey and a Brautigan [Richard Brautigan] poem, a Robert Stone piece about Kesey, just a whole lot of stuff that eventually acquired a kind of reputation. That came out just before I went to Montana.

Then came the honky-tonk episode. We had a contract for that book with Random House, but it never became anything except a chapter in *Famous People*. We got back to Kentucky, and I continued to tinker with this old fiction. In the school year '79 to '80, I taught for a year at NKU, Northern Kentucky [University], just as a visiting lecturer, and thought that I was going to be hired to stay on. That was within driving distance of Henry County; I could commute. At the last minute, somebody else was hired instead. I got affirmative-actioned out of a job. It was okay, though. I was sorry at the time, because I thought I desperately needed a job. Anyway, almost simultaneously with that, I got a letter from Pat Strong, an editor at Farrar, Straus, and Giroux, which had held the contract (they had taken the contract for my book from the Dial Press, that had bought it many years before that), telling me that if I didn't write this book within a year, that they were going to cut my contract loose. Well, of course, that didn't mean anything. I'd long since spent the little advance that I got, but I would no longer be able to say, "I have a book under contract with Farrar, Straus," which would have been a blow to my ego at least.

My wife and I had a bad year that year because we lost a set of twins. They were stillborn, premature. So I was facing a real dark winter, kind of in the dark night of the soul, very early in '81. At that point I had a draft of *The Natural Man* probably eighty percent finished, but it still didn't feel right to me. There was something wrong. In my heart I knew what it was, and it was that the book *was* in first person. I had never been able to shake myself loose from the notion that, in some way or another, the story was so autobiographical and so personal, that if I didn't write it in first person, it would falsify the subject. But I knew that the fact that it was in first person was not serving it well.

Gurney [Norman] called me up not long after we had lost these babies and when things really looked grim, and at that point I had about five or six months left on my grace period. Gurney said, "Look, I need to go to New York, and I've got spring break coming in March." He said, "Let's go to New York, and you take your manuscript and deliver it by hand to Pat Strong, whoever that is." I said, "You're on. Okay, let's do." That very day we made plane reservations, three months in advance for March, the Ides of March, March fifteenth.

The next day I went back to page one of the draft of *The Natural Man*—I think I was calling it that by that time—and started recasting it sentence by sentence, recasting each sentence in first person. I wasn't two pages into it until my spirits were lifted immensely. It was just like going in a musty old house and opening up the doors and windows. It let light and air into the book just instantly. I knew, from that moment on, that I had done the right thing, and it changed the tone of the book immeasurably. I just sailed through the revision, and by March fifteenth I had a complete draft. Everything was there except a little bit of the epilogue.

BEATTIE: So the story of *The Natural Man*'s being written over twenty-two years is really not the case. It was set aside for a long while.

McCLANAHAN: Except I never stopped thinking about it, I never stopped tinkering with it. In the fall of 1969 I came back to Kentucky and holed up in a little cabin that my wife's mother owned down on Cumberland Lake, and I spent four months just working on it. That's all I did for that four months. And there were other periods when I would take it up and try to belabor it into life, and then give up and go on to something else.

I forgot to mention that the other two major things that happened to me both had to do with *Playboy* magazine, in the early seventies. As a friend of Kesey's, I happened to know some people in the Grateful Dead rock band. *Esquire* asked me to write a profile of the Grateful Dead, which I took a year to do. I wrote this great, long—it was sixty-eight pages long—looping kind of thing, very personal journalism kind of stuff.

BEATTIE: Did you travel with them to do it?

McCLANAHAN: Yes, I hung out with them. We didn't travel, but I lived with Jerry Garcia for a couple of weeks, and I hung out backstage a lot when they played San Francisco. The piece was about hanging out with the Grateful Dead as much as anything. Anyway, *Esquire* wanted to cut it, and by that time I was so sick of it that I couldn't bear the thought of getting back into it. I said, "No, I don't want to cut it." I wanted to try it somewhere else. So they killed it, and my agent started shopping it around, and it found a home at *Playboy.* They published it pretty much intact, although I had a quarrel with them after the fact about one or two little editorial alterations they made. But they published it and gave me their award as the best new contributor of nonfiction of the year. That was a thousand bucks and a trip to New York and a little trophy-like thing, and a great deal of pats on the back.

Then the year that I taught for Wendell, in the early seventies, at UK, I reencountered my old friend Little Enis, the Lexington rock and roller, who had once been the subject of my master's thesis. I was going to do a thesis for a folklore professor at UK, Bill Jansen, on this rock and roll musician, and in 1972 when I was back here, purely by chance, I reencountered this guy whom I had known back in my graduate school days. He was down and out, and playing out at this rough old place called Boots's Bar, with a lot of go-go girls. During that year I spent the whole year teaching for Wendell and writing a piece about Little Enis. It, too, was a great big long piece of writing. It was about fifty pages long. I sent it to *Playboy,* and they bought it in three days and gave it the best contributor of nonfiction award for the year. So I got two of those awards.

I was already thinking about a book called *Famous People I Have Known* that was going to be about people who were actually anything but famous, but whom I had known. So that piece, of course, became a kind of centerpiece in the book, the piece about Enis. I originally wrote the Grateful Dead piece thinking that it was going to be for that book, too. In fact, I called it "Grateful Dead I Have Known." But, in the end, I didn't like it well enough to include it in the book. It had become kind of dated and passé. So, that's my career in a nutshell.

BEATTIE: In a recent review of what that newspaper referred to as a Kentucky classic, in this case *The Natural Man,* critic Robert Kaiser wrote in the *Lexington Herald-Leader,* "McClanahan's gift is an ability to see and describe clichés in an entirely new light. His prose is breathless, free, and self-confident, but it is his use of apt familiar imagery rooted in rural Kentucky life that makes his writing strike a chord." What do you think of those comments?

McCLANAHAN: Well, I'm hugely delighted that he perceives it that way, but my prose is, in fact, anything but, "free and self-confident and breathless and . . ." Well, that's an illusion. That's a trick. I work very hard for that effect. I tinker endlessly with my prose. I am delighted that people can read it that way. But I think of my prose as working in a kind of point-counterpoint manner. What I like to do is play off highly literary, florid, overblown, rhetorical rotundity. Against real earthy, raw, language. I like to see what sparks I can strike when I knock those two elements together. I love taking a reader to the extreme of one of those and then pulling the rug out from under him or her with the other. So I try for a kind of admixture of the two things. It's like if you get the chemistry right, it works, and if it's not right, you know it right away. I'm constantly reworking sentences. I don't write fluently at all. My writing is very labored, and when it's missing, it feels labored. You can tell it. But fortunately, I feel it first, usually; I don't turn loose of it until I get it to where I think it's right. But that's a generous thing for him to say, and I was grateful for it.

BEATTIE: When that book first came out, the review in the *New York Times* was a rave review, and your book was compared to *Catcher in the Rye*. How do you feel about those comparisons?

McCLANAHAN: Oh well, *Catcher in the Rye* and *Huckleberry Finn,* I mean, I could not be traveling in any company that could delight me more, because *Catcher in the Rye* was an immensely powerful influence on me when I was an undergraduate. In fact, when I read that book I thought, "Well, there's just no point in anybody ever writing any more books; it's all been said right here.

BEATTIE: Was there any conscious comparison in your mind as you were writing?

McCLANAHAN: Yes. I thought a lot about Holden Caulfield. But I also thought quite consciously about Huckleberry Finn. In fact, at the end of the novel, Monk McCormick says to Harry, how he's cutting out, you know? Well, I was thinking about the line about Huck leaving civilization and so forth, and heading for the territory, "lighting out for the territory," he says. Even more specifically, the appearance of Dr. Rexrote and Nurse Ratliff, that's the Duke and the Dauphin right from Huck Finn. I thought of that quite consciously, about the similarities and so forth. But Monk McCormick, for me, is Huck Finn.

BEATTIE: And also yourself.

McCLANAHAN: And, of course, I'm Harry, and Harry is also Tom Sawyer. You know, he's a little more civilized than Huck, and so, those connections were very meaningful to me, and I was immensely delighted when Ivan Gold said that about the book.

BEATTIE: Have you ever thought about writing a sequel to it?

McCLANAHAN: I have thought specifically about that connection, yes. But in a way, I'm writing a sequel to it right now. That is, not literally a sequel to it, but I'm working on three long stories, one of which is finished, and which was in *Esquire* in December of '88, a story called "The Congress of Wonders," which is set in a carnival side show in 1944, and involves Dr. Rexrote and Nurse Ratliff, who reemerge. I'm doing two other long stories to accompany that one, in what I hope will be a book. Dr. Rexrote and Nurse Ratliff make cameo appearances in both of them. I haven't rejuvenated Harry, but I've rejuvenated these minor characters. In fact, one of these two long stories, for a little while, was going to involve a return by Harry to Needmore. He was going to come back and teach in Burdock County Community College. I may try that, yet, sometime.

BEATTIE: That I'd like to read. What have you been writing since your publication of *Famous People I Have Known*?

McCLANAHAN: I spent a long time writing "The Congress of Wonders," that short story, which is not a short short story, it's forty-five pages long. I'm a very slow writer, as you no doubt figured out. The first thing I really undertook after *Famous People* was published was a screenplay, which I was working on with a fellow whom I didn't know when I began this, but who's become a good friend, Paul Wagner. He's a filmmaker from Louisville. He's been a documentary filmmaker. We undertook to write a screenplay about some high school rock and roll musicians of the fifties. We were going to do it together, and he wanted to make a dramatic film for the first time. He's an accomplished documentary maker. He won an Academy Award a few years ago, in fact. But that didn't pan out because I just wasn't comfortable writing for the screen. I didn't know how to do it and was kind of at a loss for how to approach it. So I gave it up after six months or so and began working on "Congress of Wonders," which turned out well, and which I'm very happy with.

Then, as I said, I am working on these two long stories to make a book with "Congress of Wonders." The story is called "The Congress of Wonders," and I would like to call the book *A Congress of Wonders*. One of the stories is very long, it's a hundred pages or so, and it's about eighty-percent finished. What it is, is a revamp of the story about the school bus wreck that I spent my year at Stanford on, thirty years ago. The other story is about a character from my home town—Bracken County—who, believe it or not, had two noses. Seems highly improbable, but it's true. This is a guy that was there when I was a kid, and who manufactured and employed a bomb for another man. Blew this other man to smithereens, basically. He didn't kill him actually, but in my story he does. I wrote a draft of the story about this man with two noses when I was an undergraduate. I only have a certain number of stories. I just have to keep working on them. Students always say to me, especially sophomores and people who are just beginning, they say, "Well, we're so young, we don't have any experience, we don't have anything to write." I say, "What the hell are you talking about? I spent thirty years writing this story about when I was fifteen. You've been fifteen, you know."

BEATTIE: The three stories that you're working on now that you're hoping to have published as a book, do you have a publisher waiting for these?

McCLANAHAN: Farrar, Straus has an option on my next book. Whether they'll exercise it or not, I don't know.

I forgot to finish a thread that I was following at one point. I mentioned that I was having this correspondence with this editor at Farrar, Straus named Pat Strong, whom I envisioned as a sort of Pat Buchanan-type, a beefy, red-faced young Irishman. When I went to Farrar, Straus with my manuscript in hand, when Gurney and I made that trip to New York in 1981, I went in with my manuscript and I said, "I have an appointment with Mr. Strong." They said, "No, no. You mean Mrs. Strong." Then the door opened, and out came this absolutely beautiful young woman who looked like Diane Sawyer. She was an absolutely wonderful editor to work with. She worked with me on both my books, on *The Natural Man*, and then on *Famous People*. I was just crazy about her. Unfortunately, she has left Farrar, Straus. She's at the *New Yorker* now; she's a fiction editor there.

BEATTIE: You've talked a little about this in conjunction with your books, but I was wondering about your method of composition, where you write, when you write, the tools with which you write.

McCLANAHAN: Well, I'm not a very regular sort of person. Right here [home office] is certainly where I write. But in another sense, I kind of write all the time. I think all the time about whatever it is that I'm working on. I have said a lot of times that after spending all those years on *The Natural Man,* when I finally finished it, I put myself to sleep every night by thinking about the next line or the next phrase in *The Natural Man,* in whatever draft of it I was working on. When I finally finished it and published it, it was kind of like losing an old friend. I felt kind of lonely for it in a funny way. I'm persistent, obviously, but I'm not diligent. The one time that I ever forced myself to write a certain number of pages each day was when I was writing the first draft of *The Natural Man,* and I wrote that in a white heat. I was teaching three sections of freshman comp. and two sections of creative writing, one of which was eighty miles away in Portland, Oregon. The freshman comp classes had thirty people in them, each one, three of those, so that was ninety, and then probably fifteen in each of the writing classes. Despite that, I wrote five hundred words a day, every single day. I was sleeping two, three hours a night. I was drinking twenty-five cups of coffee a day. I lost forty pounds in about five months. In a way, I could recommend it, because I never was happier in my life. I was absolutely wildly excited, because it was a major breakthrough for me, and it just felt so good to be doing it. I knew, ultimately, it was not a successful piece of writing in that version. But it had good things in it, and I knew I was onto something, even then.

BEATTIE: Do you compose directly on a word processor?

McCLANAHAN: I do. This is a new thing for me, though. I've resisted this for many, many years.

BEATTIE: But now that you're doing it, is it a good thing or a bad thing?

McCLANAHAN: Oh, I think it's a really good thing, in my particular case, because my tendency to tinker with the prose is made so much simpler.

BEATTIE: Would you comment on what you think the nature of creativity itself is?

McCLANAHAN: I can only speak from my own experience, but for me it's like finding the right amalgam of history and imagination. I'm not interested in stuff that's made up whole-cloth, very much. I shouldn't say I'm not interested in it, but I have no interest in writing that way. If it doesn't spring from my experience, then it doesn't send me. I'm interested in examining my own experience to see if I can't learn something from it. Every story that I've ever done, every piece of writing that I've ever done that's been any good, has, in some fashion or another, sprung from that.

BEATTIE: Do you think creativity is part nature, part nurture?

McCLANAHAN: I think so. There has always been something in me that sought expression, and I've been a word freak all my life. I love language just for the sound of it. For me, the fact that I'm singing is as important as the song. I have an absolutely flat ear, a tin ear, as they say, and no capacity for music at all, and yet writing is a kind of singing to me. It's like literally composing. I like to get every word as right as I can get it, because otherwise, I hear clinkers. It's got missed notes.

BEATTIE: How do you think being a Kentuckian has influenced your work?

McCLANAHAN: Well, I think the whole oral tradition thing, that's kind of a given. For instance, my favorite passage in *The Natural Man,* I don't know if you would ever have noticed that it's all one sentence, but it's an eight hundred word sentence that has all those dirty jokes in it, all those punch lines of dirty jokes. Well, of course all those jokes have rattled around in my head all those years, because I've heard them a thousand times and told them a thousand times. I think if you're not a part of a tradition that values the ability to tell stories, then something is missing. I don't imagine that I heard one of those jokes anywhere outside the confines of the state of Kentucky.

BEATTIE: What writers have particularly influenced you?

McCLANAHAN: Well, Flannery O'Connor is, to me, the real capstone of American fiction. And, of course, I was immensely impressed by Faulkner, when I was a student, especially. In fact, I do readings, and I should have said this before, I do a lot of readings. I do readings at the drop of an invitation. The truth is, I really write for the readings.

BEATTIE: Readings give you a goal?

McCLANAHAN: Yes; my writing doesn't actually seem to really come to life for me until I've read it aloud. I hear it in my head being read aloud by me all the time when I'm working on it, but when I get it to the point that I can nail some friend of mine to a chair somewhere and make him or her listen to me read, then it becomes real for me.

BEATTIE: You had mentioned your writers' conference you do annually in Augusta. Could you talk a little bit more about that?

McCLANAHAN: Sure. It's gone on now for four years. I don't know if you're familiar with Augusta, but it's a lovely little town. It's right on the bank of the Ohio. The first year we had a keynote speech by Sallie Bingham. We had poetry, fiction, and drama workshops that year. George Ella Lyon—she's, by the way, a very fine Kentucky writer—did the drama workshop, I did the fiction workshop, and who did the poetry workshop that year? I can't remember. We have also a keynote speech and a roundtable discussion that follows that. We have literary readings, and as I mentioned, now we're doing video screenings and experimental work, mostly in video. The second year John Egerton did the keynote speech, and we had a reading by Nikki Finney, a black woman poet who was teaching at UK. Over the course of the weekend there are usually, in terms of the total number of people who show up for the whole thing, the events, the roundtable and so forth, the total attendance is approaching five hundred people for the weekend. People come from all over.

BEATTIE: When is this conference held every year?

McCLANAHAN: The first weekend in October. I go to the Hindman Settlement School Writers' Conference [Appalachian Writers' Workshop] every other year. That's a great little conference. It's wonderful, and having a week is really better than having a weekend, because you can really get to know people.

BEATTIE: What is the most important thing for people to know about you?

McCLANAHAN: From my point of view, that I'm a good guy. I like people a lot. I like socializing. I like human society. I find it incredibly rich and rewarding, and that allows me to be interested in just about everybody I talk to. I think that's basically who I am.

May 29, 1992

BOOKS BY ED MCCLANAHAN

Stanford Short Stories, 1964. Edited by Richard Scowcroft and Wallace Stegner with the assistance of McClanahan. Palo Alto, Calif.: Stanford University Press, 1964.

One Lord, One Faith, One Cornbread. With Fred Nelson. New York: Doubleday/Anchor, 1972.

The Natural Man. New York: Farrar, Straus, Giroux, 1983.

Famous People I Have Known. New York: Farrar, Straus, Giroux, 1985.

A Congress of Wonders. Washington, D.C.: Counterpoint Press, 1996.

JIM WAYNE MILLER

MILLER: My name is Jim Wayne Miller, and I was born on October 21, 1936, in Buncombe County, North Carolina. My home community is Leicester, North Carolina. My father's name is James Woodrow Miller. He was born in 1912, and his middle name reflects an enthusiasm on the part of his parents for Woodrow Wilson, I believe. My mother's name was Edith Smith. My father had many, many jobs. At various times he worked for the Southern Railroad in Asheville. But for most of my growing up years, he settled in with the Firestone Tire and Rubber Company in Asheville, North Carolina, and he was a shop foreman. Later on, for about the last fifteen years of his employment, he was a service manager for the Firestone Tire and Rubber Company in Asheville. My mother was a housewife all those years. I have five brothers and sisters; I am the oldest.

My paternal grandparents, my Grandmother and Grandfather Miller, lived about five miles from our house in an old twelve- or thirteen-room house that was three stories climbing up the side of a hill. He was a landed farmer; he had enough land to have sharecroppers, so he was a gentleman farmer, really. They were not really wealthy, but they were comfortable, and they were progressive. He tended to get all the government publications on agriculture. He was probably the first person in that community to have running water in the house, and electricity, telephones. I remember when I was a little boy, I was fascinated with the old crank telephone. He was also the fire warden for his end of the county.

My Grandmother Miller, her maiden name was Wells. I use that name in my novel, and often times, with my characters. She was a housewife, but an extraordinary woman. I would say just extremely intelligent, and she expressed herself with great forcefulness. She could have gone on stage, I believe. She's the person who, in my earliest memories, was always reciting stuff remembered from her school days. She was a great encourager of her grandchildren as far as schooling was concerned. I believe I wrote somewhere that after my grandparents, my paternal grandparents, passed away, and the house was emptied of all the contents and parceled out amongst the children, they found in an unused room, in bureau drawers, the schoolwork of her grandchildren all rolled up and tied with red ribbon. It looked like the red tape from a congressional archive or something.

BEATTIE: Maybe it'll be more valuable. Were your grandmothers similar in personality and character to the ones in *Newfound*?

MILLER: Yes. And you see, the other side of the family, my Grandmother and Grandfather Smith, I simply used their names, you know, in the novel. So, you can see to what extent it's autobiographical. They were of a different class. They were sharecroppers. Although my Grandmother and Grandfather Smith never were sharecroppers on the Miller farm, they were on other farms. It seemed right for me just to telescope all that stuff. My Grandfather Smith, for instance, was an illiterate man. He did not read or write. My Grandmother Smith did read, but she read mostly the Bible and just utilitarian things like that.

After my father got his farm, he continued to work, as we would say, "on the public works" in Asheville. But we had about seventy acres. We had a tobacco allotment. We had cows and chickens and ducks. So my grandparents, at about age sixty-five, came and built a little house on our place, which was in hollering distance practically, and lived there, and my grandfather ran the farm. My father always, just like a landlord, bought the fertilizer, bought the seeds, made the cash outlays for everything, and then they split them down the middle at tobacco sale time.

BEATTIE: Did he mostly farm tobacco?

MILLER: That was the cash crop, but of course we had huge gardens. We had corn. We had a mule, cows. I milked two cows morning and evening for most of my growing up days.

BEATTIE: What about aunts or uncles? Were they influential in your life at all?

MILLER: Oh, in many different ways. And again, the difference was reflected in the families. My aunts and uncles on my father's side, that is my paternal uncles, I didn't come into contact with as much. They were usually some distance, they were working away, often Baltimore or Detroit or someplace like that. But it was on the other side, it was my mother's brothers and sisters, my Uncle Clinton, and my Uncle Roy, and my Uncle Van, and all these people were right there in the community. They followed along in their father's footsteps in that they were fox hunters and farmers. We would go berry picking to my Uncle Clint's house or they would be in the group in the evenings when we'd go out and sit and fox hunt half the night. So I would say they were more of an influence. And in terms of just affection and familiarity with the grandparents and with the uncles and aunts, that was really on my mother's side, simply because of their proximity. They were there.

BEATTIE: You write in your essay in *Contemporary Authors,* and you've just spoken about your paternal grandmother reciting poetry to you, you quote Saul Bellow saying, "A writer is first a reader who has been moved to emulation." You add that you believe a writer is first a listener. Do you think that listening to your paternal grandmother was what helped develop your interest in reading and writing?

MILLER: Oh, yes, because it was alive. It brought it alive.

BEATTIE: Did you have family members read to you as a child?

MILLER: No. My mother and father, they did not read to us. By the time I was aware of it, there were already too many of us. We talked. We told stories. But, we listened to the older people on the porches and out in the yard when we would have a watermelon sliced or something, you know, on a Sunday afternoon.

BEATTIE: So you think it might be more the oral tradition, the storytelling tradition?

MILLER: It was an oral thing. Of course, I brought books home from school. But we were not bookish people, except visiting the paternal grandparents. They had books all over the place. But even there, it was my grandmother's recitations more than reading with a book in your hand. I'm thinking, in my case, you're first a listener. We listened to and told these long, involved stories that might be interrupted by somebody else dropping in or by having to go do some chore, but you would come back and pick it up again, you know, these epics.

BEATTIE: Which would certainly do more for the imagination and for close listening, and later for close reading and analysis, than what most children get today who aren't exposed to reading or listening.

MILLER: Right. These are slowly developing things; you have to pay attention. Something that's mentioned early on in the tale or the narrative is going to be relevant, but you can't chop the mind, the attention, up into little bits. If you do, you'll miss the whole point of it. The other thing, of course, is I was pre-TV.

But we had radio. I listened in the afternoon after school. There were two or three little fifteen-minute programs in a row that I always listened to. I knew that I had to listen to these programs when they came on, and then I would go do my milking and do all the other things. But you listen and you imagine the situations just from the little sound. People still listen to the radio, obviously, but that whole world is gone. There is very little radio drama now.

BEATTIE: You also wrote about the archaic speech that you grew up hearing, of course not calling it that or realizing it was that then, but you talk about scholars coming in to research the Elizabethan traces of the language.

MILLER: Yes. That was awareness that came later, looking back on it. I would walk across the mountain and go visit my Aunt Vashti, and sometimes I would stay two or three days or a whole weekend with them. Aunt Vashti might be sitting on the porch, and as I'm walking into the yard she'd see me, and she'd say, "Well, light down." And my Grandmother Smith, when I would go up to her house—as I said, it was very close by— I liked to run barefoot onto the porch at six-thirty on Saturday morning, and she would say, "Hmph. Did you come to borrow fire?" Which, in an earlier time, could have been a real question. She was simply using it in a jocular way. I was always giving her fright, or giving her a start, because it never occurred to me, you know, I'm me, I'm here, and I might walk up behind her like that while she'd be working at something and she'd go "Umph," and then she'd look around and realize who it was. She'd say, "I thought you was somebody."

BEATTIE: What sort of childhood did you have?

MILLER: It was, in many ways, idyllic, I would say a wholesome childhood. Here I was, after all, living on a small farm with my brothers and sisters within sight of one set of grandparents and within ten minutes' drive of the others, and we usually would go out on a Wednesday evening and visit, and then sometimes on a Sunday, have Sunday dinner with the paternal grandparents. It was a coming and going of all the aunts and uncles and cousins and relatives. We were always strapped financially for things that cash would buy, but we did not want for basics. We had food, clothing, and shelter, and we grew a lot of our own food, including meats.

BEATTIE: Where did you attend school and what was that like?

MILLER: I attended the Leicester Grade and High School, all one big building, a big red brick building built by the WPA, the Works Project Administration, in the thirties, as part of the government effort to recover from the recession. The school still stands; it's in pretty good shape, and it was quite an elaborate school for that place and time. There were remnants on the lower campus of the old school that my father had gone to, which was a wooden building, and it was as gray as a hornet's nest by the time I went through there and it was used as a shop.

There was a continuity in that, in that school, and in that community. My father and my mother had both been students of my seventh grade teacher. That was a peculiar thing, too, in that our teachers, for the most part, were teachers who were there in the community. They knew the community and they had some depth to their familiarity with it. That, of course, was both a positive and a negative thing for any little kid coming through, because if you had had an older brother or older sister who had not been a good student, or who was from a family that was considered a not nice family, then your identity was ascribed to you in advance. But if, on the other hand, your teachers had had a positive experience with your family members or thought well of them, then they were disposed towards you. If you got in trouble, and we all got in trouble, they took an interest in you and their interest was to help get you through this trouble, not to kick you out of school. I find that that's different nowadays. Teachers don't always know that much about their communities, or care, and it has happened, oddly enough, through one of the things that was supposed to be an improvement, and that's the big consolidated school. What it does is it pulverizes and homogenizes all these communities, and the school represents no community in particular, but all of them. I'm sure there are many, many advantages to this sort of thing, but one of the disadvantages, I find, is that there is not that kind of personal sense of community and knowing who a person is and where they come from.

BEATTIE: You wrote about being a teaching assistant when you were in the third grade. Would you talk about that?

MILLER: Sure. My teacher at that time was a Miss Duckett. Her method was simply to delegate, to designate two or three students in the room; I think we had six rows of bolted down seats all over the oil-saturated, wooden floors. She would take three of her students she figured were reading very well, and give them two rows of students to be responsible for, and anyone in those two rows, if they had a question about pronunciation or the meaning of a word during silent reading period, they raised their hands, and we went to them and helped them out. I don't know how conventional an arrangement that was for that time, again I say the forties. I don't know that much about the history of education and the pedagogical fads and fashions at the time. But that was my first stint as a teaching assistant. Then, in addition to that, and I don't know how this came about, but it's a tie-in with that paternal grandmother, my third grade teacher would let me leave the room and be gone for a couple of hours. She would send me to other classes in the school to tell stories.

BEATTIE: Do you remember anything else about early schooling in terms of what subjects emerged as favorites?

MILLER: Well, we had a writing assignment in the fourth and fifth grades, I think. It might have been in the fifth and sixth. We had a little state-approved spelling book, in the state of North Carolina, and it was a very thin little blue-backed speller. Each chapter would introduce fifteen or twenty new words. The standing assignment was to write a sentence in which you used this word, and you underlined the word, and you'd write a sentence which demonstrated your understanding of the meaning of that word. That meant you could do that, write fifteen or twenty sentences on the front and back of lined notebook paper. The other option was to write a story or a paragraph, an essay or something like that, in which you worked these words in, and again you had to underline the words that were being used for the first time. I responded very positively to that, and I usually wrote the little essay or the story and underlined my words, because to me it was just a nice game to see how you could do this. I would try to work little variations on it. I'd try to see how many words I could get into one sentence.

BEATTIE: You wrote that one summer you were inspired by a radio play to write something similar. Do you remember that as one of your first desires to do creative writing on your own?

MILLER: Well, it was not the first. The first was a poem. I had read a poem in a book from school; it was a poem about dark woods. It was not Frost's "Stopping By Woods on a Snowy Evening," but it was something like that. I simply composed a poem, which was very derivative and imitative of that, and I showed that to my grandmother, and she praised it and I think she kept a copy. It was one of those things bound up in the red ribbon. But the radio drama thing, it was just a regular program that came on in the early afternoon in the summer. It consisted of mystery stories, and I remember what the plot was. A man worked in a radio station, and he plotted to murder his wife. What he was going to do was, he was going to record his voice, this was his alibi, he was recording his voice at the radio station and playing that, and while he was playing, he was off killing her. That was his alibi; everybody could hear that he's on the radio. But just toward the end of his radio presentation, the record stuck, and it kept going around and around and around. So that gave him away.

BEATTIE: How old were you at the time of these two incidents, the poem and the radio play?

MILLER: Oh, the poem, I would have been in the second grade. I would have probably have been seven years old, because I started school when I was five, in August or September, and I was coming up on six. As far as the radio drama, I might have been eight, going on nine.

BEATTIE: Did you write much more on your own?

MILLER: It was sporadic, and I wrote less in high school than I did in grade school, because writing was not a thing to do.

BEATTIE: What was your high school experience like?

MILLER: It was not so much that I was caving in to peer pressure; I just did what I needed, really. I played baseball. I did things with my buddy, like making whiskey. I hunted and fished. I was not a poor student. I was a good student, and I was elected again and again for all those offices that none of the other kids wanted. They figured, "Let Miller do it." President of the class, student council, that sort of thing.

BEATTIE: Was English your favorite subject in high school?

MILLER: I think I would have to say it was, yes. I was salutatorian at the eighth grade graduation. But then in high school, my grades went down, and I was not even in the academic running. There was about thirty-five or thirty-six of us in my graduating class. Very small. Two of us went off to college.

BEATTIE: Will you tell me about your time in Berea, and did you go straight from high school to Berea?

MILLER: Yes. Dr. Willis Weatherford, Sr.—who was a member of the Berea College Board of Regents—lived at Black Mountain, North Carolina, about twelve miles to the east of Asheville. In the spring of the year he took some time out and he'd go out in the mountains. It was partly excursion for him. It was a good time of year to travel around. He would go around to small schools and go into the senior classes and tell the Berea story, and encourage students to consider going to Berea. So, I got application forms and simply applied. And, you know the callowness of youth, it didn't really make much difference to me one way or the other. I got accepted. Looking back on it, I think I should have been a little more apprehensive about it, because obviously it's the most important thing that ever happened to me, really. It changes your whole life.

I went up to Berea in September of 1954. And I simply went through in the mid-fifties a typical situation at Berea, where all the students worked. But it was so easy to do because it's unlike many other colleges where students have to work also, but the college doesn't acknowledge this, the college doesn't care. The only difference at Berea was that there were people who were half-time students, that is, who worked a lot more because they had no money whatsoever. There's no tuition, just room and board, essentially. We had money for that. Then, after a couple of years, I started getting even those charges dropped from some anonymous donor I never knew. The stipulation was that teachers at Berea could put forward names of students who might receive these things, but the donor was to remain anonymous. It would be like a hundred-and-seventy-five dollars a semester or something like that for this room and board. I would get that remitted.

BEATTIE: I assume your family was supportive of your going to college?

MILLER: Oh, yes, very much so. It's just amazing. I went up there at seventeen. You know how old my mother was at the time? Thirty-four. My mother was sixteen when I was born, and we grew up together.

BEATTIE: What was your Berea experience like?

MILLER: Well, I simply went up there and did my work, my labor assignment, and went through the classes. When I told my parents that I had decided to become an English major, they did not question this. They thought that was all right; whatever I wanted to do was fine with them.

By my sophomore year I was interested in getting into the literary organization on the campus at Berea, an organization called Twenty Writers. It was so-called because at any given time that was the limit, and it was competitive getting into that. I submitted some material. I was already seeing a lot of this girl whose student labor at the time was teaching laboratory courses in German. I was studying German. And that was Mary Ellen, my wife. She was a member, already, of Twenty Writers. She called me one evening on the phone. She was calling me as a representative of Twenty Writers to tell me that the group had met, and had taken in a couple of new members, and I was one of them.

BEATTIE: How did the group function? Were faculty members involved?

MILLER: There was a faculty advisor. In those days, his name was Thomas McRoberts Kreider, a member of the English department. He was later department head, and a couple of years ago, he retired. I'm still in contact with him and his wife, Janet. She taught journalism at Berea. So he was the faculty advisor, and we met on a regular basis. We had an agenda; we'd know going into the meeting who was going to be presenting work, because usually they would have, in those days, mimeographed it and given everybody copies, and we would have read them in advance. Then the person would get up and read their piece, or their poem, story, whatever, and we would critique it.

BEATTIE: So it was a workshop method?

MILLER: It was a workshop method, yes. We also had an annual publication, a publication of Twenty Writers.

BEATTIE: Was that the literary magazine for the campus or a separate publication?

MILLER: It was a separate one. It was just for that organization, because there was another publication put out by Miss Emily Ann Smith's prose writing class.

BEATTIE: I remember [Kentucky poet] Albert Stewart talking about Emily Ann Smith and how influential she was for him.

MILLER: Oh, yes. For generations. Miss Smith passed away last week. I think she was eighty-nine. She was a wonderful teacher of both literature and of writing.

BEATTIE: Do you think Twenty Writers taught you critical skills as much or more than your classes, or was it just an additional help?

MILLER: There was a reciprocity to it. You certainly got experience critiquing a piece of work like that and, of course, I think we looked at our fellow students' work, bringing to that task the criteria that we got out of the classroom. We would look at it just the way we would look at something we were asked to read that might be a classic. Often times, we would allude to our learning.

BEATTIE: You met your wife at Berea. When did you marry?

MILLER: We married in August of 1958. She had graduated in 1957; she was a year ahead of me.

BEATTIE: And her major was . . . ?

MILLER: English.

BEATTIE: You had also majored in English at Berea.

MILLER: Yes. Between my junior and senior years—that is as a rising senior, in that summer—I did a home stay in Germany under the auspices of the Experiment in International Living—which is headquartered in Putney, Vermont—and they always encourage Berea College to send someone from that group. They tried to bring in some geographic diversity in the groups they sent over. So, I had done that, and while I did not have technically a major in German, I had maybe a minor in German, plus this experience. It was on the strength of that that I went to Fort Knox Independent School System as a kind of combination English and German teacher. I taught there two years. I would teach one class every semester of English, but mostly I taught skill-level German.

It was a pleasant experience in many, many ways, and the two years were very different. The first year, Mary Ellen and I lived in Elizabethtown and commuted. Then, she substituted that year for a woman who was on a sabbatical leave, and she worked with the seniors. She was the senior class advisor, and that meant she had the business of supervising the class annual and all the special things seniors do. And, you know, she made less money than I did. It was just like the old *Mary Tyler Moore Show,* when Mary Tyler Moore goes in and asks Mr. Grant for a raise. And why are these other people making . . . ? And he just says flat out rough, "Because they're men and you're a woman." They sat right there in the offices, Mary Ellen and I side by side on chairs, and said, "We're going to give him more money than you because he's a man." We encountered the same attitude originally when we came here [Western Kentucky University]. But it has changed, it has changed.

Mary Ellen then just taught that one year, and she made arrangements to go back to graduate school at the University of Kentucky. So, in the summer, we set her up with an apartment in Lexington, and I stayed on another year at Fort Knox, but I lived on the base that year. I lived in the bachelor officers' quarters at Fort Knox. I was there taking my meals in the cafeteria with all of these first lieutenants and people ambitious to make it as officers in the United States Army.

BEATTIE: I read you had written that when you went to the Fort Knox schools, even though the person who hired you had had your résumé for some months, he saw right before you started teaching that you hadn't had any education courses, so he asked you to go back and take some.

MILLER: That's true. Because there was a teacher shortage, the education department in Frankfort had emergency certificates and ways in which they could get around it. So when we did go over to Fort Knox in the beginning, we had a week of orientation. Teachers came to the school every day, Monday through Friday, for a week. I think it was on a Friday afternoon, the last day of that orientation, that a message came for me that I should go by the superintendent's office before I left the base that day, very important. I went over and they confronted me with the fact that I had no education courses. I simply said, "Well, you've had my dossier since April, and I never pretended to have these." He said, "Well, this is a very serious problem." So he provided the forms and I projected a plan of study over the next, I believe, seven years it would take me just taking courses in summer school. In order to go back and teach that next year, I had to begin my plan, which I did down at Western Carolina College. Then, the next year following, I went back to graduate school, and it became a moot question. I never completed my education courses.

BEATTIE: And you decided to go to Vanderbilt and ended up majoring in German instead of English?

MILLER: Yes, and that decision was made at a pay phone in the bachelor officers' quarters there, because I submitted my application for the English department at Vanderbilt, because I had learned about the Fugitive Agrarian literary group while a student at Berea, and I thought that those people were keen and neat and all that. Robert Penn Warren, Allen Tate, and John Crowe Ransom were probably the best-known names in the group. I wanted to just go down there and study and be associated with Vanderbilt. In my naïveté I felt that probably those people were still there. I didn't know they had long since departed. The only member of the Fugitive Agrarian group who was still there at the time was Donald Davidson. I eventually did study with Donald Davidson and Randall Stewart, who was a well-known Hawthorne scholar, and who was department head. But, I was only offered an assistantship at Vanderbilt.

But my materials were seen by this fellow from the Department of Germanic and Slavic Languages. He noted that I had been on this Experiment in International Living, that I had been teaching German, that I was, at the time, teaching German at Fort Knox. He simply called me on the telephone with the purpose of persuading me to change my area of study, and he had some very tempting incentives. He was, in effect, offering me one. An NDEA [National Defense Education Act] Fellowship, which did not require me to teach and would allow me to carry a full program. Well, even though I was teaching German, I thought that would be a very high-powered program, and it was, and I wasn't at all confident about it. But more than that, I did not want to go into that field; I wanted to study English. So, we had conversations by telephone while I was there, and he was very persistent. Dr. Joseph Rysan, born and brought up in Prague, Czechoslovakia—what really clinched it was his final point that I could still study under these people in the Vanderbilt English department. I could take a kind of minor in that, and at the same time study with him. So I agreed that we could do that, after having discussed it with Mary Ellen. We did move to

Nashville, again leaving in August, by which time we'd been married two years. That's when she found work at the Methodist Publishing House as a copywriter for *Together* magazine, and I began that program at Vanderbilt, a three-year residency.

Then we came here to Bowling Green. I chose to come to Bowling Green and Western Kentucky University because I had met, by that time, a lot of people who had gone to school here. It was Western's proximity to Vanderbilt's library that attracted me, because I'd only completed my residency and the course requirements, and then I had to do the dissertation, and I thought it would be an advantage to be close. I came here and found that this school was just growing by leaps and bounds, and there was plenty of work to do. At the end of my second year here, three people retired out of this department. One of these people was a German teacher and all of his courses opened up for me. If I had gone to some other place, I guess I would have had to teach as a junior member seven or eight years before I could have gotten courses that were suddenly thrust upon me.

BEATTIE: So you were able to teach German literature courses as well as language classes?

MILLER: Right. Mary Ellen joined the English department. We got so busy, we didn't think about going anywhere else, and there was nothing to push us out of here and there was nothing, really, to pull us anywhere else, so we've had no regrets about this place. It's been a very good place for us.

BEATTIE: Do you find, or have you found in the past, that you've had English students wanting to work with you?

MILLER: Yes, and a lot of people here think I am in the English department. This is, to me, a sad thing, in a way. They think, "He writes, so he must be in English," as if nobody but an English department person would write. Sometimes a member of the English department here will ask me to come and make a presentation in a class that they're teaching, but I've not taught any English classes here as part of my official load. This is just something I do. When I've taught outside of my field, it has been in Western's honors program, where I would make up a kind of a theme course, or a topical course. The other thing is, the way our department is structured here, it is a department of modern languages and intercultural studies. That includes minority studies, women's studies, black studies, and also our folklore program, which is one of the best in the country. I have taught, and still do teach, when it comes up on a rotation basis, a course in Appalachian folklore and folk life. But again, the tie-in is there, to some extent, in the rationale and methodology, because there were so many early Germans who were theorists of the whole notion of folklore. The very word "folklore" is a translation from Johann Gottfried Herd's German word "Volkskunde." You just take the two parts of the term, "volk" and then "kunde," meaning knowledge or lore. Because before that happened, people who were interested in folklore in England, and in the English speaking world, referred to is as popular antiquities, and that was a kind of galumphing phrase that was not going to go anywhere.

BEATTIE: Were you writing when you were teaching at the Fort Knox Schools and while you were in graduate school?

MILLER: Yes, I was writing all the time. I have written, from time to time, my best stuff, I think, and turned out the most, when I had the most work to do teaching. That is, it's that old notion that the task expands to fill whatever time you have for it. Then, the opposite of that is, if you feel an urgency, you can get it done somehow.

BEATTIE: Sheer adrenalin, maybe?

MILLER: Yes, you have to. I mean, in journalism you don't wait for an inspiration, do you? You almost always have a deadline. I began writing a bunch of little poems at Vanderbilt in the spring of 1963, at a time when the demands on time were just really tough, because I was getting ready for my oral examinations to be admitted to candidacy and all of that, and there was just logically no time to do anything else. But these poems were coming, and I had to do something with them, and also, they were a kind of a diversion from . . . You know, you need a little break from whatever it is you're doing, no matter how much you're devoted to it. So I started writing those, and I sent away eight or ten of them in March, maybe, of 1963, to Maxine Kumin, who was conducting "The Writer's Workshop," a column in the magazine the *Writer,* and promptly forgot all about them. It was not until July when, accidentally, I picked up a copy of the *Writer* from a bookstore rack in Nashville, opened it up to her column because I read it whenever I thought of it, and there was my poem discussed.

BEATTIE: That must have been a wonderful first experience.

MILLER: It sure was. That was my first stuff in print that was outside of an academic publication.

BEATTIE: Would you talk about your publishing career after that?

MILLER: Well, the appearance of those poems in that column certainly greased the skids. About six weeks later, after those poems appeared in the July, 1963, number of the *Writer*—I got a big manila envelope from the *Writer,* and it was filled with cards and letters from the editors of literary magazines. They all said pretty much the same thing, "We noted the poems that were discussed in Maxine Kumin's column. If you have other poems like that, we would certainly be interested in seeing them." So that's an entrée, isn't it? That's a foot in the door. I did not send poems out to all of the places that responded like that, but I did to some, and it's helped.

BEATTIE: Wasn't that unusual, to have magazines request your work?

MILLER: Oh, yes. It was just a stroke of colossally good luck.

BEATTIE: Were they little magazines, poetry magazines?

MILLER: Little magazines, that's right. And from that point on, I would simply get the *Directory of Little Magazines and Small Presses,* and look around in it and send poems and stories and essays out to places that looked like they were publishing the sort of stuff I had. Over the years I must confess that I have narrowed my range. I don't send out material blind much, anymore. My problem has come to be to resist the temptation to send out a poem that's not particularly good. I've learned that I write in jags. That is, I might write six or seven poems that would deal with the same theme or that would be working with the same imagery, and I might write five or six poems before I write *the* one. Or sometimes, I'll write past the poem that I am looking for. I won't even recognize it. It may be the third attempt would be *the* one, but then I'll go ahead and write three or four more that are not as good as that, and editors will help me to see this. Jerry Williamson, who edited *The Mountains Have Come Closer,* helped me to see this. So, what I don't need to do nowadays, is to send out derivative poems that are parodies of my best work.

BEATTIE: Are you saying that you have to be your own best editor, because you're afraid your own name recognition will get you published, even if you don't think it's your best work?

MILLER: That's right. People will publish poems of mine that I will not allow to be published, because I don't always write good poems. Who does?

BEATTIE: *The Mountains Have Come Closer* is what you won the Thomas Wolfe Award for.

MILLER: Yes. That book still tends to be more or less the one that if someone asks what of mine they should read, I will tell them that that's, essentially, it.

BEATTIE: Would you talk about your publishing career in terms of each book, and what you're working on now?

MILLER: My first poems were published in a little book called *Copperhead Cane,* published in a series by Robert Moore Allen in Nashville. He was one of the people who got in touch with me after my poems appeared in the *Writer.* He said, "Do you have a collection?" I said, "I don't have at this time, but I project having a number of poems that would make a collection by thus-and-such a date." So in 1964 he published this little book called *Copperhead Cane,* so-called because there was an image of a walking cane, the handle of which is carved into a snake's head. Then I came up here [Bowling Green].

After that I devoted myself for a while to finishing a dissertation. It was printed in 1965. Then I began teaching here and publishing in all kinds of little magazines, mostly having to do with the Appalachian region, because my work, from the very beginning, was connected with place, or perceived as being an expression of place. I did not publish another book until 1971, which was a little collection of ballads from Whippoorwill Press having to do with political activism, mostly in the East Kentucky coal fields, and that was done by a press that Lee Pennington had suggested to me. The collection was called *The More Things Change the More They Stay the Same.* That was in 1971.

In 1974 I went back to the material that had the poems of *Copperhead Cane* and added another section to it, and submitted it to the University of Georgia Press. They liked the manuscript and wanted to include it in their contemporary poets series. But the editor, oddly enough, wanted me to lengthen my manuscript, because they wanted it approximately the same length as the other things in their series. I said, "I don't believe I have other poems that belong with these." The editor said, "Send me what you have and let me take a look." Out of the poems that I sent, he made a selection for a third section of the book, and as a consequence, showed me a relationship between my poems that I'd never seen before. Oddly enough, though—and this was *Dialogue with a Dead Man,* 1974, University of Georgia Press—the reviewers of that book separated almost equally as to whether or not they thought the third section was appropriate or whether they thought it was inappropriate. It was just a toss up.

Well, by that time I had already been on sabbatical leave, in the spring of 1970, in which I went to Austria with the express purpose of becoming more acquainted with contemporary German and Austrian literary poets. I made acquaintance with lots of people, and I read some stuff by another fellow that I liked, and located him in Salzburg. I began translating his work. His name is Emil Lerperger. He won an Austrian national prize for poetry. I translated selections from various of his books and published them with the Green River Press in a book called *The Figure of Fulfillment.* But, you know, you don't really translate poems, you just make other poems that sort of parallel the originals. That was in '75.

Dialogue with a Dead Man was quickly sold out at the University of Georgia Press, and I had a letter that I showed when it came. It said, "Your book has been our best seller in the poetry series. We will not be reprinting it." They said, "I know this sounds strange, but it has to do with the circumstances of university press publication, so we remit to you the rights. Good luck." I showed this letter to Raymond Tyner, who was the publisher of the *Green River Review* and of the press who just published my translations. He took the book and reprinted it in 1978 and kept it in print a long time so that people became acquainted with it.

In 1980, with the Appalachian Consortium Press, I published *The Mountains Have Come Closer.* They kept the book in print a long, long time. Then in the mid-eighties I published with Seven Buffaloes Press two or three little things. First of all, *Vein of Words,* a group of poems almost exclusively dealing with the writing of poetry. In '86, I published *Nostalgia for 70* with them, also.

Then I made the acquaintance of Jonathan Greene and his Gnomon Press. I published the little chapbook, the short story, *His First, Best Country* with Gnomon, followed by *Brier: His Book,* a collection of poems involving the persona of a Brier who is just a kind of representative Southern Appalachian person.

So, that's where I stand. All along during this time, of course, I published reviews, I published articles in these mostly regional magazines, but sometimes little, fluffy pieces. I did a piece on language for the *New York Times Magazine,* a piece on language for the *Houston Chronicle*; I wrote journalism on the side. I told you about six articles that I have published on the occasion of James Still's eightieth birthday. And, of course, I've done editorial work for the Jesse Stuart Foundation, bringing out Stuart's out-of-print books. Then, of course, I edited James Still's collected poems. In addition, I wrote a little book— and it is a book—called *The Examined Life: Family, Community, and Work as Reflected in American Literature,* as the culminating item in a three-year seminar that we conducted down at Boone, North Carolina, for the Southern Highlanders Institute for Educators. It was for secondary school teachers coming back in the summer. I directed that institute, and we published a book out of that.

BEATTIE: Do you enjoy going back and forth between different genres and different types of writing?

MILLER: Right. And, see, I never intended to write this little novel, *Newfound.* It came in '89. What happened was, it's this networking of these connections. Some of my poems were used in Bradbury Press's anthologies for young people. In fact, I told George Ella Lyon, the Lexington writer, about Bradbury Press and their needing things, and she published things there, too. And once, after she had been in contact with Richard Jackson, an editor for Bradbury, she sent word to me that Jackson had said, "Miller's poems also have a narrative thrust to them. Why doesn't he write us a real narrative? Why doesn't he write us a novel?" I was working with her at the Hindman Settlement School Writers' Workshop [Appalachian Writers' Workshop] when she brought me that news. So I took a short story I had and submitted it along with an outline as to how I would develop it, and the short story became the first three chapters of *Newfound.* I would say I wrote the novel, while teaching here and doing everything else, in about six weeks.

BEATTIE: You were talking about *His First, Best Country,* which is about to be produced at Horse Cave Theater here in Kentucky this summer for the state's bicentennial. Will you talk about the origin of that and about how it has evolved from other genres?

MILLER: Well, I originally wrote a short story about a fellow, and I was again doing it on the premise, "What if a person, such as myself, tried to go back to the community where they were born and brought up? What kind of problems would there be, what kind of complications?" The story, then, is about this fellow, Robert Jennings Wells, who is the grown-up version of the Robert Wells in *Newfound,* taking Roma Jean Livesay, this disturbingly beautiful woman, and his cousin, Edna Rae, to a Conway Twitty concert. That's what it's about, and it's about the social gaffs he makes.

Now, I had another bunch of fictional material in progress that involves a boy whose mother has brought him back and left him to be raised by his grandparents while she's off living in the American fun house. So now I have added to the story of the Conway Twitty business this boy and the grandparents and the house, and that's what *His First, Best Country* as a play is about. What I'm doing here is I'm constituting a family. They don't know it yet, but here's Robert Jennings Wells, and he's back after all these years, and here's Roma Jean Livesay, who's had two husbands in this place, and they've both been no-accounts, and she's worked for the welfare office or something, and here's this boy whose grandparents had to move out of this old house because it's been impounded by the Army Corps of Engineers. Well, the play is about how those people get forged into a family; a father, a mother, a son; or a husband, a wife, and a kind of blended family. That's what it's about.

BEATTIE: So it has come from a short story to a play.

MILLER: And it's going on out into novel form. And the thing that has impressed me in doing all of this is using the same material, essentially, the different possibilities and impossibilities of these two genres. For instance, I think some of the best effects are gotten in prose by the interior monologue. You can get inside of somebody's head and you can see the world from their point of view. You can't do that with a play. With those people on the stage, one viewpoint is as valid as another, depending on what you do with them.

BEATTIE: Do you find that your heroes or heroines or protagonists vary from genre to genre, or that the sympathy level or identification level varies, or the message itself varies, perhaps?

MILLER: As I said in the *Courier-Journal* not long ago, I think drama is the most demanding form. You can't meander. In a short story even, or certainly in a novel, you can meander, you can take little side trips and come back to the main theme. This has got to be straight down the track. Otherwise, if there's not any conflict, it just comes to a screeching halt.

BEATTIE: Do you still feel that your natural bent is poetry?

MILLER: Yes, I really do.

BEATTIE: And the other genres are things that you can do, but they don't come as naturally?

MILLER: Right. I think I can do them and do a workman-like job, but I've noticed something as I've been rewriting this play. The very places that I've been asked to delete things are places that are a little lyrical moment. They do not work in the play or you've got to mention them very briefly and get on with it.

BEATTIE: What other things are you working on now, and what future work do you have planned?

MILLER: What I like to do, I like to write something that just bubbles up out of me and that's my own agenda. I don't have any place to publish it, I'm not thinking about publishing. I write it because I like to do it. The other thing is, I like to take something as a job of work and say, "This is what these people need, it's what they say they need, it's what they want," that's appropriate for where it would appear without any particular enthusiasm about it, just sit down and see if can I do this, say the way a man might make a cabinet to go in the kitchen. Craft. I mean, the business of writing as being able to do something; that's what you do. It may not be exactly the thing that you're most enthusiastic about, but you can do it. In some ways, I'm prouder of being able to do that, on occasion, than I am of the other, more mysterious fiction.

BEATTIE: Some people look at creativity as a response to a deficit. I don't know if it's a gift or a response to a deficit.

MILLER: It's a quest for me and it's a discovery with me. It just amazes me, and forever does again and again and again, that I can sit down, and I'll have this thing that maybe I want to write, and I'll play with it a little, and something happens. A thing that I hadn't thought of at all comes up. It's like the old German proverb, "Der Appetit kommt beim Essen—the appetite comes with eating." You can start out cold and you just don't have any particular urge, and you warm to it. You get involved with it, and suddenly you think of something that you hadn't thought of, but it was there, and you sort of teased it out. Well, to me, that's an ever-fresh kind of thing to do. It never cloys; it's just as much fun as it was the last time.

BEATTIE: You wrote something which I could relate to very well, that it's the process of writing that's important, and not the product.

MILLER: Yes, because you don't think it all out. I don't know of anybody who does think it all out ahead of time. The process drags up the rest of what you need. In retrospect, you see that you wrote that thing really in order to get to something else. Sometimes you have to write a thing not because you are going to sell it, or you're going to place it or publish it or anything like that, but you have to do that in order to get on to something else. You don't really get exactly what it was until you're already there.

BEATTIE: I've been asking writers what they think the nature of creativity is. Is there anything that you can add to that?

MILLER: I think it's a pulling together of things.

BEATTIE: Although people talk about poems and writing that sometimes come as gifts, they can't explain them. But the rest of writing is hard work. Do you experience the same thing?

MILLER: I experience that, and some things come easier than others, but even when they come easy, I look back in time and I have been able to understand why it came easy. That is, there had been a long preparation that I didn't know anything about, and in *The Vein of Words*, I've got a little poem called "Something" in which I say, often times this poem that you write is something that you sent away for years ago, and now it is arriving like a package that comes in the mail. That is, there'll always be a background to it, especially, if it does just coalesce with a surprising degree of ease.

BEATTIE: In your essay in *Contemporary Authors* you write, "Freud says somewhere that writing has it's origin in the voice of an absent person. Many of my early poems, like the ones Maxine Kumin commented on, were eulogies to an absent person spoken in a voice that was not quite mine. After writing the poem 'Meeting,' the absent person, my grandfather, began to speak in his own well-remembered voice as if answering because he had been spoken to." Was writing your poem 'Meeting,' then, a turning point for you in developing your own poetic voice?

MILLER: Yes, and it was an anchor point in that collection, *Dialogue with a Dead Man,* because up to that point only the live man was speaking and, of course, you've got to have two people for a dialogue. So, once that happened, I got the other side of the conversation. I think that whether Freud is right in that speculation, this kind of writing is about the absence of something, whether it's a human voice or it's a way of getting things right. I've thought of it as dieseling. You know, when your car is not firing just right, you could pull into the driveway and turn off the switch, and the car keeps going, keeps running. My mind typically, after I've been involved in situations and new experiences, will diesel. I won't just go on to something else, I will ruminate on that and I'll go back over it and over it and over it. And in the process, I think it's Wright Morris who says, "Fiction begins with the act of remembering." As soon as you begin to remember something that's happened to you that you've been involved in, you are remembering in a selective way. The way to test this, and I've done this with members of my family, with my sister and my brothers, we'll be together at Christmas, and we'll recall something that happened in the family years ago. We were all right there. I will remember it one way and usually my sister will take violent opposition to it . . . you know, that it wasn't that way at all, or, "You're leaving out what really started it," and I may be. It's just that we all have these different viewpoints from the way we come at things, and that's another little juncture where fiction diverges from the active facts.

BEATTIE: But, in a sense, you're writing about an absence in order to become more whole yourself, to fulfill something.

MILLER: To fulfill it, yes. In those poems I was writing about the absent grandfather because I wanted him to be there. That's one way I could hear him again.

BEATTIE: Or you're trying to find a way of coming to terms with or to understand something.

MILLER: I know that those poems are therapeutic to me, and I was so pleased one time to learn that over in Indiana at a mental retardation facility, I got word that someone was using them in a grief therapy program. To me that was better than a positive review.

BEATTIE: You write in your poem "A House of Readers," "I saw myself as essentially a farmer raising a crop of kids," writing about yourself. You haven't talked about your own children yet, but I want to ask you about them, and is that farming or Appalachian connection still, do you think, the strongest aspect of your identity as a person as well as a writer?

MILLER: I think so. I don't know why people have difficulty admitting or considering that who they are has something to do with where they are or with where they've been. Yes, here I was, well into my work here at Western, my kids growing up, one of them lying on the floor reading his book, another one lying on the floor in a pile of books about magic. That's when Fred [Miller's son] was literally studying magic and doing magic tricks. And I remembered an anecdote, an old joke about a man who's up in this rocky field with three big strapping sons, and his neighbor passes along and stops to pass the time of day with him. And he says, "Well, John, why are you having those boys pick all them rocks up out of that field? That land is so poor and steep it won't raise anything." The farmer puts his hand over his mouth so the boys won't hear and says, "It'll raise boys." He knows that he's just got a discipline going there, you see. We didn't have anything more than a garden plot, and I was away from all of that, and yet that rural imagery and that imagery of agriculture was creeping into my poem. It all culminated in that notion of being a grower of children, if not of corn.

BEATTIE: A related question: you define the Brier as a quintessential Southern Appalachian person struggling to remain free of an ascribed identity, determined to be himself. Do you relate to struggling to remain free of an ascribed identity, or do you embrace that identity?

MILLER: Yes, I have difficulty with it. I think that, in some ways, I don't have any difficulty, as I said a moment ago, considering that who I am has to do with everything that I have been and everything that I've experienced. That's why I used Thomas Wolfe's observation, "Each of us is all the sums he has not counted," as a little statement to put in the front of *Newfound*. I'm not reluctant to count those sums, but because the Appalachian region has associated with it so many negative stereotypes, I do know people of my approximate age and background who are uncomfortable talking about that, who want to falsify, who don't want to admit that they've come from humble circumstances, or that they were deprived in lots of ways. I don't feel reluctant to talk about that, especially in terms of literary reception. Because, you see, Appalachia, in the public mind, in the popular American mind, we're very ambivalent about it. We have a very positive image of it and also a very negative image, and we use these depending upon what we're after. If you take on a long-running television series like *The Waltons*, that's the positive image of the South, generally, of the southern mountains, because they live over there at the foot of Walton Mountain, and they're just the best people you could imagine, and they live this, in some ways, idyllic existence.

The same subset of people, the same general area, will give you these southern gothic stories like [James] Dickey's *Deliverance*, where for no apparent reason, these toothless savages just want to do in these nice folks from the suburbs of Atlanta. My own experience is that, sure horrible things and violent things have happened and do happen in the southern mountains, and there are poor people, and there is a low rate of educational attainment, and all of those things that we're living in. Yet I have never been particularly afraid in those places; I've been much more frightened in the Washington airport.

BEATTIE: Maybe it's human nature just to be afraid of what's foreign.

MILLER: I think it is. It's not unrelated to the notion that sociologists have found that when we talk about violence, the violence we really fear is the violence that is anonymous, it's the person we've never seen before in our lives who mugs us on the street. But if we're talking about violence in our community and we're sort of familiar with the people who perpetrated it, it doesn't bother us in the same way. We're more tolerant of it, somehow. It's common around here for people to say, after learning that somebody got shot, well, "He needed shooting." You know, they know him.

BEATTIE: It's interested me in the last two decades how what was previously put down, regional writing, has become all the vogue since, maybe, *Foxfire*, to the point where instead of such an association's being terrible, it has become so glorified that it's not real, either.

MILLER: Precisely, and I don't want to be in either camp. I don't want my writing to be automatically put down because it's about the South or the Mountain South. On the other hand, I don't want it to be automatically glorified as good writing.

BEATTIE: Some of the Kentucky writers that I have been interviewing have a very definite sense of place in their writing that has to do with geography or region, whether it's Western Kentucky or Eastern Kentucky or the Bluegrass or even the state's urban areas. Others, I think, their place in their fiction is a psychological state far more than a geographical state.

MILLER: I think that place is one factor, one of many factors, that have to be considered in talking about the way you write or in talking about the product and the end, and these things are cyclical. The attachment to place, or the focus, the high definition of one particular place in the country, this varies from time to time. This argument was going on in the nineteenth century in the time of William Dean Howells, who was infusing into the genteel literature of the Northeast something a little rougher and wilder and woollier. Some New England critic, whose name escapes me right now, carried this to its logical extreme and showed how too much emphasis upon this would result in a determinism, to the point, he said, that any writer who came from a mountainous area would have to identify himself as such on the frontispiece of his book, and that we could condemn his work unless it gave us a sense of sublimity.

BEATTIE: What about writers who have influenced you? Can you talk about who they may be?

MILLER: Well, I was an English major as an undergraduate. I'd come through a good English program at Berea College, and we studied the Greek classics, we studied the novels and the poetry of the writers who, in the fifties, were a part of the cannon. I studied American literature and, of course, I made my own special study, out of school, of southern American writers. I told James Still one time, "I've gone to school to you; you never did know it." That is, I just read him with a special interest, the way I read Harriette Arnow, or Jesse Stuart, because these people were folks who were writing about a place and a culture, or a subset of our culture, that I came out of myself. So I read them with special interest, and also that interest was heightened in consideration that these people made these books. These are made things. How did they do it? I would look and see how the story was crafted, how the poem was put together. So, obviously, those people have influenced me.

But I would say also that there are some German writers, since I have taught German literature and continue to teach it, who have influenced me, and one is a woman, a nineteenth-century poet that I did a dissertation on, with the imposing name of Annette Von Droste-Hülshoff. I studied her work in great detail. Some other nineteenth-century poets—Edward Moerike, Theodor Storm—these people tended to be regional writers of their place. There's a phenomenon in German literature that's known as *Heimatsliteratur, heimat* meaning homeland. So *Heimatsliteratur* is writing that is sort of consciously regional, and I've been influenced by people like that.

BEATTIE: What about contemporary Kentucky authors? Are there any you particularly admire?

MILLER: Oh, I admire something about just about every writer that is working right now. Whenever I do a spoof of somebody, when I do a satirical send-up of somebody, it's because I have become so familiar with their work from having liked it and read it and read it and read it, that it's almost like a baseball pitcher who telegraphs the particular kind of pitch. I can see it coming after a while, so I can imitate them. It's the old notion that imitation is a form of flattery. I've done a spoof of Bobbie Ann Mason, for instance. I think I called it, "Bobbie Ann Mason Writes Little Red Riding Hood." I wrote a spoof of Wendell

Berry. I think it's called "Wendell Berry Comes Up from the Fields." There's just all sorts of things that I like about different writers who are working. [Ed] McClanahan, for instance, I remember when his *The Natural Man* came out, he was giving a reading over at Centre College, at the bookstore there. I'd already read the book, and I had trepidations because I didn't know, even in this day and time, what might happen there, and I knew that it's just a raunchy book. So, he said, "I have a clean reading and a dirty reading for this book, and I'm going to give you the clean reading." I thought, "Oh, great," because of those little under-graduates. He proceeded to read the dirtiest stuff I had ever heard.

McClanahan is a slow writer; he's not written a lot, but he waits till he gets it right, whatever the circumstances of his life are. When that book appeared, there was a little article in the back of a *New York Times Book Review,* and I clipped it and gave it to him, that he held the prize for having delayed a novel's publication the longest. Gurney Norman, I reviewed *Divine Right's Trip* in the early seventies when it came out, for the *Courier-Journal,* and I thought it's an interesting kind of a thesis novel, but Gurney is wiser than he seems. That is, he does his best work as a writer, and those little simple stories, *[Kinfolks: The Wilgus Stories],* they're just as clear as spring water, but there's a lot of depth to them, too.

BEATTIE: When were you at Yaddo with James Still, and was that on more than one occasion?

MILLER: We were there for about three weeks at a time in the summer of '83 and again in the summer of '84. And, of course, the setup there is, I had my own accommodations, he had his. He had his living quarters and his workroom. I had my living quarters and workroom, and we saw one another at meals.

BEATTIE: He talked about one time when he was there, Sallie Bingham's being there, too.

MILLER: Yes.

BEATTIE: Was that at a time when you were there?

MILLER: Yes, and we frequently conversed at mealtime with Sallie. Sallie was on a slightly different schedule; she may have already been there when we arrived and then she left before we did, because people were coming and going all the time. Then, I think, from there she went on to MacDowell.

BEATTIE: How do you find such places, as places to work?

MILLER: I don't like them at all.

BEATTIE: You're, I think, the only person who has said that. Why is that?

MILLER: It makes me self-conscious to go to any particular place, a special place, to write, because writing is not a special thing for me; it's something I do all the time. I could write anywhere, but if I'm staying over in a motel or something on my way to someplace else, and I need to write something, I set up right there and do it. To me, it was especially daunting there because, well, you go ahead and you get settled and then you come to lunch. "Oh, where are you staying?" This is some stranger over there. "Oh, I'm staying in West Hall." "Which apartment?" "Well, the one on this end, I think it's A-6, or something." "Oh, yes. That's where William Carlos Williams stayed."

BEATTIE: So, it's really the artificial demand put on you to be the writer versus the concentration on writing itself.

MILLER: Right. To be The Writer. It threw me off my pace somehow. Of course, the other thing was that both times I was there with Still, I was working on my own stuff, sure, but this was a time when I was supposed to be Boswell to his Johnson, you know. In fact, a rumor started at Yaddo that I was James Still's biographer. That, too, annoyed me. I have done these things with Still, and I may do more, but I just don't want to lock myself into doing anything like that.

BEATTIE: In *Vein of Words* you have several poems about poetry workshops and about teaching. Could you comment on how you think creative writing should be taught and how writers' workshops should be run?

MILLER: Well, W. H. Auden has said the thing that has stuck in my mind about this: "You hang around writing until you get the hang of it." I had already been hanging around writing a long time before I came across that observation and realized there's something to this. One of the frustrations in working with people who come to writers' workshops is that I run into too many people who are interested in the writing, but they aren't interested in reading anything. I don't think that that will work. I think you've got to read all kinds of things and not for duty, but because, darn it, you're interested in them. I don't see much good writing. So, I work, as far as teaching writing—to the extent that I do it, and I do it only briefly here and there—I always work from models. I never get up and talk about writing, even if that's the announced topic.

BEATTIE: The model is more than the examples that come out of the workshop?

MILLER: Oh, absolutely. Published literature. I have a kind of loose-leaf thing that constantly changes and evolves. I'll throw out things and I'll add other things, whatever I find interesting or useful. Typically, I like to work with transparencies. I don't care if I've got something that's several pages, we will read that thing. We'll read it in the way a writer ought to read things . . . how it's made, how it gets its effect. Then, people may have already brought manuscripts to the workshop. Sometimes, depending on the format, they will have sent them in in advance. If I've had them in advance, I will already have read them and commented on them using as a background that piece of writing we looked at, which we know is successful, so that we've got a gauge. Remember what so-and-so did here and how they handled that, and look what you've done here. You've given us two paragraphs of the mountains as a static wall hanging; now how does James Still do this in the opening of "The Run for the Elbertas?" Something's happening, you see. He's given you the description of the mountains way down in the story somewhere. So that's the way I go at it.

BEATTIE: I was impressed by your recent essay in the first issue of *Thinker Review* from Louisville. I was wondering if you would discuss that essay?

MILLER: Well, it may be two or three essays. In the opening part, I think I call it "Reading, Writing, and Region: Notes from an American Periphery." In the first part of that essay, I talk of historical poetry looked at in the English-speaking world from somewhat of a historical perspective, how the function of poetry has changed in the last couple hundred years. Whereas poetry used to be a medium that was as common as MTV, now it has been moved off to the margin and it serves a narrower audience and perhaps a narrower function. Because poetry used to be an all-purpose medium, it gave people their "daily dose of narrative," and we've got to get it one way or the other. We're going to get our narrative, even if it's just gossip, or if it's out of the *National Enquirer.* But we have so many different sources for that now it has meant that poetry can be a pure thing; it can be just poetry, but it has definitely narrowed the audience, and people are almost specialists who read poetry, anymore. The other part of that article has to do with this whole business of place and region, and what I'm trying to do there is to point out we have collectively, in the United States, been so afraid of being anything less than national. Of course, nation is a political entity. It's a thing that's defined by history and things like that, but within any nation, as we are seeing, within any political entity, there are other kinds of more organic entities, ethnic groups, people who've lived in one place a long, long time and many, many generations. Those realities, we move so fast down the interstate of contemporary life that we don't see them. These are the little side roads, these are the blue highways of literature. I'm simply trying to call attention to that, and I'm trying to place it now in an international or global context. I thought it was a good time to do it, because we have talked about Russia, the Soviet Union. Well, who are the Russians? Different ethnic groups, you see. All of them one, with their separate subnational identities and languages. And foods. And folkways. The reality of the thing is there. Now, they were all yanked by main force into this political entity. It lasted a while, and it's come apart, and now they're going back. There was a kind of pax Soviet Union imposed upon these people. They were peaceful because somebody stronger had a boot on their necks. Now, are we going to ever learn? Or are we to just go back to the same old kinds of bitter fighting between these groups, or are we going to learn how to maintain these little group identities and get along with one another? I don't know. I'm not sanguine at all about the future there, or even in this country, because we're fragmented into factions and groups and everybody's a zealot on this or that subject. But what I'm looking for and what I'm hoping that writing in some way could contribute to, is the notion that you can hold these identities, but you've got to hold them in an informed and intelligent way and realize that somebody else can hold an identity proudly, or with confidence, at least, but that their doing so doesn't necessarily endanger me. It seems that in reality, once you look at history, it's always the lowest common denominator that prevails. I'd just like to ratchet up the denominator a little.

June 18, 1992

Books by Jim Wayne Miller

Copperhead Cane. Nashville, Tenn.: Allen, 1964.

The More Things Change the More They Stay the Same. Frankfort, Ky.: Whippoorwill, 1971.

Dialogue with a Dead Man. Athens: University of Georgia Press, 1974.

The Figure of Fulfillment. (Translations from the work of Emil Lerperger). Saginaw, MI.: Green River Press, 1975.

The Mountains Have Come Closer. Boone, N.C.: Appalachian Consortium Press, 1980.

Vein of Words. Big Timber, Mont.: Seven Buffaloes, 1984.

Nostalgia for 70. Big Timber, Mont.: Seven Buffaloes, 1986.

Brier: His Book. Frankfort, Ky.: Gnomon, 1988.

The Examined Life: Family, Community and Work in American Literature. Boone, N.C.: Appalachian Consortium Press, 1989.

Newfound. New York: Orchard, 1989.

His First, Best Country. Frankfort, Ky.: Gnomon, 1993.

Copperhead Cane. Bilingual English-German edition. Translated by Miller and Thomas Dorsett. Middletown, Ky.: Grex, 1995.

SENA JETER NASLUND

NASLUND: I am Sena Catherine Jeter Naslund. I was born June 28, 1942, in Birmingham, Alabama. My father's full name was Marvin Luther Jeter. He was born in 1892 in south Alabama in an area known as Helicon, which I always liked, since Helicon is the traditional home of the muses. My mother's full name is Flora Lee Easter Sims; actually, her name is Jeter. She's dead, too, now. She was born April 8, 1901, in McFall, Missouri.

My father was an M.D., and my mother had a bachelor of music degree from the American Conservatory of Music in Chicago. During my lifetime, she mainly played the piano. She taught music at home and in the public schools in Birmingham after I became about eight years old. My father's M.D. degree is from Emory University in Atlanta.

BEATTIE: Would you also tell me about what you recall about your grandparents or aunts or uncles?

NASLUND: All but one of my grandparents died before I was born. Actually, this would take a whole novel to discuss, and *is* taking one. It's a novel I'm working on, in fact, because I've gone back to writing some southern stuff after not doing it for a long time. But I only knew one of my grandparents, and this was my father's mother, whose name was Sena Sewanee Carter Jeter. I'm named for her, Sena. She was the first child in the family born right after the Civil War. When her father came back from the Civil War, he let it be known that he'd been befriended by a Yankee soldier whose last name was Sena. Just what this Yankee did for him isn't known, but when my great-grandfather got back home, he named his first child after his friend-enemy, Sena. I think it might have happened around Sewanee, Tennessee, since that was part of my grandmother's name, but I don't know that.

So, she's the only grandparent I remember, and she died when I was five years old. This grandmother lived next door to us with two of her daughters. The two daughters were the oldest surviving member of the family and the youngest surviving member. The oldest one, who was known as Pet, had been married and had a son who had disappeared, I think deserted, from the army during the Second World War. The youngest daughter's name was Kumi, and she never married. She was devoted to my father and to the family and to taking care of her mother. Her name was actually Myrtle Kumi, but she always went by Kumi. She taught mathematics for almost fifty years at Phillips High School, which was the big central high school in Birmingham. She actually had an M.A. in English from Auburn University. When she was hired, they wanted somebody to teach math and she was a math whiz, even though she'd chosen English. She, I think, was a frustrated writer. She did write a little bit of poetry, and she was devoutly, but eccentrically, religious. Kumi read the Bible all the time, but found no church compatible.

My other aunt, Aunt Pet, was a great storyteller. She had arthritis and was in bed most of the time, and she would tell me stories of mad dogs in south Alabama, and of "haints," ghosts. I loved to hear her stories, and she was unfailingly kind to me. The other aunt was impatient with me; she much preferred my older brother. I have two older brothers, Marvin Dock Jeter, who's an archaeologist, and John Sims Jeter, who is an engineer.

BEATTIE: What sort of childhood did you have and where was it spent?

NASLUND: It was spent largely in Birmingham, across the driveway from my grandmother and aunts, or then just my aunts, and then finally just my aunt, as people died off. But occasionally, we didn't live there, in Birmingham. My father worked as the company doctor for a coal mining company in West Virginia. When I was going on six years old, we spent the summer there, in Laredo, West Virginia, which was an exotic and interesting town to me. Then, when I was about eight, we spent a similar summer living in the state insane asylum in Jackson, Louisiana, or on the grounds of it. So, those were the places where I grew up.

I went to Norwood Grade School for the eight years I was there. It was seven-tenths of a mile to school, and the sidewalk ran beside a very lovely boulevard in front of older, richer, and more distinguished houses than ours. It was a picturesque walk. I enjoyed my sense of neighborhood quite a bit. I was an extremely good student and was conscientious about school work and cared about it and worked hard at my studies. I took up the cello when I was about nine, and this was a focal point for me from about nine to nineteen. I also became a fanatical Christian when I was nine, and it lasted about as long as the cello, about nine to nineteen.

I was a fierce little child and I felt very guilty about it. I was a very good fighter and I would beat up other children, and my brothers would have me race their older male friends, who I could usually beat. In fact, I beat them all.

BEATTIE: Did you find that having brothers made you want to do more traditionally tomboy types of things?

NASLUND: Absolutely. I was a pretty rough and tumble kid and, as I say, I did feel guilty about this, because after I beat somebody up, it'd be necessary to lie about it to their parents. So I had a huge head of guilt, which the neighborhood religious fanatic helped me with, telling me it was all gone, it was simple belief.

BEATTIE: This was the appeal of Christianity?

NASLUND: Exactly. I knew I was wicked and something needed to be done about it. My parents were not particularly religious people, or if they were, they were privately religious. I think they were agnostics, and religion was not a big concern of them. My father supported my Christianity, acknowledged it, and seemed pleased with it.

BEATTIE: Does this mean that you started going to church when you hadn't before?

NASLUND: My parents had always taken me to Sunday school, but it wasn't extreme enough to answer my extreme need of guilt. Nobody at Sunday school was talking about my wickedness. This was a fairly liberal Methodist church, and they weren't fundamentalist enough to suit me. I needed something bedrock, simple, and absolutely clear that addressed my issue, and I didn't find that in my Sunday school. But after I became a fanatic about the basement church of my neighbor, then I did become devoted to going to Sunday school. I noticed that someone else had gotten a one-year perfect attendance pin, so I said to myself, "I want one of those." But I wasn't content with one year; I ran it up to ten years. So I had a definite obsessive-compulsive streak about my growing up.

I read a great deal and enjoyed reading a great deal. That was one of the most enjoyable things I did as a child. I enjoyed playing the cello, too, but reading was finally more satisfying, much more satisfying.

BEATTIE: Did you pick up the love for reading on your own, or through school, or through family?

NASLUND: Both of my parents read to me, my father when I was fairly little, and my mother on for years. I simply loved to hear her read to me. Often it would be summer, the attic fan would be on, the bed had been moved over to the window so we'd get a breeze, and we'd be lounging there and she would read to me. But one summer when I was about, I don't know, ten or eleven, I was reading one of the books by myself, curled up in a chair. It was a hundred degrees in Birmingham, no air-conditioning. But I noticed that I was shivering, and I realized that the power of the language had transported me to a different physical condition. I was very impressed by this. I stopped and took note of it and thought I would like to be able to do this with language. It was a kind of moment of revelation, as far as my becoming a writer was concerned.

I did write as a child. I wrote some poetry. I wrote a newspaper when I was very small. That was my first thing, made-up newspapers about the imaginary world that I had. I was about six, I guess, when I started doing that. But I had insomnia, I had trouble sleeping, and I would entertain myself at night by telling myself stories. They were continuing stories; they went on forever. My newspaper was sort of about that world. I was always a male character in these things, because it seemed more exciting. I had a dear friend, who's still a wonderful friend, who would act out these things with me during the day. So we lived in a kind of prolonged fantasy where good triumphed over evil.

And I did feel guilty about not being able to sleep. I felt that good girls went to sleep at night and this was more evidence of my errant ways.

BEATTIE: What about school? What subjects did you like best?

NASLUND: Reading was my first special interest at school, and in about the fifth or sixth grade, that began to transfer into writing. I did have a teacher, Grace Montgomery, who thought I wrote good book reports. I remember doing one on a Richard Halliburton travel book that she thought had good descriptive words in it, so I was encouraged that way by her.

I had two influential grade school teachers. One was Gladys Burns, who was the geography teacher from grades three through eight. She struck me because she was beautiful and she was a lady, and I'd never seen anyone so beautifully mannered and warm and affectionate as she was. She also had an imagination; her approach to geography was imaginative. Then her best friend was Claudia Houston, an ex-WAC [Women's Army Corps], who I felt had everything together for herself. She understood the sort of nervousness that I had, and she gave me, in a way, a moral center. Between the two of them, I felt sort of wonderfully taken care of—the side of me that wanted to, I guess, be able to relate to other people, and the side of me that said you have to be right with yourself in some way.

In high school I had a teacher who very much encouraged my writing; her name was Leslie Moss. She later married, and was Leslie Moss Ainsworth. She ran the school newspaper. I had her as an English teacher as a sophomore, and she was an absolutely brilliant, imaginative teacher, who very much encouraged my writing.

BEATTIE: Sounds like you related to your teachers exactly the same way I did, in terms of remembering all their names.

NASLUND: Oh, yes. I was once shocked to be talking to somebody that couldn't remember some of the names of their teachers. I know all of their names and what they wore. I can describe their clothes.

BEATTIE: So how a teacher related to you personally was extremely important to you.

NASLUND: Yes, it was more important to me than how I got on with my peers. This became less true when I got in college. But, I mean, my peers became more important to me as a group after the twelfth grade. It was my teachers who seemed to give me what I needed. I didn't particularly fit in with my peers.

BEATTIE: In your story "Ice Skating at the North Pole" you refer to a child's living for, or adoration of, a teacher, and that's pretty much what you're talking about now. I was thinking from the way you put that in your story how important that must be to you.

NASLUND: It was very important to me, growing up. Teachers really were far more important than just transferring certain information or teaching certain skills; they were possibilities for being. And if their possibility for being supported me, it was very much something I needed.

BEATTIE: What was your education like beyond the elementary and high school levels?

NASLUND: I went to Birmingham Southern College, which was also in Birmingham, and I mostly lived at home. I wanted to go off to college, but we couldn't afford it—it was the best college in the state, and probably the best college in a number of states in the region. It's always ranked as one of the best buys in education, and they graduate a tremendous number of people who turn out to be professionals. It turned out to be excellent for me, a wonderful school. It was intellectually stimulating and attracted other students who were highly congenial.

I majored in English. I didn't start in English. I started in pre-med, and flunked chemistry three times. This eventually convinced me that God didn't want me to be a medical missionary, and that I'd better do something I enjoyed.

BEATTIE: Is that what you intended to be, a medical missionary?

NASLUND: Yes.

BEATTIE: Was this about the time that you were changing your mind about religion?

NASLUND: Yes, I went to college when I was seventeen, so, by about age nineteen, my zealotry had pretty much worn away. I didn't have a big crisis over religious belief; it just eroded, rather painlessly. But finding a career that I could satisfy myself with was a big question for me, and one I wrestled with quite a bit. I couldn't justify to myself going into something I simply enjoyed, English. I had to do good. So, I wrestled with that, and there was actually a moment of conversion in that question, too.

I was sitting next to a friend of mine, Dwight Isbell, who was shortly after killed in an auto accident, and he was probably the most brilliant person I've ever known. I was very, very fond of him. But I was sitting in class and we had discussed this question of career, as college students do. And the professor, Cecil Abernathy, suddenly posed this question, "In what way are Huckleberry Finn and Pip of *Great Expectations* alike?" I was electrified by the question. I didn't know the answer, but I knew that whatever the answer to that question was, was of extreme importance to the psychological growth and well-being of Dwight Isbell, who sat next to me. I knew this all in a flash, and I was just breathless to hear the answer. Nobody in the class knew the answer to the question. The professor said, "They're both boys in search of a father," and I knew that exactly defined my friend. And I knew with that, that although literature might not save masses of people, that it could save individual people, that there was something there that was offered that would benefit one's life if you understood. When we walked out the door, my friend turned to me and said, "Sena, how can you say that literature isn't good for a person?" And he referred exactly to this incident in exactly the terms that I've told you. He, as well as I, instantly recognized it, and recognized this relevance to my question. So, I thought, if it happens once, it's likely to happen more than that.

BEATTIE: Why and how do you think you became a writer?

NASLUND: Well, I have answered it in part, and I think that the simple answer is my great love of reading and being enamored of that world aesthetically. I think also that my mother probably wanted me to be a writer, although she never said so directly. She, too, loved reading, and was a great reader. She'd been a musician. There was a little question about whether I might not be a musician. I was offered a college scholarship to play the cello at University of Alabama, which I turned down, even though I had no money, because I didn't want to be bound to the cello. I felt I had reached my technical limits; I wasn't going to get better, and it wasn't good enough. But I have a great love of music, and there's a lot of music in my writing. Music does seem like a spiritual force to me.

So, I became a writer most definitely from compulsion about it. I didn't know when I was in college that that was for sure what I wanted to do. I mean, even going into English didn't necessarily mean being a writer. I might have been a professor of literature.

Then I was out of school for a little while. After Birmingham Southern, I lived in San Francisco. I lived there with someone I'd known from college, a man named Jon Brock, and we were there for about nine months, scrounging around different ways. I finally ended up being a clerk-typist for the state of California. We lived on a houseboat part of the time and in a slum part of the time. This was after I graduated from college, in early '64.

Then I taught high school in Alabama for a year and sort of was mulling all this time, you know, "What am I going to teach like my Aunt Kumi?" Get into something and stay in it for fifty years. But Birmingham Southern didn't have an extensive writing program. I had written a play that took place over a whole year, and I had taken one creative writing class, and I'd written four short stores in that class. So I had begun to get the feel of writing.

When I was teaching at E. B. Erwin High School, a textbook came through, *Literature of the United States,* with some color photos in the front. One of them had a caption under it, "This is the University of Iowa. This is Paul Engle. At the University of Iowa you can get a Ph.D. with a creative dissertation." It occurred to me that this was for me, that I wanted to learn to write better. So, even when I left graduate school, I was uncertain about what my teaching future would be. No one had told me that your dissertation defines you, and since mine was a creative writing one, then I was so defined.

So, for a while I wrote stories, partly drawing on my own experiences and past, and trying to learn technique. I think I was a fairly slow learner in all of this. But after I had Flora [Naslund's daughter] in 1980, I had enough technique so that now I wanted to write about things that mattered more to me. I wanted to write about what had been of sustaining value to me personally, when things were difficult, so I had another change in my writing.

BEATTIE: How was the University of Iowa for you? Did you go straight there from Alabama where you were teaching high school?

NASLUND: Yes, I did, and I did an M.A. with a creative thesis, and then I taught for a year at Muscatine Community College. Then I continued with the Ph.D. program with a creative dissertation.

BEATTIE: How did you find the atmosphere of the Iowa program in terms of competitive feelings or feelings of encouragement with peers in the program?

NASLUND: I made some friends in the program who are still my friends. I did not find this huge competitiveness that people sometimes speak of with the Iowa Writers Workshop. I was, I would say, oblivious to it. In a way, I was near the top of the heap, and that's probably why I got fellowships and teaching assistantships and the goodies that people seem to want so much. I was one of the few women students there at the time; my consciousness about that was so low I didn't even notice.

I got married after I was there for a year. That marriage lasted five years. I was married to a student, but he was a student in the philosophy program, which suited me very well, and he was very supportive of my writing. His name was Michael Callaghan. I loved doing philosophical talk, and we talked endlessly. He loved classical music, as well, so we had many shared interests.

I think my Iowa experience was rather atypical. It was atypical in another way, and that was that I was in the academic programs as well as the workshop. By and large, the workshop people didn't know I was in the academic programs doing all these scholarly papers, and vice versa.

That was very different from the typical M.F.A. student. They were almost antiintellectual. At first it worried me a great deal that the people in workshops never wanted to discuss what something was about. They never would mention the theme. I felt that they were afraid they would be wrong and be felt stupid. When Angus Wilson came in, that was one of the great differences that he made. He said, "I not only want to talk about what this is saying, but whether I believe it or not, whether I think it's right or wrong." That was a very refreshing change.

BEATTIE: You have a definite writing style.

NASLUND: I guess so. But for such a long time I seemed like such an amorphous person to myself, that I felt I never became an adult, really, until I had a child. Marriages, sexual experience, deaths, they didn't make me into an adult, but having a child did. So, you know, I'm only eleven years old, and now I have a self to write out of, having become mature.

BEATTIE: You're also a teacher, a professor. Does that role help or hinder your work as a writer, do you think, and will you describe your teaching role as distinguished teaching professor at the University of Louisville?

NASLUND: Being a teacher of both literature and writing has helped me, I think, to be a better writer. What I see in other people's work that succeeds or fails, in general terms, eventually teaches me something that I can use about my own writing. I very much like teaching at Vermont College, where I teach as well as at U of L, and I've also taught at other places. I've taught at the University of Montana, where I went right after Iowa, and I was visiting professor at University of Indiana-Bloomington for a year. Those teaching experiences have all added to my sense of myself as a teacher.

I think I'm a good teacher and I like to teach, but it's also very time-consuming, and that's the down side of being a teacher for a writer. I've gotten so much gratification from it that I might better have gotten from doing my own work, that it's been something of an impediment, in that way. And since I'm beginning to come out with books, I more and more want time for myself.

BEATTIE: How many years have you been teaching at the University of Louisville, and where were you teaching, and for how long, before that?

NASLUND: In '72-'73 I was at University of Montana as assistant professor. I've been at U of L from '73 until the present. I've had a couple of sabbaticals. I had a leave of absence for teaching at I.U.-Bloomington in '86-'87. Actually, it was an unpaid leave of absence from U of L. It was supposed to be a sabbatical, and then I was actually offered this job at I.U. I didn't apply. They called me up because some of my former students had gone to school there, and they were on the committee for recruiting somebody, and they all insisted I be hired. I knew Maura Stanton who was there, and I'd known her at Iowa, and she likes me and my work, also. I was quite astonished to be offered this job at a prestigious university at a better salary than U of L's, and I didn't even have to apply.

I didn't really like the town of Bloomington. When I was driving back to Louisville, and the Louisville skyline rose up south of the Ohio River, it seemed like heaven to me. It was absolutely gorgeous. I can't describe it, how celestial the city seemed. Likewise, my little house here; that seemed absolutely right for me.

But I liked the graduate students and I liked my colleagues there at IU quite a bit. There was a larger creative writing program than at U of L, and I enjoyed a lot being a part of a number of professionals.

BEATTIE: Leon Driskell, who teaches with you here at U of L, wasn't he one of your professors in Alabama?

NASLUND: He was. He taught at Birmingham Southern College. He was one of my literature professors. He didn't teach creative writing there, but he was very hospitable to it, and he supported literary magazine endeavors. I remember he talked to me a long time about a poem I had written. I guess, at that time, I seemed as likely to go into poetry as fiction. In fact, Leon said that he was later surprised that I had been a fiction writer rather than a poet. But I was astonished by Leon's generosity then and now, his willingness to give incredible amounts of time to individual people. He was certainly that way about my poem. I couldn't believe anybody would have so much to say about my work.

Leon also helped me to attend Breadloaf [Writers' Conference]. He decided I ought to have some wider influences, so he got me to apply and rustled down some money from the college. It was a wonderful experience for me to get to go there.

So, Leon was a very encouraging figure in my life. I know when I was in graduate school I lost track of Leon for a number of years. I would even sometimes have imaginary dialogues with him. When I was in a tight fix, I would think of what I would say to Leon and what Leon might say back to me. It was a sort of imaginative therapy that really worked very well. He was a powerful and important and encouraging force in my life. I feel our writing is rather different now, that I've become, in a sense, more aesthetic, and he's, I think, more interested in the regional approach. In many ways we overlap, but I think that we certainly respect what each other has to do and offer.

BEATTIE: Before you came to U of L, when you were at Montana, is that where you met your second husband?

NASLUND: Yes. Alan Naslund was a student at the University of Montana. In fact, he was a student in my class. He came here with me and we were married in Louisville in '73. He had an M.A. from the University of Montana. U of L had him sort of do an M.A. again, and then he entered into a Ph.D. program. He got his Ph.D., I believe, in 1980, and he taught at U of L as a graduate teaching assistant or as a part-time lecturer off and on during that time.

BEATTIE: That was the year that your daughter Flora was born, and you named her after your mother?

NASLUND: Right, and her middle name, Catherine, comes from my name.

BEATTIE: You had started talking a little bit about the Vermont College program. How long have you been teaching there?

NASLUND: I started doing that when Flora was turning three. She always has her birthdays at Vermont College, so that's kind of how I keep track of them. But I have trouble with arithmetic sometimes, so I guess that's 1983. In '84 I first taught there. The M.F.A. program had been going maybe three or four years before I joined it. Roger Weingarten, who's the director of the program, came through Louisville, and did a reading here, and he interviewed a few of my students who were vaguely interested in going to Vermont College. They were wonderful students, and when he finished, he offered me a job. I was a little skeptical. I felt, you know, what is this? Writing by correspondence? Bennett Cerf's school-of-famous-writers kind of thing. So I went into it a little skeptically. But I just loved the program and became addicted to it. I think it's the ideal thing for writers to do. It's a low-residency program, which means that everybody's together twice a year for eleven or twelve days, and then the time in between, a student has an advisor and corresponds with that advisor about both reading and writing. While we're at the residency there are many work-shops, such as one has all over in various writing programs, so every student's work is put through a workshop. There are also lectures given by faculty and graduating students. There are readings given by graduates and graduating students and faculty, and visiting writers as well. It's the kind of writing program that one would describe as a studio program. The thing that pleases me about it is that you get to know the person or the five people you correspond with very well, so one gets much more personal attention out of the Vermont College program as a student than out of any of the traditional workshops that I've been acquainted with—Iowa, Montana, Indiana, or U of L. It's intense and personal.

BEATTIE: Have you maintained any kind of relationship or correspondence with former students from that program?

NASLUND: Yes. Some of the former students have become faculty members there. Vermont College does hire its own graduates, which is sane to me, and unusual. I have a lot of friends who are former students, whether at U of L or at Vermont College.

BEATTIE: While we're on the subject of teaching, would you discuss your thoughts concerning the nature of creativity, where it comes from, and to what extent you think creative writing can be taught? And what do you think is the best way to teach creative writing?

NASLUND: It seems to me that there is a large genetic factor in creativity. So, one starts with a certain gift. Whether you use the gift or not, there are many factors involved in that. Has the nurture been right for it? In my case, I was read to as a child. I had a gift for language, and that was developed by my parents reading to me. I recognized the pleasure in it and wanted it for myself. I think that the right environment gives what one has inherited a chance to flourish.

I very much do think creative writing can be taught. I think I've taught it numbers and numbers of times. I've seen students who were very mediocre writers become good writers through the interaction of the teaching process and what they wanted to learn. To me, creative writing can be taught as much as anything else can be taught.

What is the best way to teach creative writing? I think that what I try to do is to see what is unique about an individual writer and to encourage that, to see what is the very best thing, and to help that to grow. At the same time, I look for what is the biggest impediment to this person, and I try to stay away from that. So, I move from the extremes toward the inside. I think that the biggest requirement is flexibility on the part of the instructor. You don't want to make your students write like you or write like each other, but that initial tuning in to what's wonderful about what the student has done is, to me, the beginning of effective teaching in creative writing.

BEATTIE: You've also taught in summer creative writing workshops or institutes. Will you talk about that experience?

NASLUND: Well, I like doing that, too. It's almost too tiring for the money. But, you know, you meet exciting new people that way, and sometimes you see real talent. You see people there who are all making an earnest effort. They don't have to do this, and they have some desire and talent or they wouldn't be there. So, I find it a nice change of pace to get to do that occasionally.

BEATTIE: Which ones have you taught?

NASLUND: I've taught twice at Indiana University-Bloomington, the summer conference, and I think that's a great conference. I went to Stony Brook, New York, and worked in a conference at University of Tennessee in Chattanooga. Last summer I taught in the Stone Coast Writers' Conference in Portland, Maine. I think that the best conference is the I.U. in Bloomington, of those that I've directly taught in.

I generally see possibilities in the work of the people who come to these conferences. Some of them are a little on the self-indulgent side; they're not, in a sense, critical enough of themselves. They think they have accomplished more than they have, they think they're further along than they are. But often, they do have something. To communicate with them, you have to get through their view that they're already practically arrived to help them start work.

BEATTIE: Will you tell me a little more about your personal life, about your marriages and about your daughter?

NASLUND: As I said, I was married to Michael Callaghan for five years, and to Alan Naslund for about seventeen years. And Flora is eleven. In both of the marriages, I was married to people who were supportive of my writing and with whom I had a lot of congeniality. I was sorry that each of the marriages ended. Flora is the light of my life and she's very bright, multitalented, and a wonderful child, wonderful companion. I guess I would say that Flora is the best thing that ever happened in my life.

BEATTIE: What about your own writing? You've been published in a number of prestigious literary and little magazines, such as the *Paris Review* and the *American Voice*. Will you trace your publishing career?

NASLUND: Of course, I was self-published at age six with my newspapers, and in high school I wrote journalistic articles, but also a short story that was published across the front of a newspaper for Christmas. That meant a lot to me. My special teacher saw to that. It's called, "Then Peal the Bells More Loud and True." It was, as I say, a Christmas story. It had some good writing in it. It won some sort of scholastic prize later on.

In college I published in the college literary magazine both poetry and fiction. And my play, *Boadicia,* was produced in college. Then, in graduate school, I really didn't publish much. I was focused on getting the degrees. As I was leaving the University of Iowa, the *Iowa Review* carried a piece of one of my stories, and I published another piece in the *New Orleans Review* that I'd written when I was a graduate student. It was called "Burning Boy."

Things sort of chugged along; a story a year or so would come out. I felt I had a hard time breaking into publishing, and I was writing rather traditional stories, sometimes music-centered. I was reading, and I felt some frustration about not publishing more. So I said to myself, "I know what they want, and it's a zany voice. I can do it."

So I wrote "The Animal Way to Love" out of a voice that was totally different from anything else I'd done. Friends who had liked my writing a lot hated this piece. It was too callous for them. I sent it a couple of places and it got rejected, just mediocre literary magazines, *Sheraton Review* was one. Then I had taken my mother to the library, and I was waiting for her, and I picked up the *Paris Review* and read a story by Alice Adams and I thought, "The Animal Way to Love" is a lot like this, but better. So I popped it off to the *Paris Review,* and within two weeks I got a letter from George Plimpton just raving about it. So I was right. I had outguessed them. I knew what they wanted, and this was the breakthrough in my publishing. I later won an NEA [National Endowment for the Arts grant] with the same story, and won a Kentucky Arts Council grant with the same story. I got an invitation to submit to the *New Yorker* with this story. So, I had been really right, and I somewhat resented this, but I also learned a lot from being able to do something so different.

So I wrote a bunch of these stories, and they began to connect, and I began to try to work them into a novel. In fact, the novel that's going to come out from Ampersand is *The Animal Way to Love.*

But after Flora was born, as I mentioned, I grew tired of this assumed voice, and I wanted to write what I alone needed to write. These stories, too, were published, and they benefited from the earlier experiment in doing something different; I gained a lot of control and perspective from doing that. Also, the women's movement benefited me a great deal; I was able to leave stories that were male-centered, like "The Death of Julius Geissler," which was the thing that appeared in *Iowa Review,* and "Burning Boy," which was about a black boy in Birmingham. I was able to write stories that were more from a female perspective, and I felt very at home doing that. These stories published well, too. I think I learned a certain daring about honesty from *The Animal Way to Love* set of stories.

BEATTIE: Which reminds me of what you were talking about in your own childhood about dealing with honesty and punishment and wanting to play the male roles because they were more exciting.

NASLUND: Yes, it does; it was part of that. So, I'm grateful to the women's movement for having raised my consciousness, and kind of letting me come into my own, although I'm involved in this "Tink" novel. But I wanted to see what I could do with commercial writing, so I set myself to write a Sherlock Holmes spin-off, which I've just finished, as you know, having been so kind as to read the manuscript for me. So now I'm trying to market that. I feel that I'll never write another big commercial book, at least not on that level, and I want to go back to my "Tink" story.

The first chapter was published in the *American Voice*. It's called "I Am Born," which is a spin-off from the first chapter of *David Copperfield*, also titled "I Am Born." There's a lot of allusion to Dickens in my work, because he was such a transporting writer for me. My mother did not read Dickens to me; he was the first writer I read on my own. I just relished the roll of his sentences, his many clauses, which I have a character say in one of my stories. It's in "Madame Charpentier," I think. So, I have tried other things than was my natural bent, and I think I've benefited from all of them.

What I've learned from *Sherlock* is something about plotting. I'm not a very naturally plot-oriented writer; I'm in the Virginia Woolf camp. Virginia Woolf has been a terrific influence on me, and very liberating, and very wonderful. *To the Lighthouse* is probably my all-time favorite novel.

BEATTIE: Eudora Welty is a big influence on you, too, isn't she?

NASLUND: Less so than Katherine Anne Porter and Flannery O'Connor. Flannery O'Connor's humor and sense of dialogue were very important to me. One of my friends when I first came to Louisville was Bonnie Cherry, who helped me start the *Louisville Review*. She once said to me, "Your writing is at the intersection of Virginia Woolf and Flannery O'Connor," and I thought, "Yes. Yes." I've always held onto that, and I've said it a number of times.

BEATTIE: Nice intersection and nice place to be.

NASLUND: It combines the red clay on my feet from the South with the sort of aesthetic sensibility I also have.

BEATTIE: I can see that, particularly in "Ice Skating at the North Pole," that magical realism.

NASLUND: Yes. Well, magical realism, it's another phase of my writing that's come on a little bit later, and I never expected to take that turn. I disliked fantasy in fiction, I was very much a realist, and I especially disliked the revamping of Greek myths or Greek characters. I especially disliked Updike's *The Centaur*. I was lying in bed one night, angry that one of my friends was divorcing his wife after seventeen years of marriage. Ironic, isn't it?

BEATTIE: That particular number, yes. [Naslund's second marriage lasted seventeen years].

NASLUND: And I had an image of a perfume bottle with perfume flowing into it rather than out of it, and I woke Alan up and told him, "I can't sleep. I've got this damn bottle in my head." I described the bottle in some detail, and he said, "You need to write a story. Get up. I'll fix you some coffee." He got up, too, and was very supportive, and I wrote "Essence for Miss Venus." That was the breakthrough into the fantasy mode. Then I began to use magical realism as a concluding mode, rather than the pervasive mode, of the whole story.

BEATTIE: Do you think that was a dream influence of your own, or was it influenced by magical realists that you had read?

NASLUND: It was dream influence of my own. I don't feel very congenial with the South American magical realists; they're too chauvinistic to suit me, and I find them difficult to read. So it was something that came out of my own need. I see that now as expressing some sort of ardent wish on the part of the character. I don't see it as wish fulfillment or a cop-out, but as a sort of psychological turn in which you know more fully the pressures that are on the character, as in the end of "Ice Skating at the North Pole," or in "The Perfecting of the Self, Ambrose Number 14."

BEATTIE: When I was rereading that book just the other day, what strikes me more than the magic of those stories, or perhaps what is the essential magic, is their music. In your story "Five Lessons from a Master Class" you write, "Obviously there was nothing to talk about, nothing high-flown or theoretical about the art of music until there was music." Will you comment on the importance of music in your work? I think you have commented some, but I'm interested in whether or not you think this influence may also speak to the dominance of sound over the other senses in your work.

NASLUND: I think I write about music partly because it's something that I know a little bit about in a technical sense, having been an orchestral cellist and having played the piano and heard my mother play every day while I was growing up, and she played classical music. She didn't talk about it much, and I don't know if you know that my mother lived here [in Naslund's Louisville home] with me for twelve years. She spent the last three years of her life in a nursing home; she had Alzheimer's, but she did live with me for a long time. So again, and more recently, I heard playing as I had when I was a child.

So there's that practical thing that I know something about; and, in a sense, playing music is something for my characters to do. But also, I am just personally terrifically moved by music, and although I'm not at all a good performer and was never a high-level performer, the act of listening to music is a spiritual act, when it's good, for me. The music rouses certain things and satisfies certain things for me, and these are rather unworded questions and unworded answers. But nonetheless, they suffice. They are one of the things that have been of sustaining value to me. So when I gave myself the challenge to write of what had been of sustaining value, I naturally had to include music, since traditional religious faith was not of sustaining value as far as I was concerned.

BEATTIE: It seems to me that writers who are theme instead of plot oriented, as you are, that the sound of the words themselves, the essence of meaning, comes down to language and the music of that language far more than in plot-oriented writing.

NASLUND: Yes, this has been, I'd say, largely unconscious on my part. One of the very helpful comments that you made about *Sherlock* was about the way the alliteration makes the style work. I've become more aware of that since you've said that. I am aware of sentence rhythms. I mentioned loving that about Dickens when I was a child, and I think that that's a kind of carry-over from my response to music. The music in music.

BEATTIE: Virginia Woolf is very prose-poetry oriented.

NASLUND: Yes. I've thought about writing as being voice or vision oriented, and I wouldn't call myself a voice writer by and large, although all the Trixie stories are voice stories. But to me, that was the change in my style, to go from trying to let language be transparent and conjure up a visualized world, to an awareness of the writer's voice in one's ear.

I do enjoy being read to so much, and I feel like now I'm beginning to get voice and vision into some kind of balance with things. I also think that there are a lot of important visual items in my story. The image of ice skating at the North Pole is visual. So, I think that I have a real compulsion to include music in my stories, and it's tucked into a lot of stories where one wouldn't think of them as being primarily musical stories. I don't know as much about painting; I don't have any talent in that direction, so it's less available to me as an analogue for the creative process.

When I was working with plot in *Sherlock,* I did think of the whole thing as cinematic. I mean, I was writing it for the movies as well, so that helped me to become more plot oriented. I also like food in stories quite a bit, and there's a big eating scene in the "Chopin" story. But in the last story too, there's an eating scene when the characters come home. I like food in Virginia Woolf a lot, the meal that's prepared in *To the Lighthouse,* the beef dish.

BEATTIE: In reading the manuscript of your soon-to-be published novel, *The Animal Way to Love,* I felt that your themes of individual human isolation and loneliness resolve themselves somewhat in your last sentence, "I took Wanda's hand, I laced my fingers into her fingers and squeezed, felt my bones woven into her bones and into our strength," more than they do in most stories in *Ice Skating at the North Pole.*

NASLUND: I see this whole progress of the novel as being a novel about friendship, about women becoming friends. The first section of the novel is about a failed friendship; one of the women commits suicide. Then Trixie, my main character, does learn to be Wanda's friend, and somewhat against her nature. In some ways, she wants to protect herself by maintaining her isolation and not responding to Wanda's need. There's a lot of explicit heterosexual behavior described in this, and I see that as secondary. I've done this very much on purpose. Usually, you know, novels are about finding compatible men, and the women's friendships are secondary. But for me in this book, and I think that's the revolutionary thing about this book, the main topic is how one woman becomes a friend of another. It's not a lesbian relationship; we're talking about friendship. And there is a heterosexual exploration, and mistakes, and adventures on both their parts, with a variety of men.

BEATTIE: You talked about *Sherlock in Love.* Since it's very different from anything else of yours I've read, will you comment on the origin of that?

NASLUND: Well, as I say, I had the yen to make money, and I happened to read Nicholas Meyer's The *Seven-Per-Cent Solution* and very much enjoyed it. Freud was an interesting figure to me, and he had Holmes meet Freud. Up until that time, I had read maybe one Sherlock Holmes story. But I was talking to friends, Rick and Corie Neumayer, and I talked about how I would like to do a book on Sherlock Holmes' smarter sister. This was before "Sherlock Holmes's Younger Brother" came out. It was quite some time ago. They were quite interested in this idea, and they encouraged me.

I decided I would read all of Holmes, so I got the big, two-volume, I think it's Barin-Gould edition of Holmes. I read all of the stories and all of the criticism included in that. I felt I didn't want to violate the canon, although I wanted to expand on it. Then, during one of my sabbaticals, I had company for Thanksgiving. My brother Marvin and his family came, and during that time I was domestic. I did nothing but cook and clean up for four days, which I didn't mind doing; I was glad to have them as company. But I was tired of it. And Alan and I—this was before Flora was born—went out for dinner Sunday night at the end of that long Thanksgiving weekend with Rick and Corie. Corie turned to me and said—Corie's a painter—when I was mildly complaining about all this cooking and cleaning up, she said, "Well, you could begin your novel tomorrow." And I thought, "It's just that simple."

So, I came home and wrote the first chapter and read it to Alan, who was very encouraging about it, and I set myself a schedule to get it done. I would write six hours a day or ten typescript pages, whichever came first. I would not be interrupted during that time by any phone call or any interaction. I typed it on the typewriter. The paper was across the room, so that at the end of each page I stretched my legs by getting a piece of paper. It was an entirely disciplined effort. I wrote for five days a week. I did not write on the weekend. I wrote whether I had an idea in my head or not. I sat down at the keyboard and literally said to myself, "Hands on keyboard. Type." And I wrote a sentence and then I said to myself, "Great, you did it. Now, another one." But always within half a page, I would be back into the story and fascinated and enchanted by it. So discipline led me to some sort of fun. I wrote *Sherlock* from Thanksgiving to Valentine's Day. I never missed a single day of my schedule. I was always on my schedule, because I was on sabbatical. That was what allowed writing six hours a day.

So then I messed around with revising it, and I couldn't quite get the plot to be plotty enough. I lost interest in it and got interested in other things, so it sat in a drawer for a while. Then this last summer, when I was recovering from the divorce with Alan, I had to read at Vermont College, and everything was too close to me, everything was too raw. I looked at "Ice Skating at the North Pole" and I felt, "You thought that was pain. You know nothing about it." But even so, those stories were too painful to read. So I went back to *Sherlock* as a place to hide, and I got interested in revising it.

Again, friends supported me, different friends this time around. So, I spent the whole school year then revising *Sherlock,* and it's ready to go again. Whether it makes me rich or not, you'll have to add as a postscript. Not rich, just a little bit of money, please.

But my other way of working is through inspiration. Sometimes a story simply seizes me. I told you the story of writing "Essence for Miss Venus." I was angry, an image came and seized, and Alan helped me to write it. "Ice Skating at the North Pole" was a story that seized me. I stayed up all night one night when I couldn't sleep again, and remember, childhood insomnia was a time for doing fiction. There have been a number of stories that have come out of not being able to sleep.

In *Sherlock,* I realized if I was going to write a Sherlock Holmes story, the only thing I knew enough about to make central to it was music. So my female protagonist is a wonderful violinist, and of course it is in the canon that Holmes played the violin and had a Stradivarius, which was highly unlikely, even then, for Conan Doyle to give him.

I'm sure that music is going to figure big in my "Tink" novel. It's already in the first chapter, although I've written a hundred and sixty pages into it that are not particularly musical. But I think that it will be her art. Maybe I could make her a writer. I'd like to.

BEATTIE: *The Animal Way to Love,* I was thinking how this is written in the form of a musical composition.

NASLUND: It is almost subtitled "A Partita," which is the name for these unaccompanied box suites for cello. They may have five or six or so separate parts, and they're marked gavotte or courante, allemande, or something like that, jig. And at one time I was so conscious of that that I wanted to put that in the title.

BEATTIE: Even the paragraphs (the form) and the white space between them make me feel that. Although many of your stories in *The Animal Way to Love* are set in places you've lived, if your writing has a sense of place, it strikes me that that place is more interior, more psychological, than simply geographical. Would you agree with that?

NASLUND: Absolutely. I think that that's one of the most important features of my writing. The story I'm trying to write now—which just was one of those that seized me, and I hope I can finish it and make something of it—is called "In the Anteroom." It grows out of an image of being at the Paris Opera. We had a box there, and it was close to the Chagall ceiling, which is very incongruous with the baroque and classical nature of the building in general, and I was very taken with having the luxury of this box. But not only was there a box, there was an anteroom to the box, which seemed like a dead space to me, with chairs kind of scattered around in it. I don't know how to describe it, but the story is kind of about the nonimportance of geography. It's exactly about the issue that you're talking about. It came out of my reading of a book that a friend lent me called *The World is a Room,* and it seems to me the mind is a room or the mind is a world. So I do have sometimes a sense of connection with other people. I don't mean to sound overly mystical, it's just that there seems to be a connection that's transdimensional.

BEATTIE: But even though your stories are filled with references to Birmingham and Louisville, and even though you write about your mother being born in Missouri in one of your stories, there's no real sense of regionalism.

NASLUND: No, there isn't, and that's one of the ways that I mentioned that Leon [Driskell] and I are different. His strength grows out of his strong sense of regionalism, and I don't mean to be limiting when I use that term in connection with him. One of my favorite quotes is from Shakespeare, "And give to airy nothingness a local habitation and a name." A sense of naming things to somehow have their essence—that seems ungeographical to me in an interesting way—and a name is something that blooms out of the mouth; it's a breath, it's air, it's life itself.

Moving up a little bit from Virginia Woolf would be Flannery O'Connor, whom I mentioned, and Katherine Anne Porter. I tend to be more influenced by, I would say, modern, rather than contemporary, writers. Faulkner is another big influence on me. Among contemporary writers, work that I've particularly admired has been by Jane Smiley, not *Thousand Acres,* which won all the prizes, but *Ordinary Love and Goodwill,* I liked a great deal. I have enjoyed Maura Stanton's fiction. *The Country I Come From* is a collection of hers. And Stewart Dybek's *A Childhood in Other Neighborhoods,* which I think has a beautiful title. I love that title. Those are some recent contemporary things that have spoken to me in the way of fiction writing. As I was coming along I was fascinated by Richard Yates's work, who did become my teacher, at Iowa.

Poets have been influential for me, too. The British Romantic poets meant a lot to me. Walt Whitman meant a tremendous amount to me when I was about eleven or twelve. The expansiveness of his ego was very liberating to me, his catalogs of things, his rummaging around through his mind and finding all the things he wanted to name and say and including them all. I much preferred him to Carl Sandburg, which represented good taste at an early age, I think. Robert Frost has meant something to me. His use of the colloquial, and yet his pretty formalized statements. Wallace Stevens was sort of the person whose writing gave me permission to embrace the aesthetic as the spiritual.

BEATTIE: Cerebral, as well as aesthetic.

NASLUND: Very cerebral and very imaginative, and his work has been tremendously important to me. The American poet who was plenty intellectual in his stance, Theodore Roethke, and his student, Richard Hugo—who I knew at Montana, who hired me to teach there—have been very interesting poets for me. Also, Emily Dickinson meant a great deal to me in terms of the originality of metaphor. And my friend Maureen Morehead's poetry—and she was my student at one time at U of L—has been extremely important to me. I can't read Maureen's work without not wanting to write.

BEATTIE: What sorts of writing projects do you have planned for the future?

NASLUND: I have started "In the Anteroom," which is going to be short and complete, I hope, soon, and I have this "Tink" novel that I need to go back to. I haven't worked on it for a year now while revising *Sherlock Holmes.* So those two things are kind of in a holding pattern. I've been thinking lately of a new story that would be a kind of relief from this first-person female point of view, called "A Shepherd's Calendar," which is about an old man and a boy who live in a shepherd's wagon in Montana. I've thought some about writing that. But, I've had in mind these two titles for a long time. One is called "Passage to Indiana" and the other is called "Connoisseur of Clouds." It may be that this "Tink" novel will eventually be titled "Connoisseur of Clouds." Right now its tentative title, which nobody likes, is "Mirror Window, Mirror Door."

"Connoisseur of Clouds" and "Passage to Indiana" were both intended to be stories about my relationship to my mother. I was very close to her. Another story about her that I have a title for is called "Bach-Busoni." Busoni was someone who wrote piano transcriptions of Bach pieces that were intended for other instruments. I might try to write that some time. I have an image or an event that it's centered around.

Another story I had in mind was one that was tentatively called, or labeled, "Farm Pond," which was about swimming in a pond with Flora and the farm family of one of my students in Vermont. That story wouldn't be literally about them, of course, but just springing from that exhilarating, wonderful experience. It was a skinny-dipping experience, which I'd never done before, and I didn't know these people well. It was mixed sexes. But it was a wonderful rebirth kind of experience, and I feel that it echoes off Lawrence's story, "The Horse Dealer's Daughter," which has a descent into a murky pond, and then a sort of coming up out of the grave. This experience was sort of something that was helpful to me in terms of recovering from this marriage with Alan. So, I have two titles of things that are midway finished, and about five titles of things that don't exist at all.

I have another collection of short stories that's unpublished, although all the stories have been published in it, called "In the Free State." I need to turn my attention to salvaging it at some point, but I'm getting tired of salvage; I want to do some new stuff. I also have a play called "Bombingham," which is about Birmingham during the civil rights era in the sixties. It's written, and I'd like to salvage it.

BEATTIE: It interests me when you say "a play," because to me it's such a different way of thinking to write a play than to write any other type of prose.

NASLUND: It really is, but I find the limitations of virtually all dialogue and some action and confined setting and so forth, to me that, in a sense, makes things easier than when you have the whole world open to you, the whole world of the mind, or room of the mind open to you. My plays tend to be sociological, as the title "Bombingham" suggests.

My fiction tends now to be more inward and psychological. But I would like to write some more plays.

BEATTIE: Do you read reviews of your work?

NASLUND: I do read reviews, and *Ice Skating* has largely been reviewed very positively. I have read a negative review of it, and even that was interesting and instructive to me. Some of the ones that are positive seem a little bit maybe slightly off, and others make me think of things I hadn't thought of before, so I enjoy them.

BEATTIE: It's refreshing to find a writer that has respect for reviewers. So many say, "Oh, I never read reviews."

NASLUND: I know they don't. They don't want to read them, and I don't understand that. Why don't you want to know how somebody who is giving you a serious reading has responded to your work? I don't know why people don't want to know that.

BEATTIE: How long have you edited the *Louisville Review,* and will you discuss the nature and origins of that publication?

NASLUND: The *Louisville Review* was founded in 1976 by Bonnie Cherry, whom I mentioned earlier, and Tom Willett, who's now Tom Broughton-Willett, who were both undergraduate students at U of L, and myself. We three did the first year of it. They said, "We're seeing so much great stuff, it's a shame it's not published. Let's start a publication, exporting some of the U of L stuff and importing other stuff." I very much agreed with them, and that's how it's gone. The editors have changed over the years, the students have come and gone at U of L. I'm the only professional person who regularly works on it. Sometimes we have a guest editor. When Robin Lippincott was living here and teaching at U of L, he was the guest fiction editor. Millard Dunn's been a guest poetry editor, so has Paula Rankin, who's a pretty well-known poet who happened to be in Louisville. So we've had a number of guest editors.

The *Louisville Review* has been cut from the university foundation budget, and so we're struggling to survive now. We run national contests with entry fees of ten dollars in order to pay our printing bill. If you know anybody who wants to be an angel to the *Louisville Review,* please, please let them flutter down. People have helped us. We've asked former contributors for donations, and a number have come in. We publish poetry and fiction. Occasionally we publish drama, not too often, and about once a year we include children's poetry and fiction. We've published some very well-known and successful writers, as well as people who are publishing for the first time. Sometimes there's not a lot of difference in the quality, but the first-time publishing person may have a story or a poem that is just as fine as anything can be, in my opinion.

I wished that I had named the magazine "High Horse" instead of the *Louisville Review.* There's a line from Yeats, "And shall poetry, that high horse, go riderless?" And, of course, I take poetry in the broad sense to include fiction. You know, you have a little bit of the Kentucky flavor, but at the same time it would be a more portable title if I should leave the University of Louisville.

BEATTIE: Is there anything that you think is particularly important about yourself or your writing that we haven't discussed?

NASLUND: Well, I feel that, like the members of Bloomsbury, the two most important things to me are aesthetic form, as embodiment of the human and the spiritual, and personal relationships. That includes, say, my relationship to Flora, to family, as well as to friends. I do think friends are terrifically important. I feel that my identity is kind of along those lines, both personally speaking, and as a writer. I think that I'm a loyal person in my relationships to other people. I think that's a gift I have to offer, not particularly to my credit; I mean, it's just my nature, and I think that I'm a patient person, in terms of my writing, and my willingness to try to improve it, and to try to be open about it.

May 12, 1992

BOOKS BY SENA JETER NASLUND

Ice Skating at the North Pole. Bristol, R.I.: Ampersand, 1989.

The Animal Way to Love. Bristol, R.I.: Ampersand, 1993.

Sherlock in Love. Boston: Godine, 1993.

The Disobedience of Water. Boston: Godine, 1997.

Zoya Tereshkova

Marsha Norman

NORMAN: My name is Marsha Norman, and I was born in Louisville, September twenty-first, 1947. Mother's name was Bertha Connelly, and my father's name was Billie Lee Williams. He was an insurance agent and she was a homemaker. I grew up on Bourbon Avenue, which is between Audubon Park and the airport.

BEATTIE: What was your childhood like?

NORMAN: It was kind of an isolated childhood. Mother was not one to have an active interest in her child's social life. Quite the contrary, she really thought it was better if I played by myself. And she had a suspicion of other kids. I thought, at the time, she was quite restrictive. It turned out to be sort of a fabulous way of developing a writer. There was no television, because she thought it was sinful, so there was only reading; she just didn't know quite the extent of sin one could find in books. I spent a childhood, really, that prepared me for the life I lead now, where I can tolerate, and indeed need, a great deal of isolation and quiet and privacy. She was very supportive about what I wanted to do. I mean, her credo, really, was "You can do whatever you want." I've really benefitted from that extraordinary gift of confidence she gave me.

Dad was gone a lot. He was an insurance agent of the old school; he was out every night selling people their car and their home owners' and their fire insurance. And when the boys [Norman's brothers] were old enough to go hunting with him, he did a lot of things with them. I have two brothers; Mark, who is three years younger than I, and Stewart, who is six years younger than I. Then I have a sister, Ruth, who is nine years younger than I am.

We had a really quite fabulous extended family. My grandfather lived on the next street. My great-aunt, Bertha Toole, whom I adored, and at whose home I spent a lot of my time, was really kind of my patron saint and protector. Much more a person of my ilk than Mother was. Bubby was one of those bourbon-drinking Baptists. All the pictures of her, you see her in a red strapless dress leaning against the bar with five handsome men. She really just knew how to have a good time, and she didn't have children of her own. I was her kid, and that was the best thing in the world for me.

BEATTIE: Were you raised a Baptist?

NORMAN: No. Mother was a Methodist. Later in my parents' lives they went to a church called the Christian Missionary Alliance, which is a far more serious brand of religion. There's a whole missionary theme that runs through my life. There were always missionaries at our house. Every Wednesday there was a meeting of a thing called "the Prayer

Band," which is a group of old women, really, who come over in flowery dresses to kneel on the floor and pray for people in faraway lands. I mean, my whole life there was this funny little box from the World Gospel Mission, and this box always had one of those goitered, starving children on the cover. This little box, about the size of a box of baking soda, was for coins that children would put in to help these children. God knows where these World Gospel Mission monies went, ultimately.

So, I really have a kind of lifelong fascination, indeed obsession, with religion and its effect on people. I rebelled against all this religion as a kid, and as soon as I got out of the house, basically, I didn't want anything to do with it. I mean, I actively hated it. Yet I find that there was a great boon to me in the hearing of those biblical stories at an early age. I find that the presentation of moral dilemmas, this is a good thing to do for a writer kid, you know. If Mother had known she was raising a writer, she couldn't have done it any better. You know, fill somebody up, separate them from all of their friends, don't let them play with anybody else, and fill them all full of these ancient stories of conflict over moral issues. As it was, when I decided to become a writer, she couldn't have been more upset. I mean, she was horrified.

BEATTIE: Why was that?

NORMAN: She was not happy with the kind of stories I decided to tell. Clearly, if I had decided to tell stories about people's salvation, people finding the Lord, she would have been happy about that. But the fact that I wanted to write about prisoners who used foul language, this didn't make her happy.

BEATTIE: Did 'night, Mother make her happy?

NORMAN: No, 'night, Mother did not make her happy at all. 'night, Mother upset her deeply. In fact, when she finally agreed to go see it, which was when Kathy Bates did it in Louisville, she took Bubby, my great-aunt, with her, and she took Dad, and I arranged for the tickets, and the night came and went, and the next morning there was no phone call. Mother was like the master of not communicating. But about two weeks after that, I was talking to Bubby on the phone, and she happened to mention that, oh yes indeed, they had gone to see this play. I said, "Well, what did you think?" Bubby said, "Well, you know, I could hear every word they said." And my mother, literally to the end of her life, never made a comment about seeing the play. I mean, she decided, I think, after a certain point, that rather than try to change my mind about what I was doing, or correct me, or sort of get on me about it, which she did in the early days, she just decided not to say anything, which was kind of hard to take.

I think, in a sense, all writers work from some kind of need to express. What produces that need, you don't know. In my case, I think it was this lifetime of secrecy. In our household, you didn't say anything unless it was a nice thing. If you didn't have something good to say, you didn't say anything. And you went around with a smile on your face. This was required. That builds a lot of internal monologue. You know, I sat around smiling, thinking about what I would be saying if I weren't sitting there smiling.

BEATTIE: Do you think your mother felt that *you* were Kathy Bates, that *she* was the mother?

NORMAN: No, I think even in the plays in which she is clearly the character, like in *Getting Out*, where she is clearly the mother, she didn't recognize herself at all, even when the mother in the play walked in the door. When the mother in *Getting Out* walks in the door with a basket full of cleaning supplies, I was convinced that Mother would know that this was a picture of her, because all she ever did was clean. I mean, it's a religious activity, I think. Sort of trying to get the dirt out, getting rid of the sin and the evil, that's masquerading as the dirt on the floor. But you know, she wasn't able to do that. Now, in *The Fortune Teller*, which I dedicated to my mother, this was a thing that caused one of the greatest splits in our relationship, because she did recognize some of those events.

BEATTIE: Your mother is Fay's mother in *The Fortune Teller*?

NORMAN: Right.

BEATTIE: In the novel, Fay comes to terms with her mother.

NORMAN: Well, I don't think mother got far enough in reading the book to know that. I think that she read probably up to the part about the fourth birthday party where the kid gets the umbrella, and then she knew that I was taking stories from my life and, as she said in the message she left me on the telephone answering machine, "turning them into this vulgar filth."

BEATTIE: Did you get an umbrella for your birthday?

NORMAN: Yes.

BEATTIE: That must have been hard to take, your mother's lack of approval.

NORMAN: No, it was conditional approval. And it wasn't just me. If we did the things she liked, then everything was great. If we did the things she didn't like, then it was just . . .

BEATTIE: Well, your choice was to get approval or be who you are.

NORMAN: Right. And strangely enough, of the four kids in my family, two of us were the bad kids, my brother Stewart, who's really a woodworker and just a master carver, is now making boats, and I. We were the bad kids, and she was constantly on us. Mark and Ruth were the good kids. When Mother died—she had a stroke, just one of those sudden, kind of lightening-bolt-out-of-the-sky kind of strokes—and she was in a coma in the hospital, Mark and I stood there beside her, and Mark was praying, or talking to her, saying goodbye to her. I realized that he was saying goodbye to a person that I didn't know. Who was he talking to? He wasn't talking to *my* mother. Who's he talking to? That's clearly the truth of relationships between parents and children. Every child has his own parent, and whether it happens to be also the parent of that child's siblings . . . You know, it's a very special, idiosyncratic relationship.

But what I said earlier is true: even though our lifetime together was fraught with all of these difficulties, and there was a lot of screaming, and there was a lot of this antagonism and difficulty, what my mother did that was good was very, very good.

BEATTIE: What was that? What do you think she gave you?

NORMAN: What I said before, confidence. I know that she read to me constantly until I could read for myself.

BEATTIE: What did your father think about your writing? Did he go to see your plays?

NORMAN: Oh, I think he was very proud. He did see my plays. Dad is a very social creature. He likes to show up and be friendly, and that's how he's approached his whole life. He would come to see anything. You know, Dad really only needs an invitation and he'll be there. He'll laugh and he'll have a wonderful time and he will give you a big kiss and he will say it was fabulous and he will go away and you won't have a clue what he thought. But maybe he didn't think anything. He doesn't live in a very complex world, I don't think. I just don't know him very well.

BEATTIE: Is he still living?

NORMAN: He is. He is remarried and he's still living in Kentucky and still hunting and still winning senior citizens' moto-cross races, and is a great guy.

BEATTIE: You talked about your mother having read to you as a child. Did you know how to read before you went to school?

NORMAN: I don't think so. You know, there are these films where I was sitting there on the sofa reading out of a book to my brothers and sisters, and I was five, but I think that what I had done was to memorize the book.

I went to Prestonia Elementary School. I remember it as this idyllic and wonderful thing. I was in a terrible fight in the third grade with a girl named Brenda, because Brenda said that my dress was ugly, which I agreed with. I thought it was ugly, too. I had had a fight with Mother earlier in the day about this dress, but I couldn't let Brenda say this, you know. So, I had to have a fight with Brenda and stand behind the cloak room. Other than that, it was an uneventful elementary school experience. I was kind of a star kid. I did great. I couldn't draw, still can't draw. But you know, it was wonderful. I wish I could find an elementary school to send my children to that was as good as that school.

BEATTIE: What made it so good?

NORMAN: Well, just the level of commitment of the teachers and their kind of eccentricity. I remember a teacher named Gladys Lackey who always wore great flowery, purple dresses and hats, like the woman in the Magic School Bus series. I remember the teachers as that old-style American teacher. You know, here's the person who's in it for life, who knows it absolutely, and who feels respected and appreciated by the community, and who regularly produces a crop of kids that can do whatever it is they're supposed to do by the end of the fifth grade.

BEATTIE: Did you have a favorite subject then?

NORMAN: Oh well, I always liked to read better than anything.

BEATTIE: Did you start writing on your own at that time, or was that later?

NORMAN: No, I liked writing. As a matter of fact, a couple of years ago, my first-grade teacher showed up and gave me something that I had done for her class that she had saved all these years. That's what I mean about those old-style teachers. I really came under the spell of, oh, probably ten or twelve extraordinary teachers. Extraordinary, not just good. People who spotted me and who knew that I would respond if they came over.

BEATTIE: And you felt probably more understood there than you did at home?

NORMAN: Absolutely. There's a funny film. Dad was this amateur photographer and took all these movies. There's this funny film of me on the first day of school, and here I am walking up the street, only Dad's battery was running down in the film, so that what happens when you play it back, it's at super speed. So, here am I, this little kid, going off, and I start out at regular speed and then suddenly I'm running, a sort of slap-stick sort of running, and waving like "I can't wait to get out of here. I'm gone, I'm gone, I'm gone. Gone to the first grade." And I know that's how I felt.

BEATTIE: What about junior high and high school?

NORMAN: I went to Durrett. It was the beginning of a thing in the [Jefferson] county schools called the Advanced Program. I was in the first year of that. Again, it was a great stroke of good fortune for me. There was a man named Bob Neill who was a kind of eccentric genius educator, who had put the whole program together. In the eighth grade he came into the room and was drawing carbon chains. It was sort of that Sputnik era about "we have to educate our children so that they can beat the Russians to the moon," or whatever. It was great. That was also the age of new math, and it was fabulous.

In the eighth grade I met Martha Ellison, who proceeded to take me in hand and to say to me, "You are a writer, you have always been a writer, you are going to be a writer, and you're going to write for me."

BEATTIE: You dedicate your book *Four Plays* to her.

NORMAN: Right. She was one of those people who, like Bubby, came along and provided a haven for me and a challenge for me. These surrogate mothers that really, in my whole life, I was lucky enough to find. You know, people who wanted me exactly as I was, and didn't want me to do any other kind of thing, like work for the airlines and marry a doctor. No, they really wanted me to write.

BEATTIE: What made her say that you were a writer? Had you written something particularly good, or did she just like all of the things you had written?

NORMAN: Well, I think that there was chat among the teachers in the advanced program. And Sarah Merrill, who was the eighth grade teacher, had alerted Martha to what I had written. So Martha invited me to be a part of the newspaper staff, as a freshman. That was really all it took. Martha was one of those just gorgeous, charismatic creatures. She was tall and slim and wore lots of jangly bracelets and great-looking clothes and flirted with the football coach and, at the same time, she had this great mind and a wonderful command of English, and she did a lot of work on the National Council of Teachers of English. Once I was in her tribe, it was very much a kind of Dead Poets Society, very much that kind of thing. You were one of Martha's kids, and Martha would make sure that you did your writing and that you got better and that you did your reading. Then she would enter your writing, and you would win contests. And you would get the newspaper out. She was an ally, in a basically alien world, in the alien world of high school.

My junior year was the year that I won the state writing competition with an essay called "Why Do Good Men Suffer?" That's what I'd been writing about my whole life, clearly a theme that relates back directly to the Bible things we talked about before. I mean, this is what I write out of: I write out of those essential mysteries of suffering and salvation. I was always writing on assignment. I didn't think of myself as a writer. I just knew it was something I could do. I think because my family was not a literary family, I had the impression that I could not write for a living, that I was going to have to teach. Even all through college I didn't think I could be a writer. Even until I wrote *Getting Out* I didn't think I could be a writer. I think this was a useful thing, too. I think it's really dangerous for people to think of themselves as writers too early. It puts you too early into that observation mode. You stop living and start watching.

I went to Agnes Scott College and there was another extraordinary teacher named Merle Walker. I was a philosophy major there, and Merle was great. I think she thought I was quite unlikely as a philosophy student. You know, I didn't come with the kind of . . . Hmm. Well, I don't know. Maybe she thought all philosophy students were odd. I really responded to it.

The English department was not a place I felt comfortable, and it's a particular joy of mine now to go back and be welcomed with such open arms in the English department. It's almost as though they invented me, that they knew all along that I was their writer, it's just they were letting me, you know, have my little fling with philosophy. They're quite proud of me now, and that's amusing. But in college I didn't have a great academic experience. I had a great human experience there. Again, it was a situation of isolation. Agnes Scott is a small girls' school in the South filled with mainly girls from wealthy families. I went there on a music scholarship and played for the dance group every afternoon.

BEATTIE: What did you play?

NORMAN: I played all kinds of show tunes, basically. I mean, that was the beginning of my life in the musical theater, sitting there and playing "Edelweiss" while people did pliés. I'd started playing the piano at age five, and I played all the way through school. I was terrific on the piano.

BEATTIE: Is this something you had thought of as a career?

NORMAN: Yes. I had thought that perhaps that might be something I could do. What I found out about practicing the piano was that I couldn't sit in a room and play the same thing over and over and over again. I could sit in the room, but I didn't want to be playing something I already knew. But I had a great piano teacher as well. I mean, this woman, Olga Hanz, brought me from age five to age eighteen at the piano. And she did some great favors for me. She entered us in these state competitions every year, and she would let me go in, even if I was unprepared, even if I decided that I was cocky and cool now, and I didn't have to practice, and I could just go in there. She would let me go in and be humiliated by these horrible examiners that would come to see about your fingering and your touch and your whatever. So, these were the lessons that she taught me.

She was a great, great enormous woman whose husband, Frank, paced in the back of the apartment and cooked sauerkraut and sausages. She was also an oil painter. I mean, I just was really privileged to grow up around women of passion. I caught that from them, that you could have a life that was driven by that.

Well, what happened when I got out of Agnes Scott, I needed a job, and, with a philosophy degree, you can't do anything. So, I was hired by Bill Main. He had been a teacher at Durrett, and he was then head of the school program at Central State Hospital, which is a state mental hospital [in Louisville], on the grounds of which there was a children's unit. So, I saw Bill and he always thought I was sort of smart and everything, and he said he would like to have somebody out there. It was that era of that late sixties kind of idealism. So I went, and I had the most profound two years of my life working there. I was completely unprepared. The Binghams [Barry Bingham, Sr., and Mary Bingham, then-owners of Louisville's *Courier-Journal*] had set up this model program, and part of what Bill could use the money for was educating the person who turned out to be me, who would direct this program. So, he sent me to school.

I would go out and I would spend the whole day with these wild little children, and then I would get in the car and drive back to U of L [University of Louisville] and go to school. Those two years of looking at people who had real trouble taught me more than I could have ever learned anywhere else about how people deal with trouble and what symptoms mean. I could see that the kid that was beating his head against the wall was not beating his head against the wall to make me unhappy or drive me crazy; he was doing it because that made it feel better. Somehow that act, which looked so bizarre, was actually simply that kid solving that problem that minute. That's critical learning for a dramatist and a human, you know. That the suffering in the world is not, by and large, aimed at you. These people are not trying to make you unhappy or miserable: they are really just trying to solve their problems. You can see this in *'night, Mother.* Clearly, here is Jessie, who is killing herself to solve the problem of her life. She is not doing it to get revenge on her mother, to do any of the other things that one might expect.

I loved that time of watching kids. There was a kid there who was, from time to time, bitten by imaginary bees. This was a big, strong kid who was thirteen. You can imagine this group of us, we were all these believers in these innocents, and we would gather up all of these very sick children and put them on a bus and take them to Mammoth Cave. We were in the middle of Fat Man's Misery in Mammoth Cave. And sure enough, there he was, bitten by this bee. He just clawed his way over all the other ordinary folk to get out of Fat Man's Misery, and I actually felt kind of the same way. I wasn't bitten by an imaginary bee, but I really wanted out of there, just like he did. I continue to see this in life, where people are bitten by imaginary bees. I understand that. And I'm grateful to Bill for hiring me so that I could learn those things.

BEATTIE: Did you decide, after those two years, that that's not how you wanted to spend your life, working with such children?

NORMAN: Well, what I felt was that I left brokenhearted. In fact, I realized that the kids that were there were going to grow up not to be like me, but like the person across the room with his head in his soup. You know, they were in the system, and they weren't going to get out. And I think that that kind of heartache about that arrives full-blown in plays like *Getting Out.* I mean, the difficulty of freeing yourself from whatever prison you find yourself in. I left feeling that I couldn't do anything, and that that wasn't where I needed to be.

I went from there to teaching in the Jefferson County Public Schools' Advanced Program. Heddy Glen hired me to come back and teach the fifth grade, which I was also unqualified to do.

BEATTIE: At which school?

NORMAN: At Prestonia again. I went right back to where I had been. It was now in a different building. It was good, it was interesting to go and look at what my education had been. It was a kind of personal archaeology in that way. It was also really interesting to deal with a group of really smart ten year olds. I was really lucky that I was able to have so much contact with children over my life, and now the same thing is true. Watching them is infinitely more interesting than watching adults, it's infinitely more revealing about humans as a group, and they are our only hope. So, it behooves all of us to be involved with them to whatever extent we can. I'm really fortunate that I was able to have my own children after this, but I have always been drawn to them as a group. They're not like us, you know. They are not like adults. I'm convinced that the very old are not like us, either. We use this word *humans* really loosely to enfold the whole group, but there are really quite a number of different species that exist. I think the same thing is true of men and women. This is not the same group, either.

BEATTIE: How did you find your experience in graduate school at U of L? Did you find it wildly different, your classroom education versus your daily experience with the children you were working with?

NORMAN: Well, yes. I thought it was kind of useless. I was happy to have the reading lists, you know, but with the exception of studying under Gerhard Hertz, who I took music courses from, and Dr. Kane, who I took *Ulysses* from, I just didn't find that it was a useful place to be. I didn't really get anything from graduate school, didn't learn anything.

BEATTIE: After you taught in the Advanced Program, what did you do?

NORMAN: Then Martha Ellison intervened, again, and she said, "Don't you want to come teach at the Brown School?" I said, "Oh, that sounds like fun." Because by then I'd gotten into this difficulty with Heddy Glen, and, curiously enough, the difficulty was over a book, a biography of George Washington Carver, which the students were required to read. I forget what it's called, some kind of reading program that required you to read out loud seven books a year to the kids. One of the books you had to read was this biography of George Washington Carver, which was this terribly biased, just hideous book. It was totally outdated in terms of its view of him and his life and its references to him. I mean, there would be things like "George's Aunt Mariah was so clean." Well, please, you know. So I said to Heddy Glen, "You know, we can't keep reading this book. This is not a good book." She said, "Well, what other biography of George Washington Carver would you recommend?" I thought, "Come on." I thought I'd left the mental hospital.

So, I knew I needed to move on. Again, clearly, I was searching for the place where I belonged, and always, at the end of these periods of two years, I would feel I was somehow assigned to the wrong room. So, I kept looking.

Well, Martha said to me, "Why don't you come do this, then?" She said, "The Kentucky Arts Commission has this really great program called 'Filmmaker in the Schools,' and I think they would like you a whole lot, and they will train you to be a filmmaker in the schools." Because, of course, I wasn't qualified to do that, either. So I met Nash Cox [director of the Kentucky Arts Commission], who became like the guide for the next part of my life, and Nash Cox hired me to be the "Filmmaker in the Schools" and sent me to New York, that next summer, to study film.

Then, for the next two years, I taught at the Brown School, teaching kids to make little eight-millimeter films about robberies and fish tanks, and that was interesting. That was fun.

After that two years, Nash Cox said, "There are these new grants available called the Special Arts Project. Why don't you write a proposal for the grant for the Special Arts Project and let's see if we can get the money?" So, I did that, and we got the money. So Nash said, "Well, listen, you wrote the budget; why don't you direct the program?" I said, "Okay." So I did that for two years.

Now, it's thrilling to me that the Special Arts Project still exists in the Jefferson County Schools. But it was the first time that anybody had put two hundred thousand dollars' worth of artists and arts programs in the schools, and I was happy to do that. But I'm not an administrator, and ultimately, it was not satisfying to me. I was nearing the place where I was indeed haunted by this need to write, and I was at the place where I had to find out if I could or not. I reached this point and knew that I had to try it, that I had to have the answer to the question, "Can I have a life as a writer?"

So what I did, that last year at the Special Arts Project, was to take a job writing "The Jelly Bean Journal," which was the children's section of the newspaper. I also took a big job for KET [Kentucky Educational Television] doing the workbook for an educational television series that they did, a remedial reading series. So, I had three jobs that year. I collected enough money so that I didn't have to work for a year. I knew that one of the answers might be, "No, you can't have a career as a writer." But I was ready to hear that. I was ready to know the truth, whatever it was. If the world had said "no," well, I don't know what I would have done. But, as it turned out, the world didn't say no at all.

The first thing I sat down to write was a book and lyrics for a musical. This was in '78. I quit working in September of '76; I did not go back to work, and I wrote the book and lyrics for a musical, which I quickly realized was not something you could do by yourself. Then John Jory [producing director of Actors Theatre of Louisville] called me and said he had heard I wanted to write, and would I come in and talk to him? I went in and talked to him, and he offered to pay me five thousand dollars to take a tape recorder around to talk to people in the city and collect their thoughts about busing. Then he and I and various other people would put all of those thoughts from the tape recorder together into a play about busing, and for this he would pay me five thousand dollars.

BEATTIE: How did he know you?

NORMAN: From the Kentucky Arts Commission work. I went home and I thought about his offer, and I thought, "Well, you know what? I don't want to do that." I couldn't believe that I was actually thinking, "I don't want to do that," but I felt I had bought my freedom with this intense year of work, and I was not going to sell it to somebody, even for five thousand dollars. So, I went back in to John the next week and I said, "Thanks for this offer, but I don't want to write about busing." He looked at me and he said, "Well, what do you want to write about?" And that was really the beginning of my career. John and I had three lunches in which he talked to me about the mistakes you don't have to make as a first-time writer for the theater, and then I sat down to write *Getting Out*. John read *Getting Out* and loved it, and it won the Great American Play Contest, and he put it on at Actors Theatre, and he cast Susan Kingsley in it, and the world came to see it, and the rest is history.

BEATTIE: When did you start writing screenplays? Was that right after *Getting Out*?

NORMAN: After *Getting Out*. When you have a big hit, the offers come in. The first one I did, I think, was "Children with Emerald Eyes."

BEATTIE: How did you find the experience of writing screenplays?

NORMAN: Oh, I thought it was horrible. But the money . . .

BEATTIE: It allowed you to get the money to do what you wanted to do in the theater?

NORMAN: Well, this is how the reasoning goes, but in fact what happens is, the money buys you the lifestyle that you then have to support by continuing to write screenplays. Not that this is a bad thing. It is not the business of the theater, unfortunately, to provide writers with a living. If it were, there would be a lot more writers left in the theater. But, in fact, the theater does not even offer to pay you for what you've done. The theater says, "Well, you know, write it, and we'll see what we pay you. Maybe we'll pay you a million dollars. Maybe we'll pay you two dollars and fifty cents. Maybe we'll pay you nothing." And it doesn't matter how long you've worked on it. In the movies they say, "If you write this, we will pay you this." You know that going in, and this is how the adult world functions, and this is what writers need, this kind of guarantee.

BEATTIE: Did you look at that experience as just a job to get money, a job that didn't have the ego involvement of other writing that is more your bailiwick? Sometimes, I know, in screenplay writing, whatever you write may be changed, or seven people may work on it, or seventy people may work on it, before it's over.

NORMAN: Well, certainly you can't look at screenplays as pieces of individual work. You can't see it as your vision. You can't go in with that kind of hope. On the other hand, if any parts of you should survive to the final product, so many millions of people will see it that it has to be interesting for writers.

BEATTIE: Is there any screenplay that you're particularly proud of?

NORMAN: Well, the one that I just finished, which I think maybe has a chance of actually being done. It's a piece called "Cross My Heart" that I did for Amblin, for Steven Spielberg and Kathy Kennedy. It's a remake of a French film. It's about a little boy whose mother dies, and his friends help him bury her, and help him evade the law for a while. That, I think, has real possibilities.

But, you know, it's been fifteen years that I've been writing screenplays, and the only one that's been made is 'night, Mother. Now the piece I did for Jean Whelans and Tyne Daly, the TV piece, *The Face of A Stranger,* I think they finally called it, I was quite proud of that. But it's very, very difficult to do this work, because quite often what the studios want, or what the executives want, is for you to read their minds and write what they would have written if they had been writers. And, you know, I don't have any idea what is in their minds.

BEATTIE: It seems to me that most of your work, your plays and your novel, are in large part about people feeling and actually being trapped, and about their eventually finding a way out, whether that is through death, or a solution in life, or simply a different perspective or understanding. Would you agree with that, and how have you felt trapped by critics or by success or by genre?

NORMAN: Well, certainly I agree with you that they're all about being trapped. Who knows whether this is environmental or genetic? I have always had a sense of claustrophobia. I have it when I'm in elevators, I have it in cars, I have it in conversations. But I think it probably comes from a kind of spiritual need to be loose, not tied down, in a way. And, as I've gotten older, I've seen that much more as a state of mind, rather than as a physical state.

Clearly, when I was a child, I felt very much trapped and locked into that family situation. One of the things that would happen as a child is that Dad liked to drive, so our vacations were these events where he would put us in the car, all six of us, and lock the doors and drive to Miami, which is a long way. We were constantly in this world of our parents and our family, and that was it. I really wanted very much to be in that other room; it was again this sort of assigned-to-the-wrong-room thing.

I'm fortunate in that I have this as a kind of life issue, and apparently a lot of other people feel it, too, because they respond to my work. I'm sure that there are people who would feel, for example, trapped by two children in a household and all this stuff that's in my life now. I don't feel that way about it. I feel like this is a great, great gift. Ultimately, I think I felt confined by my own isolation, you know? I really wanted out of that into the world of family life and life itself. I think that's what makes me think that it isn't so much any particular physical entrapment, but it was a kind of way of seeing things and a response. I didn't want to be locked up. I don't really know whether that's a result of my childhood or some genetic code, some little chromosome that says, "Okay, she's in the doesn't-want-to-be-locked-up crowd."

BEATTIE: Do you think your art is a trap, as well as a way out, in that once you're a success, you need to continue to be successful?

NORMAN: There are certainly times when I've felt very much in competition with myself. Certainly in the years between *'night, Mother* and *The Secret Garden* I felt very trapped in the world of the tragic drama, and I wanted out of there. I tried to get out by writing funny plays, and the world said, "We don't want these funny plays; we want you to write those great, serious things." But I didn't want to write those great, serious things. I'd already done that. I was through.

BEATTIE: But your serious plays are filled with humor as well.

NORMAN: Yes, they are. But in fact, it took a break as complete as *The Secret Garden* for the world to kind of let me out. I mean, I think I've spent my life writing my way out of corners. And that's great. It's great to be in a corner and have some mechanism for getting out of it. I mean, clearly, a lot of people don't have that way out.

BEATTIE: Sure. And *The Secret Garden* itself, was that you working out some of your own childhood, in a way?

NORMAN: Well, I don't know. I didn't put anything into the story, but I read it with *my* eyes. In working on *The Secret Garden*—and you will see again in *The Red Shoes* I've done the same thing—was just to make it more clearly the story of the person who was at the center of the story. In *The Secret Garden,* the major thing that I did was to keep it Mary's story all the way through, and thank Mary at the end. I mean, Frances Burnett didn't thank Mary. In fact, she kind of lost interest in Mary about halfway through. I think this is a problem for girls, that people lose interest when a sick boy shows up. I was angry about that, and I thought that this ought to be corrected, and I was able to do that. Fortunately, the rules of the theater assisted me in that. You can't change central characters halfway through. So, it wasn't that I was on this tirade to fix this book, which is loved by millions. I just needed to make it fit the theater better, which means we have to have one star.

BEATTIE: In what ways do you think your plays are similar, despite the fact that you're obviously interested in experimenting with different themes and devices in each play?

NORMAN: Well, I think they are all about people of great courage. They are about people who get to a certain point, where it is either go on or die, and the people ultimately find a way to go on. That moment, to me, is very thrilling. That is the reason to write, to pass along that kind of survival information. This is how we meet those moments of crisis and get through them. I'm not doing it as a polemic; I'm not interested in teaching the world how to do this. I really just want to give examples. I think that that's been the function of storytellers throughout history, to provide the culture's wisdom by example. And if people see in it something that is familiar to them, and is instructive to them, then that's good. But I don't think of these things I've written as moral fables. They are simply stories of one person's experience that's recorded. I mean, I think it's a great privilege of the storyteller to nominate certain people for permanent memory by the human race. If we're lucky in our lifetime, we will in fact be able to get a couple of people into the record. If you are Shakespeare, then you get a whole lot of people into the record. But, you know, if you're me, maybe you get Arlene, maybe you get Jessie, maybe you get Mary Lennox. That's exciting.

BEATTIE: Another way of phrasing my question is, what is the most important thing you feel you're doing in your work?

NORMAN: Dramatizing these moments of courage, moments of courage belonging to people you would not suspect were equipped to deal with it.

BEATTIE: The everyday heroes, the quiet heroes.

NORMAN: Right. The people that you never see. I mean, 'night, Mother, really the image that was on the poster and all the graphics was the image that I told to those people: "This takes place in a house on a country road that you would drive right by and you would never know that anything was going on in this house."

In *Third and Oak: The Laundromat,* here are people in a laundromat in the middle of the night. I used to see that laundromat on my way home in Louisville, after nights of parties at the theater. I would drive home, and there would be this laundromat in the middle of the night, at two, three o'clock in the morning, there would be two people in there.

BEATTIE: You once said, in another interview, that you write about what bugs you. What inspired *'night, Mother*?

NORMAN: At that time there were five or six people that I knew well whose children had killed themselves. It was kind of epidemic, I felt. I was stricken by it. I wanted to know why they did it, and whether there was anything I could have done. And I wanted to know if I were ever to be in that situation, whether there was any way that I could be saved. That was on the content side.

On the form side of the issue, I had seen two plays that purported to be about this topic. One was *Whose Life Is It, Anyway?,* which is just a kind of glorified tantrum—"Why won't they let me die?"—and the other was a play by a writer at Actors [Theatre of Louisville] who had read an article in the newspaper, that I had also read, about two men who spend a weekend together, and at the end of the weekend one man goes off to buy milk, and the other man kills himself, and that's agreed upon in advance. The play was *The Weekend,* and at the end of the play, the friend goes off to buy the milk and the curtain comes down. And I thought, "What?" In the program notes it says, "After the man goes off to buy the milk, the other one kills himself."

Well, I'm sorry, but you know, we're dealing with real people, and this is a real problem, and we don't do this by putting the information in the program notes. What we do is, we do this like the heavyweight bout. We put a person who wants to kill herself in a room with the person most likely to save her—even with someone who loves her—someone who has a claim on her. What I thought was wrong with *Whose Life Is It, Anyway?* is that it's about all these hospital people that the protagonist doesn't know. You know, what's at stake here? The protagonist can be mean to these people; they don't care. He doesn't care about them.

But with Momma and Jessie this is a deep, long, complicated relationship of great, intense love. Even though they misunderstand each other all day long, Momma has that line in which she says, "Well, Jessie, I was with you all the time. How could I know you felt that way? How could I know you were so miserable? I was here the whole time." And she really means that. So that's where it came from.

The third thing it takes to write a play like *'night, Mother* is the opportunity to write it. It doesn't just take the thinking of it. I mean, I think it takes three things. You have to have the content, and then you have to have the form, and then you have to have the time. I came to New York in the summer of 1981 and promptly was fired from the job I had, which was doing the lyrics and book for a musical called *Orphan Train.* I was fired almost instantly, and I thought, "Oh, now what? Oh, this is good. I'm in this city where I don't know anybody or don't have any real pals, and it's summer time, and I don't have a job." So, suddenly this time opened up. I'm a great believer in the nature-abhors-a-vacuum school of life, really, that that vacuum created by being fired is almost always a good thing, because what rushes in to fill that up is something unexpected, something nonlinear, something new, a kind of wildness. And when there's wildness, there's life and possibility.

So that's what happened. I sat down then to write *'night, Mother,* and I would go out every day into the city and ride the bus. I would be stuck about what Momma was going to say. I knew the Jessie character well, because the Jessie character was those people I knew who had killed themselves. The Momma character, the savior, I didn't know. So I would go and sit on the bus, and I would have these silent conversations with these women on the bus. I'd say, "Okay, now Jessie's just said this; what do you say back?" And instantly I would know what they would say. So, I felt very much that I had collaborators, in a sense: all of those women on the bus, who would have done the same thing, none of them any more remarkable than Momma, and all of them just as tenacious and just as fierce.

BEATTIE: In your novel, *The Fortune Teller,* you write, "Nobody likes a sacrifice." How does that apply to your career and to your private life?

NORMAN: Oh, I think that has to do with my mother. She did a great deal of sacrificing for us. She sacrificed her pleasures, her time, her youth, her nights, days, everything. And she thought that we would thank her. I don't think we did.

BEATTIE: Do you see sacrifice as something that's controlling, even when it's not intended to be, at least consciously?

NORMAN: Well, I don't know about that. I don't think that she did it in order to be thanked. But she thought she would be. She thought that there was a promise, you know, that had been made to her, that if you raise these children and give them your whole life, they will be grateful. And that is not what happens.

BEATTIE: You've won numerous prizes and awards, including the Pulitzer Prize and the Tony Award. What have these meant to you? Has any meant more than any other?

NORMAN: The Tony, I think. They're quite different. The Tony means, "Welcome to the club. Come, sit down, and have a few drinks. Let us tell you some stories." The Tony is a big public ceremony. The year I won the Pulitzer there was no ceremony at all. I mean, my doorman handed me the check. But the Tony is an overwhelming rush of approval unlike anything I have ever felt in my life. It hits you, it knocks your breath out. So many people get up there and can't breathe and clutch their chests and all that. There is really a feeling of breathlessness about it. It was fun to win the Tony. It still is fun to have won one. I would like to win some more Tonys. The Pulitzer, on the other hand, is a grave responsibility. The Pulitzer can have a kind of strange effect that people figure, "Well, you know, okay, that's yours. Now you are dead, or on the pedestal, or whatever."

Among us writers, it's common knowledge that the play after the Pulitzer is the one that the critics are going to destroy, because the expectations are so high. I think Wendy [Wasserstein] is really the only person I can think of whose play after the Pulitzer was well-received. The Pulitzer does put you in competition with yourself, in a way. And it's envied. And the thing is, you know, the Pulitzer is just as much luck as any of the rest of these prizes.

BEATTIE: But, of course, you have to have substance to back up any luck.

NORMAN: This is true, but there are a lot of extraordinary plays that have never won the Pulitzer and, of course, now can't. And there are a lot of major writers that have been denied their Pulitzers. And I think it would be great if Pulitzers were given for a body of work instead of for individual plays. I think it would be really great.

BEATTIE: What do you think is most important for people to know about you?

NORMAN: Oh, boy. I don't have any idea. I mean, I suppose it depends on who they are. I like what I do. What's been wonderful about it as a life for me is that even on the days when it's been most depressing, either a bad review or a lack of response or trouble with something I was trying to write or trouble with the other people around or whatever, writing is still the only thing I want to do at ten o'clock in the morning. I still would rather be here in my study than any place else in the world, in the morning. I still love the feel of the paper on the side of my hand. I am so fortunate in that the thing I most wanted to do in my life is the thing that I, in fact, do.

When I was working on *The Fortune Teller* I thought a lot about this business of past lives, and multiple lives, and I remember one day having the thought, "Oh, great. This is the life where I get to be the writer." You know? I think that for me, identifying what it was I wanted to do . . . I mean, that's really kind of how I operate. I say, "What is it that I want to do?" I don't say, "Well, I can't do such-and-such because of this." I don't start out with obstacles. I don't start out with the how; I start out with the what. I also operate in that world of, "Okay, this is what I'm going to do, and it's clear that I have no choice except to be a writer, so I will."

And I've been very fortunate in finding wonderful people to work with and to be my friends over the long haul. I mean, John Jory just commissioned a new play from me yesterday. We sat there and thought, "Isn't this fabulous? This is sixteen years of friendship and work together in the theater, in a world that increasingly sees people cut off from their colleagues and their long-term associations."

BEATTIE: Will you talk about your family for a minute?

NORMAN: My family. Tim Dykman is my husband and I have two children, Angus Dykman and Catherine. Catherine is one and Angus is five, and they're wonderful children. We adore them. Another gift from the gods is children.

BEATTIE: What does your husband do?

NORMAN: He's a painter, he's an artist. We live here [Brooklyn, N.Y.] and we have a house on the ocean [Long Island]. I love the ocean. When you grow up in Kentucky, of course you're going to love the ocean. It's just something about the perspective that the ocean gives, you know. "Okay, here is a really large force. So, please don't think of yourself as a large force, Marsha. Here is the ocean. *This* is a large force."

June 2, 1993

Books and Plays by Marsha Norman

Getting Out. New York: Dramatists Play Service, 1979.

Third and Oak: The Laundromat. New York: Dramatists Play Service, 1980.

'night, Mother. New York: Dramatists Play Service, 1983.

Third and Oak: The Pool Hall. New York: Dramatists Play Service, 1987.

The Holdup. New York: Dramatists Play Service, 1987.

Sarah and Abraham. Unpublished. Produced at Actors Theatre, Louisville, 1988.

The Fortune Teller. New York: Random House, 1987; London: Collins, 1988..

Four Plays by Marsha Norman [Getting Out, Third and Oak, The Holdup, Traveler in the Dark]. New York: Theatre Communications Group, 1988.

The Secret Garden. New York: Theatre Communications Group, 1992.

The Red Shoes. Produced in New York, 1993.

CHRIS OFFUTT

OFFUTT: My name is Christopher John Offutt, and I was born on August 24, 1958 in Haldeman, Kentucky. My mother's name is Jody—Mary Jo McCabe Offutt. She was a housewife until all the children left home. Then she went back to school, and now gives tests and does some teaching at Morehead State University, where I went, as did all of my brothers and sisters. My father is Andrew Jefferson Offutt. He sold insurance until 1972, and then quit to become a full-time writer, which he's done ever since.

BEATTIE: He writes science fiction?

OFFUTT: And fantasy. Sword and sorcery fiction and science fiction.

I have a brother and two sisters. I have a sister, Scottie, in Somerset, who works for the paper. She's a journalist. She's worked for a bunch of papers in Kentucky. My brother, Andrew Jefferson Offutt VI, lives in Fairfax, Virginia, and teaches at the college there. My sister, Melissa, is in San Diego and is in sales. I'm the oldest.

BEATTIE: So the stories in your memoir about your family, particularly the anecdotes of events at the dinner table, were those written exactly as they occurred?

OFFUTT: That's a tricky question, because you're dealing with memory. Once you remember one thing, then the next time you remember it, you don't remember the event, you remember the memory of the event. So if you remember something ten times, you know you're remembering a memory of a memory of a memory. Ultimately, I think that the reader finishes a work of art, finishes a piece of writing, and each person's interpretation, how can that be disputed? Certainly the writer, I feel, has absolutely no business to try to inform or reinform a person on how to interpret his or her work. Same with a painting. If you see a beautiful painting, whatever it touches in you, it touches. It's like snowflakes. There's no reaction to a work of art that is the same.

BEATTIE: What was your childhood like?

OFFUTT: It was a very free childhood. There were several families who lived on a hill. What I'm from is an unusual place. It was a clay-mining company town until the late twenties when it began to go into decline. It finally petered out in the forties after the war. In the sixties, a charcoal-manufacturing company took over the old brickyard and used it to make charcoal. This was a town that in the twenties had been thriving. It had a baseball team, a doctor, a saloon, a barber shop. When I grew up, there were about two hundred people there, and there was nothing but a store and a school and a post office and the church. So most of the families that had lived there had been there a long time and had been employed, one way or another, with that concern. But the majority of the people had left.

So I grew up with several boys. There were no girls, really, but my own sisters. Another family had sisters, but they were older. Mine were younger. So as a kid, there was just boys. There were the younger girls, who were my sisters, and there were the others, and so there was about six or seven or eight of us boys, and we just had a real free kind of a childhood.

BEATTIE: Do you remember the kinds of games you played, or things you did?

OFFUTT: Sure. We rode our bicycles all the time. We rode them in the woods. I played a lot of board games with my family because we were fairly isolated. In the evenings, my friends and I played basketball on a dirt court, and we got into a lot of mischief. It was a pretty rough and tumble way to live. As long as we were home by six to eat dinner, it didn't matter what we did.

BEATTIE: What about your early education?

OFFUTT: My elementary school was built in 1934 by WPA [Works Progress Administration]. They're closing it this year, which really hurts me. That's the final nail in the coffin of that community. The store is gone. The final store closed when the man died who ran it, and closing the school . . . there'll be nothing but a post office, and that may well close.

BEATTIE: How many people still live in the area?

OFFUTT: About two hundred. A little less. I walked to that school. I walked to grade school every day for eight years. It was at the foot of the hill. [That school] went up to eighth grade. There was no middle school. We were bused about nine miles to the county high school. All the high school kids got bused to town for school.

My first grade teacher was Mary Alice Jenks. I go visit her whenever I'm home. She taught me to read and write. She's a little upset about some of the language in my books; she told me she wanted not to stare at a sentence too long. She also was quite adamant about the fact that she did not teach me some of those words. I was lucky to have Mrs. Jenks as a teacher.

I had a fourth grade teacher who was very supportive of reading, Jackie Hardin. She appreciated the fact that I was a big reader and let me dispense with the textbook because after a week, I'd read everything in it, and I was bored. I was always bored. You asked me about childhood and school. I was always bored at school. I did well at it, but I was bored. If we had to read something in class, I was done half an hour before everybody else.

I taught myself rudimentary reading skills. My mother helped me a lot with just rudimentary skills, with matching letters and words and realizing what words were.

BEATTIE: Were you read to a lot by your mother?

OFFUTT: Not that I recall. There was always plenty of books around.

BEATTIE: Was reading something, when you got to school, that you really enjoyed doing?

OFFUTT: Yes, I loved to read. I still love it. I read all the time.

BEATTIE: When did your interest in writing first develop?

OFFUTT: I have a manuscript from the second grade. I might be able to recite part of it. I can't remember when I was born, but I can recite from my own works all the time. It said, "Once upon a time, in a town called Bubbletown, there lived a man named Kenny Clark." Now I remember choosing that name, because it was Clark Kent and it was Superman, so Kenny Clark. "And one day, his neighbor came to him and said, 'People are coming to kill you.'" So those are the first two lines of that story, denoting the necessary paranoia for the writer, even at age seven. And that story has a beginning and a middle and an end. At the end, he has a shoot-out, and he shoots the guys and throws them in the back of his car and takes them to the police station and then lives happily ever after.

In spelling class, you could either define the spelling words or write a story using them, to prove that you knew the words and you knew how to spell them. Well, the first time I defined them, and the teacher didn't like that. See, I constantly ran afoul of teachers. This teacher didn't like it because mine weren't dictionary definitions. So right off the bat, I started to learn that authority figures wield authority with rules and not with reality. What she wanted me to do was to open the dictionary and copy out what it said. So I began writing stories to use my spelling words. Nobody else ever did, but that was something I then always did. So in a way, my first writing was an act of rebellion.

Writing is a form of rebellion. I really think it is, at a certain level. You know, that's what you choose to do. You're withdrawing from life. You sit in a room all the time with your mind, make little marks on paper, and hope they add up to something. It's not how most people live, so therefore, it's a form of rebellion. Anyway, it's a ridiculous way to live.

BEATTIE: Would you say your writing is to understand life better, though? I mean, instead of just rebelling against it, you're almost trying to capture it in a deeper way by understanding it?

OFFUTT: Yes, I'm very interested in understanding life. I'm constantly disappointed, actually, by people. But I'm very interested in living and understanding the whole thing. Well, sometimes I think life is not all it's cracked up to be.

BEATTIE: What was high school like for you?

OFFUTT: It was awful.

BEATTIE: What about any teachers that might have been influential?

OFFUTT: I took a class with Diana Walk, an English teacher, three out of four years, and I worked for the school newspaper. I was the sports editor, and had a little column called "The Cranny." I drew cartoons for it, and Diana Walk was the sponsor. But I lived so far out. I could never get a ride home. Where I'm from was looked down upon by the rest of the county because of the old clay plant and then because of the brick factory. There were drag races there. There were regular poker games out there. The big bootlegger was there, and there were occasional shootings. You put a bunch of white people together and they're going to work out their own pecking order. That's essentially what Eastern Kentucky is; I don't know what the percentage is, but it's almost all white. You want to talk about understanding life—well, that's what life is, you know. Everybody wants to be better than somebody else.

Well, anyhow, kids from Haldeman who went to the high school right off the bat were suffering because of the way they were viewed by the rest of the county. There were few of us. It was the smallest community. People made fun of us because our clothes smelled of smoke from the charcoal plant.

I was four-feet-eleven when I was fourteen years old, and I had long hair. Well, the high school administrators said, "You can't have long hair. You have to cut your hair." I said, "No, I won't do it. I refuse." So, I just went to school. Everybody had to get all their hair cut off by the following Monday or whatever, and everybody else did, but me. They called me into the office—and this is the first week of high school for me—and they said, "We'll take you to go get your hair . . ." I said, "No, I don't want to cut my hair." They said, "We'll call your parents," which was no big threat. I said, "Great." So they called my father, and about five minutes later, the principal said, "You don't have to cut your hair." So I was the only person in school, the only boy, who had long hair. This was in 1972. It was a big deal. So my rebellion worked. My high school never had the dress code again. It failed right there.

BEATTIE: Do you know what your father had said to change your principal's mind?

OFFUTT: Yes. He told me years later, that he paid taxes in this county, and that kept the school going, and not to ever bother him about me unless it was about my behavior. He said that I got good grades, and to leave him alone unless my behavior was bad, which, of course, it did become later. So that was the beginning of high school for me. Nobody liked me. Then I cut my thumb with a knife that I got for my birthday, and was all messed up. I couldn't participate in sports right off the bat.

I had a creative writing class with Mrs. Walk, and I wrote some stories there. I read all the time. I read constantly. I read ten to fifteen books a week. There was no library at my high school. My mother was very instrumental in getting a public library set up in Morehead. At the time, you weren't allowed to check out books from the college library. The townspeople couldn't get a card, because the college sets itself apart from the community, and it did much more so then. Of course, the college library didn't have children's books anyhow, but my mother got this library set up, and they allowed me to check out all these books in the summer. I'd check out thirty books in a week, and read them. Then one day—the Cincinnati Reds had a big season, they were winning—and I was a little league catcher. I went and asked the librarian for books on baseball, because I'd pretty much read most of what was there. She said, "What are you interested in?" I said, "I'm a catcher." She said, "Okay." So she went to the card catalogue, and she led me to the aisles, and she handed me *The Catcher in the Rye.* I stayed up all night reading that book when I was twelve years old. I never read another juvenile book after that. Ever. That book just . . . I couldn't believe that book. Up until then, I'd been reading all juvenile fiction, and I'd read a lot of adult fiction that was lying around the house. But they didn't have the same effect on me as that book. It just was a different kind of writing altogether.

BEATTIE: Was Holden Caulfield your alter ego?

OFFUTT: No. I mean, I have very little in common with Holden Caulfield, right? He's a guy who's a flipped-out rich kid in New York City. Well, that didn't have anything to do with me.

BEATTIE: The rebellious part of Caulfield's character, though?

OFFUTT: Well, yes, I guess. It was just the writing itself, see. It wasn't the characters or the event; it was that writing could be that way. That you could write that way. That you didn't have to write about Tarzan of the Apes or the Hardy Boys.

BEATTIE: You realized you could write about real people?

OFFUTT: Write about real people and real stuff, and a book could be written in first person. The only first person I'd read was *Huck Finn.* That was a very different book, too, you know. It was a great book. But this book just tore my head off. I just could not believe that you were allowed to write that way, see. That book and then Dad's book, *The Castle Keep,* were the two biggest, single books in my life. *The Castle Keep* is a novel of my dad's that's set in Haldeman in the house I grew up in, about a guy who's a writer, who has two sons and two daughters and wants one of his sons to be a writer.

BEATTIE: Did your father talk to you about writing as you were growing up?

OFFUTT: He didn't talk to me about writing. He marked my manuscripts. Every manuscript I ever wrote, he marked. Every story for school. Every paper that I wrote for school, he always read it and gave me support on it and helped me. He never rewrote it, but he could always help me with it. He was a tutor. I mean, I had a tutor throughout grade school and high school. I knew English grammar inside and out by age ten and eleven. I learned it the hard way, you know. I learned it by making mistakes and being constantly corrected. I mean, I knew the difference between *as* and *like,* and *further* and *farther,* plus everything else. I had an instinct for grammar and for writing, and I knew what really worked.

BEATTIE: After you read *Catcher in the Rye,* did you experiment on your own with writing similar types of things? Did you try to imitate Salinger?

OFFUTT: I never really tried to imitate anybody. I didn't believe in it. I still don't. I know it's advice given to a lot of writers, but I never took it, and I would never give that advice to anybody. If I read six books by one writer, my writing will maybe reflect that influence a little bit, unconsciously. But I think everything I've read influenced me, and I never tried to copy anybody. So no, I didn't try to write like him. I just stopped reading juveniles.

BEATTIE: What sort of books did you read, then?

OFFUTT: I don't remember. I just moved from the juvenile section of the library to the adult section. I read everything I could get my hands on.

BEATTIE: You must have been different from your classmates or peers in terms of reading so much.

OFFUTT: Oh, yes. I read more than anybody.

BEATTIE: What did you do after high school?

OFFUTT: I tried to join the army. I failed the physical. I hated high school. That last year, I'd fallen apart. I was involved with drugs. There were always drugs in the school, and the school was unprepared for them. The teachers had no experience with them. There were three different principals through my four years there. So things were really a mess, and ours was the biggest freshman class that went through. They canceled the senior trip after our class.

I decided that I was going to just join the army and not have to go to school anymore. I wanted out. I really wanted out of the hills. But I failed the physical. I got a general degree, whatever it's called. There are three different levels of degrees you can get, high school degrees. I got the bottom-level degree, with no distinction.

BEATTIE: But your grades were good, right?

OFFUTT: Well, yes. I didn't do so well in typing and math. I never got anything less than an A in English. I was a little upset in high school when they didn't give me the English Award. But by that time, there was no way they were going to give me anything because of my attitude. Anyhow, I failed the army physical. There was some paperwork and some fast stuff done so I could have a degree. I got a job at a hardware store, which I hated. In Morehead. Then, at the last minute, I just decided to enroll at Morehead State because I didn't like working at that hardware store. That was in the fall of 1976.

BEATTIE: Did you spend the next four years at Morehead?

OFFUTT: Well, not exactly. I quit quite a few times and traveled. I quit to be an actor in New York. I hitchhiked there to be an actor. I quit again, and went out west and hitchhiked around out west. I had a hard time breaking free of the hills. A real hard time, actually. I was very curious about the outside world, but it just didn't do me much good out there. The first time I went out, I came home with my leg in a cast. So I went back to college, but I changed my major. I changed it from theater, which I'd been involved in before, to art, because I'd seen paintings in New York, and I wanted to be a painter. Then I changed my major again. I just kept on shifting things around and quitting. I always had jobs. I always had to work during the summer. I worked every Christmas and every spring break and every summer. Sometimes I had a part-time job while I was in school, and sometimes I didn't.

BEATTIE: Your memoir, *The Same River Twice,* reads as though you were gone for ten years and came back. But you came back periodically?

OFFUTT: *The Same River Twice* time is sandwiched a little bit. There are big pieces of my life that I did not include. But I began leaving home when I was nineteen. It took me about six years until I was fully gone. I graduated from college; I had a girlfriend and she just seemed to think I should graduate, so I did. Then I had nothing to go back to.

BEATTIE: What did you major in at Morehead?

OFFUTT: My degree is in theater, and I have a minor in art.

BEATTIE: As you write in *The Same River Twice,* you sound as though you weren't quite sure what you wanted, but you knew that whatever it was, it was in the arts.

OFFUTT: Right.

BEATTIE: Do you know what experience you were looking for? Was it a matter of getting out of Eastern Kentucky to find something particular, or just to see what was in the rest of the world, or what?

OFFUTT: I don't know. I always thought I was looking for something, something intangible. I didn't really know what I was looking for, but I felt that I was. My brother, one time, told me that he didn't think I was looking for anything. He thought I was running away. At the time I denied it, but I think he was right. I was running away. And I was very, very, very, very curious about the rest of the world out there, and I still am, although I know quite a bit about it now. I covered it. I covered the country. I lived in a lot of places in this country, at a bottom level of existence, and I really saw a lot of it.

BEATTIE: You write in *The Same River Twice* about being in Massachusetts and returning to New York because it was very much like Eastern Kentucky.

OFFUTT: I felt like New York was . . . I know that other people pointed out that this is an unusual similarity, but I really felt like, in some ways, New York City and Eastern Kentucky are similar, because you can sort of just do whatever you want, and people leave you alone. In Eastern Kentucky, people leave you alone. You can live however you want. As long as you don't seriously mess with somebody else, nobody messes with you. People are the same in New York. All I ever wanted was for people not to mess with me. Of course, I have a habit of messing with people, too.

BEATTIE: Sort of a conflict there, yes. Is there a place outside of Kentucky that you felt was more home than other places?

OFFUTT: No, nowhere. I felt like an alien everywhere. I feel like an alien in Lexington now, actually. I've been here for three days. It's just another medium city in America and it reminds me of . . . that's the thing about America. Wherever you go, there's going to be McDonald's, chain hotels, chain restaurants, malls, chain stores in the malls . . . You drive two thousand miles and eat the same meal and sleep in the same bed, manufactured by the same company in the same exact hotel room that you did two thousand miles back. And that makes me feel like a foreigner. Eastern Kentucky is the only place I ever felt truly comfortable, either at home in the hills or by myself.

BEATTIE: Do you still feel that way about Eastern Kentucky?

OFFUTT: Yes.

BEATTIE: Is it a place you'd like to return to live?

OFFUTT: Sure. Classic. You leave when you're young, and you go back when you're old.

BEATTIE: Do you have specific plans to do that?

OFFUTT: I don't have specific plans beyond now, today. Right now, I just want to go home and see my family. See my kids. My wife and I got married and moved to Kentucky in the late eighties, and we were there for just under a year. We used all our money up from our savings trying to fix up a house to live in. Our plan was to go there and buy this house, and we were going to have kids there. We were going to raise our kids right where I grew up, on the same hill. Our neighbors were people that I grew up with, who now had kids.

But I couldn't find a job. My wife couldn't find a job. We ran out of money. I applied to graduate school. I didn't really have any interest in going to school, but it was a means of getting out. It was like joining the army again. I had to get out. I was once again in the situation of being in the hills and not being able to get out, except I was older. It was just really strange. So I applied to six schools, and they all took me, but I didn't know that. The first one that called me and said, "We'll take you," was Iowa, and I said, "Okay, okay. I'm coming." I borrowed money from a bank. I couldn't even borrow money from a bank in Rowan County. No bank there would lend me money. So I had to go out of the county to Sandy Hook, and they lent me money so we could move. We had to borrow money to move to Iowa. We rented a van and moved into a condemned building in Iowa. It's gone now. I mean, you could see daylight through the walls, and the ceiling fell in two rooms while we were living there.

Well, I hated Iowa. It was flat. Everybody was blond. Really, there are a lot of blond people out there. People dressed well. I just didn't like it. I didn't like being in school much at all. I had never liked being in school. My whole relationship with formal education is really twisted because I always excelled at it. It was the only thing I excelled at, really. The only thing I consistently did well was apprehension of knowledge. But I just never liked it—the classrooms, the teachers—none of it. Even graduate school, which was a wide-open situation. You didn't even have to go to school; I didn't go a lot. I started skipping school in grade school. In graduate school, at one point, I just quit going altogether. But, we had a baby in Iowa. We had a baby there, and I got a grant, right after graduation.

BEATTIE: Was this the Michener Grant?

OFFUTT: Yes. So my short story collection, *Kentucky Straight,* I got a little bit of money for it. I hadn't finished it or anything. That's a really long story about how that came about. But anyhow, we got a little money. There wasn't any money to go anywhere, but it was enough money if my wife, Rita, worked. We lived really carefully. I could continue to write, and I could try to finish *Kentucky Straight,* or what became that. So we did, and by that time, we had a baby. We were just in a situation where we couldn't afford to leave.

Now we have another baby. We have two children. I used to travel with a backpack. But I can't do that anymore. I have all these other things I have to carry around. So, we've been in Iowa City five years. As soon as I got out of graduate school, I started liking Iowa a little bit more. I realized that I didn't like the school, and I was taking it out on the state. Now I see Iowa City as a small town and very efficient. There's plenty of work. It's clean. It's safe. And we have two kids. You know. We're there, we know a bunch of people there. So I don't know what's going to happen. I like it better now. Let's just put it this way: I am less uncomfortable in Iowa than anywhere else I've lived except Haldeman. Everywhere else I felt incredibly uncomfortable. Iowa, I have the most tolerance for it.

BEATTIE: You talked about your wife. When did you meet and marry her? She's from New York, is that right?

OFFUTT: She's from Manhattan. She grew up in Manhattan and Brooklyn. She had moved from Manhattan to Boston to be in a theater company, and she was living in a group house, as they called it up there at the time. In Boston, they had all these old, big mansions that people were cutting up into apartments, but they were trying to preserve them. In Rita's case, there were three men and three women all in their thirties who were sort of pitching in and living together in these huge mansions. They all had two rooms apiece and a bunch of common rooms, and it seemed like an interesting way to live if you could stand living with five people. It wasn't for me.

My best buddy who had gone to school at Morehead, for graduate school in painting, he came to visit me, and he lived in this house. I used to go over and visit him, and Rita was one of the women in that house. I always liked her, and I got to know her pretty well. I was interested in her, but I knew that if I asked her out, it would just be a disaster. I would then not feel comfortable going to visit my buddy. So, I didn't ask her out in order to protect my relationship with Dave, because at that time, I was living in a rooming house. I'd just begun a manuscript that became *The Same River Twice.* Another girlfriend had dumped me. I'd been evicted from an apartment. I was working three days a week, and I was pretty vulnerable. I knew that I needed that relationship with Dave. I could not cut myself off, and I knew that if I asked this woman out, it would just go all to hell.

BEATTIE: Did you think your backgrounds were too different?

OFFUTT: No, it was just that everything had always gone to hell with me and women. I thought Rita was terrific. She seemed really smart, really interesting, and I'd never met anyone like her. But my relationships with women just had been such a sequence of mishaps. Women always wanted me to get a job. They always thought, "Wow, this guy's really smart. He's got a lot of potential. It we could just clean him up a little bit, get him to wash his hair more often. Maybe get nicer clothes on him. Get him out of those flannel shirts. You know, this guy could make some money. He'd make it. He's real smart. He could go out there and be a good provider." Well, my old girlfriend, she was always leaving those matchbooks around that said, "Learn electricity in your spare time," and all this stuff. At that time I was recognizing and trying to come to grips with the fact that I would be single all my life. Because good God, that would be a lot easier. So anyhow, I didn't ask her out. But I got to know her really well.

Then pretty soon I used to go over to visit Dave when I knew he wasn't there, and I knew she was there, because they had this great big house, and we'd sit and watch movies together. They had a video room. It was like Herman Munster's house, this big, old, gigantic place. Then she told me she was moving back to New York, so I thought, "Perfect." She was leaving in a month, so I asked her if she wanted to have a date that day. I knew she was leaving, it was finite, it was going to end. There was no risk involved. I wouldn't damage my relationship with Dave. I could have a quick romance with her. She'd be gone. It had a tragic ending all set up. She's going to go to New York. I'm going to stay. And maybe in the meantime, we could have a lot of fun together. So we spent the entire next month together. Every day. She went to work with me. A couple of times, I went with her.

BEATTIE: Where were you working?

OFFUTT: It was an awful job. I took pictures of children in malls. I had this portable studio, a backdrop and a camera and tripod and some lights. I had to go set up, and I would drive to these malls around New England three days a week and just prop these kids up on the table and take their pictures. So Rita could come with me. That was a hard job, but in some ways it was one of the better jobs I've had. We spent all our time together, and then she moved, and I started flying to New York, and taking the train, and she'd come back and forth. I moved to New York. I gave up the first nice apartment I had. I'd moved into a nice apartment. I had just begun to have some friends. This job as a photographer seemed like the best job I'd had, even though it was awful. It was still better than being a dishwasher.

BEATTIE: You say Rita is a psychologist?

OFFUTT: Well, yes. She was working in a theater company. Things had gone bad for her in New York, and she just needed to get away from her situation. So she moved to Boston and got a job in this theater company. Then she went back to Manhattan and began working as a social worker, and I moved back and we lived in Manhattan. Two months after she left, I left.

BEATTIE: You have been together ever since?

OFFUTT: Yes. As a matter of fact, right now's the longest time we've been apart. This trip to Kentucky.

BEATTIE: That's not very long, is it?

OFFUTT: No, I've called her every day.

BEATTIE: Is your wife working in Iowa now?

OFFUTT: Yes. She works with the homeless and the mentally ill. That's her specialty. She worked in New York with the mentally ill. In Iowa, they give her the hard cases. She saves people's lives. They try to commit suicide, and she takes care of them. She dragged a guy off a bridge on Christmas Eve once, in this bad snow. I couldn't do what she does. She's a perfect partner for me. There's not much bothers her.

BEATTIE: You had stories that appeared in a lot of literary magazines, and you said that the story of *Kentucky Straight*'s publication is a long story. Will you tell me what that is?

OFFUTT: Well, yes. It has to do with a lot of luck. For one thing, I never had any stories get printed until the book was accepted. It doesn't look that way. One would assume they were all published beforehand. Nobody wanted to publish these stories. I have over a hundred and thirty rejections at home.

BEATTIE: Just for the stories in *Kentucky Straight*?

OFFUTT: Yes. Nobody wanted these stories. They're set in an unusual place. The people, the characters, are unusual characters, and the events of the stories are unusual. I don't have a famous name. I didn't go to fancy schools. I'm not well connected. I'm not from the prevailing ruling class, you know. I'm a white guy, and that's about it. I'm not from the upper class, and I don't write about it. The majority of the reading public, you know, is upper-class white people. Mainly women, actually. So anyhow, I couldn't get in print, and I know that had to do with the material, because the stories aren't bad. I always felt like they were written well, as well as I could write them. But as a matter of fact, the magazines in the South would reject those stories sooner than any other magazines.

BEATTIE: Because those magazines and journals were afraid of stereotypes?

OFFUTT: I think that a lot of stories in the literary magazines of the South, a lot of them, if they're about rural characters, there's an implicit agreement between the writer and the reader that we're talking about "them." You know, we're talking about "those people." My stories are very much about "us." I don't make any deals that way with the reader. These are my people. These are me. This is me. And a lot of the South has a real class consciousness. Now this is all speculation on my part, but for whatever reasons, they weren't getting in print.

My attempt in this book was to destroy the stereotypes. The stereotypes are Li'l Abner, Dukes of Hazard, Barney Google, and Snuffy Smith. Beverly Hillbillies. Those are very negative stereotypes. Now then there's that, the flip side. The other negative stereotype is the simple-but-happy poor mountaineer. You know, the guy who's ignorant and at home with the woods and just has this wonderful little . . . Now, I don't know anybody who is ignorant but happy. I know very few people who are simple. I think the people in Eastern Kentucky have incredibly complicated lives, very rich lives. So one of the things I wanted to do with that book was to blow out of the water all of the clichés, all of the stereotypes. Eastern Kentucky is a unique situation. It's had all these efforts to help it. Somebody's always trying to help it or trying to protect it, and I wanted to try to be honest about it. It's a really hard world. I mean, I'm a writer. I'm not an Appalachian writer. You know? I write. I write books. *The Same River Twice* isn't an Appalachian book.

I couldn't get in print. I'd never sent anything out until I was in graduate school. The woman who came to be my editor has a brother who went to a private college in Iowa. She wanted to visit it. She worked a deal to where she could come down to the Iowa [Writers' Workshop] program, give an hour-long question-and-answer thing, and get her trip underwritten. So I gave her three stories, and she didn't like them. She said, "Send me more." I was pretty belligerent, and I said, "If you don't like them, why do you want more?" She says, "Well, I like the writing. I don't like the stories." Okay. So I sent her more, and I didn't hear from her for about six months. So I wrote her a letter, and she called me back and said, "I'm really sorry I haven't written. I meant to write you. You sent me six more stories. I liked two of them." I said, "Oh, great." She said, "Send me more." So I thought, "Okay."

In the meantime, Rita had gotten pregnant, and I was just writing fanatically all the time. Every time I'd finish a story, I'd sent it to this editor in New York. Then I got out of school and my wife had the baby. I got a job as a carpenter, and I was supposed to put up a mailbox one day, when this editor called and said, "We'd like to make an offer on the book." Well, I got really choked up. I started crying. She said, "Would you like me to call back later?" I said, "Yes." Then I pretty much said yes to everything, which was a mistake. I probably should have immediately called an agent and said, "Look, I've got an offer; can you help me?" But I didn't. The whole manuscript had been rejected by an agent. Even an agent wouldn't look at it. Then, as soon as I added a cover letter to each story in *Kentucky Straight,* stating "This story is from a collection coming out with Random House," oh man! Magazines and journals suddenly wanted to publish one. So that whole business was backwards, for me. Then I got a grant. Wow!

BEATTIE: That was the Michener Grant?

OFFUTT: Yes. It's a private grant through James Michener. That Michener Grant allowed me to write these two books, essentially. It gave me the jump I needed. So over the next two years, I wrote more stories, and then I had ten. I just arranged an order that I thought would lead up to the tenth one, then I dropped the last one. Which is the way I write, you know. Always cut the last few pages. I finished that book and was sick of writing about Kentucky. I didn't know what to do. I was burned out. So I went back to *The Same River Twice.* I had a manuscript form of draft three that my parents had typed for me about three years before. It was really short. It wasn't very good, but I wanted to go back to it. Everybody said, "Don't go back to it. Never go back. Always go forward. You're a better writer. You're not the same." So naturally, as soon as somebody started telling me what I should do, I decided I would do the exact opposite, and I went back to it.

I went to New York and got an agent, because my editor was getting tired of me. I was always asking her all these questions, so she said, "Look, I'm going to get you an agent, and you can call her."

BEATTIE: So your editor got your agent for you?

OFFUTT: Well, she set up appointments with six agents. By this time, they all wanted me, because the work was done. The first book was the hard work. The leg work and labor were over. I interviewed all these agents, and I just picked the one that I laughed the most with. I went with Virginia Barber because she had a Ph.D. in English, which nobody else did.

One woman who worked at the agency, her best friend from high school was going to school at Iowa, and was getting ready to finish and go to Mexico and do some kind of weird research. So the agent, Mary, went to visit her mother in Indiana where she's from, and then shot out there to Iowa to see her best friend. She did not like her best friend's husband at all, and her best friend had to work all the time, so she didn't know what to do, so she called me and said, "Look, I'm from your agency," and I spent the next couple days just hanging out with her. I didn't know what to do. She was buying lunch and dinner, and I was entertaining her and telling her stories and whatnot. Then, right before she left, she said, "What are you working on?" I said, "Well, I'm working on this book that deals with all these stories I've been telling." She got really excited. She said, "Wow! Can I have it? Can I see it?" I said, "No, this is not for publication yet. This is based on my journals. This is something that I do between projects, to just keep it alive. It's very personal and it's just for me." I said, "No, you can't take it." She couldn't believe it. She said, "What is it? Notes?" I said, "No, it's draft twenty-four." So I talked to Rita about it, and I realized if I didn't give my own agent my manuscript in my own house, I would never put it in the mail. So I did. I gave it to her.

I called Becky, the editor, and said, "Look, you know Mary's got the manuscript. She's going to send it." Becky was really excited, too. In the meantime, Becky left Random House and went to Simon & Schuster. I called her, and when she told me, I couldn't believe it. I said, "Well, look. If you're going, I'm going." She said, "Okay, we'll take his manuscript over here." Well, they didn't like it. The Simon & Schuster people did not like the manuscript.

So I went to New York to Simon and Schuster. I sat in a room with four editors at Simon & Schuster. What happened was, I stayed with my wife's parents. I couldn't eat in the morning I was so nervous. I mean, a lot was riding on it. By this time, we were running out of money. I'd received another grant from the Kentucky Arts Council, which had helped. I'd taken the train into the city, and the meeting was early afternoon. I was walking, and I realized I should probably eat a little bit because the meeting could last long, and I didn't want my stomach to growl. So I stopped and I grabbed a sandwich off the street. I was going to carry it over to the Simon & Schuster building, and I figured I'd eat in the lobby. I got there and there was this huge building and it says Simon & Schuster on it. I was completely floored. I couldn't believe it. So I went over and I sat on the street and just ate my sandwich and stared at it. Then, when I went into the building, there was a security guard. He looked at me, and he said, "Oh you want that door." And I thought, "All right! This guy knows who I am. They recognize me. They know I'm coming. These guys are on the ball." So I went to the door, and there were steps going down, and I went down the steps, and there was a guy back there, and he said, "Okay, where is it?" I said, "Where's what?" He said, "Where's the package? You're the messenger, right?"

I went back upstairs, and I went to the security guy, and I said, "I have an appointment upstairs." So, I get upstairs and the elevator opened. It doesn't open in the hallway, but it opens in an office, and right in front of me, behind her desk, is obviously an actress or model who's working as a secretary, because she is the most beautiful woman I had ever, ever seen in my life. The door opened and I just stared at her. She's wearing five hundred dollar clothes and there's this beautiful office with a glass desk. I'm standing there, you know, coming up from the basement, and she says, "Oh yes, it'll be a few minutes. Will you have a seat?" She points to a chair right there beside her. So I sit, and I am so intimidated I keep staring at her; I don't know what to do. Then I realize that I've got a piece of this sandwich stuck in my teeth. I feel it with my tongue, so I get up and ask for the men's room. So I go to the men's room and I'm in there, with a piece of cardboard, taking stuff out of my teeth. I don't even want to go back in that room with this woman, she's got me so intimidated. I go back in, and I say, "I better go to the bathroom." You know, just in case. So, I urinate, and I go back out, and then I think, "Well, just in case, I better go back in and see if I need to do anything else." So I go in, and so by this time, I'm a complete wreck. I'm sweating. I'm essentially hiding in the bathroom of this building. I realize on the toilet, I realize I've got to go back in there. So I get up, and I pull my pants up with such force that I rip my underwear off the band, half of it around. I'm standing there and half of my underwear is hanging off of me. I just ripped it right off, and I can't believe it. I have to go in. I realize I'm running out of time, you know. I can't change clothes. I don't have any extra underwear. I don't want to go in there without wearing underwear. I realize if I start taking my pants off—I'm in a little booth—that I don't have time for this. So I just stuff my underwear down one side of my leg of my pants, and hope nobody will notice. I walk into this office where these editors are sort of waiting to decide whether they're going to take this book or not by this . . . person, and all I can think about is my underwear is down one whole side of my leg.

So I sit down, and we start talking, and they start asking me these questions. I'm just so preoccupied I just say whatever, the whole time hoping they won't notice that I'm trying to sit so they won't see this big . . . Afterwards, they leave, and I said to the editor, to Becky, "Well, what do you think? She said, "Well, Chris, I think they liked you. You were just flaky enough to where they think you're the real thing."

In the meantime, I'd had a lucky feather I was wearing under my shirt, and it was starting to itch me. So I pulled that out, and they're sitting there, and I'm pulling out a lucky feather and they said, you know, they're kind of making a joke, "Do you have anything else?" And I say, "Well, yes, I've got stuff in all my pockets. I've got a lucky rock. I've got a little bag of dirt from Kentucky. I am loaded with lucky stuff. And my underwear is falling off."

BEATTIE: That reminds me of the dirt that you spread before you got married.

OFFUTT: Yes, it was a pinch of that same dirt that I'd taken with me for luck. I guess I'm superstitious. Anyhow, I went back to Iowa and they called, and the rest is history. But we're still broke. We ran out of money again, but this year I got an NEA [National Endowment for the Arts] grant, so we have enough money to go another year.

BEATTIE: What are you working on now?

OFFUTT: A novel. I'm not real happy with it. I think I prefer short stories. But I have a contract with Simon and Schuster to write a novel. See, they would not publish *The Same River Twice* unless I promised to write another book, because I'd already left one company. They called me a maverick and a renegade. They thought that I might be a loose cannon, a one-book crazy man, and they wanted a commitment. So, I agreed. I think it was a lousy thing, actually. But that's what I'm working on. A novel that's set in Kentucky.

BEATTIE: And your publisher said it needed to be a novel, not another collection of short stories?

OFFUTT: A novel sells more than short stories. You know, they're very commercial. I mean, that's all they think about, is dough. They're a bunch of cheapskates, too, if you ask me. Even if they have a big building with glass desks.

BEATTIE: They have to pay for the big building and glass desks, I guess. Is the novel you're working on autobiographical?

OFFUTT: I think everything is, really. It's autobiographical. The short stories are autobiographical, even though none of the families in there are my family. I'm not actually a functioning character in any of the stories. I still consider them very autobiographical. I'm in every one of those stories. I'm all those people, in a way, and those stories certainly are emotionally autobiographical. *The Same River Twice*, that's straight-out autobiographical. I don't want to write that way anymore. It's too constricting. Really constricting. When I started writing *The Same River Twice*, I thought if I could change, if I could write my life and transform it from being this long system of errors and bad decisions and bad luck and disastrous situations and stupid things—if I could transform it, if I could write it—it would validate it, and it would rationalize winding up in a rooming house alone at thirty years old. That's why I started it. It was never intended for anything but for me, for my efforts at understanding myself and what had led me to this situation.

BEATTIE: Do you feel as though your finishing your memoir, completing it yourself, in terms of writing it or having it published, got you to arrive at some conclusion about that?

OFFUTT: Maybe. I don't know.

BEATTIE: The end of that book reads as though you have come to terms with something, yourself or with your life.

OFFUTT: Well, yes, I guess so. You see, the pregnancy thing wasn't in there for awhile. I mean, obviously I wasn't married when I started *The Same River Twice*, so I had all the back stories, I had all the events. At one point, it was six hundred pages. You should see what I cut out. Well no, you shouldn't. But I cut out a lot of material. It wasn't working very well. It had big structural problems, as a book. I didn't know what to do. I mean, it was autobiographical. You can't go in and fix it.

BEATTIE: Change your life.

OFFUTT: I couldn't change it. I couldn't, you know, jazz it up. So what I did was, I found all these notes that I'd written while Rita was pregnant that I'd completely forgotten about. Then I went back to the diary. See, that's what I did. I went back to diaries again, and realized it would take an incredible amount of work to try to do this, and I didn't know if I could do it. But if I could do it, I could lay in the story of pregnancy and then write the birth, and it would solve my structural problem. I tried several techniques, different ways of telling the story, and it just wasn't working out. But I realized that this would do it. Then I realized that I had two stories, a past and a present.

BEATTIE: It certainly works in terms of softening the experiences in the beginning of the book.

OFFUTT: See, I missed that. See, that's the thing. When you say did I come to a conclusion, I don't know. I mean, what I'm facing now is a life of relative boredom. I had a very intensive, exciting lifestyle for a long time, and I liked it. I got used to it.

BEATTIE: That was while you were traveling around?

OFFUTT: Yes. I got used to it. When I started stopping, I didn't like stopping so much. It was hard. It was really hard. I wasn't as resilient, you know. My body couldn't take it. My mind started getting a little crazy at the edges, and I didn't like that. I didn't know how to get out of it. I essentially got out of it through writing stories that made up *Kentucky Straight*. That was how I got out. I just stayed in one place and did something else for two years. So now, I'm in a situation where I have two children. I have two books out. I never thought anything like that would happen. I have a car now, you know. I never had a car. I have to somehow assimilate myself to this lifestyle, which is very staid. And a writer's life . . . . you just stay by yourself. Sit in a room. So the only place I can find any excitement right now is in playing poker.

BEATTIE: Are you the kind of writer who would prefer to work at some physically more active job and write, or just write?

OFFUTT: I don't know. What do you mean, physically more active?

BEATTIE: I mean something other than sitting in a room.

OFFUTT: Every job I ever had was very physical, even that photography job. I was always with the kids. I kept in shape that way. I kept in physical shape and I got exercise and worked that part of my body. I don't know what I'm going to do now, actually. I joined a gym and I never went. I couldn't stand it, actually.

BEATTIE: It seemed artificial?

OFFUTT: It seemed very artificial.

BEATTIE: Is it going out and actually accomplishing something, or being around other people—that kind of action—that you want?

OFFUTT: Yes, just something that is exciting. Writing is very exciting, but it can be real lonely. But I don't have anything that's as exciting as it used to be. And that's fine. I used to drive real fast. Then I realized that I had to stop that because I have these two kids. I had to be careful. I've had to place myself at less risk, and I really put myself in peril over and over and over when I was in my twenties. Part of it was fun. Part of it was I didn't really care at all. I didn't care if I lived or died.

BEATTIE: Do you think you were testing something?

OFFUTT: Who knows, you know? I was frightened to understand something, I guess.

BEATTIE: Are you in a position now where you stay at home to do a lot of taking care of your children?

OFFUTT: Well, yes and no. I'm certainly involved with them and I want to be involved with them. I have a very close relationship with both boys. I call Sam every day if I'm on the road and talk to him. He always says the same thing.

BEATTIE: Which is?

OFFUTT: "When you coming home, Daddy? I need you to come home, Daddy." Today he wanted me to go with him to his friend's house. I said, "I can't, Sam. I'll be home in a couple of days." He said, "Oh, a couple is two." But I write. I approach writing as a job. I can't just hang around the house with the kids all the time. Rita works part-time, and I work. We have different arrangements with each other, and some daycare, and a baby-sitter comes in. Rita's involved with our children more than I am. I just try to be there. I'm always home, is the thing.

BEATTIE: So you do your writing at home?

OFFUTT: Oh, yes.

BEATTIE: What are your writing habits?

OFFUTT: I get up and I write the first thing in the morning. Let me amend that. I sit down at a computer with a cup of coffee or with one cup of double espresso within thirty minutes of getting up every day. So that means, maybe I get up at ten. Maybe I get up at eight. Maybe I get up at two. It doesn't matter. Soon as I get up, I sit down and within half an hour, I've got it all worked out to where I can eat breakfast, fix coffee, take a shower, brush my teeth, take my vitamins, and sit down to work within thirty minutes of getting up. I write a little bit in a journal to start out, to get myself geared towards thinking in narrative fashion, because I frankly think that writing is an unnatural act. I don't think my mind works that way. My mind does not work in a logical progression of narrative. My mind works in little hops and skips and jumps and images. My mind really works with images, so it's like boom, boom, boom, boom. Then I'm way off over in left field. We don't talk in sentences. Nobody converses in sentences. We don't think that way. It's all artificial. So I start out writing a diary to get myself back into the unnatural way of using my mind, which is pretty pathetic when you consider that you sit around all day in a room using your mind in an unnatural fashion. Then I work a minimum of four hours. There are times when I want to get up immediately, but I sit there for four hours at least. I'm very process oriented. I care very little about product when I'm working. As long as I'm working, that's all that matters. If I write one page or twenty pages, it doesn't matter. It's that I sit down and I'm doing it. That validates me. It's my identity. It makes me feel good. It makes me okay. Otherwise, if I don't, I'm just a bum again, and I was a bum for a long time.

I also write poetry, too.

BEATTIE: I wanted to ask you about that, because your diction, your syntax, and everything about *The Same River Twice* is so poetic, I was wondering if you had written or want to write poetry?

OFFUTT: I write it all the time. I constantly steal everything from my own material. I went through my poems and robbed my poems for the book, and of course, *Kentucky Straight*'s the same thing. I mean, descriptions, especially, can come from any place in my writing. Sometimes my journal or poetry or sometimes letters. Or from a story that just is a failure as a story, but there's some stuff in there I can salvage.

BEATTIE: Will you talk about your title, *The Same River Twice*?

OFFUTT: It's from a quote by Heraclitus. He was a Greek philosopher. He's called Heraclitus the Obscure. He was the second oldest Greek philosopher that we know about. None of his writings survived, which makes me kind of interested in that.

BEATTIE: I was going to say, is this your alter ego?

OFFUTT: Maybe. But we know about him through the references from other writers. Later philosophers would say, "Oh, Heraclitus." So we know there was this guy who wrote. His quote was "You can never step into the same river twice." I lived by the river when I wrote that book. I had a strong relationship with the river, and it just seemed perfect.

BEATTIE: Sort of like, "You can't go home again."

OFFUTT: You can't go home again, but who knows what his full intention was with that title? For me, it worked on a number of levels. Life is a river, and sort of looking back at it—I was stepping into it, actually. By writing about my life, I jumped right into the mud of it.

BEATTIE: How important do you think sense of place will be in your future writing?

OFFUTT: I think it will be crucial, because it's crucial to me. It's not important to my writing for its sake; its because it's important to me. I get very interested where I happen to be in the local history. Place is important to me. Where I write, the room that I write in, the space . . . places are all very important.

BEATTIE: Many contemporary novelists set stories or novels in a place, but it's only for the sake of giving a city a name because they're really writing about an internal landscape. You don't see yourself writing that way at all? Not that your stories don't have internal landscapes, but your surroundings, your settings, are almost characters.

OFFUTT: That's because my internal landscape is the woods.

BEATTIE: That's what I mean. It's almost a character.

OFFUTT: For me, it's the same. It's one and the same. I have one story that's told from the woods's point of view. I think the story is called "From the Woods." So yes, my internal landscape is the woods. I just write about the woods, and I'm willing to surrender myself over to the writing.

BEATTIE: Do you have any views on where creativity itself comes from?

OFFUTT: I always knew I was really creative, even when I was a kid. And I always was. I drew constantly. When I was a child, all I did was draw. I wrote stories, but I was much more interested in drawing. I made up games, and I invented everything. I invented board games. I invented card games. I invented a deck of cards and invented a game to be played with this deck of cards. It wasn't real sophisticated, but I was always doing that. I put on plays and shows with my brothers and sisters.

I got really interested in the nature of creativity when I was in college. I started taking some psychology classes. I considered myself as having deep insights naturally. There's nothing worse than a college freshman taking a psychology class. First of all, I thought I was crazy. Then, I thought everybody else was. I read a lot about creativity, and I read a lot of biographies of great writers and great artists, hoping for insight. Of course, all I got was insight into them, not into me. I don't know if there's a blanket answer for everybody. It's something, though, that's intangible.

I think children are very creative. Essentially I think that the education system beats creativity out of kids. In my day, it was a real beating. Now, it's more metaphoric. I think now, they're not allowed to beat the kids so much. But constantly, you're told not to think for yourself. Not to invent things. You're told to stay between the lines on a piece of paper, to color between the lines, to use brown for tree bark, to use green for the leaves. Don't use blue for the leaves. Children are constantly having their creative impulses blunted by formal education, and also by peer pressure.

My family did not do that. My family supported my creative impulses. Like I said, I was bored all the time. I either talked or caused trouble, just out of my own boredom, or I drew. I drew pictures a lot in class.

For me, there's a real active rebellion in being creative. You do what you want to do. Nobody tells you what to do. There are no rules, and there's no boss. Hah! That goes dead against the grain of American society. There are rules here and you have to have a boss. Somebody's got to tell you what to do. If you're making art, or you're engaged in the process of making art, you're completely on your own, you're not contributing to society. You're not working. You're not making money. You're not doing anything but essentially entertaining yourself in a little room.

BEATTIE: Of course you *are* contributing to society, ultimately.

OFFUTT: Maybe. Maybe not. You never know. I have validity as a contributor now. Four months ago, I didn't. Four years ago, I was a bum and a failure, even though I'd already begun this book [*The Same River Twice*]. I was entertaining myself in a room. For me, that is an act of rebellion against society. But also, creativity is ultimate freedom. Nothing I've ever done grants me as much freedom as writing, and I've tried a lot of different art forms. Writing fiction is the one that gives me the greatest form of freedom.

BEATTIE: And satisfaction?

OFFUTT: Well, it's never very satisfying. I'm never satisfied.

BEATTIE: Not even in the midst of the writing process itself?

OFFUTT: Sometimes a first draft can be satisfying, but what's satisfying is when the time goes by. See, for me, I'm not really talking about creativity. I'm talking about the process of writing. I'm very process oriented. Writing makes big chunks of time go by. Nothing else makes big chunks of time go by as rapidly except playing poker. I mean nothing else. Not sex. You can't have sex six hours a night every night. But you can write six hours a night every night. Or you can play poker six hours a night every night. I'm bored all the time and I want time to go by. Life is very slow to me. Very, very slow. John Berryman, the poet, said, "Life is boring, but we must not say so," and we don't. We don't say so. We do all these other things to hide and combat our boredom.

Now the nature of creativity, I think it has to do with being damaged, frankly. The writers that I've met, the majority of the writers that I've met, are people who are damaged.

Not so badly damaged that they can't function, and not so undamaged that they can get by. Most people are damaged, but writers . . . there's a little area there where they're damaged a little bit more than most people, but not as much as true sociopaths. You know, writers are this side of . . .

BEATTIE: Neurotic but not psychotic?

OFFUTT: Well, maybe. Neurotic but not completely blind to it. Able to function with support. I need support to write. I need a real stable world, a real stable place. A real consistent pattern. And I can make stuff happen. Writers . . . our creativity comes from that, and it may come from wanting to re-create. For me, it's moving time fast and making myself heard. Screaming into the wind of the culture. I screamed loud and I screamed long enough, and now, people are interested.

My father said something really interesting when I called him to tell him about the contract with Random House for the short stories. There was a pause, and I told him. He said, "Well, son, I'm sorry. I blame myself." I said, "What are you talking about, Dad?" He said, "I didn't realize that I had made your childhood bad enough to produce a writer."

I had an interesting dream last night.

BEATTIE: Which was?

OFFUTT: I went to visit my neighbor at home. My best buddy who's lived all of his life on this hill. He had moved to town and he was miserable. While we were there, a fox attacked his cat, then turned into a wolf. The fox did. I ran down to try to save the cat. The wolf grabbed my arm, my left arm, and started clawing at it and ripping at it with its teeth and its claws. I was bleeding freely from . . . from this arm. It was pulling me in that direction. Then it suddenly appeared on my right side, latched onto my right arm, and began pulling me in that direction, clawing. By this time, I was bleeding openly from both arms. So I kicked this wolf over a cliff that suddenly appeared, and it fell. As it fell, it latched onto my right hand and would not let go. Its claws were diggin' deeper and deeper into my hand. So there I was, on a cliff with my arm over the edge and a wolf hanging off it, bleeding from both arms after being pulled in two directions, waiting for my neighbor, who had moved to town and was unhappy, to shoot the wolf. Then I woke up. I woke up and I decided this morning that you're the last person I'm going to talk to. I'm not going to do interviews anymore.

April 24, 1993

BOOKS BY CHRIS OFFUTT

Kentucky Straight. New York: Vintage/Random House, 1992.

The Same River Twice. New York: Simon & Schuster, 1993.

LEE PENNINGTON

PENNINGTON: My full name is Royce Lee Pennington. I was born in 1939, May the first, in a little place called White Oak, Kentucky, one of probably twenty-five or thirty White Oaks in Kentucky. It's just back up there with my granddad's place. My mother and dad lived there on three different occasions, and they were there when I was born. The old home place is no longer there, and the well's been filled in to keep kids from falling in it. I was back up there this past week, and it's amazing how a place where one grows up, one thinks in terms of the rather large size of fields and whatnot, and the place itself where the house was is hardly as wide as this room [Pennington's Middletown, Kentucky, living room].

BEATTIE: What was your childhood like?

PENNINGTON: I had a very sick childhood. By the time I was four or five years old, I had pneumonia every winter. When I was three years old, I had double pneumonia and diphtheria at the same time; I was hospitalized for twenty-nine days.

I can remember being in the hospital very, very vividly. Mom went in the ambulance with me, but they didn't let her sit beside me. They stopped her at the waiting room, and she never was able to make contact with me again that whole twenty-nine days I was there. My family came to see me, and they couldn't come in the room where I was, but they could come to this little window and raise the window up a little bit and talk in to me.

I remember playing peek-a-boo with another little kid that was there. We were in cribs. They had sheets or something hanging around the crib, but there was this big hole in the end of them, and I can remember hollering "peek-a-boo" and looking around . . . twisting my head around, even though I was strapped down.

I remember, when I was getting ready to come home, singing at the top of my voice, "I'm going home, I'm going home." That was the first thing Mom said she heard when she walked into that area, she heard me singing at the top of my voice. I had to learn to walk again, because after being strapped down for twenty-nine days, I couldn't walk.

BEATTIE: How old were you at this time?

PENNINGTON: I was three years old. My parents bought a little tricycle, and I could sit on that tricycle and pump the tricycle around the house, and build up enough strength to learn to walk again.

But all the time growing up, until I was probably nine or ten years old, Mom just came up with an idea. She heard about this commercial tonic called Father John Medicine. Mom said it was the awfullest smelling stuff and the awfullest tasting stuff that there ever was, but she started giving me that, Father John. After that, I never had pneumonia again.

None of them expected me to survive, the doctors or any of them. Odd thing about that Father John Medicine, the main base of it was cod-liver oil. To this day, I crave that stuff.

My younger years, child years, I was probably extremely mischievous. I can remember doing all sorts of things, scaring girls with snakes; there was hardly anything that I wouldn't try. Mom told me later, she said she reached that point that if I weren't hurting myself or I weren't hurting somebody else, then she let me go.

BEATTIE: What about siblings?

PENNINGTON: When I was growing up, there were four or five of us around. There were eleven in the family, but all of them were not around when I was growing up. I had my sister "Boots," Laura, and I had my sister Mary Lou, who died when she was twelve years old. And I remember my brother Leonard, who was killed in World War II at Iwo Jima.

BEATTIE: What about your parents? Are they still living?

PENNINGTON: My mother's still living. My father died in 1963. My mother still lives, and she's ninety-one years old, extremely alert. My father was, by his own admission, an alcoholic. I always thought, looking back on the stories, that he wasn't an alcoholic, that he just drank a lot. The last seventeen years of his life, which was most of the time I knew him, he didn't drink any. He was a gambler.

But I didn't know him during that period. The time I knew him, he had joined the church and become a Baptist minister, like my grandfather, and like five generations of them. And my brother is a minister, so there are now six generations going along that line.

BEATTIE: So your father went from farming to being a Baptist minister?

PENNINGTON: Well, where I grew up, the Baptist ministers were nonpaid ministers, so he didn't quit farming; his livelihood was farming. But he did preach. Both my parents worked incredibly hard. Dad, I know, would be up at three or four o'clock in the morning, getting out and loading the truck, to take stuff off, and then he'd get home maybe seven or eight o'clock that night, and then he'd have to be loading the truck again. Mom did the majority of loading the truck, and the children there at home worked in the fields. We all worked the fields. You were always in the fresh air and you always ate well. I remember it as a vigorous kind of life, if physically hard.

BEATTIE: Will you tell me a little bit about your early schooling?

PENNINGTON: From the earliest time I can remember, I was always fascinated with books and reading.

BEATTIE: This is before going to school?

PENNINGTON: Before going to school. And even before I started to school, even before I could read, I'd be carrying books around. There's something about them that just fascinated me.

BEATTIE: So your house was one that had books in it.

PENNINGTON: No, not while I was growing up. It had the Bible in it and then a few old books that my sisters had pitched back. These books I remember carrying around were just throwaways that my sisters had used in school. They were hardbacks, and they had these interesting lines and words that I didn't know, but I was just fascinated by them.

Then I went to a little one-room school up at White Oak up on the other leg of the valley. I had to walk about a mile each way every day. I remember being so excited about being able to make out words in the first grade. I don't know anything in all of my life that excited me more than seeing these words and feeling the magic of being able to figure out what they were and the sounds of them.

We couldn't keep any teachers at that school. A teacher would come in and teach for two weeks and quit, and then we wouldn't have another teacher for four or five weeks.

BEATTIE: Why would they keep quitting?

PENNINGTON: Well, it would be so far away from where they were trying to get to, and they didn't like what they were doing, and the teachers they could attract there, even much later on when my sister taught up there, when I was in the sixth grade, I think she only got fifty-eight dollars a month for teaching.

BEATTIE: And this was in the 1940s.

PENNINGTON: Yes, this was in the forties. It was just a matter of somebody deciding, well, they thought they'd teach, and so they'd go out and they'd try it for a couple of weeks and say, "No, this is not a life for me," and they'd run off and leave it.

BEATTIE: They'd have to teach, what, six grades at once?

PENNINGTON: Eight grades. All eight grades, all subjects, during the day. But the fourth grade I had to do twice, because my mother sent word, even though I had straight A's, that I hadn't gone to school enough that year to be passing. So, they failed me in the fourth grade. Mom failed me. I remember in the third grade, Miss Billups really didn't teach any grades; she just sat and made hook rugs. But I think that probably what she did was one of the more innovative and spectacular things in education. She had the classes teaching each other. When I was in the third grade, I taught first grade the whole year. I had three students, and one of them I double-promoted from the first grade to the third grade, a real good student. I gave the students their grades and taught the whole thing. Taught all first grade. All subjects. Of course, in the first grade, you didn't have too many. You had your arithmetic, we called it, your spelling, and your reading, and that was about it.

The fourth grade was the first contact with any kind of history that I remember. It was a historical novel, in fact, and later on I got involved with my writing as a result of that historical novel. I remember the content of it. It was about a family that came to this country with the beginnings of the country, the first settlers, called the Farnham family. The book was about this family going from colonial times on up into the end of the 1800s. The first writing I ever remember doing was as a result of my being somewhat disturbed that generations of this family didn't continue on into the 1900s and the twentieth century. I remember creating two more generations of Farnhams. I can remember it was about eighty pages long, but I finished that book out. I don't know whatever happened to that manuscript. It was handwritten.

BEATTIE: That's the first writing you remember?

PENNINGTON: That's the first writing I ever remember doing, yes. I can remember learning to make letters, the old cursive-style writing, but I don't remember creating anything up to third grade.

The big turning point in my wanting to become educated occurred when I was in the seventh grade, although my sister, I think, put the seed in my mind. She wasn't much older than I was, three or four years, but she taught me in the sixth grade, and she said, "Some day you're going to go to college," and I laughed at her. That was the last thing on earth I wanted to be involved with. I wanted to be out in the woods, and so I'd perceive myself as going to be a sheep farmer.

I doubt if anybody had a college degree, who taught at that school. You got certificates to teach. I think there were three different levels, first class, second class, and third class. I think third class was the lowest you could get. You took a test to see if you could get that certificate, and if you could, then you get a third-class teacher's certificate.

But in the seventh grade, there's a teacher came out to that school, Bob Waddell, and my whole world changed that year. After the seventh grade I knew, whatever it took, I'd be going to college. I was curious at that time, really I could almost look back and use the word *profoundly* curious. And not only did Bob Waddell whet that curiosity, but he also directed me toward finding answers. We'd take walks on the lunch break, and I was curious about fossils, and I always thought Indians did these things to rocks. He was telling me how old these things were, millions of years old. This is the beginning of the seventh grade. When I got time off, on Sunday, from the farm, I'd go out into the woods and dig around in rocks and split rocks open and find things out about them. Then I'd take them to Bob Waddell, and he'd say, "Well, you know, you can go to the library over here in Portsmouth, and you can get a book out on those kinds of fossils and figure out what it is." I also became extremely interested in the stars and the planets and astronomy in general, and he would direct me.

I remember he told me once when he was younger he had made a radio, and I decided I was going to make a radio. He told me how he had done it—he just told me what he had used—and I made one. By the time I'd finished the eighth grade I'd already read Darwin's *Origin of Species*.

BEATTIE: Did that teacher inspire most of the students?

PENNINGTON: I don't think he inspired anybody else. I seemed to be the only one, and I expect that's the way it happens, that you have a one-to-one relationship. But from that time on, I knew I was going to go to college. I was the first one in our family to go away to college, and we can trace our family back to 1132 in England.

All through high school, and I went to McKell High School, my big interests were in writing. I was writing stories and poems by the time I was in high school, and in the later years in high school, the junior and senior years, I was very much involved with journalism and news writing—making money—what I thought was big-time money. Well, I made enough money in my junior and senior year in high school to pay for my high school expenses, for things like class rings, and I bought a suit—my first suit. God, it was an awful-looking thing. Looked like a gangster suit. It was a light gray, and I bought that for a prom. I paid twenty-one dollars for it with money I'd made from articles. I'd covered all the ball games my junior and senior year. Jesse Stuart got me that job.

BEATTIE: Jesse Stuart was one of your teachers?

PENNINGTON: He was principal of my high school. Jesse went to the *Portsmouth Times* and said to the people over there, "Why don't you let me get one of our students to write articles about the school?" They said, "Well, have you got one?" And Jess told them yes, he had one, and came back over and told me I was it.

I'd never written an article for a newspaper. But I used models. I cut some ball games out of the newspaper, reports of ball games. This was my junior year, and I went out to our ball games and the first few articles I did, all I did was change the names of the teams and the scores. I left the other words exactly as they were. I took my stories over and gave them to the sports editor and he said, "These are well written," and the fact is, he wrote them, except you know, I was just changing names of teams and scores, and everything else was staying the same. But I learned to do it on my own after that, and learned to be kind of innovative. When I got to my senior year, I even managed to get a column going, which I wrote on the Eastern Kentucky ball teams: football, and baseball, and basketball.

I was really interested in writing, and I was very interested in the physical sciences. I was doing chemistry experiments, on my own, at the high school in my junior year, by myself. Jesse gave me a key to the high school so I could come in on weekends and use their library and work with chemistry. I was doing some pretty spectacular stuff, according to my teachers.

Then I made my own telescope. Never will forget, got lens and this, that, and the other, and made it, and got out in the yard one night with it, and got it set up, and pointed it out to this sort of semibright star out there in the sky, and got down and got it in focus, and nearly cried, because the first thing I ever saw looking through a telescope was the rings of Saturn. It was just such an incredible experience.

After that, everything had to do with nature, up in the sky or on the ground, I was just curious about and interested in. In 1958, I was the first in Kentucky, Ohio, Tennessee, or any of those places—it got on the Associated Press—I was the first to spot the Arend-Roland Comet. And I once saw a meteor come all the way into the ground. There are probably not ten people in the United States, or the world, who've ever witnessed that.

When I started to college, I was still split, wanting to major in science and wanting to write. I started out majoring in astronomy. I went to Baldwin Wallace College for a semester, and that was way too expensive for me. With Jesse Stuart's help I transferred to Berea College in Kentucky, and wound up getting a B.A. degree there. When I switched from Baldwin Wallace, I'd picked up six hours in astronomy. But when I transferred to Berea, they didn't offer an astronomy major, and I transferred to geology. There was only one person in the whole geology department, a man with a master's degree, and here I was studying under one person, and that didn't make sense. It was my junior year before I declared a major in English. Still, today, I'm fascinated by the physical sciences. I have a telescope now, and I still get out and I look at Venus and Saturn and Jupiter and still look at craters in the moon.

BEATTIE: I'd like to go back for a minute to your relationship with Jesse Stuart. It sounds like a particularly close one. How did that develop and what was it like?

PENNINGTON: It was indeed a very close relationship, and Jesse had a way of making everybody he came in contact with feel a close relationship with him. My first contact with Jesse was when I was a junior in high school. I knew about Jesse and knew of his writing. Jesse had that major coronary in '54, and I heard that Jesse was going to come and be principal, and I thought, "There's no way in the world a man can have the massive heart attack that Jesse had in '54, and come back two years later and be principal of rough-house McKell High School." But I heard that Jesse was going to do it. I wanted to pick up Latin with the other courses that I was taking, and I had to see the principal to get permission. Jesse came into the assembly and talked to the students and then, after the assembly was over, he was out in the hall. I walked up to him and I said, "Mr. Stuart, I want to take an extra course, and I want to take Latin, and I need to get your permission." He said, "What's your name?" I said, "Lee Pennington." He said, "You've got straight A's." He said, "You can take anything you want." That was before the school even opened. That was the first day. I mean, we didn't have any classes or anything, and Jesse had already come in and looked at the record. I think he may have had ulterior motives; Jesse couldn't get enough teachers to teach the classes, and I think he went in and looked at the students who had good grades and pulled them out. I know there were half a dozen of us.

I had a semester my junior year that I didn't go to a single one of my classes. I taught eighth grade and came in the evenings and took tests for my classes. But Jesse needed teachers, and he got about a half a dozen of the students and put them in the classroom, and filled up positions. At that time I was quite fascinated with Jesse's *Man With a Bull-Tongue Plow*, early on a very influential book on me. Not so much the book as the poems in it.

BEATTIE: When had you read those?

PENNINGTON: Well, I'd read those probably as a sophomore, but when I was a junior and senior, by then it had came out in paperback, and I could get hold of that, and I carried it around. The poems in there just fascinated me. They had a simplicity about them, yet they had some depth and human meaning to them. They were about things I knew and was aware of.

From that time on, Jesse and I were always close. First of all, as teacher and student—that kind of relationship—pretty much remained, even though Jesse and I became colleagues. But a very close relation. We—Joy [Pennington's wife] and Dean [Stuart's wife] and Jesse—traveled together, and we taught a lot together, and we carried on an enormous correspondence, Jesse and I did.

Jesse and I taught together in a writing workshop at Murray State University for ten summers. This would have been from about '68, '69 through ten years, and that was three weeks every summer. Jesse taught the short story and I taught poetry. Different teachers, Harriette Arnow taught the novel, L. J. Horton taught the articles-writing and journalism every year, and Wilma Dykeman was there for one year teaching the novel. Alvin Tresselt taught children's stories writing. He's the dean of the children's institute you see in the writer's magazines all the time. He's got about sixty books he's written, sixty children's books.

But I think the main thing, when the Stuarts came here, meaning Louisville, or wherever we were, the Stuarts always stayed with us, and I'd take Jesse out to autographings. And we often went to W-Hollow [Stuart's home]; for Joy and me that was always our getaway place when reality was setting in too much. When civilization was overwhelming us, we'd go to W-Hollow, and there was always the peacefulness, and the relaxing, and the good time, and the talks there.

But the correspondence Jesse and I had was fairly substantial. At one period Jesse wrote more than I did on the corresponding. He was, I think, one of the great corresponders in the writing field. There have been weeks I've got as many as seven or eight letters, and I have in my collection somewhere in the neighborhood of four thousand letters that Jesse wrote and, in addition, I probably have about a fourth that many carbon copies of what I wrote. So, in one sense, there exists both sides of the correspondence, which is fairly unusual, I think, in letters.

BEATTIE: Tell me a little bit about your book, *The Dark Hills of Jesse Stuart*.

PENNINGTON: I knew right off it was a book, but I did it as my thesis at the University of Iowa for the master's degree. But I wrote it as a book. What I wanted to do was to go back to some of Jesse's very early writings, and I used *Harvest of Youth*, his first book, which he privately printed back in 1930. I wanted to go into that book and find out themes and vision and whatnot that had attracted Jesse at the outset, and to see if those themes and that vision had any sort of path or track that he had followed throughout his fiction. What I was able to find was that, at least I thought, and some others thought, too, later, that very early on Jesse had particular themes that he'd like to work with, and he had a particular vision that he maintained throughout his writing career, and it, in particular, exhibited itself in his fiction. It first showed itself in his poetry.

BEATTIE: What were some of those themes?

PENNINGTON: I don't know if it was true, or if it was part of Jesse's public mask, but Jesse always had the appearance of being in total innocence. [Poet] Bill Cohen said about Jesse one time, he's the only man he ever saw that wasn't kicked out of the Garden of Eden. But Jesse always had that innocence about him.

Jesse's image and his public appearance seemed to me not to match what he was saying in his fiction; there were two different visions. Let me take one theme. Jesse, in his fiction, indicates that the best comes from mixing, whether it be races or cultural levels or what else. Jesse will invariably have contrast between one culture and another, and the combining of those cultures then produces something greater.

Jesse constantly looked upon Appalachia as a dying culture. Not many, I think, perceived that, but it wasn't so much that the culture was dying, but Jesse recognized that, and said that it was over and over and over, dying. But what Jesse was interested in, I think, was that from this death will be a rebirth, and that rebirth is what is important. So it doesn't matter where you look in his fiction, you're going to see the darkness and the death, but you need to look just beyond that to where the vision is pointing.

I think Jesse Stuart and Ernest Hemingway had the same vision, but for one exception. Ernest Hemingway, for him it was always important as to how you fought the battle, but you would always lose, and there was no such thing as a winner. I think Jesse was just the opposite of that on the conclusion; how you fought the battle was important, but also, Jesse wound up optimistic, always a winner. Sometimes it seemed sentimentally outrageous that the person would win, but Jesse ended up with a winner. So, from the darkness and death came the rebirth. And you can see that in his poetry. You can see it in his fiction, in just one work after another. It's always that child or that whatever is next; it's that next generation.

Many people thought Jesse was poking fun at Appalachia. He was never doing that; although Jesse was a great humorist in the vein of Mark Twain, but he was never poking fun at people. He just saw the humor and exaggerated it sometimes a little bit, but some things were just very funny.

Jesse, in his fiction, presented equality that would put most of us to shame—equality across cultural lines and equality across racial lines. Though Jesse didn't, especially on the racial aspect of it, exhibit that in his personal conversations or his life. But his fiction certainly did.

BEATTIE: You've alluded to Stuart's personal vision being different from his poetic vision.

PENNINGTON: Well, I think all of us have masks, and sometimes we put on a public mask or even a personal mask that is different, somewhat, from what we believe deep down.

BEATTIE: How do you think Jesse Stuart's personal mask and his persona differed?

326 / Conversations with Kentucky Writers

PENNINGTON: Personally, with Jesse, there was that business of the racial problem, which maybe was so deeply embedded in the South, and the North and East and West, that for some people I don't think they were ever able to get over, personally, the concept of the mixing of the races, or even the integration of the races. He would be happy if there were two runners out there and one was black and one was white, if the white one won. But his books didn't exhibit that at all.

BEATTIE: Do you think he was aware of that dichotomy?

PENNINGTON: I doubt it.

BEATTIE: How did he react to your book?

PENNINGTON: He was very fond of the book. As a matter of fact, he saved my back a couple of times. When I was working with the thesis committee at the University of Iowa, very often they'd say, "Well, this point's outrageous." In the meantime, I would have written Jesse and said something like, "Well, you know, I know nobody's come up with this idea before, but I'm just wanting your reaction on it," and Jesse, on several occasions, wrote back and said, "You're the first to hit on this and it's exactly right; it's exactly what I was trying to do," and so often, when the thesis committee would say something like that was outrageous, I would just simply take Jesse's letter and say, "Well, I want you to read this." I remember a couple of times the head of the committee said, "Well, if the author says it's right, there's no reason we should say it's wrong." So they'd let it pass, let it go on through. As I say, I began that as a book, and it was done as a thesis, and then shortly after that I added one chapter, because there was a book that came out after my thesis came out, and I added a chapter to it.

BEATTIE: What year was this?

PENNINGTON: 1967. I did my thesis in '65; the book came out in '67.

BEATTIE: How did Stuart's vision influence your writing vision, or did it?

PENNINGTON: Well, I don't think it did. I think what influenced me early on was the subject matter and style and form of *Man With A Bull-Tongue Plow.* I think maybe style more than anything. But Jesse and I wound up, I think, being curious and excited, sometimes about different kinds of things, different areas.

If I had to take my whole life, as to who the most influential writer would have been, it would have been the Spanish poet, Lorca. Federico García Lorca, I think has had, and I think still has, the most influence on my perception of the universe.

A friend of mine when I was in graduate school said, "Have you read Lorca?" And I said, "No." He said, "Read Lorca; he'll change your life." So, I got Lorca's poems in translation. Some of the translations I don't think are very good. But the kinds of things that Lorca did, of immersing . . . And I think that's where it's connected, that wherever we go and whatever we do, we become immersed, and part of the whole universe. We're just merely cells of a gigantic body, and, if you want to do it spiritually or physically, it's the same manner.

I think the thing that fascinated me about Lorca was his simplicity, which has such a depth to it, and his image-making, his image- and metaphor-making. The line, about the ocean in that great poem "Casida, the Reclining Woman," the translation, I think, of that poem is really well done. But there's a line, "the ocean cannot see the light of its own face," because of the immenseness of the ocean, it's impossible for the ocean to see it's own light. That same poem has a line that I love, "You cannot know where the heart of the toad or the violet hide." I think Lorca's probably the only one around who would have ever even thought to put the violet and the toad in the same natural concept.

So, I still read Lorca a lot, and even poems that I almost know by heart, I go back and read them again. I would say that would be a major influence. I think, fiction-wise, probably Albert Camus, and in particular, his novel *The Stranger*. Something about the removal of the writer. Something about, I think, the indifference of the writer. I guess I see myself as some of the fiction . . . I have nothing as a writer to invest or say message-wise, that I am just depicting here . . .

BEATTIE: You're a vehicle.

PENNINGTON: Yes. Something is of interest here, something has attracted me to it, and maybe that's my message, what I'm attracted to is my message, but once the attraction is made, I don't want to maneuver the characters into convincing you of this or convincing you of that. It's just simply here they are, and I think that opening of that novel, *The Stranger,* says "Mother died today, or maybe it was yesterday. The telegram doesn't say. It just says, 'Your mother died today.'" That kind of indifference, almost, seems to me nothing that Camus is trying to sell; there's no "I want you to feel this way" or "I want you to feel that way."

BEATTIE: But in choosing what to write about, you're presenting the reality that you want to show.

PENNINGTON: No question about that. I'm doing some work now with video, which is just as exciting to me as writing a short story or a novel. I'm doing a piece on my mother. My mother was famous locally, over the years, for a song she sang, a special song she did in church, called "The Gospel Ship." I recorded Mom on video, and it occurred to me, some of the lines of the song, "The gospel ship has long been sailing, bound for Canaan's blissful shore. Thousands there have gathered, there is room for thousands more." The metaphor of that song seemed to me to represent my mother in a lot of ways. She is the gospel ship.

So, I went back, and I had a tape recording of her singing that song, and I'm blending that together with some of the video itself. But it's my attraction to some of the things that she says I'm interested in, and I merely want to present them. Who knows? Nobody else may be interested in them.

BEATTIE: But you make those connections in your writing so that readers can make, perhaps those same, or perhaps other, connections.

PENNINGTON: I'm a presenter, not a judge.

BEATTIE: While we're talking about your writing, could you comment on your book of poetry that was nominated for a Pulitzer Prize?

PENNINGTON: That was *I Knew a Woman* and again, that's as close to a visionary point as I could perceive myself. I think the creative process is feminine. I really think that the reason probably, historically, that there are more male artists than female artists, is a result of that. First of all, the epitome of creation, for me, is life. Life pretty much, in all areas and categories and ways, is a sacred sort of thing, from a snake to a fly to a person. One time I was even probably fairly close to the Buddhists, though I didn't wear a screen to keep from breathing in living things and killing them. But I look upon life as incredibly sacred, and I don't make a distinction between plants and animals. I'm not a vegetarian. I eat meat, but I also eat plants. I don't make a distinction on one and say, "I don't do this because I'm killing something." I think only the female can create life. She, in some levels of species, has some help, but once the contact is made, she's on her own, and she creates. I think, in a lot of ways, males are, I don't want to use the word "jealous," but they can't do that, so what they do is create what they can. I think the urge is there, whatever your sex. I think living things are creating things, and to the extent the male must be secondary, mimic. Mnemisis, the Greeks said, life itself. I think that's what art is, is a mimicking of life, of the creation. Did you ever note how much satisfaction a woman has in having a child?

BEATTIE: *Some* women.

PENNINGTON: Just think about it. I mean, here is not something new. But think of the reaction to a new baby. You'd think, as many times as it's been done, folks would quit getting excited about it and they would say, "Aw shucks, my sister did that last year," you know. It's absolutely like the first time it's ever happened on the planet. That's the epitome of creation. I think that spirit, that urge, that whole thing, is permeating throughout the universe.

I suspect God is a woman. I suspect God is feminine. God is the creator, God is the creation, the creative process. *I Knew a Woman,* the vision of that was, I wanted to focus in on that creative process. I used woman as my symbol to indicate that process, and it goes through various levels in the book. There are some very sensual kinds of creativity, there are some very spiritual kinds of creativity. There are real characters who are symbolic characters; there are deified feminine characters who represent things. All my life, I think, I wanted to make that statement, and I finally decided at one time I would do it, and the book itself covers quite a long period of writing time. The distance between some of the poems in the book run twenty-some years. Some poems were done twenty-some years ago, and then some very recent kind of poems were written at the time the book came out.

BEATTIE: Was it a project that you kept working on over the years, or did it become a book after several poems were incorporated?

PENNINGTON: When I started working on the book, I worked a couple of years actually putting the book together, but I made use of poems that had been written over twenty-some years. This is a concept I think I had had for a long time, even before I could perceive of the concept.

BEATTIE: What year was that book published?

PENNINGTON: '77.

BEATTIE: Is your view, then, that of an androgynous life, or that most people are composed of male and female elements?

PENNINGTON: Yes, I think that has always been a part of my vision. I consider myself very much a male, but I'm very comfortable with my feminine aspects, too. And I think that would be true of a female. I think the female ought to be very comfortable of her male aspects. We're getting into some of that, I think, with the various movements that have been taking place over the years. Right now I have no trouble of being sentimental and weeping in places where they say a male shouldn't be doing that. I have no uncomfortable feelings about emotional things that they say, "That's feminine, you shouldn't do that, you shouldn't exhibit your emotions." Likewise, I think if a woman wants to use a sledge hammer, she should. You know, she should be comfortable in that aspect. Yes, I think there's probably a third concept that we're the combination of male and female. I think the process, as we know it now, is feminine. I think the announcing of it is masculine.

BEATTIE: So, like Jesse Stuart's vision, the third thing that comes out of it is superior to either independently?

PENNINGTON: I think the combination is always better than the separate. I think anyone a hundred percent feminine or a hundred percent masculine is probably out of control. If I could say one thing that I think is the way I feel, I think the whole universe is only understandable in relation to opposites, and it's the combination of those opposites that we ultimately can understand. I don't think you can understand good without understanding evil. I think our very own bodies, if a laser cut us in two, we're opposites. We're this side against this side; even though they have similarities, they are opposite of each other. Everything I know, everything I know about the universe, is opposites. I think that's very clearly a thing one needs to look for in my writing. There will be that opposite. I can't think of anything I've ever done in my life that doesn't say, "Here's this side; here's this side." I guess that's what I was saying earlier of not being the judge. I don't want to write only one side. I want both sides.

BEATTIE: Was it journalism that taught you the discipline of writing, do you think?

PENNINGTON: Journalism, to me, was always as creative as any other kind of writing. It's different, but it's not different. Some really great creative kind of pieces have appeared in journalism. Some of the most lasting, I think. After all, you know, that "Yes, Virginia, there is a Santa Claus," was a piece of journalism. But unless you're into features, if you're just doing news kind of articles, it's almost that you only have a few minutes to capture this, and it's only going to last a few minutes, and it's only going to survive a few minutes, you know. People are going to be wrapping fish in it in just a little bit. But there have been a number of things that I did that have lasted with me. I was editor of the college paper and I wrote an editorial, couldn't have been more than three or four paragraphs long, that had as much effect as any writing I've ever done.

BEATTIE: What was it about, do you recall?

PENNINGTON: Yes, very vividly. Berea College has a motto, "God hath made of one blood all nations of men." I think pretty much they practice that. Oh, I ran into some racial things here and there, but the whole policy was pretty much the heart of the college. And we had a soccer team, and we had some people on the soccer team from Africa, and they were down to Carson Newman College to play a soccer game. This would have been 1960. Carson Newman, a Baptist college, Southern Baptist, would not let the two guys from Africa on the soccer field, and Berea College pulled the soccer team and forfeited the game.

I wrote an editorial on it, that here was a college training missionaries to go to Africa, to teach the Africans about Christianity, and here are two Africans come to this college, and they won't let them on the field. I wound up saying I agreed with Berea College that God had made of one blood all nations of men.

Copies of that were sent to Carson Newman, and the student body got up in arms, not opposing the editorial, but got up in arms with their own policies. As a matter of fact, with the administration's policy. By that time it wasn't the students' policy. The young people of 1960 would have—the majority of them—in fact, I'm sure it was the young people, those vigorous people on the civil rights marches and whatnot, that broke down the barriers. But ninety-eight percent of the student body voted to totally integrate Carson Newman instantly, and the faculty also voted.

That editorial was carried on the convention floor of the Southern Baptist Association meeting, and at that time it was proposed it was defeated, but that was the first time it was proposed that all Baptist public facilities—schools, hospitals—be fully integrated. So that little two-or-three paragraphs piece of journalism had a major effect at the time. It stirred up a lot of stuff. Who knows? It may have been like a little breeze of wind that starts on one end of the country, and it's a major storm when it's on the other end. I don't know. How do you figure out those connections?

So journalism has been important. I think I got it in my blood back in high school, and I think once you get it in your blood, I don't care what you do, it'll come out on you sometime. You know, you'll just break down in the middle of the road and write something; you can't stand it. And that happened, and still happens to me. There's not a month goes by that I don't do an article strictly for a newspaper that has no extension beyond the few seconds of its importance then, and then it'll disappear. I don't know. Maybe these things get back in a file, but they don't have the immortality about them as a poem or as a story. But I think they're equally valuable.

BEATTIE: So you graduated from Berea in what year with what major?

PENNINGTON? Graduated from Berea in 1962 and majored in English, had a B.A. in English.

BEATTIE: So you never got the science major, but you minored in science?

PENNINGTON: Yes. I've got all sorts of hours in science. I've got, I think, about twenty, twenty-one hours in astronomy; I've got several hours in geology; a few hours in chemistry and physics; and, a scattering here and there of the physical sciences.

BEATTIE: Is Berea where you met your wife?

PENNINGTON: Yes. Joy and I met early on. We knew each other, but we didn't date until . . . I hitchhiked to California one summer while I was in school, and Joy went to the East Coast to baby-sit. Berea had a program where they could get some of the students—girl students, I think primarily—into baby-sitting jobs, in-house baby-sitting jobs in some of the more ritzy areas of the country. They'd go up for the summer and they'd get Berea's tuition, plus room and board, for the following year. Anyway, this one summer I wanted to hitchhike to the West Coast and just see what the country was like. I got back to Berea a week early. I was editor of the newspaper, and I wanted to get back a week early and get the paper out right when the college opened up that first week. Joy was a director of one of the dormitories, student director, and she had to be back a week early. We were the only two on campus. We kind of wanted to date, and we didn't have much choice, if we followed through on it, which we did, and that was in the fall. That was in the fall of '61, and we were married in January of '62.

BEATTIE: What was her maiden name and where was she from?

PENNINGTON: Joy's maiden name was Stout, an English name. Joy's from east Tennessee, up in the mountains, right on the border of North Carolina, not far from Boone, North Carolina.

BEATTIE: Iowa is where you got your master's in English?

PENNINGTON: I started out at the University of Iowa. I went there for the Writers' Workshop, and it didn't quite turn out to be what I thought it was, or what I thought it should be. Six weeks along into the program, I dropped out of the Writers' Workshop and went into the regular English program. I had to get down on my knees and beg to a few professors to let me in that late into the semester, but they did. Joy and I got our master's there. By the way, we both did our theses on Jesse Stuart. I worked with the fiction, and Joy worked with the poetry, and she got her degree a little bit later. We went to Southeast Community College in Harlan County [Kentucky] and taught there a couple of years.

BEATTIE: And all this time you were continuing to write?

PENNINGTON: Oh, yes, I published a great deal while I was in graduate school, almost totally poetry. I had a magazine article or two, but I published two hundred pieces of poetry when I was in graduate school.

BEATTIE: Probably more than any of your professors.

PENNINGTON: Yes, that was the case, and the reason I did it that way. When I got out at the University of Iowa, I was told along with the rest of the students not to send anything out for publication. I thought that was the most absurd thing I ever heard. If you're going to write, you ought to be sending stuff out.

BEATTIE: What sorts of places did you publish your poetry?

PENNINGTON: It was pretty much every place going then, but mainly smaller magazines, the so-called little magazines, but they were good magazines. Different ones around the country. I think I got in about fifty of the magazines during that particular time.

BEATTIE: Was this your first published creative writing?

PENNINGTON: No. I had been published before I got out of undergraduate school. I had a short story published in *Mountain Life and Work,* and I had a couple of poems—this is while I was an undergraduate—in some anthologies that came out. There used to be a publisher over in Virginia that published anthologies, and I had a couple of poems in that. *Mountain Life and Work* was the first magazine that I made with a piece of fiction.

One of the articles I published while I was in New York, that was also published in *Mountain Life and Work* was about book collecting. But more than that, it was about the importance of books, and it was called, "Some Day I'm Going to Buy a Book." That article had as much effect as anything else that ever happened, I think. I had a contest with my high school students at Newburg; the one who put together the best personal library with the least amount of money, I was going to give him fifty dollars.

BEATTIE: How did you judge that?

PENNINGTON: Well, it was a rather subjective kind of thing, of saying, "Okay, I've got a hundred books, and I spent four dollars for them," or whatever, "And here are the classics, and here are the whatever." I made the final judgment, or made the total judgment. But anyway, what they had to do, they had to get their collection together, and keep a record of how much they spent on it, and then they had to bring the collection to me and actually show it to me, bring their books in in boxes. This one boy came in, and he said to me in the middle of this, a little black boy came in, and he handed me two or three books, and he said, "These ain't mine." He said, "These are my dad's." He said, "But someday, I'm going to buy a book." And I said to him, "Do you have a penny?" He said, "Yes, I've got a penny." I said, "Well, give it to me," and I handed him a copy of *Huckleberry Finn,* Mark Twain's *Huckleberry Finn,* and told him, the time is now, he's now just bought a book.

Well, that article was on the importance of book collecting, and that thing must have been reprinted twenty-five times. I mean, I think it got every place except *Reader's Digest.* It just ran and ran and ran, and every once in a while somebody would send me a clipping, and I didn't even know it would be reprinted. I know it got in some of the New England newspapers and magazines.

When I lived in New York, I published probably fifteen or twenty pieces. Then in Iowa, I published close to a couple hundred pieces in graduate school. The biggest year I ever had, I set out to see if I could get a piece a day—one piece of writing a day—accepted. I built up to it, and I didn't make it, but I had accepted more than I ever had accepted in my life any other year. Like to killed me. I mean, I was keeping four or five hundred pieces in the mail all the time, and I had three hundred and twenty-one pieces accepted.

BEATTIE: In one year?

PENNINGTON: In one year.

BEATTIE: Probably a world's record.

PENNINGTON: Well, I don't know. I know I missed my three hundred and sixty-five, but I know, also, I'd never had that many accepted at one time.

BEATTIE: Your *Writer's Digest* article, when did you write that?

PENNINGTON: That I wrote after . . . I used that illustration, the information of that, in a lot of talks around to writers, and I was up in Indiana, and the *Writer's Digest* editor was up there. I gave that talk at a dinner with a bunch of writers, and she heard it. She said she'd love to see that as an article, so I wrote it and sent it to her. I wrote it on the back of a rejection slip. I had several of them around, so I could have me another thing to talk about, rejection slips. Some of them had come on eight-and-a-half-by-eleven sheets and the backs were clean, so I put the copy on that. I guess *Writer's Digest* kept that. I guess they've still got that. The editor told me later that that article got more letters than any article they had had in *Writer's Digest*. I guess there were a lot of people out there that had been rejected.

If you write, you're going to get rejected; that's just part of it. The real sad thing, I think, is an awful lot of people take rejections personally, and I think an awful lot of people are stopped mid-road by rejections. They send a manuscript out two or three places, and it's rejected, and they say, "Well, I'm worthless, I can't write, so I give it up." But rejections, that's just part of it. It's a little like saying, "Okay, we're going to have a big rain, but we're not going to have any water in the yard." You know, if it rains, you'll have water in the yard, and if you write, you'll have rejections, if you send pieces out. Rejections don't really mean anything other than you've not picked out the right place at the right time to send it. After all, it doesn't have a whole lot to do with the quality of your writing, whether it's rejected or accepted. Just simply read all that's being published, and you're going to see some great writing, and you're going to see some of the worst writing in the world. And it's still being published. So, publishing is just merely, again, the connection. If you connect what you've got with what somebody wants, they're going to take it. It may be the worst piece in the world, or the best piece in the world, it doesn't really have any connection.

BEATTIE: When you went back to Kentucky from Iowa, what did you teach at Southeast Community College?

PENNINGTON: I taught the first creative writing course, I think, ever taught in Harlan County. The very system [Kentucky Community College System] just hadn't had any creative writing courses taught. And I taught the first writing of poetry class ever taught in Kentucky.

BEATTIE: How long were you at Southeast?

PENNINGTON: I was at Southeast two years, and it was an incredibly exciting time. Harlan County excited me very much. It's kind of odd, when I graduated from Berea College, I had a job offer at a high school in Harlan County, and I thought that was the last place I wanted to be. Harlan County had the reputation, I knew about it, "Bloody Harlan Kentucky," and I didn't want to go there. Oddly enough, three years later, that was the place I wanted to go most. I'm not sure why the change of attitude, although I think part of it had to do with the major amount of publicity going around on Appalachia, that you had the worst students in the world, you had the worst schools in the world, and I may have even been a part of that information being passed around, till I suddenly paused to say that I was from Appalachia, and I went to Appalachian schools, and I was an Appalachian student. And suddenly, I wanted to go back to Appalachia and see what would happen if Appalachian students were given the opportunity and the freedom to create, to sense an appreciation of things around them.

And what happened was pretty astounding to me. With the four little books that my students produced, and the poems that they had published, and the short stories and articles that they published in magazines all over, they published over a thousand pieces of writing in the two years that I was in Harlan County.

BEATTIE: How many students did?

PENNINGTON: I had thirteen students in each class, and I don't know why that number happened, I didn't have a limit on it, up or down. They just simply wound up there; there were thirteen students in each of the classes. In fact, one of the books they published was called *Thirteen,* and that was in the spring of '66. They published a little book called *Thirteen,* which had thirteen poems by each of the thirteen students in the class.

BEATTIE: And they published it themselves?

PENNINGTON: They published it themselves; I was pretty much behind it. As a matter of fact, I personally did the financing of it. The first book was called *Spirit Hollow,* a book primarily of fiction, and the second one was called *Thirteen.* The third one was called *The Long Way Home,* and it was a book of fiction. The last one, of course, was called *Tomorrow's People,* and this book attempted to say, I thought, "What about tomorrow's people?" You know, "Here is the hope." It was dedicated to Harlan County, and that was a book I didn't have to finance. We had five hundred copies, and except for a few that were sent out . . . in fact, I sent them to Jesse Stuart, about twenty copies . . . A lot of things happened politically, a lot of explosions took place, and I sent these twenty books out because, frankly, I thought the book was going to be confiscated, and I wanted some copies on the outside of Harlan County when it happened. But otherwise, the five hundred copies sold out in five days.

BEATTIE: What made it so popular?

PENNINGTON: Well, I think the fact that some of the power structure got pretty upset about it, and were rather verbal in their being upset, and a little bit more than verbal. I think, in that book, the students took a good look at their environment, at themselves, at Harlan County, and in a lot of ways, in some instances at least, depicted it fairly honestly.

BEATTIE: As was going on elsewhere in the sixties, at that time.

PENNINGTON: Right. No different from any place else, I suppose. May have been the first time that it had happened creatively right there. I don't know. The sheriff, he got upset, some of the power-structure people got very upset because they didn't quite know how to react to the distance fiction should give to literal life. They were more inclined to think in terms of these poems being newspaper accounts of what they were doing right at that instant, and they didn't want anybody to know that they were doing it. Then, the president of UK [the University of Kentucky], John Oswald at that time, called me and said he wanted me out of Harlan County. He said, "I want you to get out of there." For my safety. I said, "No, I'm not going to leave." I never will forget, he said, "I am your boss." He said, "I am the president of the University of Kentucky. I am your boss. I am giving you, as your boss, a direct order, and that order is, get the hell out of Harlan County." I said, "You named it," and we got in the car. It was on a Friday, and we had an armed-guard car in front of us, and an armed-guard car in back, and I was carrying the magnum on my lap. We drove out about midnight.

I think we had enormous support from Ellis Hartford, dean of the community college system. In fact, the reason we wound up in Louisville, I'm sure, is because Ellis Hartford, he told me, "You can go any place in the community college system you want to." And I said to him, "Where do you want me to go?" He said, "We got a new college opening up in Louisville, and I'd like you to go there." That's why we wound up here in Louisville.

A couple of things that were difficult for me: One, you know if you live your life thinking you're one thing, and you discover instantly you're not, you know it's hard to handle. You think your whole life is in that direction and suddenly it's not the case. You're not what you believe you are. That happened to me, because I thought I was a pacifist, and I found out I really wasn't. Pacifists don't carry guns, especially don't carry magnums, especially don't carry magnums with steel bullets that'll shoot through V-8 engines, but I was. And for a couple of years, I really had trouble with that, really internal, psychological trouble being able to handle that. My statement, I think, on Harlan County, writing-wise, is my book of poetry, *Songs of Bloody Harlan*. That came a couple of years after the experience.

BEATTIE: It sounds like the brunt of the furor fell on you, instead of on the students.

PENNINGTON: Yes, the furor was focused, and it was toward me, and it was misguided and, you know, the citizens of Harlan County, they were behind me, they were behind the students, even though, from a distance you look at it and you say, "What a terrible place," because Harlan County has done this kind of thing to a teacher or whatever. It was narrowed down to three or four people who happened to be in power-structure positions and didn't, somehow, want the exposure they thought they were getting, which they certainly weren't getting that much. They got exposures after the *Courier-Journal* came out. The *Courier* article went Associated Press, and it appeared in four thousand newspapers in the United States and, you know, such an odd thing as somebody getting run out of town over poetry, that hasn't happened a whole lot in the United States. It was just amazing. It was like some kind of Fellini dream or something. It was taking place, and we were right in the middle of it, but you'd look at it and you'd say, "No, this is not happening. This is not taking place. This can't take place." Even after it was over and took place, you still look back and say, "No, that really didn't take place. That's impossible." The people right in the middle of it would have said the same thing.

BEATTIE: Have you been back to Harlan County since?

PENNINGTON: No, and I probably won't, though I've long since, I think, passed the stage of worrying about something physically happening to me if I did.

BEATTIE: What year, then, did you move to Louisville?

PENNINGTON: We got into Louisville in '67, and were here in the fall of '67; that was a semester before Jefferson Community College opened. It was my best semester teaching. I just put out notices that I was going to teach a creative writing class over in Ahren's Trade School, and had people to sign up, and I think a hundred and fifty people signed up for that class. But the class held, I believe it was fifty-one students, that we were able to get in the room. And Joy, at that same time, taught a speech class over there, so we both taught. That's probably unusual, too, that we taught a semester at the college before it was a college.

BEATTIE: Will you tell me about being at JCC, the courses you teach?

PENNINGTON: Well, I've taught a number of different kinds of courses over the years at JCC. I've taught the world humanities courses, world literature courses, taught composition courses, creative writing courses. At one time, I was teaching, primarily, creative writing. Now, I'm teaching totally writing courses, more composition . . . freshman comp, than anything. Found in my older years that that's the area that seems to be more fun now.

BEATTIE: You also taught storytelling there, didn't you?

PENNINGTON: Joy and I taught storytelling for a couple of years there. We had four different classes in storytelling, back at the time Jefferson Community College was sponsoring the Corn Island Storytelling Festival. The classes were really successful in whole bunches of ways. They taught the oral tradition, they made the jump . . . the relationship between the oral tradition and the written word, the literary. Students who were in those first four classes, there are probably half a dozen or a dozen of them who have continued on as professional storytellers.

If you can think in terms of storytelling being visible, it was a very visible class. Those storytellers did much in the community, going into places and telling stories, elderly places, places where the handicapped were. They were just simply good classes. When Jefferson Community College dropped the sponsorship of the Corn Island Festival, the administration told us that we could teach the storytelling, but we would have to do it above our regular class load.

BEATTIE: Will you talk a little bit about how you became interested in storytelling, how you became a storyteller, and what the Corn Island Festival is?

PENNINGTON: Well, storytelling had been totally a part of my own existence, and probably everybody's existence, whether we recognize it or not. In growing up, I heard stories, but I didn't know they were stories. There was recognition of them as stories, or as storytelling much later on, but storytelling from a cultural, from a ritualistic, from a tribal, and tribal being much broader than just the name of some tribe, like community or like family point of view. Stories always gave us examples of how to live, of how to be whoever we were. We learn by example. I grew up around storytelling. Looking back, I can recognize when my mother and father were telling me some stories from the old McGuffey readers, and some stories that they had heard, and stories that said significant things that we could be or become, things happening in my own life, and stories connected in my own life, and my own experiences, and I think even later creating my own experiences.

BEATTIE: You started telling stories when you were very young, didn't you?

PENNINGTON: The first time I remember creating a story was one to get me out of trouble. Way back at the beginning of this interview, you remember I said the old home place had an old well that had been shoved in to keep kids from falling in it. Well, when I was growing up, that well was still there. My brother built a house there, even after the old home place disappeared, and my brother used that well. But he also used the well to keep things cool in; that was the country way of doing it. You'd take your well bucket and put your milk or your Cokes or whatever you'd have that you wanted to keep cool, sometimes butter was kept that way. My brother had some Cokes in the bucket in the well, and I got them out and drank them, and I got caught at it. Didn't get caught taking them, but got confronted with taking them by my mother. And I created a story right on the spot as to this thing that had come along and gotten these Cokes out of there. And Mom was pretty sharp, still is. She didn't believe me then and I don't think she believes me now.

That was the making of a story, taking a few facts and pitching them out the window and creating them. But I always was around storytellers, like the neighbors down from us, Aunt Lonnie, Perlina Moore. She told me stories, and sang songs to me, and told me little jingles, and her husband, Jim Moore, made up stories all the time. I still remember those stories, very vivid ones. Hunting stories, going out and catching three animals out of one tree, I remember. And I remember his getting some animals up a tree and saying that he smoked them out with a cigarette, a hand-rolled cigarette. He'd blow smoke up in the tree, and this animal would come out and he'd knock it in the head. He'd bring a ground hog out and knock it in the head. He'd bring a ground hog out, and then he'd bring a rabbit out, and then he'd bring a squirrel out. And he'd talk about getting two animals with one shot, two squirrels with one shot, those kinds of stories. Then he would have big, tall tales, things that you just couldn't possibly believe, but also couldn't stay away from listening to, because it wasn't so much that you needed to believe him, it was just the magic that the images they talked about created. I don't think anyone, you know, who heard, even way back, the Davy Crockett stories or the Daniel Boone stories, I doubt if anybody believed those literally. I doubt if anybody believed that Davy Crockett actually stood and stared the bark off a tree. He had the reputation of being able to stare a raccoon out of a tree, and he saw this one up in a tree, and he started staring at it, and he never got it to fall. Finally, he climbed up the tree to see why it wouldn't fall, and found out it wasn't a raccoon, but a big old knot on the tree, and he had stared all the bark off the tree. I don't know if anybody literally believed that, but they believed maybe what the story meant, that here was a character who had such power that if he were confronted with that kind of situation, that might be the way it happened. After all, I expect that's the way stories are, not that they happened or will happen, but if they did occur, this might be the way they took place. Especially mythology, and local mythology, as well as classical kinds of mythology.

But storytelling has always been a part of what I can remember and look back on, the way we sat around and told each other just what had happened to people, what had happened to animals, strange things that took place, stories that not only entertained and informed us, but gave us examples, models, literally, to live by.

I see a direct correlation between the oral story and the written story. I think there are differences, but they're only differences in their dress, in the clothing that they have. What they do, and the examples that they set for us, and the pleasures they give us in our association with them, are pretty much the same. And one's relationship to them is probably more related to mood or whatever else than it is to something strikingly different.

I'm as excited at hearing a rather special kind of oral story as I am of reading a very special kind of literary story. Ultimately, the experience is the same. What they do to the culture, they're ultimately the same. It's just a different form.

So, professionally, if you say my first association, I was getting paid for what I did orally before I knew it was storytelling. I didn't think in terms of it being storytelling. To me, it was the fabric of life. It was the culture that I grew from. It was the life that I knew and had learned things from, and all I figured I was doing was I had learned these things, I had come in contact with these things, many other people had not, and if I could tell them about it, then suddenly they had that connection, they had that contact that wasn't there before.

Storytelling back in the early seventies, folks thought it simply meant telling lies. It took the general public a while to realize that storytelling is as much connected to telling the truth as it is to telling lies. It's these really intense truths that come out of these stories, I think, that's been part of the attraction to it.

The National Storytelling Festival started in Jonesboro, Tennessee. The second year, I was down there, and they had three or four storytellers. The first year at the National had only one storyteller, and that was Jerry Clower. The second year they had three or four storytellers, and I was one of them. I emceed the whole program that weekend.

The Corn Island Storytelling Festival was a spin-off from the national. At the time we thought we'd have the National Festival and then we'd have regional festivals going on at other times during the year. I was a member of the first board of directors for NAPPS [National Association for the Preservation and Perpetuation of Storytelling; now NASA, National Storytelling Association], and we talked about establishing regional festivals. I said, "Well, I'd like to do one in Louisville," and that's the way the Corn Island Festival got started.

There are a whole bunch of them around now, a whole bunch of festivals. There are probably, right now, festival and festival kinds of activities, storytelling activities, probably between four and five hundred such events annually throughout the United States. The National Festival is first, we were second, and then just a proliferation of festivals and story events. The International Order of EARS [a secret acronym], which now sponsors the Corn Island Festival, we produce half a dozen to eight events a year, all of which are bigger than that first Corn Island Festival by a long shot.

The big year that the Festival took off in audiences was our first year of holding the ghost tales at Long Run Cemetery; that would have probably been in '82. We expected maybe four or five hundred people to show up to that event, and we had about twenty-five hundred people to show up to it. So that was really the take-off of the large audiences that now attend the Corn Island Festival.

One year after that, I guess it was, well, it went '82 and then it went '83, and then by that time the Festival had reached too-large proportions, the administration at Jefferson Community College felt, for them to continue sponsoring it. They dropped the sponsorship.

Joy and I, in '83, formed the International Order of EARS. The original purpose of the organization was to support the Corn Island Festival. EARS became much broader than that later on, with the development of other events: storytelling in the state parks and the storytelling celebration at Iroquois Park. And we've done the storytelling events at Locust Grove, and we do a spring ghost tales, and Halloween horror tales, and beyond that, we've also developed a storytelling resource center here in Middletown, which is only one of half a dozen throughout the whole world.

Our storytelling center is quite workable in that we have more than three thousand tapes, audio and video, of storytellers telling stories, and we have books on the storytelling, and magazines on the storytelling, and articles—individual articles—on storytelling. The books and the magazines and all of the tapes are cross-referenced on computer, so that if you know the name of a story, then you can go in and punch it in the computer, and we can draw up how many tellers we've got who have told that story. We've also, for the last few years, been videoing and audioing everything that we're doing, in addition to the rather wide range of tapes and whatnot we have from storytellers throughout the country and the world.

It's not unusual now for us to get a letter or phone call from foreign places requesting information on certain kinds of storytelling, or certain aspects of storytelling, where can they look to find this, where can they locate a particular storyteller. So far, we've been able to fulfill those requests successfully.

June 25, 1991

BOOKS BY LEE PENNINGTON

The Dark Hills of Jesse Stuart. Cincinnati, Ohio: Harvest, 1967.

Scenes from a Southern Road. Smithtown, N.Y.: JRD, 1969.

Poems and Prints. Louisville, Ky.: Greenbow, 1969.

Wildflower . . . Poems for Joy. Brooklyn, N.Y.: Poetry Prevue, 1970.

April Poems. Brooklyn, N.Y.: Poetry Prevue, 1971.

Appalachia, My Sorrow. Louisville, Ky.: Love Street, 1971.

Songs of Blood Harlan. Fennimore, Wis.: Westburg Associates, 1975.

Spring of Violets. Louisville, Ky.: Love Street, 1976.

Coalmine. Louisville, Ky.: Love Street, 1976.

The Porch. Louisville, Ky.: Love Street, 1976.

The Spirit of Poor Fork. Louisville, Ky.: Love Street, 1976.

Creative Composition. Lexington, Ky.: University of Kentucky Printing, 1976.

I Knew A Woman. Louisville, Ky.: Love Street, 1977.

Ragweed. Louisville, Ky.: Aran, 1980.

The Janus Collection. Louisville, Ky.: Louisville Graphique, 1982.

Foxwind. Louisville, Ky.: Aran, 1984.

Appalachian Quartet. Louisville, Ky.: Aran, 1984.

The Scotian Women. Louisville, Ky.: Aran, 1984.

Thigmotrapism. Louisville, Ky.: Green River Writers/Grex, 1993.

BETTY LAYMAN RECEVEUR

RECEVEUR: I am Betty Layman Receveur. My birth name actually was Betty Arline Layman. I believe I was named for Arlene Francis, the television personality, but my legal name now is Betty Layman Receveur. I was born here in Louisville. I'm a seventh generation Kentuckian. I was born October twenty-fifth, 1930. My father's name is Russell Hamilton Layman. My mother's maiden name was Georgia Pauline Heyser. I was raised by my paternal grandparents. My grandfather was Frank Fuller Layman and my grandmother was Addie Shelton Layman, Shelton being her maiden name. They were incredible people. Everything I am, that is good, I owe to my grandparents. I owe them a great deal.

BEATTIE: Are they also native Louisvillians?

RECEVEUR: No. They were born down in the state. The Laymans came to Kentucky very early, before 1800, about 1795, from Pennsylvania. They floated down the river on flatboats after the Revolutionary War. My great-great-great grandfather had fought in the Revolutionary War. His name was Joachim Layman. They took up land down in what was then Hardin County, in what finally became Grayson County. They owned six hundred acres down there. All of my Layman ancestors came from there. Before I was born they had moved to Louisville. I was born here.

BEATTIE: When you say your grandparents raised you, from what age?

RECEVEUR: Virtually from birth. I was born, as I said, in 1930. The times were very hard for people, and very often the younger people would live with the older people in order to survive. So my real parents were living with my paternal grandparents at that time. They moved away when I was three. But I was always pretty much in the care of my grandparents, and when my parents moved away, I stayed with them. I have two younger brothers who were raised by our real parents. So we were separated as children, so far as living together, but I always saw them. I care very much for my brothers now. I love them, we're close.

My real family unit was with my grandparents, who supported me totally, who made all decisions about me. For all intents and purposes, they were my parents to me, and I still feel that they were. I miss them very much. They both died in the sixties. The older I get, I think the more I realize how very much what I am has been affected by my grandparents and their views about life, and their feelings about what one does and how one behaves. I owe a great deal to my grandmother, who literally was a woman born in Victorian times; both my grandparents, of course, were. As I was a little girl growing up, women were simply not encouraged to do the kinds of things that little girls are encouraged to do now, because to be successful, you needed to marry a man who would take good care of you and have your family and raise it. But my grandmother would say to me—and I find it remarkable now—my grandmother would say to me almost every day of my life, "You are pretty, you are smart, you can do anything in the world you want to do." I think that gave me the courage to try to do things that by rights I probably had very little expectations in, and yet, I was stubborn enough to try, and to succeed in some of those things.

BEATTIE: Did your grandmother possess that spirit herself? Did she feel she could do pretty much what she wanted to do?

RECEVEUR: Yes, I think she did feel that way. Neither of my grandparents, I think, had much schooling, but they were the brightest people I ever knew. People with more common sense than I ever knew in my life. They had a great capacity for love. They were both storytellers. There was a very strong oral tradition in the family. They could have been writers, but they didn't write their stories down, they just spoke them. They told me wonderful stories of the old days and of our pioneer ancestors and of all the people they'd known, their grandparents, their great-grandparents. They had been handed down, complete with dialogue, these stories. I've had people say to me, "How did you research all the language that's in *Oh, Kentucky!*?" I'd say, "My lord, I grew up listening to a lot of that, so it was very easy for me."

BEATTIE: Did your paternal grandmother come from Kentucky? Did she have the same kind of heritage that your grandfather had?

RECEVEUR: Absolutely. She had the heritage of strong women. In fact, in some ways, I feel that Kitty Gentry of the book *Oh, Kentucky!* is a composite of all my female ancestors. My grandmother was a tremendously strong woman, physically and emotionally. The most emotionally stable person I ever knew in my life was my grandmother. She would talk about her mother, who died, actually, before I was born. She died as a rather young woman. But my grandmother always said, "My mother was afraid of nothing." I have a tintype of my great-grandmother, that I keep along with my other pictures that mean a lot to me, on my cherry chest in my bedroom. You can look at this woman's face and know that she was a strong woman. I think that women in the old days did not feel inferior to men. Women on the frontier were very equal to men. It was only later in the Victorian era where women started to feel like fluttery little creatures who couldn't do very much, if anything.

BEATTIE: As I was reading *Oh, Kentucky!*, I thought the appeal to contemporary women of that book would be the fact that the female characters are so strong, and yet romance is still there.

RECEVEUR: I think that's true, and I think that's quite possible in the world. When I was going on tour, after the original publication of *Oh, Kentucky!*, very often I was asked by interviewers in various places to comment on the modern-day woman and how I felt the modern woman relates to the pioneer woman. Of course, pioneer women just had very hard lives, in many ways, very demanding kinds of lives, but I think that modern women, too, have demanding lives in other ways. I think that maybe we all try to do more than we can, and I think that maybe priorities need to be set. If there's anything that we've let get away from us, it is what's most important in our lives. I think sometimes we try to do so much that we forget that there are priorities.

BEATTIE: What did your grandfather do for a living?

RECEVEUR: My grandfather did several things. He had worked on the railroads for a while. At one time he farmed before he came to Louisville. As he got older, he worked for the old Honeycrust Bakery. That's the job I remember most, because he worked there for many years until he retired. He worked until he was seventy-five. He was part Cherokee Indian. He was six-feet-five, with wonderful long legs, and a marvelous face—high cheekbones and a beautiful roman nose. I have a brother who really looks very much like my granddad, and my younger son looks very much like my grandfather. It pleases me very much to see those features still in my family. He was a very strong man, very proud.

We were always poor. It's become a cliché, almost, to hear people say, "Well, we were poor, but we didn't know it." But it was true. In my case, I never thought of us as being poor. We had enough to eat. There were a lot of things that we could not afford, but we just had so many other things. We did things together, the three of us, and it was probably as good an upbringing as a child could ever have, really. I lived down close to St. Louis Bertrand Catholic Church at Sixth and St. Catherine; the whole neighborhood was poor. It was a very nice neighborhood. I hadn't even heard of air conditioning. I'm not sure if anybody had, or if it was even invented. But on summer evenings we would sit out on the porch, and neighbors would walk up and down the sidewalk, and sometimes come in and sit and talk. Sometimes the priest from over at the priest house would come and sit on the porch, or we would walk down to the neighbor's house and sit and talk. It was lovely, and it was a mixed neighborhood. There were all sorts of people there. It was a good upbringing for someone who wanted to be a writer when she grew up.

My first experience with real romance came from this little old Italian couple who lived about three doors down from us. I mean, we're not talking about Sir Lawrence Olivier and Katherine Hepburn in that charming movie they made together. Their name was Tedechi, and Mr. Tedechi was a little fellow about five feet tall and really round. His wife towered over him, and she had dyed black hair. Bless her heart, she was a good woman, but Mrs. Tedechi had a face like a potato, she really did. But he just adored this woman, he adored her. I remember once as a little girl being over there and she had gotten some oil-cloth for the table. It had flowers on it, and she was showing it to me, and he was standing in the door watching this. She looked up at him and she said, "I like this tablecloth," and he said, "I like you." It was clear; they just adored one another. I really knew what true romance was at that time. It wasn't too long after that before Mrs. Tedechi was taken ill, and she was taken off to the hospital and she died. Mr. Tedechi lived for about another year and died. They said that he'd had a stroke, but even as this kid that I was, I said, "Mr. Tedechi died because his heart was broken after she was gone." I really still think that is true.

BEATTIE: It sounds as though that same example was set by your grandparents.

RECEVEUR: Absolutely. My grandfather lived to be ninety years old. He would have been ninety-one in a few months from his death. He died at home. He went to sleep one night in his own bed. He was an active man up to that time, and simply did not wake up the next morning. He loved my grandmother and she loved him, very much. They were devoted to one another. I'm a great one for family. I believe deeply in families and in how important they are, and I believe in family ties.

BEATTIE: Your childhood, what was it like?

RECEVEUR: It was really wonderful. One of the things I remember most about my childhood was how much I loved to read. The one thing we did not have in our house was books. But I can never remember a time when I couldn't read. Before school, even, I seemed to be able to read. I loved words. I loved the look of them, and I loved the sound of words. I remember trying to read tin-can labels and church bulletins, which were almost the only words I came in contact with, and, of course, newspapers.

When I went to school, that was wonderful, because books were there. But when I was about in the fourth grade, I found a little lending library in the back of a dry-goods store. Now, it wasn't part of the city system. At that time we lived out in the South End. We moved around a bit, because we were renters. I know that the lure of those books was so strong that I would go and borrow the books and take them back home. It was maybe four blocks or so from the house, and I felt it was a perilous way to go by myself. But I wanted those books so badly, the lure was so great, that I would brave that.

Then, very soon after that, we moved down around the St. Louis Bertrand Church, and I went to St. Louis Bertrand School. I owe a lot to that school, because the Dominican nuns taught there, and I would not be the person I am today if I hadn't been taught by the Dominican nuns. Excellent, excellent teachers. I graduated as valedictorian of my class. This was from the eighth grade. I won a scholarship to the old Holy Rosary Academy, which was down near Central Park then. It was a school that my grandparents could never have afforded to send me to. So, that was really a great thing to happen. My grandmother had encouraged me to go on to school and to go to college, and she said, "I know that you can win a scholarship to college. I know you can go."

I'm sure that it was a great disappointment to her when one semester into high school I ran off and got married. I was fourteen years old. Don't ask me why. Whenever I go and lecture now where there are young people, if I go to colleges or if I go to grade schools, I say, "Don't do that, because it limits your life in such a way that it takes a lot of doing to overcome that. You really need to be a person yourself before you think about getting married. You need to wait until you're established." It was pretty foolish, on my part.

BEATTIE: How old was the man you married?

RECEVEUR: Seventeen. His name was Donald William Receveur, which is where my Receveur name comes from. Having gotten that name at fourteen, and having three sons who bear that name, it has become my legal name through the courts.

BEATTIE: How long did you stay in that marriage?

RECEVEUR: I stayed in that marriage thirty years. It was not a marriage made in heaven. My first husband is certainly a very nice man, and he's the father of my children, and that certainly is something very special, but by the time I had gotten to be twenty years old, I started to realize that we were not very well-suited for one another. He was, in a very well-meaning way, very authoritarian, even though he was only three years older than I. Because I'd been fourteen when we married, it was almost as if he thought he could keep me fourteen for the rest of my life, to the point that he controlled the purse strings, so that I didn't even have grocery money. I mean, I couldn't go to the grocery. He bought groceries. Again, he is not a horrible man. We are friends now. But sometimes now he will say, "My goodness, I don't know what I was thinking of back then."

After many years, my first husband and I went into the antique business, but, my goodness, I had grown sons by that time. I worked in the antique business, and I worked really hard, and finally I started to push to become a grown-up human being. I think that one thing that started this whole process was that I did start to write early on. I started in my early twenties. I had two little boys at that time.

BEATTIE: What age were you when they were born, and what are their names?

RECEVEUR: My oldest son is Donald William Receveur, Jr. He was born in 1946. Then I have Richard Lewis Receveur, my middle son, who was born in 1950. When they were sixteen and thirteen, my third son was born in 1963. His name is Brett Andrew Receveur. I'm very proud of my sons; I love them very much indeed.

BEATTIE: Are they all in Louisville?

RECEVEUR: No. The oldest is a doctor of psychology and he's in Denver. The other two are in Louisville. Rick, the middle one, is a most respected attorney here. My youngest son, Brett, is in the antique business now. He works with his father, who is still in the antique business. They own The Midas Touch on Bardstown Road.

BEATTIE: Were you able to finish high school after you got married?

RECEVEUR: No, I never was able to go back to school. But I always read a lot, and, as I said, the Dominican nuns had given me a very good education. I read and continued to educate myself. I feel that books open up the world to you in a way that nothing else does.

When I was in my early twenties, a neighbor was throwing away an old typewriter. I said to him, "Do you mean you're going to throw that away?" He said, "Well, yes. Would you like to have it?" I said, "Oh, yes. I would love to have it," and I carried it home. It was heavy. I carried it about a block home. I believe that my footprints are probably in the asphalt out there still. But I decided I was going to try to write. I said to myself, "I'm going to make this sound like a book if it's the last thing I ever do." I started with a historical romance because, being out of school, I was a very undisciplined reader. I read *Ulysses,* so I read good things, but I also read historical romances, and I just loved them. I thought, "That's what I'm going to write." So, I did. I started in. We moved from that area of town, and we moved, actually, to this house [on Huon Drive] right here. I've been in this house for over thirty years.

I met a woman who belonged to a writers' club. Up to that time, I had had no contact at all with other writers. I had certainly not had any writing classes or anything. The club is about forty years old now.

BEATTIE: This is the Louisville Writers Club?

RECEVEUR: Yes. I came to the club when I was in my late twenties, very shy, and still very much under the control of my husband, who wasn't pleased at all with my writing, and he wasn't pleased with my going to this club.

BEATTIE: Was that because he was afraid he might lose some control over you if you had other interests?

RECEVEUR: I do think so, yes. As I look back on it now, I'm sure that's what it was. I think that I was interested in things that he wasn't, and that made him feel uncomfortable. It made him feel that he would lose me. But, I went to my writers club meetings every other week, and other club members were very encouraging to me about this book I was writing. I started with an historical novel. I read somewhere that beginning writers should never try to write historical works first because they're simply too complicated. I thought, "Well, I've put in too much work on this to back out now." So I kept on. I certainly wasn't writing full-time, but I would get my manuscript out and work on it, and then I'd put it away. Finally, ten years later, I had finished this book. I sent it off to Putnam's, because at that time, there were no original paperbacks. They were all reprints. So I sent it to Putnam's, as I say, and of course, I didn't have an agent. I didn't even know about agents. I just sent this off, and I got back a letter from the editorial staff. I didn't know that that was unusual. I didn't know that in all likelihood the first reader would just ship it back to me. They wrote a letter to me, a very nice letter, and they said, "You write very well; this is a good book. But there's no market for this book at all. Romance is as dead as the dodo." Well, I didn't know about markets, either. I just wrote what I wrote. So there I was, with this book.

BEATTIE: What was the title of the book?

RECEVEUR: I called this book "Sable and Gold," because it was set in the Gold Rush days. It was six-hundred-and-thirty pages in manuscript. I sent it out a couple of other places, and they said the same thing. So, I considered it a labor of love. I put it up on my closet shelf, wrapped it up carefully and just put it up there. I wrote short stories. I published in some little literary magazines. Over a twenty-year period I had made a grand total of a-hundred-seventy-five dollars as a writer, so I certainly wasn't a pro by any stretch of the imagination.

I had always thought I would be interested in the theater, and by the time I got to be about forty, I thought, "Well, maybe it's now or never." My children were growing up by that time. Even my youngest son was beginning to get old enough that I could do things like that, and I was beginning to be more independent myself. I had made that push to become a grown-up woman instead of staying a fourteen year old, as my first husband had kept me.

BEATTIE: What do you think instigated that change in you?

RECEVEUR: Probably taking home that typewriter was the very beginning. A very strong push was joining the writers club and having comrades who encouraged me greatly, some of whom had published books and told me that I had talent. I think, too, when we got our own business and I started to work in that business, I saw that I could do these things. I at one point had learned how to drive, and I did have a car, and I could get out in the world and do things. I was no longer at home with little kids. I just made a push and insisted that when I worked in the business I was going to have money of my own to spend however I pleased. I had never had money to spend however I pleased. I made the statement, "I do not work for nothing, not for anybody." It caused considerable upheaval in my marriage. I'm not sure my first husband ever really accommodated himself too well to that. He is a fine man, he really is. He simply had his way of doing things, I had mine, and finally that didn't do and we parted. We separated and divorced.

It was maybe twelve or thirteen years before I finally got my first book manuscript down and sent it out again. I sent it out finally again in '77.

BEATTIE: The same book, without any changes?

RECEVEUR: The same book without any changes. I was encouraged by writer friends of mine, people who knew that I had that manuscript all those years ago, to send it out, because they said, "You know, there are these original paperbacks on the stands now and they're romances." I kept saying, "Nobody would want it." So finally, a dear friend of mine said, "You've got to send it." I said, "I don't have a box." She said, "I will get you a box if you'll send it." So here she came with the box, and almost just to placate her and get her off my back, I said, "Okay, I will send it, but I know they don't want it." So, I got it down. I looked at it. The paper was not yellowed, but the corners were curled. I still had the same old manual typewriter that I'd typed it on. I took each sheet, and I put each one on the ironing board, and I steam-ironed the corners flat, and I sent it off. And I went on with my life. I was in the antique business, you know. I was busy, I was doing things. I'd been doing some theater for a while. That's amateur theater. I just kind of forgot about it. Four months went by, and I'd sent it to Avon Books, which is one of the top five paperback houses. Again, without an agent. I just sent it through the slush pile.

I came home one day from work and I found an executive size envelope in the mailbox with the return address of Avon Books. I looked at it, and I remember very clearly what I thought. I thought, "Inside it says, 'Sorry, we can't use your manuscript. We're returning it under separate cover.'" I opened it and it was from Nancy Coffey, the executive editor of Avon Books, and she said, "We love your book. We would like to publish it, if you would accept an advance of five thousand dollars against royalties of eight percent up to a-hundred-and-fifty-thousand copies, ten percent thereafter." Well, I had to read it through twice to really believe what I was reading, and I started to hyperventilate. I felt ill for three days. It was as if a truck had hit me. I'm not sure I can ever quite live through anything as astonishing as that was again. I knew that I was always going to be writing one thing or another, because writing simply validates me in a way that nothing else in my life, perhaps, does. But here I was with a manuscript that was going to be published, and it opened up a whole new world for me.

Before that book came out, my first husband and I were divorced. The book did not cause that. The selling of the book did not cause that. That was in the works. In some ways, my book's acceptance almost made my divorce harder, and it made me probably hold off longer than I would have. But getting my first book accepted changed my life, and I realized then that what I needed to do was to go ahead with another novel, because that's what my publisher wanted. The truth is, I had started another historical romance all those years back, and I had several chapters of it written. Then when they said, "No, there's no market for this," I just put it aside. I went digging into old papers and found it, and it became *Molly Gallagher,* which really, up until I wrote *Oh, Kentucky!,* was my best-selling book. In fact, it still sells in Germany. They love me in Germany, for some reason or other. It's been in paperback over there.

BEATTIE: How did the first book sell? How was that received?

RECEVEUR: It sold very well. It made some of the best-sellers lists at B. Dalton and Waldenbooks, which just surprised me greatly and gratified me a lot. Then *Molly Gallagher* did even better. *Molly Gallagher* made number six on the *L.A. Times* list, which was nice. Then I wrote *Carrie Kingston,* which was another historical romance. I've made a living from writing since 1979. My publisher changed the title of "Sable and Gold." The protagonist's name in this was Sable Flanagan, hence the sable and gold for the Gold Rush days. They liked the name Sable Flanagan, and they titled the book *Sable Flanagan.* So all three of those books made a living for me. They sold in the United States and Canada, and they also have been sold in a good many countries in Europe.

But then things changed. The editor that I'd been with all the time, who worked directly with me, moved to edit at Ballentine Books. The only change I had to make in *Sable Flanagan* was to add two pages. I had to make a love scene more explicit. I've never been that lucky since; I've always had to do more rewrites. So, when *Sable Flanagan* was ready to go to the printers, I got a call from my editor, Pam Strickler [Pamela Dean Strickler], who had, as I said, done it all, and she told me she was moving over to Ballentine, but not to worry because my book was all ready to go. Meanwhile, I had gotten a New York agent, who is really a power agent at Writers House in New York. His name is Albert Zuckerman, and he's Ken Follett's agent. He's big time, and he is a sweet, sweet, sweet man. I really owe him a lot, and I appreciate everything he does for me. Also, Pam Strickler, the editor, has done so many things for me. I owe a lot to these two people. She always has believed in my work.

My agent called me after a while, and he said, "Guess what? Guess who's interested in Betty Receveur's new book? I just got this note from Ballentine Books saying they would like to see Betty Receveur's new book." Of course, I had only published with Avon. So, it turned out that I did go with Ballentine then, and I had the same editor, Pam Strickler. I have had her throughout my career.

Very often when publishers have an author who writes in a certain genre, and they can make money, they do not let you change. They don't want you to change into another kind of writing. I always pushed at the perimeters of the historical romance. I was never quite happy stuck in it. I always wanted to do more, and in some ways, I think probably my books didn't make as much money as some books do. Some romance writers are rich. I think I'm not because I always put other things in my books. I recall one historical romance that I read, and its protagonist must have taken a-hundred-and-fifty baths in the course of this book. It always seemed to be just a ploy to show how beautiful she was without her clothes on. Her would-be lover was hovering around, and he would almost come in on her or something. I couldn't write a book that just centered on the love between these two people. I always realized there was a world going on, and I had to try to portray that world. So I always pushed a little bit against that. Finally, my editor came here; she'd never been to Kentucky. Pam visited me, and she fell in love with Kentucky. I was working on the last historical that I did, *Carrie Kingston,* and at the time I said to her, "What would you think about setting a book in Kentucky?" She said, "Oh, I just think, it would be wonderful." So I kept thinking about that, and after I had finished *Carrie Kingston* I had remarried, and my husband and I would go jogging around the Bellarmine [College] track. I was jogging around the Bellarmine track one day, and the whole plot for *Oh, Kentucky!* just came to me. I knew Kitty Gentry and I knew what was going to happen to her. I knew she was going to have two husbands. I knew she was going to have children by both these men.

BEATTIE: It surprises me to think that there would be anything negative or contrary to sales in terms of your pushing the romance genre, because to me that makes a book all the richer.

RECEVEUR: But see, I think *Oh, Kentucky!* is historical fiction; it's a historical novel, even though it has some romance in it. There are historical romances, and this is a romance set in historical times, essentially, rather than the other way around. I always had trouble putting the romance, or sex if you will, in books. I always had trouble putting that first. I could only put it in in the context of the story I wanted to tell. So, I think that some people liked that, and other people did not like it.

BEATTIE: What gave you the ideas for your first novels?

RECEVEUR: I don't know. I never had any problem at all thinking up stories. Plotting is the easiest part of writing for me. My problem is stopping. The truth is that the original manuscript for *Oh, Kentucky!* was fifteen-hundred-and-twenty-seven pages. It ended up taking me five years to write *Oh, Kentucky!*, and I never stopped researching the whole time. Now, I would qualify this whole thing by saying that I became very ill in the middle of writing *Oh, Kentucky!*. I think it would have taken me four years in any case, but I was ill for eighteen months. I had a failing thyroid and didn't know it. When the doctors found that out, they started to do tests, and it turned out that I was really in danger of dying. I was in danger of going into a coma at that point. My thyroid had just virtually ceased to function. They said that if I had gone into a coma and been taken to a hospital, unless they figured out very quickly what was causing the coma and reversed that, I would have died. But fortunately, we caught that, and it was easy enough to take care of. I take a tiny little synthetic substance, a tiny little pill every day.

Within two weeks, I was perfectly fine. It was as if I had been asleep for eighteen months and woke up. I did get right back to work. I really lost work during that time, because I worked every day, but I would go and read it the next day and tear it all up. So, it slowed me down considerably. As I said before, it finally took five years to complete *Oh, Kentucky!*, and the research went on every day of those five years. I sent it to my publisher in two big cardboard boxes. My editor called me and said, "My God, Betty, look at this manuscript." She loved the manuscript, but they really felt that even though it was physically possible to publish this whole thing in one book, it was going to be a very big book. So, we together decided to cut it off at statehood, because that was a natural stopping place. I'm taking the rest of the material that was leftover and fleshing it out, and that is the basis for the sequel. The sequel will begin at just about the place where *Oh, Kentucky!* leaves off, which is where Roman Gentry has been elected to the United States Senate, and they're going off to Philadelphia. This book will pick up with them arriving in Philadelphia, and, of course, ultimately they will come back home. There were some very exciting things that happened in that next period in Kentucky, including the Aaron Burr treason trial.

BEATTIE: You talked about Kitty Gentry being a composite of your female ancestors. Was there a historical character that paralleled Roman Gentry or anybody elected about that time that is a similar character in *Oh, Kentucky!*?

RECEVEUR: Roman was based on several different people. Roman is a fictional character, but I borrowed from real characters, from their adventures, many times. I had wanted to put a list of those people in the author's note in the back, but there was so much paper matter in this book already, that my editor encouraged me to keep my author's note as brief as possible. But certainly Roman was based a little bit—that part of his life at least—on John Brown of Kentucky, who was one of the two first United States Senators sent off to Philadelphia.

BEATTIE: I was impressed by the author's note, because it's rare that a reader gets to know how much is fact and how much is fiction in a book. I certainly wondered that with real characters in the book, such as Daniel Boone, which of these adventures really did occur?

RECEVEUR: Well, almost everything with Daniel probably did occur, because there are so many things that we know about that he did. We know exactly where he was and how his adventures came out. I tried to be very true to Daniel, indeed. Daniel was a most interesting character for me. I didn't know what I was going to think about Daniel when I researched him, because I had grown up hearing about Daniel Boone, the great hero of Kentucky. Then later revisionist historians came along and said, well, he really wasn't all that great after all. He didn't deserve all this fame. So, I didn't know what to think. I researched and researched and researched Daniel and the family, and I came to love Daniel. I feel this deep kind of love and regard for Daniel, who was not a perfect man by any means. He certainly had flaws, if you want to call them that. But he did a lot for Kentucky, there's no question about that. I feel that we need to take our hats off to him periodically. I think, after my research, I came away believing that Daniel was probably as much Indian as any white man could be who had no Indian blood whatever, so far as I ever could determine. He was, of course, from English parentage, and he had been born in Pennsylvania, and where he lived there was an Indian tribe nearby.

Daniel, instead of going off to school as he was supposed to, would go off with the Indians. They were very friendly, and they just kind of took Daniel under their wing. He learned so many things from them. I really feel that he came to admire the Indian way of life and was, at heart, himself essentially an Indian. So that when he was captured and taken off and became the son of Chief Blackfish, I think it was probably an extraordinary thing. I'm not at all sure that he couldn't have escaped earlier than he did. I think perhaps he could have. Daniel was very clever, and I think he might have been able to escape sooner. But once he knew that fort was going to be attacked, it seems to me that there was this crisis of conscience and he could not do anything except go back to the fort.

BEATTIE: Did he have an Indian wife, as well as his caucasian wife, Rebecca?

RECEVEUR: Absolutely. It's sure that he was given an Indian wife, as the son of the chief would have been. He was only there for four months, mind you. But I think it was an important time in his life and, as I say, I think that he must have been terribly torn, because here, finally, was probably the life he really had always admired. But it was true that people had written to tell Rebecca. After all of this came out in the trial, he was court-martialed, and there were people who made it their business to write to Rebecca and tell her that he had had an Indian wife. Most people think that's why Rebecca would not come back with him, for it was almost a year before he could persuade her to come back. Now, there have always been rumors that Rebecca married, herself, during that time. I could find no histori-cal basis for that, and other historians who hold Ph.D.s can't find any basis for that at all. So, I don't believe that.

BEATTIE: Will Daniel Boone figure at all in your sequel to *Oh, Kentucky!*?

RECEVEUR: Yes, a bit. Of course, he'd gotten older. He was so extraordinary be-cause he finally ended up losing all of his lands. Even though he owned land, I think he almost had that Indian concept of owning land, and he never could quite go to the trouble to secure his holdings in some kind of legal way. So he ended up losing everything as a really old man. I think he was about sixty when he went to Missouri and took Callaways and other Boones along with him. I'm always really touched because there's one account of his going to Missouri that states that a lot of the women and children and some of the men and their supplies were loaded into boats, but some went overland. I'm not sure exactly why, but some of them went overland, including Daniel, and there was a journal kept on that trip. In this journal the man says, "And the old man walked all the way." I just get choked up every time I think of Daniel walking all the way to Missouri.

BEATTIE: Are you planning other Kentucky books after your sequel to *Oh, Ken-tucky!*?

RECEVEUR: Some people have said to me, "I think that you should follow the Gentrys and the Claibornes all the way up to World War II." I've said, "I don't think I'm going to live long enough to do that." Right now I will be very content to finish this story. It will please me very much. I'm proud of *Oh, Kentucky!*, and I think that it's what I wanted to do probably my whole life, but had to wait until I had the skill to do it and was ready to do it, was mature enough myself.

BEATTIE: Because of your living in Kentucky, has *Oh, Kentucky!* been the most satisfying book that you've written?

RECEVEUR: No question about it; I wrote this book because I loved my grandparents. The book is dedicated to my grandparents. It says they were true Kentuckians, and I think that's absolutely true. They epitomized, for me, what Kentuckians should be. And I myself feel a very true Kentuckian; I love this state. I love the land, I love it's history, I love it's people. I really wanted young people today to know what a marvelous state they live in. It's the most beautiful place in the world for me.

BEATTIE: After you divorced your first husband, when did you remarry?

RECEVEUR: My second marriage was in 1980. I married John Birkett. John is a mystery writer. He lives here in Louisville. We were married eight years. We are still very close to one another, very committed to one another, as a matter of fact. We just do better living in separate houses. So we have a strange, but very good, relationship. I met him through the Louisville Writers Club. We had known one another for many years.

BEATTIE: I'm interested that since you have been so successful as a writer, that you're still a member of the Writers Club.

RECEVEUR: There was a period when I wasn't. I was so into other things. Some of my oldest and dearest friends I met through that club, so I was always in close touch. But now I go back, and I find it really nice. I like associating with writers. I do some teaching now, and I like that. I do workshops; I've taught at writers' conferences. I have come to enjoy it very much. I particularly like it when I can work really closely with a small group of students. The [Louisville-based] Green River Writers Novels-in-Progress Workshop is probably the most satisfying thing that I've done. Some of those people are very talented, and it's really nice to work with that. I love to find people who have talent in writing. I love that and I love to do whatever I can.

BEATTIE: You talked about having done some acting locally. Where was that?

RECEVEUR: I went over to Heritage Theater at the Jewish Community Center. A friend took me to one of their productions, and I thought it was handsomely done, very professional. And the theater's little program said, "We're having try-outs for such-and-such a play." I thought, "I'm going to do this. I'm going to go do this." I was forty by that time, and I thought, "It's now or never." So, I went over and I tried out, and they called me and said, "You've got the part of Miss Krumholtz in *How to Succeed in Business Without Really Trying.*

BEATTIE: You'd never done any acting before?

RECEVEUR: No, I'd never done any acting. But when I was really a kid, I didn't think I was going to be a writer; I thought I was going to be in the theater. I didn't know as a kid that you couldn't get married and be a writer or be an actress. At least, for a long, long time you couldn't. This was kind of my last stab.

BEATTIE: What do you think the nature of creativity is?

RECEVEUR: I think that we're born with that. I think that there are people who are simply born with the ability to dance, say. I think, in the same way, you're born with the ability to write, to plot, to think up stories, to be filled with stories. There certainly may be some genetic thing here. I think that's proven over and over again. I'm a firm believer in genes. I think the fact that my grandparents were so filled with stories certainly has some part in my creativity. I think that I had the right blood for it, too, because I am part Cherokee, I am part Welsh, I'm part Scot, all these storytellers. I don't know. The stories, the images, the characters were always in my head, always. I know they just finally had to come out.

BEATTIE: Would you say that you have always felt compelled to write?

RECEVEUR: I think that's true, yes. I get unwell when I go for long periods without writing. I start to feel really jittery and not good. It's something that is a part of me that I need to do. I do think creativity is a gift, and I'm very grateful for it. I think it's a gift, not a curse, and I think it makes me more, not less. Not in any way am I trying to brag, but I think that I had such a good heritage, and I am very lucky to have had that. I think that I have some of the common sense of my grandparents, and they certainly taught me how to love. They taught me how to be a good parent and a good grandparent. They taught me how important family is. I feel filled with good things, and I feel I've had an extraordinary life. If I die tomorrow, I couldn't complain, because I do have this feeling that there's this great continuity of life that is passed on. My grandparents will never be dead as long as I'm alive, because there's so much of them in me that I know I have passed on to my children, who pass it on to their children. I just think that we're not really gone, ever.

What I tried to do in *Oh, Kentucky!* was recreate a way of life. That did spark enormous research, because I had to find out how Kentuckians of that era did everything. They went out in the wilderness with essentially nothing. How did they survive? How did they do those things? I found it very interesting that they gathered wads of buffalo hair, and treated dead nettles like flax and came up with a substitute for linsey-woolsey, because they had neither linen nor wool.

BEATTIE: Where did you do most of your research, for that book and for others?

RECEVEUR: Everywhere. I haunted places like the Filson Club, and, of course, I examined materials from the Kentucky Historical Society and materials from the Kentucky section of the library. Then I begged, borrowed, and bribed old rare book dealers to get me things that were out of print that I needed. I never stopped. I love research. I almost love research for it's own sake, because you just come upon things that are so extraordinary, and there are times when you will make a connection that you hadn't expected to make. It's just like finding gold. It's wonderful.

BEATTIE: Have you discovered things in your research that you don't believe people are aware of generally, including historians?

RECEVEUR: I don't know. This really is an ego-trip for me in some ways, but I think that I understand Daniel Boone probably as well as anybody who's ever studied him. It's as if there's some kind of link between me and Daniel. John and I used to go down to Harrodsburg. I had heard that the Harrodsburg Historical Society has one of the original paintings that had been done by Chester Harding, who painted Daniel just a few months before he died. Daniel was an old man. Those works were the only works done from life. All the other things you see of Daniel were just an artist's kind of idea of him, and the Harrodsburg Historical Society had one of those paintings. The historical society was among the row houses down there, and every time John and I would go, it would be locked up and nobody there. I kept just desperately wanting to see that painting. So finally, over at the Beaumont Inn, I talked to one of the proprietors, and I explained who I am, and I told him my mission and said, "Is there any way?" He said, "Why, yes." You know how little towns are. "Why, yes. I'll call Miss Sally So-and-so. She'll just come right here. I know she will." He put me on the phone to Miss Sally and she said, "Well, I'll meet you right over there. Be over there in twenty minutes and I'll take you in." So John and I went over, and I saw the painting of Daniel. I just stood there and I looked at him, and tears started running down my face. I said, "Oh, Daniel. I'm so sorry." So many things happened to him that were really sad. I'd come to love him so much and to feel a kinship with him. There's some kind of bond. It's strange, but I feel that I knew him.

Very often, if I get over to Frankfort, I go up there where at least part of him is buried. I think his spirit's there, in any case, his and Rebecca's. It's one of the most beautiful spots in Kentucky, high up, overlooking the Capitol and the Kentucky River. An interesting story can come out about that, too. Fully a year after I'd been working on *Oh, Kentucky!*, I went out to see a great-aunt of mine, who is the youngest sister of my grandmother who raised me. She had a photograph that I had never seen of my great-grandfather. She loaned it to me so that I could have it copied. When I brought it home, I turned it over, and found on the back, in this old, browned ink, a listing of the family tree going back, and where the families had lived. With each generation it would say where they lived, and the earliest ones said Boonesborough. Goose bumps just popped up, and still do, every time I remember that. I really, firmly believe that it's why I felt so drawn to that spot, and it's why I felt so pulled to the Kentucky River.

BEATTIE: You say you now write on a word processor?

RECEVEUR: Yes. I was using the same old typewriter, and after I started *Oh, Kentucky!*—I had maybe three hundred pages done—I got the computer, and it took me two weeks to teach myself the word-processing system. It was like going from a horse and buggy to a jet.

BEATTIE: Do you write first drafts directly onto the computer?

RECEVEUR: Oh, yes. I can never write longhand. I'm very much a print creature. I need to see that print. Longhand just doesn't give me the idea of what I'm doing in the way that print does.

BEATTIE: Do you discipline yourself to producing a certain number of hours or pages at a time?

RECEVEUR: I never demand a certain number of pages, because it simply won't work that way for me. There are some times when a certain portion or certain segment of a manuscript will go very easily and very quickly, and will be fewer pages than I thought it was going to be. I never know how many pages anything's going to take, even after all this time. Other times, it takes me infinitely longer, and I'm just tickled to death if I get through two pages. I work very hard, and I work the way other people work at a job, because if you write as a living, you really have to do that. I can remember back at the time when I was still an amateur writer, not making a living. I would think, "My muse is not with me today, so I just am not in the mood to write." Well, if you're bucking a deadline, you just go ahead and write. There have been times when, even with the flu or something, I've sat there bleary-eyed and sick and tried to put some things down, and some days are better than others. Maybe some terrible thing has gone wrong in your life—you're grieving or you're upset. I have found that the work that I do on those days is just as good as the work I do on my best days. I used to think, "Oh, none of this is going to be any good." I think that most professional writers get to that point where you write because it's your job to do it. If I'm behind on a deadline, as I am now, I will be working Saturdays and sometimes Sundays as well, though I love to kind of keep Sundays and say, "Okay, this afternoon I can do what I want to do." But through the week I keep a really good schedule. I work many hours a day, and I often work at those times when other people are having vacation time, or it's evening, or it's a holiday. I can't tell you how many times I've had to correct galleys over Christmas.

BEATTIE: What do you think is the most important thing for people to know about you?

RECEVEUR: I know there are just so many people who are very much like me. I've always felt that if I could reach one person and they would read something I'd written and identify with that at once and say, "Yes, I know how that feels," I would feel very successful.

June 28, 1992

BOOKS BY BETTY LAYMAN RECEVEUR

Sable Flanagan. New York: Avon, 1979.

Molly Gallagher. New York: Ballentine, 1982.

Carrie Kingston. New York: Ballentine, 1984.

Oh, Kentucky! New York: Ballentine, 1990.

Kentucky Home. New York: Ballentine, 1995.

JAMES STILL

STILL: My full name is James Alexander Still, Jr. I was born on a farm very near Lafayette, Alabama, on July 16, 1906. My father was a horse doctor; that is, a veterinarian without formal training. He was also a farmer. Altogether, there were ten of us. There were five girls first and then five boys. After my mother passed on, my father married again and had another boy, so I'm including him as well. I was the first boy that came after the five girls. I think all in our family were welcome. I grew up in what I would call a very happy home. We children, none of us could remember an unkind word spoken between our parents.

We lived in various places. First, we lived at Double Branch Farm, which was, as I said, very near Lafayette, Alabama. I think we left there after about five years, but I remember it very well. After Grandma Still died rather suddenly, we went and lived awhile with Grampa in his place at his big farm—at Marcoot [Alabama]. It's still a place down there. There's little more than a store and a church. My grandparents on my mother's side, though, they were Lindseys. They were Scotch-Irish.

BEATTIE: What was your mother's full name?

STILL: Her name was Barcelona Anadora, and she was called Lonie. She was born in Georgia, up in horsefly country. When she was maybe fifteen or sixteen they moved to Alabama. Both of my grandpas were from never-the-twain-shall-meet sort of families. My Grandpa Still was a veteran of the Civil War. In fact, he was wounded twice. When I was growing up, the Civil War was sort of yesterday, and I knew several war veterans. They used to come to the school on Confederate Day and talk to us.

My grandfather had rather a large plantation. My grandpa never owned slaves himself, but his parents did, my great-grandparents owned slaves. To think I've come, you know, across this length of time to now. Don't mistake me; I have very liberal ideas, and I concern myself with the civil rights of all people. I'm as good as anybody and better than nobody. I am, however, proud of my southern boyhood, and I don't know of any substitute for it. But I had to leave home. I would have gone to sleep there. I could never have done anything there.

BEATTIE: Do you recall a particular age when you felt you wanted to, or needed to, move on?

STILL: No, I never thought about that. I just wanted to go to college, which was impossible. There was no precedent in my family, but I intended to go. I didn't know how.

BEATTIE: Do you know where that desire came from?

STILL: Well, I knew other people who went, and I knew about college. I was a reader.

BEATTIE: When did that start? Were you read to as a child before you knew how to read yourself?

STILL: I believe I could read before I went to school. My sister, she taught me to read. There was a little book we had on the Eskimo, and I remember that book particularly. I loved that book. They'd read it to me. I knew every word in it. I could recognize those words. They were taking me to school sometimes before I was ever enrolled, and the teacher welcomed these little visitors. In fact, I was told that the teacher asked me why I didn't come more often. I said, "I would, wouldst Momma would let me."

The best teacher I ever had was the first grade teacher. She was a hands-on teacher. She was the kind of teacher that Foxfire has. I was the smallest person in the class. I was the only child who had to stand on a box to reach the chalkboard. We did things, like the first day of school she handed me an ear of corn and she wrote my name on the desk, and I was to shell off grains and outline my name, which I did, over and over. Very soon that day I could write my name; I knew it's shape.

We planted things. We brought eggshells to school, and each one of us had a grain of corn, which he planted, and we learned about growing things. We acted out. I recall *Hiawatha*. We acted *Hiawatha*. I remember I was a squirrel.

I had several teachers in grade school who were average, I would say. One, as I remember, in the fifth grade, read stories to us nearly every day from a magazine that's long-discontinued for children.

Then we moved to Lafayette and lived in Judge Norman's house, which was a grand home. It's not there anymore; too bad.

BEATTIE: What was it like?

STILL: Well, it was a bit like some of the antebellum homes that are still there in Lafayette, Alabama. You know, with the chandelier, great hall, and roof. I know that it was so big that, although we'd come from a big home, we still didn't have enough furniture to fill it up.

First we lived in another house—it was sort of a compound—adjoining that first house, and we'd play school. We moved back to the farm after being there a while, but there was a mortgage on the farm, and we had to leave it again. We moved into Chattahoochee Valley which has five or six great cotton mills. In fact, the Lanett Cotton Mill was in that day the largest one, perhaps, in the world.

Then we moved to Shawmut, on Lanier Avenue, Boss Row. In those days, the people lived in the factory homes. Those on Boss Row, where the bosses lived, lived in nicer homes, you know. We lived in one of those.

BEATTIE: Was your father working for the factory?

STILL: No. My parents wanted to move there because nearly everybody had a cow in their backyards. And anyway, there were a great deal of other animals—horses, mules, and things like that, down there. When we lived up in the county there, of course it was mainly cows, horses, and so on. Little by little my father's practice became a small-animal practice as tractors took over. Also, he looked after dairy cattle. He was appointed by the state as a rabies inspector. That is, every dog had to be inoculated. And, as we lived almost on the Georgia line, and there was a lack of veterinarians, he worked both for the states of Georgia and Alabama for a while. Also, we were very near to Auburn University where he used to go down and take short courses. There they would send up interns and veterinary students to travel with him and go with him in his work, toward the end.

We lived there and then we moved—I don't know why—to Girard Station just outside of Fairfax, still in a line down there. I went to high school there and graduated, and then later I went off to school and I never lived with my family again. My mother died and my father moved out in the country about four miles.

BEATTIE: How old were you when she died?

STILL: Well, she died in 1935. She was fifty-five years old. Then my father married again, and he married a girl who was the same age as my older sister. Naturally we just resented it, not knowing her, and when we got to know her, we liked her very much. It astonished all of us. She died in childbirth within a couple of years. Several years passed, then my father married still a third time.

BEATTIE: Did your mother die from a terminal illness or an accident?

STILL: It was a malignancy. I was at the University of Illinois at that time.

BEATTIE: So your father married a third time, then? There were not children by that marriage?

STILL: Oh, no. He was older then. His wife had a son about seventeen, eighteen. In a way we liked him all right. But I never felt welcome at home again. She somehow felt threatened, by me, especially. And if I went home, she made it unpleasant for me. That was a great source of pain for me for several years, and something I couldn't do anything about.

BEATTIE: You were talking about the teachers in elementary school that were so good. Did you have the same experience in high school?

STILL: I had only one man teacher, the principal at Shawmut, Alabama, Carl Lappert. He was a good teacher, but he taught to the tune of a hickory stick, as the old saying goes, and all the students were frightened of him. We studied, because we were afraid not to, which is not the best way. I regret to say that I did not have, except for this man, well, there was a geometry teacher who I'm sure was a good teacher. I mean, she meant well, but I've always been a dumbbell in math. I think she was probably good. But aside from that, I cannot think of a teacher who did anything for me, really, or for anybody else.

BEATTIE: Did you have a particular interest in reading or writing at that point?

STILL: Not much. I remember in high school I started a novel.

BEATTIE: Ambitious, for high school.

STILL: I know I had never seen the ocean, but it was a sea story, and I used to write it every night. I was just enjoying doing it, you know. I was living it as I wrote it. When I was somewhere in the grades, I don't know when, I wrote a story on a tablet, which I still have, with a hard pencil. It is now hard to read. Of course, I wrote it on acid-free paper, or it wouldn't exist today. I found it not long ago. It was called "The Gold Nugget." I read that with some difficulty; it was pretty faint. But I could see then that whoever wrote that would be writing again. I only stopped when the paper ran out.

BEATTIE: As you read it now, what do you see in that story that was so promising?

STILL: I saw my future in it. Everything I was to do and be was right there. I saw it between the lines.

BEATTIE: You're talking about style as well as philosophy, content?

STILL: I don't know anything about style, because style is me. I have no more idea what my style is than anything. I can't even imagine what my style is. I just write the way I can write. In our home we had three books that I recall. One was the Bible, which I don't know whether people looked in or not. Then there was a book called *The Anatomy of the Horse*. And my father got the *Veterinary Journal,* which I used to try to read, with no success, but there was another book. The back was off of it. It was a big, large book called *Cyclopedia of Universal Knowledge.* It had a little of everything in it you could imagine, and some things you can't. It had some short history of every country, population, size, products, a few things like that of every country. It had social correspondence, it had business correspondence. It had samples of maybe ten or twenty or twenty-five words of several foreign languages, and how to pronounce them. I'm sure that I was the only person in that state, or child, who knew twenty-five words of Arabic. Then there was a section of poetry—Byron, Shelley, Keats, great poetry—and Shakespeare. I memorized them. It was my first introduction to poetry. I remember Wordsworth.

I recall one day a student brought to school a copy of the *National Geographic,* and I remember he let me borrow it. Here was an article on Alaska, "The Valley of Ten Thousand Smokes." I was fascinated by that. That started me on my journeys around the world, right then. I knew I had to go to Alaska someday. Well, I never did, and it's very low on my priorities now. No matter. And once in a while I might see a copy of the *Geographic.* As you know, we used to have here copies going back to 1897 or '98, when it was founded.

BEATTIE: At the Hindman Settlement School?

STILL: Yes. I don't know what became of them. But I went to high school in town, in Lafayette. We walked two miles, I believe. My high school had once been a college, one very large building. Unusual for a schoolhouse, in those days. More than that, we didn't have the usual county teachers. It was a city school, so we had better teachers, generally, than there usually would be. In fact, our teachers, like mine, came from somewhere else in the state. They always referred to it as *The* College.

BEATTIE: Did you live in the state at all after high school?

STILL: I was office boy in the towel mill, Fairfax Towels. There wasn't anything else to do.

BEATTIE: This was in Alabama?

STILL: In Fairfax, Alabama, where I went to high school.

BEATTIE: How long did you work there?

STILL: Oh, just that summer. But I was home one summer and couldn't go back to school; I needed the money. They gave me a job and didn't give me anything to do. Nobody pointed out anything. What I did, I learned the styles of towels, numbers and names, and I found out what was happening, and went and sat down in all the offices and saw what was going on. That's what they wanted me to do. But I knew it wasn't for me. And I couldn't go back to school. I left. It was the Depression, and I couldn't get any job with nobody. I went to Texas. I picked cotton. I rode the rails. I went to Atlanta, Sears and Roebuck. I went through Rome, Georgia, tried to get a job with the ironworks.

On the roads there were people everywhere. How I made it, how I got along, I don't know. The thing about it is, I don't remember, except one time, in which I kind of got downhearted. That was in Rome, Georgia. I remember one time and I remember what I wanted to do about it, but I didn't. Now, don't get me wrong, I'm very optimistic. I'm not self-destructive.

BEATTIE: What year did you go to college?

STILL: I went in the fall of '24. I had sixty dollars. I went to Lincoln Memorial University, and that's all the money they ever got out of me. And when I graduated, say five years later—I was out a year—they owed me seventy-five.

BEATTIE: How did that happen?

STILL: I worked everything. I had nothing. This was Depression, and there was no money, nobody could do anything for me. And that meant work scholarships; everybody worked. It was sort of a Berea situation. I worked in a rock quarry the first year. Eventually, I was a janitor. Had all kinds of jobs. My grades were poor the first year because I was so tired. You went to school in the morning, worked in a rock quarry in the afternoon. At nine o'clock at night in the library, I was the janitor, and I swept the library and scrubbed up the tables and emptied the wastebaskets. I was too tired to sleep, to study. I wanted to sleep.

But after the first year, when I was out of the rock quarry, my grades picked up. I had a double major, English and history. I stayed an extra year. I graduated in 1929.

The college had a magazine called the *Lincoln Herald,* which they still have, a college publication in which the doings of the college were recorded, and you'd send it out to donors and people like that, to alumni. Nowadays it's mostly for alumni notice.

Anyhow, I had a good teacher in classical literature there. I had a wonderful teacher in biology and a good history teacher. Aside from that, it was a lost cause. But I will tell you, I needed that place. You see, my high school training wasn't what it ought to be. I think maybe they were doing remedial work, in a way. But what Lincoln Memorial did for me was the library. I discovered the publishing world, all these magazines, and I discovered, no thanks to any teachers, the writer Thomas Hardy.

BEATTIE: So, you spent a lot of time in the library on your own?

STILL: I lived there. I just went mad; I didn't know what to read first. I discovered the *Atlantic Monthly,* and I knew it was a most prestigious publication. I decided I was going to write for it. And while in school there, I reckon my sophomore year, there was a magazine there called *American Speech.* It's a scholarly study of language. Still going. I wrote two articles for them, and I was a sophomore, and they published it. In time, H. L. Mencken wrote his *American Language,* and he used both those articles, and gave me credit. I have a copy of the one volume. James A. Still, you find me in the index.

BEATTIE: What were your articles about?

STILL: One was on Christian names in the mountains, the Cumberlands, and then the other was on place names.

Then I had nothing. Not a dime, nothing. The school was in trouble financially, and we students had a very spartan living. We ate everything off the table every day. The school had a marvelous apple orchard, and plenty of walnut trees. They have a great acreage there, or did. It's, to my notion, the most beautiful natural campus in America, and I've seen an awful lot of them. Notice I said natural campus.

BEATTIE: What happened after college? What did you do as soon as you were graduated?

STILL: I began to write little things for Sunday school magazines, and I'd get two dollars, three dollars. I don't know how many articles there were. Even later, after I came here [Hindman, Kentucky], I wrote things for the Sunday school magazines for adults, because my sister subscribed to them. I wanted her to see something I'd written. I remember I wrote an article about the Hindman Settlement.

BEATTIE: Had you grown up going to a particular church that these magazines related to, a particular denomination?

STILL: My father's people were Missionary Baptists, attended the Rock Springs Church, where all my people are buried going back in time. The old cemetery. I've got a book that lists all of the graves in the county. There they are, lined up. My mother's people are Primitive Baptists, and they attended a church about a mile beyond. Each met once a month, and we attended both of them. Grandpa Lindsey was an elder in the Primitive Baptist Church.

I went to Sunday school all those years. I can remember the preacher once, in the church at Fairfax, heard that I was going away to college, and before the service he came and sat down beside me and told me to stay at home and do something for my parents. Well, anyway, I did go. Grandpa Lindsey thought I shouldn't be running off, thought I should be working, because that's what children were supposed to do. But before he died, he sent me word he'd changed his mind, I'm glad to say.

BEATTIE: So, after college you were writing these articles. Where were you living at the time?

STILL: I went to Lincoln Memorial, then I went to Vanderbilt University. Actually, I'd won all these awards. There were six essay awards available, different judges.

BEATTIE: At Lincoln Memorial.

STILL: Yes. I entered five writing contests and I won all five of them. Well, there was a man who gave work scholarships to students. Also, when he used to visit there—of course, I didn't meet him or anything like that—he noticed we were pretty poorly dressed, so he left money to buy a suit for about a dozen of us. They cost about fifteen dollars then, and somebody measured us up on campus for suits. I went to the librarian who was in charge of this and I told her I wanted to write him a letter and thank him. She said, "He doesn't want any communication." He was a man who gave things to Berea and other places. He was a man about eighty years old, a philanthropist. But I said, "Could I just write him a letter and you send it to him?" "Yes, all right."

Well, he got this letter, so this is probably the first letter he'd ever permitted, and the next time he came down, he got acquainted with me and others he was helping. He had us over at Middlesboro, Kentucky, to a luncheon, kind of got acquainted with us. When I graduated, I sent him an invitation. He had never been invited. He came down and spent the whole week, went to the class day and everything, and then I won all these awards. They dedicated the Duke Hall of Citizenship. Benjamin Duke of Duke Power Company had given the money for this building they still use, a big auditorium and classrooms and so on. He was actually on his deathbed, he was ill, but his wife and daughter came to the dedication. Well, this little magazine I spoke of, *Lincoln Herald*, spoke about my winning all these awards, and he read it, and he wrote them and told them that he would send me through graduate school at Duke University, all expenses paid. He sent two hundred dollars to one teacher to bring me to Duke. So, I went and had my subject already picked out for a thesis, and Duke was just a building. They'd taken over Trinity College, which they still use there.

BEATTIE: Those prizes you'd won, were they in English?

STILL: They were just for essays. One was the gold medal given in all the colleges in Tennessee called the Rush Strong Medal for Truth, an essay on the value of truth. Solid gold. I always called it my liar's license.

Well, then this man arranged it so I'd have this scholarship. I was going, and then this other fellow said he would send me to graduate school anywhere in the South. I went to Duke, and I wasn't favorably impressed. It was just a building, you know. They hadn't used that new campus. But anyway, I knew about Vanderbilt, so I went to Vanderbilt instead.

And there [at Vanderbilt University] were the members of the southern literary movement Fugitives, and this is what happened. I had John Donald Wade in American literature, and the first week or so in the class, we students didn't know each other. We came from California, Yale, all over, all graduates. The Fugitives were our teachers. Wade said he wanted to find out just where we stood in American literature before he started class, so he gave us all a card, and we numbered one through twenty on each, ten on each side. He read one sentence from the writings of authors from the beginning of the Civil War period to that day. No, it went back before that, because they had Emerson and Thoreau and Longfellow and whoever. He told us that he did this every year, and nobody'd ever passed it yet, not to be concerned. Nobody did except me, and I made a perfect score. Well, I was totally unknown when I went in that classroom. When I came out, I was famous. It's partly a fluke that I got them all, but that tells you what that library did for me.

BEATTIE: So it was your own self-education, you think, as much as anything else that caused you to know so much?

STILL: Yes. I was a mad man in that library. I wanted to know. And I do today; I still want to know.

BEATTIE: What other Fugitives did you have as professors?

STILL: Well, John Crowe Ransom was there. There were others there that I didn't have. Robert Penn Warren was at Oxford at that time. Another one was in Sewanee teaching, I think. He came back and read to us all. But I had those two. You see, they read their chapters from *I'll Take My Stand,* which was published the next fall, to us. If you read them singly, you're not impressed with them.

I did my thesis under Walter Clyde Curry, the Chaucer scholar, who wrote the book called *Chaucer and the Mediaeval Sciences,* which was a textbook for years. I wrote on the function of dreams and visions in the Middle English romances, which meant that I had to learn to read Middle English, which I did. There are a-hundred-and-six volumes of the Early English Text Society I had to peruse. I wrote this thesis and really should have thought about sending it to Freud, who was alive in those days. I wish I had. It was right in his line of thinking.

BEATTIE: How much Freud had you read before writing your thesis?

STILL: I just knew he existed, that's all. Anyway, we were just learning what psychiatry was. I also made a dream book out of it, too. It's kind of an appendix. I don't know how I came on that subject. But Curry was the first true scholar I ever had, and some people'd say he was cruel and demanding. I needed him, let's put it that way.

BEATTIE: For the discipline of scholarship?

STILL: I did. I got it there. Ransom was a great teacher and has been noted; he's in a book called *Ten Great Professors.* But Walter Clyde Curry . . . the thing is, Chaucer is the only author that I feel I sort of identify with, to this day.

I graduated then in 1931, and here was this scholarship to the University of Illinois. There were no jobs, so I went there. And this philanthropist, up until then, as I understand it, had never given a scholarship, except a general one, like a work scholarship. He had never given a specific scholarship to a man. He only gave them to girls with the idea that they would be school teachers. But the librarian there got him to give it to me.

I went to the University of Illinois and got a degree in one year, a degree in library science. I never had the slightest desire, inclination, to go for a doctor's degree. I didn't even think about it, never. My history professor at Vanderbilt, after I had turned in a paper on Gustavus Adolphus, I remember he called me up the day after he read it. He suggested that I come and work on a doctorate in history, and he would be my advisor. But I didn't have the slightest interest in getting my doctor's degree.

BEATTIE: At that time, did you think you were going to spend your life as a librarian?

STILL: Who knows? I had taken enough courses, thinking I might have to teach school, to qualify to teach school. I had education courses, which, I'm sad to say, were a waste of my time and everybody else's time. They taught methods, no content. Or little content. Illinois, though, was very strenuous.

BEATTIE: In what way?

STILL: It was never hard, the work, but there was too much of it. A good many students already had master's degrees, you see, and nearly everybody had had some training, had worked in a library.

BEATTIE: Was this a second master's [for you]?

STILL: No. It was a B.S., and I found it very tedious, cataloging and so on. But I loved reference, I'd have made a good reference librarian.

If I had to go again, I'd probably be a biology student, or a botanist or something. That's a field I never gave up. I'm right into that even now. I'm learning still. I'm still reading and so on. I'm still going at that, because I'm just curious. I have these wonderful conversations here at the Hindman Settlement School with the extension director who lives on campus. He knows so many things I want to know. And I take a magazine called *Science News*. It's a weekly for people like me with very weak backgrounds in chemistry and physics and astrophysics and medicine and behavioral sciences and so on, and it also gives a list of the new books in the fields that you never see anywhere else. So, if you read that over thirty years, you pick up considerable knowledge and awareness of the earth. Everything from the weather to geology, and so on.

BEATTIE: All that goes into being a writer.

STILL: Well, I always say anything somehow comes to bear on what you're doing. I'm not an educated person. I don't like the word *educated*. That's an arrival, and education is a trip, it's a journey. You never really arrive, you know; you're on your way.

BEATTIE: Education doesn't end when the degree ends.

STILL: Yes. And to this day, including last night, at midnight, I was reading a history of Sears and Roebuck from the beginning. I once tried to get a job with them. Anyway, but I just had to turn the light out I don't know how many times. Reading wakes me up. I keep four or five books going at a time. I just go from one to the other. They're mostly nonfiction, except these studies I've been doing. One of the French writers, Daudet—I love Daudet, Alphonse Daudet, I just love him. I read him in French first when I was studying French. I had five years of him. I used to read French. But it's gone awful rusty now, and I have to read translations. But he survives translations. As a person, I liked him. Henry James said he knew Daudet and Turgenev, and he kept saying several times in his biography that he loved them both. I know what he meant. He was ideal. He was exactly the kind of person that I would like to be.

BEATTIE: What is it about him that attracts you?

STILL: There's no way to tell. His little book called *Letters from My Mill,* which overnight made him famous, this was during the era of Napoleon the Third, he wrote a book of poems first and got the attention of the Empress Eugenie. The first part of that is a book called *La Petite Chous.* I noted in 1920 Little, Brown published all of his works in translation. They have disappeared from the earth, almost. I sent out a search for *La Petite Chous.* It's easily available in any library in France, but not in translation. They found one, a copy in the Anderson, Indiana, public library, and it's on its last legs, I assure you. I had to patch it as I read it. It was one of the great reading experiences. I wish I had read it years ago. This was just a year or two ago. The first half of that book is a masterpiece. He wrote it before he went to Paris. The last half he wrote later. It's excellent.

I'll jump ahead a little bit to say the greatest novel ever written by a Kentuckian about Kentucky is *The Time of Man* by Elizabeth Madox Roberts. The first half of that book is a masterpiece. The rest of it is excellent. But that was a slacking off. She wasn't able to sustain it all the way through. No matter. It's a great book. I have a few little quarrels with it.

You see, I think there are two kinds of novels. One is a told story, the author's telling. You know, this man is writing this story. You may just sort of forget it or lose it. He's there at your arm. That's one novel. The ones I like to read are those where there are no authors there; you can imagine it existing in nature. I like to think *River of Earth* is one that exists in nature. James Still is not there and never has been.

BEATTIE: Which is why the style, to you, is something that should be irrelevant.

STILL: It's not irrelevant; it's itself. You know, I have no idea whether I can look at myself. I don't remember writing much of it. It should be timeless. It doesn't date. Timelessness is what saves it. I wish some publisher would let me choose some books that I think they ought to bring into print again.

BEATTIE: What happened after graduate school, then? Where did you go after that?

STILL: I came back in June; I stopped in Nashville. There was a student there that I'd gone to school with, John West. He was in the school of religion; he was going to be a preacher. He was working, still going to school, and he was working at the Settlement House. I went out there and he was not there, but expected. I remember sitting there quite a while and he didn't come, and I remember there was a big clock up there and I thought, "I'm going to wait ten minutes, and if he doesn't come, I'll leave," and he came within that time. Otherwise, I wouldn't be sitting here.

Well, he was coming here to start a vacation Bible school—he and his wife—and he wanted me to come out with him. His brother-in-law was from here in Rockcastle County, and we were to establish three Boy Scout troops and three baseball teams, which we did. We came and we camped and played all summer long. We had nothing to do with vacation Bible school itself. At the end of that time the librarian here left, and they needed a librarian, so they hired me, but they couldn't pay me anything. They couldn't pay anybody. They had an endowment as now, but it wasn't paying off, and they were having a hard time, feeding the students here and keeping them. So I worked three years with no pay. Then, times had gotten better, but don't ask me what I did in summer. There was no work.

BEATTIE: Did you stay here, though?

STILL: No. I figured that out. Having nothing, not a dime, after the fourth year, I was going to leave, and some donor offered to give them fifteen dollars a month to pay me, so that I got for nine months, fifteen dollars a month. Then there was the summer with nothing, and then it got a little better, and I was paid a little bit more. But after six years— I averaged it up once—I had averaged six cents a day, for six years. Toward the end of that I began to write little verses and poems. I was not alone here; there were a number of teachers. For the most part, though, the women teachers were from wealthy—mainly, Mount Holyoke, Smith—colleges and other such institutions, and they were generally people who were doing voluntary work. I think I was the only one who wasn't getting anything at all. They did pay the woodworking man some after he was married, they paid the gardener, they paid the workers coming in, the hired people here. They paid partly the principal. But then I had a story or two in the *Atlantic*.

BEATTIE: That you wrote while you were living here?

STILL: Yes. I started at twenty-six years old, and one day I sat down, I had written some poems, and I sent them to the *Atlantic*. Eventually, they took one. After that the editor always looked at my stuff, and then he published about two stories.

BEATTIE: So really, you started at the top in publishing.

STILL: That's what I intended to do. Back at Lincoln Memorial, in college days, it was a school where they say only missionary barrels came, you know, clothes and things like this. But they also took old books and magazines and back numbers, years of them, and they used to get back numbers of say, the *Atlantic*. I was supposed to check the files for missing numbers, and burn the rest. But I saved them. I have years of *Atlantic*. I took them home, and I spent the summer reading them. I intended to write for the *Atlantic*. It can be said if I learned the art of conversation, I learned it from the *Atlantic*, from the best writers of America and England of that day. That made all the difference. Anyway, I then published three poems and ten stories over the years. Then Viking published a book of poems from me, called *Hounds on the Mountain*. Beautifully made book. In fact, it won a graphic arts award for bookmaking that year.

BEATTIE: What year was that published?

STILL: 1937. It's a letterpress book. If you ever see it, you can open it; it stays open, you know. Beautiful paper. An edition of seven-hundred-and-fifty copies, none were autographed. After then, they asked, didn't I have a novel? Well, yes, I did, I was writing one. "Well, let us see some of it." I sent them the first section and the last section. I hadn't written the middle. And they sent a contract.

BEATTIE: Viking.

STILL: Yes. Later, I asked my editor, Marshall Best, who was also at the same time the editor of Elizabeth Madox Roberts, and who was at the same time riding herd on John Steinbeck, but wasn't his direct editor . . . Well, I had these marvelous letters from him, as I think anybody writing for him would. At least twice he sent a story back and said he was sorry, there's something about it, you know. They liked it and all like that, but in each case I looked at it, and looked at the ending, made a few minor changes, and sent it back. A story called "The Run for the Elbertas," which is very long, as long as most magazines want to publish, while I was writing it, somehow or other *Esquire* learned that I had this long story, and they wrote and said they would like to look at it, no matter how long it was. But already, at that time, the *Atlantic* accepted it. They sent it back to me and asked me to shorten it.

They said if I couldn't, then they would try to do it. Well, what I did, I added some sentences to it. I thought we should know, specifically, how old this boy was, in two, three little lines. So they published it as it was. They couldn't do anything, either. I met, several years ago, the poetry editor of the *Atlantic,* at the University of Kentucky, and he said to me, "We remember the day 'The Run for the Elbertas' arrived at the *Atlantic.*"

They gave me four hundred dollars for that story, which was a lot in those days. Then, when it was set up in galleys, he sent another hundred dollars, saying they liked it even better than when it was submitted. Behind every little story you write, there's something behind it somewhere, the little adventure on my part. I read about all these unhappy authors, you know, struggling. I think the one thing that saved me was, I never had unrealistic expectations. If something came back, well, I already knew where it was going next.

BEATTIE: It sounds as though when you started sending out manuscripts, you started with a positive attitude that this was where you were going to send it, it was what would be accepted, and it was.

STILL: Listen, anything literate can be published.

BEATTIE: I mean published in good places, reputable places. Places that set the standard instead of ignoring it.

STILL: Most look at current magazines and so on for that. You know, I look for the classics. People have some idea I just whittled. That isn't the way I work. The way I work, if you call it work, is I play, really. A story takes on a life of it's own, after a while. Until that time, you're not getting anywhere with it until it's working on itself. In the meantime, I'm enjoying writing it, playing with it. I know where I'm going. I don't have a story otherwise, do I? I don't know how I'm going to get there. So, I can write the first paragraph and I play with it a while, and play with it. Type it over and just play. It's like stirring concrete. Ideally, I think every line of prose ought to have the values of a line of poetry. I'm not talking about poetry, actually, but anyway, it should have the longevity, it should have the essence, in every line. Most of my stories start going from the first word. Any single line that impedes that flow should come out, no matter what it is. You drive toward the end.

BEATTIE: Some writers think that with prose, especially novels, or with longer prose work, that more irrelevancies can be included because of the space you have to work in. It sounds as though you don't believe that.

STILL: Well, with a novel, you've got more elbow room. The novel's a lot more fun to write, because you can knock around and do a lot of things with a novel. Every sentence must belong there, or it shouldn't be there. Just look at the great writers, every one of them. They're going somewhere. Every sentence is advancing, almost unbeknownst to the writer.

BEATTIE: You mentioned that you know from the beginning, before you start a story or a novel, what the end is going to be.

STILL: Well, I don't know about the ending. I never just say I'm going to write a story or something. It just grows in my head, I just think about it a while. I just keep playing with the idea until it gets imprinted, and I write something down. I say you've got to start somewhere, and I just start right quick and dash off that paragraph then play with it. If I get stuck, I like to go right to the end then and—this is no method, I want you to know. I just do it every time and catch off that last one.

BEATTIE: So, the concept you might have at the beginning could change by the time you play with it.

STILL: Oh, yes. They're all surprises, every sentence. Every paragraph surprises me, otherwise what fun would it be writing it? When I get through, if I feel I've done something, it's a feeling that I can't get from anywhere else. Even when it's published, usually by the time it's published, I don't feel anything. The book is on its own, nothing to do with me anymore.

BEATTIE: It's the creativity that causes the pride and the sense of accomplishment, you're saying?

STILL: I like to think of a story in this way, till you touch a nerve somewhere, you know? Make a contact someway. Till I jump myself, almost. No, I just play my way through. If you get stuck on the way, go to the last paragraph and play with it. Eventually, I can get it almost to work anywhere, and I did. Then, of course, when I get to that point, I usually throw it out. Then revisions: I don't know what you are going to revise for; I've already done it. When I get through, I'm through.

BEATTIE: So you revise as you write.

STILL: I play with it. I play with it until it comes true, till I believe it myself and the characters are talking to me.

BEATTIE: But do you find it difficult to move on in the story until the part that you've already worked on comes true?

STILL: No, I can hardly wait, because in the meantime, another part of my mind is already doing . . .

BEATTIE: So you can focus on several things at once.

STILL: Oh, sure. Everybody does. You are every person in that story, you are simultaneously one person and another. You're in their body-skins. You know everything about them, everything. Every character has no secrets.

BEATTIE: Before you start writing do your characters reveal themselves, or do they do so as you write?

STILL: Eventually you know everything about them.

BEATTIE: Eventually. So, that could be while you're writing.

STILL: Yes. A story makes itself as it goes. Frost said it very well; with a poem it's like ice in a skillet. It grows on its melting. That's what he said. It's very well stated. Sometimes I've been asked, a student'll say, "How do you write a poem?" Well, what can you say? But I finally found the answer to that.

BEATTIE: Tell me.

STILL: The first time I related this was in the Humana Building at Louisville. I had never been in that magnificent structure, and there were several of us who were going to do a little talking. They got around to me, and I said, "First, I can't help remarking what an extraordinary room this is. I never would imagine such a wonderful place. I like it in here." I said, "Also, there is only one other structure that's more beautiful than this building, and," I said, "it's my log house back in Knott County." Then I said, "I'm sometimes asked how do you write a poem, and not just by children, either." Well, I found out. Some years ago, Eleanor Clark, who is Mrs. Robert Penn Warren, I knew her. In fact, I knew her before Robert Penn did. Up at Saratoga Springs, New York. She spent a good part of her life in Italy and so on, was very mature, just a marvelous . . . Has a book about oysters or something, I can't think of the title. She told me what to do if you were attacked by an octopus, and were all wrapped in these many arms. There is just one thing you can do. What you do is you poke your hand in his mouth and get a handful of something and turn it wrong-side out. And that's how you write a poem. The attack has to be there. You can't escape that that poem has got you there. You've got to do something about it. How can you get rid of it? The subject has to be turned wrong-side out to see the inside of it. A great many poems are written about the tentacles drawing circles. The insides of the octopus is what you're going to write. Anyway, the interior of a poem has to be exposed. That's how you write a poem.

BEATTIE: I think that's a great answer. Did you get your first contract with Viking on the strength of your poems in the *Atlantic*?

STILL: Yes. And other places—poetry in the *New Republic,* the *Nation*—places like that.

BEATTIE: You didn't have an agent?

STILL: No, I didn't have an agent for a long time. Agents don't handle people who can't make them money, you know. There wasn't any money with me.

BEATTIE: You went directly to Viking with your manuscript, then?

STILL: Well, a friend of the founder of Viking, connected me with Viking Press.

BEATTIE: The first novel of yours that they published was *River of Earth.*

STILL: 1940.

BEATTIE: When did your military service come into play? Was that before this?

STILL: After, at the beginning of World War II.

BEATTIE: You were drafted, weren't you?

STILL: Yes. I knew I was going to be drafted. I was older for a soldier; I was about thirty. The average soldier was about twenty, twenty-one years old, in my outfit. I was the oldest man in my outfit except the colonel, and I wouldn't have been drafted, except for the politics. I didn't have any voters here, you know what I mean, no family here. Parents did everything in the world to keep their boys out of the army, and I had nobody to do this for me. In fact, I didn't want anybody to try.

I was in Florida when the superintendent of schools, a friend here, learned that I was going to be drafted from his brother-in-law, and he told me I'd better come back, and I did. But when I got back here, he'd gone over there and talked to his brother-in-law and said, "This man, you know, his age, you shouldn't be drafting this man." He got me off. But when I learned that, I went over there and told him that I didn't want anybody taking my place.

BEATTIE: So you wanted to go.

STILL: No, I didn't particularly want to go. I didn't want anybody taking my place. He asked me, "You really want to go?" I said, "Yes, I do. I don't want anybody taking my place." Well, there was a woman that's sitting in there and she's trying to get her son off. I remember what she said; it's in the book. She said, "Let them that want to go go, and them's that want to stay stay." I remember someone said, "Well, we couldn't fight much of a war if we did that." So I went.

BEATTIE: At the time when you were drafted, where were you? You say you were in Florida.

STILL: You see, I nearly froze over here. I spent two winters over here and nearly froze in that, so when I sold a story to the *Saturday Evening Post,* I lived off them several years. I just sold them one story a year. After then I went to Florida, and that's what I was doing in Florida.

Then the army, all those years, it seems like a blip on the screen now, but I shipped out of here and went to Fort Thomas, and after a week there, we shipped down to San Antonio. There was a train-load of us. It was March, cold. Got off the train in New Orleans, and they took us in trucks into the Duncan Field, which is part of the big field complex, Lackland Air Base. They left us in the street to freeze all night, the rest of the night. I remember how cold it was. Next morning, they came, they called the roll, they called two names of these couple of thousand of us. One was mine and one was another fellow. They told me to report to a certain headquarters, which I did.

We went to the first sergeants of the headquarters squadron. He was an old Irishman, an old retread from World War I. He was a regular soldier; hard-drinking, red-faced, gambling, mean as a snake. He could barely read and write, and he wasn't going to have anybody in there had more education than he had. So, he refused me. He sent me to the main headquarters, where I should have been in the first place.

Well, as soon as I got there, the sergeant-major was an old retread, First World War, and he was going to be discharged, retired, but they had retained him. He'd belonged to the Book-of-the-Month Club, and he knew about me. My book was in the catalog, and he remembered that. He told me to sit there by him and he said, "You're going to have this job someday; see what's going on." I'll never forget that headquarters. All these men were torn from their homes. It was an unhappy place, and there was cursing, language I'd never heard. Nobody ever said anything civil or decent. Sergeant Jacobs, this first staff sergeant-major, had me sitting there by him, and I had contracted from my niece chicken pox. But I didn't tell anybody that I was sick, and I thought I was going to fall off that bench. Another thing was, as a private, I would have to line up in a long line, and it would take a long time for me to get in, get something to eat, and then get back to the office. So what he did, he immediately made me a private first-class, got a stripe so I could be in another line, in another dining room where it couldn't take so long. But in time I wasn't eating lunch, because about everything I ate came up.

I got acquainted with myself. I really didn't know myself till I got in the army. There are things I won't do and nobody's going to push me around. I didn't know that. I wouldn't take anything off anybody.

BEATTIE: How many years were you in the army?

STILL: Three-and-a-half. I had some unbelievable exploits.

BEATTIE: Have you ever written them down?

STILL: No.

BEATTIE: You think you will?

STILL: I don't know. I don't think so.

BEATTIE: What happened when you returned from the army, what did you do?

STILL: It was rough. It was bad. I came home and I couldn't keep food in my stomach. I'd had malaria twice, almost died once. I'd had the dysentery that kills you. I got it in Ethiopia, in Eritrea, is where I got it. I ate something there I wasn't supposed to eat. And I'll never forget that. Terrible. Anyway, I was just skin and bones, really.

BEATTIE: What did you do career-wise when you returned from the war?

STILL: What did I do? I didn't do anything for a year. I sat in that door over there by the creek, day by day. I remember I was having trouble keeping food down, and I wasn't going to the Veterans Hospital, so I went to Lexington Clinic. Dr. Kirkpatrick was there. He became a friend. He knew about me; he'd read my things. He talked to me, and then they had about a day to go through everything, heart and everything. When I came back to him he told me that, "There's nothing physically wrong with you; you're just like an old clock, you've been wound up too tight. You're going to have to wind down. How are you spending your days?" So, I told him. He told me, "Whether you want to or not, you get out and go where people are, where things are doing." And I did.

BEATTIE: Is there a book that you would like to have written and haven't yet?

STILL: No, there isn't. I like the old, great ones.

BEATTIE: Jim Wayne Miller has observed that in your poems, novels, and short stories, your characters, he says, "journey out into the world like Jack, get their barrel full, and return gladly home." Are your characters returning to something innately Appalachian, do you think, or do you think most people want to return to their place of origin, wherever that may be?

STILL: We're all homing pigeons, you know; I think we all are. And although I live here, and will never live anywhere else, I still feel like homing to a place that doesn't exist anymore, really.

I remember the writer Johnny Cheever saying toward the end of his life—I didn't know him, but I used to see him at Yaddo—he said, on his life, when he was dying, "I want to go home, but I don't know where home is."

BEATTIE: The quest, the constant seeking, do you think that's something we all do?

STILL: It's seeking, but there is a spot, a place. It's not just the seeking. There was a place, you know. I feel that more as I get older. And I would go. If it was there, I would go. But the trouble is, I go there and I can't bear it for more than two days. Too much nostalgia, it's just too much.

BEATTIE: You're talking about a literal place.

STILL: Literally, I can't bear it.

BEATTIE: Where is that?

STILL: In Alabama where I was born. I lived a very different life from this, in a sense, which I wish I could write about.

BEATTIE: In your poem, "River of Earth," you speak of "the thing laid open, the hills translated." You've translated the hills as well as or better than anybody, but is there anything about Appalachia that you believe remains untranslatable?

STILL: Of course. How do people describe the Great Plains? I have all these books, and everybody's trying it. They never quite make it. Nobody quite makes it. I used to be a Civil War buff. I still occasionally read a book. I mean, I have read on the Civil War, several biographies of Robert E. Lee, but nobody has ever made him come alive to me. He's a paragon. You simply cannot. Nobody's been able to do it for me. The nearest to it was Robert [Charles B.] Flood's book, *The Last Years of Robert E. Lee* [*Lee—The Last Years*]. He came as near as anybody is ever going to do it, I think, but not quite. When I read Leon Edel's *Henry James,* I feel like I know him now. He became a human being.

I recall reading in the *New York Times* some time ago, there was an actress, I didn't know her name, but I should have known maybe, she was ninety-eight, she was quite old. They gave her a reception at the Waldorf Astoria Hotel, I believe, a small group of the famous actors of this day, and some they talked to a little afterwards and they said, "What would be your advice for, let's say, a young lady who had it in her heart to be an actress, who had come to New York and went to acting school, and really means it?" She said, "Go home. Go home and live a normal life." Your chance of succeeding in this business is practically minuscule, nil.

BEATTIE: Would that be your advice to writers?

STILL: I would say in the first place, "Don't write. But if you can't help it, maybe, all right, go ahead and do it." I don't find many people willing to work.

BEATTIE: Do you think that's a drive that comes from within? Don't you think that writers, real writers, know that that's what they are?

STILL: I don't think they have any choice. I understand there are preachers who, in a sense, would rather not be preachers, that they felt called or something. I don't feel called. But I don't know why that answers something that I have a need to do, and why I get something out of it that I can't explain to anybody. I never particularly admired writers. I mean, I know a lot of them in a way, and I rather liked them and so on, but the lives of writers never interested me, particularly. They always seemed to me so unhappy and tragic, and so far as the world'll let me, I'm pretty optimistic. I've been happy with it. I didn't, as I've said, have unrealistic expectations. But maybe I did, I sent work to the *Atlantic*; I started there.

BEATTIE: Well, I don't think it's unrealistic if that became a reality. Your writing got published.

STILL: But then there are a lot of good surprises in the world. There is something called, I'm sure, networking that anybody . . . you can hardly go it alone. Somebody, for example in my case, got two Guggenheims for me. There has to be somebody. But then you've got to have what it takes, otherwise it doesn't do any good. You've got to be ready. Sure, there's something called damn fool luck; apparently I had what the *Atlantic* could use.

BEATTIE: Doesn't sound to me like luck; it sounds like you had the talent and you knew what you wanted.

STILL: No, it wasn't luck, is what I'm trying to say. It's something. But even so, then what would have happened if I hadn't, some way through this professor who introduced me to the publisher, for example, who asked me if I had a manuscript . . . You know all these little . . . I can see many, many things.

Well, when the American Academy of Arts and Letters gave me the Peabody Award, I learned later that there was a committee of three people and one was a famous southern writer who died recently. He insisted that I get it. I never had any connection with him whatsoever, wouldn't have imagined he'd ever read anything of mine. He wouldn't give up. He insisted that I get it, so that finally the others just said okay. They gave it to me. They each had their own candidate and was putting him forward. One of the others agreed with him, so I got it.

BEATTIE: Is there anything else that you would like to mention about yourself?

STILL: No, I think I've said too much already. I believe I've told you more than anybody.

August 2, 1991

BOOKS BY JAMES STILL

Hounds on the Mountain. New York: Viking, 1937.

River of Earth. New York: Viking, 1940.

On Troublesome Creek. New York: Viking, 1941.

Way Down Yonder on Troublesome Creek: Appalachian Riddles and Rusties. New York: Putnam, 1974.

The Wolfpen Rusties: Appalachian Riddles and Gee-Haw Whimmy-Diddles. New York: Putnam, 1975.

Pattern of a Man and Other Stories. Lexington, Ky.: Gnomon, 1976.

Sporty Creek: A Novel about an Appalachian Boyhood. New York: Putnam, 1977.

Jack and the Wonder Beans. New York: Putnam, 1977.

The Run for the Elbertas. Lexington: University Press of Kentucky, 1980.

River of Earth: The Poem and Other Poems. Lexington, Ky.: King Library Press, 1982-83.

The Wolfpen Poems. Berea, Ky.: Berea College Press, 1986.

The Wolfpen Notebooks. Lexington: University Press of Kentucky, 1991.

Index

creativity, 29, 76-77; in childhood, 314-15; and
circumstance, 199; effects of judgment on, 168;
essence of, 128; and formal education, 315; as
genetic ability, 271, 351-52; as gift, 271, 352;
and lack of completeness, 128-29; nature of,
13, 54, 76, 147, 168, 183-84, 199, 217, 236,
254, 315, 351-52; teaching, 178
Crescent Hill Baptist Church (Louisville), 122
Crescent Hill Library (Louisville), 41
criticism: constructive, 147; course, 226; editorial,
93; from nonwriters, 166
Crockett, Davy, 336
cruelty of children, 165
Cuban Revolution, 66
Cuba (Ky.) School, 190
cultural activities, community, 69
culture shock, 139, 193
Curry, Walter Clyde, 363; *Chaucer and the
Mediaeval Sciences,* 363
Curtin, John Robert, 128
Cyclopedia of Universal Knowledge, 360
cynicism, 165

Daly, Tyne, 292
Danforth Fellowship, 45, 47
Dartmouth College, 47, 50-51
Darwin, Charles: *Origin of Species,* 322
Daudet, Alphonse, 364-65; *La Petite Chous,* 365;
Letters from My Mill, 365
Davidson, Donald, 248
Davidson, William, 63
Dayton Daily News, 192
deadlines, 52, 169, 211, 250, 354
death: as essential nature of things, 109; of father,
39; life comes from, 112; of lover, 145; of
mother, 49, 86-87; of son, 49-50
Deep South, 65, 67
Democratic Party, 40, 65
DePauw University, 155
Depression, 24, 59, 360-61
desire to write, 29, 35
dialect, writing, 56
dialogue, creating, 135
diaries, 129, 154, 203, 205, 312
Dickens, Charles, 273-74; *David Copperfield,* 273
Dickey, Frank, 33
Dickey, James, 123; *Deliverance,* 256
Dickinson, Emily, 278
Dillon, John, 69
Directory of Little Magazines and Small Presses, 250
Disciples of Christ, 175
discipline, 108, 168, 276; of scholarship, 363
Disney, Walt, 28
dissertations, 67, 120-21, 159, 177, 193-94, 251,
267; creative, 178, 268
divorce, 87, 90, 105, 208-9, 229-30, 347
Dominican nuns, as teachers, 344
Donadio, Candida, 102
Dorris, Abel, 47-50, 53
Dorris, Asa, 50

Dorris, Jim Leonard, 39
Dorris, Madeline, 50
Dorris, Michael, 39-57; adoption of children, 47-
48, 51; and anthropology, 41; childhood, 39,
41; courtship and marriage, 50-51; on
creativity, 54; death of father, 39; death of son,
50; education, 40, 43-45, 47; and Erdrich, 42-
44, 48, 50-51, 53, 55-56; extended family, 39-
40; and Fetal Alcohol Syndrome, 42, 48-49;
mixed-blood background, 45; and Native
Americans, 39, 43, 45-47, 50, 52-53, 57; on
other authors, 41,43-44; on reading, 46; on
sense of place, 53-54; on woman's point of
view, 55; on writing, 41-42, 52-57
—works: *The Broken Cord,* 41-42, 47, 49-50, 56;
The Crown of Columbus, 46, 48, 53, 57;
"Groom Service," 52; *Morning Girl,* 43, 52;
New Native American Novel in Progress, 55; *A
Yellow Raft in Blue Water,* 55, 57
Dorris, Mary Bridget Burkhardt, 39
Dorris, Pallas, 50
Dorris, Persia, 50
Dorris, Sava, 48, 50
draft, military, 66, 226-27, 369
Driskell, Dennis Halman, 59
Driskell, Laura, 64
Driskell, Leon, 59-79; childhood, 59-60; on civil
rights, 65, 67; on creativity, 76-78; extended
family, 59-61; marriage, 64; military service,
64, 66; on other authors, 63, 68, 70, 72, 74-78;
on sense of place, 72; on stereotypes, 75; and
Sue Driskell, 64, 66, 71, 73, 77-78; on
teaching, 67-70; and University of Georgia, 59-
62; and University of Louisville, 63, 67-68; on
writing, 61-63, 66, 71
—works: "Before Dinnger," 78; "The Blue You
Thought in Kentucky," 75; "Bright Star," 78;
"Dun-Roving," 75; *A Gift of Time,* 72; "He
Heard the Nickel Go Down," 74; "Hester's
Keep," 72; "The Hollow," 76; "Hoodwinked,"
73; "The Note," 72; "The Other," 72; *Passing
Through,* 74-76, 78; "Signing across the Dark,"
78; "To Flannery O'Connor, 1925-1964," 78;
"To Sue," 77
Driskell, Mae Frances Curtis, 59, 76
Driskell, Michael, 64
Driskell, Sue, 61, 63-64, 66, 71, 73, 76, 78
drugs, involvement with, 303
Duke, Benjamin, 362
Duke University, 191, 362-63
Durrett High School (Louisville), 286-87
Dybek, Stewart: *A Childhood in Other Neighbor-
hoods,* 277
Dykeman, Wilma, 324

Early English Text Society, 363
EARS, International Order of, 337
eating scenes, 275
Edel, Leon: *Henry James,* 371
editors, 28-29, 102